ENGLAND IN EUROPE

English Royal Women and Literary Patronage, c. 1000–c. 1150

Queen Emma, wife of King Æthelred II and of King Cnut, receives the book *Encomium Emmae reginae*. British Library Add. 33241

England in Europe

English Royal Women and Literary Patronage, c. 1000–c. 1150

ELIZABETH M. TYLER

UNIVERSITY OF TORONTO PRESS
Toronto Buffalo London

Toronto Buffalo London
www.utppublishing.com

ISBN 978-1-4426-4072-6

Library and Archives Canada Cataloguing in Publication

Tyler, E.M. (Elizabeth M.), 1965–, author
England in Europe : English royal women and literary patronage, c.1000–c.1150 / Elizabeth M. Tyler.

(Toronto Anglo-Saxon series; 23)
Includes bibliographical references and index.
ISBN 978-1-4426-4072-6 (cloth)

1. Emma, Queen, consort of Canute I, King of England, –1052. 2. Edith, Queen, consort of Edward, King of England, approximately 1020–1075. 3. Encomium Emmae Reginae. 4. Vie d'Edouard le Confesseur. 5. Women – England – History – Middle Ages, 500–1500. 6. Literary patrons – England – History – Middle Ages, 500–1500. 7. Politics and literature – History – Middle Ages, 500–1500. 8. European literature – English influences. 9. Queens – Great Britain – Biography. 10. Normans – Great Britain – Biography. I. Title. II. Series: Toronto Anglo-Saxon series ; 23

DA160.T95 2017 942.01'90922 C2017-900131-0

University of Toronto Press gratefully acknowledges the financial assistance of the Centre for Medieval Studies, University of Toronto, in the publication of this book.

University of Toronto Press acknowledges the financial assistance to its publishing program of the Canada Council for the Arts and the Ontario Arts Council, an agency of the Government of Ontario.

Canada Council for the Arts **Conseil des Arts du Canada**

Funded by the Government of Canada | Financé par le gouvernement du Canada | Canada

In memory of my grandmother, Mary Elizabeth Reed, and my mother, Kathleen, and for my aunts, Mary Elizabeth, Louise, Rosi, Barbara, Patricia, and Helen

Contents

Note on Translations and Referencing

Published translations have been used where available and emended as necessary. The aim is to facilitate, for readers who may be familiar with one or two of the languages (Latin, Old English, or Old French used), access to the full texts. Full details of a translation are provided in the bibliography following the reference to the edition of the original text. To facilitate cross-referencing between the original text and the translation, I have provided, where possible, references to books, chapters, and line numbers (in preference to page numbers, which are used only when necessary).

Acknowledgments

It is a great pleasure to acknowledge the many debts I have incurred in the writing of *England in Europe*. This book has taken me far into new areas and would not have been possible without the intellectual generosity, insights, gentle admonitions, and patient listening of many friends and colleagues. Julia Barrow, Stephen Baxter, Timothy Bolton, Stephen Church, Catherine Clarke, Richard Dance, Marilynn Desmond, Ziad Elmarsafy, Richard Gameson, Simon Gaunt, Jane Gilbert, Joanna Huntingdon, Ellen Joyce, Matthew Kempshall, Simon Keynes, Clare Lees, Roy Liuzza, Rosalind Love, Nicola Morato, Carole Newlands, Máire Ní Mhaonaigh, Bruce O'Brien, Emma O'Loughlin Bérat, Monika Otter, Christine Phillips, Lucy Pick, Christian Raffensperger, Geoff Rector, Felicitas Schmieder, Pauline Stafford, Eric Stanley, Carol Symes, Nicholas Watson, and Bjorn Weiler have all helped me to learn new material and listened to the arguments developed here. Christopher Baswell and Elaine Treharne offered encouragement at crucial points in the early stages of this project, helping me to see the argument of the book and its significance. In the final stages Elisabeth van Houts, Wim Verbaal, and Jocelyn Wogan-Browne read a full draft and convinced me that it was finished; I will always be grateful for that. Angela Wingfield's and Laura Napran's care with the typescript saved me from many errors and much frustration. At University of Toronto Press Andy Orchard and Suzanne Rancourt backed this project from the start, and I remain grateful to them for their continued support as the book grew in length and depth, and deadlines passed; and I am grateful for the care with which Barb Porter shepherded the book from typescript to publication. The incisive comments of the readers for the press guided my final revisions. Many thanks are also due to the Centre for Medieval Studies at the University of Toronto for meeting the cost of the book's subvention.

I was very fortunate to write this book at the University of York, which provided a rich and supportive intellectual environment and valued a book that took many years to write, following many detours and finding new destinations along the way. Friends and colleagues in the Department of English and Related Literature and the Centre for Medieval Studies (CMS) have nurtured the twin loves of poetry and history writing on which this book rests. I am especially grateful to Derek Attridge, Tim Ayers, Henry Bainton, John Barrell, Jacques Berthoud, Katy Cubitt, Helen Fulton, Hugh Haughton, Amanda Lillie (and Michael Fend), Linne Mooney, Mark Ormrod, Richard Rowland, Michele Vescovi, and Sethina Watson. Thomas O'Donnell, Nicola McDonald, Alastair Minnis, Felicity Riddy, Matthew Townend, and Jocelyn Wogan-Browne will, I am sure, recognize their incalculable influences on the book's intellectual landscape. I am grateful to graduate students from both the Department of English and CMS who have taken my "England in Europe" course over the years; I have learned much from their probing questions, fresh perspectives, and occasional dissatisfactions.

My research has been deeply shaped by long collaboration with Lars Boje Mortensen. Our shared interests in medieval literature across languages and political boundaries led to the establishment of, first, the Interfaces Network and, then, with Christian Høgel, the Centre for Medieval Literature, funded by the Danish National Research Foundation. The wide European horizons and challenges of Interfaces and the Centre for Medieval Literature underpin every chapter of this book. I have been especially grateful for the intellectual companionship of Panagiotis Agapitos, Henry Bainton, Paolo Borsa, Venetia Bridges, Kenneth Clarke, Rita Copeland, Jeroen Deploige, Jane Gilbert, Mayke de Jong, Karla Mallette, Máire Ní Mhaonaigh, Francine Mora-Lebrun, Thomas O'Donnell, Francesco Stella, Wim Verbaal, David Wallace, and George Younge.

I have benefited from substantial leave, in addition to regular research terms, over the course of writing this book. The award of a university anniversary lectureship in 2004, which brought a year's research leave, allowed the project's foundations to be laid. Arts and Humanities Research Council (AHRC) leave enabled a first draft to be finished in 2009–10, just as the new manuscript of the *Encomium Emmae reginae* and the lost poem from the *Vita Ædwardi* appeared; my thanks are also due to the AHRC for its acceptance of the subsequent deferred completion of this book. The final years of writing were supported by the Danish National Research Foundation (project number DNRF102), via the Centre for Medieval Literature.

Friends and family have been great company and sustenance over the years: Elizabeth Gatland, Stephanie Hanson, Ellen Joyce, Nicola McDonald, Lars Boje Mortensen, Thomas O'Donnell, Felicitas Schmieder, Chris Teesdale, Jocelyn Wogan-Browne, my brother, Sam Tyler, and my father, Richard Tyler, and *all* my cousins. My sons, Ben and Hugh, have been loving and funny and only occasionally exasperated, while growing up with this book. Most fundamentally, the dedication of this book to my grandmother and her daughters (especially my mother) acknowledges their love and their teaching me to notice women and the family knowledge that they pass from generation to generation. Given the subject matter of this book, I must acknowledge the Sisters of the Sacred Heart and of the Dominican Order, in whose schools I happily began my education, and the teachers at the public Philadelphia High School for Girls; they opened my eyes from an early age to the value of women's communities in educating girls to value the life of the mind and to think far beyond the confines of their own time and place. Our own experiences inevitably shape what we study; my own fascination for women's family connections and education was formed early.

Finally, this book rests on hours of conversation with Thomas O'Donnell and Jocelyn Wogan-Browne; I am indebted in equal measure to their insight, patience, and generosity.

I thank *Early Medieval Europe* and *Viator* for permission to reprint substantially revised versions (chapters 2 and 3) of earlier articles, and *Anglo-Norman Studies* (chapters 4 and 5) and *Review of English Studies* (chapters 1 to 5) for permission to use some material presented in earlier articles.

Abbreviations

AASS	*Acta sanctorum Bollandiana* (Brussels and elsewhere, 1643–)
AB	*Analecta Bollandiana*
ANS	*Anglo-Norman Studies*
ApT	*Apollonius of Tyre* (Old English)
ASC	Anglo-Saxon Chronicle
ASE	*Anglo-Saxon England* (journal)
ASPR	*Anglo-Saxon Poetic Records*
CCCM	Corpus Christianorum Continuatio Mediaevalis
CCSL	Corpus Christianorum Series Latina
CHP	Guy of Amiens, *Carmen de Hastingae proelio*
CSEL	Corpus Scriptorum Ecclesiasticorum Latinorum
EAA	*Epistola Alexandri ad Aristotelem*
EETS	Early English Text Society
EHR	*English Historical Review*
EME	*Early Medieval Europe*
Enc.	*Encomium Emmae reginae*
Epistolae	*Epistolae: Medieval Women's Letters*, ed. Ferrante (electronic resource)
Ety.	Isidore of Seville, *Etymologiae sive origines*
GG	William of Poitiers, *Gesta Guillelmi*
GND	*Gesta Normannorum ducum* (William of Jumièges, Orderic Vitalis, and Robert of Torigni)
GRA	William of Malmesbury, *Gesta regum Anglorum*
HA	Henry of Huntingdon, *Historia Anglorum*
HAp	*Historia Apollonii regis Tyri*
HE	*Historia ecclesiastica* (Bede, Hugh of Fleury, or Orderic)
HSJ	*Haskins Society Journal*

JMH	*Journal of Medieval History*
JML	*Journal of Medieval Latin*
LAA	*Letter of Alexander to Aristotle*
LC	Goscelin, *Liber confortatorius*
Meta.	Ovid, *Metamorphoses*
MGH	Monumenta Germaniae Historica Auct. Ant. – Auctores Antiquissimi Briefe d. dt. Kaiserzeit – Briefe der deutschen Kaiserzeit DD – Diplomata regum et imperatorum Germaniae Ldl – Libelli de Lite imperatorum et pontificum QQ zur Geistesgesch. – Quellen zur Geistesgeschichte des Mittelalters SS – Scriptores SS rer. Germ. – Scriptores rerum Germanicarum
ODNB	*Oxford Dictionary of National Biography*
OE	Old English
OMT	Oxford Medieval Texts
PL	Patrologiae cursus completus, series latina
QEQE	Stafford, *Queen Emma and Queen Edith*
RES	*Review of English Studies*
RS	Rolls Series
S	Sawyer number
Thy	Seneca, *Thyestes*
TRHS	*Transactions of the Royal Historical Society*
VA	Asser, *Vita Alfredi*
VE	*Vita Ædwardi*

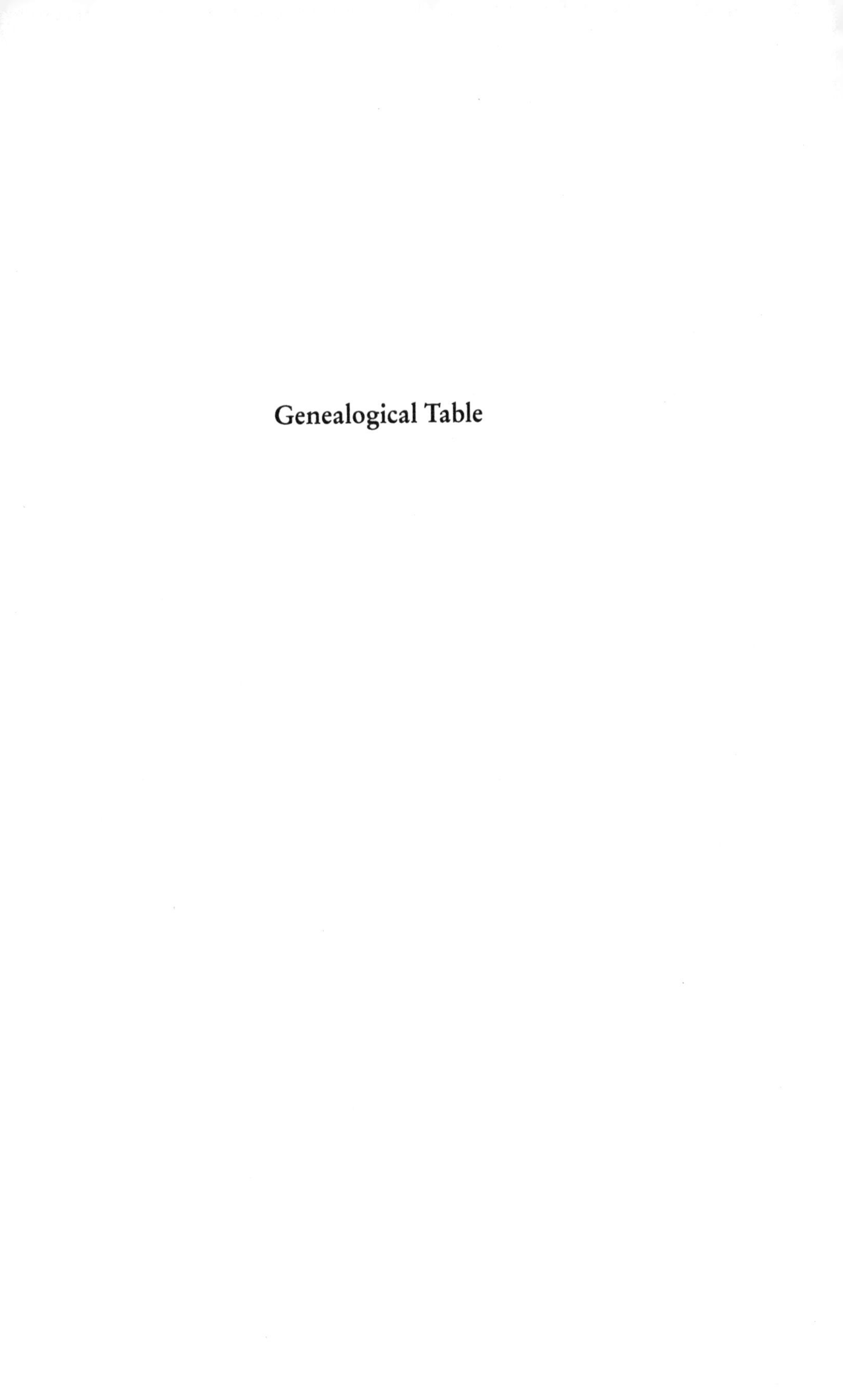

Genealogical Table

Genealogical Table
Adapted from P. Stafford, *Unification and Conquest*

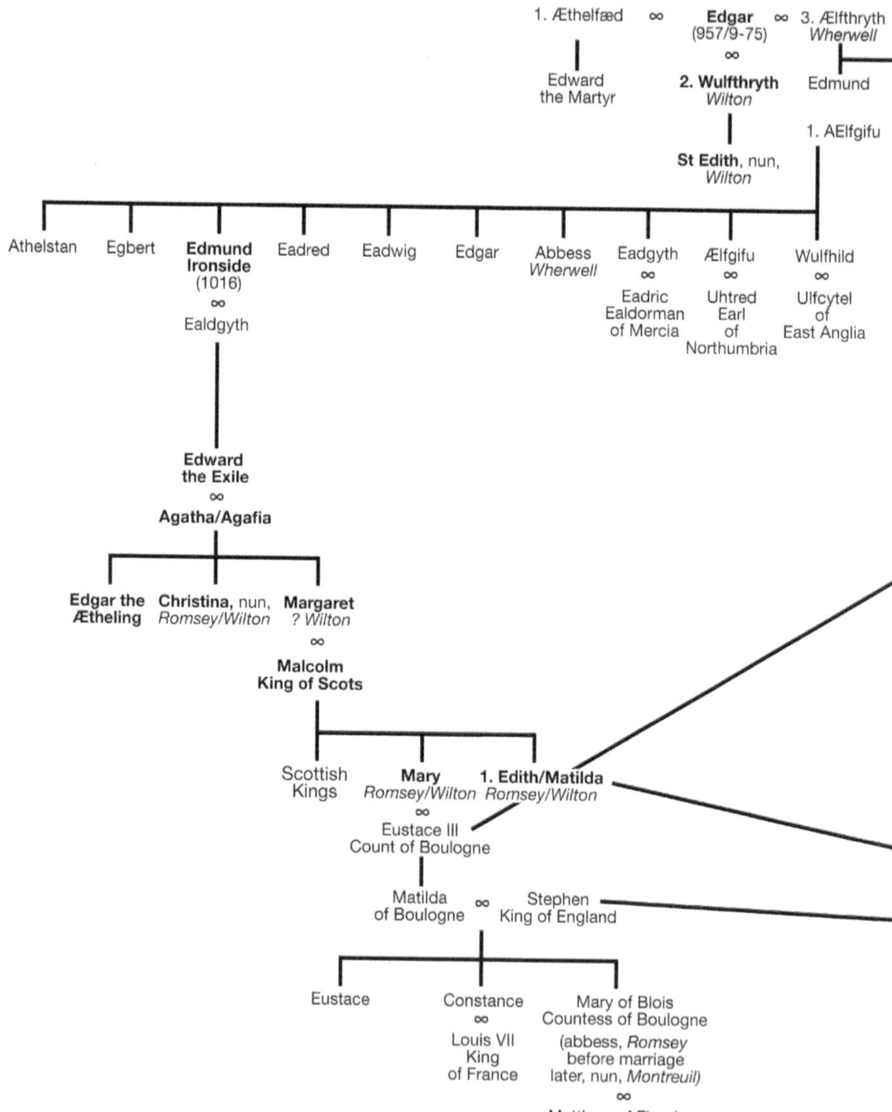

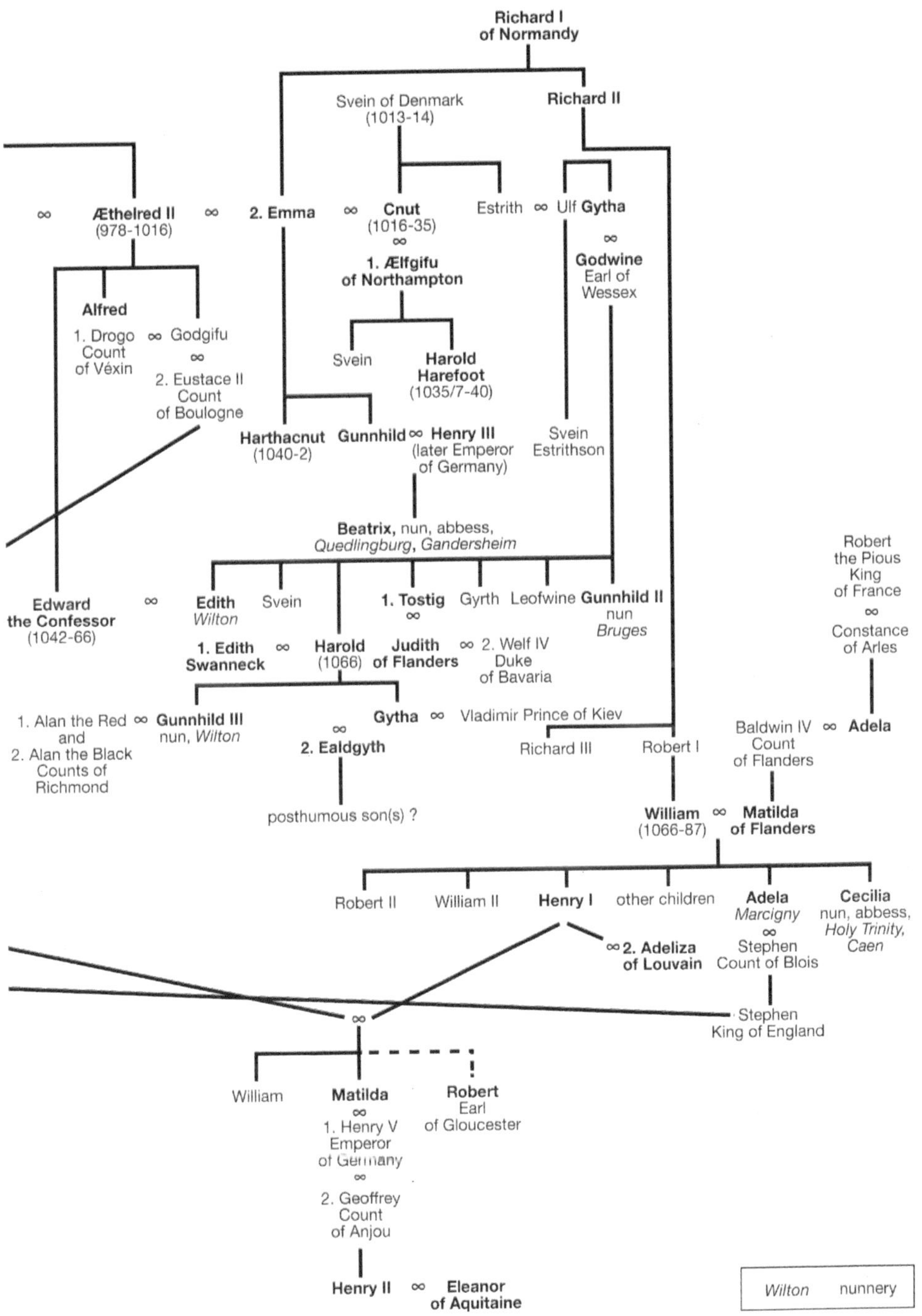

Richard I of Normandy
Svein of Denmark (1013-14)
Richard II
Æthelred II (978-1016)
2. Emma
Cnut (1016-35)
1. Ælfgifu of Northampton
Estrith
Ulf
Gytha
Godwine Earl of Wessex
Alfred
1. Drogo Count of Véxin
Godgifu
2. Eustace II Count of Boulogne
Svein
Harold Harefoot (1035/7-40)
Harthacnut (1040-2)
Gunnhild
Henry III (later Emperor of Germany)
Svein Estrithson
Beatrix, nun, abbess, *Quedlingburg*, *Gandersheim*
Robert the Pious King of France
Constance of Arles
Edward the Confessor (1042-66)
Edith *Wilton*
Svein
1. Tostig
Gyrth
Leofwine
Gunnhild II nun *Bruges*
1. Edith Swanneck
Harold (1066)
Judith of Flanders
2. Welf IV Duke of Bavaria
1. Alan the Red and 2. Alan the Black Counts of Richmond
Gunnhild III nun, *Wilton*
Gytha
Vladimir Prince of Kiev
2. Ealdgyth
Richard III
Robert I
Baldwin IV Count of Flanders
Adela
posthumous son(s) ?
William (1066-87)
Matilda of Flanders
Robert II
William II
Henry I
other children
Adela *Marcigny*
Stephen Count of Blois
Cecilia nun, abbess, *Holy Trinity, Caen*
2. Adeliza of Louvain
Stephen King of England
William
Matilda
1. Henry V Emperor of Germany
2. Geoffrey Count of Anjou
Robert Earl of Gloucester
Henry II
Eleanor of Aquitaine
Wilton nunnery

ENGLAND IN EUROPE

English Royal Women and Literary Patronage, c. 1000–c. 1150

Introduction

Uideres quoque delphinos electro fusos, ueteremque rememorantes fabulam de eodem metallo centauros.

(One might see dolphins moulded in electrum, and centaurs in the same metal, recalling the ancient fable.)

Encomium Emmae reginae 1.4

These lines describe Svein's ships as the Danish king sets off to conquer England. The *vetus fabula* is Virgil's *Aeneid*. Thus a Flemish cleric, the Encomiast, invoked the Trojan foundation of Rome in his history of the Anglo-Danish dynasty written for Queen Emma, Norman princess and widow of both the Anglo-Saxon King Æthelred and Svein's son, King Cnut. The Encomiast's allusion to Troy asserted a bold and intertwined political and literary vision. This vision, developed through a web of overt and subtle allusions, figures Emma's text as a foundation legend on the model of the *Aeneid*, itself a still compelling point of origin for western European literary culture in the twenty-first century.

This current book began with a very specific question, which I posed to myself the first time I read the *Encomium*: how did this allusion to the *Aeneid* make sense in the Anglo-Danish court of the early 1040s? That is, how did referring to Virgil's epic make meaning in that court where no one, I thought, knew anything about Latin literature? Trying to understand how a classicizing Latin text could work for Emma in the multilingual Anglo-Danish court, where English, Norse, and French competed, led me to take a long view chronologically and a wide view geographically. The search for understanding entailed reaching back to Alfred the Great's vernacular educational program for the laity and his establishment of the first of the late Anglo-Saxon royal nunneries, Shaftesbury, where his daughter Æthelgifu became abbess. In turn, it required looking forward, into the twelfth century, to the literary culture of the court of Henry I and his wife, Edith/Matilda, a nunnery-educated princess of the West Saxon dynasty. Equally, answers were not to be found exclusively in England, and extending to Flanders, Normandy, and Denmark proved insufficient. The frame had to be widened to include Northern France and the German Empire. From this wider view, a rich set of relationships emerged between the English royal women of the Anglo-Saxon, Anglo-Danish, and Anglo-Norman dynasties, from Emma to Edith/Matilda, and the literary cultures whose patronage they made an essential part of the exercise of queenship.

In calling these women English – be they Anglo-Saxon, Anglo-Danish, Anglo-Scottish, or Anglo-Norman – I am deliberately following the example of Goscelin, who, c. 1080, considered Eve, a nun of Danish and Lotharingian parentage who was raised in the West Saxon royal foundation at Wilton, to be English. Situating the Norman Conquest amidst migrations that include biblical and classical examples, he writes:

> Transferuntur denique gentes et regna, … hodieque Normanni in Angliam, Britanniam, in qua te quoque cum Anglica gente constat fuisse aduenam: sed et patre Dano et matre Lotaringa a claris natalibus filiam emersisse Anglicam.
>
> (Moreover peoples and kingdoms suffer migration … and today the Normans into England, Britain, in which it is agreed that you also were a foreigner among the English people: but it is also agreed that from a Danish father and a Lotharingian mother, a daughter grew from that noble birth who was English.)[1]

In later chapters of this book Eve's place at Wilton and her move to the nunnery of Le Ronceray in Angers will shed light on the literary culture of English queens. English royal women is a deliberately wide category, which includes the women in the families of all the kings of England from Æthelred to Henry I, including Cnut, Harold Godwineson, and William the Conqueror. These women were connected to each other by genealogy, marriage, and conquest. Moreover, they knew each other or were known

1 Goscelin, *Liber confortatorius* (hereafter cited as *LC*), 41 (trans., 117).

to each other and shared, passed on, and followed each other's cultivation of dynastic literature.

In the process of my trying to answer a specific question about the *uetus fabula* on Svein's ship the question that drives this book came into focus. How did English royal women across the eleventh and twelfth centuries use Roman myth, legend, and history to negotiate conquest, both Danish and Norman? This question does not provoke a simple answer but rather draws our attention to the complex intersection of dynastic politics, female patronage, lay literacies, multilingualism and internationalism, the attraction of classicism, and theorizing about fiction in the literary culture of the English court across the eleventh and twelfth centuries. When this intersection is opened up, the integral place of Anglo-Saxon England within high medieval western European literary culture begins to come into focus. As this book argues, we can only see this integral place in Europe if we radically revise our established understandings of eleventh-century English literature by including women and changing our chronological and geographical parameters.

The eleventh century was a period of dramatic change in Anglo-Saxon England. The marriage of King Æthelred to Emma of Normandy at the beginning of the century, Cnut's conquest in 1016 and his marriage to Emma, the restoration of the English royal dynasty with the reign of francophone Edward the Confessor, Edward's marriage to the Anglo-Danish Edith, the brief rule of her brother Harold Godwineson, the Norman Conquest itself, and the marriage of Henry I to Edith/Matilda in 1100 all stand out as pivotal events in England's relationship with Europe. While recent scholarship has reshaped our understanding of the social and political history of the period anchored by the Danish and Norman conquests, its literary history has not come into focus.[2] Attention has been directed at what went before (the learning of the Benedictine Reform, and the production of the great codices of Old English poetry, including the *Beowulf* manuscript) and what came after (the explosion of Latin and French writing that characterized the renaissance of learning and culture in the Anglo-Norman realm). As a result of this focus, linguistic and political upheaval is thought to have imposed a period of inactivity, creating a fundamental discontinuity between Anglo-Saxon and Anglo-Norman literary cultures. In recent years foundational work, led by Elaine Treharne,

2 See for example, Stafford, *Unification and Conquest*.

on the continued vitality of English as a written language across the conquests of 1016 and 1066 has challenged this periodization, drawing attention to monastic centres – focal points of written literary culture throughout the Anglo-Saxon period – as sites for the continued cultivation of English into the thirteenth century.[3] When we shift our attention from the dazzlingly obscure Latin of the Benedictine Reformers, which fell out of popularity as the eleventh century progressed, to the Latin that became the language of history writing in the late Anglo-Saxon court, the study of Latin has a major contribution to make in rewriting cross-conquest English literary history.[4]

Far from being an interlude, the eleventh century marked a rich, vibrant, and fast-paced period of creativity for English literature, particularly in the court. The historiographical culture of the late Anglo-Saxon court – with its often contradictory accounts of conquest, factionalism, and near civil war – was extraordinarily lively as clerics and patrons, most especially women, grappled with what it meant to give a true account of events. At the heart of much of this history writing lay innovative responses to classical Latin epic poetry, especially that of Virgil, Lucan, Statius, and Ovid. The political engagement and European currency of this poetry made it especially valuable when events in England repeatedly redrew the map of Europe and placed European dynastic politics at the centre of literary culture. Courts and literature had a long history of association in England, as they did elsewhere in Europe, which can be seen most notably with kings Alfred and Edgar. The difference in the mid-eleventh century is the orientation of Latin literature, written for queens, towards dynastic politics. This move brought politics to the centre of even such apparently literary matters as the nature of fiction.

England in Europe focuses on two histories, both neglected by literary history. Both were written in Latin, likely by Flemish clerics for eleventh-century queens at the centre of the period's turbulent political life and court culture: the *Encomium Emmae reginae* for Queen Emma and the *Vita Ædwardi regis* in verse and prose for Queen Edith. Norman-born Emma's queenship (1002–52) extended across the rule of her first husband, the Anglo-Saxon Æthelred; that of her second husband, the Danish Cnut; and the reigns of her sons, Harthacnut and Edward the Confessor. She

3 Swan and Treharne, eds., *Rewriting Old English*; Da Rold, et al., eds., *The Production and Use of English Manuscripts*; and Treharne, *Living through Conquest*.

4 For a preliminary discussion of eleventh-century and early-twelfth-century Latin and French literature in England see my "From Old English to Old French."

thus simultaneously forms a bridge between Anglo-Saxon England, Anglo-Danish England, and Normandy and vividly illustrates that internationalism was a feature of the English court decades before the Norman Conquest. Her literary patronage needs to be understood in the context of her multiple political identities and the multiple linguistic communities in which she, as a speaker of French, English, and Danish, participated. She also reminds us of the importance of the patronage and reception of Latin literature by non-Latinate lay people. In the next generation her daughter-in-law Edith, said to be fluent in English, Danish, French, Irish, and Latin, took on a similar role, from her marriage in 1043 until her death in 1075. Edith was the daughter of the Anglo-Saxon magnate Godwine and his Danish wife, Gytha; the wife of Edward the Confessor; and the sister of Harold Godwineson; and she remained in England after 1066. Like her mother-in-law Emma, she embodied the political complexity and linguistic richness of eleventh-century England. Furthermore, she was the highly educated product of the Anglo-Saxon royal nunnery of Wilton and, throughout her life, moved between this nunnery and the court. Attention to her literary patronage reveals the crucial role that nunnery-educated, polyglot, royal women continued to play in the production of English history writing into the twelfth century, when William of Malmesbury claimed the Wilton-educated Queen Edith/Matilda as the instigator of his *Gesta regum Anglorum*.

Courts, especially since Bezzola's groundbreaking multivolume study *Les origines et la formation de la littérature courtoise en occident (500–1200)*, published in the middle of the last century, have long been recognized as sites of literary culture.[5] This current study is particularly indebted to Bezzola's tracing of lay appropriations of classical texts and their stories, his emphasis on the close ties forged by the Normans and Angevins between England and France, and his attentiveness to the active role of women as literary patrons and in the processes of vernacularization. His identification of Edith/Matilda as the first woman to use Latin literary culture to project a political image helps to bring into focus the importance of Emma's and Edith's pre-conquest use of classicizing texts to put their own cases before the court. His perception of Edith/Matilda's patronage of Latin for political ends as a new departure brings into sharp focus that the literary culture of eleventh-century Anglo-Saxon queens has been left out of established narratives of the development of court literature.

5 Bezzola, *Origines*, esp. 2.2: 422–6.

C. Stephen Jaeger's work, especially his *Origins of Courtliness* with its debt to Norbert Elias's *The Civilizing Process*, is also a starting point for this study.[6] Jaeger locates the origins of courtliness in tenth-century Germany in the efforts of ecclesiastics, specifically bishops, to civilize secular rulers. His argument, like my own, brings Latin, rather than vernacular, literature, into the heart of the discussion and finds its centre of gravity in the period before the twelfth-century renaissance. While building on Jaeger, this current study gives greater weight to lay people alongside clerics as the agents in this civilizing process by examining the way in which lay readers and audiences, in dialogue with clerics, claimed the classical past for themselves. Among those lay people were women, who were almost entirely excluded by Jaeger's model of the court and its literary culture as a male space.[7] In contrast, my study, with its emphasis on the place of the queen at court and the frequent exchanges between the court and the royal nunneries, in which both secular and religious women were educated, will argue that women were key players in the cultivation of literature. The work of Sarah Foot, Pauline Stafford, and Barbara Yorke has made the Anglo-Saxon royal nunneries better known to us in the last two decades.[8] Here I will move from this historical work to argue for their literary importance, as Stephanie Hollis and Katherine O'Brien O'Keeffe have so insightfully done in their recent work on Wilton.[9] Work on the German royal nunneries, by Katrinete Bodarwé and others, provides important models for looking at the West Saxon nunneries and also provides evidence of the specific connections between these two sets of foundations.[10]

Both Bezzola and Jaeger, as their titles indicate, search for courtliness. I have deliberately avoided using the term *courtly*. This book aims to open up the nature of the literary culture of the English court over the hundred or so years between the *Encomium* and the *Gesta regum*. Although it has an eye towards later literary developments, especially vernacular romance, the book does not aim to use this period to tell a story about the birth of courtly literature. Although there will be moments when what women did with Latin texts in the eleventh and early twelfth centuries is directly

6 Jaeger, *Origins of Courtliness*.

7 Nelson, "Gendering Courts."

8 Foot, *Veiled Women*; Stafford, *Queen Emma and Queen Edith* (hereafter cited as *QEQE*); Stafford, "Queens, Nunneries"; and Yorke, *Nunneries*.

9 Hollis, ed., *Wilton Women*; and O'Brien O'Keeffe, *Stealing Obedience*.

10 Bodarwé, *Sanctimoniales litteratae*.

relevant to later romance, and although romance can act as a useful lens in looking at earlier Latin writing for women, I want to avoid the distortion of such teleology and to step away from diminishing the eleventh century as a prequel to the better-known twelfth century. Such an approach, perhaps counter-intuitively, serves only to enforce a gap between Anglo-Saxon England and European literature of the twelfth century by claiming for post-conquest literary culture what was already flourishing in the late Anglo-Saxon period.

Given widespread scholarly interest in medieval European court literature, the sidelining of the *Encomium* and the *Vita Ædwardi* from English literary history is of great consequence to understanding the European context of English literature and the English contribution to European literature. Recent work by Andy Orchard, Victoria Jordan, Monika Otter, and me has begun to redress the neglect of the literary qualities of these two texts, but it has not yet placed them in relation to each other or drawn out the challenge they pose to established literary history, with its often national preoccupations.[11] Both of these works have been overlooked as texts written by foreigners for women. Their absence from literary history is particularly ironic because internationalism and female patronage are so celebrated as driving forces for literary innovation in the twelfth century, as we see most clearly, in looking ahead to the Angevin realm, in the place of Eleanor of Aquitaine and Marie de Champagne in literary studies.[12]

Neither Emma nor Edith, and certainly not the Encomiast or the anonymous author of the *Vita Ædwardi*, seems sufficiently English to belong to pre-conquest English literary history. The dynastic imperatives of their texts are as much the concern of Denmark and Normandy as of England, further distancing them from English literature. While our conception of Anglo-Saxon literature has space for an international clerical Latin literary culture stretching from Theodore of Tarsus to the Frankish Lantfred, we have expected the literature that is concerned with the secular aspects of life to be vernacular and Anglocentric, even to the point of forgetting, at times, that *Beowulf* is about Scandinavians. Recent critical interest in the contribution of Anglo-Saxon vernacular literature to the creation of an

11 Orchard, "Literary Background"; Jordan, "Chronology and Discourse"; Otter, "1066"; Otter, "Closed Doors"; Tyler, "Fictions of Family"; Tyler, "Talking about History"; and Tyler, "*Vita Ædwardi*."

12 For an early and sharply insightful setting out of an international model of English literary production from the twelfth century onwards, see particularly Salter, *English and International*, esp. 1–28.

English or Anglo-Saxon identity, while making important contributions to seeing the investment of literary culture in politics, has further intensified the nationalizing tendencies of literary history.[13]

Yet current interest in global literature invites us to see the limitations of national literary history and to embrace the internationalism of the *Encomium* and the *Vita Ædwardi*.[14] Likewise, current interest in the French literature of high and late medieval England, led by the groundbreaking work of Ian Short, Jocelyn Wogan-Browne, and Ardis Butterfield, points us away from any easy associations of language and nation or kingdom, as does the important contribution of Bruce O'Brien in looking at the languages of England from c. 800 to c. 1200.[15] In the multilingual context signalled by the linguistic proficiences of Emma and the Encomiast, and Edith and the Anonymous, Latin became a bridge between the vernacular literary cultures of Anglo-Saxon England and Anglo-Norman England. This bridging role of Latin breaks down periodizations based on language, Old English versus Old French, and thus enables us to see that the early, and distinctively insular, use of English as a written language nourished European literary culture more broadly in the High Middle Ages.

Part of the difficulty in seeing the wider European significance of pre- and post-conquest English literature lies with the underdevelopment of the literary history of the eleventh century generally, except when it can be pulled into the long twelfth century. The recent collection of essays, *Latin Culture in the Eleventh Century*, edited by Michael Herren, C.J. McDonough, and Ross G. Arthur, marks a new, broader interest in eleventh-century European literature.[16] I hope that this current book will contribute to the way in which we study aspects of Flemish, French, Norman, and to a lesser extent German literature in this period, as well as the texts associated with England that are my main focus. In this regard, it is worth highlighting that the object of my study is less the multilingual nature of English literary culture, which has been much discussed in recent years, but rather English literary culture as part of a wider European context, which would not be

---

13 See for example Howe, *Migration and Mythmaking*, which has made a major and rightfully influential contribution to the literary history of Anglo-Saxon England.

14 Leersen's *National Thought in Europe* includes many examples of the impact of nationalism on literary study, with specific reference to medieval English literature; Georgianna, "Coming to Terms."

15 Short, "Patrons and Polyglots"; Wogan-Browne, *Saints Lives*; Wogan-Browne et al., *Language and Culture*; Butterfield, *Familiar Enemy*; and O'Brien, *Reversing Babel*.

16 Herren, McDonough, and Arthur, *Latin Culture*.

the same without it.[17] Fundamentally, literary studies do not yet have a language for talking about literary history in non-nationalizing ways. The terms *international* and *post-national* simply instate the "national" in a way that is inappropriate to the counties, duchies, kingdoms, and empires of the High Middle Ages. European – or, even more narrowly, Western European or Latin European – models for literary history have only begun to move substantially beyond the methodologies that simply connect existing national narratives. One of the aims of this book is to contribute to new, more European frameworks for studying medieval literary culture.[18]

Turning from foreigners to women, the failure to take seriously women's learning and the agency it engendered has led to both the *Encomium* and the *Vita Ædwardi* being considered, if at all, in terms of the education of their authors rather than as intimately related to the expectations and literary cultures of the women who commissioned them. They have thus been detached from the English court. Neither Emma nor Edith was the passive recipient of her text; rather, each woman was patron, informant, and potentially a proponent of her text, as Stafford's rich and important historical work has shown.[19] From a literary perspective, as this book reveals, it is equally important that each woman played an active and high-profile role in the use of the classical past in these texts. Several decades of scholarship on women in the early and high Middle Ages underpins this argument. Especially important has been the work on women as cultural ambassadors by Susan Groag Bell, on women and literary culture by Joan Ferrante, on female patronage brought together by June McCash, on women as keepers of dynastic history and as subjects of Latin poetry by Elisabeth van Houts, on women's role in the Romanization of barbarian courts by Janet Nelson, and on female reading communities, including matrilinear, by Felicity Riddy, Jocelyn Wogan-Browne, and D.H. Green.[20] Given the chronological and geographical focus of this

17 My edited collection, *Conceptualizing Multilingualism*, takes the intertwined literary and linguistic history of England as its focus.

18 Borsa et al., "What is Medieval European Literature?" 13–17; and Wallace, *Europe*.

19 Stafford, *QEQE*.

20 Bell, "Medieval Women"; Ferrante, *Glory of Her Sex* (and especially her discussion, pp. 90–105, of texts, which are the subject of this current book); essays by Huneycutt, McCash, and Parsons, in McCash, *Cultural Production*; Nelson, "Gender and Genre"; Nelson, "Gendering Courts"; Nelson, "Dhuoda"; Van Houts, "Women and the Writing of History"; Van Houts, *Memory and Gender*; Van Houts, "Latin Poetry"; Riddy, "Women Talking"; Riddy, "Mother Knows Best"; Wogan-Browne, "'Reading is Good Prayer'"; and D.H. Green, *Women Readers*.

book, van Houts's work has been especially fundamental to my narrative at every turn. Throughout the development of my argument I have aimed to be alert, following Judith Bennett, to the continuities as well as the discontinuities of women's experience amidst political and social change. Women crossed the conquests of eleventh-century England differently than did men, especially, though not solely, because marriage to an Anglo-Saxon woman could bestow legitimacy on a conqueror, as, for examples, the marriages of Cnut and Emma, and Henry I and Edith/Matilda.[21] The way in which women crossed conquests in the eleventh and early twelfth centuries had a very significant impact on European literary culture.

The *Encomium* and the *Vita Ædwardi* both claim that their queen specifically commissioned their production, and thus these texts fit securely within the most narrow definitions of patronage. Such narrow definitions, as for example that of Karen Broadhurst, which are sceptical of claims of lay patronage and wary of reading dedications as evidence of patronage, are valuable in their appeal for rigour.[22] However, such a tight view of patronage is not attuned to the ways in which the writers of the texts that are considered in this study – even though almost all of them were commissioned – characterize their relationships with their patrons. While the material nature of the relationship is not ignored, these writers give primary emphasis to the creative sphere, and it is this intellectual relationship that I will explore in looking at English royal women's literary patronage.

Following Joan Ferrante and D.H. Green, I emphasize that patronage includes not only commissioned texts that are rewarded materially, practically, or professionally but also texts that are the result of the intellectual or emotional support of a woman or the result of a woman's searching for knowledge that is answered by the production of a text.[23] These are the terms that our writers use to explain their relationship with their patrons, and these are terms that acknowledge rather than efface women's active roles in the *creative* dimensions of literary production. Even when they address a very present political problem on behalf of a royal woman, or mention material support, these writers *always* engage with her intellectually, with one telling exception, the Empress Matilda, which will be explored in the conclusion. Engagement on the part of female patrons

21 Bennett, "Confronting Continuity"; Searle, "Women and the Legitimisation"; and Stafford, "Chronicle D."

22 Broadhurst, "Henry II."

23 Ferrante, *Glory of Her Sex*; and D.H. Green, *Women Readers*, 189–217.

profoundly shapes the literary nature of each text, which is thus, in varying degrees, the result of a collaboration between writer and patron. From the perspective of a concern for active collaboration I do not draw a sharp line between dedicatee and patron, as Green does, since a woman's known patronage of writers, as we shall see with Edith/Matilda, can actively influence the production of texts that may strictly speaking be said to have been the result of a speculative dedication. From this perspective the discounting of texts for which there is only evidence of dedication entails the serious underestimating of women's influence on literary culture (as it would also for men). At the same time, it gives too much weight to the act of commissioning and material reward, which does not necessarily involve an intellectual relationship between writer and patron.

The view of literary patronage as entailing creative influence over a text shapes the methodology of this book.[24] In looking at the *Encomium* and the *Vita Ædwardi*, I begin by not simply accepting the Encomiast's and Anonymous's claims that they wrote at the behest of Emma and Edith, but rather working through each text to see if and how queenly patronage shaped these texts. The *Encomium* and the *Vita Ædwardi* offer evidence in abundance of their patron's direct intervention in the production of the texts. As the very different educational backgrounds of Emma (not Latinate), and Edith (convent educated to a high level) illustrate, a range of lay people, with or without direct command of Latin, could not only participate in but also exert control over literary culture. Following on from the *Encomium* and the *Vita Ædwardi* to look at later texts, such as Hugh of Fleury's writing for Adela of Blois and the Empress Matilda, I will look not only for dedications and claims of commission but for the influence of female royal patronage on texts, considering the ways in which authors responded to the known concerns and literary tastes of dedicatees and commissioners. At the same time, the wider social context of a text's patronage and reception will be fully in the frame. Throughout this study, while a rigorous approach to female patronage will be taken, a higher standard of evidence for female rather than male lay patronage will not be imposed.

A close focus on active female literary patronage within the intensely multilingual context of the English court provides insight into the nature of lay literacy in the early and high Middle Ages. The bulk of my

24 Tyson ("Patronage of French Vernacular History," 184–5) considers a range of elements that must be identified in accepting a claim of patronage, and I am indebted to her thinking here; however, we disagree on the weight given to material support.

enquiry lies with the lay use of Latin literary culture, a topic that Rosamond McKitterick has opened up for the Carolingian Empire with her arguments for a maximalist view of literacy among a lay elite who continued to speak Latin.[25] The approach to lay literacy taken here steps away from the two intertwined dichotomies – orality and literary, and Latin and vernacular – that shape much scholarship, in order to look at the talk around the text. This talk around the text ranges from the talk of a non-Latinate lay informer to the talk of a highly learned cleric explaining a difficult text. The contrast between the learning of Emma and the learning of Edith underscores the point that the varied Latinities of the laity and the very quickly shifting multilingualism of the court (with the place of Danish and French changing quickly as a result of marriages, conquests, and exiles) required a highly developed culture of explanation – talk – which crossed both written and spoken languages. This culture of explanation was not limited to Latin, because English texts, such as the *Old English Boethius*, equally required explication. While Brian Stock's highly influential concept of "textual community" is an essential starting point for this study (as for so many), it cannot fully capture the dynamic within the English court in which the relationships between literate and non-literate were not straightforwardly hierarchical, but multiple and multidirectional, inflected through gender, social status, and vernacular literacy as well as Latin learning.[26]

The structure and methodologies of this book are designed to use the *Encomium* and the *Vita Ædwardi* to look into the Anglo-Saxon court during the Danish and Norman conquests and, from this vantage point, to reassess late Anglo-Saxon England's place in European literary history. Each of these central texts is studied in two paired chapters. In the first of each pair I attend closely to the text, particularly the author's engagement with the Roman epic and with the tradition of late antique commentaries on classical poetry. Roman history writing, especially Sallust, and late antique Christian poetry are also important intertexts for both the Encomiast and the Anonymous, but it is the Roman epic that captures their imaginations and those of their patrons and audiences. Troy, the Roman Civil War, the figures of Dido, Cleopatra, and the warring brothers of Thebes, and Ovidan metamorphoses are all central to the discussion as intensive and extended close reading reveals the Encomiast's and the Anonymous's

25 McKitterick, esp. *Written Word.*
26 Stock, *Implications of Literacy.*

improvised and often wavering explorations of the boundaries between history and fiction.

My approach to the classicism of the *Encomium* and the *Vita Ædwardi* has been formed by the the classicist T.P. Wiseman's concept of the Roman story world in his *Myths of Rome*. Wiseman's concept of the story world recognizes and encompasses a fluidity between myth, legend, and history in antiquity; it was precisely this fluidity that made epic poetry attractive in negotiating conquest, as new dynasties required foundation legends and as partisan narratives became political tools – situations that also shaped the history and poetry of ancient Rome. Furthermore, Wiseman's concept of the Roman story world insists that the history, myth, and legends of Rome were the domain of both the educated and the non-educated, and thus the term makes space, when brought forward, to encompass both the learned classicism of the male cleric and the investment made by the laity in using the classical past to explore secular experience.[27] In addition to Wiseman, my reading of eleventh- and twelfth-century classicism has drawn on the work of Charles Martindale, whose *Redeeming the Text* brings reception theory to bear on our understanding of the very nature of a classical Latin text, which can draw our attention to the manner in which Latin poetry was read in the Middle Ages.[28] Stephen Hinds's capacious understanding of allusion in classical Latin poetry, in his *Allusion and Intertext*, has been defining for this book in the model that it provides for moving beyond spotting allusions to the classics in medieval poetry to considering the complex intertextuality forged by medieval poets between themselves and the ancients.[29]

Specific studies of medieval and early modern classical reception also underpin this book. From an early stage Alastair Minnis's work on the commentary tradition was formative for my approach to the medieval reading of classical texts, as was Lawrence Nees's book on the classical tradition in the Carolingian court.[30] Long before this current project had

27 Wiseman, *Myths of Rome*.

28 Martindale, *Redeeming the Text*.

29 Hinds, *Allusion and Intertext*. On a more practical level, my close reading across classical and medieval texts is supported by the excellent notes in Alistair Campbell's edition of the *Encomium* and Frank Barlow's edition of the *Vita Ædwardi* and by two databases: *PoetriaNova*, which enables electronic searches of classical and medieval Latin poetic texts up to 1250, and the Brepols *Library of Latin Texts*, which includes prose and verse texts from antiquity and the Middle Ages.

30 Minnis and Scott, *Medieval Literary Theory*; and Nees, *Tainted Mantle*.

begun, I learned much from David Quint's study of the political poetics of the early modern reception of classical epic; what I learned from Quint has also been extended to encompass gender through the work of Margaret Ferguson, Suzanne Hagedorn, and Marilyn Desmond.[31] Among medievalists, the most instrumental in shaping the methodology of this book is Christopher Baswell, whose *Virgil in Medieval England* taught me much about the Middle Ages' reading of classical Latin poetry and the fusing of intertextual close reading and historicism. When I first read Baswell's book in 1995, I wished for a chapter on late Anglo-Saxon England; I hope that this current book offers something of a worthy prequel.

Fiction is, of course, not a self-evident category, and I have drawn on the work of many medievalists in teasing out the ideas about fiction that are present in the *Encomium* and the *Vita Ædwardi* and the texts indebted to them. The writing of Hanning, Partner, Dronke, Mehtonen, Morse, Otter, and Kempshall, among many others, has been particularly important, especially in considering the relation between history writing and fiction.[32] However, seeing the debates about the nature of fiction that took place in the late Anglo-Saxon court is impossible without a mode of approach to the classical past that acknowledges both lay and clerical efforts to shape history with fiction, and which has room for the place of reception in the production of fiction. In terms of frameworks for analysing how eleventh- and early-twelfth-century writers and audiences theorized fiction, the work of D.H. Green has been essential. Green's emphasis on the complicity of author and audiences regarding the made-up status of a story takes a deeply social approach that allows agency to lay audiences as well as to clerical authors.[33] The social and political nature of the fictions of the *Encomium* and the *Vita Ædwardi* eludes models that are more fully bound within literary theory.

In the second chapter of each pair, drawing on more historical approaches, with particular debt to Stafford's *Queen Emma and Queen Edith*, I show that social contexts and reception are key to understanding why the Roman story world was attractive and why ideas of fictionality were pressing. This requires peopling the English court through the use

31 Quint, *Epic and Empire*; Ferguson, *Dido's Daughters*; Hagedorn, *Abandoned Women*; and Desmond, *Reading Dido*.

32 Hanning, *Vision of History*; Partner, *Serious Entertainments*; Dronke, *Fabula*; Mehtonen, *Old Concepts and New Poetics*; Morse, *Truth and Convention*; Otter, *Inventiones*; and Kempshall, *Rhetoric and the Writing of History*.

33 D.H. Green, *Medieval Romance*, esp. ch. 1.

of a range of texts, both narrative and documentary, and modern scholarship (including the database of PASE, Prosopography of Anglo-Saxon England) to build a picture of the patrons and audiences who had a determining impact on the production and reception of the *Encomium* and the *Vita Ædwardi*. Both the people at the English court and their political allegiances directly shaped late Anglo-Saxon literature. Throughout the paired chapters, close reading of densely textured literary works is situated within imagined social and political contexts. Neither the literary nor the political is visible in isolation, requiring an interdisciplinary approach to see either. Integrated textual and contextual study shows that the dynamics of writing for women who found themselves in threatening circumstances and surrounded by people who knew their stories is essential to the experimentation of the *Encomium* and the *Vita Ædwardi*; this experimentation is a political and social, as well as a literary, phenomenon, and my explication of this experimentation is deeply informed by Gabrielle Spiegel's powerful ideas about the "social logic of the text."[34]

These four main chapters, textual and contextual, aim to show that the *Encomium* and the *Vita Ædwardi* were tied into a literary culture that was created and shared throughout England, Normandy, Northern France, Flanders, and the Empire. The wider European network of texts within which the *Encomium* and the *Vita Ædwardi* ask to be read includes the hagiography of Saint-Bertin; the poetry of *The Cambridge Songs* and the Loire School; Guy of Amiens's *Carmen de Hastingae proelio*; the histories of Dudo of St Quentin, William of Poitiers, and Hugh of Fleury; Turgot's *Vita sanctae Margaretae*; historical writing and poetry from Reims; and the Old French *romans d'antiquité*. These textual relations were created by the movement of elite people in both directions between England and the Continent and thus show a dimension of elite social mobility that was an essential element in the "making of Europe," as Robert Bartlett has shown.[35] The movement of women, in dynastic marriage, and of the clergy was of greater direct consequence for literary culture than was the movement of lay men across political boundries. Lay men's crossing of political boundaries in war and exile has become the stuff of history, both medieval and modern. The mobility of women, especially but not

34 Spiegel, *Romancing the Past*; and Spiegel, "History, Historicism."
35 Bartlett, *Making of Europe*, 24–59.

solely in marriage, and of clerics had greater direct effect on literary culture and thus on the keeping of history and the development of poetics.

It is central to the argument of this book that the literary culture fostered by Emma and Edith was connected both to what came before and to what came after. To set the scene, the four main chapters are preceded by a shorter chapter, "Vernacular Foundations," which suggests that the way in which the Anglo-Saxon vernacular culture of the tenth and eleventh centuries made English and Latin history writing unusually accessible to the laity contributed to the environment in which texts like the *Encomium* and the *Vita Ædwardi* could not only be written but also find patrons and audiences. For all the Europeanness of the *Encomium* and the *Vita*, their production in England and the connection that this had to vernacular literacy need to be probed. Key texts considered in this chapter include the *Old English Boethius* and the *Old English Orosius*, the Anglo-Saxon Chronicle, *Apollonius of Tyre*, and the *Letter of Alexander to Aristotle*. These texts all illustrate the centrality of the Roman story world to written secular literary culture. This preference for the Roman exists alongside the Germanic story world, even though the latter has been seen as more characteristic of Anglo-Saxon literature. The first chapter thus begins this current study with a substantial revision of Anglo-Saxon literary history and argues that this revision is essential to understanding later eleventh- and twelfth-century literature.

The final two chapters of the book move forward from the Norman Conquest into the early decades of the twelfth century. The first of these chapters, "The Women of 1066," begins by looking at the way in which the women of the West Saxon and Godwine dynasties took the literary expectations of the Anglo-Saxon court with them when they fled to Scotland, Flanders, and Denmark. I then turn to the new royal women of England to look at the disjunctions and surprising links between the literary culture of the late Anglo-Saxon court and the poetry and history written in the circles of the women of the Conqueror's family: his wife, Matilda of Flanders; his daughter Cecilia, abbess of Holy Trinity, Caen; and his daughter Adela, Countess of Blois, addressee of Hugh of Fleury's *Historia ecclesiastica* and Baudri of Bourgueil's poetry. The final main chapter, "Edith Becomes Matilda," follows Edith/Matilda from her birth as the child of the learned West Saxon princess Margaret and the Scottish king Malcolm, through her education at Wilton, and into her marriage to Henry I. Her representation in poetry by Hildebert and Marbod, and William of Malmesbury's claim that he wrote his history of the kings of England because Edith/Matilda wanted to know about her West Saxon ancestry, shows her maintaining and perpetuating a model of queenship that was established by Emma and Edith. We conclude, with Adeliza of Louvain, Edith/Matilda's successor as Henry I's wife, by considering the ways in which the model of queenship that was forged by Emma and Edith and continued by Edith/Matilda contributed to the context in which this francophone queen from the western borders of the German Empire acted as a focal point for the production of some of the earliest poetry and history written in Old French. Placing women at the centre of non-nationalizing literary history enables us to move Anglo-Saxon literary culture from the periphery to the centre of Europe and to show that its impact continued as a constitutive role in European literary culture well beyond 1066.

1 Vernacular Foundations

In the century and a half before English royal women began to patronize the writing of classicizing history that engaged with the Roman story world, some Roman myths, legends, and histories were already known in the written vernacular in England. The translation, copying, and circulation of Boethius's *De consolatione philosophiae* (*Consolatio*), Orosius's *Historiarum adversum paganos libri septem* (*Historiae*), the *Epistola Alexandri ad Aristotlem* (*Epistola Alexandri*), and the *Historia Apollonii regis Tyri* (*Historia Apollonii*) reveal a desire on the part of the Anglo-Saxons not only to know more about pagan antiquity but also to use this knowledge in turn to shape and explore their own experiences.[1] The Latin texts in this diverse group are the products of late antiquity, both Christian and pagan; they are not the classical Latin texts that will become newly influential, throughout western Europe, in the eleventh and twelfth centuries. However, each of these late antique texts passes on accounts of pagan antiquity. Moreover, the *Consolatio*, the *Historiae*, the *Epistola Alexandri*, and the *Historia Apollonii* were not set aside in the face of increased interest in classical texts from the middle of the eleventh century onwards. Rather, each became more popular, exerting critical influence on developments in philosophy, on history writing, and on the emergence of

1 Latin texts: Boethius, *De consolatione philosophiae* (hereafter cited as *Consolatio*); Orosius, *Historiarum adversum paganos libri septem* (hereafter cited as *Historiae*); *Epistola Alexandri ad Aristotelem* (hereafter cited as *EAA*); and *Historia Apollonii regis Tyri* (hereafter cited as *HAp*). Old English translations: *Old English Boethius* (hereafter cited as *OEBoethius*); *Old English Orosius* (hereafter cited as *OEOrosius*); *Letter of Alexander to Aristotle* (hereafter cited as *LAA*); and *Old English Apollonius of Tyre* (hereafter cited as *ApT*).

romance.[2] Read and copied throughout the eleventh century (and, in the case of the *Old English Boethius*, into the twelfth century), the Old English versions of these late antique texts stand as important testimony to the vitality of the written vernacular literary culture that preceded and continued alongside the promotion of Latin historical writing by queens of England, as initiated by Emma's commissioning of the *Encomium Emmae reginae* in the early 1040s.[3] The importance of Boethius's *Consolatio*, Orosius's *Historiae*, the *Epistola Alexandri*, and the *Historia Apollonii* in the twelfth century, including their importance to literary developments as significant as Neoplatonic literary theory and the "birth of romance," forcefully reminds us to attend to their presence, in the vernacular, in late Anglo-Saxon England.[4]

Although *Beowulf* and other heroic verse seem emblematic of Anglo-Saxon secular literature and have received extensive scholarly attention, more Anglo-Saxon material comes down to us about Alexander the Great than about Germanic heroes, though the latter defines the field of Old English studies.[5] While we cannot know how representative of Anglo-Saxon literary culture, written and oral, the manuscript evidence is, the presence of Old English translations of late antique texts does underscore the importance of the Greco-Roman inheritance. The translation of this material into the vernacular marks a distinction between the literary culture of England and that of her Continental neighbours.[6] This chapter raises the question of the connection between the presence of the Roman

2 See the manuscripts catalogued in Mortensen, "Diffusion of Roman Histories," 119–65; *EAA*, ed., Boer, iii–xxi; *HAp*, ed., Kortekaas, 14–22 and appendix 1, 413–18. For Boethius see Courcelle, *Consolation de philosophie*, 301–32, and, for Britain in the first volume of the catalogue of Boethius manuscripts, Gibson and Smith, *Codices Boethiani*.

3 On the manuscripts of the Old English translations: *OEOrosius*, ed. Bately, xxiii–xxvi; *OEBoethius*, ed. Godden and Irvine, 1:8–43; *Klaeber's Beowulf*, ed. Fulk, Bjork, and Niles, xxvii (*LAA* is in the *Beowulf* manuscript); and *ApT*, ed. Goolden, xxxiii; and Wormald, *Making of English Law*, 1:206–10.

4 Wetherbee, "From Late Antiquity," 132–3, and, for one among many accounts of romance in the twelfth century, D.H. Green, *Medieval Romance*.

5 This takes into account the sustained narratives of Alexander in *LAA* and *OEOrosius* (3.7, 9, and 11) that tell the deeds of Alexander, his father, Philip, and his successors. Alexander is also mentioned repeatedly in *The Wonders of the East* (ed. and trans. Orchard), like the *LAA*, in the *Beowulf* manuscript. The garbled reference to Alexander in "Widsith" (line 15) indicates that there were limits to the popularity of this Alexander material (*Minor Heroic Poems*, ed. Hill, 61).

6 With the exception of Notker Labeo's late-tenth-century Old High German translation of the *Consolatio*.

story world in English and the active engagement with the stories of Troy, the Roman Civil War, Thebes, and metamorphoses that so conspicuously marks the Latin history written for English royal women across the eleventh and twelfth centuries. Lay learning comes sharply into focus in connection with both Alfred's and Æthelred's courts.

Boethius's *De consolatione philosophiae*

Both the *Old English Boethius* and the *Old English Orosius* are the products of King Alfred's educational program (whether directly as a result of being translated in his court or indirectly as a result of increased vernacular literacy), which explicitly sought to extend book learning to the laity as well as to raise standards among the clergy by making the books "ða ðe niedbeðearfosta sien eallum monnum to wiotonne" (that are the most necessary for all men to know) available in the vernacular.[7] As Alfred wrote, or had written, in the preface to the translation of Gregory the Great's *Pastoral Care*, it should be arranged

> ðæt[te] eall sio giogud ðe nu is on Angelcynne friora monna, ðara ðe ða speda hæbben ðæt hie ðæm befeolan mægen, sien to liornunga oðfæste, ða hwile ðe hie to nanre oðerre note ne mægen, oð ðone first ðe hie wel cunnen Englisc gewrit arædan: lære mon siððan furður on Lædengeðiode ða ðe mon furðor læran wille & to hieran hade don wille.
>
> (so that all the free-born young men now in England who have the means to apply themselves to it, may be set to learning (as long as they are not useful for some other employment) until the time that they can read English writings properly. Thereafter one may instruct in Latin those whom one wishes to teach further and wishes to advance to holy orders.)[8]

The vernacular had a role to play in the education of the laity and the clergy, and, as Asser's *Life of Alfred* allows us to see, Alfred, whose own mother had introduced him to vernacular literacy, included girls among those educated at his court.[9]

---

7 *Old English Pastoral Care* (hereafter cited as *OEPastoral Care)*, preface, 7 (trans. 126).

8 *OEPastoral Care*, preface, 7 (trans. 126).

9 Asser, *Vita Alfredi* (hereafter cited as *VA*), 23 and 75. For recent extensive discussion of the Alfredian educational program, see Pratt, *Political Thought*, 113–350. For doubts about the Alfredian character of many of these translations, see note 23 below.

Neither Boethius's prosimetrical, Neoplatonic *Consolatio* nor its Old English translation was in any sense primarily engaged with the Roman story world. However, to Boethius, writing for an educated audience in the early sixth century, the myths, legends, and histories of Rome constituted a shared language. Alfred and his circle, translating in the Anglo-Saxon court of the late ninth century, did not seek to efface the text's rootedness in the Roman world, as revealed by their treatment of classical myth, which was potentially challenging material for a Christian king. By rendering in the vernacular Boethius's accounts of Jove's battle with the giants, Ulysses's encounter with Circe, and Orpheus's attempt to rescue Eurydice from the underworld, the translator expands, moralizing and at times even boldly reworking his Latin model.[10] In so doing, he turns the myths found in the Latin *Consolatio* into occasions for teaching. His retelling of Boethius's account of the story of Ulysses and Circe will be our orientation point in looking at what the *Old English Boethius*, read and copied into the early 1100s, taught its readers over the centuries following the reign of Alfred.

Conscious that Ulysses may not have been familiar to his audience, the translator contextualizes his wanderings within the aftermath of the Trojan War. Significantly, while he needs to add material about Ulysses to sustain his moral message and simply to inform his audience about this figure's identity, he offers no details of the Trojan War. Troy is the already familiar, interpretative framework that the translator deploys to enable his audience to understand new material about Ulysses. The kinds of explanation offered in the Old English translation reveal an expectation of basic knowledge of the Roman story world as transmitted in a few well-known Latin texts – at the very least, of the broad outlines of the legendary Trojan War. In this regard, it is significant that Ulysses, who figures only tangentially in the *Aeneid*, though he is at the centre of the unknown Greek *Odyssey*, has to be placed within the Trojan context.[11]

Later in his work the translator offers fascinating insight into how his audience may have come to know the Trojan legend. Where Boethius

10 Jove and the Giants: *OEBoethius* (B Text) 35; and *OEBoethius*, ed. Godden and Irvine, 2:407–9. Ulysses and Circe: (B Text) 38; and *OEBoethius*, ed. Godden and Irvine, 2:442–6. Orpheus and Eurydice: (B Text) 35; and *OEBoethius*, ed. Godden and Irvine, 2:415–23. S. Irvine, "Ulysses and Circe."

11 Tyler, "Trojans."

records Nero's savage burning of Rome, the translator, incorporating material from a widely transmitted Latin gloss, draws a comparison to the earlier burning of Troy. Troy thus glosses or explains what happened in Rome. When the versifier subsequently turns this section into poetry, he imagines that Nero knew about Troy because the Romans talked about its destruction. In other words, he assumes that stories about Troy circulated orally, independently of the written text such as the *Aeneid*.[12] This assumption may point to the way in which knowledge about Troy circulated in the court of Alfred and that of his descendants.[13] Given the presence of a range of scholars at the court, and the expectation that learning was not to be the preserve of a Latinate clerical elite, there is no reason to think that stories from the *Aeneid* did not become part of the storytelling culture, if they were not already.[14] The translator's addition of a reference to Virgil, where Boethius had only Homer, alerts us to the status of the Roman poet in Alfredian circles. He writes of "Omerus se goda sceop þe mid Crecum selest was, se was Firgilies lareow (se Firgilius wæs mid Lædenwarum selest)" (Homer the good poet who was best among the Greeks, who was Vergil's teacher [this Vergil was the best among the Latin speakers]).[15] Homer is here identified through his relationship to Virgil, who is in turn singled out as the best Latin poet. Paradoxically, the Alfredian additions to Boethius's account of Ulysses suggest not an absence of knowledge about the Roman story world but a desire to build on and expand what was already there.

In telling the story of Ulysses's seduction by Circe and the transformation of his followers into animals, the translator engages in a metapoetic consideration that reveals his concern for the truth value of *fabulae*, an issue that will again become pressing in the *Encomium* and the *Vita Ædwardi*. He labels this story, as well as the stories of Jove and the giants, and Orpheus and Eurydice, as false ("leasum spellum"). In the case of the account of Ulysses, this term translates and brings into the text the gloss *fabula* that is found in commentaries on the Latin *Consolatio*.[16] *Lease*

12 *OEBoethius* (B Text) 16 and (C Text) Metre 9; and *OEBoethius*, ed. Godden and Irvine, 2:315 and 505.

13 For a Carolingian example of the oral circulation of material from the *Aeneid*, see Innes, "Memory, Orality," 13–18.

14 Asser, *VA* 77 and 89, and *OEPastoral Care*, preface, 7 (trans. 126).

15 *OEBoethius* (B Text) 41 and (C Text) Metre 30.

16 *OE Boethius* (B Text) 35 and 38; *OEBoethius*, ed. Godden and Irvine, 2:442. S. Irvine, "Ulysses and Circe," esp. 389; and S. Irvine, "Wrestling with Hercules," esp. 179–80.

spell, while not affirming language, is not especially harsh in comparison to the more condemnatory words related to *beswican*, for example. *Fabula* and the shifting concept it denoted would come, over the course of the following centuries, to be at the centre of urgent theorizing about fiction, including that by the Encomiast and the Anonymous.[17] In attempting to understand why searching questions about fiction were asked in the eleventh-century court, it is important to look back and recognize that the nature of *fabulae* had engaged an earlier English court, although Old English scholarship has not focused on issues of fictionality. The resolution of the question of the value of *fabulae*, as expressed in their translation of Boethius, would become both authoritative and, because it was written in English, more accessible.

Although the translator of Boethius's *Consolatio* and his circle were not worrying about a theory of fiction, as the Encomiast would begin to, they were concerned to teach their audience how to read classical myth in a Christian world. In this context, the designation of a story as *fabula* in no way stripped it of value. In recounting the myth of Orpheus and Eurydice, the translator, while using the language of falsehood to translate *fabula*, follows Boethius in asserting that the myth taught the truth – that those fleeing hell should not look behind them lest they return to their earlier sin.[18] Just as we still find it later in the twelfth century, the language of lying is used before a language of fiction has been elaborated.[19] Although the translator takes steps to make sure that his audience will not mistake pagan myth for truth, he equally seeks to prevent its dismissal.

Finally, the Alfredian treatment of Ulysses illustrates the remarkable confidence with which Alfred and his circle approached the classical past. As Susan Irvine has shown, the translator radically revised the story of Ulysses not because he misremembered or misunderstood it but because he wished to portray the Greek wanderer as a king, led astray by his immoderate lust for the goddess. Thus the story is transformed into a space for exploring the nature of good kingship, a major Alfredian preoccupation that runs throughout the *Old English Boethius*.[20] Similarly, Irvine has argued that the concern to represent Hercules as unequivocally morally admirable, and the nature of the expansions of Boethius's brief references to this divine ancient hero, reveals the desire to turn him into a model for

17 See chapters 2 and 4 herein.
18 *OEBoethius* (B Text) 35.
19 See chapter 2 herein.
20 S. Irvine, "Ulysses and Circe."

Alfred's own kingship.[21] This reworking of Boethius's *Consolatio* shows Alfred and his circle turning to Rome in order to frame their own experience, as they sought to shape Anglo-Saxon kingship in the ninth-century context of expanding West Saxon hegemony and Viking threat.[22] The translator's bold revision of Circe's seduction of Ulysses and other myths also draws our attention back to his understanding of the *fabulae* of classical antiquity. The nature of their authority and truth did not preclude his own desire to invent and imagine.

Malcolm Godden's recent questioning of Alfred's direct authorship of the *Boethius* translation, and Godden's emphasis on how difficult this philosophical text remained even in translation, demands that we not readily accept the text's claims that it was made by the king himself or assume that the text was intended to be widely disseminated among lay readers.[23] However, Godden's sense that Boethius's *Consolatio*, even in translation, would be too difficult for lay audiences might, on the contrary, be taken as evidence of an astonishing ambition on the part of Alfred and his advisers, or of later translators if that is the case. Moreover, there was no requirement that a text, having been translated into the vernacular, no longer needed to be accompanied by learned discussion to be accessible. Simply rendering a text into the vernacular written word need not remove it from the kind of culture of clerical explication that Asser represents as surrounding the king.[24] It is not only Latin texts that require interpretation. As Nicholas Howe illustrated in arguing for the integral nature of textual communities to reading in Anglo-Saxon England, the Old English word for "to read," *rædan*, is associated with the oral acts of giving advice and taking counsel. Vernacularity does not remove the need for a textual community.[25] Nor does vernacularity imply a text that is intended to become widely available; it can remain, as the *Old English Boethius* surely did, the preserve of a social and educational elite.

Alfred's desire to extend learning to the laity can also be situated within the context of the evidence of lay and royal intellectual ambition among the Carolingian elite. Within the Carolingian Empire, for example, we find not only kings, such as Charlemagne's grandsons Louis the German and

21 S. Irvine, "Wrestling with Hercules."

22 S. Irvine, "Idea of Rome."

23 Godden, "Did King Alfred Write Anything?"; and Godden, "Alfredian Project," esp. 107–14. For a counter view see Pratt, *Political Thought*, 113–350.

24 Asser, *VA* 77.

25 Howe, "Cultural Construction."

Charles the Bald, but also other laymen and women attaining high standards of learning.[26] Dhuoda, an educated woman with close connections to the court of Louis the Pious, not only wrote a handbook for her son but also read a no less demanding text than Augustine's *De civitate Dei*, which was so misunderstood, even by Orosius.[27] However, while Rosamond McKitterick in her groundbreaking study, *The Carolingians and the Written Word*, has developed a maximalist view of lay literacy within the Carolingian Empire, others are more cautious.[28] That caution and the difficulty of the *Old English Boethius* remind us that, even when we are looking at vernacular texts, lay learning, especially as distinguished from the more functional kinds of literacy required to read documents, was restricted to a small elite. But this small elite, even if it included only the king and some of his counsellors (the Old English word for this group, *witan*, emphasizes the centrality of wisdom to their role), could be highly influential in determining how the kingdom was ruled. Alfred's vision of widespread lay literacy, set out in the preface to the *Pastoral Care* and by Asser, did not have to be fully achieved to be influential. Even a modest expansion of lay literacy, facilitated by the use of the vernacular, would have had an impact on the literary culture of the court and those in contact with it. Later in this chapter other known literate laymen of the late tenth and the early eleventh century will come into view. The impact of their reading may suggest possibilities for lay literacy earlier in the tenth and the late ninth century, when it is harder to identify literary laymen (and lay women).

Alfred's sense of the enormous potential for the vernacular to enable lay access to learning is illustrated precisely by his choice of text, Boethius's *Consolatio*, a difficult text that had only recently begun to circulate in Latin in Carolingian contexts, where it did not attract lay readers like Dhuoda.[29] The translation emphasizes Boethius's own status as a layman by incorporating material from a Latin *vita* into the text, making it the first chapter.

26 McKitterick, *Written Word*, 211–70; Nelson, *Charles the Bald*, 82–5; and Goldberg, *Struggle for Empire*, 32–9 and 165–71. On lay intellectuals, including the anachronism of the term, see the introduction and contributions to Wormald and Nelson, *Lay Intellectuals* (esp. Kershaw, "Eberhard of Friuli"; Nelson, "Dhuoda"; Pratt, "Authorship"; and Ashley, "Lay Intellectual").

27 Riché, "Bibliothèques," 88–96; Dronke, *Women Writers*, 36–54; McKitterick, *Written Word*, 223–5; and Nelson, "Dhuoda."

28 McKitterick, *Written Word*. For critique see, for example, Noble, "Secular Sanctity," 28.

29 *OEBoethius*, ed. Godden and Irvine, 1:4–5. Dhuoda does not appear to have read the *Consolatio*, which also does not figure in the lists of books owned by three Carolingian lay people, as studied by Riché, "Bibliothèques."

This foregrounding of Boethius as a lay author may point to some of the attraction of the text to Alfred and his circle of scholars as they set out to challenge expectations for lay learning.[30] Perhaps, as Godden argues, Alfred's confidence in the vernacular was misplaced when it came to Boethius. However, as we shall see when we look at the *Vita Ædwardi*, a text that was very much indebted to Boethius's *Consolatio* in Latin could find educated lay readers and could attempt to influence court politics.[31]

Orosius's *Historiarum adversum paganos libri septem*

Boethius's *Consolatio* was not the only text translated in the late ninth or the early tenth century, just the most challenging. The *Old English Orosius* and the Anglo-Saxon Chronicle also show us an Anglo-Saxon elite who were informed about the world of antiquity and eager to understand their own world in relation to it.[32] Orosius's *Historiae*, as its title indicates, was fully engaged with the polemics of the late antique world. In response to Augustine's request (or so he claims) Orosius rolls out a providential view of history to defend Christians against claims that the abandonment of the pagan gods threatened the survival of the Roman Empire.[33] In the process of developing his argument that current barbarian attacks on Rome were minor compared with the suffering experienced by Rome (and its Macedonian, Carthaginian, and Babylonian imperial predecessors) before its conversion to Christianity, Orosius provides a far-reaching history of the ancient world. Widely circulated in the Middle Ages, this history was particularly valued for its synthetic account of Rome from its foundation to the fifth century AD. Such accounts contrasted with the more limited scope of the works of various classical historians. Equally, it was valued for its distinctively secular rather than ecclesiastical subject matter. In presenting a rewriting of the history of four empires from a Christian perspective, it created a new genre, a Christian history of the secular world, which contrasted with histories of the Church such as Eusebius's.[34] The

30 *OEBoethius* (B Text) 1. *OEBoethius*, ed. Godden and Irvine, notes 2:248–57.

31 See chapters 4 and 5 herein.

32 On the *Old English Orosius* see my forthcoming "Writing Universal History" and the works cited there, especially Godden, "Anglo-Saxons and Goths"; Godden, "Sources"; and Godden, "The Old English *Orosius* and Its Context."

33 Orosius, *Historiae*, prologue.

34 Mortensen, "Diffusion of Roman Histories," 101–14; Fear's introduction to his translation of the *Historiae*, 13–14; and Kempshall, *Rhetoric*, 64–78.

Old English Orosius, though both abridged and supplemented, is largely faithful to its late antique source, conveying the breadth of Orosius's vision of antiquity and his capacity to think comparatively across the histories of four successive empires.[35] Its foreshortening of Orosius's seven books reveals not exhaustion or inadequacy in the face of Orosius's at times unruly and not always coherent text, but rather a serious rereading of the text in light of the needs of an Anglo-Saxon audience.[36] Significantly, this abridgment does not separate it from contemporary approaches to the Latin text. In the ninth century, when the Latin text was being most intensively read, it was often shortened.[37] Thus, its treatment in Old English mirrors closely the parallel treatment of the Latin text in the Carolingian Empire.

The interest of lay readers also puts the *Old English Orosius* in an analogous position to the place of the Latin texts within the Carolingian Empire. The presence of Orosius's *Historiae* among the books owned by Eberhard, Count of Friuli, and his wife, Gisela, whose surviving will has made them famous examples of learned Carolingian lay people, underscores the value that lay readers placed on access to an account of the history of Rome.[38] That Gisela, who died in 874, and Alfred were rough contemporaries and that on two occasions as a child Alfred had visited the court of her brother, Charles the Bald, illustrates that the West Saxon court was using English to participate in a wider Latinate literary culture.[39] The circulation of Orosius's *Historiae* in the vernacular in Anglo-Saxon England, however, would have made it potentially more accessible to lay audiences than was the text in the Carolingian heartland.

The *Old English Orosius*'s treatment of the story world of pagan Rome, mythic, legendary, and historical, offers insight both into what an elite group of Anglo-Saxons knew about the classical world and into the attitudes they were beginning to form towards the issue of its value. Its

35 *OEOrosius*, ed. Bately, xciii–c; and Kempshall, *Rhetoric*, 76–8.

36 Whitelock, "The Prose of Alfred's Reign," 90; Godden, "Anglo-Saxons and Goths"; and Godden, "The Old English *Orosius* and Its Context," 12–13.

37 Mortensen, "Diffusion of Roman Histories," 113. On the possibility that the Old English translator was working from an abridged text of the *Historiae*, see *OEOrosius*, ed. Bately, lx; and Godden, "The Old English *Orosius* and Its Sources," on the likelihood of a glossed East Frankish exemplar.

38 Riché, "Bibliothèques," 96–101; La Rocca and Provero, "The Dead and Their Gifts"; and Kershaw, "Eberhard of Friuli."

39 Asser, *VA* 11 and 13.

chapters on Alexander and Troy, subjects that would become the stuff of romance in the twelfth century, reveal that already the capacity of these stories to breach the boundaries of history was being recognized.[40] The Alexander of the *Historiae* is a securely historical figure and, given Orosius's providential theme, one destined to be not a hero but a figure of destructive pride, a perspective that is deliberately enhanced by the Old English translator.[41] As Orosius says when he first introduces Alexander, he was "uere ille gurges miseriarum atque atrocissimus turbo totius orientis" (truly a whirlpool of sufferings and ill-wind for the entire East).[42] Alexander dominates the Old English narrative of the Macedonian empire, just as he did in the Latin original. Thus the reader of either text stands to be well informed about the ancient Macedonian conqueror and is clearly told that he deserves to be condemned, not celebrated.

Orosius also uses the Alexander material to develop a theme that will run throughout his work: that of *historia* turned to *fabula*.[43] After he finishes his account of Philip, and as he turns to Alexander, Orosius pauses to criticize those who treat the terrible disasters of the past – in this context, the conquests of these two Macedonian kings – as though they were praiseworthy. Such a stance, he complains, turns accounts of Philip and Alexander into *dulces fabulas* and obscures the fact that the pagan past was much worse than the Christian present.[44] Orosius's point about the danger of turning history into *fabula* is not lost on the Old English translator, who renders *dulces fabulas* as praise poetry when he writes:

> Ic nat, cwæð Orosius, for hwi eow Romanum sindon þa ærran gewin swa wel gelicad 7 swa lustsumlice on leoðcwidum to gehieranne, 7 for hwy ge þa tida swelcra broca swa wel hergeað, 7 nu, þeh eow lytles hwæt swelcra gebroca on becume, þonne gemænað ge hit to þæm wyrrestan tidum 7 magon hie swa hreowlice wepan swa ge magon þa'ra' oþra bliþelice hlihhan.[45]
>
> (I do not know, said Orosius, why the earlier conflicts are so well liked by you Romans and so willingly listened to in poems and why you praise so well

40 See the essays on Alexander in *Conter de Troie et d'Alexandre*, ed. Harf-Lancner, Mathey-Maille, and Szkilnik, for recent discussion.
41 Orchard, *Pride and Prodigies*, 120–5.
42 Orosius, *Historiae* 3.7.5.
43 Kempshall, *Rhetoric*, 76.
44 Orosius, *Historiae* 3.14.8.
45 *OEOrosius* 3.7.

the times of such afflictions, and now, although some small affliction happens to you, then you complain about it as the worst of times, and you can weep as miserably about it as you can laugh happily about those others.)

Earlier in the Latin, Orosius denigrated stories of the pagan gods as agents by using the language of *fabula* when he rejected the opinion of those who claimed that the god Phaeton had caused a drought:

grauis aestus incanduit, ut sol ... uniuersum orbem non calore affecisse sed igne torruisse dicatur ... ex quo etiam quidam dum non concedunt Deo ineffabilem potentiam suam, inanes ratiunculas conquirentes ridiculam Phaethontis fabulam texuerunt.

(unending heat blazed up so that it is said that the sun ... did not merely warm the entire world with its heat but roasted it with fire ... Some authors who do not grant God His ineffable might, looking for empty excuses, have weaved out of this event the ridiculous story [*ridicula ... fabula*] of Phaethon.)[46]

The Old English translator conveys the full force of Orosius's original by rendering *fabula* as "to worde 7 to leasungspelle" (story and as lying tale).[47] For Orosius and his translator who follows him, history must be kept separate from legend and myth in order to explicate the place of Rome within God's providence.[48] In a work of history rather than philosophy, like Boethius's *Consolatio*, we find a less sympathetic view of pagan myth. A reader familiar with both texts would have inherited from late antiquity not a monolithic view of *fabula* but a debate in which genre was a key element in distinguishing lies from truthful stories.

The treatment of Troy in the *Old English Orosius* is further revealing of perceptions within the Anglo-Saxon court of the dividing line between what we would term history and term fiction. In a typically late antique move, while situating it within his narrative of the foundation of Rome, Orosius severely and explicitly curtails his account of the Trojan War and the city's fall. He excuses himself from recounting these events, because

46 Orosius, *Historiae* 1.10.19.

47 *OE Orosius* 1.7.

48 Other examples of Orosius's interest in the relation between *fabula* and *historia* include *Historiae* 1.12.3, 1.12.6, 2.18.5, 2.19.4, 6.17.7–8, and 7.26.3. Some are lost in the abridgement of the Old English.

they are so well known: the war, from Homer's poetry; and the fall of Troy and Aeneas's exile, from the literary study of the school room that was dismissively referred to as "ludi litterarii disciplina" (school exercises). Writing when the fall of Troy had become a newly powerful symbol of the disintegration of the Roman Empire, he passes over in total silence Virgil's dominant and alluring account, relegating it to the education of children and unwilling to mention the poet by name. The role played by the pagan gods in the *Aeneid* was too antithetical to his own narrative of Rome's place within providential history.[49]

Superficially, the Old English translator follows Orosius, likewise excusing himself from giving more than the scantiest details, because the story is well known. Given the treatment of Troy in the *Old English Boethius*, we should not discount his expectation that Aeneas's flight from the ruins of Troy was familiar in Alfredian circles. However, it quickly becomes evident that the translator's attitude to Troy presents a direct challenge to Orosius's own. Rather than deriding Troy as the stuff of a child's education, he twice invites his reader, if they should be unfamiliar with the story, to learn more about Troy from books.[50] There is no sense that Troy is a dangerous or trivial *leasungspell* like the myth of Phaeton. Orosius's evasiveness is transformed into an occasion for learning in the Old English because the translator, while remaining on one level true to his original by not telling the story of Troy, authorizes his readers to find out more if they do not know about it. Given Virgil's central place in the grammatical curriculum, and the Boethius translator's addition of reference to him, we should also take seriously the Orosius translator's prompting of his audience.[51] And, as the reference to the fall of Troy as an oral story known to Nero suggests, we should register the likelihood that the story of Troy was available in Alfred's very international court both in the form of a text of the *Aeneid* and as stories derived from this poem but told from one person to another.[52] For the translators of Boethius's *Consolatio* and Orosius's *Historiae*, the story of Troy, while associated with poetry, had been assimilated into history. Orosius himself, though scornful, does not label accounts of Troy as *fabulae*, and he does fit the events, however briefly recounted, into the chronology of his narrative. From early on, Troy was

49 Orosius, *Historiae* 1.17–18; Coumert, *Origines*, 267–70; and Tyler, "Trojans."

50 *OEOrosius* 1.11.

51 On Virgil and the grammatical curriculum, see chapter 2 herein.

52 See above on page 24 and chapter 2.

both poetry and history; we will see this ambiguity becoming a fruitful space for the poetic and the political imagination in the eleventh century.[53] Here, that space has not yet been activated, though the ground had been laid.

Finally, before turning to the manuscripts of the *Old English Orosius*, we need to take into account not only what the text suggests about the knowledge of Virgil in late-ninth-century or early-tenth-century elite West Saxon circles but also what it shows about the limits of their access to the classical past. When confronted with reference to the Theban disaster of Oedipus and his sons, or with Medea's sowing of serpents' teeth that grew into soldiers, the translator simply skips over them entirely although Orosius had paused to label both as *fabula*.[54] Statius's *Thebaid* and Ovid's *Metamorphoses* as yet meant nothing to Anglo-Saxon audiences (and in this they are no different from those elsewhere in Europe north of the Alps).[55] The silence about the best-known stories from Statius and Ovid, texts that were not yet widely known, highlights the meaningfulness of the translator's invitation to the *Aeneid*. Later, in the mid-eleventh century, the reception of Statius and Ovid would transform Anglo-Saxon literature.

Although translated at the end of the ninth century or at the beginning of the tenth century, the *Old English Orosius* continued to be copied and used throughout the late Anglo-Saxon period. In addition to the earliest surviving manuscript dating from the first half of the tenth century, a further full text and two fragments, all from the first half of the eleventh century, have been preserved.[56] If manuscript survival is in any way indicative, the vernacular version eclipsed the Latin original until the middle of the eleventh century, when Latin history writing came to prevail in the Anglo-Saxon court.[57] For over a century and a half, from Alfred's reign onwards, English was the dominant language of history – not restricted to the history of England but suitable too for the history of antiquity. Contemporary Anglo-Saxon history, in the form of the various versions of the Anglo-Saxon Chronicle, which developed from the Common Stock,

53 Tilliette, "*Troiae ab oris*."

54 Orosius, *Historiae* 6.17.7 and 7.26.3.

55 Reynolds, ed., *Texts and Transmission*, 394 for the *Thebaid* and 276–82 for the *Metamorphoses*; discussed further in chapters 4 and 5 herein.

56 *OEOrosius*, ed. Bately, xxiii–xxvi.

57 Gneuss and Lapidge, *Bibliographical Handlist of Manuscripts*, entries for Orosius's *Historiae* and the *OEOrosius*.

was also firmly within the realm of the vernacular.[58] There are, moreover, connections between the vernacularity of the Chronicle and the *Old English Orosius*. The Common Stock was produced within the Alfredian education program, to which the *Old English Orosius* also had connections. Looking ahead to the tenth century, Malcolm Parkes has argued, and Janet Bately has cautiously accepted, that the second scribe of the "A" version of the Anglo-Saxon Chronicle (Cambridge, Corpus Christi College 173), based in Winchester, also made the oldest surviving copy of the *Old English Orosius* (London, British Library, Add. 47967), suggesting that these two texts continued to share an audience (one that was likely close to the court) in the decades after Alfred's reign.[59] This sense of an intimate relationship between Roman and contemporary history will be strengthened when we look forward into the eleventh century, into the decades around the production of the *Encomium Emmae reginae*.

In the mid-eleventh century, version "C" of the Chronicle was carefully added to the early-eleventh-century copy of the *Old English Orosius* to form what Katherine O'Brien O'Keeffe has called a "book of histories" (London, British Library, Cotton Tiberius B. i).[60] Orosius's secular subject matter, interpreted within a Christian frame, made it an attractive partner for the Chronicle. The purposeful combining of the *Old English Orosius* and the Chronicle brings ancient history up to the present day. The way in which the Chronicle begins, with Julius Caesar's conquest of Britain, while creating a chronological overlap between itself and Orosius's account, also illustrates how well the two texts fit together. For the Chronicler, as for Bede on whom he drew, history is a Roman genre, and thus Anglo-Saxon history begins not with the pre-migration experience of various Germanic peoples on the Continent but with Caesar's incorporation of Britain into the Roman Empire some five hundred years earlier.[61] Although the representation of Rome in the *Old English Orosius* as almost undisturbed by the gentleness of the Gothic sack of 410 clashes with the Anglo-Saxon Chronicle's vision of an event so cataclysmic that the

58 Pratt, *Political Thought*, 117. Although the Latin manuscripts of Bede outnumber the English, the vernacular makes a strong showing in this period with 4:7. Gneuss and Lapidge, *Bibliographical Handlist of Manuscripts*, entries for Bede's *HE* and the *OEOrosius*.

59 *OEOrosius*, ed. Bately, xxiii; Parkes, "Palaeography of the Parker Manuscript," 156–7; Dumville strongly disagrees, in *Wessex and England*, 55–139.

60 ASC "C," ed. O'Brien O'Keefe, xlii; and see further my "Writing Universal History."

61 Bede, *HE* 1.2; and ASC "C" *s.a.* B.C. 60.

Romans withdrew from Britain, making way for the Anglo-Saxons, fundamentally both texts share a compatible view of history writing.[62] Bede's comment that King Æthelbert's production of written law codes early in the seventh century, shortly after his conversion to Christianity, was done in the Roman manner, even though those law codes were written in English, makes the point that genre (in this case written law) and the act of writing (rather than the language of writing) can determine a Roman horizon of interpretation.[63] Within the expectations of written history, the Anglo-Saxons are encouraged to see themselves in Roman terms.

Given the structure of Orosius's *Historiae*, which combines a narrative of one empire overlapping with and succeeding the next in a steady *translatio imperii* from east to west, with a repeated instruction to those living in the Christian present to compare their own experience with that of the pagan past, the combining of the *Old English Orosius* with the Chronicle shows Roman history, especially of the pagan period, being actively related to Anglo-Saxon history. The manuscript compiler, by chronologically overlapping his account of Britain with that of the Roman Empire in the *Historiae*, perpetuated Orosius's own method of telling intermingled or interwoven history.[64] Orosius's *Historiae*, in Latin as much as in English, cannot be understood as a classicizing text that would forge a link through emulation between the present and the pagan past of classical Rome (indeed that past is rejected). Rather, the Christian present and the pagan past are brought into dialogue, a dialogue based on knowledge of that past. Classicism will come to replace condemnation with admiration, but crucially Orosius's text, in English as well as in Latin, has already taught the habit of using Rome to think with. Indeed even in the twelfth century, for all their confident classicism, writers still turned to Orosius's *Historiae* to obtain a broad sweep of Roman history.[65]

Looking at the social and political context in which version "C" came together with Orosius contextualizes this move to see Anglo-Saxon history in terms of Roman history and reveals lay as well as ecclesiastical

---

62 Godden, "Anglo-Saxons and Goths."

63 Bede, *HE* 2.5. *Old English Bede* (hereafter cited as *OEBede)* 2.5 carries over this notion of written law as Roman.

64 Kempshall, *Rhetoric*, 67–8, 74, and 77–8.

65 Mortensen "Diffusion of Roman Histories"; and Mortensen, "Working with Ancient Roman History," 416–18.

investment in this move. In the mid-eleventh century the different versions of the Anglo-Saxon Chronicle that grew from the Alfredian Common Stock came to be associated closely with the different factions who struggled for dominance in Edward the Confessor's England. Version "C" supports the House of Leofric, Earl of Merica; version "E" (Oxford, Bodleian Library, Laud misc. 636) supports the House of Godwine, Earl of Wessex; and version "D" (London, British Library, Cotton Tiberius B. iv, fols. 3–9, 19–86) takes a more court perspective.[66] This investment of versions "C," "D," and "E" in the factional politics of the period illustrates that, although chronicle writing was a monastic activity, the resulting chronicles were not monastic chronicles; indeed Brooks has recently strongly emphasized their royal character.[67] The full engagement of the various Anglo-Saxon Chronicles with secular history and with competing accounts of contemporary events suggests that the keeping of history was an active part of mid-eleventh-century political discourse.

Leofric, who died in 1057, provides a vivid example of a layman at the meeting point of monastic and royal concerns. Appointed by King Cnut, the earl was known as a benefactor of Benedictine monasticism (as well as remembered for some monastic depredations) and as a loyal supporter of Edward against the Godwines in the 1040s and 1050s.[68] This meeting of monastic, aristocratic, and royal interests is neatly mirrored by the two texts that link, rather than divide, the *Old English Orosius* and the Chronicle in Cotton Tiberius B. i. The *Menologium* is a calendar poem, indebted to computus and concerned with the cycle of the ecclesiastical year. Its final lines ally this monastic perspective with royal power and the ambition of the West Saxon dynasty:

Nu ge findan magon
haligra tiida þe man healdan sceal,
swa bebugeð gebod geond Brytenricu
Sexna kyninges on þas sylfan tiid.

66 For a recent discussion, with references to earlier scholarship, see Baxter, "MS C," 1189–94; and Keynes, "Manuscripts," 547.

67 Brooks, "Why Is the *Anglo-Saxon Chronicle* about Kings?"

68 Baxter, *Earls of Mercia*, 32–43; and Williams, "Leofric."

(Now you are able to discover the saints' feast days that are to be observed wherever the command of the Saxons' king extends throughout Britain in this present time.)[69]

Meanwhile, *Maxims II* seeks to place a series of proverbs that are largely preoccupied with secular aristocratic life, including advice on good kingship, within a vision of God's providence consonant with the *Old English Orosius*.[70] The choice to link the two historical texts with poetry extends the quasi-prosimetrical mode of the Anglo-Saxon Chronicle of the tenth and eleventh centuries to the entire manuscript and thus represents poetry and history writing as intimately related. The Encomiast and the Anonymous author of the *Vita Ædwardi* both interrogate the relation of poetry and history as ways of recounting contemporary politics.

Returning to Leofric, the coming together of these four texts suits his role well as royal supporter and monastic benefactor and encourages us to look seriously at figures like Leofric, if not the earl himself, as readers of or listeners to all the texts of Cotton Tiberius B. i. As the work of James Campbell and Simon Keynes has stressed, there is much evidence for substantial literacy, especially in the vernacular, among the late Anglo-Saxon lay elite in the areas of law and administration, and Campbell's work also considers the role of this elite in the production and reception of literary texts.[71] The Chronicle is not the only vernacular text associated with the earl. The *Visio Leofrici*, written in English shortly after his death, finds Leofric by Edward's side, protecting the king's interests militarily and in prayer. The earl's close support of the monastic way of life, which might have encouraged him to cultivate book learning, whether by reading or by listening, is illustrated by the *Visio*'s account of his appearance in priest's vestments and his custom of praying at Dunstan's tomb.[72]

Just as the abbreviation of the *Old English Orosius* was fully in step with the latest Carolingian developments in the ninth century, its combination

69 *Menologium* lines 228–31.

70 *Maxims II*. Robinson links the two poems with the Chronicle but not with the *OE Orosius* ("Most Immediate Context," 27–8).

71 Keynes's "Royal Government" and, from among Campbell's many articles, "England c. 991" (esp. 6–8, 10–11, and 14–16) most explicitly make the link between the levels of literacy needed to govern the kingdom and the literary culture. Both Keynes and Campbell build on, but disagree with, Wormald's seminal articles ("*Lex Scripta*" and "Uses of Literacy"), which see less evidence for personal literacy among the laity.

72 *Vision of Leofric*. Baxter, *Earls of Mercia*, 1–4.

with the Chronicle is not a weak vernacular echo, several centuries later, of a Carolingian practice but an early example of a new and important phenomenon in the use of Orosius's *Historiae* in the eleventh and twelfth centuries. It is in this period that the *Historiae* first began to be brought together with other historical texts, whether to range more fully across antiquity or to bring the account more closely up to the present day.[73] This use of the *Historiae* is part of a growing interest in the period in the Roman past and its relationship with the present that so marks our notion of the twelfth-century renaissance. Rather than cutting off the Anglo-Saxons from such intellectual developments, the presence of Orosius's *Historiae* in the vernacular may have encouraged such thinking.[74]

The *Epistola Alexandri ad Aristotelem*

With its wild tales of an overweening king, the *Letter of Alexander to Aristotle* (*Letter of Alexander*) continues Orosius's representation of pagan antiquity as not fit for emulation. The Old English version was probably translated from the Latin between the late ninth and the late tenth century, and the Latin itself was translated from an earlier Greek text by the seventh century at the latest.[75] Although its view of Alexander is less harsh than that found in the translation of Orosius's *Historiae*, it remains condemnatory.[76] The intimate relationship between the Old English translation of the *Letter of Alexander* and *Beowulf* throws into high relief the association of *fabula* with the Roman, rather than the Germanic, story world. Not only does *Beowulf* immediately follow the *Letter of Alexander* in the manuscript, but, as Andy Orchard has persuasively suggested, "the tissue of echoes and parallel, both verbal and thematic, that links the *Letter of Alexander* and *Beowulf* is perhaps explained by the notion that the author of the *Letter* knew the poem at first hand, and consciously developed hints in his original text in a way which deliberately drew on aspects of *Beowulf*."[77] Thus the divergence of the *Letter of Alexander* from *Beowulf*

73 Mortensen, "Diffusion of Roman Histories," 119–65; and Mortensen, "Working with Ancient Roman History," 416–18.

74 Tyler, "Writing Universal History."

75 Powell, "*Alexander the Great*"; Stoneman, "Latin Alexander," 168; and Stoneman, "Medieval Alexander," 238.

76 Orchard, *Pride and Prodigies*, 120–4.

77 Orchard, *Critical Companion*, 25–39, esp. 35.

in its commentary on the representation of the unbelievable is particularly striking.

The Old English *Letter of Alexander* takes over the Latin *Epistola Alexandri*'s concern to defend itself against the charge of being made up, as either a *fabula* or lies. Early on in the *Letter*, Alexander raises the problem of credibility, assuring his tutor:

> Þa ic þe write 7 cyþe, 7 æghwylc þara is wyrðe synderlice in gemyndum to habbanne æfter þære wisan þe ic hit oferseah. Ne gelyfde ic æniges monnes gesegenum swa fela wundorlicra þinga þæt hit swa beon mihte ær ic hit self minum eagum ne gesawe. Seo eorðe is to wundrienne hwæt heo ærest oþþe godra þinga cenne, oððe eft þara yfelra, þe heo þæm sceawigendum is ætewed. Hio is cennende þa fulcuþan wildeora 7 wæstma 7 wecga oran, 7 wunderlice wyhta, þa þing eall þæm monnum þe hit geseoð 7 sceawigað wæron uneþe to gewitanne for þære missenlicnisse þara hiowa.
>
> Ac þa ðing þe me nu in gemynd cumað ærest þa ic þe write, þy læs on me mæge idel spellung oþþe scondlic leasung beon gestæled. Hwæt þu eac sylfa const þa gecynd mines modes mec a gewunelice healdon þæt gemerce soðes 7 rihtes.
>
> (These things I write and tell you, and each of them is individually worth bearing in mind exactly as I observed it. I would not have believed the words of any man that so many marvelous things could be so before I saw them myself with my own eyes. The earth is a source of wonder first for the good things she brings forth, and then for the evil, through which she is revealed to observers. She is the producer of well-known wild beasts, and plants, and stone and metal-ore, and of wondrous creatures, all those things which are difficult to comprehend for those who look and observe because of the variety of their forms.
>
> But now I will write to you about those things that come first to mind, in case I can be accused of empty talk and shameful lies. Look, you yourself know that the nature of my mind is always such as to keep me continually within the boundaries of what is true and right.)[78]

Idel spellung and *scondlic leasung* render the Latin *fabula* and *turpe mendacium*.[79] The sheer length of this insistence on truth brings it into the

78 *LAA*, 226–7.
79 *EAA*, 205.

foreground. Admitting that Alexander's adventures may not seem credible alerts the reader that the classical pagan past has become a place in which the suspension of disbelief is invited, a critical element of fiction.

As Orosius warned, tales about Alexander teeter between history and legend, and the association with Hercules, which is made explicit in another text from the *Beowulf* manuscript, the *Wonders of the East*, draws them close to myth.[80] Significantly, it is in the *Letter of Alexander*, not in *Beowulf* – which could equally stake a claim to narrate the unbelievable and which may have supplied the language for some of the most fabulous descriptions in the *Letter of Alexander* – that the issue of credibility is raised.[81] The Roman story world becomes a space for the imagination, a place of *fabula*, although the possibilities that this presents are not yet articulated as they would come to be later in the eleventh and the twelfth century.

Not incidental to our present discussion, the representation of Alexander will become fully implicated in the process whereby, from the twelfth century onwards, history and romance come to define themselves in opposition to each other. Indeed, the Latin *Letter of Alexander* would be found, through its inclusion in the *Historia de preliis*, among the sources of the earliest romance of Alexander, the influential late-twelfth-century *Roman d'Alexandre*.[82] The matter of Alexander, just like the matter of Troy, lent itself to both historical and fabulous representations, which were sometimes contained in the High Middle Ages within a single manuscript, pointing to medieval awareness of this contradictory variety.[83] The possibility for this awareness is present even within the restricted field of the Anglo-Saxon vernacular with *Old English Orosius*, the *Letter of Alexander*, and the *Wonders of the East* offering different perspectives on Alexander and other Latin accounts. These texts, evidently known at least to the *Old English Orosius* translator, were all available, even if in limited circulation.[84] In answer to the question of how a reference to the *vetus fabula* (ancient fable) could make political meaning in Emma's *Encomium*, the *Letter of Alexander* illustrates that vernacular literary culture had already

80 Orchard, *Pride and Prodigies*, 131.
81 Orchard, *Critical Companion*, 35.
82 Alexander of Paris, *Roman d'Alexandre*; and Cary, *Medieval Alexander*, 15, 29–32, 38, and 43–4.
83 Baumgartner, "Formation du mythe."
84 Orchard, *Pride and Prodigies*, 116–39 (esp. 118–20).

worked to accustom late Anglo-Saxon audiences, lay as well as clerical, to enjoying, and even at times consciously considering the value of, made-up and at times contradictory stories of pagan antiquity. The political preoccupations of the *Letter of Alexander*, with lordship and conquest, were not remote from those of the reigns of Æthelred and Cnut. Moreover, the *Letter*, with its depiction of Alexander writing to his tutor Aristotle, represents lay people fully engaged with the issue of what makes a narrative credible; this subject would become pressing as the Anglo-Danish realm collapsed and again as different accounts were offered of the causes of the Norman Conquest.[85]

Historia Apollonii regis Tyri

Among the many copies, reworkings, and retellings of the Latin *Historia Apollonii regis Tyri* is an Old English translation dating from the late tenth or the early eleventh century.[86] The *Historia Apollonii*, like Boethius's *Consolatio*, Orosius's *Historiae*, and the *Letter of Alexander*, is a late antique text. Although there is no scholarly consensus as to whether the *Historia Apollonii* was composed initially in Greek or in Latin and whether it was composed in a Christian or a pagan milieu, the world it purports to portray is that of pagan antiquity.[87] In distinction to Boethius's *Consolatio*, Orosius's *Historiae*, the *Epistola Alexandri*, and their Old English translations, the *Historia Apollonii* focuses on family life, including romantic love. The contrasting fortunes of two eastern Mediterranean dynasties are narrated as the intersection of family life and dynastic politics are scrutinized. In the first dynasty, order is perverted by incest and the king loses his throne, while his daughter remains unredeemed within the text. In the second, exemplary marriages of chaste and dutiful daughters to suitably aristocratic suitors ensure dynastic continuity. Antiquity becomes a space within which to explore the interconnectedness of proper relations between fathers and daughters, marriage, good kingship, and dynastic stability. In this vision of antiquity, though there is no conflict with Christian values (the chastity of daughters and the faithfulness of spouses

---

85 *LAA*, 224–7.

86 *HAp*, ed., Kortekaas, 14–22, and appendix 1, 413–18; and *ApT*, ed. Goolden, xxxiv. For extensive discussion of the *Apollonius* see Archibald, *Apollonius of Tyre*.

87 *HAp*, ed. Kortekaas, 97–131; Hexter, Review of *Historia Apollonii*, ed. Kortekaas; and Schmeling, "*History of Apollonius*," 143–5.

are rewarded), the fundamental interest lies in secular life. The most pagan episode, the discovery of Apollonius's lost wife in the temple of Diana, brings no uneasiness.[88] The deliberate consonance of the behaviour of Apollonius and his family with Christian teaching, especially about sexual continence, as well as the absence of condemnation of paganism, means that the text lends itself to an exemplary Christian reading. Behind this consonance, moreover, lies a willingness to use pagan antiquity to explore Christian values – a willingness that cannot be reduced to the figurative, for instance the temple to Diana being read simply as a nunnery.

The way in which the story of Apollonius, in Latin and Old English, simultaneously provides a space to consider the secular world away from the overtly pastoral concerns for salvation, and allows just such religious concerns to be taught, may account not only for its popularity but also for the ecclesiastical transmission of its many manuscripts and versions. The absence of conflict between Christian and pagan values within *Apollonius* means that both antiquity and paganism, and thus the Roman story world, open up an imaginative space. This space will become fully exploited over the course of the eleventh and twelfth centuries as the classical past is turned to for new models, especially for secular experience. *Apollonius* presents a sharp contrast to *Beowulf*, the *Letter of Alexander*, and the *Orosius*, in all of which paganism, whether Germanic or Roman, provides negative rather than positive exempla. The *Historia Apollonii*, a text whose manuscript transmission suggests that it found new popularity from the eleventh century onwards, offers a markedly different way of viewing the paganism of the Roman story world, and one that was shared by its Old English translation.[89] In later manuscripts the proximity of the *Historia Apollonii* to Trojan material alerts us to the importance of this new outlook in allowing the story of Rome's foundation from the ruins of Troy to become a powerful poetic and political language in the eleventh and twelfth century.[90]

88 *ApT* 36 (trans. 295).

89 *HAp*, ed. Kortekaas, 14–22, and appendix 1, 413–18.

90 Florence, Biblioteca Medicea Laurenziana, Plut. lxvi.40, fols. 62r–70v, from Monte Cassino (s. IXex); Leiden Universiteitsbibliotheek, Voss. Lat. F. 113, fols. 30v–38v, probably from Tours (s. IXmed); Oxford, Magdalen College, 50, fols. 88r–108r, probably of English origin (s. XIIin), all discussed in *HAp*, ed. Kortekaas, 24, 37–8, and 41–2. Tilliette, "*Troiae ab oris*."

The manuscript context of the surviving copy of the Old English *Apollonius* indicates that this positive view of the Roman story world was authorized at the highest levels of the Anglo-Saxon Church. The Old English *Apollonius* appears in Cambridge, Corpus Christi College 201, probably a New Minster, Winchester, manuscript. In this manuscript, from the centre of West Saxon ecclesiastical and political power, *Apollonius* comes at the end of a series of homiletic and legal texts that were written by or closely associated with Wulfstan. Patrick Wormald thinks it likely that these texts, which he labels a "Wulfstanian primer of Christian standards," came together in York, where Wulfstan was archbishop from 1002 until his death in 1023.[91] Wulfstan, adviser to both Æthelred and Cnut, had been at the heart of the English court since his elevation to the bishopric of London in 996. As such, he wrote laws in the name of the king and, as we see in his famous *Sermo Lupi*, unflinchingly preached repentance and Christian behaviour to both these successive kings, their courts, and their followers.[92] In a period when the Church was exerting greater control over the institution of marriage, *Apollonius*, with its faithful marriages and sexual continence, was well suited for use as an exemplary text by Wulfstan or those within his orbit. The regulation of marriage recurs throughout this section of Corpus Christi College 201, and yet, as Pauline Stafford writes, Wulfstan kept "tactful silence on issues of divorce, concubinage and polygamy."[93] The nature of Christian marriage must have been an especially live issue in the court of Cnut, a king who maintained two consorts, Ælfgifu of Northampton and Emma.[94] Perhaps the indirectness of using *Apollonius* to censor a king offers us some insight into the delicate position occupied by courtier bishops, who were vulnerable to the king's power, yet accountable before God for the king's soul. Wulfstan himself chastises bishops who shirk their pastoral responsibilities, in a text, *The Institutes of Polity*, which is found in the same section of Corpus Christi College 201 as *Apollonius*.[95] The bringing together

91 Wormald, *Making of English Law*, 204–10; and Anlezark, "Reading 'The Story of Joseph,'" 92 (note Anlezark's caution regarding when and where *Apollonius* joined the Wulfstan material).

92 Wormald, "Archbishop Wulfstan"; and Wormald, "Wulfstan."

93 Stafford, *QEQE*, 229; Lees, "Engendering Religious Desire," 36–9; Morini, "Old English *Apollonius*"; and Heyworth, "*Apollonius of Tyre*."

94 Stafford, *QEQE*, 73–4, 86–7, 229, 233–4, and 243–4; and Stafford, "Ælfgifu." See also chapter 2 herein.

95 Wulfstan, *Institutes of Polity*, 59–77 (trans. 108–10).

of *Apollonius* with law codes, homilies, and a treatise on the order of society was a bold and inspired choice, whether on the part of Wulfstan himself or of another cleric, to turn to the positive representation of pagan antiquity and a new type of story – a tale of adventure and love – to teach the Church's new values on marriage in a court whose king flagrantly disregarded them. Perhaps it is precisely to this difficult situation that we owe the survival of the Old English *Apollonius*. That a need to communicate with the Anglo-Saxon lay elite about family life shaped the ways in which church men used, wrote, and preserved literary culture reminds us that lay audiences are a critical component of the recourse to antiquity as a site of emulation rather than condemnation.

Where the *Apollonius* of Corpus Christi College 201 allows us to see clerics at the highest level of the Anglo-Saxon Church turning to the Roman story world to carry out their pastoral responsibilities, the reference to a copy at Burton Abbey may allow us to see that the interest in the Roman story world could also come from the laity. Potentially, both lay and clerical interests worked to make *Apollonius* popular. The text, which appears as *Apollonium anglice* among a small number of Old English texts in the monastery's late-twelfth-century library catalogue, may have come to the foundation in the eleventh century.[96] Strong thematic connections between the life of nobleman Wulfric, the founder of Burton Abbey, and the text of *Apollonius* suggest that his status as benefactor may not have been coincidental to the text's presence at Burton (although we cannot press this possibility too far given that the manuscript is part of a monastic library and not certainly from the eleventh century). Monastic and lay interests, especially in the period of the Benedictine Reform when laymen like Wulfric supported monks, are not opposed, as we have already seen clearly in the person of Leofric. From this perspective, *Apollonius*, a text suited to both lay and clerical appropriation, reveals the role that the laity played in influencing the texts created and preserved in monasteries.

From the mid-tenth century Wulfric's family were close allies of the West Saxon kings as these kings sought to extend their power north into Mercia and the formerly Viking-controlled Northumbria. The foundation of Burton Abbey (by 1004), the only Benedictine house in central Mercia at that time, illustrates well Wulfric's support for a royal dynasty whose efforts to unify England had gone hand in hand with the promulgation of

96 Lapidge, *Anglo-Saxon Library*, 72; and Sharpe, et al., *Benedictine Libraries*, 33–42.

reformed monasticism.[97] Æthelred's charters show that Wulfric was regularly at court in the company of a group of leading noblemen who were distinguished by their learning and their promotion of the Benedictines. These men included Æthelweard and Æthelmær, Ælfric's very active patrons who not only provided funding for his monastery at Eynsham but also pushed him to make translations, including from the Bible, even when he was reluctant. Laymen, as well as clerics, took pastoral care seriously, and agency in the provision of texts could lie with both groups. Æthelweard, who translated the Anglo-Saxon Chronicle from Old English into Latin for his cousin the Abbess Matilda of Essen, was exceptionally learned. Also in this group was Ordulf, uncle of Æthelred, who owned a text by Rabanus Maurus and who may have retired to Tavistock, the abbey that he founded.[98] Literate associates do not make Wulfric himself literate, but he stands out as a man who was part of a world that was focused on the king, in which learned laymen actively promoted the use of the vernacular. Thinking about these men, when we turn to consider what may have attracted them to *Apollonius*, we cannot help but be struck by the thematic importance of literacy, among both men and women, within the text (as was also the case in the *Letter of Alexander* and the *Old English Boethius*). We should not overlook the affinity of the noblemen of *Apollonius*, who become *ealdormen* in the English translation, with men like Wulfric. Without insisting on a direct connection between Corpus Christi College 201, whose copy of *Apollonius* may come from York, and the Burton copy, we notice that Wulfstan, archbishop of York, was at court at the same time as Æthelweard, Æthelmær, Ordulf, and Wulfric and that Ælfhelm, ealdorman of southern Northumbria (York), was Wulfric's brother.[99] These men are among the potential audiences of *Apollonius of Tyre* in York, in Winchester, and at Burton.

The women of the story of Apollonius also draw our attention back to the family of Wulfric. In *Apollonius*, kingdoms twice pass through a female heiress to her successful suitor. Not only Apollonius, but also his son-in-law, inherits the throne in this way, and the incestuous desire of King Antiochus for his daughter results in the loss of his kingdom. The

---

97 Sawyer, ed., *Charters of Burton Abbey*, xxxviii–xliii; Sawyer, "Charters of Burton Abbey," 30; Stafford, *Unification and Conquest*, 153–4 and 158; and Insley, "Family of Wulfric Spott," 122–3.

98 Keynes, *Diplomas*, 188–93; Cubitt, "Ælfric's Lay Patrons," esp. 171; and Gretsch, "Historiography."

99 Sawyer, *Charters of Burton*, 45–53 (S878 and S906).

text also emphasizes the role that these women play in choosing their own husbands. Wulfric, who is, unusually, referred to as his mother's rather than his father's son (*Wulfrune sunu*), may well have inherited his own position through her.[100] His mother was sufficiently important that her kidnap by Vikings in 945 is recorded by the Anglo-Saxon Chronicle, a text that is notoriously uninterested in women. While his father remains unknown, his mother left her mark on the written record, which remembers her endowment of a secular foundation at Wolverhampton, a town that still bears her name. Wulfric, who appears to have had no son of his own, may have been doubly aware of the attractiveness of a rich heiress, all the more because his own daughter (described as *earm* in his will, and resident in the nunnery at Tamworth) did not take on this role. His will makes careful provision for her and seeks to protect her interests; she may have been an invalid and not suited to marriage.[101]

Wulfric was dead by c. 1004, and his brother, Ælfhelm, fell from favour in 1006 when Æthelred had him murdered and his sons blinded. However, in the next generation, the family of the founder of Burton may have continued to find the story of Apollonius topical, as well as good entertainment. The continued power of this family is illustrated by their successful maintenance of their political influence even after Ælfhelm's demise.[102] Cnut's first consort, Ælfgifu, was Ælfhelm's daughter and Wulfric's niece. Her strategic alliance with Cnut, through which he sought to gain control of the Midlands, and her effective support of her son Harold Harefoot's claim to the throne after Cnut's death (in the face of Emma's counter-efforts on behalf of her own sons) would have made her and those around her keenly aware of women's roles in dynastic politics. The promotion of monogamous faith to one spouse in *Apollonius* may have had particular resonance as Harold, Harthacnut, Alfred, and Edward, the sons of Cnut and of Æthelred by Emma and Ælfgifu, respectively, vied for the throne and tore the kingdom apart. Across three generations, from Wulfrun to her granddaughter Ælfgifu, the family of Wulfric Spot would have been well aware of the political impact of dynastic marriage.

100 Sawyer, *Charters of Burton*, xxxviii; and Kelly, ed., *Charters of Abingdon*, 1:126 (S886).

101 See Whitelock, *Anglo-Saxon Wills*, for a text, translation, and full notes, 46–51 and 151–60. Sawyer, *Charters of Burton*, xxxviii–xliii; and Barlow, *English Church*, 316.

102 Stafford, *Unification and Conquest*, 158.

Meanwhile, the monks of Burton Abbey may have found the text useful in teaching new ecclesiastical values about marriage to a wider circle of laymen. In this regard, we can note that Leofric, Earl of Mercia, whose father had been at court alongside Æthelweard and other learned laymen and whose own investment in vernacular literary culture was suggested earlier, was among the benefactors of Burton in the reign of Edward. He may have been a relative of Wulfric's family.[103] The story of Apollonius seems especially well suited to the situation of the men and women of Wulfric Spot's family and reminds us to see it as a text that lay people may have sought, as well as a text to which monks turned to teach them. In this sense it shares important affinities with some twelfth-century romances. Most obvious are two romances of antiquity: the *Roman d'Eneas*, an Old French recasting of the *Aeneid* that was likewise engaged with the intersection of women's affections and dynastic politics, which will be discussed in the context of Emma's *Encomium*; and the *Roman de Thèbes*, a reworking of Statius's *Thebaid* that also reveals women's place within a dynastic politics that was torn apart by fratricide and incest, which will be discussed in the context of Edith and the *Vita Ædwardi*.[104] Given the nature of the evidence, this reconstruction of the context of Burton's *Apollonius anglice* can only be highly speculative. But its consideration within this chapter serves a specific purpose: to highlight the connections between *Apollonius*, both in Corpus Christi College 201 and in the Burton booklist, and Anglo-Saxon court circles in which the imperatives of secular life and lay learning combine to impel a new, positive version of pagan antiquity among a small but influential elite.

Daniel Anlezark's rich codicological approach to the unity and context of Corpus Christi College 201 reminds us also to keep women readers in view. The manuscript, in its mid-eleventh-century form, begins and ends with texts gendered for women. His powerful suggestion that the manuscript may have been shaped for a female audience such as Nunnaminster draws attention to Anglo-Saxon royal nunneries whose communities often brought together religious and secular women who moved freely between court and cloister.[105] Later chapters will argue that the *Vita Ædwardi*, with its deep investment in the Roman story world, was written for just

103 Sawyer, *Charters of Burton*, xliii and 30; and Stafford, *Unification and Conquest*, 158.

104 *Roman d'Eneas*. See chapters 3, 4, and 5 herein.

105 Anlezark, "Reading 'The Story of Joseph,'" 93–4.

such an audience at the royal nunnery of Wilton. This reading community might have included women who were prepared for the Anonymous's radical turn to Roman epic in his search for ways of narrating the chaos of Edward's reign by the earlier vernacular *Apollonius*.[106]

Finally and less speculatively, *Apollonius* allows us to step back and look at the English vernacular literary culture of the early eleventh century in a larger European context. In a Northern Italian chronicle in the 1020s, almost contemporary with Wulfstan's period as courtier bishop, we find a king who had slept with his daughter-in-law being rebuked by reference to the bad king Antiochus.[107] Meanwhile, the Latin *Apollonius* was known to the Norman court in the early eleventh century. The text appeared together with poems that, according to Elisabeth van Houts, satirized the marriage of Emma and Cnut, and with poems that were closely associated with the patronage of Emma's mother, Gunnor. Emma may have been familiar with the story of Apollonius on both sides of the channel, in Latin and in English.[108] In their will Eberhard and his wife, Gisela, had left a copy of the *Historia Apollonii* to their married daughter Engeltrud in the ninth century.[109] But thereafter manuscripts of the text and references to the story disappear from view until the beginning of the eleventh century, when the *Historia Apollonii* seems to have found new relevance, perhaps created by concerns to implement the Church's new teachings on marriage.[110] From this perspective its English translation is not an example of vernacular literary culture lagging behind Latin, but rather we see it fully in step with the latest developments. Kortekaas, the text's most recent editor, characterizes the *Historia Apollonii* as a *texte vivant* – appearing in many different recensions, open to editorial intervention, abbreviation, and wholesale reworking; the Old English text (itself shortened from the Latin), which comes very early in the text's high medieval revival, should be placed firmly within that *texte vivant* tradition.[111]

106 See chapters 4 and 5 herein.

107 *Chronicon Novaliciense* 5.3 (Archibald, *Apollonius*, 219, includes an excerpt and a translation).

108 Paris, Bibliothèque nationale de France, lat. 8121A. *Jezebel*, ed. Ziolkowski, 29; and Van Houts, "*Jezebel* and *Semiramis*."

109 Kershaw, "Eberhard," 105.

110 *HAp*, ed. Kortekaas, 15–22.

111 *HAp*, ed. Kortekaas, 3–146, and Hexter's review, 186.

Conclusion

The *Old English Boethius*, the *Old English Orosius*, the *Letter of Alexander*, and the story of Apollonius, each in their own way, reveal that the vernacular literary culture of England was not only in step with but also on the cutting edge of the latest developments in continental Latin literature. Their strong engagement with secular life, the prominence of lay learning within all but the *Old English Orosius*, and the likelihood that these texts found lay audiences, if not lay readers, all stand out. Together these features suggest that the laity played a role, similar to the pressure exerted on Ælfric by Æthelweard to translate the Bible, in the ambitious expectations that translators, compilers, and scribes had for the vernacular in late Anglo-Saxon England. While these texts, which arose in their Latin forms in the world of late antiquity, were not classicizing, they did in various ways pave the way for an openness to the intellectual project of classicism, which had at its root an emulation of antiquity that would shape poetics, vernacular literature, modes of persuasion, and politics in the next century. The *Old English Orosius* would have left Anglo-Saxon audiences with a basic grasp of the chronology of Roman history. As we shall see when we turn to the *Vita Ædwardi*, Boethian thought would become a major influence as poets, from the mid-eleventh century onwards, sought to justify their new-found appreciation of the Roman story world.[112] Even though the Latin and English versions of Orosius's *Historiae* and the *Epistola Alexandri* take hostile views of pagan antiquity, they witness a fascination with this past and a desire to understand the present in relation to it. In contrast, Boethius's *Consolatio* and the *Historia Apollonii*, and their translations, insist on the exemplarity of the pagan past. Distanced from Boethius's neoplatonic rather than Christian stance, the Alfredian translators negotiated and (in the case of Hercules) even expanded on the exemplarity of the myths of pagan Roman that they found in their model. Key to this move was the incorporation and development within the translation of the ideas about the nature of *fabula*, which they found in the glosses that accompanied the text by the late ninth century.[113]

112 See chapters 4 and 5 herein.

113 *OEBoethius*, ed. Godden and Irvine, 1:5–8. The only use of the term *fabula* occurs twice in Boethius's *Consolatio* 3.12 (prose and meter).

From the twelfth century the Latin texts of the *Epistola Alexandri*, Orosius's *Historiae*, and the *Historia Apollonii* became increasingly popular and occasionally circulated together.[114] This newly found shared readership underscores the connections between the pre-conquest, secular, vernacular literary culture of England and aspects of the Latin literary culture of the twelfth-century renaissance. These texts were not only ancillary or preparatory to classicism but also part of a broader range of ways to access the Roman story world. From this perspective the accessibility of the Roman story world in English appears as an important factor in Emma's turning to *fabula*, to the *Aeneid*, to make sense of dynastic struggle and to protect her position amid the dangerous factionalism that followed the death of Cnut. In so doing, she and the English royal women who followed in her footsteps built on vernacular foundations to forge a new relationship between the present and the classical past that would contribute to a reshaping of the literary culture of medieval Europe for centuries to come.

114 Specifically, *HAp* and *EAA* circulated together, as did Orosius's *Historiae* and *HAp* (see the manuscripts listed in Mortensen, "Diffusion of Roman Histories," 119–65; and *EAA*, ed. Boer, vi–xxi). Excerpts from Orosius's *Historiae* appear together with *HAp* and *EAA* in Vatican City, Biblioteca Apostolica Vaticana, Vat. lat. 1869.

2 Fictions of Family: The *Encomium Emmae reginae* and Virgil's *Aeneid*

Introduction

The *Encomium Emmae reginae* is a highly crafted account of the Danish conquest and then rule of England in the first half of the eleventh century. The author of the *Encomium* was probably a monk from the Flemish monastery of Saint-Bertin in Saint-Omer; he may, however, have been a canon from the collegiate church of Our Lady in the City. He wrote, as he tells us, to support Queen Emma's interests amid the complex dynastic politics of the early 1040s – the fallout from conquest and from divisive rival claims to the kingdom.[1] The Encomiast's version of events begins with Svein Forkbeard's reign as king of Denmark and his efforts to conquer England in the second decade of the eleventh century. Then he tells how, after defeating King Æthelred II, Svein's son Cnut finally achieved a more lasting conquest of England. The Encomiast goes on to attribute Cnut's long and peaceful rule in part to his marriage to Emma, widow of Æthelred. A period of instability, much lamented by the Encomiast, followed the death of Cnut in 1035. The Encomiast recounts in the final section of his text that this unrest was not resolved until 1040 when Harthacnut, Emma's son by Cnut, succeeded to the kingdom and shared its rule with his half-brother, Edward the Confessor. In fact this period of tranquillity being celebrated by the Encomiast was illusory, and he had to

1 On the identity of the Encomiast, *Encomium Emmae reginae* (hereafter cited as *Enc.*), ed. Campbell, xix–xxiii, and Keynes, introduction, xxxix–xli. On specific links between Saint-Bertin, Saint-Omer, and England and their wider context see chapter 3 herein, pages 110–11, and work cited there.

revise the ending when Harthacnut's death brought Edward to the throne in his own right. The newly discovered revision to the ending of the *Encomium* (preserved in a late-fourteenth-century manuscript (Copenhagen, Kongelige Bibliotek, Acc. 2011/5)), which greets Edward as Æthelred's legitimate heir, stands at odds with the whole of the text preceding it.[2] The effect is to expose the deeply tendentious nature of its account. The *Encomium* actively masks the factionalism threatening Emma's position when the period of Danish rule in England was drawing turbulently to a close. The Encomiast is thus presenting a particular picture of past glory and present peace as part of a deliberate attempt to intervene, on Emma's behalf, in the politics of the Anglo-Danish court.

The *Encomium* has proven to be a difficult text to interpret because of uncertainties about its context, style, and content. What was its intended audience: the court at Bruges, where Emma spent time in exile in the late 1030s; Emma herself; her sons; or Harthacnut's court? How is its artificial, overtly literary style suited to the writing of history? And why does it contain so many evident falsehoods? In reading the *Encomium*, I pay close attention to context, style, and content as integrally linked aspects of its meaning. Current scholarship has convincingly argued that the Encomiast wrote not only for the Anglo-Danish court of Emma's son Harthacnut but also from within that court. This argument is now further strengthened by the discovery of the Edwardian recension and the hastiness of its revisions.[3] Writing a text that supported Emma, from within the court at a time of fast-paced political change, was a difficult task. Emma had led a complicated life, and a straightforward account of her *vita et mores* would have done her no favours. As the Encomiast realized, her life was not the stuff of exemplary history, especially when many of the participants were still alive and formed the audience for the text. The Anglo-Danish dynasty, rather than Emma, is the Encomiast's subject, but even within this larger context her representation presented the Encomiast with difficulties.

---

2 Bolton, "Newly Emergent"; and Keynes and Love, "Earl Godwine's Ship," 195–7.

3 Stafford, *QEQE*, 28–40; Keynes, introduction, xxxv–xxxvi, xxxix–xli, lix, and lxix; and Orchard, "Literary Background," esp. 158–9, 166, and 169. In contrast, Gameson, looking at the *Encomium* from the perspective of manuscript study, writes that the text and manuscript were most likely produced in Saint-Omer; "Angleterre," 165. The manuscript is generally accepted to be Flemish or Norman and to date from the middle of the eleventh century; see, for example, Keynes, introduction, xli–xlv; and Gneuss and Lapidge, *Bibliographical Handlist*, 219.

Indeed, I will argue that it is precisely because the composition of the text is so little removed from the place and events it records that the Encomiast makes a fascinating, if tentative and pragmatic, turn to fiction.

Although fiction has long frustrated historians' attempts to use the *Encomium* as a source for the Danish conquest of England, recent interest in the text from literary scholars suggests ways of looking at that fiction more productively.[4] In this chapter I will examine the fictionality of the *Encomium* with two interrelated goals in mind: to understand more clearly the meaning of the text itself and to explore the relationship between fiction and historiography in the eleventh century. In order for this to be done, the intellectual virtuosity that the Encomiast displays in his text needs to be brought to the fore. The learning and the style of the Encomiast's writing place his work firmly within a distinctively medieval historiographical tradition. His rhyming prose is typical of Continental historiography in this period.[5] The impressive Saint-Bertin book list of 1104 further underscores that the Encomiast, if he was from this foundation, came from a library that was well-stocked with works of medieval historiography, as well as with classical and Christian writers such as Cicero, Macrobius, and Isidore, authors whose works shaped medieval views of history and whose influence is evident throughout the *Encomium*.[6] The situation of Saint-Bertin within the archdiocese of Reims alerts us also to its potential connections with the wider world of the cathedral schools of Northern France. From the ninth century and especially from the time of Gerbert of Aurillac's archiepiscopacy in the last decade of the tenth century, Reims was known for the study of classical literature and

4 *Enc.*, ed., Campbell, xlvi, l–lxix; Southern, "Classical Tradition," 186–7; Stenton, *Anglo-Saxon England*, 697; M.W. Campbell, "Personal Panegyric"; John, "Riddle"; Lifshitz, "Political Pamphlet"; Keynes, "Æthelings," 184–5; Keynes, introduction, lv–lxxi; Morse, *Truth*, 39; Tyler, "Eyes of the Beholder"; and Orchard, "Literary Background."

5 *Enc.*, ed. Campbell, xxxix–xl; Smalley, *Historians*, 13; Janson, *Prose Rhythm*; and Guenée, *Histoire*, 218–20.

6 The booklist (Becker, *Catalogi*, 181–4) postdates the *Encomium* by some sixty years and, since there was a fire in 1033, cannot be assumed to represent the library known by the Encomiast. However, the list remains a useful indication of the calibre of the library, and of the standards of learning within the community when the *Encomium* was written. On Saint-Bertin as a centre of learning see *Enc.*, ed., Campbell, xx–xxi, and Keynes, introduction, xxxv–vi. For a discussion of intellectual life in eleventh- and twelfth-century Flanders see de Moreau, *Histoire*, 249–305.

for the cultivation of history writing, rhetoric, and poetry.[7] Although the Encomiast appears to have written his text in England away from the library of Saint-Bertin, his intellectual formation was exceptional and allowed him to approach fiction in terms that would only become fully conceptualized in the course of the twelfth century. Finally, in considering the *Encomium* and Saint-Bertin, it is important to emphasize that the Encomiast is atypical when compared to other Flemish writers of the eleventh century. These writers, including those from Saint-Bertin, were largely preoccupied with the writing and rewriting of hagiographical texts. From this perspective the *Encomium* requires that we revise our understanding of the intellectual life of Saint-Bertin, but also that we see the Encomiast's intellectual formation as shaped by factors outside of Flanders, whether in Reims or in England. Although our much greater knowledge of Saint-Bertin encourages us to locate the Encomiast there, we should not dismiss the possibility that he was a canon from Saint-Omer.[8]

The concept of fiction needs to be examined at the outset in order to make plain why and how I am using this term in relation to the *Encomium* and to avoid the distortion of applying a modern category to a medieval text. At the same time, however, I do not want to efface the lack of clear conceptualization that characterizes notions of fiction before the twelfth century, since it is my contention that this very lack of clarity makes fiction attractive to the Encomiast. Although scholars have associated the emergence of developed notions of fiction with the flourishing of vernacular romance in the twelfth century, recent work has drawn attention to the self-conscious use of episodic fiction in Latin historiographical texts of the eleventh and twelfth centuries. When discussing the *Encomium*, however, the term *fiction* needs to be kept loose in order to make space for the inconsistencies and improvisation involved in the Encomiast's eleventh-century experience of fiction. In using the term *fiction* in connection with the *Encomium*, therefore, my concern lies, in the first instance, with the content of the text and, in the second instance, with its production and reception. In terms of content, *fiction* refers to an element of a text, or a whole text, that is made up (often referred to as *ficta* or with the verb *fingere*). The Encomiast, as we shall see, inherited concepts for understanding the nature of a made-up narrative both from the classical rhetorical

7 J.R. Williams, "Cathedral School"; Glauche, *Schullektüre*, 62–83; Riché, *Gerbert*; Riché, *Écoles*, 179–81; Lake, "Truth"; and Lake, *Richer*, 1–29, 71–80, and 185–98.

8 See chapter 3 herein.

tradition and from the study of poetry. In terms of production and reception meanwhile, audience and in particular a complicity between author and audience play an integral role in fiction; an account is not fiction but a lie if the author knows it is not true but the audience does not, and if the author is trying to persuade his audience to believe rather than to make-believe. The Encomiast shows a keen interest in issues of complicity, although it suits his pragmatic ends to let fiction and lies (a notion to which he explicitly refers) remain indistinct categories.[9] Writing for the men and women who are his subject matter, moreover, foregrounds issues of complicity. He is not informing them about events unknown to them but offering an account of events in which they, or their relatives and associates, took part.

The fictionality of the *Encomium* is a large topic, potentially shaping every layer of the text. I will begin by looking at the text's two prefaces, a prologue addressed to Emma herself and an argument addressed to the reader, in order to demonstrate that the Encomiast's understanding and use of fiction is indebted to traditions of classical rhetoric. At the same time, these two prefaces, as well as the main text, also reveal that the Encomiast was profoundly drawn to poetry since all three are full of allusions to Virgil's *Aeneid.* What the Encomiast does with Virgil and what he learns from him stand as key indications of the way he understands fiction to be working within his own text. The *Aeneid*, like the *Encomium*, is a text that provides an account of the origins of a dynasty in order to forward current political aims. One of the ways in which Virgil served Octavian's interests was by creating fictions about Aeneas and his family. In this regard the Encomiast finds in the *Aeneid* a useful model for the fiction that he produces for Emma, especially when those fictions concern her family and her place within it.

Emma's Family: Facts and Fictions

Emma was a powerful political figure during the Danish conquest of England and throughout the reigns of Æthelred II, Cnut, Harthacnut, and Edward the Confessor.[10] Her power rested on her various roles within the

9 Bäuml, "Varieties," 249–65; Nykrog, "Literary Fiction"; Fleischmann, "Representation"; Haug, *Vernacular Literary Theory*, 91–106; Mehtonen, *Old Concepts*; Otter, *Inventiones*, esp. 1–19; and D.H. Green, *Medieval Romance*.

10 Stafford, *QEQE*, 209–54.

family: daughter, sister, wife, and mother. Queenship, as Pauline Stafford writes, was "an office exercised by those who retained strong family identity and whose authority and power could still be conceived of in family terms."[11] A second but no less important point is that, even by medieval standards, Emma had to negotiate her power within an extraordinarily complex set of family relationships, as a thumbnail sketch of Emma's place in early-eleventh-century English history makes clear.

Emma, daughter of Richard I, Duke of Normandy, and sister of his successor, Richard II, was married first to Æthelred II, king of the English, in 1002. She bore him two sons, Edward the Confessor and Alfred. Æthelred II had had sons by his previous marriage (or marriages).[12] After the Danish conquest Emma married Cnut, by whom she had one further son, Harthacnut, and a daughter, Gunnhild. Her sons with Æthelred II went into exile in Normandy. Cnut had an earlier English wife, Ælfgifu of Northampton, and he continued his relationship with her after his marriage to Emma. When Cnut died, Harold Harefoot, his son by Ælfgifu, succeeded to the English kingdom in part because Harthacnut, his son by Emma, was away in Denmark. After a period of dispute and then of joint rule Harthacnut became sole king on Harold's death in 1040. Towards the end of his reign Harthacnut recognized his half-brother, Edward, as co-king, and Edward became sole king on Harthacnut's death in 1042. It was during this period of co-rule that the *Encomium* was written, with the new ending added after Harthacnut's death. Emma's relationship with Edward appears, not surprisingly, to have been difficult. This difficulty has been attributed to the long separation when he was in exile in Normandy, and her possible role in the murder of her other son, and Edward's brother, Alfred. In 1043, after he had gained sole rule and married Edith, daughter of Earl Godwine, Edward stripped his mother of both land and treasure because, in the words of the Anglo-Saxon Chronicle, "heo wæs æror þam cynge hire suna swiðe heard. Þæt heo him læsse dyde þonne he wolde ær þam þe he cyng wære. 7 eac syððan" (she was earlier too harsh with the king, her son, in that she did less for him than he wanted, before he was king, and also afterwards). Emma remained a marginal figure until her death in 1052.[13]

11 Stafford, *QEQE*, 192.

12 Stafford, *QEQE*, 72.

13 ASC "D," s.a. 1043 (see also "C"); Stafford, *QEQE*, 249–53; and Keynes, introduction, lxxi–lxxviii.

In many places the *Encomium* offers a very different version of early-eleventh-century history than the one just recounted. For example, among the text's fictions of family, are Cnut's wooing of Emma (the Anglo-Saxon Chronicle tells us that she was unceremoniously fetched, and poetry composed for the Norman court is scathing about the marriage);[14] the impression that Cnut is her first husband;[15] Cnut as the father of Edward;[16] fantastic Virgilian ships;[17] Ælfgifu of Northampton as Cnut's concubine; and Harold Harefoot as the son of a serving girl.[18] Within the text the Encomiast acknowledges that some of his material may be perceived as fiction and lies, and he is interested in issues of credibility. Indeed, the opening words of book 1 admit that the Encomiast knows that some among his audience may find it hard to believe his characterizing of Svein as "omnium sui temporis regum ferme fortunatissimum" (practically the most fortunate of all kings of his time). Defensively he asserts that he has ascertained this from "ueridica ... relatione" (truthful report).[19] He keeps this issue of credibility in the foreground when, at the end of his first chapter, he returns to the question of truth: "At ne me credat aliquis hec falsa fingendo alicuius amoris gratia compilare: recte animaduertenti in subsequentibus patebit, utrum uera dixerim an minime" (And lest any man think that I am lying, and concocting what I say from regard for any person's favour, in what is to follow, it will be plain to any one paying due attention, whether I am telling the truth or not).[20] Fascinatingly, in these lines he does not assert that he is telling the truth; rather he shifts the ground, writing that his audience will know whether or not he is. He flags his own consciousness that writing for an audience in the know shapes his work.

14 *Enc.* 2.16–17 and ASC "C," "D," and "E," s.a. 1017; *Jezebel*; and *Semiramis*. Keynes, "Æthelings," 183–4; Van Houts, "*Jezebel* and *Semiramis*"; and Stafford, *QEQE*, 33–4 and 225–31.

15 *Enc.* 2.16–18. *Enc.*, ed. Campbell, xliii and xlvi, but see John, "Riddle," 61–4.

16 *Enc.* 2.18. *Enc.*, ed. Campbell, xlvi, but see John, "Riddle," 64–5.

17 *Enc.* 1.4 and 2.4. Tyler, "Eyes of the Beholder," 257–65; and Orchard, "Literary Background," 160–6.

18 *Enc.* 3.1. Stafford emphasizes that the designation of Ælfgifu as *concubina*, a term of abuse, was meant to cast doubt on the throne worthiness of her sons (*QEQE*, 233). On Emma's spreading of rumours about Harold's low birth see John, "Riddle," 82; and Stafford, *QEQE*, 237.

19 *Enc.* 1.1.

20 *Enc.* 1.1.

His approach accords well with a notion of fiction that requires audience complicity. He knows that the reader will find incredible his account of the magic raven banner, which the Danes carry into battle.[21] Later he insists that the notion of Harold being Cnut's son is *falsa aestimatio* (false estimation), while, of his account, "quod veritas credi potest" (this can be believed as the more truthful account).[22] Credibility runs as a theme throughout his account of the letter, quoted verbatim, which summoned Alfred from exile and resulted in his death. According to the Encomiast, Harold forged the letter in Emma's name to lure Alfred to England. Although scholars have not believed the Encomiast's version of events, opinion has been divided on whether he made up the whole episode to discredit Harold or whether Emma actually wrote the letter and the Encomiast pinned it on Harold in order to exonerate her for playing a part in her son's death. In either case, it is interesting to note that within the context of a made-up story the Encomiast lays heavy emphasis on issues of deception, falsehood, and credibility in describing how Alfred was deceived by the forgery. Thus, at a key moment in his text he draws attention to the process whereby fabrication works.[23] It is this self-conscious view of made-up stories on the part of the Encomiast that I would like to underline. While many of his fictions have long been recognized as such by scholars, I do not think we have recognized how *openly* and *deliberately* fictional the *Encomium* is. And yet the members of Harthacnut's court, more than any other audience, would have recognized the flagrant nature of many of these fictions. Edward, for instance, knew that Cnut was not his father.[24] The immediate audience of the *Encomium*, in other words,

---

21 *Enc.* 2.9.

22 *Enc.* 3.1.

23 *Enc* 3.2–4. John and Stafford view the letter as Emma's, while Campbell and Keynes see it as the Encomiast's work. *Enc.* ed. Campbell, lxvii; John, "Riddle," 85–6; Keynes, "Æthelings," 196; Staffford, *QEQE*, 35–6, 239–40, 242–5; and Keynes, introduction, xxxi–xxxiv and lxiii–lxv.

24 Campbell considers audience reception of the Encomiast's misrepresentations, and Keynes the effect of the audience on the Encomiast's account of events, *Enc.*, ed. Campbell, xlvi, and Keynes, introduction, lix–lx. Orchard attributes the Encomiast's misrepresentations to responsiveness to his audience's political "sensibilities" ("Literary Background," 158–9). John is also sensitive to audience in his reading of the *Encomium* but argues in contrast that the Encomiast could not have been presenting Edward as the son of Cnut, because the audience (which included Edward) would not have believed this; see "Riddle," 63. For Lifshitz, the lies and misrepresentations of the text are evidence that it was written in 1039 to influence the Flemish court during

would have recognized that part of the text was not true, and obviously so. Rather than chastising the Encomiast for not being a reliable source, this audience would have asked what that fiction was doing, what meaning it created. The fiction and lies of his text could not be suppressed given this audience. What is fascinating to watch, within both the text and its prologues, is how the Encomiast seems compelled to work through these issues on a theoretical level. In the process he reveals both hard thinking and a playfulness and delight in raising these questions as he simultaneously writes in support of Emma and explores the contradictions of his task.

Why Virgil?

Like the language of so many medieval writers, that of the Encomiast is infused with Virgil's poetry, to such an extent that we might even be tempted to see the use of Virgilian allusion in the text as simply a part of its language.[25] But Virgil is not, as Campbell suggests, simply a linguistic "veneer."[26] While this is undoubtedly so in some places, it remains the case that right from the start the Encomiast announces that his use of the *Aeneid* is integral to both the production and the meaning of his text. He is openly using the Roman story world and calling on his audience to do

---

Emma's exile. She suggests that the Encomiast, unfamiliar with English history and reliant on Emma, did not know that he was not always telling the truth ("Political Pamphlet," 39–50). Smalley thinks that the Encomiast avoids outright lies in deference to his readers' knowledge of the facts (*Historians*, 75). Southern's view that the historicity of the *Encomium* is unproblematic when viewed from the classical historiographical tradition, while seminal, does not consider audience ("Classical Tradition," 186).

25 Comparetti's study first published in 1885 remains the classic introduction to the subject; see *Vergil in the Middle Ages*. For more recent discussion see, among others: Munk Olsen, "Virgile et la renaissance," esp. 31–8; and Baswell, *Virgil in Medieval England*.

26 Campbell describes this influence of classical writers on the Encomiast's language but not on how he conceptualized the task of writing for Emma (*Enc.*, xxiii–xl, esp. xxiv, xxix, xxxiv, and xxxv). Orchard also disagrees that the Encomiast's debt to the classics can be understood as simply linguistic ("Literary Background," 159). Searle suggests a more profound influence of Virgil on the Encomiast, but her interest lies with Dudo's use of Virgil ("Fact and Pattern," 126–7). John sees the invocation of Virgil as an important marker that the text is about Emma, but does not pursue the role of Virgil in the text; on the contrary, in a casual aside he questions whether the Encomiast would have read the *Aeneid* ("Riddle," 59). Southern places the work firmly within the classical historiographical tradition as represented by Sallust and Suetonius ("Classical Tradition," 186).

the same. In the prefatory argument he expresses his fear lest the reader accuse him of not praising the queen, because he is recounting the deeds not of Emma but of her family. This concern runs throughout the argument, and it is to Virgil that the Encomiast appeals in order to answer potential criticism that he has left out Emma:

> Atque ut ad hoc intuendum nulla erroris impediaris nebula, a similibus atque a penitus ueris hoc tibi habeas theorema. Aeneida conscriptam a Uirgilio quis poterit infitiari ubique laudibus respondere Octouiani, cum pene nihil aut plane parum eius mentio uideatur nominatim interseri? Animaduerte igitur laudem suo generi asscriptam ipsius decori claritudinis claritatisque in omnibus nobilitare gloriam. Quis autem hoc neget, laudibus reginae hunc per omnia respondere codicem, cum non modo ad eius gloriam scribatur, uerum etiam eius maximam uideatur optinere partem?
>
> (And that no cloud of error may hinder your understanding of this, you may take the following as an illustration from similar and entirely true matters. Who can deny that the *Aeneid*, written by Virgil, is everywhere devoted to the praises of Octavian, although practically no mention of him by name, or clearly very little, is seen to be introduced? Note, therefore, that the praise accorded to his family everywhere celebrates the glory of their fame and renown to his own honour. Who can deny that this book is entirely devoted to the praise of the Queen, since it is not only written to her glory, but since that subject occupies the greatest part of it?)[27]

This explicit invocation, not just of Virgil but of Octavian and the *Aeneid*, is arresting and should indeed make us stop and think. At the very outset of the text the Encomiast firmly and explicitly places his narrative in a Virgilian framework. By way of contrast, the Encomiast is also deeply indebted to other classical authors, especially Sallust and Lucan, as well as Ovid, Horace, Juvenal, and Lucretius, but it is only Virgil whom he explicitly, and (as we shall see) repeatedly, invokes.[28]

A brief consideration of the Encomiast's use of Lucan illustrates the distinctive nature of his debt to Virgil. Lucan is most in evidence as the *Encomium* comes to a close, when Harthacnut and Emma return to

27 *Enc.*, argument.
28 *Enc.*, ed. Campbell, xxix–xxxiv; and Orchard, "Literary Background," 159–60.

England from Bruges. As Campbell has discussed, Lucan's portrait of Cornelia, Pompey's virtuous and loyal wife, departing with her husband (defeated at Pharsalia) from Lesbos, stands behind the Encomiast's depiction of Emma's departure from Bruges. The city's inhabitants lament Emma's leaving, just as those of Lesbos lamented Cornelia's.[29] Later, in the final lines of the *Encomium*, Lucan's chilling indictment of the possibility of shared rule, made with a reference to Romulus's killing of Remus, is recalled as the Encomiast celebrates the joint rule of Harthacnut and Edward, united by Emma.[30] Both these allusions profoundly disrupt the optimism of the Encomiast's Virgilian framework and reveal his own disquiet at the factionalism that this joint rule could not quell. But neither is announced. Although they might be recognized by other learned readers of the *Encomium*, Lucan's disturbing *De bello civili* is not presented to the audience, the Anglo-Danish court, as an overt warning. The allusions to Lucan cannot, however, be dismissed as linguistic veneer (any more than his Virgilian language was); they are too apt. Rather they reveal just how far from reality was the Encomiast's Virgilian vision and how aware he was of that gap. From the standpoint of 1042, Cnut might have looked more like a defeated Pompey than the founder of a dynasty, while Harthacnut and Edward evoked fratricide rather than fraternal harmony. It is worth registering as well that, while the reference to Cornelia strikes a dark note, it does not undermine Emma's position, either overtly or covertly, since Pompey's wife is wholly admirable within Lucan's epic. Similarly, the reference to Romulus and Remus implicates the brothers, not Emma, in strife. His debt to Lucan reveals the Encomiast's strong loyalty to Emma. Returning to the *Aeneid*, the explicit appeal to Virgil in the argument, in contrast to the quiet allusions to Lucan, indicates that it is the optimism of this epic that shapes the Encomiast's understanding of his task in writing for Emma and of the place of fiction within it.

Rhetorical Historiography and Poetry in the Eleventh Century

The turn of the Encomiast to Virgil and fiction does not necessarily put his work beyond the bounds of *historia*; to understand why it does not, we

29 *Enc.* 3.12; Lucan, *De bello civili* 8.147–58. *Enc.*, ed. Campbell, xxxii.
30 *Enc.* 3.14; Lucan, *De bello civili* 1.96. Keynes and Love, "Godwine's Ship," 217.

need to look briefly at the relationship between rhetorical historiography and poetry.[31] The nature of history writing was hard to pin down in the eleventh century. Historiography was an auxiliary, rather than an autonomous, discipline in the Middle Ages; thus historical texts, though central to both a grammatical and a rhetorical education, were not studied as history. Educational practices in the Middle Ages encouraged history to be seen as a branch of both poetry and rhetoric since rhetoric was included in a grammatical curriculum that was largely devoted to the study of poetry. This tradition of grammatical rhetoric contributes to widespread notions of a specifically rhetorical historiography and to a lack of distinction between poetry and rhetoric, both of which leave their imprint on the notion of history. Looking within the ecclesiastical world of the Encomiast, it is also notable that, although poetry was generally not included in the study of rhetoric until the twelfth century, this practice was influentially introduced into Reims in the late tenth century by Gerbert of Aurillac.[32] Moreover, and keeping an eye on the Encomiast's preoccupation with Virgil, the designation of Virgil by the fifth-century Latin writer Macrobius as both poet and orator reminds us that intimate connections between poetry and rhetoric informed understanding of the *Aeneid* itself.[33] As we shall see, the Encomiast powerfully deployed the *Aeneid* for a very rhetorical end: to persuade Harthacnut's court of the value of the Anglo-Danish dynasty.

The Latin rhetorical tradition, which stretched back to Cicero's *De inventione* and the *Rhetorica ad Herennium* (basic rhetorical treatises that were widely known in the Middle Ages), placed history as part of a triad: *historia*, *argumentum*, and *fabula*.[34] Isidore wrote in his influential *Etymologies*: "Inter historiam et argumentum et fabulam interesse. Nam

31 For general accounts of the nature of medieval historiography see Smalley, *Historians*; Ray, "Medieval Historiography"; Ray, "Triumph"; and Guenée, *Histoire*. Further relevant material is cited in note 33.

32 Richer, *Historiae* 3.47; and Glauche, *Schullektüre*, 64.

33 Macrobius, *Saturnalia* 5.1. Curtius, *European Literature*, 82 and 145–6, esp. 148; Southern, "Classical Tradition," 177–83; Smalley, *Historians*, 12 and 15–18; Guenée, *Histoire*, 19–20 and 26–7; Ray, "Medieval Historiography," 51–8; Ray, "Triumph"; Partner, "New Cornificius," 5–22; Ward, "Some Principles," 103–65; Woodman, *Rhetoric*, 98–101; Haug, *Vernacular Literary Theory*, 8–9; Morse, *Truth*, 7–10, 33–4, and 85–124; Mehtonen, *Old Concepts*, 11–61; D.H. Green, *Medieval Romance*, 3–4; and Kempshall, *Rhetoric*, 121–264.

34 Mehtonen, *Old Concepts*.

historiae sunt res verae quae factae sunt; argumenta sunt quae etsi facta non sunt, fieri tamen possunt; fabulae vero sunt quae nec factae sunt nec fieri possunt, quia contra naturam sunt" (It is different between history, argument, and fable. For histories are true matters which happened; arguments are matters which, although they did not happen, could have happened, but fables are matters which neither happened nor could have happened, because they are contrary to nature).[35] According to this classification, *historia* is concerned with truth and with recounting events that actually happened, *argumentum* with recounting events that, although they did not happen, could have happened, and *fabula*, which is often linked to poetry, with events that neither happened nor could have happened.

In practice, *historia* did not remain as distinct from *argumentum* and *fabula* as Isidore suggests.[36] The less constricting formulation, of Cicero and the *Rhetorica ad Herennium*, that *historia* was "gesta res, sed ab aetatis nostrae memoria remota" (an account of actual occurrences remote from the recollection of our own age) is more of a piece with medieval practice.[37] *Historia* and *argumentum* share features with our understanding of fiction. Classical rhetoricians, concerned with persuasive oratory and the demands of the courtroom, and the historians who wrote under their influence, direct or not, taught medieval historians to supplement their often scanty facts with "the imaginative creation of verisimilar materials" (to quote Roger Ray) in order to produce a credible account. Both the *Rhetorica ad Herennium* and Cicero's *De inventione* taught the art and application of verisimilitude.[38] According to the *Rhetorica ad Herennium*:

35 Isidore of Seville, *Etymologiae sive origines* (hereafter cited as *Ety.*) 1.44.

36 For example, both Martianus Capella and Priscian add a further element to the triad, thus underscoring the fluidity of the conceptions of history and fiction that the Encomiast would have inherited. See Martianus Capella, *De nuptiis Philologiae et Mercurii* 5.550; and Priscian, *Praeexercitamina* 2.

37 *Rhetorica ad Herennium* 1.8.13; and Cicero, *De inventione* 1.19.27.

38 Ray, "Triumph," 68; Partner, "New Cornificius," 16; Morse, *Truth*, 6–7, 60–1, 86–7, 97, 101–2; and Kempshall, *Rhetoric*. For discussion of the relationship of rhetorical and poetic verisimilitude see Mehtonen, *Old Concepts*, 97–102. On knowledge of *De inventione* and *Rhetorica ad Herennium* in the Middle Ages see Dickey, "Some Commentaries"; Bliese, "Study of Rhetoric"; Ward, "Commentator's Rhetoric"; and Ward, *Ciceronian Rhetoric*, esp. 74–167. On the medieval transmission of these rhetorical texts see Munk Olsen, *L'étude des auteurs*, 1:99–350; and L.D. Reynolds, *Texts and Transmission*, 98–100.

> Veri similis narratio erit si ut mos, ut opinio, ut natura postulat dicemus ... Si vera res erit, nihilominus haec omnia narrando conservanda sunt, nam saepe veritas, nisi haec servata sint, fidem non potest facere; sin erunt ficta, eo magis erunt conservanda. De iis rebus caute confingendum est quibus in rebus tabulae aut alicuius firma auctoritas videbitur interfuisse.
>
> (Our Statement of Facts will have plausibility (verisimilitude) if it answers the requirements of the usual, the expected, and the natural ... If the matter is true, all these precautions must nonetheless be observed in the Statement of Facts, for often the truth cannot gain credence otherwise. And if the matter is fictitious, these measures will have to be observed all the more scrupulously. Fabrication must be circumspect in those matters in which official documents or some person's unimpeachable guaranty will prove to have played a role.)[39]

Verisimilitude plays a vital role in making credible accounts both of events that have happened and of events that are made up. It contributes to breaking down the sharpness of any distinctions that might be made between *historia*, *argumentum*, and *fabula*. Behind verisimilitude stand the modulated and pragmatic views on truth telling that were to have a strong influence on historiographical writing and to play an important role in the development of ideas of fiction. Cicero's *De inventione*, introduced into the curriculum by Gerbert, was known at Reims, where Richer's *Historia* illustrates that it shaped contemporary history writing.[40]

The debt of historiography to poetry also contributes to the fluidity of the categories *historia*, *argumentum*, and *fabula*. Poetry taught that fable could be true, although it emphatically did not recount the deeds that actually happened. However, because so much poetry, including Virgil's *Aeneid*, was historical in nature, the truth of poetry could be hard to distinguish from the truth of history.[41] In light of Lucan's status in the Middle Ages as both poet and historian, the Encomiast's recourse to Lucan, and his use of allusions to Lucan, points to his deep interest in the ambiguous relationship between history and poetry. Although history and poetry would eventually go their separate ways, this was a long process that only

39 *Rhetorica ad Herennium* 1.9.16; see also Cicero, *De inventione* 1.21.29–30.

40 Lake, "Truth," 26–7; and Lake, *Richer*, 71–80.

41 Mehtonen, *Old Concepts*; and Morse, *Truth*, 85–124, esp. 98–9. For a discussion of the aesthetic and formal similarities of historical and fictional narratives in the Middle Ages see Partner, *Serious Entertainments*, 194–211.

gathered real force in the course of the twelfth century. In the eleventh century it was far from being the case. The difficulty of negotiating the boundary between history and poetry therefore particularly troubled historians of the eleventh century, as the two discourses were only just beginning to be distinguished from each other.[42] To take one example, in his *Gesta Guillelmi*, an account of the deeds of William the Conqueror written shortly after 1066, William of Poitiers articulated a clear unease about the dividing line between history and poetry: "Parturire suo pectore bella quae calamo ederentur poetis licebat, atque amplificare utcumque cognita per campos figmentorum diuagando. Nos ducem, siue regem, cui nunquam impure quid fuit pulchrum, pure laudabimus, nusquam a ueritatis limite passu uno delirantes" (Poets were allowed to imagine wars so that they could write about them, and to amplify their knowledge in any way they liked by roaming through the fields of fiction. But we will purely and simply praise the duke or king, to whom nothing impure was beautiful, never taking a single step beyond the bounds of truth).[43] William associates poetry with fiction, *per campos figmentorum*, and sets up an opposition between poetry and history. The Encomiast may have aligned his work differently, but, as we shall see, he too struggles to keep poetry and history distinct.

Reading Carefully: Rhetoric

The Encomiast's sophisticated engagement with issues of truth in the writing of history is evident in his two prefaces to the text. The prologue, addressed to Emma, recounts the circumstances of the text's production and vividly portrays its author's anxiety that his text is not history. The argument then confidently puts forward the Virgilian framework and gives the reader a brief summary of what follows. In these two prefaces the Encomiast overtly explores the potential that fiction offers him as he tries to write in praise but also in defence of Emma. We can only see this, however, if we avoid assuming, as many have done, that the Encomiast is defending himself as a writer of history. Although both prefaces clearly show that the Encomiast wrote from within the tradition of rhetorical historiography inherited from the classical tradition, the *Encomium* is not just

42 Southern, "Classical Tradition," 196; and Guenée, *Histoire*, 221–2.

43 William of Poitiers, *Gesta Guillelmi* (hereafter cited as *GG*) 1.20. Mora Lebrun, *L'"Énéide" médiévale*, 42–4; and Shopkow, *History and Community*, 132–3.

another medieval historical text that does not negotiate a prominent gap between its theoretical position on the nature of true history (as set out in the prologue) and the practice of history (as played out in the text). Something much more interesting is going on here, but it only becomes clear if we read the prefaces carefully and remain alert to the ways in which the Encomiast uses many of the rhetorical topoi common to other medieval prologues.[44] The Encomiast does not trot out these topoi in order to present a conventional case for the truth of his work. Medieval texts, whether Latin or vernacular, rarely reject the conventions of their genre; rather, authors use conventions, and the expectations they set up, to convey their own specific and often original meaning.[45] The tension between the conventional use of the topoi and the Encomiast's use of them to express his own particular meaning serves to highlight the original and, at points, radical case that he is making for fictional historical writing.

The Encomiast begins by professing his devotion to Emma. He tells her that he closely identifies with her interests and perspective on the happenings of the early eleventh century.[46] This is not merely a rhetorical stance aimed at gaining Emma's goodwill.[47] Rather this sense of close identification, expressed in especially emotional terms when the Encomiast recounts the murder of Emma's son Alfred, runs throughout the text.[48] Thus from the start, the Encomiast creates an authorial persona that overtly claims to

---

44 *Enc.*, ed. Campbell, xxiv and xl; Simon, "Untersuchungen zur Topik"; Janson, *Latin Prose Prefaces*, 24–6; Vessey, "William of Tyre," 435–45; Smalley, *Historians*, 75; Gransden, "Prologues"; and Morse, *Truth*, 107–24.

45 Haug, *Literary Theory*, 11–12.

46 "Salus tibi sit a Domino Iesu Christo, o regina, que omnibus in hoc sexu positis prestas morum elegantia. Ego seruus tuus nobilitati tuae digna factis meis exhibere nequeo, quoque pacto uerbis saltem illi placere possim nescio. Quod enim cuiuslibet peritiae loquentis de te uirtus tua preminet, omnibus a quibus cognosceris ipso solis iubare clarius lucet. Te igitur erga me adeo bene meritam magnifacio, ut morti intrepidus occumberem, si in rem tibi prouenire crederem." (May our Lord Jesus Christ preserve you, O Queen, who excel all those of your sex in the admirability of your way of life. I, your servant, am unable to show you, noble lady, anything worthy in my deeds, and I do not know how I can be acceptable to you even in words. That your excellence transcends the skill of any one speaking about you is apparent to all to whom you are known, more clearly than the very radiance of the sun. You, then, I esteem as one who has deserved of me to such a degree, that I would sink to death unafraid, if I believed that my action would lead to your advantage.) *Enc.*, prologue.

47 On *captatio benevolentiae* see *Rhetorica ad Herennium* 1.4.6–1.5.8; and Cicero, *De inventione* 1.15.20–1.16.22.

48 *Enc.* 3.6.

be on Emma's side; he makes no attempt to hide the partisan nature of his account or the role of Emma's patronage in shaping the narrative. The Encomiast does not go on, in the following lines, to claim that he is going to transmit *memoria rerum gestarum* – with all its associations with history as a narrative of events that actually happened in the past.[49] Instead, he tells us that he longs to write this sort of history but doubts his ability to do so.[50] Of course, this sentiment and his profession that he lacks sufficient eloquence are modesty topoi; however, their use is not conventional, and, for reasons that will become apparent, I think we should read these lines as the Encomiast's profession that telling it "like it happened" would be of no help to Emma.[51] This association of *res gestae* with the past, as Cicero and the *Rhetorica ad Herennium* make so clear, also reminds us that history may be problematic for the Encomiast because he brings his account into the present.[52] The Encomiast's rewriting of the text after Harthacnut's death forcefully illustrates just how rooted in the present this text is and underscores the difficulties that contemporary history poses when the participants comprise the author's audience.[53]

Latin prefaces to historical works conventionally address the nature of history and the importance of truth. The Encomiast is no exception, and

49 *Rhetorica ad Herennium* 1.8.13; Cicero, *De inventione* 1.19.27; Isidore, *Ety.* 1.41. Janson, *Latin Prose Prefaces*, 149–50; and Simon, "Untersuchungen zur Topik," (4), 78–81 and (5–6), 94–111.

50 "Qua ex re, mihi etiam ut precipis, memoriam rerum gestarum, rerum inquam tuo tuorumque honori attinentium, litteris meis posteritati mandare gestio, sed ad hoc faciendum me mihi sufficere posse dubito" (For this reason, and furthermore, in accordance with your injunction, I long to transmit to posterity through my literary work a record of things done, things, which, I declare, touch upon the honour of you and your connections, but I am in doubt concerning my adequacy for doing this). *Enc.*, prologue.

51 *Rhetorica ad Herennium* 1.5.8 and 3.6.11; and Cicero, *De inventione* 1.16.22. Modesty topoi are frequently discussed; for example, Curtius, *European Literature*, 83–5, 159–62, and 407–13.

52 Simon, "Untersuchungen zur Topik," (4), 88–9; and Gransden, "Prologues," 56.

53 Orchard argues, on stylistic grounds, that the revised ending (which was known before the discovery of the full Edwardian recension in the abbreviated version found in Paris, Bibliothèque nationale de France, lat. 6235) is the work of the Encomiast. This further supports his view that the text is written from Harthacnut's court. Orchard, "Literary Background," 167–9. The full Edwardian recension makes clearer still the stylistic unity of the revised ending and the main body of the text. Keynes and Love, "Godwine's Ship," 197–8.

he accordingly moves on to explore, in a key passage, what is required by the writing of history:[54]

> Hoc enim in historia proprium exigitur, ut nullo erroris diuerticulo a recto ueritatis tramite declinetur, quoniam, cum quis alicuius gesta scribens ueritati falsa quaedam seu errando, siue ut sepe fit ornatus gratia, interserit, profecto unius tantum comperta admixtione mendatii auditor facta uelut infecta ducit. Unde historicis magnopere cauendum esse censeo, ne ueritati quibusdam falso interpositis contraeundo nomen etiam perdat, quod uidetur habere ex offitio.
>
> (This quality, indeed, is required in history, that one should not deviate from the straight path of truth by any divergent straying, for when in writing the deeds of any man one inserts false elements in the truth, either in error, or, as is often the case, for the sake of ornament, the hearer assuredly regards events which happened as events which did not happen, when he has ascertained the introduction of so much as one lie. And so I consider that the historian should greatly beware, lest, going against truth by falsely introducing matter, he lose the very name which he is held to have from his office.)[55]

Throughout these lines the Encomiast's stance is highly impersonal as he deliberately avoids suggesting that his own work is history writing. History, as a narrative of *gesta*, should have nothing false added to it. He sees two sources for such falsehood: error and ornament. In using the term *mendatium* here the Encomiast is very clear that he is not considering the way in which medieval notions of historical truth extend to what we would call fiction, nor is he even considering the truth that can be expressed by fable. He is certainly not worrying about verisimilitude. Rather he is drawing attention to the problem of mixing history and lies; the problem with inserting lies, he tells us, is that the audience then comes to view as false even what is true within a text: "auditor facta uelut infecta ducit." This phrase *facta uelut infecta* is key, and we will return to it when we consider what Virgil tells the Encomiast about truth mixed with lies. The Encomiast finishes this section by commenting on the interconnectedness of credibility and truth, a point underscored by the syntax of his sentence: "Res enim ueritati, ueritas quoque fidem facit rei" (The account

54 Janson, *Latin Prose Prefaces*, 66–7; and Vessey, "William of Tyre," 440–3.
55 *Enc.* prologue. Discussed briefly by Morse, *Truth*, 139.

or event itself, to be sure, wins belief for the truth, and the truth does the same for the account or event).[56] Here we see the influence of the classical rhetorical tradition that stressed the need for facts to be presented in a credible fashion.[57] The Encomiast, who needed to persuade his audience, as much as any classical orator in a courtroom ever had to, was keenly aware of the importance of credibility to the writing of history and of the techniques involved in effective persuasion. The Encomiast's deployment of the term *res* in this line, moreover, highlights his delicate sense of the complex semantic field of this seemingly ordinary word. *Res* can denote an actual event or fact, as well as an account of that event or fact. By using *res* no fewer than eight times in his prologue, the Encomiast exploits its semantic ambiguity to explore the relationship of his account of Emma's life to events that actually took place.[58]

The Encomiast's association of ornament and falsehood is, perhaps, not so transparent. The artificial rhyming prose of the *Encomium* was not a simple style. Moreover, the Encomiast's style is highly ornamented, marked by the use of alliteration, paronamasia, and the repetition of words and phrases.[59] Thus the Encomiast seems to write in a style that he himself would see excluded from historiography. Bernard Guenée sees many medieval historians as torn between the view that a simple style is better suited to the expression of historical truth, and the desire to produce an elaborate Latin. Especially evident in the eleventh and twelfth centuries, such Latin displayed the erudition of the author and pleased those elite patrons who were keen to appear cultivated. In such contexts the preference for plain style was often a mere topos.[60] But this is not what the Encomiast does. He tells us that the style of his own text is not appropriate

56 *Enc.* prologue. See note 58 for the complexity of *res* that makes translation of this sentence difficult. Campbell's translation reads: "The fact itself, to be sure, wins belief for the veracious presentation, and the veracious presentation does the same for the fact."

57 *Rhetorica ad Herennium* 1.9.16; and Cicero, *De inventione* 1.29.46. Ray, "Triumph," 72–3; Morse, *Truth*, 83; and D.H. Green, *Medieval Romance*, 148–9.

58 In examining Augustine's use of *res*, Roger Ray writes that by *res* "Augustine does not mean 'the sheer facts' ... *Res* expresses not the literal occurrence but the edifying shape of the actual happening"; see Ray, "Bede, the Exegete," 131; see also Ward's application of Ray's point about *res* to John of Salisbury's notion of history, "Some Principles," 108.

59 Orchard, "Literary Background," 159.

60 Simon, "Untersuchungen zur Topik," (5–6), 79–80 and 89–94; Janson, *Latin Prose Prefaces*, 140–1; Vessey, "William of Tyre," 443–5; Ray, "Medieval Historiography," 48–51; and Guenée, *Histoire*, 214–26.

to history. Indeed, the Encomiast seems to have backed himself into a corner with his discussion of error and ornament. First, he does not use the language of fiction that can express truth (for example, *fabula* or *figmentum*), but the language of lies and falsehood; *falsus*, which he uses twice, does not denote some incipient but positive notion of fiction. Nor can these lines be read as an example of the language of lying being used in the absence of a developed theory of fiction. Rather, as we shall see, the Encomiast is acknowledging that he faces the dilemma of presenting as true what is not only false but also *known* to be false by his audience.[61] Second, his view of ornament as encouraging lies reveals that he is working within a much less flexible framework than that offered by much classical and medieval thinking on the relationship between history and fiction. The Encomiast seems to have adopted, at this point in the prologue, a rather austere view of history. But perhaps this is because he views some (though not all) of what he has to say about Emma as outright lies rather than what is acceptable within the norms of exemplary history or the kind of fictional truth that fable can convey. Certainly some discomfort is apparent when he then goes on to express his sense of shame that so few live up to his strict vision for maintaining the office of historian: "Hec mecum aliaque huiusmodi me reputante rubor animum uehementer excruciat, cum pariter considero, quam pessime in talibus sese humana consuetudo habeat" (Having reflected upon these and similar matters, shame powerfully afflicts my spirit, when I likewise consider how very imperfect the customary behaviour of mankind is in such matters).[62]

He displaces this shame by saying that he is distressed by the general state of the writing of history. We might wonder, however, if his distress is not more personal. The shift from *me* to *humana consuetudo* does not fully mask his personal implication. Indeed, what I would suggest is that he is actually drawing attention to the fact that he has consciously abandoned the office of historian in his attempt to write in praise of Emma.[63] He is aware that, in writing in defence of Emma, he is engaging in a partisanship that undermines the status of his work as history and leads him to write a narrative that is neither literally nor figuratively true.[64] Indeed,

61 D.H. Green, *Medieval Romance*, 8 and 12; and Mehtonen, *Old Concepts*, 124–8.

62 *Enc.* prologue.

63 See pages 76–7 on panegyric and historiography.

64 On the antipathy of partisanship to Ciceronian notions of *historia* see Lake, "Truth," 233.

even though his account of Svein and Cnut might be framed as exemplary history, with Harthacnut and Edward as intended audience, the Encomiast nowhere invokes this mode with its notion that events and people should be presented not as they were but as they might best be imitated.[65] On the contrary, he insists his work is praise of Emma.

The Encomiast moves on to engage further in issues of style. He mentions two kinds of account: one that is restrained and hides what is open, and the other that is both loquacious (and this does have a negative force) and yet interested in expressing the truth of the matter.[66] He writes: "Uidens enim aliquis quempiam pro exprimenda rei ueritate uerbis indulgentem, uanae loquacitatis eum mordaciter redarguit, alium uero, quem dixi blasphemium fugientem et aequo modestiorem in narratione, cum operta denudare debeat, aperta oc[c]uluisse dicit" (In fact, when a man sees somebody giving the rein to words to express the truth of a matter, he blames him bitterly for loquacity, but another, whom I describe as one avoiding reproach, and more restrained in his equitable account, he declares, indeed, to hide what was open, when he ought to uncover what was concealed).[67] The Encomiast's play on *operta* and *aperta* calls to mind the advice of classical rhetoricians to aim for clarity, in Cicero's language, *narratio aperta*. In both the *Rhetorica ad Herennium* and Cicero's *De inventione* clarity is explicitly associated with brevity, whereas the Encomiast declares that he will pursue clarity through loquacity.[68] His use of wordplay, furthermore, draws attention to his departure from rhetorical norms as he continues in this vein. The Encomiast's subsequent statement, in lines that are now strikingly personal, that despite the negative connotations of loquacity it is according to this second category that he is going to write *historia* also reveals his conflicted attitude about producing history for Emma: "Tali itaque angustia circumseptus ab inuidentibus loquax dici timeo, si neglecta uenustate dictaminis historiam scripturus multiplici narratione usus fuero" (And so, hedged in by such difficulty, I fear to be called loquacious by the envious if neglecting elegance of form, I adopt a *multiplex narratio* when addressing myself to writing history).[69]

65 For a medieval *locus classicus* see Bede, *HE* preface.

66 Isidore, *Ety.* 10.155.

67 *Enc.* prologue.

68 *Rhetorica ad Herennium* 1.9.14–15; and Cicero, *De inventione* 1.20.28–29.

69 *Enc.* prologue.

The Encomiast's embrace of loquacity can be interpreted as a conventional claim that the writer does not have the eloquence required by his subject; this topos is familiar from classical rhetorical treatises and medieval historiography.[70] Yet, in choosing the term *loquacity*, the Encomiast flaunts his rejection of brevity that, even if *brevitas* is a topos more often honoured in the breach than observed, was widely seen in the Middle Ages as a characteristic of effective historical writing.[71] In denoting his text as *historia*, the Encomiast seems to have stepped back within the confines of history, but this is not an unequivocal move. He hedges his bets and opts for a style that is not associated with historical writing, at least in its ideal form. And, as will become apparent when we look at allusions to Virgil in this passage, he evades history again in designating his work as *multiplex narratio*, as will be discussed further below.

In the final lines of the prologue, the Encomiast now tells us that what his envious enemies call *loquacity* is the *only* way in which he can make known the truth of the memorable affairs of Emma's life:

> Quoniam uero, quin scripturus sim, euadere me non posse uideo, unum horum quae proponam eligendum esse autumo, scilicet aut uariis iudiciis hominum subiacere, aut de his, quae mihi a te, domina regina, precepta sunt, precipientem negligendo conticessere. Malo itaque a quibusdam de loquacitate redargui, quam ueritatem maxime memorabilis rei per me omnibus occultari. Quocirca, quandoquidem iubentem dominam magni pendens hanc mihi elegi uiam, excusabiles deinceps occasiones posthabens hinc narrationis contextionem faciam.
>
> (Since, indeed, I see that I cannot avoid writing, I aver that I must choose one of alternatives which I am about to enunciate, that is either to submit to a variety of criticisms from men, or to be silent concerning the things enjoined upon me by you, Lady Queen, and to disregard you, who enjoin me. I prefer, accordingly, to be blamed by some for loquacity, than that the truth of so very memorable a matter [*res*] should be hidden from all through me. Therefore, since I have chosen this way for myself, greatly esteeming the lady

---

70 Janson, *Latin Prose Prefaces*, 125–8.

71 *Rhetorica ad Herennium* 1.9.14–15; and Cicero, *De inventione* 1.20.28–9. Curtius, *European Literature*, 85 and 487–94; Janson, *Latin Prose Prefaces*, 6–7 and 154–5; and Ray, "Medieval Historiography," 52.

> who commands me, I will set aside one after the other affairs from which I can excuse myself, and proceed to the composition of my narrative.)[72]

Here the Encomiast seems to have, again, stepped away from, if not quite rejected, history in favour of the truth of fiction; note the contrast between the *veritas maxime memorabilis rei* of this section and the *memoria rerum gestarum* that he longed to transmit at the beginning of the prologue. He seems to have moved towards a less restricting notion of historical truth than he espoused when writing about lies and ornament and is perhaps coming to the point where he can admit the truth of fiction into his text.

His use of the term *narrationis contextio* in this passage certainly suggests that he sees his text as having as much to do with fable as with history. Medieval writers used the language of weaving to emphasize the consciously creative aspects of historiography.[73] But the Encomiast's reference is more specific and points not just to creativity but also to fiction. The phrase *narrationis contextio*, which is not a common expression, also occurs in a well-studied passage from Macrobius's commentary on the *Somnium Scipionis*, where it is associated not just with fable but with the worst kind of fable that philosophers never include in their writing:

> Fabulae, quarum nomen indicat falsi professionem, aut tantum conciliandae auribus voluptatis, aut adhortationis quoque in bonam frugem gratia repertae sunt. auditum mulcent vel comoediae ... Hoc totum fabularum genus, quod solas aurium delicias profitetur, e sacrario suo in nutricum cunas sapientiae tractatus eliminat. Ex his autem quae ad quandam virtutem speciem intellectum legentis hortantur fit secunda discretio. In quibusdam enim et argumentum ex ficto locatur et per mendacia ipse relationis ordo contexitur ut sunt illae Aesopi fabulae elegantia fictionis illustres, at in aliis argumentum quidem fundatur veri soliditate sed haec ipsa veritas per quaedam composita et ficta profertur, et hoc iam vocatur narratio fabulosa, non fabula ... Ex hac ergo secunda divisione quam diximus, a philosophiae libris prior species, quae concepta de falso per falsum narratur, aliena est. Sequens in aliam rursum discretionem scissa dividitur: nam cum veritas argumento subest solaque fit narratio fabulosa, non unus reperitur modus per figmentum vera referendi. Aut enim contextio narrationis per turpia et indigna numinibus ac monstro similia componitur ... quod genus totum philosophi nescire malunt – aut

72 *Enc.* prologue.
73 Ward, "Some Principles," 103, 107, 118–19, 120, 136, 137, and 140.

> sacrarum rerum notio sub pio figmentorum velamine honestis et tecta rebus et vestita nominibus enuntiatur: et hoc est solum figmenti genus quod cautio de divinis rebus philosophantis admittit.
>
> (Fables – the very word acknowledges their falsity – serve two purposes: either merely to gratify the ear or to encourage the reader to good works. They delight the ear ... This whole category of fables that promise only to gratify the ear, a philosophical treatise avoids and relegates to children's nurseries. The other group, those that draw the reader's attention to certain kinds of virtue, are divided into two types. For in certain ones the argument may be spoken from fiction, and the order itself of the narrative is woven through lies, as are those fables of Aesop, famous for the elegance of their fiction; in others, however, the argument is grounded in the solid foundations of truth, but this very truth is made known through what is contrived and made up, and this is now called fabulous narrative, not fable ... Of the second main group, which we have just mentioned, the first type, with both setting and plot fictitious, is also inappropriate to philosophical treatises. The second type is subdivided, for when truth lies under the argument and only a fabulous narrative is made, more than one way of representing truth through fiction is discerned. Either the weaving together of the narrative [*contextio narrationis*] is composed of matters shameful to and unworthy of the gods, and even resembling a monstrosity ..., a type which philosophers prefer to disregard altogether; or else a decent and dignified conception of holy truths, with respectable events and characters, is presented beneath a modest veil of allegory [*pio figmentorum velamine*]. This is the only type of fiction approved by the philosopher who is prudent in handling sacred matters.)[74]

If the Encomiast did know this passage (Macrobius is listed in the Saint-Bertin book list), then, in using the term *narrationis contextio*, he signals his awareness of the potential complexity involved in thinking about the relationship of fable and truth, when that truth is both historical and fictional.[75] Certainly, Macrobius's views on *fabula* became key to twelfth-century theories of fiction.

---

74 Macrobius, *In somnium Scipionis* 1.2.

75 Campbell notes the allusion to Macrobius, *Enc.* prologue (note 6). Dronke, *Fabula*, 25–30; Reynolds, *Texts and Transmission*, 223–32; Minnis and Scott, *Literary Theory*, 118–19; Lapidge, "Schools, Learning," 41; Lapidge, "Abbot Germanus," 395–6; Haug, *Vernacular Literary Theory*, 230; Kelly, *Conspiracy of Allusion*, 13–35; and Mehtonen, *Old Concepts*, 120–1.

A consideration of the use of Macrobius in Wipo's *Gesta Chuonradi* can help us to appreciate the delicate and strategic case that the Encomiast is making for the fictional quality of his work. Wipo, an imperial chaplain, presented his *Gesta Chuonradi* to Emperor Conrad's son, the future Emperor Henry III, in 1046, only a few years after the *Encomium* itself was written.[76] Portraying himself as following in the footsteps of both biblical and classical writers of exemplary history in writing Conrad's life, Wipo sets up an implicit contrast between history writing and the other ways that ancient philosophers advised the res publica. Drawing directly on the same passage from Macrobius that was such a touchstone for developing ideas about fiction, and mentioning the late antique writer by name, Wipo identifies these other ways as "somnia probablia" (credible dreams) and "fabulosas narrationes" (fictional narratives) that were "honestis rebus et nominibus velatas, cum huiusmodi figmenta nil philosophiae refragentur" (veiled with noble affairs and names, since *figmenta* of this sort gainsay no philosophical question).[77] He values *figmenta* as tools for advising kings but does not position them within history writing. This concern shapes his text. In recounting the coronation of Conrad, he acknowledges that some of what the king did that day had a mystical significance ("mysterio"). However, because the *Gesta Chuonradi* are written as "historia publica," he acknowledges that readers attend more "ad novitatem rerum quam ad figuras verborum" (to the new turns of events than to the figurative meaning of the words).[78] Wipo is emphatically not hostile to representations of events that are figuratively rather than actually true. But that is the proper concern of poetry, such as he himself included at the end of the *Gesta Chuonradi*, and such as his *Tetralogus*, written for the instruction of the young Henry.[79] Where Wipo keeps poetry and history apart, the Encomiast lets them spill together – not accidently but purposefully.

Returning to prologue of the *Encomium*, we find that throughout the discussion of the loquacity with which he will praise Emma the Encomiast brings alive what could have been a merely conventional denigration of his opponents.[80] When he writes of his loquacity and his fear of being accused

76 Wipo, *Gesta Chuonradi*. Bresslau's introduction (xvi–xxii) for date.

77 Wipo, *Gesta Chuonradi*, prologue.

78 Wipo, *Gesta Chuonradi* 5.

79 Wipo, *Gesta Chuonradi* 40; and Wipo, *Tetralogus*.

80 *Rhetorica ad Herennium* 1.5.8; and Cicero, *De Inventione* 1.16.20. Haug, *Literary Theory*, 9.

of loquacity, he mentions other possible competing accounts of Emma's action that would be more restrained (*modestior*) but less truthful. This comment, when considered in the context of Harthacnut's court, may refer to specific arguments and discussions about Emma.[81] The mention of his envious detractors appears to be, then, not just an empty rhetorical stance but a reference to others at court who might be jealous of his close relationship with Emma. All this underscores the attractiveness of rhetoric, both in its epideictic form (concerned with praise or censure of an individual) and in its forensic form (concerned with the accusation or defence of individuals in law), to the Encomiast as he tries to use history to praise Emma and to make a case for her amid the infighting of Harthacnut's court.

Turning from the prologue to the argument allows us to see the Encomiast continuing to struggle with the nature of his text. In addressing the reader, rather than Emma, the Encomiast appears to have left behind his anxious critique of *historia*. Indeed, *historia* is no longer mentioned, and his concern turns to asserting that his text should be read as praise of Emma. Although much panegyric did masquerade as history writing, what is interesting here is that the Encomiast is open about his aim to praise. Indeed the reader cannot help but wonder what the Encomiast thought of the compatibility of *laus* and *historia*. The desire to praise, as the tradition of rhetorical historiography recognized and as the Encomiast was well placed to know, often led the historian to lie.[82] But praise was more positively part of Virgil's aim in writing the *Aeneid*, as the Encomiast will tell us.

In his concern to defend himself from the charge that he does not praise Emma sufficiently, the Encomiast draws attention to the artistry of his text by flagging its carefully designed structure. First, he advises the reader that a comparison of the beginning, middle, and end of his text illustrates that praise of Emma is always his purpose: "Quod ita esse ipse fatebere, meque ab eius laudibus nusquam accipies deuiare, si prima mediis, atque si extima sagaci more conferas primis" (But you will admit that this is the case [that the book is devoted to praise of Emma], and allow that I nowhere deviate from her praises, if you wisely compare the beginning with the middle,

81 Stafford, *QEQE*, 6–12; and Keynes, introduction, lxix–lxx.

82 Guenée, *Histoire*, 58–65 and 363; Morse, *Truth*, 130; Wiseman, "Lying Historians"; Mora-Lebrun, *L'Énéide*, 27 and 42–4; and Nelson, "History-Writing."

and the end with the beginning).[83] In a showy display of learning he then further labours the artifice of his work with reference to the construction of a circle, before returning to the structure of his own work: "Simili igitur continuatione laus reginae claret in primis, in mediis uiget, in ultimis inuenitur, omnemque prorsus codicis summam complectitur" (By a similar connection, therefore, the praise of the Queen is evident at the beginning, thrives in the middle, is present at the end, and embraces absolutely all of what the book amounts to).[84] The Encomiast alerts his reader to the patterned and artificial nature of his narrative. As Horace wrote of Homer, "Atque ita mentitur, sic veris falsa remiscet, / Primo ne medium, medio ne discrepet imum" (And so skilfully does he invent, so closely does he blend facts and fiction, that the middle is not discordant with the beginning, nor the end with the middle).[85] Horace, using the language of lying for fiction, represents pattern as a marker of fictionality. The Encomiast will offer a narrative that, like history writing and unlike the *Aeneid*, follows the chronological order of events, but he instructs his audience to read with attention to form. He thereby indicates that his meaning lies in part in the structure of his work. With his overt artistry the Encomiast places his text at the margins of historiography.[86] His knowledge of Horace, moreover, indicates that he has, again, aligned his work with poetry rather than history.[87]

The Encomiast ends his second preface with the phrase *explicit argumentum* (hence the editorial designation of the preface as an "argument"). *Argumentum* can mean simply a summary of the text, and this is in part an accurate description of this section of the *Encomium*. However, aware of the Encomiast's engagement with rhetoric, it is hard to banish entirely the rhetorical meaning of the term *argumentum* as denoting a narrative that stands between *historia* and *fabula*. The Encomiast's last word, *argumentum*, before he moves from his prefatory material to the body of his text, calls to mind a narrative that recounts events which could have happened, even if they did not.

83 *Enc.*, argument.

84 *Enc.*, argument.

85 Horace, *Ars Poetica* lines 151–2.

86 D.H. Green, *Medieval Romance*, 93–133.

87 *Enc.*, ed. Campbell, xxxiii. Horace was well known in the Middle Ages, especially from the tenth century onwards; his work is listed in the Saint-Bertin book list.

Reading Carefully: Virgil

Caught between irreconcilable views of historical truth, buffeted by dangerous infighting at court, the Encomiast's own views of the methodology of history appear contradictory and changeable. In trying to negotiate the place of historical truth in a defence of Emma, the Encomiast turns not just to the tradition of rhetorical history but also to poetry. Allusions to Virgil's *Aeneid* in the prologue and the argument show that a particular understanding of fiction offered the Encomiast some sort of solution and clarity as he tried to conceptualize his task. The first phrase to consider is *ut morti intrepidus occumberem*. The Encomiast assures Emma that he will risk death in order to further her cause. This line alludes to Virgil's account of the Greek soldier who was captured by the Trojans. The Greek vows that he will persuade the Trojans to admit the wooden horse (stuffed full of his armed compatriots) or die in the attempt. As we all know, he was successful. Virgil writes:

> "Ecce manus iuvenem interea post terga revinctum
> pastores magno ad regem clamore trahebant
> Dardanidae, qui se ignotum venientibus ultro,
> hoc ipsum ut strueret Troiamque aperiret Achivis,
> obtulerat, fidens animi atque in utrumque paratus,
> seu versare dolos seu certae occumbere morti."

> ("Meanwhile, lo! some Dardan shepherds with loud shouts were hailing to the king a youth whose hands were bound behind his back. To compass this very end and open Troy to the Achaeans, stranger though he was, he had of free will placed himself in the way of their coming, confident in the spirit and ready for either event, whether to ply his crafty wiles or to meet certain death.")[88]

This may not initially seem very interesting, but a little further on in this episode the Greek soldier, Sinon, draws attention to issues of truth and lying:

> "'Cuncta equidem tibi, rex, fuerit quodcumque, fatebor
> vera,' inquit: 'neque me Argolica de gente negabo:

88 Virgil, *Aeneid* 2.57–62.

hoc primum; nec si miserum Fortuna Sinonem
finxit, vanum etiam mendacemque improba finget.'"

("'Surely, O king,' he says, 'whatever befalls, I will tell thee all truly, nor will I deny that I am of Argive birth. This first I own; nor, if Fortune has moulded Sinon for misery, will she also in her spite mould him as false and lying.'")[89]

Servius's influential fourth-century commentary on the *Aeneid*, almost certainly known to the Encomiast, offers insight into the Encomiast's reason for turning to Virgil's account of Sinon.[90] In discussing this passage, Servius focuses on the process by which the Greek persuades the Trojans to let the horse in: "Et utitur bona arte mendacii, ut praemittat vera et sic falsa subiungat. nam quod de Palamede dicit verum est, quod de se subiungat falsum" (And he makes use of the valuable art of lying, so he says first what is true, and then he adds what is false. For what he says about Palamedes is true, but what he says about himself is false).[91] He notes that Sinon begins with what is true and what the Trojans will also recognize to be true. Only once he has established his credibility, therefore, does he go on to tell his very effective lies. Like the Encomiast, Servius is interested in the relationship between speaker and audience and the establishment of credibility.

The relevance of the reference to Sinon for the Encomiast's consideration of the nature of the narrative he is producing for Emma comes into even sharper focus when we recall the soldier's association with Palamedes. Among his lies, Virgil's Sinon falsely identifies himself as a kinsman of Palamedes, who was unfairly accused of betraying the Greeks. Servius explains that Palamedes was stoned to death after Ulysses used a forged letter (said to be from Priam, king of the Trojans) to frame Palamedes for treason. There is, obviously, no direct correspondence between Alfred and Palamedes, though both were killed as a result of forged letters. Given that accusations surrounding a forged letter lie at the heart of the Encomiast's attempts to exonerate Emma, his allusion to Sinon in his preface suggests that the letter included in the *Encomium* is a source of disquiet for the

89 Virgil, *Aeneid* 2.77–80.

90 Servius, *In Vergilii carmina commentarii.* On the Encomiast's knowledge of Servian commentary tradition see pages 92–7 herein.

91 Servius on *Aeneid* 2.81.

Encomiast. It is important to underline here that, in moving from the Encomiast's allusion to Sinon, to Palamedes and the letter, we are not overreaching: the episode is commented on not only by Servius but also by Cicero at the end of his *Topica* and by Boethius in his commentary on the *Topica*; both authors draw attention to the way that circumstantial evidence (in this instance the letter) can make a falsehood seem true.[92] Gerbert's introduction of these texts into the curriculum at Reims reminds us of their presence within the archdiocese of which the Encomiast's foundation was a part.[93] Staying with Reims, later in the eleventh century the Sinon episode would catch the eyes of the poet Godfrey of Reims who, like the Encomiast, was drawn to the story of Troy and conscious of its value for negotiating political conflict.[94]

What is the Encomiast doing with this set of echoes to Sinon, and also to Palamedes? Has the Encomiast here allied himself with the lying Greek soldier at just the point when he is professing his devotion to Emma? If this is the case, we are presented with two alternatives. Either he is going to work subversively against Emma, or he is alerting his audience that, in order to work for her, he is going to have to tell lies as well as fiction. I think we can safely dismiss the former because it is difficult to see anything subversive, in relation to Emma, going on in this text. Therefore, we are left with the latter: the Encomiast is telling his audience that not all of his account will conform to the standards of historical truth. In aligning himself with the Greek Sinon, the Encomiast indicates some of his anxiety about lying. But, more important for considering the fictionality of the *Encomium*, the audience – and here we must be referring to its learned members – that recognizes the reference to Sinon becomes complicit in the Encomiast's move away from history.

The sense that the Encomiast is preoccupied with lying is reinforced by the phrase to which I drew attention earlier: *facta uelut infecta*. This phrase is again significant and drives home the point that I have been making about fiction and lies. *Facta uelut infecta* – these words allude to the memorable passage in book 4 of the *Aeneid* where Fama takes flight to spread

92 Servius on *Aeneid* 2.81; Cicero, *Topica* 20.74; and Boethius, *In Ciceronis Topica*, book 6, p. 388.

93 Richer, *Historiae* 3.46. Lake, "Truth," 230.

94 Godfrey of Reims, "Sompnium de Odone," line 261; and Godfrey of Reims, "Ad Lingonensum," 397. Verbaal, "Homer," 331.

the news that Dido and Aeneas have slept together while sheltering from a storm in a cave:

> Extemplo Libyae magnas it Fama per urbes,
> Fama, malum qua non aliud velocius ullum.
> mobilitate viget viresque adquirit eundo;
> parva metu primo, mox sese attollit in auras
> ingrediturque solo, et caput inter nubila condit.
> illam Terra parens, ira inritata deorum,
> extremam, ut perhibent, Coeo Enceladoque sororem
> progenuit, pedibus celerem et pernicibus alis,
> monstrum horrendum, ingens, cui, quot sunt corpore plumae,
> tot vigiles oculi subter (mirabile dictu),
> tot linguae, totidem ora sonant, tot subrigit auris.
> nocte volat caeli medio terraeque per umbram,
> stridens, nec dulci declinat lumina somno;
> luce sedet custos aut summi culmine tecti,
> turribus aut altis, et magnas territat urbes,
> tam ficti pravique tenax quam nuntia veri.
> haec tum multiplici populos sermone replebat
> gaudens, et pariter facta atque infecta canebat:
> venisse Aenean, Troiano sanguine cretum,
> cui se pulchra viro dignetur iungere Dido;
> nunc hiemem inter se luxu, quam longa, fovere
> regnorum immemores turpique cupidine captos.

> (Forthwith Rumour runs through Libya's great cities – Rumour of all evils the most swift. Speed lends her strength, and she wins vigour as she goes; small at first through fear, soon she mounts up to the heaven, and walks the ground with head hidden in the clouds. Her, 'tis said, Mother Earth, provoked to anger against the gods, brought forth last, as sister to Coeus and Enceladus, swift of foot and fleet of wing, a monster awful and huge, who for the many feathers in her body has as many watchful eyes below – wondrous to tell – as many tongues, as many sounding mouths, as many pricked-up ears. By night, midway between heaven and earth, she flies through the gloom, screeching, nor droops her eyes in sweet sleep; by day she sits on guard on high roof-top or lofty turrets, and affrights great cities, clinging to the false and wrong, yet heralding truth. At this time, exulting with manifold gossip, she filled the nations and sang alike of fact and falsehood, how Aeneas is come, one born of Trojan blood, to whom in marriage fair Dido deigns to

> join herself; now they spend the winter, all its length, in wanton ease together, heedless of their realms and enthralled by shameless passion.)[95]

Virgil's Fama spreads both truth – what was done – and falsehood – what was not done – about Dido. This is just what the Encomiast does for Emma. Admittedly he only makes up lies that make her look good, which is not at all what Fama does for poor Dido. Nevertheless, in using this phrase, the Encomiast associates himself with Fama in a complex gesture, as a glance at the wide semantic field of *fama* indicates. Medieval notions of *fama* "meant public opinion, idle talk, rumor, and reputation as well as fame; both a good name and a bad one were called *fama*; and while *fama* denoted information or news, at the same time it meant the image formed of a person by that information."[96] At the centre of *fama* lies public opinion. This is not, however, beyond the scope of history, as indicated by Bede's influential view that *fama vulgans* lies at the heart of the *vera lex historiae*.[97] However, while it might appear that the Encomiast is here associating himself with this acceptable historical sense of *fama*, his account of Emma's life, as we have seen, flies in the face of public opinion. Members of Harthacnut's court would have recognized this instantly. Therefore, the Encomiast is perhaps better understood as signalling his hope that his version of events will mould public opinion at court. Furthermore, by alluding to Virgil's Fama at this point in the prologue, the Encomiast raises doubts about the veracity of all the accounts of Emma, not just his own, that were circulating at court and further afield; his allusion to Virgil makes the point that public opinion was not necessarily true or agreed on, and one often had to play for it.

The Encomiast, moreover, does not just cast doubts about public opinion and leave it at that. Rather, by recalling Virgil's Fama, he leaves the door open to fiction – a point that Chaucer can help us to see. The Encomiast's allusion revealingly prefigures Chaucer. In *The House of Fame* Chaucer is also drawn to Virgil's account of Fama, and, as he explores when he rewrites the story of Dido and Aeneas from a perspective that is more sympathetic to Dido, Dido is very much Virgil's own creation, rather than a historical representation. It is not, of course, just Chaucer who

95 Virgil, *Aeneid* 4.173–94.

96 Fenster and Smail, *Fama*, 2 and 11.

97 Bede, *HE*, preface. Ray, "Bede's *Vera Lex Historiae*"; Wickham, "Gossip."

does this; he is part of a tradition of creative responses to Dido,[98] and recognizing that tradition helps us not to overlook the importance of the Encomiast's allusion to Fama and Dido. We can see him circling around the issue of lying and what it means for his text; we can also see a glimmer of fiction on the horizon.

This passage from book 4 of the *Aeneid* may, finally, also help us to understand the Encomiast's use of the term *multiplex narratio* to describe his own text. Earlier I suggested that this phrase does not really denote history writing in a straightforward way. Is the Encomiast here thinking of Fame's *multiplex sermo* (4.189), which mixes truth and fiction? Is *this* the kind of text that he is writing, one that mixes history with fiction and lies? To answer this, we need to look at just how closely Virgil's description of Fama is recalled in the argument. The Encomiast still has Fama in mind when he concludes the argument: "His enim animaduersis, o lector, uigilique, immo etiam perspicaci, oculo mentis perscrutato textu, intellige, huius libelli seriem per omnia reginae Emmae laudibus respondere" (Noticing these matters, O Reader, and having scanned the narrative with a watchful, nay more, with a penetrating eye, understand that the course of this book is devoted entirely to the praise of Emma).[99] The language of this final sentence closely recalls the lines earlier in the argument in which the Encomiast explicitly invokes the model of Virgil and Octavian:

> Aeneida conscriptam a Uirgilio quis poterit infitiari ubique laudibus respondere Octouiani, cum pene nihil aut plane parum eius mentio uideatur nominatim interseri? Animaduerte igitur laudem suo generi asscriptam ipsius decori claritudinis claritatisque in omnibus nobilitare gloriam. Quis autem hoc neget, laudibus reginae hunc per omnia respondere codicem, cum non modo ad eius gloriam scribatur, uerum etiam eius maximam uideatur optinere partem?
>
> (Who can deny that the *Aeneid*, written by Virgil, is everywhere devoted to the praises of Octavian, although practically no mention of him by name, or clearly very little, is seen to be introduced? Note, therefore, that the praise accorded to his family everywhere celebrates the glory of their fame and renown to his own honour. Who can deny that this book is entirely devoted to

98 Courcelle, *Lecteurs païens*, 1:281–378; and Desmond, *Reading Dido*.

99 *Enc.*, argument. See pages 71–2 herein.

the praise of the Queen, since it is not only written to her glory, but since that subject occupies the greatest part of it.)[100]

The *animaduersis* of the closing sentence brings us back to the earlier *animaduerte* with which the Encomiast calls on his reader to notice that praise for his family is praise of Octavian. *Laudibus respondere* takes us back to the same place because he used these words, first to describe Virgil's praise of Octavian and then his own praise of Emma. So this final sentence emphasizes, through verbal repetition, that the Encomiast is indeed intending to do for Emma what Virgil did for Octavian. But there is a twist. If we dare align ourselves with the perspicacious reader, the phrase *vigilique ... occulo* brings us straight back to Virgil's description of Fame and her many eyes (*vigiles oculi* at *Aeneid* 4.182). Here the Encomiast is effectively issuing a warning to his complicit reader, one last time before taking up his story, that his text is full of fiction and even lies. And, further, that truth and lies may be equally (*partier* at *Aeneid* 4.190) and indistinguishably mixed. The close juxtaposition of the episode of Dido's fame and the identification of Emma with Octavian pushes away any unfortunate identification of her with the fallen queen, but not before this association has been admitted into the text. Thus the Encomiast acknowledges the rumours that circulate about Emma, which, as poems from the Norman court illustrate, could be as salacious as any gossip about Dido.[101]

Throughout the prologue and the argument the Encomiast is thinking about history in a sophisticated, though not tidy or entirely consistent, way. He keeps changing tack, reworking and deliberately obscuring the boundaries between history, fiction, and lies. It is here that we can see an author working in an intellectual and aesthetic context that is engaged with fictionality and the nature of history but which has not yet developed coherent theoretical frameworks within which to understand these concepts. The Encomiast's sophisticated inconsistency is reminiscent, once more, of *The House of Fame*. At the very least, Chaucer's unfinished poem encourages us to take the Encomiast's inconsistency seriously, rather than dismissing it as the result of the unthinking reproduction of various topoi about the writing of history, or even of the desire to deceive his audience. That audience would not have been so easily fooled. Rather, the prologue and the argument are a careful and densely allusive response to the

100 *Enc.*, argument.

101 Van Houts, "*Jezebel* and *Semiramis*."

difficulty of praising Emma when the audience was intimately familiar with the details of her life. There is, in short, nothing abstract or purely theoretical about the Encomiast's turn to fiction. It is the task of writing for Emma that has caused him to reassess the nature of *historia*. From this perspective, moreover, the *Encomium* appears as a significant text in the history of the development of fiction because its fiction is a response not only to intellectual and aesthetic developments but also to social and political necessity.

Playing Out in the Text

The Encomiast's invocation of Virgil subsequently informs the construction of the main body of the text. The entire text is not by any means structured according to that of the *Aeneid*, and Christian paradigms of the piety of the king are also a powerful thematic concern alongside engagement with the Roman story world. Many of the text's Virgilian echoes remain on the level of language rather than being deployed as allusion. Likewise, a Virgilian framework does not account for many of the text's more blatant fictions of family, such as the slandering of Ælfgifu and Harold. Nonetheless, the *Aeneid* does create a climate in which such lies make sense: Virgil rewrote family history, and the Encomiast follows in his footsteps. The influence of Virgil is most evident in the memorable accounts of Svein's and Cnut's conquests of England, where we find a clustering of Virgilian allusions that serve to represent Cnut as Aeneas, and Svein as his father, Anchises.[102]

The Encomiast gives very little information about Svein's campaign to conquer England and, instead, dwells on Svein's fleet:

> Aggregati tandem turritas ascendunt puppes, eratis rostris duces singulos uidentibus discriminantes. Hinc enim erat cernere leones auro fusiles in puppibus, hinc autem uolucres in summis malis uenientes austros suis signantes uersibus aut dracones uarios minantes incendia de naribus, illinc homines de solido auro argentoue rutilos uiuis quodammodo non inpares, atque illinc tauros erectis sursum collis protensisque cruribus mugitus cursusque uiuentium simulantes. Uideres quoque delphinos electro fusos, ueteremque rememorantes fabulam de eodem metallo centauros. Eiusdem preterea celaturae multa tibi dicerem insignia, si non monstrorum quae sculpta inerant me

102 Tyler, "Eyes of the Beholder," 257–65; and Orchard, "Literary Background," 160–6.

> laterent nomina. Sed quid nunc tibi latera carinarum memorem, non modo ornatitiis depicta coloribus, uerum etiam aureis argenteisque aspera signis? Regia quoque puppis tanto pulcritudine sui ceteris prestabat, quanto rex suae dignitatis honore milites antecedebat; de qua melius est ut sileam, quam pro magnitudine sui pauca dicam. Tali itaque freti classe dato signo repente gaudentes abeunt, atque uti iussi erant, pars ante, pars retro, equatis tamen rostris, regiae puppi se circumferunt.
>
> (When at length they were all gathered, they went on board the towered ships, having picked out by observation each man his own leader on the brazen prows. On one side lions moulded in gold were to be seen on the ships, on the other birds on the tops of the masts indicated by their movements the winds as they blew, or dragons of various kinds poured fire from their nostrils. Here there were glittering men of solid gold or silver nearly comparable to live ones, there bulls with necks raised high and legs outstretched were fashioned leaping and roaring like live ones. One might see dolphins moulded in electrum, and centaurs in the same metal, recalling the ancient fable [*ueteremque rememorantes fabulam*]. In addition, I might describe to you many examples of the same celature, if the names of the monsters which were there fashioned were known to me. But why should I now dwell upon the sides of the ships, which were not only painted with ornate colours, but were covered with gold and silver figures? The royal vessel excelled the others in beauty as much as the king preceded the soldiers in the honour of his proper dignity, concerning which it is better that I be silent than that I speak inadequately. Placing their confidence in such a fleet, when the signal was suddenly given, they set out gladly, and, as they had been ordered, placed themselves round about the royal vessel with level prows, some in front and some behind.)[103]

The description of these very royal ships being prepared slides into a description of the ships at sea and then into a brief account of the ease with which Svein subdued England.

The description of Svein's fleet is echoed later in the Encomiast's equally attention-grabbing but fact-free account of Cnut setting sail on his own conquest of England:

---

103 *Enc.* 1.4.

Tantus quoque decor inerat pupibus, ut intuentium hebetatis luminibus flammeae magis quam [l]igneae uiderentur a longe aspicientibus. Si quando enim sol illis iubar inmiscuit radiorum, hinc resplenduit fulgur armorum, illinc uero flamma dependentium clipeorum. Ardebat aurum in rostris, fulgebat quoque argentum in uariis nauium figuris. Tantus siquidem classis erat apparatus, ut, si quam gentem eius uellet expugnare dominus, naues tantum aduersarios terrerent, priusquam earum bellatores pugnam ullam capescerent. Nam quis contrariorum leones auri fulgore terribiles, quis metallinos homines aureo fronte minaces, quis dracones obrizo ardentes, quis tauros radiantibus auro cornibus necem intentantes in puppibus aspiceret, et nullo metu regem tantae copiae formidaret? Praeterea in tanta expeditione nullus inueniebatur seruus, nullus ex seruo libertus, nullus ignobilis, nullus senili aet<t>ate debilis; omnes enim erant nobiles, omnes plenae aetatis robore ualentes, omnes cuiuis pugnae satis habiles, omnes tantae uelocitatis, ut despectui eis essent equitantium pernicitates.

(So great, also, was the ornamentation of the ships, that the eyes of the beholders were dazzled, and to those looking from afar they seemed of flame rather than of wood. For if at any time the sun cast the splendour of its rays among them, the flashing of arms shone in one place, in another the flame of suspended shields. Gold shone on the prows, silver also flashed on the variously shaped ships. So great, in fact, was the magnificence of the fleet, that if its lord had desired to conquer any people, the ships alone would have terrified the enemy, before the warriors whom they carried joined battle at all. For who could look upon the lions of the foe, terrible with the brightness of gold, who upon the men of metal, menacing with golden face, who upon the dragons burning with pure gold, who upon the bulls on the ships threatening death, their horns shining with gold, without feeling any fear for the king of such a force?)[104]

Although there are similarities to Svein's ships in the form of the lions, the human figures, the dragons, and the men, as well as in the references to pure gold, the focus has shifted to the arms (specifically the shields) of Cnut's men and their nobility. The Encomiast's message is clear: Cnut is terrifying, and terror is a positive attribute for an early medieval king.

The *Aeneid* lies behind both of these fleets, and the Encomiast overtly tells us so when he writes of Svein's ships: "Uideres quoque delphinos

104 *Enc.* 2.4.

electro fusos, ueteremque rememorantes fabulam de eodem metallo centauros" (One might see dolphins moulded in electrum, and centaurs in the same metal, recalling the ancient fable).[105] The fable is Virgil's account of a boat race – one of the games held to mark the anniversary of the death of Anchises. Indeed, the Encomiast's description of Svein's fleet is full of verbal echoes from this boat race.[106] What this does is to represent Svein as Anchises, the father who fled Troy with his son but died before the Trojans reached Italy. Allusions to Anchises's funeral games are highly appropriate here; Svein, of course, arrives in England and becomes king. However, his rule does not last long, and Cnut must reconquer the kingdom. The striking aptness of this paralleling assures us that the Encomiast knows what he is doing and that he very carefully deploys classical allusion in creating his dynastic legend.

In the account of Cnut's fleet Virgil is not explicitly mentioned, and, as has been shown by Andy Orchard, the focus shifts to presenting Cnut as a Christian king, with the ornamental beasts recalling the symbols of the four evangelists.[107] But the emphasis on the armour and weaponry of the soldiers, which flash in the sun like flame, also recalls the shield of Aeneas.[108] Indeed, the message that Cnut stands as both a Christian king and an Aeneas figure is a critical feature in the construction of the dynastic myth. Virgil portrays the sun glittering on Aeneas's arm, including the shield, as Aeneas discovers this gift from his mother, Venus. To unwrap the significance of this allusion we must look at the context of the shield in the *Aeneid.* The shield and other weapons are a gift from Venus to her son as he prepares for the campaign against Turnus, war leader of the Italians. Victory in this battle ends the wandering of the Trojans. Aeneas's subsequent marriage to Lavinia, daughter of the king of Italy, leads eventually to the foundation of Rome by their descendants. Depicted, and thus foretold, on Aeneas's shield is a major component of the Roman story world: the history of Rome from the birth of Romulus and Remus to the triumph of Caesar Augustus, the first emperor – and the same Octavian to whom Emma is explicitly paralleled in the argument. The battle of Actium, in

105 *Enc.* 1.4.

106 See Tyler, "Eyes of the Beholder," 260–2, for the specific linguistic parallels between the *Encomium* and the *Aeneid.* Note also that Isidore discusses centaurs as an example of *fabula* in *Ety.* 1.40.

107 Orchard, "Literary Background," 164.

108 Tyler, "Eyes of the Beholder," 261.

which Octavian defeated Mark Antony at sea and gained sole rule of the Roman Empire, dominates Virgil's depiction of the shield and provides much of the imagery and language of the fleets of the *Encomium*. As he sets sail to conquer England, Cnut is thus figured as a second Aeneas, destined to found an enduring and glorious empire, but Octavian (and thus Emma) is not forgotten. Cnut's ships are similar to Svein's and so closely modelled on Aeneas's shield that it is not necessary for the Encomiast to label them too as *fabula*, especially given his advice in the argument to compare the beginning, the middle, and the end of his work.

Even within the context of the finely crafted prose of the *Encomium* and its broad linguistic debt to the pagan classics, the fleets of Svein and Cnut stand out in high relief. Dense with Virgilian echoes, Virgilian figures of speech, and Virgilan mythic beasts, the accounts of these two fleets that describe their ornament are literally ornamented themselves. According to the Encomiast's own strictures in the prologue, this is just the kind of writing that blurs the line between things done and things not done. He makes this point directly when he refers to his source for these ships as the *vetus fabula* (ancient fable). These ships are far from what the Encomiast would have classified as history, but they do not claim to be credible as facts; indeed, they are openly fictional, explicitly make-believe. In engaging with Virgil, one of the great conduits of the Roman story world into the Middle Ages, the Encomiast found a space to explore his own understanding of fictionality.

There is another fleet of ships in the *Encomium*, those that Harthacnut takes with him to visit his mother in Bruges.[109] The Encomiast recounts that, during the reign of Harold Harefoot, Emma summoned Harthacnut to come to her in exile. Like the description of the fleets of Svein and Cnut, the passage describing Harthacnut's setting sail is full of Virgilian echoes. Unlike the earlier descriptions, however, here the echoes come from throughout the *Aeneid* and do not allow us to draw a parallel between Harthacnut and any one figure in the poem.[110] On one level this illustrates what a good source the *Aeneid* is for the language of sea voyages that can be plundered with little thematic consequence. From this perspective the close ties between Svein's and Cnut's ships and specific well-chosen episodes in

109 *Enc.* 3.9–11.

110 *Enc.* 3.9. Echoes include *Aeneid* 1.35, 1.37, 1.520, 3.277, 5.768, 5.836, 6.901, 9.484, and 12.736.

the *Aeneid* thus come into even sharper focus. Yet the account of Harthacnut's fleet, when read in the context of the ships of Svein and Cnut, still has much to tell us about the Encomiast's negotiation of history and fiction, as well as shedding light on his more thematic concerns.

There is nothing particularly heroic about Harthacnut. Svein's ships projected royalty, Cnut's ships projected terror, but Harthacnut's were caught in a storm on the way to Flanders. In the midst of the storm he has a reassuring vision, not that he will reconquer England but that Harold Harefoot will conveniently die so that, as the Encomiast says, "regnum patriis uiribus domitum sibi iusto heredi iustissima successione incolumne rediret" (the kingdom conquered by his father's strength would return safely by most rightful succession to himself, the rightful heir).[111] Even after this vision he does not head off to conquer England (as Aeneas would have done) but is "cum matre morante et memoratae uisionis promissa expectante" (with his mother expecting the events promised by the vision).[112] It was not until after the arrival of messengers to announce that Harold was dead and that the English nobles wanted Harthacnut that "his Hardocnuto materque animati repetere statuunt horas auiti regni" (encouraged by these things, Harthacnut and his mother decided to return to the shores of the ancestral realm).[113] In terms of the Encomiast's thematic concerns, his downplaying of Harthacnut's military might lays heavy stress on his succession as rightful heir to Cnut, rather than as conqueror. Throughout the *Encomium*, rightful succession, and its association with Emma as wife and mother, remains a major concern.[114] This description of his fleet shows us Harthacnut firmly outside the Virgilian paradigm that encompassed both his father and his grandfather before him. The account of Harthacnut's fleet makes it clear, too, that the young king is no Octavian. Svein and Cnut participated in a mythical, heroic past into which it would have been easy to fit Harthacnut as comparable to Silvius, son of Aeneas and Lavinia. But Harthacnut, who comes to the throne as rightful heir, not conqueror, is part of the present. In the present he is certainly no Octavian, victor of that famous sea battle at Actium, because that parallel has been reserved for Emma. Having to fit a powerful woman into the picture ultimately disrupts the Virgilian framework.

111 *Enc.* 3.9.
112 *Enc.* 3.10.
113 *Enc.* 3.11.
114 John, "Riddle," 60–1, 78–9, 82, and 91–3; and Stafford, *QEQE*, 30.

The Encomiast also has to face the problem of history and fiction in recounting Harthacnut's fleet. Although he has used Virgilian language to describe Harthacnut's ships, these distinctly unfabulous ships are credible. The Encomiast's language in this passage is much more like the unornamented writing that he associated with history in his prologue. Yet his combination of rhetorical verisimilitude and Virgilian allusion is motivated just as much by his desire to use form to convey meaning, as was his representation of the fleets of Svein and Cnut. In the argument the Encomiast told us to pay attention to form, and indeed, structurally, the *Encomium* is a very carefully balanced text. If we read the text according to the Encomiast's advice and compare the ships of Harthacnut, recounted at the end of the text, with those of his grandfather and father from the beginning and the middle of the text, we find that, in the present, Emma emerges as a more important figure than Harthacnut. Furthermore, the juxtaposition of Harthacnut's fleet with Svein's and Cnut's fleets, whose fictionality was so ostentatiously announced, also highlights the way in which the Encomiast's acceptance of fiction (although perhaps set in train by his rather strict view of history, coupled with his worries about outright lying) becomes a more positive move. He uses overt fiction and the Roman story world as a way to glorify Svein and Cnut – a move with a Virgilian sanction.

Subtle echoes of Lucan in this passage support the sense that Harthacnut is an anticlimax in comparison to his grandfather and his father and also hint that all is not well behind this facade of rightful succession. Three echoes of Lucan's grim epic recall the eerily becalmed sea and then terrifying storm that prevent Caesar from returning to Italy, thwarting for the time being his destructive desire for war. Significantly, these echoes, all from one episode of *De bello civili*, are not scattered fragments of language.[115] Comparison, however veiled, to Lucan's Caesar, a megalomaniac, further distances Harthacnut from Virgilian hopes of dynastic glory and admits a counter-narrative that evokes civil war. The contrast between the quietness of these echoes and the Encomiast's concern to make sure his audience recognized those to Anchises's and Aeneas's ships underscores the point that Lucan is not used in the *Encomium* to speak directly to Harthacnut's court. No occasion for teaching is created here, where an audience unfamiliar with Lucan's poem might be encouraged to ask about

115 *Enc.* 3.9 and Lucan, *De bello civili* 5.416, 429, and 511 – all noted by Campbell, *Enc.*, xxxii.

it. And yet, as with the other Lucan allusions previously discussed, these are strikingly apt and show that the Encomiast used Lucan in his thinking. Perhaps he was even engaging more learned audience members, away from those whom he was trying to persuade of an Anglo-Danish Virgilian golden age, in recognizing that Lucan had more to offer in understanding the politics of Harthacnut's court than did Virgil. It was not just lies about Emma that made him worry about the truth of his history but equally the instability of the very Anglo-Danish dynasty that he celebrated. From this perspective too, attending to the Encomiast's use of Lucan further underscores his consciousness of the fictionality of his vision of the Anglo-Danish dynasty.

The Encomiast's use of fiction places him within the intellectual environment that in the twelfth century produced much more assured and positive views of the value of fiction than did those offered by rhetorical theory or even Macrobius. For example, earlier we looked at how the Encomiast's use of the term *narrationis contextio* to denote his own text suggested that his thinking on history and fable may have owed a significant debt to Macrobius. By using the term *narrationis contextio*, the Encomiast associated himself not with the truth of *narratio fabulosa* but with the worst kind of fable that is based on falsehood. When the Chartrian scholar William of Conches (c. 1080–c. 1154) comments on the same passage from Macrobius, he goes even further than Macrobius does. In developing the case for the legitimacy of poetic fiction, he rehabilitates even these worst fables.[116] Viewed from this perspective, the Encomiast's association of himself with the truth of fiction is not just a negative rejection of history as a form unsuitable for Emma but also a recognition that fiction too can be useful *and* truthful.

Virgil, Servius, and History

The centrality of the *Aeneid* to the fabric of the *Encomium* that is revealed through the close reading of Svein's and Cnut's fleets shows us that the relation of history and fiction that so concerned the Encomiast in his prologue continued to engage him in the course of writing the remainder of his text. The tradition in which he is likely to have read the *Aeneid* will

116 Dronke, *Fabula*, 13–30; Minnis and Scott, *Literary Theory*, 118–19; Baswell, *Virgil in Medieval England*, 97–101; and Mehtonen, *Old Concepts*, 14, 50, and 143–4. See pages 73–4 herein.

allow us to consider further the Encomiast's perspective on the complicated and ever-shifting relationship of history and fiction and what this might mean for his own narrative.[117] In the eleventh century Virgil was read within the commentary tradition, and, as such, most early medieval copies of Virgil came with an "apparatus of prefaces, lives of Virgil, prefatory poems, glosses and commentary." At the centre of the critical apparatus was some version of Servius's commentary on Virgil. The importance of Servius for the reception of Virgil in the Middle Ages cannot be underestimated – especially before the end of the eleventh century, the period from which new commentaries on the *Aeneid* began to be produced.[118] The book list from Saint-Bertin records that, at least in 1104, the library had a manuscript designated as Servius, in addition to texts of Virgil's poems. A ninth-century complete Virgil in the library of Saint-Amand offers us a surviving example, from a Flemish foundation, of a Virgil accompanied by extensive glosses and commentaries, including those by Servius (Valenciennes, Bibliothèque municipale, 407). Looking at the text of the *Encomium*, it is not difficult to prove that the Encomiast's conception of Virgil was formed by the commentary tradition. For example, the Encomiast quotes the couplet: "Nocte pluit tota, redeunt spectacula ma(ne);/ Diuisum imperium cum Ioue Cesar habes" (It rains all night, but the public games duly take place in the morning; / You, Caesar, hold divided empire with Jove).[119] That the Encomiast knows these lines and attributes them to Virgil indicates that he read Virgil within the commentary tradition. The couplet is attributed to Virgil in accounts of his life. Such texts often circulated with Servian commentaries.[120] Fundamentally, a Servian

117 With different emphases, D.H. Green also discusses medieval understanding of the historicity of Virgil (*Medieval Romance*, 14–15 and 153–62).

118 Comparetti, *Vergil in the Middle Ages*, 56–61; Munk Olsen, "Virgile et la renaissance," 38–42 and 48; M. Irvine, *Textual Culture*: 118–61, esp. 118 (from which the quotation is taken) and 126–41; Mora-Lebrun, *L'Énéide*, 12–20; Baswell, *Virgil in Medieval England*, 47–53; Fowler, "Virgil Commentary"; and Marshall, *Servius*, esp. 12 and 14.

119 *Enc.* 2.19.

120 For the couplet see Donatus, *Vita quae Donati aucti dicitur*, in *Vitae Vergilianae*, ed., Brugnoli and Stok, 111. For a range of lives of Virgil see Ziolkowski and Putnam, *Virgilian Tradition*, 179–403; and Stok, "Virgil." The couplet does not appear in the surviving lives of Virgil that circulated before the twelfth century, but it is attested in later medieval manuscripts of lives of Virgil (*Vitae*, ed. Brugnoli and Stok, 73–4). However, as Comparetti shows, this and other couplets were already associated with the biography of Virgil when the poems in Codex Salmasianus were copied in the

view of the purpose of the *Aeneid* shapes the Encomiast's understanding of his task. According to Servius, Octavian asked Virgil to write the *Aeneid* in order to praise him through his ancestors: "intentio Virgilii haec est: Homerum imitari et Augustum laudare a parentibus" (this is Virgil's intention: to imitate Homer and to praise Augustus through his ancestors).[121] As we saw earlier, this is just what the Encomiast says he will do for Emma, his own Octavian.

How then might the Servian commentary tradition have informed the Encomiast's understanding of fable and its relationship to the writing of history? Servius held that the *Aeneid* contained truth alongside fiction: "est autem heroicum quod constat ex divinis humanisque personis, continens vera cum fictis; nam Aeneam ad Italiam venisse manifestum est, Venerem vero locutam cum Iove missumve Mercurium constat esse compositum" (Moreover, it is heroic because it is composed of divine and human characters, containing truths with fictions; for, while it is evident that Aeneas came to Italy, it is certain that Venus having spoken with Jove, or Mercury having being sent, are made up).[122] Later Servius explains that in his account of the Trojans Virgil "ab hac ... historia ... discedit" (departs from this history) but that he does this not "per ignorantiam, sed per artem poeticam" (through ignorance, but through poetic art).[123] For Servius, poetic fable could represent the truth of history.[124] Furthermore, Servius drew a distinction between fable and history that does not rest on whether or not something happened but on whether it *could* happen. He writes that "fabula est dicta res contra naturam, sive facta sive non facta" (fable is a matter recounted against nature, whether it happened or not), while "historia est quicquid secundum naturam dicitur, sive factum sive non factum" (history is something recounted according to nature, whether it happened or not).[125] Put alongside the *Encomium*, this passage makes it clear that, by turning to Virgil, the Encomiast was seeking to place his text

late eighth century (*Vergil in the Middle Ages*, 144). Campbell notes that the couplet is not Virgilian and suggests that the Encomiast may have had a manuscript with introductory material and the life of the poet; it is now clear that he did (*Enc.*, xxiii–xxiv). On the relationship of Donatus and Servius see M. Irvine, *Textual Culture*, 118, 121–6, and 129.

121 Servius, preface to the *Aeneid*.

122 Servius, preface to the *Aeneid*.

123 Servius on *Aeneid* 1.267.

124 M. Irvine, *Textual Culture*, 131–2, 135–6, and 240.

125 Servius on *Aeneid* 1.235. Wiseman, "Lying Historians," 130.

within a tradition that neither expected history to tell what actually happened, nor judged fable as "untrue." Servius conceptualizes *fabula* and *historia* in a way that obscures the rhetorical distinctions between *historia*, *argumentum*, and *fabula* that are focused on events which happened, events which did not happen but could have happened, and events which could not have happened.

The irrelevance of the actual existence of the fleets of Svein and Cnut comes into sharper focus when we look at what Servius says about the boat races to mark Anchises's death. These boat races are, as we saw, the Encomiast's acknowledged model for Svein's fleet, and he told the reader that Virgil's account was fable. Servius interprets these funeral games as a reflection of the games given by Octavian in honour of Julius Caesar, and, taking a stricter view of history than that we have just looked at, Servius comments that Virgil often wanders away from history: "magni frequenter, ut diximus, ad opus suum Vergilius aliqua ex historia derivat: nam sic omnia inducit, quasi divini honores solvantur Anchisae quos constat Iulio Caesari tribuisse Augustum" (Very often, as we have seen, in his work Virgil deviates somewhat from history: thus, for example, he represents the whole matter as if the divine honors, which, it is well known, Augustus bestowed on Julius Caesar, were paid to Anchises).[126] In Servius's view, Virgil's account of the past did not tell what actually happened, but it advanced the current political aims of his patron Octavian. The Encomiast, in short, inherited a paradigm that consciously confuses the line between history and fiction, as we would see them, in its search not so much for exemplary models as for political utility.

The contrast between Servian and more rhetorical ideas of history and fable (not to mention the range of approaches to *historia* within Servius's own commentary) highlights that the Encomiast was exposed to a rich and fluid, rather than clear and systematized, set of ideas about history and fable. His own discussion of history, his flagging of Virgil as fable, and the style of his text (including as it does sections of high ornament) show that he was well aware that history and fable were complex and contested ideas to be negotiated. From Virgil, mediated through the commentary tradition, the Encomiast inherits a licence to invent (and indeed to abandon) history, to use fable to create an Anglo-Danish dynasty by giving it mythical origins, and to decide who was in the dynasty (Edward the Confessor)

126 Servius on *Aeneid* 5.45.

and who was out (Harold Harefoot) regardless of their parentage. Perhaps Virgil even offers the Encomiast solace as he worries about lies. Ultimately, even though he does worry that he is more like Sinon, the lying soldier, or even Fama, I think the Encomiast would like to see himself as doing for Emma what Virgil did for Octavian.

The account of Fama reminds us that Virgil's depiction of Dido exposed the ancient poet to learned medieval readers as no historian. Looking briefly at the reception of Virgil's Dido in the Middle Ages allows us to finish considering what the Encomiast might have thought of the *Aeneid* as history.[127] It is not by chance that the Encomiast should have alluded to Dido in a prologue that is so preoccupied with the relationship of history and fiction. Servius tells us that Virgil based his Dido on Medea from Apollonius's *Argonautica* and that the historical Dido was a chaste widow. In contrast, Virgil's fictional Dido throws herself onto the pyre when Aeneas leaves her to found Rome – this Dido is not the stuff of history.[128]

127 M.L. Lord, "Dido"; Courcelle, *Lecteurs*, 1:376–8; Desmond, *Reading Dido*, 23–73, esp. 55–8, and 81–3; and Foehr-Janssens, "Reine Didon." In connection with the Encomiast's perception of the historicity of the *Aeneid*, it would be interesting to explore whether he knew the prose of Dares the Phrygian, *De excidio Troiae historia*. Although the text is spurious, Dares's claim to offer an eyewitness account of the fall of Troy was widely accepted in the Middle Ages, and his depiction of Aeneas as the treacherous betrayer of his city was considered to have greater value as history than Virgil's version. The increasing popularity of the *De excidio* from the early eleventh century onwards reminds us that the Encomiast wrote during a period in which Virgil's poetic account of the fall of Troy was contested. It is not impossible that the Encomiast knew Dares. Isidore mentioned Dares as the first historian of Greek and Trojan matters (*Ety.* 1.42). Mora-Lebrun argues that the *De excidio* was integral to Dudo's *De moribus et actis primorum Normanniae ducum*, a text produced at the beginning of the eleventh century; among its dedicatees was Emma's brother Richard II. The Saint-Bertin library held a copy of the *De excidio* in 1104. On the manuscripts of Dares, see Munk Olsen, *L'étude des auteurs*, 1:363–78. For discussions of the influence of Dares in the Middle Ages, in addition to Courcelle and Desmond see Guenée, *Histoire*, 275–6 and 303–4; Singerman, *Clouds of Poesy*, 147–9; Morse, *Truth*, 97–8; Mora-Lebrun, *L'Énéide*, 20–1, 28–40; and Baswell, *Virgil in Medieval England*, 18–21.

128 "Despectus Iarbus rex Libyae, qui Didonem re vera voluit ducere uxorem et, ut habet historia, cum haec negaret, Carthagini intulit bellum; cuius timore cum cogeretur a civibus, petiit ut ante placaret manes mariti prioris, et exaedificata igitur pyra se in ignem praecipitavit" (Rejected Iarbas, King of Libya, who in the truth of the matter wanted to marry Dido, as history has it, when she refused this, he waged war on the Carthaginians. When she was compelled [to marry him] by the citizens, who feared him, she asked that first she might placate the spirit of her first husband, and having built therefore a pyre, she threw herself into the fire) (Servius on *Aeneid* 4.36).

Given the stories and counter-stories circulating at court about the twice-married Emma, we can see that a passage about Dido, wronged by Virgil, might attract the Encomiast, even if he is otherwise actively resisting any paralleling of the two queens. Macrobius develops Servius's point to incorporate issues of style, a subject that troubled the Encomiast, as we have seen. In the *Saturnalia*, large sections of which are devoted to the literary criticism of Virgil's works, Servius appears among the guests at a fictitious dinner party.[129] Putting the words in Servius's mouth, Macrobius writes that Virgil's Dido is not historical. Macrobius then goes on to think about the power of a well-told, but made-up, story. He writes:

> sed bene in rem suam vertit quidquid ubicumque invenit imitandum; adeo ut de Argonauticorum quarto, quorum scriptor est Apollonius, librum Aeneidos suae quartum totum paene formaverit, ad Didonem vel Aenean amatoriam incontinentiam Medeae circa Iasonem transferendo. quod ita elegantius auctore digessit, ut fabula lascivientis Didonis, quam falsam novit universitas, per tot tamen saecula speciem veritatis obtineat et ita pro vero per ora omnium volitet, ut pictores fictoresque et qui figmentis liciorum contextas imitantur effigies, hac materia vel maxime in effigiandis simulacris tamquam unico argumento decoris utantur, nec minus histrionum perpetuis et gestibus et cantibus celebretur. tantum valuit pulchritudo narrandi ut omnes Phoenissae castitatis conscii, nec ignari manum sibi iniecisse reginam, ne pateretur damnum pudoris, coniveant tamen fabulae, et intra conscientiam veri fidem prementes malint pro vero celebrari quod pectoribus humanis dulcedo fingentis infudit.

> (but wherever he had found material worthy of imitation he has turned it to good use for his own ends. Thus he has modelled his fourth book of the *Aeneid* almost entirely on the fourth Book of the *Argonautica* of Apollonius by taking the story of Medea's passionate love for Jason and applying it to the loves of Dido and Aeneas. And here he has arranged the subject matter so much more tastefully than his model that the story of Dido's passion, which all the world knows to be fiction, has nevertheless for all these many years been regarded as true. For it so wings its way, as truth, through the lips of all men, that painters and sculptors and those who represent human figures in tapestry take it for their theme in preference to any other, when they fashion

129 M. Irvine, *Textual Culture*, 141–7; and D. Kelly, *Conspiracy of Allusion*, 36–78.

their likenesses, as if it were the one subject in which they can display their artistry; and actors too, no less, never cease to celebrate the story with gesture and in song. Indeed, the beauty of Virgil's narrative has so far prevailed that, although all are aware of the chastity of the Phoenician queen and know that she laid hands on herself to save her good name, still they turn a blind eye to the fiction, suppress in their minds the evidence of truth, and choose rather to regard as true the tale which the charm of a poet's imagination has implanted in the hearts of mankind.)[130]

In this passage Macrobius draws attention to precisely the role of beautiful writing in the triumph of fiction over fact, and, as D.H. Green's discussion of this passage emphasizes, Macrobius also draws attention to the way in which the audience consciously chooses to believe in Virgil's Dido, even though it knows better.[131] This passage raises the intriguing question of whether the Encomiast was trying to produce a text that would use well-wrought fiction to make his audience forget the real Emma, or at least aspects of the real Emma.[132] Has Virgil's use of fiction, presented in ornamental writing, in order to praise Octavian, given the Encomiast licence to do the same for Emma? Ultimately the Encomiast does not step so far away from history, and he deliberately produces a work in prose – a choice that separates the *Encomium* from the *Aeneid*, as the Encomiast himself emphasizes by calling his work *prorsus codicis*, at just the point in the argument when he associates himself most explicitly with Virgil.[133]

Although we cannot make out the precise contours of his conception of history, fiction, and lies, perhaps because the Encomiast did not know them himself, we can see him using the *Aeneid* to explore their limits. It is only once he has explored fully the possibilities of history that the

130 Macrobius, *Saturnalia* 5.17.

131 Desmond, *Reading Dido*, 55–6; Baswell, *Virgil in Medieval England*, 19; and D.H. Green, *Medieval Romance*, 15.

132 The Encomiast need not have known the *Saturnalia* to make such a connection between Virgil's poem and his own work; his access to Servius, as well as to the general intellectual milieu in which he wrote, could have been sufficient. Campbell's note 2 to *Enc.* 2.8 registers a possible linguistic parallel with *Saturnalia*. On the transmission of the *Saturnalia* see L.D. Reynolds, *Texts and Transmission*, 233–5. On knowledge of the *Saturnalia* from the twelfth to the thirteenth century, with some comment on earlier centuries, including eleventh-century manuscripts, see D. Kelly, *Conspiracy of Allusion*, 13–35.

133 *Enc.*, argument.

Encomiast, newly confident of its diversity, can step back within its permeable boundaries. The Encomiast's improvised and often confused, though never unsophisticated, exploration of the boundary between history and fiction shows us that he wrote within an intellectual climate which in the twelfth century would produce powerful conceptual arguments for the truth of fiction. The integral place of Virgil within the Encomiast's bold movements towards fiction illustrates clearly that for him the *Aeneid* was no longer a schoolroom text studied from a grammatical perspective for what it taught about language rather than its content. Rather, it and the Roman story world it conveyed, had become powerfully attractive both in terms of literary theory and as a political tool. From this perspective the *Encomium* is a deeply classicizing text that finds the Roman story world to be fit for emulation. In this the Encomiast's concern is far away from Orosius's anxiety about the need to include the Trojans in his history.[134]

New Ending

The ending of the recently discovered Edwardian recension of the *Encomium* powerfully underlines the fast-changing social and political imperatives behind the Encomiast's improvised Virgilian theorizing about the nature of *historia* and the place of the text in the court. After Harthacnut's death the image of the half-brothers – united with their mother and ruling the kingdom – has no value for the future as the Encomiast moves forward, recounting events almost as they happen. Emma, Edward, and the whole land grieve deeply over the death of the king's brother. Then, as he does in the argument, the Encomiast turns and addresses the reader, writing:

> Nunc, o lector uigil, tua appareat sollicitudo atque reduc ad memoriam in prohemio quidnam dixerim de circulo. Memini quidem dixisse me in faciendo circulo ad unum idem punctum fieri reductionem quatinus circulus rotunditatis accipiat orbem. Sic quoque factum est in anglici regni administrando regimine.

> (Now, O watchful reader, let your careful attention show itself and bring back to recollection what I said in my preface about the circle. I indeed

134 Orosius, *Historiae* 1.17–18. See chapter 1 herein.

> recollect that I said that in making a circle there must be a returning to one and the same point so that the circle may attain the orbit of its round form. So likewise it was brought to pass in the arranging of the rule of the English kingdom.)[135]

In the argument Emma was at the centre of this circle, but now the circle refers to the return of the West Saxon dynasty, and the Encomiast moves on to celebrate Æthelred as the foremost king of his time, and Edward as his legitimate heir, for whose return the land had long yearned. As Simon Keynes and Rosalind Love have pointed out, this ending is bizarre given that the Encomiast had so conspicuously written Æthelred out of his history, even effacing his parentage of Edward and Alfred. The ending also utterly undoes the carefully crafted Virgilian history of the Anglo-Danish dynasty. Commemoration of Æthelred negates Cnut as a second Aeneas. Strikingly, Emma is no longer the centre of the circle and no longer Octavian, even though the Encomiast has carefully based his new ending on the beginning in which she was the central figure.

The absence of Virgilian allusion in the new ending confirms that the Encomiast was unable to recuperate the Virgilian framework in which he had so deeply invested his work, both conceptually in his understanding of history and in terms of the story it told. An Anglo-Danish dynasty with an illustrious future no longer made any sense, and his polemical text was effectively in tatters. The flagrant contradictions between the new ending of the *Encomium* and the rest of the text meanwhile suggest that in the fast-moving political environment of 1042 there was no time for a radical reorientation and rewriting of the text, though he and Emma remained committed to using the text to protect and forward her now even more precarious position. All he can do is to associate Emma with Edward as two figures weeping over the death of a son, a brother, and a dynasty, and to herald the glorious restoration of the West Saxon dynasty. Remembering the subsequently difficult relationship between Edward and Emma, we strongly suspect that Edward was not receptive to his mother's efforts to persuade him that his and England's future lay with the Anglo-Danish dynasty in which she featured centrally.

---

135 Keynes and Love, "Godwine's Ship," 195–6.

3 Talking about History: The *Encomium Emmae reginae* and the Court of Harthacnut

Introduction

The *Encomium Emmae reginae* testified in the previous chapter to the advanced learning of its author and to the stimulus that the politics of the text's court audience exerted on his theorizing about the relationship of history and fiction. From this perspective the *Encomium* is a prime example of a Latin text that was produced in order to have a particular impact on a lay audience, whose members were not learned. This chapter will focus accordingly on the social and linguistic contexts of the *Encomium* in order to consider the strategies available for communicating a Latin text to lay audiences in the specific context of Anglo-Danish England.[1] In other words, I want to pose the questions of how and why Emma and the Encomiast conceived of a Latin text as an effective way of protecting her vulnerable position. By exploring both the production and the reception of the *Encomium* within the distinctively multilingual context of Harthacnut's court (where English, Danish, French, Dutch, and Latin all interacted), I aim to contribute to our general understanding of the way in which lay people staked claims to Latin literary culture in the Middle Ages, especially in the period just prior to widespread vernacularization.

1 On lay audiences and Latin historiography see, for important examples, Nelson, "Public Histories"; Nelson, "History-Writing"; McKitterick, *Written Word*, 236–41; Mortensen, "Stylistic Choice"; and Innes, "Memory."

Harthacnut's Court

Harthacnut's short rule was unpopular, and his court was riven by factionalism. The court, a group of people rather than a place, included the men and women who regularly attended the king, among whom were the most influential warriors and clerics, thegns in royal service, and importantly the queen and her household. The make-up of the court and of royal assemblies, the *witan*, was overlapping.[2] The complex and shifting alliances that resulted from both the Danish conquest and the bitter succession disputes after Cnut's death left the court a potentially violent group made up of men who had been supporters of Harold Harefoot, of Harthacnut, and of Edward and Alfred. Harthacnut, branded a pledge breaker for the murder of Earl Eadwulf and criticized for having had Harold Harefoot's body thrown in the Thames, was himself implicated in this violence. His invitation to Edward the Confessor to rule jointly with him may have been an attempt to quell the disquiet stirred by his rule. Among those who appeared at court was Earl Godwine, one of the new earls who had risen to power under Cnut. He had switched allegiance from Harthacnut to Harold Harefoot, and then back again to Harthacnut, and was, in the interim, implicated in the death of Alfred – actions that hardly recommended him to Harthacnut, Emma, or Edward. Also recorded at court was Godwine's old enemy, Earl Leofric of Mercia (whom we saw in chapter 1 as associated with the "C" version of the Anglo-Saxon Chronicle, which survives copied together with the *Old English Orosius*). Leofric, who had backed Harold Harefoot's claims and may have been a kinsman of Ælfgifu of Northampton, was now among the followers of Harthacnut. He would go on to become a strong supporter of Edward in the king's struggles against Godwine.

The politics of Cnut's conquest continued to shape attitudes in Harthacnut's court where, for instance, Harold, son of Thorkell, was earl. Thorkell's savage harrying of Æthelred's kingdom had occurred in recent memory, as had his switching of sides from Svein to Æthelred and back to Cnut. Despite his changeable loyalties Thorkell later ruled Denmark for Cnut and kept custody there of the child Harthacnut. Harthacnut and

---

2 Keynes, *Diplomas*, 156–62; Stafford, *QEQE*, 97–122; Cubitt, *Court Culture*, 1–15; J. Campbell, "Anglo-Saxon Courts"; Reuter, "Assembly Politics"; Insley, "Assemblies and Charters"; and Roach, *Kingship and Consent*, 1–44.

Edward may have viewed Thorkell's son from different perspectives. As we saw in the previous chapter, discord also extended to the relations between Emma and Edward that, despite what the Encomiast says, were uneasy. The fundamental difficulty of presenting Edward with an Anglo-Danish dynastic origin legend is starkly evident in the Edwardian recension's celebration of him as Æthelred's son.[3]

The tensions of Harthacnut's court and its leading men are very carefully negotiated by the Encomiast. Thorkell, who is of special concern to him, is represented as having been steadfast in the Danish cause, and the text is cagey about Godwine's role in Alfred's death, blame for which is assigned to the now-dead Harold Harefoot.[4] And the Encomiast, as we have seen, depicts perfect harmony between Emma, Harthacnut, and Edward.[5] His expertly delicate treatment of the potential sources of division among those now loyal to Harthacnut is central to the important arguments put forward by Simon Keynes and developed by Andy Orchard that the *Encomium* was written both *for* and from *within* Harthacnut's court.[6] Moreover, both the Encomiast's prefaces and his text overtly express his anxiety that his version of events will not be accepted by those around Emma.[7] In vindicating Emma for Alfred's death, he imagines someone hostile to her objecting to his account: "Sed fortassis hic mihi quilibet clamabit, quem liuor huiuscae dominae liuidum onerosumque reddit" (But perchance at this point someone, whom ill-will towards this lady has rendered spiteful and odious, will protest to me).[8] The mark left on the *Encomium* by the tensions of Harthacnut's court, along with the text's hasty revision for Edward's court, is a strong indication that it was written as a means of intervening in debates within that court, and more broadly among the political elite, about Emma; further, it heavily underscores the fact that the *Encomium* was meaningless if it failed in this goal. This understanding of the intentions of Emma and the Encomiast brings us firmly back to the question of how Latin texts were communicated to lay audiences.

---

3 Bolton, "Newly Emergent," and chapter 2 herein.

4 For Thorkell: *Enc.* 1.2, 2.1, 2.2, 2.3, 2.6, 2.7, and 2.9. For Godwine: *Enc.* 3.4. For Harold: *Enc.* 3.5.

5 *Enc.* 3.14.

6 Keynes, introduction, xxxix–xli, lix, and lxix; Orchard, "Literary Background," esp. 158; and chapter 2 and the works cited there.

7 See chapter 2 herein.

8 *Enc.* 3.7.

To begin, we need to return to the kind of Latin text that the *Encomium* is. The *Encomium* is a classicizing work whose pages reveal the influence of a range of Latin authors, including Sallust and Lucan, as well as Ovid, Horace, Juvenal, Lucretius, and Virgil.[9] In his open acknowledgment of Virgil, the Encomiast signals to his audience that recognition of his debt to the Roman story world is central to the meaning of his text. His use of Virgil to figure the Anglo-Danish dynasty as the founders of Rome is an essential aspect of the text's ideological meaning in that it asserts an imperial and civilized European identity for Cnut.[10] Importantly, this meaning could have been appreciated by a lay person who had some exposure to Latin literary culture but who could not actually read Latin; both the oral circulation of the Roman story world, as imagined in the *Old English Boethius*, and its strong presence in the vernacular written word come into play here.[11]

Although we saw in the last chapter that the Encomiast's exploration of the nature of fiction was intellectually sophisticated, this need not distance the text from Harthacnut's court and the elites connected to it. On the contrary, it is precisely the meeting of the two different experiences of the fictionality of his account that generates his theorizing. The Encomiast is deeply interested in the distinction between the lies that are told to trick an audience and the untruths that both author and audience recognize as such. In the context of the current discussion of the audience of the *Encomium*, what is most significant is that, although the Encomiast's arguments about the nature of *historia* are highly learned and would have required an educated reader to be apprehended, they are intimately connected to his concern to sway the opinions of the uneducated members of Harthacnut's court. That is, the Encomiast's intellectually sophisticated exploration of the boundary between historical narrative and fiction was a response to a social and political problem: the need to present a version of events that defended Emma to an audience that had participated in those events and would have had definite views about her reputation. This audience in particular would have recognized that parts of his text were untrue, and obviously so. It would have asked what that fiction was doing, what meaning it created. Thus, in order to make sense of the text rather

9 *Enc.*, ed., Campbell, xxix–xxxiv; and Orchard, "Literary Background," 159–60. On knowledge of Virgil in Anglo-Saxon England, see note 19 below.

10 Tyler, "Eyes of the Beholder," 257–68, and chapter 2 herein.

11 See chapter 1.

than simply dismiss it, the least intellectual members of Harthacnut's court would also have had to ask the same questions about the nature of fiction that the Encomiast was unable to resist posing in his prefaces (if not in the same terms). His foregrounding of his attempt to be Emma's Virgil draws his audience, learned and unlearned alike, to his recourse to the Roman story world as a space in which to explore the political potential of fiction. The Encomiast's use of Virgil alerts us to the way in which his text might have appealed to people with different kinds of, and access to, Latinity, and it invites us to look at the interaction of these different Latinities.[12]

Talking around the Text

An assessment of the central role that talk played in shaping and disseminating the substance of the *Encomium* can help us to see how a Latin text could have been envisaged as contributing to political debate in Harthacnut's court. The language of the two prefaces makes clear not only that the Encomiast intended his written Latin text to intervene in spoken debate about Emma but also that this text was given its form in an environment in which the oral and the written interacted. As Stafford writes, talking was a central means of governing in late Anglo-Saxon England, and a premium was placed on controlled speech.[13] Controlled speech is governed by rhetorical rules, whether written in the Ciceronian treatises that influenced the Encomiast or expressed as part of the decorum of court behaviour. In the prologue, addressed to Emma, the Encomiast conceives of history as written down in order to be heard. Indeed it is precisely the situation of having the text he has written (*scribens*) heard by its audience (*auditor*) that leads him to worry about the relationship of *facta* and *infecta*.[14] In the argument the Encomiast addresses himself not to the listener (*auditor*) but to the reader (*lector*). Back in the prologue, he associates his much-criticized loquacity with both the written and the spoken word, and the term he uses for the bitterness with which his enemies assail him, *mordaciter*, neatly brings to mind the real mouths that argued about Emma and the Anglo-Danish legacy in Harthacnut's court. The Encomiast's repeated allusions to Virgil's figure of Fama, who was spreading rumours, both true and

12 Banniard, "Language and Communication"; and McKitterick, "Latin and Romance," 135–7.

13 Stafford, *QEQE*, 106.

14 See chapter 2 herein.

false, about Dido, also reveal his concern for the way in which conversation, counsel, debate, and gossip make and break reputations, especially Emma's. Alongside various oral and written traditions, these highly social activities were influential factors in shaping the *Encomium*.[15]

In looking at the impact of literacy in the Middle Ages, scholars (most especially Michael Clanchy, Franz Bäuml, and Brian Stock) have emphasized that the function of literacy within a society is of greater importance than the ability of the individual to read; thus a few literate people, be they members of the clergy or of the laity, can have a disproportionately significant impact on lay access to written texts by discussing and explaining the content of those texts to others.[16] Precisely because it is rooted in social relationships, Brian Stock's influential notion of the "textual community" has been immensely productive in opening up the subject of the ability of the non-learned secular aristocrat to access and make use of Latin literary culture.[17] At the same time, however, Stock's view of literacy as widening the gap between the literate culture of the learned (who came to see literacy as "identical with rationality") and popular culture (which remained primarily oral and thus of lesser value in the eyes of the learned) entails a situation of "cultural diglossia" (in Walter Ong's terminology) that poses problems for understanding the *Encomium* within Harthacnut's court.[18] The focus on how texts are mediated to the illiterate leads to a view of literacy in which authority accrues to literate writers and interpreters of texts (who are generally male clerics), and consequently hides from view the ways in which the spoken words of lay people, including lay women, could shape the conception, production, and reception of written Latin texts. In a court context (as also in wider political assemblies) – in which the clerical and lay elites, both male and female, mingled and in which learning conferred authority, but in which there were other kinds of power, including that of an active patron – the issue of who had control over the written

15 For the Encomiast's interest in Virgil's Fama, see chapter 2. On gossip and orality see the articles in Fenster and Smail, *Fama*; Wickham, "Gossip"; and Innes "Memory," esp. 19.

16 Clanchy, *From Memory to Written Record*; Bäuml, "Varieties," esp. 237–49; Stock, *Implications of Literacy*; and Stock, *Listening for the Text*.

17 Stock, *Implications of Literacy*, 522.

18 Stock, *Implications of Literacy*, 31; Ong, "Orality, Literacy"; and Ziolkowski, "Cultural Diglossia."

word was potentially a very complex process with communication and the dissemination of knowledge taking place in many different directions.

Functional models of literacy provide a useful starting point for seeing how stories from the *Aeneid* might have been available to lay aristocrats – an important element for understanding the *Encomium* in Harthacnut's court. If a medieval reader's Latinity extended beyond rudimentary knowledge of the Psalms, he or she was likely to have been exposed to the *Aeneid*.[19] The basic nature of glosses in many manuscripts suggests that, even within the schoolroom, the *Aeneid* was surrounded by a developed culture of explanation.[20] This tradition of teaching the *Aeneid* to the young would, I think, have made it more natural for a figure such as the Encomiast to tell stories from the *Aeneid* in a court context and to explain the use of a Virgilian framework for the *Encomium*. Many portions of the *Aeneid* are, after all, simply good stories whose potential value could be apprehended without direct access to the text (which, as the place of Troy within Old English prose texts indicates, was certainly the case).[21] If members of the audience did not already know it, and this might be particularly so for the Danish incomers, the *Encomium* would become an occasion for teaching about Troy. In this regard the text was evidently effective because, in the next generation, not only is the story of Aeneas central to the *Vita Ædwardi*, but it parodies the Encomiast's attempt to represent the Anglo-Danish dynasty as heirs of this Trojan legacy.[22]

The Roman story world played a fundamental role not only in the education of clerics but also in the way clerics taught and guided secular aristocrats in the eleventh century.[23] However, in looking at, for example, the desire of many European ruling dynasties for Trojan origins, one sees that, even if the initial impulse may have been clerical, the laity would come to have their own, very secular stake in the *Aeneid* and in accounts of Troy

19 On the importance of Virgil throughout the Middle Ages and in Anglo-Saxon England, see chapter 2, pages 59–61, and the work cited there. Despite the scarcity of surviving manuscripts of the *Aeneid* from this period, texts reveal an intensive knowledge of the poem in learned circles in late Anglo-Saxon England: see Gneuss and Lapidge, *Bibliographical Handlists* for manuscripts of the *Aeneid*; Lapidge, "Study of Latin Texts," 101; and Baswell, *Virgil in Medieval England*.

20 L.D. Reynolds, *Medieval Reading*, 11 and 28–33; Lapidge, "Study of Latin Texts," 99–140; and Wieland, "Glossed Manuscript."

21 Baswell, *Virgil in Medieval England*, 30–40, and chapter 1 herein.

22 See chapter 4 herein.

23 Jaeger, *Envy of Angels*, 139–64

and Rome.[24] The early leap of the *Aeneid* from Latin into the vernacular, when it was rendered into Old French as the *Roman d'Eneas* in the mid-1150s, further illustrates the draw of the *Aeneid* for lay audiences.[25] Looking specifically at England in the decades before the Danish conquest and continuing after, we have evidence of knowledge of the Roman story world among the laity, with vernacular translations attesting to its currency; they just as often assume knowledge of this material as transmit it.[26] Thus we should recognize as well the presence of Latinate men and women among the lay elite, including the ealdorman Æthelweard, whose Latinity shaped the Anglo-Saxon understanding of their own past. For example, using Virgilian echoes, Æthelweard recalls Aeneas's momentous arrival in Italy, when he recounts the arrival of Hengest and Horsa in England in his Latin translation of the Anglo-Saxon Chronicle.[27] Literate aristocrats such as Æthelweard were the exception rather than the rule; there is no reason to assume, however, that these exceptions were isolated and that these aristocrats did not *speak* with other noblemen and women about what they had learned in Latin books. Catherine Cubitt's recent work on the agency of Ælfric's lay patrons, Æthelweard and his son, is critical here too in highlighting the confidence with which they engaged in shaping the production of their commissioned texts.[28] We must not assume, in approaching the *Encomium*, that the *Aeneid* was only known as a scholarly text. Christopher Baswell's characterization of the move of the *Aeneid* into the vernacular as "explosive" alerts us to see in the *Encomium* not just the preparation for that vernacularization but the signs of growing lay claims to the content of the *Aeneid* in eleventh-century England.[29]

---

24 Baswell, *Virgil in Medieval England*, 2, 7, 10–14, and 40; Southern, "Classical Tradition," 170 and 189–95; Guenée, *Histoire*, 275–9; Ingledew, "Book of Troy"; and Innes, "Teutons or Trojans?" 248–9.

25 *Roman d'Eneas*.

26 See chapter 1 herein.

27 Æthelweard, *Chronicon* 1.3; and xlix in Campbell's introduction. Winterbottom, "Style of Aethelweard"; J. Campbell, "England, c. 991," 164–5; Gretsch, "Historiography," 224 and 241; and Tyler, "Trojans."

28 Cubitt, "Lay Patrons"; and on lay literacy generally see herein chapter 1, page 45, and the works cited there.

29 Baswell, *Virgil in Medieval England*, 2, 10–16, 62, and esp. 168–219.

Multilingual Pre-conquest England

In thinking about how the *Encomium* and the *Aeneid* might have been known at Harthacnut's court, we need to remember that the talk surrounding the *Encomium*, the *Aeneid*, and other Latin texts in the Anglo-Danish court was not just in *the* vernacular, or *a* vernacular, but in *several* vernaculars: English, Danish, French, and Dutch. Looking forward to the complex linguistic situation of post-conquest England suggests ways of approaching the linguistic consequences of the earlier Danish conquest of England and how they may have shaped the *Encomium*. The centrality of trilingualism to the vibrancy of the literary culture of Norman England has been highlighted by recent work, especially by Ian Short and Jocelyn Wogan-Browne. The long-established use of English as a written language encouraged the flourishing of French as a written language. As a consequence, the first written French historiography and proto-romance were the products of a distinctly insular, Anglo-Norman, literary culture.[30] Scholars have also noted that the growing confidence of written vernaculars in the twelfth century changed the environment of Latin texts. Moreover, in this environment the interplay of oral and written, Latin and vernacular, played an influential role in the emergence of fiction while the authority and truthfulness of written narratives was seen to be undermined by their move into the vernacular.[31] Ian Short's insistence that the "vernacularisation of culture" was "one of the most important, and one of the least widely recognized, aspects of the new intellectual vitality of the twelfth century" prompts me to ask if some of the sophistication of the *Encomium*'s interaction with its audience results from its production in a polyglot context, which included a written vernacular.[32]

The linguistic and cultural complexity of the Anglo-Danish court, especially in the reign of Harthacnut, far outstrips that of post-conquest England.[33] This point is strikingly made if we simply consider the languages spoken by those figures who are pictured in the *Encomium*'s

30 Short, "Patrons and Polyglots"; Wogan-Browne, *Saints Lives*, 118; Tyler, "From Old English to Old French"; and O'Donnell, Townend, and Tyler, "European Literature." See also Clanchy, *From Memory to Written Record*, 199–225.

31 Bäuml, "Varieties," 249–65; and D.H. Green, *Medieval Listening and Reading*, 237–69.

32 Short, "Patrons and Polyglots," 231; Tyler, "From Old English to Old French"; and Tyler, "Crossing Conquests," 173–4.

33 For recent incisive discussion see O'Brien, *Reversing Babel*, esp. 1–121.

frontispiece (see frontispiece herein): Emma, Harthacnut, Edward, and the Encomiast. The Norman Emma, raised in Rouen and married to Æthelred II, certainly spoke French and English; being the daughter of the Danish Gunnor, and the wife of Cnut, she may also have spoken Norse.[34] Emma may further have acquired Old Dutch (a language very close to Old English) while in exile in Bruges. Her son Harthacnut, who was raised in England and Denmark, would most likely have spoken both English and Norse. Her son Edward the Confessor, raised in England and Normandy, would have spoken both English and French. When he returned to England from exile, he was accompanied by Leofric, who was English but likely educated in the French-speaking part of Imperial Lotharingia; by the Norman Robert, abbot of Jumièges; and by Herman, who was also likely a Lotharingian (though it is not clear whether he was French or German speaking).[35] Any, or all three of these clerics, could have been a learned interpreter of the *Encomium* for Edward and others at court, underscoring that a key member of the text's audience, though apparently not himself Latinate, was well positioned to gain access to the text's meaning.

The last figure in the frontispiece, the suppliant Encomiast, was obviously literate in Latin, and even before he came to England he may have been familiar with contexts in which two vernacular languages were in contact. His rendering of personal and place names indicates a Germanic speaker, making it likely that he spoke Dutch. However, the closeness of Saint-Omer to the permeable (social as much as geographical) linguistic frontier between French and Dutch, as well as the position of the city within the archdiocese of Reims, increases the likelihood that he spoke or was familiar with both languages and was aware of the social and political issues involved in negotiating language contact.[36] His reference to the Flemish court, and in particular to the Countess Adela, daughter of the French king Robert the Pious, underscores his awareness of language contact and politics in the highest levels of Flemish society – and not incidentally suggests that Emma and Adela may have spoken to each other and

34 Stafford, *QEQE*, 214.

35 On Leofric see Tyler, "German Imperial Bishops." Given that the others who are thought to have returned to England with Edward were francophone (Leofric; Robert; and Ralph, son of Edward's sister Goda and Count Drogo of the Vexin), we may surmise that Herman was too (Barlow, *Edward the Confessor*, 50).

36 *Enc.*, ed. Campbell, xxxvi–xxxvii; Milis, "French Low Countries," 347; Milis, "Linguistic Boundary"; de Grauwe, "*Olla vogala*"; and van Houts, "Flemish Contribution," 121–2.

those around them in French as well as, or instead of, Dutch.[37] Meanwhile, turning to contact between English and Dutch, we find the Encomiast well placed to have experienced this before his arrival in England. Some of the earliest written Old Dutch is found in contexts of Anglo-Flemish interaction. There are Old Dutch glosses, likely by an English scribe, in a Saint-Bertin copy of Orosius's *Historiae* dating from the first half of the eleventh century.[38] This final example of the Encomiast's range of linguistic experience makes the further point that he came from a city or a foundation that experienced a wide two-way exchange of intellectual culture between Saint-Bertin and England, which is evident also in the presence of Anglo-Saxon scribes and artists at Saint-Bertin; there, especially during the abbacy of Odbert (986–1007), they influenced the style of manuscript illumination. The exchange is also evident in manuscripts of Flemish origin in Anglo-Saxon libraries, and vice versa.[39] These artistic, intellectual, and linguistic exchanges between Saint-Bertin and England were part of wider social and political links between Flanders and England that go back at least as far as the presence of Grimbald of Saint-Bertin in Alfred's court in the late ninth century and the marriage of Alfred's daughter Ælfthryth to Baldwin II, Count of Flanders (879–918).[40] Dutch speakers and English speakers had long experience of communicating with each other, and Dutch-speaking clerics were intimately aware of the status of English as a written language, which they had themselves imitated.

The Anglo-Danish court must have been characterized by much explaining across linguistic boundaries, and the *Encomium* reflects this. In such a multilingual and increasingly European context, Latin, which was not associated with Anglo-Saxon or Danish parties or with the French of Emma and Edward, would have had a political and a linguistic utility as a suitable medium for a text that sought to transcend factionalism. Precisely because Latin was nobody's mother tongue, it could circumvent the entrenched divisions in Harthacnut's court that stemmed from the Danish conquest of England more than a generation earlier. Such a perspective

37 *Enc.* 3.7.

38 Boulogne-sur-mer, Bibliothèque municipale, 126, fol. 96 ff. Milis, "French Low Countries," 346–7; van Oostrom, *Stemmen op schrift*, 98; and van Houts, "Contrasts and Interaction," 4–5.

39 Wilmart, "Livres"; Gameson, "Angleterre," 172–3 and 181–9; Gameson, "'Signed' Manuscripts," 33–5; and Vanderputten, *Monastic Reform*, 69–70 and 144.

40 Grierson, "England and Flanders"; J. Campbell, "England, France, Flanders and Germany"; and Ortenberg, *English Church*, 21–40.

encourages us to think about the Latin of the *Encomium* as facilitating rather than hindering communication, and then the symbolic value of Latin, with its Roman story-world associations, becomes part of the text's social meaning. We should likewise register that the *Encomium* is not written in the cliquish and abstruse Latin of the Benedictine Reformers, which had so dominated the Latin produced in England; rather it is written in a still stylized but much more communicative Latin suited to the expression of the increasingly European aspirations of the court's secular elite.[41] The importance of courts and assemblies broadly in Europe reminds us too of some of the shared behaviours and goals of such political groups and meetings in which symbolic actions were used to communicate in indirect but persuasive ways in order to contribute to the creation of consensus.[42] This framework helps situate the *Encomium*'s highly symbolic mode of invoking the Trojans, as a parallel, but not an ancestor, of the Anglo-Danish dynasty.

Each of the vernaculars present even in Harthacnut's court alone would have interacted differently with Latin literary culture. Both Emma and Edward were francophone, and likely the Encomiast was as well; that is, the text's patron, a key member of its audience (which also included Edward's clerical advisers Robert of Jumièges and Leofric), and its author all spoke French.[43] Sandwiched between the Carolingian era, when spoken Latin could be understood by the West Franks, and the emergence of historical writing in French in the twelfth century, the eleventh century would seem to be a low point for lay engagement in historical narrative. However, facets of the role that Janet Nelson ascribes to historiography in the ninth century were retained. Drawing attention to the social role of history writing and the centrality of the *spoken* word to that role, she writes: "History writing was the special mode in which the learned participated in counsel: it was associated with, not alternative to, speaking, and speaking out."[44] The self-presentation, as "translators," of the first generation of historians to write in French indicates that there was a continuity between the Latin historiography of the Carolingian Empire and

41 Lapidge, "Hermeneutic Style"; Tyler, "From Old English to Old French," 168; Stephenson, "Byrhtferth's *Enchiridion*"; Stephenson, "Scapegoating"; and van Houts, "Flemish Contribution," 119.

42 Reuter, "Assembly Politics," 201–3.

43 Lewis, "French in England"; and Porter, "Earliest Texts."

44 Nelson, "History-writing," 438; Nelson, "Public Histories."

the production of French texts in the twelfth century. We may need to envisage an intervening stage during which the history writing aimed at the laity was written in Latin with the understanding that it would be read aloud or explicated in the vernacular, a process made easier by the linguistic proximity of Latin and French. In observing Emma's choice to commission a Latin text, we need to be aware that the ways in which Latin texts functioned in French-speaking environments may have influenced her expectations.[45]

When we turn to look at England, in contrast to the French-speaking areas of the Continent, we find that history writing was emphatically a vernacular activity to the extent that William of Malmesbury, writing in the 1120s, complained that there had been no history in Latin in England since Bede, other than Æthelweard's translation of the Chronicle from English into Latin.[46] William's exaggeration draws attention to the unusual (and thus, in the context of Harthacnut's court, marked) role that the English vernacular played in preserving a record of the past. In the decades after the *Encomium* was written, we saw that the activities of both Godwine and Leofric (rival earls in Edward's reign, as they had been in Harthacnut's court) were followed in two different versions of the Anglo-Saxon Chronicle, while the perspective of Edward's court shaped a third.

45 On the relationship between Latin and French up to the tenth century see Banniard, "Language and Communication," and his important monograph, *Viva Voce*. See also the work of Wright, especially *A Sociophilological Study of Late Latin* and "Translation between Latin and Romance." On twelfth-century French historians as translators see Damian-Grint, *New Historians*, 17–18. Wright's argument that literary translations between Latin and French did not occur before the twelfth-century renaissance – they were not needed, because of the "linguistic versatility and sophistication" of the users of texts – is important in considering the relationship of written Latin historiography to spoken vernacular language; "Translation between Latin and Romance," esp. 27. Even if we shy away from accepting his very late date for the final division between Latin and Romance, his argument alerts us to the strategies that facilitated extemporaneous translation from Latin into the linguistically proximate French spoken vernacular. See also Clanchy, *From Memory to Written Record*, 217–22. The views that I have presented of the consequences of the linguistic proximity of Latin and French differ from Shopkow's emphasis on Latin and the vernacular as "linguistically separate" and, in many ways, isolated from each other. This view of the relationship of Latin and the vernacular is consonant with her view of Norman lay patrons having little influence over the Latin texts that they commissioned. She views the move into the written vernacular as essential for lay control of historiography (*History and Community*, 25–9 and 246–75).

46 William of Malmesbury, *Gesta regum Anglorum* (hereafter cited as *GRA*) 1.Prologue.

The presence of three competing vernacular accounts and the manner in which version "D" conflates versions "C" and "E," revealing an awareness among Chronicle users of this competition, points to the importance of vernacular history writing as a political discourse in mid-eleventh-century England, where it intervened in, rather than passively recorded, events. Meanwhile the copying of version "C" together with the *Old English Orosius* just a few years after the Encomiast wrote his work suggests that at least some members of the original audience of the *Encomium* were accustomed to getting their history in the form of written English texts that could have been easily read aloud, and that using Rome to think with was not limited to Latin.[47] Even though it is written in Latin, Emma's *Encomium*, both in its classicism and in its partisan perspective, is enabled by the use of vernacular history writing in England as an active political discourse.

Other aspects of English in the eleventh century also inform the linguistic and social contexts of the *Encomium*. To begin with, although written English facilitated lay access to texts, there was not a direct correspondence between written and spoken forms of English. This is, of course, generally true of languages and not a specifically English phenomenon. However, the gap between written and spoken English was made greater and more apparent by the development of a standardized form of written English, based on the norms of late West Saxon, during the course of the tenth and eleventh centuries. This standardized form of English, which was used regardless of the local variety of English spoken, was a consequence of the coming together of clerical efforts to reform written English with the expansion of West Saxon political power throughout England. Thus, like Latin, written English also had a symbolic value and was not a neutral means of communication.[48]

Moreover, we must also be aware of the symbolic meaning of English to Norse speakers and the practical issues involved in their participation in English written culture. English continued to be a language of governance, the Church, and literary culture; for example, law codes, charters, homilies, and poetry all continued to be produced and copied in English.

---

47 See chapter 1 herein.

48 Gneuss, "Standard Old English"; Hofstetter, "Winchester and Standardization"; and Foot, "Making of *Angelcynn*." Clancy discusses the association of standardized English with clerical and royal authority in England of 1066, but this was also the case for the period following the Danish conquest (*From Memory to Written Record*, 213).

The use of written English during the period of Danish rule would have required strategies for explaining the content of English texts to Danish speakers, and for Danish speakers to influence the content of English texts; law codes provide a particularly good example of the outcome of this sort of dynamic process. After the Danish conquest Wulfstan produced written English law codes for Cnut, just as he had done for Æthelred II, codes that presumably required discussion in Danish as well as English in order to gain a witan's approval.[49] Emma, whose marriage to Æthelred II brought her to his court for fourteen years and who played a substantial role alongside Wulfstan in introducing Cnut to the norms of English kingship, may also have contributed to sustaining written English culture during the reigns of her second husband and their son.[50] In Harthacnut's court, information contained in written English as well as in Latin texts would have *had* to make the move from the written to the oral realm. The thinness of the Chronicle for the reign of Cnut, especially in the context of the use of English for other types of text in the Anglo-Danish period, meanwhile, suggests that the Chronicle was not only an English-language political discourse but also one associated particularly with the Anglo-Saxon ruling dynasty; in contrast, Cnut cultivated skalds, while Emma turned to Latin.[51] That the annals of the reign of Æthelred were written retrospectively, after his defeat by Cnut, confirms the Chronicle's preoccupation with the history of the Anglo-Saxon, rather than the Anglo-Danish, dynasty.[52] It was not that chronicle writing stopped in Cnut's reign, but rather that Cnut was not its subject. Moreover, the prominence of the Danes as the enemy of the Anglo-Saxons from the very inception of the Chronicle in ninth-century Wessex, and the Chronicle's disdainful representation of the Vikings as untrustworthy pagans, would not have recommended this English language genre for the celebration of Cnut's achievements.

The Danish conquest brought not only Scandinavian language but also Scandinavian literary culture to the royal court of England. Two aspects of that literary culture are relevant here: first, the place of skaldic verse in Anglo-Saxon and Anglo-Scandinavian courts and the issue of its intelligibility; second, the direct influence of Old Norse literary tradition, in

49 Townend, "Contextualizing *Knútsdrápur*," 174–5; and Townend, *Language and History in Viking Age England.*

50 Stafford, *QEQE*, 229–33; and Wormald, "Archbishop Wulfstan," esp. 245.

51 Lawson, *Cnut*, 49–54; and Brooks, "Why Is the *Anglo-Saxon Chronicle* about Kings?"

52 Keynes, "Declining Reputation of King Æthelred."

the form of oral prose narrative and Eddic verse, on the *Encomium* itself. Skaldic verse, an oral genre, was obscure, with even native speakers of Norse requiring it to be interpreted, and yet it clearly flourished in Cnut's court and other contexts associated with him.[53] The poem *Liðsmannaflokr*, a text linked to Cnut's garrison in London in the early years of his reign, appears to include a representation of Emma.[54] Not only do we need to wonder whether the English members of the Anglo-Danish court could have understood skaldic verse, but also, as Matthew Townend has discussed, skaldic verse may have remained largely incomprehensible to the Danes themselves. The Danes, who spoke East Norse, were notoriously poor audiences for skaldic verse, which, besides being highly technical, was a predominately West Norse tradition. Furthermore, it appears that skaldic verse was accompanied by a culture of talking about the text, even in West Norse contexts.[55] It seems only reasonable to suggest then that strategies for explaining skaldic verse to East Norse and English speakers existed alongside strategies for explaining Latin texts such as the *Aeneid* and the *Encomium*. At the very least, skaldic verse illustrates that we should not imagine that the Latin literary tradition, in its need for explication by a learned professional, in this case a cleric, was in a unique situation in the Anglo-Scandinavian court culture of eleventh-century England. And, as we saw earlier, even texts in English like the intellectually demanding *Old English Boethius* could require interpretation.[56]

Eddic verse and oral prose narrative, much less difficult genres than skaldic verse, may also have directly influenced the Encomiast. His depictions of the magic raven banner under which the Danes marched into battle and of the fabulous animals of Svein's and Cnut's ships find their analogues in Old Norse literature, as well as drawing on Virgilian models. At the same time we may perceive a specifically English inflection in this coming together of Norse and Roman story worlds. The text is strongly reminiscent of the close relationship, which extends back for centuries,

53 Townend, "Contextualizing *Knútsdrápur*."

54 Poole, "Skaldic Verse and Anglo-Saxon History," 286; Poole, *Viking Poems*, 86–115; Stafford, *QEQE*, 22–3; and Townend, "Contextualizing *Knútsdrápur*," 151, 162–4, and 166–7.

55 Townend, "Norse Poets and English Kings." I am grateful to Matthew Townend for discussing skaldic verse in England with me.

56 See chapter 1 herein.

between *Beowulf* and the *Letter of Alexander to Aristotle*, whose manuscript precedes the *Encomium* by only a generation.[57] The Scandinavian and Roman story worlds had long been juxtaposed in Anglo-Saxon England. The account of Svein's and Cnut's ships represents a seamless fusing of the Roman and Norse story worlds, which could not have happened without vernacular talk in England. Indeed, without such vernacular talk the *Encomium* is inconceivable. We need to account not only for lay knowledge of the Roman story world but also for a Flemish cleric's knowledge of the Old Norse literary tradition. Emma, whom we know was among the Encomiast's informants, appears as a likely source of his knowledge of Old Norse.[58] The influence of oral Old Norse traditions on the *Encomium* is direct evidence of the fluid relationship between Latin and the vernaculars and between the written and the oral at Harthacnut's court. This fluidity fundamentally undermines the ascription of the power of learning and knowledge solely to a Latinate cleric.

Although the linguistic complexity of Harthacnut's court and the long-established use of English as a written language challenge the authority of Latin, they certainly do not negate it. Moreover, the striking sophistication of the Encomiast's intellectual formation suggests a writer who could command the respect necessary to enable Latin to intervene politically. Thus, we also need to consider the expectations about history writing that the Encomiast brought with him, likely from one of the two religious foundations in Saint-Omer. Key to the attribution of the *Encomium* to either Saint-Bertin or the collegiate church of Our Lady is the Encomiast's claim to have experienced first hand, as an eyewitness, Cnut's generosity to both churches.[59] However, the mobility of Edward's chaplain, Herman, also illustrates that the cleric who witnessed Cnut's benefactions in Saint-Omer did not necessarily spend his entire career in the city. As bishop of Ramsbury, Herman spent three years at Saint-Bertin, during which time he became a monk. The anonymous author of the *Vita Ædwardi* promotes Herman as an exceptionally learned man; that learning was formed and developed in Lotharingia (if he came from there), England, and Saint-Bertin.

57 See chapter 1 herein. Orchard, *Pride and Prodigies*, 2–3.

58 *Enc.*, ed. Campbell, xxxvii and 94–7; Tyler, "Eyes of the Beholder," 263–5; and Orchard, "Literary Background," 164–6 and 173.

59 *Enc.* 2.20.

We are much better informed about Saint-Bertin than the church of Our Lady, although even with regard to the monastic community the middle years of the eleventh century are not well documented. The anonymous continuator of the *Gesta abbatum Sithiensium* for the years 960–1020 deliberately obscures the abbots in this period because they did not live up to later standards of reform. Meanwhile the continuation from 1021 by Simon of Ghent, a monk of Saint-Bertin who wrote in the final years of the eleventh century until 1145, has little to say (apart from generalities of a typical reform narrative) in recounting the period from Roderic's abbacy (1021–42) to 1081. The *Gesta abbatum* and other sources do allow us to see that the mid-eleventh century was marked by repeated disruption at Saint-Bertin, caused by reform (not entirely popular) under Abbot Roderic, a fire in 1033, the plague, and the loss of secular patronage, all of which may have led to significant departures from the community, including perhaps that of the Encomiast.[60]

Two hagiographical texts written at Saint-Bertin survive from the decade after the production of the *Encomium*, both testifying to the monks' efforts to promote the cult of their founder in difficult times. Folcard, who would later come to England, wrote a life of Saint-Bertin at the behest of his abbot, Bovo (1042–65).[61] Bovo himself wrote the *Inventio et elevatione S. Bertini* after 1052 to mark the elevation of the newly discovered relics of the saint.[62] As Monika Otter has explored, this fascinating text participates fully in the delicate negotiation that *inventiones* staged with historical credibility, an issue that was of pressing concern to the Encomiast. Of particular relevance here, however, is the ecclesiastical network within which Bovo was so anxious to situate his work. The preface includes an exchange of letters between Bovo and Guy of Châtillon, archbishop of Reims from 1033 to 1055, who performed the translation. Responding to scepticism and counterclaims about the discovery of the relics, Bovo seeks to legitimize his account with Guy's authority.[63] In the context of our concern for intellectual and literary history, Bovo's appeal to the superior learning of Guy and the canons of the cathedral at Reims is striking. Although we cannot know whether this letter exchange was

60 Simon of Ghent, *Gesta abbatum*, 635–41. Vanderputten, "Individual Experience"; and Vanderputten, "Crises of Cenobitism."

61 Folcard, *Vita quarta sancti Bertini*. See chapter 5 herein.

62 Bovo, *Relatio de inventione et elevatione sancti Bertini*.

63 Otter, *Inventiones*; and Ugé, *Monastic Past*, 72–91.

authentic or fabricated, we can register the aim of Bovo to associate the learning of his monastery with that of Reims with its famous cathedral school. It was, moreover, precisely under Guy that the school at Reims, now headed by Herimann, began to regain the prestige it had known under Gerbert of Aurillac.[64] This is evidently the world that produced or shaped the Encomiast.

Connections with Reims had long influenced the writing of history at Saint-Bertin. The *Annales Bertiniani* (*Annals of Saint-Bertin*), which cover Carolingian history from 830 to 882, were begun at the court of Louis the Pious as a continuation of the *Annales regni Francorum*; they were then kept by Bishop Prudentius of Troyes and later by Archbishop Hincmar of Reims. Subsequently the annals travelled from Reims to Saint-Bertin, where they were used by Folcuin in 962 when he initiated the *Gesta abbatum Sithiensium*. In the eleventh century a copy of the annals, now part of a compilation that began with Eutropius and extended through the Merovingian and Carolingian period, was made at either Saint-Vaast or Saint-Bertin, where it remained in the later Middle Ages.[65] As we have seen, the Encomiast shares, and indeed even goes beyond, Richer's very Ciceronian understanding of the form and content of *historia*. The Saint-Bertin book list, moreover, indicates that by the beginning of the twelfth century the abbey had assembled a substantial collection of historical works ranging from antiquity into the Middle Ages and across the kingdoms of western Europe.[66] Historical writing, however, appears not to have been produced at Saint-Bertin in the eleventh century. Not only did Simon's neglect of the period create a lacuna, but there appears to have been no history writing produced at the monastery between his *Chronicon* and Folcuin's *Gesta*. The *Encomium* potentially draws on the intellectual resources of Saint-Bertin while being very distinct in its production of not just history but secular history.

The literary preoccupations (if there were any) of the community of Our Lady in the mid-eleventh century are even harder to discern than those of its monastic counterparts. We catch glimpses of the intellectual and artistic ambitious of the canons later in the century in the stunning illuminations of a life of Saint-Omer (Saint-Omer, Bibliothèque municipale,

---

64 J.R. Williams, "Cathedral School," 663.

65 Saint-Omer, Bibliothèque municipale, 706. See Nelson's introduction to her translation of *Annals of Saint-Bertin*, 1–13 and 16; McKitterick, *History and Memory*, 50–1; and Ugé, *Monastic Past*, 62.

66 Becker, *Catalogi*, 181–4. See chapter 2 herein.

698) and in the poetry of Petrus Pictor (whose work shows affinities with that of Reims).[67] Early in the twelfth century Lambert's encyclopedic, illustrated *Liber floridus* attests to both artistic and intellectual resources in the Church of Our Lady and to Lambert's ability to access the library of the nearby monastery of Saint-Bertin. Lambert was keenly interested in the history of the counts of Flanders and of the surrounding polities (England, Normandy, France, and the Empire). One of the manuscripts used by Lambert is a mid-eleventh-century compilation including Orosius's *Historiae* and Jordanes's *De origine actibusque Getarum*. It was copied at least in part from a manuscript at Saint-Bertin and was in the collegiate library at least by the seventeenth century. If it was in the collegiate library earlier in the eleventh century, we find there an interest in the lives of secular men, parallel to that attested by some Saint-Bertin manuscripts. But it would be many decades before Lambert showed a demonstrable interest at Our Lady's in producing secular history.[68]

The absence of history writing on secular matters at either the Church of Our Lady or Saint-Bertin draws attention to the broader phenomenon, that history writing for secular patrons did not flourish in Flanders or indeed Northern France (for all the importance of rhetoric at Reims) at the time of the Encomiast's work.[69] The lives of Henry II and Conrad II were recorded in the Empire, and the *Gesta Normannorum ducum* was begun in Normandy by William of Jumièges, starting in the late 1050s. The Anglo-Saxon and Anglo-Danish court provided a secular patron, Emma, whose need to use history to negotiate the factional politics of her son's court led the Encomiast to examine and extend the function of *historia* beyond that which he had encountered in Flanders; he perhaps also

67 On the life of Saint-Omer see Denoël, "Vie," 318–19. On Petrus Pictor see chapters 4, 5, and 7 herein.

68 Lambert of Saint-Omer, *Liber floridus*. Derolez, "L'énigme"; and Derolez, *Autograph Manuscript*, 29–34. The fullest discussion of the Church of Our Lady is in the unpublished doctoral thesis of Jean-Charles Bédague, "Naissance et affirmation d'une collégiale." Ghent, Bibliotheekuniversiteit, 92 and Saint-Omer, Bibliothèque municipale, 717.

69 For Flanders see van Houts, "Flemish Contribution," esp. 112. The contrast between Helgaud's hagiographic life of Robert the Pious, which appears not to have circulated beyond Fleury, and the *Encomium* underscores the former's distance from secular biography. Helgaud insists on this distance himself: "Cetera, quae sunt de seculi militiis, hostibus devictis, honoribus virtute et ingenio adquisitis, istoriographis scribenda relinquimus" (We leave the other matters, which are worldly warfare, defeated enemies, honours acquired through virtue and ingenuity, to be written by historians) (Helgaud of Fleury, *Epitoma vitae regis Rotberti Pii*, 30).

responded to impulses from Normandy, where Emma had grown up, and from the Empire, whose rulers had been keenly watched by Emma's husband Cnut and whose clerics became royal chaplains and bishops in England. The *Encomium* resulted from a coming together of the learning of a Flemish cleric with the specific needs and patronage of Emma.

Emma in the Middle

The importance of a multilingual environment to the production and reception of the *Encomium* brings us back, time and time again, to Emma. She takes centre stage, which is just where the Encomiast in his opening argument insisted she belonged. Polyglot Emma, the Encomiast's patron, informer, and audience, emerges as a pivotal figure in the understanding of the merging of traditions in this text. Emma's probable knowledge of French, English, Norse, and even Dutch suggests that she may have been a key channel and mediator of the vernacular talk that surrounded and shaped the *Encomium*. However, what about her experience of Latin literary culture? A view of Emma in the context of her Norman background suggests that she was a non-literate lay person with an interest in Latin literature, and thus she herself becomes an example of how such people not only formed the audiences for, but also actively participated in, a Latin literary culture.

We cannot see Emma, a Norman princess in the tradition of the Anglo-Saxon royal women and aristocrats educated in royal nunneries, who will be the subject of following chapters, and there are no references to her as either learned or Latinate – this is in contrast, for example, to her successor, Edith, as queen of England.[70] Nonetheless, if Emma had been raised in the Norman court, she would certainly have been exposed to the Latin literary culture that flourished during the rule of her brother Richard II (996–1026).[71] Emma returned to his court during the period that Svein ruled in England and both she and Æthelred II went into exile. It was during Richard's reign that Dudo of Saint-Quentin completed his *De moribus et actis primorum Normanniae ducum*, which portrays Rollo, founder of the ducal dynasty, as a second Aeneas and attributes Trojan ancestry to the

70 Godfrey of Winchester's epitaphs for Emma and Edith open up the contrast: Edith is remembered as educated, Emma as not educated; *Epigrammata historica*, 2 and 4. Stafford, *QEQE*, 211–12 and 255–9.

71 *Jezebel*, ed. Ziolkowski, 37–47.

Normans.[72] The patronage and influence of Richard, as well as those of his uncle Rolf, his brother Robert (archbishop of Rouen), and his mother Gunnor, are all acknowledged by Dudo. While it is generally agreed that the Norman court was not the audience for Dudo's text, the key role played by ducal family members as sources suggests that they had an investment in its representation of the Normans as civilized and Christian leaders, and an expectation that Latin history could do political work.[73] The text of Dudo, moreover, like that of the *Encomium*, also appears to have been influenced by Old Norse oral literature.[74] Like the Encomiast, Dudo was a foreigner at the court from which he wrote; he is thus unlikely to have been directly familiar with Old Norse literary tradition or to have had the linguistic skills to access it, and he would have had to rely on his patrons. Dudo's history, furthermore, was a prosimetrical text recalling the pull exerted on the Encomiast by poetry, even though he decided to write in prose.[75]

As well as sponsoring history writing, the Norman ducal and episcopal court appears to have taken an interest in Latin verse.[76] Of particular note here are three enigmatic poems, *Moriuht*, *Jezebel*, and *Semiramis*, which are found together in Paris, Bibliothèque nationale, lat. 8121A, and show linguistic affinities, or share a literary aesthetic, with stylistically obscure Anglo-Latin poetry.[77] *Moriuht* begins and ends with dedications to Archbishop Robert and Gunnor. The other two poems appear to concern Emma directly. *Jezebel*, a dialogue between a man and a prostitute, is

72 Dudo of Saint-Quentin, *De moribus*. Southern, "Classical Tradition," 186–7 and 192; Searle, "Fact and Pattern," 125–9; Bouet, "Dudon de Saint-Quentin"; Hanawalt, "Dudo of Saint-Quentin"; Shopkow, *History and Community*, 150; and Albu, *Normans*, 12–20.

73 Searle, "Fact and Pattern"; Mortensen, "Stylistic Choice," 88–92 and 100–1; Shopkow, *History and Community*, 181–9 and 216–22; Christiansen's introduction to his translation of Dudo, xxiii–xxix; and Albu, *Normans*, 7–46, esp. 40.

74 Van Houts, "Scandinavian Influence"; Searle "Fact and Pattern," 120; *Jezebel*, ed., Ziolkowski, 42–3 and 59–60; and Galloway "Word-Play and Political Satire," 191. Christiansen, in the introduction to his translation of Dudo emphatically rejects any influence of Old Norse, xvii–xviii.

75 See chapter 2 herein.

76 Dronke, *Poetic Individuality*, 76–87; *Jezebel*, ed. Ziolkowski, 38; and van Houts, "*Jezebel* and *Semiramis*."

77 Warner of Rouen, *Moriuht*. Ziolkowski's and Dronke's editions of *Jezebel* and *Semiramis*, respectively, include discussion of style, classical and biblical learning, and literary traditions (including Old Norse) of these poems.

dedicated to Robert. Andrew Galloway reads the poem as a political satire, identifying the prostitute as Ælfgifu, Cnut's first "wife."[78] Meanwhile, Elisabeth van Houts's interpretation of *Semiramis* as a searing commentary on the marriage of Emma to Cnut presents the poem as engaged with the affairs of the ducal family; as such, it is a contribution to a debate about Emma's second marriage within the Norman court that may, at this point, have included her sons Alfred and Edward.[79] In the people and the talk, there is a continuity between the Norman, Anglo-Saxon, and Anglo-Danish courts. Like the *Encomium*, all these poems combine impressive classical and biblical learning with the influence of the Old Norse literary tradition. Their style is marked by obscurity. Consequently, for these poems to have had an audience among the members of the ducal family, they would have had to have been explained through vernacular talk.

The figure of the archbishop of Rouen, dedicatee of Dudo's work and also of both *Moriuht* and *Jezebel*, may be a key to understanding the particular contexts and processes of this culture of explanation in the Norman court. His position as both archbishop and married count reminds us that the lack of a sharp distinction between lay and ecclesiastical elites could encourage dissemination of Latin texts to those who could not read for themselves.[80] Meanwhile, the influence of Anglo-Latin verse from Æthelwold's Winchester on *Moriuht* and *Jezebel*, part of the larger cultural influence of Anglo-Saxon England on Normandy, illustrates that the *Encomium* cannot be understood simply within a paradigm of Continental influence on England. Rather it must be situated within a network of secular and ecclesiastical ties that crossed southern England, northern France, and Flanders, and which the Benedictine Reform, with its strong links to Fleury and Ghent, made especially visible.[81]

The role of Gunnor as Dudo's patron and informant, as well as her support of other Latin poets, may also have provided a powerful model for her daughter's own patronage of and engagement with the Encomiast. Although we do not know anything about Emma's relationship with her mother or what she learned from her, consideration of the connection between Gunnor and Emma draws important attention to the role of gender

78 Galloway, "Word-Play," 202–3.

79 Van Houts, "*Jezebel* and *Semiramis*"; Stafford, *QEQE*, 12 and 34; and Keynes, "Æthelings in Normandy," 185–6.

80 *Jezebel*, ed. Ziolkowski, 41.

81 Lapidge, "Three Latin Poems," esp. 211; Musset, "Rouen et l'Angleterre"; and *Jezebel*, ed. Ziolkowski, 39–41.

in Emma's decision to commission the Encomiast.[82] In particular, studies of women's literary patronage, which have identified matrilinear networks and the cultural ambassadorial role of women who married abroad, allow us to see Emma's decision to commission the *Encomium* within larger social paradigms. As the first foreign bride of an English king since Æthelwulf had married Charles the Bald's daughter, Judith, in 856, Emma may have played a distinctive and unprecedented role as a conduit between the literary traditions of the Norman court and those of the English court, thus fostering new literary developments. Janet Nelson's argument that women played a specific role in the Romanization of the early medieval Frankish courts deserves particular notice here, given the promotion of models from the Roman story world within the *Encomium*.[83] Clerical culture had, of course, long been conspicuously international, entailing the mobility of clerics, which was a prominent feature of the Benedictine Reform and Alfred's court. Emma marks an internationalization of a distinctly secular literary culture and draws attention to the particular impact of the mobility of women in contrast to that of clerics. Both her Norman background and her gender had the potential to prepare Emma to take an active part in the production of the *Encomium*. Looking forward to the generation after Emma, moreover, suggests that she established a pattern of literary patronage that influenced her daughter-in-law Edith's commissioning of the *Vita Ædwardi*. The links between the texts written for Gunnor, Emma, and Edith underscore the agency of those women who chose to use written texts to protect and extend their influence – and reinforces the important role played by women as the instigators of history writing in Latin throughout the Middle Ages.[84]

Consideration of Emma and Cnut's daughter, Gunnhild, meanwhile reveals that an ability to use Latin literary culture for political ends does not necessarily entail a desire to be Latinate. She also provides further insight into the languages of Cnut's court. Although Gunnhild is not mentioned

82 Stafford, *QEQE*, 3 and 209–13; van Houts, "*Jezebel* and *Semiramis*," 20; van Houts, "Gunnor of Normandy," 18–21; and *Jezebel*, ed. Ziolkowski, 42.

83 Bell, "Book Owners," esp. 173 and 179; McCash, "Cultural Patronage," esp. 14–17; Parsons, "Of Queens, Courts," esp. 175; Stafford, *QEQE*, 209; and Nelson, "Gendering Courts," 197.

84 Grundmann, "Frauen und die Literatur"; Clanchy, *From Memory to Written Record*, 191–8 and 253–4; McKitterick, "Frauen und Schriftlichkeit"; Geary, *Phantoms of Remembrance*, 48–80; Nelson, "Gender and Genre"; van Houts, "Women and the Writing of History"; and van Houts, *Memory and Gender*.

in the *Encomium*, which is focused on men and succession to the English throne in the period after her death in 1038, she was important to the dynastic strategy of her mother, father, and brother Harthacnut, which saw them attempt to create an allegiance with the German Empire that was strategic from both a Danish and an English perspective. Shortly after the death of Cnut, she was married to Henry III (before he became emperor), the exceptionally learned and cultured prince for whom Wipo wrote his *Gesta Chuonradi*.[85] Perhaps escorted by Brihtheah, bishop of Worcester, she arrived in the Imperial court after an expensive send-off in England, likely having travelled via Denmark, where she acquired a Danish chaplain, Timmo.[86] Her companions may indicate that Gunnhild was bilingual. After her death Timmo became bishop of Hildesheim; it is recorded, in the life of his predecessor as bishop, that while Timmo was good to his people and clergy, he was deficient in the knowledge of letters. In other words, he stood out as as not being highly Latinate amid the courtly bishops of Salian Germany.[87] Timmo's lack of learning suggests that we should see Gunnhild as an example of a royal daughter who was not Latinate, which offers precious insight not only into the kind of education that Emma and Cnut thought suitable for their daughter but also perhaps into Emma's perception that her own lack of Latinity was not a barrier to using the Roman story world to intervene in court politics. The contemporary experience of Edith, Godwine's daughter and later Edward's wife, who was educated at Wilton, forcefully illustrates that there were alternatives to Cnut and Emma's apparent decision not to educate Gunnhild.[88]

We should not imagine, however, that Gunnhild was cut off from the learned men who frequented the court of her father-in-law, Conrad II. A letter recounts that Bishop Azecho of Worms (famous for its cathedral

85 Jaeger, *Envy of Angels*, 200–2; and Wolfram, *Conrad II*, 22 and 141.

86 The marriage is recorded in many English and Continental sources, though not in the Anglo-Saxon Chronicle or the *Encomium*; for examples see Wipo, *Gesta Chounradi*, 35; *Annales Hildesheimenses* s.a. 1035 and 1046; Adam of Bremen, *Gesta Hammaburgensis ecclesiae pontificum* 2.56; *Vita Ædwardi* (hereafter cited as *VE*) I.1; *Inventio et miracula sancti Vulfranni* 18; William of Malmesbury, *GRA* 2.188. Bresslau, *Jahrbücher*, I:169–70; Schwarzmaier, *Speyer nach Rom*, 75–6; Keynes, "Giso, Bishop of Wells," 206; and Wolfram, *Conrad II*, 142–3. Disagreement as to whether Gunnhild departed from England or from Denmark can be reconciled by suggesting that she went from England to Denmark and from there to Germany.

87 *Annales Hildesheimenses*, s.a. 1038; Wolfhere, *Vita Godehardi* 33; and Adam of Bremen, *Gesta* 2.79. Bresslau, *Jahrbücher*, 1:331–2; and Wolfram, *Conrad II*, 283.

88 See chapters 4 and 5 herein.

school) was accustomed to visiting Gunnhild and bringing her almonds to ease her homesickness. The letter also tells that Emma sent envoys to her daughter to update her on the succession crisis that followed Cnut's death.[89] During her time as an Imperial queen, Gunnhild travelled as part of Conrad's itinerant court, reaching as far south as Monte Cassino, where she is recorded as receiving hospitality during a visit made by her husband and in-laws on the occasion of the installation of a new abbot.[90] Although the chronicles that recount this event give no indication of what the hospitality included, it is worth remembering that in the mid-eleventh century Monte Cassino was an exceptionally vibrant centre of literary culture where classical learning was notably cultivated and from which this learning would come to be transmitted to the north at the end of the eleventh and into the twelfth century.[91] Gunnhild thus stood at the intersection of English, Danish, and international German Imperial court culture and at the intersection of orality and literacy in a manner that recalls the example of her mother and her grandmother. Gunnhild's early death, in 1038 when she was still only a teenager, means we cannot speculate about her impact on literary culture, but her lack of a Latin education suggests that Gunnor and Emma were confident in their own formation.[92] There is no conflict between the lack of personal Latinity and the active use of Latin literary culture for political ends.

Turning away from the context of the *Encomium* to look at the text itself suggests that not only was Emma the text's patron and informant in a passive way but she significantly influenced its use of Latin literary culture. The text does not assign Trojan origins to Cnut's dynasty, an absence made all the more conspicuous because Dudo had already supplied the Normans with these illustrious ancestors. Cnut, like Rollo, is figured as a second Aeneas, but, unlike Rollo, he is not portrayed as a descendant of the Trojans.[93] Unusually among western European dynasties of this period, the Anglo-Saxons shunned such origins in favour of biblical and native genealogies.[94] Norman Emma was, moreover, in a position to know of this

89 *Ältere Wormser Briefsammlung* 5. Schwarzmaier, *Speyer nach Rom*, 72–5; Wolfram, *Conrad II*, 275–8; and Jaeger, *Ennobling Love*, 61–4.
90 *Chronica monasterii Casinensis* 2.63. Wolfram, *Conrad II*, 135–6.
91 Cowdrey, *Abbot Desiderius*, 19–27.
92 This discussion of Gunnhild is drawn from my "Crossing Conquests."
93 Ingledew, "Book of Troy," 682–4; and Mora-Lebrun, *L'"Énéide,"* 25–40.
94 Dumville, "Kingship," esp. 77–96; Ingledew, "Book of Troy," 685; and Tyler, "Trojans," 2–5.

wider prestige of Trojan origins. Looking beyond Normandy, Wipo's *Gesta Chuonradi* celebrates the emperor's Trojan descent.[95] Cnut's presence at Conrad's Imperial coronation at Rome in 1027, and Gunnhild's marriage to Henry III, would have been the occasion for their Trojan origins to have been made known to the Anglo-Danish court.[96]

A text that sought to present Cnut and his descendants to a mixed English and Danish court audience as the legitimate rulers of England might well have avoided representing Danish origins as distinct from English origins. Indeed, during the reign of Cnut the Danish dynasty continued to mark their descent from Scyld, who first appeared in West Saxon genealogies during the reign of Alfred the Great's father, Æthelwulf (839–58), when he sought to emphasize the shared origins of the incoming Danes and the English.[97] Emma's period as Æthelred II's queen would have exposed her to the West Saxon dynasty's views of its origins. The careful representation of Cnut as a second Aeneas, but not as a descendant of Aeneas, suggests that polyglot Emma was a sophisticated mediator between Norman, Danish, and English expectations and concerns. The Old English translations associated with the reign of Alfred the Great that continued to circulate in the eleventh century suggest secular elite knowledge of the Trojan legend in Anglo-Saxon England. More important, if Emma is not just a general informant but the source of the Encomiast's sensitivity to English qualms about Trojan origins, then the *Encomium* shows not just a cleric mediating Latin culture to the secular aristocracy but also a two-way negotiation rooted in face-to-face communication – in other words, vernacular talking. In this regard we should also register that Emma's expectations that Latin history writing could make a difference at court contrast with the expectations of Dudo's patrons that his history would find an audience outside of Normandy. Vernacular historiography, including Bede, Orosius, and the politically active Anglo-Saxon Chronicle, may have played a role in shaping a different situation in England.[98] Here we see the importance of identifying a range of Latinities. Emma, who appears not to have had the linguistic skills that would have allowed her direct access to the Latin of the *Encomium* or the *Aeneid*, nonetheless,

95 Wipo, *Gesta Chuonradi*. Wolfram, *Conrad II*, 18–19.

96 Lawson, *Cnut*, 108–9; and Wolfram *Conrad II*, 104.

97 Dumville, "Kingship," 95; Murray, "Beowulf"; Frank, "Skaldic Verse"; and Niles, "Locating *Beowulf*," 31–2.

98 See chapter 1 herein and my "Trojans."

through active patronage, exerts control over the Encomiast's deployment of Latin culture.

Emma as Augustus

Emma's centrality to her text's negotiation of the multilingual culture of the Anglo-Danish court placed her in an influential position vis-à-vis the Encomiast and the contents of his Latin text. In this final section I want to explore the power of that position by examining the Encomiast's representation of his patron as Octavian. I will do this through a comparison of the place of women in the *Aeneid*, the *Encomium*, and the twelfth-century vernacular *Roman d'Eneas*. From such a literary contextualization, which attends to style, characterization, and allusion, and their impact on the meaning and reception of the text, we can see clearly why the commissioning of a Latin text was itself an assertion of authority on the part of Emma, a laywoman. This discussion also challenges models that see the vernacular as key to women's active role in literary culture, underscoring even the ability of non-literate women to participate in the production and use of Latin texts.[99]

The *Aeneid*, in its story of Aeneas's flight from the ruins of Troy and his foundation of Rome, offers a vision of the past that included and legitimized secular concern for genealogy and erotic passion, in contrast to clerical preoccupations with salvation history.[100] Many of the stories of the *Aeneid* are attractive to women, particularly when their limited place in the Old English and Old Norse texts from the tenth and eleventh centuries is considered. Old English secular poems from late Anglo-Saxon England, such as the *Battle of Brunanburh* and the *Battle of Maldon*, and Old Norse skaldic verse are preoccupied with martial activity and afford little space to women.[101] Similarly, the Anglo-Saxon Chronicle is largely concerned with the activities of men.[102] Women in the *Aeneid* can be

99 Short, "Patrons and Polyglots," 236 and 244; Krueger, *Women Readers*, 14; McCash, *Cultural Patronage*, xv; Barrratt, "Small Latin?"; Wogan-Browne, *Saints Lives*, 11n17, 12n18, 15–16, and 193–9; and D.H. Green, *Women Readers*, 212–17.

100 Ingledew, "Book of Troy," esp. 670–81.

101 Women are conspicuously absent from Old English verse that commemorates events of the tenth and eleventh centuries, in contrast to poetry that recounts events from the fourth to the sixth centuries such as *Beowulf* and *Waldere*. For women in skaldic verse see Jesch, *Women in the Viking* Age, 148–68.

102 Stafford, "Chronicle D," 208.

strong; they take on active, varied, and central roles. In her marriage to Aeneas, Lavinia brings him Latium, and other women include Dido (a figure who much engaged the Encomiast, as we saw in the previous chapter), the warrior Camilla, and the goddesses Venus and Juno. In the context of Emma's experience, moreover, the *Aeneid* offers a productive model for complicated stepfamilies. The political world that was created not only by the Danish conquest of England but also by the multiple marriages of both Emma and Cnut, and their evident fertility, was nothing if not messy. Aeneas too had children by more than one wife, though, unlike Cnut, he remarried only after his first wife had died. Virgil finesses it so that Rome is founded by descendants of both Ascanius (Aeneas's son by Creusa) and Silvius (Aeneas's son by Lavinia). Moving forward to the context of the *Aeneid*'s production, Octavian was, of course, not Julius Caesar's natural son. The Encomiast's use of a Virgilian paradigm for the *Encomium* suggests that he and Emma may have found in this particular classical text a way to understand and shape an uncertain present.

However, despite its potential attractiveness to women, the *Aeneid* remains, par excellence, a tale of patriarchy.[103] Women are repeatedly cast aside as Aeneas pursues his imperial destiny: Creusa is lost; Dido is famously abandoned; and, although Aeneas's marriage to Lavinia unites the Trojan and Latin peoples, her characterization is minimal. The most active women of the text, Dido and Camilla, both behave as men (Dido in her governance of Carthage, Camilla on the battlefield) and end up dead. The women of the *Aeneid* are double edged: female agency is presented, but it is also conspicuously constrained. The representation of women in the *Aeneid* is thus problematic for a medieval woman reader whether she identifies with these female figures or takes the position of the male reader.[104]

The growth of vernacular literature, and especially the flourishing of romance, has been associated with female patronage and empowerment.[105] Broadly speaking, romance does give a place to the interests of women – love, marriage, and female interiority, which are not seen in either epic or historical writing. The *Eneas*, which is among the earliest vernacular romances, attests to this greater provision made for women. The place of women within romance can help us to see features of the *Encomium* that

103 Desmond, *Reading Dido*, 1–22.
104 Desmond, *Reading Dido*, esp. 7–12; and Desmond, "*Dominus/Ancilla*."
105 Tyson, "French Vernacular," 185 and 220–1; and D.H. Green, *Women Readers*, 212–17.

connect it to this genre and to its consciousness of a female presence in its audience. The Encomiast's representation of Cnut wooing Emma can remind us of the interest in the *Eneas* in the process whereby Lavine does fall in love with Eneas rather than Turnus. In both cases love serves dynastic ends. The concern for women's interiority, which the account of Lavine's falling in love evinces, can meanwhile draw our attention to the Encomiast's concerns for Emma's feelings, particularly regarding the death of Alfred.[106] Stepping outside the text, Gunnor's possession of a copy of the *Historia Apollonii regis Tyri*, and the presence of the Old English translation of this text in Cambridge, Corpus Christi College 201, a manuscript associated with the courtier bishop Wulfstan, suggests that Emma may have been familiar with proto-romance texts that granted agency to women's desires in the choice of a husband.[107] However, as is evident in the *Eneas*, as the women of the *Aeneid* moved out of Latin and into the vernacular, and as their lives began to command greater attention in romance, their representation had greater potential to be used to control the behaviour of aristocratic women. Although vernacularization was fostered by women, courtly romance was ultimately a genre devised by clerics to regulate aristocratic society, both male and female. Krueger, trenchantly exposing the aim of romance to control women's behaviour, discusses the association of vernacular romance with women's empowerment and the highly problematic position of women readers of romance.[108]

Emma's place within the Virgilian framework of the *Encomium* provides a marked contrast to the situation of the women in both the *Aeneid* and the *Eneas*. In reading the Encomiast's account of the marriage of Cnut and Emma as an imperial union, which brings together the Danish and the English people, the reader cannot help but recall Aeneas's marriage to Lavinia. However, this parallel only lurks; it is invoked neither explicitly nor through allusion. In comparison, Lavinia and Aeneas are much more obviously recalled when Dudo recounts the marriage of Rollo to the Frankish princess Gisla.[109] The *Eneas* brings Lavine forward only to place her more firmly within the confines of patriarchy.[110] The Encomiast does not leave Emma in such a passive position. Similarly, although he circles around the image of Fame spreading rumour about Dido in his prologue,

106 *Enc.* 3.6.

107 See chapter 1 herein.

108 Krueger, *Women Readers*, esp. ch. 1.

109 Hanawalt, "Dudo," 117; and Shopkow, *History and Community*, 150.

110 Baswell, *Virgil in Medieval England*, 168–219; and Desmond, *Reading Dido*, 107–19.

the spectre of a woman, who rules in her own right and whose desire threatens the foundation of Rome until she is spurned and dies, is appropriately not developed.[111] These problematic women of the *Aeneid* are rejected by Emma and the Encomiast when he figures her so prominently in the argument as Octavian, that is, as Caesar Augustus, first of the Roman emperors.

By presenting Emma as Octavian, the Encomiast brings her into the present and portrays her as a strong force in the contemporary Anglo-Danish political scene. Emma as Augustus may recall her unprecedented designation as *consors imperii* (indicating one who shared rule) in the *ordo* revised for Cnut's coronation and her powerful role in his reign.[112] The problematic nature of romance for the woman reader allows us to see just how strong a gesture the allusion to Octavian was. Emma is compared to a Latinate man whose authoritative rule of the Roman Empire was legendary. It is striking as well that it is Emma, rather than Harthacnut, the current ruler of the Anglo-Danish empire, who is figured as Octavian. In contrast, Harthacnut is left out of a Virgilian framework that encompasses his mother, father, and grandfather; he is not even likened to Silvius, son of Aeneas and Lavinia.[113] In the present, all the authority of the Virgilian framework belongs to Emma. In romance, as Roberta Krueger shows, references to women as patrons are often undercut by the misogyny of the text itself; this pattern finds no place in the *Encomium* – Emma's patronage was of a different order. Although within the text Emma is reliant on Cnut and then, after his death, seeks to wield power through her sons, she is not shown as contained by male dynastic concerns. For example, she is not handed over, Lavinia-like, to Cnut, but rather she shrewdly negotiates her marriage so that only his sons by her will be considered eligible for the English throne.[114] The *Encomium* ends with a compelling depiction of Emma's authority in which Emma is portrayed as central to the peaceful and strong rule of the kingdom:

> His ita peractis et omnibus suis in pacis tranquillitate compositis, fraterno correptus amore nuntios mittit ad Eduardum, rogans ut ueniens secum optineret regnum. Qui fratris iussioni obaudiens Anglicas partes aduehitur, et

111 See chapter 2 herein.
112 Stafford, *QEQE*, 175–7 and 231–2.
113 See chapter 2 herein.
114 *Enc.* 2.16.

> mater amboque filii regni paratis commodis nulla lite intercedente utuntur. Hic fides habetur regni sotiis, hic inuiolabile uiget faedus materni fraternique amoris.
>
> (After the events described, he arranged all his affairs in the calm of peace, and being gripped by brotherly love, sent messengers to Eadweard and asked him to come and hold the kingdom together with himself. Obeying his brother's command, he was conveyed to England, and the mother and both sons, having no disagreement between them, enjoy the ready amenities of the kingdom. Here there *is* loyalty among sharers of rule, here the bond of motherly and brotherly love is of strength indestructible.)[115]

Here, at the end of the text, Emma cannot be consigned to the power behind the throne as she slips out of the bounds that usually circumscribed female agency. These final lines, and the text generally, are consonant with the paralleling of Emma and Octavian that implies that support for Emma will further the peace and prosperity of the kingdom in troubled times. In this context the Latin of the text not only projects an image of Cnut, a second Aeneas, as a civilized ruler of an empire rather than as a conquering Dane, but it is also part of the social meaning of the text, with the symbolic value of the Latin working with the image of Emma as Octavian-like.

Finally, opening up what the representation of Emma as Octavian suggests about the Encomiast's understanding of the patronage of secular literature also draws us back to the recognition of Emma's agency. The new engagement with classical poetry that marks the eleventh century, in which this literary culture comes to be valued in and of itself rather than as a means to understand the Bible better, presented scholars not only with freer access to the literary heritage of classical antiquity but also with different models of literary patronage. As a result classical models of literary patronage influenced the expectations and self-understanding of poets. Reading Virgil, as we know the Encomiast did, in a context which included a life of the poet that commented on how Virgil gained and enjoyed Octavian's support, would have influenced a desire for a new kind of patron.[116] As Thomas Haye has recently written, eleventh-century poets developed ideas about their own claims to patronage (whether in a social or a material form) from their knowledge of the circumstances of classical

115 *Enc.* 3.13–14.

116 See chapter 2 herein.

poets. However, according to Haye, the laity's lack of Latin meant that these poets had to turn to bishops for patronage, and most particularly the pope and the archbishop of Reims.[117] The way in which Latin literature functioned in the Anglo-Danish court, however, challenges Haye's assumption that only a highly Latinate person, and thus an educated cleric, could act as such a patron. In this context, when we further consider the absence of secular patronage of Latin literature in Northern France and Flanders, the Encomiast's figuring of Emma as Octavian also emerges as part of a search for a new kind of patronage. Even when we look to the Empire and consider Wipo's *Gesta Chuonradi*, secular history writing that shares the Encomiast's Macbroius-inflected concern for the truth of fable, we find a very different stance towards the Roman story world, which does not attempt to find models for patronage there. Wipo, while deeply imbued with classical texts (Sallust in particular marks the *Gesta*), sets up his narrative with an Orosian move by criticizing the celebration of figures from pagan antiquity when there is silence about Christian rulers.[118] A comparison of Wipo and the Encomiast further emphasizes the latter's aspirations for a distinctive kind of patronage, and the boldness of his Augustan Emma.

The draw of a figure like Emma for a writer steeped in the poetry of Virgil and conscious of the ancient poet's relationship to Octavian comes into sharp focus, and we recognize how Emma was able to attract not a monk somehow cut adrift from Saint-Bertin, for whatever reason, but one of the best educated men of his generation, whose learning and desire for an Octavian-like patron shows strong affinities with Reims. From this perspective Emma's patronage of the Encomiast is an act of wider European importance, with ramifications beyond England. A court that could attract a scholar of the Encomiast's calibre and formation, and for whom a classicizing text like the *Encomium* could be written, aimed to rival the best of western Europe, from Normandy to France to Flanders and even the Empire.

Conclusion

Placing the *Encomium* at the meeting point of Norman, English, Norse, and Latin literary cultures underscores Emma's central, distinctive, and

117 Haye, "*Nemo Mecenus*."

118 Wipo, *Gesta*, prologue; and see chapter 2 herein.

creative role in the production of this text, and her very direct impact on the Encomiast's understanding of the nature of *historia*. In this environment Latinity could act, as it did after the Norman Conquest, as a "lifeline of communication" across a "fractured society" (to use Baswell's formulation) and as a medium that could address the competing ambitions of communities that lived in a complex political and linguistic situation.[119] Latin is not a barrier, but instead it ensures the efficacy of the *Encomium*. The use of this language contributes to, rather than detracts from, Emma's authority. Polyglot Emma, with her Latinate but subordinate cleric, was in a position to play a determining role in the oral culture of explanation that, I have argued, must have surrounded the *Encomium*. The strategies that were developed for communicating across linguistic and cultural boundaries not only allowed lay access to Latin texts but also allowed lay participation in Latin literary culture. Seen in this light, the idea that a Latin text, which makes sophisticated use of the *Aeneid*, can contribute to political debate ceases to seem absurd. Instead, the *Encomium* comes to exemplify the vitality of the multilingual court of Harthacnut in which Latin literature was only one of many literary traditions talked about across linguistic borders.

119 Baswell, "Latinitas."

4 The Politics of Allusion in Eleventh-Century England: Classical Poets and the *Vita Ædwardi*

Introduction

Writing amid the turbulence that threatened England as the childless King Edward's life drew to a close and ended, the anonymous author of the prosimetrical *Vita Ædwardi* turned to the Roman story world as he wrote to protect the position of his increasingly vulnerable patron, Queen Edith. Where the Encomiast had seen the solution as a Virgilian account of the Anglo-Danish dynasty, albeit marked with dark allusions to Lucan, the Anonymous fractured a longed-for Virgilian narrative by simultaneously invoking not only Lucan's *De bello civili* but also Ovid's *Metamorphoses* and Statius's *Thebaid*. The Anonymous uses the fratricide of Thebes, the destruction of civil war, and ideas of metamorphoses to attempt to narrate the incoherence of the events of Edward's troubled reign that he and his patron struggle to explain to others and to understand for themselves. Just as the visions of Rome that he finds in these four epics cannot be resolved, the Anonymous finds himself unable to create a stable account of Edward's life, an authorial crisis that mirrors and expresses Edith's own precarious situation. In turn, the Anonymous's struggle for coherence becomes part of his narrative as he explores the literary and moral implications of using made-up stories from pagan antiquity to shape contemporary events, which everywhere defy the imperatives of exemplarity and dynastic commemoration.

The focus of this chapter, accordingly, lies with the Anonymous's deployment of the Roman story world. Explicit invocation of the Roman story world is the stuff of the Anonymous's poetry, not of his prose. This division has obvious implications for his views of the relationship between history and fiction, and we will watch as, over the course of the *Vita*

Ædwardi, the Anonymous continues the Encomiast's exploration of this subject. Before turning to the text itself, we must consider the implications of its prosimetrical form for scholarship on the text. Historians have tended simply to ignore the poems in order to transform the text into a stable and usable source. This approach has cast the *Vita Ædwardi* as strongly supporting the Godwines in its sympathies and has allowed very little consideration of its classicism beyond comments that the Anonymous was evidently very learned.[1] An exception is a recent article by Tom Licence, which, while still reading the text as Godwinist, takes account of the poetry. Meanwhile, apart from the work of Eleanor Heningham, Victoria Jordan, and Monika Otter, the text has enjoyed little attention from literary scholars. In the 1970s Heningham argued for its literary unity. Recently Jordan and Otter have very perceptively and persuasively opened up the sophistication of the Anonymous's verse, thereby illuminating the integrity of the *Vita Ædwardi* as a text. Otter in particular has insightfully revealed the urgency and innovation of the Anonymous's metapoetic enquiry. Their focus has, however, lain largely with the *Vita Ædwardi*'s religious poetry.[2] Here I will build on the work of Jordan and Otter to present close readings of the text's more secular poetry in the context of its prose and religious verse.

These close readings, which form the substance of this chapter, illustrate that the Roman story world is fundamental to the meaning of this text. Although the classicizing of the Anonymous is startlingly overt, and this aspect is crucial to the understanding of the text as a historical source and of its place within literary history, his use of the Roman story world has so far eluded attention. Bringing the poems into the foreground, especially those engaged with the myth, legend, and history of antiquity, reveals a demanding but interpretable text whose evident instability is fully part of

---

1 Barlow gives brief summaries of each poem and comments on its form. Stafford makes bare mention of the poetry in her account of the narrative. Both note that scholars have found the work to be confusing. Barlow attributes the text's apparent incoherence to the context in which it was written, while Stafford says that the narrative finds coherence in the figure of Edith (*VE*, ed. Barlow, xviii–xxviii; and Stafford, *QEQE*, 40–8). It must be emphasized, however, that without the work of both these historians any analysis of the poems would be impossible. Licence, "Date and Authorship."

2 Heningham, "Literary Unity"; Jordan, "Chronology and Discourse"; Otter, "1066"; and Otter, "Closed Doors." Jordan assimilates the verse to the hagiographical concern of book 2 with salvation history. Otter uses the poetry to draw out the metanarrative of the text and its engagement with themes of progeny and childlessness.

its meaning. The sustained detail of the close readings offered here forcefully makes two points: one about the *Vita Ædwardi* as a historical source; the other about it as poetry. First, the *Vita Ædwardi* simply can no longer be accepted as a Godwinist account of Edward's reign, and historians must reassess its nature as a historical source. Second, the virtuosity of the Anonymous's poetry emerges strongly and requires that it be situated in the context of the famous Loire school, especially the work of the later eleventh-century poets Baudri of Bourgueil and Hildebert of Larvardin. The sophistication with which the Anonymous uses the Roman story world to explore the nature of history writing and its relationship to poetry disrupts the established paradigms that represent the Conquest as bringing English literary culture into Europe. Neither the Anonymous's poetics nor his politics can be perceived in isolation from each other.

The Key Players

The backgrounds, identities, and alliances of the key players in the *Vita Ædwardi* give initial insight into the reason the Anonymous's account of the reign of Edward might be anything but straightforward.[3] As the son of the last English king before the Danish conquest and of his Norman wife, Edward spent most of his life in Normandy and northern France and came to the throne more as Harthacnut's heir – that is as an adopted member of the Anglo-Danish dynasty – than as Æthelred's son; as such, Edward's position in eleventh-century politics was complex. His marriage in 1045 to Edith, the daughter of Earl Godwine, reaffirmed his reliance on those Anglo-Danish connections. The English Godwine had risen out of obscurity to become Earl of Wessex under Cnut and married the Danish Gytha. Save for a brief period in 1051, when Edward banished him and his sons to Flanders and Ireland and put Edith in a nunnery, Godwine remained powerful until his death in 1053. His relations with Edward were notoriously fraught; the reign was really one long power struggle between the king and the house of Godwine. Meanwhile, Gytha's brother Ulf was the husband of Cnut's sister Estrith and the father of Svein Estrithson, king of Denmark from 1047 to 1076. Godwine's children, and thus Edward's wife Edith, were not only of Danish descent; they were related to the Danish royal

3 This section draws particularly on the accounts of Edward's reign and the places of Godwine and Edith within it by Barlow and Stafford. Barlow, *Edward the Confessor*; Barlow, *Godwins*; and Stafford, *QEQE*, esp. 255–79.

dynasty. It was through Gytha that, even after the Norman Conquest, the Danes still made claim to the English throne. Edward's childlessness set all of his potential identities and allegiances against each other as he looked alternatively for an heir, in a son of his own, in a cadet line of the English royal dynasty; in William, Duke of Normandy; and in the Anglo-Danish family of Earl Godwine.[4]

Raised in the royal nunnery of Wilton and bearing a name traditional among Anglo-Saxon royal women, Edith appears to have been educated to be queen.[5] The Anonymous and other writers of the eleventh and the twelfth century attest to her literacy and learning.[6] The barrenness of her marriage, which the *Vita Ædwardi* attributes to her chaste relationship with the holy Edward, was a crisis both for Edward, leaving him with no heir, and for Edith's natal family, who had hoped, through her, to see a Godwine on the throne. It should not be assumed, however, that the barrenness was hers rather than Edward's. Infertile wives rarely survived in this period.[7] Not only the Danish Cnut but also the kings of the House of Wessex, even the pious Edgar, had shown no reluctance to set aside wives in favour of a new union that would bring better political connections or male heirs. Edward did not take another wife in 1051 when Edith was sent away with the other Godwines, and there are no records of illegitimate children. If Edith was infertile, her continued presence at Edward's side is testimony to the power that her father and brothers held over the king, or to the depths of his piety.[8] After Edward's death she appears to have returned to Wilton and to have been protected by William, after the Conquest, in a bid to project his legitimacy.[9]

Edith's brothers, Harold and Tostig, feature centrally in the *Vita Ædwardi*. The elder, Harold, succeeded his father as Earl of Wessex, and Tostig became Earl of Northumbria. Originally allies, they became rivals for the English throne at the end of Edward's reign. Tostig, as is clear from the *Vita Ædwardi*, was his sister's favourite. Edith was accused of having the Northumbrian nobleman Gospatric murdered at court on Tostig's behalf – an act that contributed to Northumbrian hostility towards their earl and implicated her fully in the subsequent violence. In 1065 the

---

4 Baxter, "Edward the Confessor."
5 Stafford, *QEQE*, 257.
6 See chapter 5 herein.
7 Stafford, *Queens, Concubines*, 81–2 and 86–8.
8 Stafford, *QEQE*, 73.
9 See chapter 5 herein.

Northumbrians revolted against Tostig. Harold gave in to the rebels' demands and was instrumental in removing Tostig from his earldom and sending him into exile in Saint-Omer, home of Tostig's wife, Judith, daughter of Count Baldwin IV. Edward died shortly after the Northern Rebellion, stricken with grief. In 1066 Harold, now king of England, was delayed from dealing with William's invasion of England by Tostig and his ally King Harold Hardrada of Norway, who had attacked England from the north. Harold killed Tostig and Hardrada at Stamford Bridge and immediately marched south to meet William at Hastings.

The Anonymous is generally identified as a cleric from Saint-Omer, either from Saint-Bertin or from the college of Our Lady. The continental Germanic forms that he gives of some Anglo-Saxon place names suggest that he came from Flanders or Lotharingia, with his interest in Flemish affairs and geography suggesting the former, and reference to Saint-Omer pointing to that city specifically.[10] His knowledge of the *Encomium* may add further weight to this identification, though he may have come to know this text in England.[11] Longstanding links between the houses of Wessex, Cnut, Godwine, and Flanders, which acted as a place of refuge amid political troubles and as an easy setting-off point for Continental journeys, ensure that the Anonymous may have had his own opinions about and insights into the crises at the end of Edward's reign. He is, moreover, particularly well informed about Tostig, whose marriage had brought him close ties to Flanders.[12] In considerations of the intellectual world of the *Vita Ædwardi*, the religious foundations of Saint-Omer, Saint-Bertin and Our Lady, will be kept firmly but not exclusively in view, as other influences and points of contact emerge. The study of the *Vita Ædwardi* has much to contribute to our understanding of the Anonymous and may, in turn, open up, in this chapter and the next, new perspectives on the clerics of Saint-Omer.

Form

The difficulty of giving an account of Edward the Confessor's reign that would support Edith in the uncertain and shifting political circumstances surrounding the king's death is embodied in the very form of the *Vita*

10 *VE*, ed. Barlow, xliv–xlvi.

11 See further on pages 151, 157, and 196.

12 Licence ("Date and Authorship") suggests that the Anonymous was close to Tostig.

Ædwardi. Made up of doublets within doublets that constantly threaten to pull apart, the *Vita Ædwardi* comprises two sections, which the editor, Frank Barlow, has labelled "books." Each book is introduced by a poetic prologue in the form of a dialogue between the poet and his muse. Book 1 is essentially a secular biography of the king (albeit a very pious one) that begins with Cnut's conquest and Godwine's rise before it loops back to Edward's birth.[13] Book 2 begins anew, attempting to redeem the Confessor's life by shaping it into an incipient hagiography.[14] The Anonymous's covering of the same chronological period in both books, but within different generic horizons, creates a tension that foregrounds issues of metanarrative, as multiple and not wholly consistent readings of Edward's life are offered within a single text.

In addition to the doubling of secular and sacred biography, the prosimetrical form of book 1, with its verse and prose versions of each episode, offers a dual perspective to which the Anonymous explicitly draws his readers' attention at the close of the first prologue. Presenting poetry rather than prose as the main form of his narrative, he highlights the different ways in which each makes meaning. The muse tells the poet:

Carmine germano germanos plenius actus
  alternans operis ordine pone modum.
Et ne continuo ledatur musica cursu,
  interdum proso carmina uerte gradu,
pagina quo uario reparetur fessa relatu,
  clarius et pateat historie series.

(Place in order by means of brotherly song [i.e., elegiac couplets]
a full account of the brothers, alternating the rhythm of the work.
And, lest monotony should spoil the tune,
Set now and then your narrative in prose,
So that with shifts the weary page revives
And the order of history more lucidly appears.)[15]

13 *VE* 1.1.
14 *VE* 2.1.
15 *VE* 1, prologue.

For the Anonymous, prose brings clarity of meaning. As the *Vita Ædwardi* progresses, however, that clarity, that apparent interpretability of events presented in prose, will be revealed as an illusion, a falsehood, which will in turn raise questions about the truth of history. Fascinatingly, the pun on *germanus*, repeated in the first line, referring first to the text's form and then to the brothers Harold and Tostig, expresses not only the centrality of their strife to the crisis of the *Vita Ædwardi* but also the Anonymous's rigorous insistence on the intimacy of form and content to the meaning of his text.[16] Finally, the doubling does not end with the verse and prose distinction. The verse itself falls broadly into two categories: classicizing secular poetry and religious verse, each offering diametrically opposed (indeed, potentially irreconcilable) perspectives on Edward, Godwine, and his sons. Only Edith remains uncriticized, though the Anonymous does admit that there is more than one way to see her. Prosimetrum is a form that resists resolution, and as such it was ideally chosen by the Anonymous to explore a political situation, Edward's lack of an heir, which had similarly resisted resolution.[17] As Peter Dronke writes with regard to Notker's prosimetrical life of Saint Gallus, form allows the poet to "shape-shift" and to use "diverse strategies for the testing of truth."[18] Both of these possibilities will be essential to the Anonymous as he narrates Edward's life for Edith's preservation in very uncertain political times.

Although the juxtaposition of history writing, religious and classicizing poetry, and hagiography creates a generically very unstable text, the Anonymous uses theme and style to impose a unity on his narrative that does not undermine its fundamental and meaningful instability. Themes of progeny, fertility, motherhood, good counsel, and madness, and the images of trees, rivers, monsters, and ships, for instance, repeat across books 1 and 2.[19] Meanwhile dense verbal repetition weaves all the text's potentially disparate parts tightly together, simultaneously allowing the Anonymous to explore the ways that truth is found in multiple perspectives and to hide himself and his patron behind a screen of doublespeak.

Multiple perspectives and disagreements about truth are, of course, a feature of the competing accounts, written and spoken, of the Conquest and its causes. We see this competition not only in the contradictions between

---

16 Newlands, *Statius*, 129–30.

17 Balint, *Ordering Chaos*, 49–50.

18 Dronke, *Verse with Prose*, 20.

19 Otter ("Closed Doors"), Jordan ("Chronology and Discourse"), and Heningham ("Literary Unity") all explore the thematic unity of *VE*.

Anglo-Saxon and Norman views about whom Edward recognized as his heir, but among accounts offered within either side.[20] Debates, implicit and explicit, about the kind of truth that poetry offers to the recording of history often mark the historiography of this period. William of Poitiers's view that poets roamed "per campos figmentorum" (through the fields of fiction), discussed in chapter 2, appears to have been specifically aimed at Guy of Amiens's poetic account of the Conquest, the *Carmen de Hastingae proelio*. Both men praised the conqueror's feats, but William thought his own prose, for all of its panegyric, remained within the "ueritatis limes" (bounds of truth).[21] Turning to the vernacular, the poetic account of Edward's death, which is included in some versions of the Anglo-Saxon Chronicle, uses archaic Old English verse to present an uncomplicatedly positive view of Edward's reign and the succession of Harold, thus belying the conflict between Edward and the Godwines that is recorded in its own pages. What is so distinctive about the *Vita Ædwardi* is that it purposefully juxtaposes starkly contradictory accounts within one text and then poses metapoetic questions about the nature of truth.

Despite its prosimetrical form and generic diversity, the different modes of the *Vita Ædwardi* are not all equal. The Anonymous insists on the primacy of poetry over prose for his work. In the dialogues with the muse he creates for himself a persona as *poeta* and writes of his art as akin to music. As he reveals when commenting on the prose of his prosimetrum, prose intrudes on the "continuo ... cursu" of the poetry, not the other way around.[22] Like the Encomiast, he does not claim that his dynastic history (denoted with the terms *gesta* and *historia* in the first prologue) is written to be exemplary, but rather to praise the queen.[23] As his predecessor in the English court also realized, even though he chose to write in prose, poetry is more appropriate to history told as panegyric.[24] Faced with the same dilemma as was the Encomiast, he comes up with a different solution. His professed preference for poetry makes his densely textured poems all the more central to the meaning and aims of his text.

20 Stafford, *QEQE*, 6–27 and 40–50; and Stein, *Reality Fictions*, 65–103.

21 William of Poitiers, *GG* 1.20. Guy of Amiens, *Carmen de Hastingae proelio* (hereafter cited as *CHP*), ed. Barlow, xxvi and xxix–xxx.

22 *VE* 1, prologue.

23 *VE* 1, prologue.

24 See chapter 2 herein.

Real-Time Narration

Before turning to the Anonymous's classicizing poetry, we must raise one other feature of the text. The Anonymous claims to narrate events from some point in 1065 in real time, as they happened, with text and context unfolding simultaneously, without authorial knowledge of the final outcome – that the strife between Harold and Tostig would become violent, leaving the kingdom open to conquest by William. Historians have been divided in dating the text's composition. Following the Anonymous's own representations, Southern points to the unusual nature of the text as one written while the narrated events are happening. Barlow concurs, seeing the *Vita Ædwardi* as being written during 1065–7 and finished by 1070; Stafford, in contrast, sees the entire text as written in hindsight, in the years just after 1066. Recent comment on the date remains divided. Keynes and Love opt for a date of circa 1068, and Tom Licence sees the text as being started in 1065 and finished before 1070.[25] The date of the manuscript (London, British Library, Harley 526), which Barlow identifies as probably copied at Christ Church, Canterbury, around 1100, further contributes to the complexity of the issue, since this manuscript may represent a version that was revised closer to the end of the eleventh century.[26] Indeed, as the successive rewritings of the *Vita Ædwardi* by Osbert of Clare, Aelred of Rievaulx, the Nun of Barking, and Matthew Paris amply illustrate, Edward's life invited revision as the events that marked the end of the West Saxon dynasty were revisited again and again.[27] Marc Bloch's refuted argument that the entire work was the product of the twelfth century also reflects a sense that the Anonymous was writing in hindsight.[28]

The tight integration of form and content across the whole of the *Vita Ædwardi*, and the text's preoccupation with prophesy, does contribute to the impression that the Anonymous knew the outcome before he wrote, and it is indeed a difficult issue, which may be further clouded by the strong possibility that, though book 1 was written before October 1066, it

25 Southern, "First Life," 385–6; *VE*, ed. Barlow, xxix–xxxiii; Stafford, *QEQE*, 40–8; Keynes and Love, "Godwine's Ship," 199; and Licence, "Date and Authorship." See also page 200 herein.

26 *VE*, ed. Barlow, xxxi–xxxii.

27 Aelred of Rievaulx, *Vita Edwardi regis et confessoris*; Anonymous Nun of Barking, *Vie d' Édouard*; and Matthew Paris, *Estoire de seint Aedward*.

28 Bloch, "Vie de S. Édouard," 17–44; Southern, "First Life," 386–95; Heningham, "Genuineness," 421–8, and *VE*, ed. Barlow, xxxiii–xxxiv. Licence also argues for an admonitory mode ("Date and Authorship").

was strategically revised later. That the text is strongly unified in a literary sense does not require that it was written after 1066, only that the Anonymous attended carefully to form as events unfolded. As his attention to the Roman story world makes clear, he consistently frames his use of themes of Theban fratricide, civil war, and monstrous metamorphosis as admonitory: a warning against letting strife break out between Harold and Tostig. Just because it came to pass does not mean that he was writing after the fact or that the text lost meaning after 1066, only that the meaning changed as the admonition came to be seen as prophecy. The Anonymous's very fine sense of the poetics of prophecy left him well placed to negotiate this change. The dangers inherent in the rivalry between Harold and Tostig were evident well before the Northern Rebellion and the Battle of Stamford Bridge.[29] If we do not accept the reality of the text's real-time narration, then we need to come up with compelling reasons that the Anonymous created this fiction (which he maintains without a slip) and that, when he is so interested in the nature of fiction, he does not characterize this aspect of his narrative as fictional.

The Muse, Her Poet, and the Roman Story World

The whole question of how to use the Roman story world in writing history for Edith is openly staged within the prologues to book 1 and book 2, each of which takes the form of a dialogue between the muse and the poet. In the first prologue the muse presses a Virgilian golden age on the poet, telling him to sing about Edward's succession as the beginning of a "secula ... aurea."[30] But by the beginning of the second prologue, the poet, now disconsolate, confronts his muse, claiming that the song she has revealed to him is one of Thebes and civil war:

> et nunc Thebaidos fedo sub scemate carmen
> hoc opus horrenti discipulo retegis.
> Rebar principium lepidum deducere textum
> de nimio caris corde meo dominis;
> nunc hostile nefas in fratrum uiscera torrens

29 *VE* 1.3. *VE*, ed. Barlow, xxx.
30 *VE* 1, prologue.

confundit letam carminis historiam;
Emathium furiis ciuili peste regressum –
heu germana nimis pectora dura – tulit.

(And now
You show your shrinking pupil that his work
Becomes a Theban song with horrid form.
I thought at first to make a pretty piece
About my lords so dear unto my heart.
But now the hate which sears the brothers' flesh
Confounds the joyful *carminis historiam*;
With raging civil war Emathian change
It got. Alas, those brothers' hearts too hard!)[31]

"Thebaidos," the title of the Statius's poem about Thebes, makes the reference to this work explicit; likewise, the reference to Lucan is overt with *Emathius* and *ciuilis pestis* recalling the opening line of the latter's grim poem ("Bella per Emathios plus quam civilia campos").

Whereas the *Aeneid* celebrates empire as the culmination of Roman history, Lucan's violent and despairing poem recounts with horror the civil war between Julius Caesar and Pompey that marked the end of the republic. We earlier saw Virgil and Lucan invoked by the Encomiast. Even more than for his predecessor, the status of Lucan as poet and historian made him particularly attractive to the Anonymous, as he himself tells us with his formulation "carminis historia."[32] The prominence of the *Thebaid*, a poem only just becoming well known in the mid-eleventh century, in the Anonymous's scheme meanwhile foregrounds the conflict between Harold and Tostig as the ultimate cause of the chaos of 1066 and underscores that this conflict, and not the Norman Conquest, is his subject.[33] Statius's poem, which recounts the conflict between Polynices and Eteocles (the sons of Oedipus) for control of Thebes, presents a grim epic of fratricide and war without winners. There is nothing subtle in the Anonymous's invocation of these competing epics: he overtly demands that his audience

31 *VE* 2, prologue.

32 Von Moos, "*Poeta* und *Historicus*."

33 On the reception of the *Thebaid* in the eleventh century see further on pages 175–80 herein.

use these classical poems as interpretative frameworks, and he highlights a conflict between Virgil and the epic poets who followed after him.

The place of Ovid within these overtly invoked frameworks is less immediately clear. In the second prologue the Anonymous refers to the way in which the ancients sang ("ut prisca canunt") about Cadmus's sowing of the seeds that grew into a horrible people ("horrida stirps"), the Thebans. With its plural *prisca*, this is most likely a reference to Ovid's account of Cadmus in the *Metamorphoses*, as well as Statius's reference to Cadmus as the beginning of the story of Oedipus's sons.[34] Ovid's *Metamorphoses* presented a coherent account of Cadmus, and, given that the Anonymous's language and imagery in much of his poetry reveal his close familiarity with a range of Ovidian verse, Ovid is likely his source here.[35] Partly, the Anonymous's reserve about Ovid may relate to his newness within the medieval poetic canon; it was in the late eleventh century that Ovid's poetry began to make a real impact on poetics. Partly too, the Anonymous shares in a widespread unease about the morality of Ovid.[36] The *Vita Ædwardi* will emerge, in this chapter, as an important witness to the process of Ovid's reception among both lay and religious audiences.

Situating an account of Edward's reign within a metapoetic dialogue of muse and poet is a complex move. In so doing, the Anonymous signals his inheritance of varied and often contradictory literary traditions, instigated by the poets of pagan antiquity and reshaped by the Christian poets of late antiquity and the Middle Ages.[37] The Roman poets whose story worlds he uses to give meaning to the disorder of Edward's final years each took a distinctive approach to the Muses, thus opening up a space in which Edith's poet could innovate. In the hands of late antique and medieval Christian poets, the Muses can be rejected as a symbol of the abandonment of the pagan stories of Greece and Rome or embraced as a symbol of the enduring power of this story world that is transformed into a source of Christian inspiration. In designating his muse as Clio, accompanied by Euterpe and Polyhymnia, the Anonymous reveals his mastery

34 Statius, *Thebaid* 1.4–17.

35 Ovid, *Metamorphoses* (hereafter cited as *Meta.*) 3.1–137.

36 Munk Olsen, "Popularité"; Munk Olsen, "Ovide au moyen âge"; and Wetherbee, "From Late Antiquity," 122–8.

37 Curtius, *European Literature*, 228–46; and Thornbury, "Aldhelm's Rejection," 74–9.

of this rich poetic inheritance. Clio is appropriately the muse of history, while Euterpe is the muse of lyric poetry, and Polyhymnia the muse of religious song, such as the Anonymous includes in the *Vita Ædwardi*.[38] The choice of Clio also alerts the reader to the Anonymous's particular affinities with Statius, who likewise called on the muse of history.[39] In selecting his muses, the Anonymous signals, from the start of his poem, the intensely self-conscious generic mix of the *Vita Ædwardi* and the tightness he has forged between form and content.

The Anonymous does not, however, place himself seamlessly into a long tradition of calling on the Muses, in the way, for example, his near contemporary Wipo, the German Imperial poet, does. In Wipo's *Tetralogus* the Muses speak of the inspiration they gave to Virgil, Horace, Lucan, Statius, and Ovid.[40] In contrast, the Anonymous models Clio, his leading muse, on Boethius's Lady Philosophy, who also presides over a prosimetrical text, and in the process he poses radical questions about the value of poetry. Boethius's Lady Philosophy was a commanding figure, whose qualities are transferred to the Anonymous's muse. The muse demands the respect and obedience of her poet and in return, in the manner of Lady Philosophy, consoles and encourages him, taking up her position on the importance of rationality over sorrow. At the beginning of book 2, when all has fallen apart, the muse responds to his disconsolate turn to Thebes and civil war with a stern command that he set aside sadness and madness.[41] In so doing, the Anonymous recalls Lady Philosophy's banishment of the poetic Muses ("poeticas Musas") whom, insulting as "scenicas meretriculas" (theatrical prostitutes), she blames for inciting uncontrolled emotion and choking off the rationality that she has so carefully taught Boethius.[42] Basing his muse, Clio, on Lady Philosophy at just the point that she banishes the poetic Muses is an unsettling and assertive move that requires the reader to figure out, as he or she reads the *Vita Ædwardi*, the judgment the Anonymous is making about his own poetry.

38 The Anonymous's choice of Polyhymnia suggests that he associates her not with pantomime, as in Ausonius's much anthologized "Nomina Musarum" (D'Alverny, "Muses," 10; and Reynolds, *Texts and Transmission*, 26–8), but with hymns, as in Horace, *Carmina* 1.1.33, or other vocal declamation as in Reginald of Canterbury, *Vita sancti Malchi* 4.335.

39 Statius, *Thebaid* 1.41. Newlands, *Statius*, 130.

40 Wipo, *Tetralogus* lines 1–112.

41 *VE* 2, prologue.

42 Boethius, *Consolatio* 1.1.

By calling up Lady Philosophy, the Anonymous boldly situates his own prosimetrum within the long debate, which goes back at least as far as Plato, about the moral value of poetry. Plato famously rejected poetry. Boethius's own prosimetrical form, the debt of his verse to the language of classical poetry, alongside his use of its legends and myths within the poetry of the *Consolatio* (for example, 5.2), illustrate that Lady Philosophy's banishment of the poetic Muses was no straightforward banishment of poetry, even if, by book 5 of the *Consolatio*, prose opens and closes the book, reversing the pattern of its book 1.[43] Likewise, the relationship between poetry and prose was pressing for the Anonymous, and he too offers no straightforward answer. Although his concerns are not so much philosophical as historical, he, like Boethius, is preoccupied by the nature of truth as he asks what kinds of truth do prose and poetry bring to the telling of history. The Anonymous's move from philosophy to history is no crude appropriation of a half-remembered, and even less understood, Lady Philosophy. The extraordinary boldness and genuine import of the Anonymous's reworking comes into sharp focus when we compare it with four prosimetra (the first of which was composed some thirty years after the *Vita Ædwardi*) that Peter Dronke has labelled philosophical allegory. Hildebert of Lavardin (1056–1133), Adelard of Bath (c. 1080–c. 1150), Bernard Silvestris (fl. 1130–50), and Alan of Lille (d. 1203), all of whom modern literary scholars recognize as working at the forefront of new literary developments, framed their prosimetra with imaginative transformations of Lady Philosophy. Godfrey of Reims (c. 1020/40–1095), though not writing a prosimetrum, made similar Boethian moves just a little before Hildebert.

These poets sought to go beyond Boethius's own position in asserting that allegorical poetry could convey meaning beyond the capacity of prose. The manifest link between the literary culture of the Anonymous and that of these more famous poets, even though they are more Boethian in their focus on man's place within the divine order, should alert us to be open to the meaning (both political and poetic, sometimes difficult, often veiled) contained within the classicizing poetry of the *Vita Ædwardi*, which participates fully in the expanding poetic horizons of the eleventh and twelfth centuries. The willingness of these late-eleventh- and twelfth-century poets to undermine and challenge a female figure based on Lady

43 O'Daly, *Poetry of Boethius*, 30–73.

Philosophy, so that she becomes a parody of the original, also alerts us that we should not expect a simple transfer of Lady Philosophy's unassailable authority onto the figure of the Anonymous's muse.[44] The inclusion of Lucan and Statius exposes a tension between the muse's Virgilian optimism and the poet's despair, which comes back to a Boethian question about the value of poetry and its proper use. As we will see, from the very first poem, while the poet ostensibly obeys the muse, he is actually quietly pulling her vision apart.

Edward's Golden Age (Poem 1)

The Anonymous begins his prose account of Edward's reign not with the king himself but with Godwine's rise to power under Cnut's rule. From the start of his story the intricacies of eleventh-century English politics force the Anonymous onto slippery ground. Although the Anonymous finds the Danish conquest of England lamentable, it provided an opportunity for Godwine to flourish. His marriage to Cnut's kinswoman Gytha ensures that his Anglo-Danish allegiances, like the Danish names of their elder children, cannot simply be forgotten even in an account of Edward's accession that was written long after the period of Danish rule. The Anonymous seeks to negotiate this messy political climate by representing Godwine as a father to all men, in other words as the protector of the native people, and by projecting a familial tie that excludes Cnut.[45] Edward's birth and return to the throne of England are hailed as the fulfilment of the prophecy that a long-preserved seed of the West Saxon dynasty would flower from ancient roots and that the *stirps* of Cnut would be cut down like a tree; at the same time, Godwine and his paternal relationship with the English remain in the foreground.

This precedence of Godwine continues to be asserted as the Anonymous moves on to his poetic account of joyous nobles presenting the new king with rival gifts after his coronation. In this first poem within the body of the text Godwine's place as leading earl and hero of the *Vita Ædwardi* is proclaimed by his gift of a gold ship complete with 120 warriors and purple sails decorated with Edward's illustrious English ancestors and their

44 Hildebert of Lavardin, *De querimonia*; Adelard of Bath, *De eodem et diverso*; Bernard Silvestris, *Cosmographia*; Alan of Lille, *De planctu Naturae*; and Godfrey of Reims, "Sompnium de Odone." Dronke, *Verse with Prose*, 46–53; Balint, *Ordering Chaos*, esp. chs. 1 and 2; and de Carlos, "Poetry and Parody."

45 *VE* 1.1.

sea battles. Until recently the damaged state of the *Vita Ædwardi* manuscript meant that less than half of this poem survived. Henry Summerson's discovery of the full poem, preserved by a sixteenth-century antiquary, allows us to recognize that it initiates a boldly unflinching exploration of the causes of the end of the West Saxon dynasty, finding refuge for truth in poetry.[46]

In depicting this ship, the Anonymous, with a dense fabric of Virgilian allusions, builds up to an ostentatiously explicit fulfilment of the muse's command to sing of a Golden Age, when he writes:

> Tunc decus armorum iungit non inferiorum,
> quanquam Vulcani referuntur in arte parari,
> regi Troiano nullo cedentia telo.
>
> (Then the earl adds the splendour of weaponry in no way inferior to the arms of the Trojan king, even though those are ascribed to the skill of Vulcan.)[47]

The Anonymous invokes Virgil's famous account of Venus's gift of the armour and weapons that will enable Aeneas to defeat Turnus, and marry Lavinia, thus paving the way for the foundation of Rome. Like the Encomiast, discussed in chapter 2, he has turned to Aeneas's shield, on which the future of Rome up to the time of Caesar Augustus is depicted and thus foretold. Some key themes in his account of Godwine's ship are obvious. The gift proclaims Godwine's status and particularly underscores his wealth. Its purple sails express the imperial and dynastic claims of Edward, as they celebrate the newly restored House of Wessex. Thus the Anonymous uses the ship to announce Godwine's position as the leading magnate in the kingdom and to suggest that Edward's position is dependent both on Godwine and on his West Saxon lineage.

The Anonymous's turning to the shield of Aeneas represents a more complex move than the earlier allusions to Virgil by the Encomiast as he

---

46 Summerson, "Tudor Antiquaries." The finding of the second half of the poem enabled Keynes and Love ("Godwine's Ship," 207–18) to confirm and develop my earlier reading of the poem as invoking Virgil, Lucan, Statius, and the Encomiast in a complex intertextual move ("Wings Incarnadine," 93–5; and "Politics of Poetry," esp. 143–9).

47 *VE* 1.1, text and translation, in Summerson, "Tudor Antiquaries," 171 and 172. See my "Poetry and Politics," 140–2, for full discussion of these allusions to the armour, especially the shield, of Aeneas.

depicted Svein and then Cnut setting off from Denmark to conquer England. In the poem the Anonymous alludes to both the *Encomium* and the *Aeneid*: there are echoes of the *Encomium*, echoes of the *Aeneid* that are also found in the *Encomium*, and echoes of the *Aeneid* that are not found in the *Encomium*. Thus, we know that the Anonymous used the *Encomium* and went back to the *Aeneid* itself, and that he recognized and responded to the Encomiast's Virgilian panegyric by rewriting the ships of the conquering Svein and Cnut as those of the restored West Saxon monarch, Edward.[48] In so doing, he effectively poured derision on the Encomiast's prophecy of an Anglo-Danish empire. The links between these two texts offer insight into the intellectual world within which the Anonymous worked. In this world he had access to the *Encomium* and had the training to read it with sophistication. This access could have been in Saint-Omer or in England, either at court or in a religious foundation. More interesting than this question of where, however, is how we catch a glimpse of the way that the Roman story world spilled out from beyond the boundaries of a text. Texts did not simply influence each other; they did so because of the social context that brought them together. The Roman story world, especially the myths surrounding the foundation of Rome, emerges as both a shared language and a site of contestation across the political divisions imposed on eleventh-century England by conquests. Given the Anonymous's acute awareness of the political meaning of Troy, I suspect that he is responding more to its currency as an active and contested political discourse in the English court than to any place the *Encomium* might have held within a Flemish library.[49]

All this Virgilian celebration of the restoration of the West Saxon monarchy that is made possible by a loyal Godwine can only be ironic in the context of the events at the end of Edward's reign. The poem could well have been written before Edward's death because the only prospects for the continuation of this dynasty lay with the young and politically weak Edgar Ætheling, and both the Godwine sons and William were actively working for its end. The poem, like West Saxon rule, is much less stable than it appears on the surface. The Anonymous even goes so far as to use Virgil against Edward. Aeneas's shield looked forward to the glory of Rome, which is the exact opposite of what we find on Edward's sails.

48 Tyler, "Wings Incarnadine," 92–6; Tyler, "Poetry and Politics," 143; and Keynes and Love, "Godwine's Ship," 211–13.

49 See pages 194–7 and in chapter 5.

Because the Anonymous is describing these sails as everything falls apart at the end of Edward's reign, the sails look backwards to what was, thus highlighting that Edward was to be the end of the House of Wessex. At the same time, the sails, with their emphasis on genealogy, suggest what could have been if only he had had children. The sails thus both mark the past glory of the West Saxon dynasty and prophesy its imminent end. They are a reversal of Aeneas's shield; there will be no Trojan renown.

Dido

Although Virgil's *Aeneid* privileges male conquest and dynastic ambition, as exemplified in Creusa's and Dido's abandonments and in Lavinia's silence, the ancient poet does not entirely occlude women's voices. The Anonymous, writing for a woman exposed by dynastic collapse, was attentive to Virgil's women and the potential they presented for exploring not only Edith's situation but the varied perceptions of her position at the close of her husband's reign. In the first poem of the *Vita Ædwardi*, Virgilian allusion functions to bring Edith into the foreground. The line "quo patrum series depicta docet varias res" (on which are shown the instructive lineage) recalls not only Aeneas's shield but also Dido's lineage, as depicted on the gold plates of her table, plates that insist on her own claim to royal splendour.[50] The reference to Dido's lineage in her first meeting with Aeneas is, of course, laden with irony because he will cause its end. Abandoned by Aeneas in favour of his imperial destiny in Italy, Dido meets a desperately sad death. Having lamented that she is not pregnant with the son of Aeneas, she kills herself. Strikingly, in his lines devoted to the queen of Carthage in book 4, Virgil admits her sorrow into his narrative and gives some sense of interiority to a woman who stood in the way of the Empire. The slaying of her husband by her brother Pygmalion will also chime with the Anonymous's presentation of Harold and Tostig's enmity as a cause of Edward's death. By recalling such a memorable figure from the *Aeneid* here, the Anonymous hints at the anguish of barrenness for Edith; childless as Edward's death approaches, she can continue neither his dynasty nor her father's dynasty. While the prose assiduously avoids associating Edith's childlessness with the crisis of 1066, here as elsewhere the poetry in contrast reminds us that because she bore

50 Virgil, *Aeneid* 1.640–2.

no children there can be no prophecy of illustrious descendants such as we find on Aeneas's shield. In raising the absence of an heir, the Anonymous is aware that some may have blamed Edith, and he is alert to her emotional anguish.

Another echo from Virgil's account of the meeting of the queen with the Trojan exile underscores that the Anonymous has Dido in mind here. He writes that Godwine's gift of the ship "supereminet omnes" (overtopped them all). In using these words, he picks up on Virgil's "supereminet omnis" that occurs as part of an extended epic simile.[51] As the queen approaches Carthage's temple to Juno, in which Aeneas stands enthralled by the wall paintings depicting the fall of Troy, the poet compares Dido to Diana who towers over other goddesses. Although the expression occurs elsewhere in classical and medieval poetry, and the syntax of the *Vita Ædwardi* instance differs from that of Virgil, Ovid's repetition of "supereminet omnis" to describe Diana underscores the memorability of Virgil's simile. That this description refers to her when she is being chased by Cadmus's grandson Acteon also brings Theban connections, reinforcing the thematic significance of the echo in the *Vita Ædwardi*.[52] The association of Dido, who so famously slept with Aeneas in a cave sheltered from a thunderstorm, with Diana, the virgin goddess, fits in with the simultaneous mourning for the absence of a child and the implication of virginity that shape the Anonymous's portrait of Edith. In Dido's position as childless woman, vulnerable widow, and spurned lover, threatened by her brother's desire for power and unable to maintain female rule over Carthage, the Anonymous finds a way to explore Edith's experience and to bring it to bear, indirectly but forcefully, on his story.

The Anonymous's circling around the figure of Dido also offers insight into his engagement with debates about the relationship of poetry to history. Like the Encomiast before him, the Anonymous is highly likely to have known Servius's commentary on the *Aeneid* and of the gap between Virgil's Dido and the chaste widow whom "habet historia."[53] From this perspective, Dido continues as a site for theorizing fiction while the Anonymous develops ideas about the truth of poetry that go beyond those of the Encomiast. Returning to a thematic level, Servius's revelation of Virgil's misrepresentation of a chaste widow as a queen driven by passion would

51 Virgil, *Aeneid* 1.501.

52 Ovid, *Meta.* 3.182.

53 Servius on *Aeneid* 4.36. Chapter 2 herein.

have made Dido even more attractive to the Anonymous as he negotiated the conflicting views of the chastity of Edward and Edith's marriage and the accusations that the queen had been an adulterer, such as those alluded to by William of Malmesbury.[54]

Civil War and Fratricide

Although poem 1 ostensibly praises him, allusion reveals Godwine coming in for sharp criticism. The words "dona ferentes" (bearing gifts) serve to compare him to the Greeks bringing the Trojan horse into Troy.[55] This reference to "dona ferentes" is not isolated but rather stands as part of a tissue of destabilizing allusions, which runs throughout the verse of the *Vita Ædwardi* and insists that the reader look askance at Godwine. Within this poem, for example, the fire-breathing dragon that adorns Edward's ship ("linguis flammam uomit ore trisulcis" (belches fire with triple tongue)) also comes, like the Greeks and the gifts, from the second book of the *Aeneid*, in which Virgil compares the Greek Pyrrhus to a snake.[56] This line occurs in the context of the massacre at Troy and the death of Priam, king of Troy, at the hands of Pyrrhus. This strikes a very anti-Godwine note for a text that calls him, in prose, the father of his country.[57] Allusion to Lucan and Statius drive home the point.

From the very opening of the poem, whose second line ends with "gaudia rerum" (joy in matters), Lucan disrupts the celebration of Edward's return. With these words the Anonymous recalls Cleopatra, bearing lavish gifts as she attempts to seduce Julius Caesar in lines that follow on from an extended explanation of how her father married her to her brother (Ptolemy) so that they could rule together.[58] The Anonymous's phrase "munere tali" (with such a gift) returns us, gruesomely this time, to the image of Cleopatra and gifts. Lucan describes Caesar's feigned grief when he was presented with the head of his rival Pompey, who was killed by Cleopatra's brother, the king of Egypt. Weeping crocodile tears, Caesar tells the messenger bearing the head that if Ptolemy did not hate his sister, he might have made a fitting return for such a gift by sending him the head of Cleopatra.

---

54 William of Malmesbury, *GRA* 2.197. Stafford, *QEQE*, 265.

55 Virgil, *Aeneid* 2.48–9. This allusion and the others are discussed more fully in Tyler, "Poetry and Politics."

56 Virgil, *Aeneid* 2. 475.

57 *VE* 1.1.

58 Lucan, *De bello civili* 10.107–10.

The situation of the Godwines in the 1060s does not seem far away: Edith and Edward have had no children, and two of Godwine's sons are manoeuvring, one with Edith's support, to succeed Edward. Yet Edith is no Cleopatra figure here, unless the *Vita Ædwardi* is written very much against her interests. Rather the Anonymous offers a contrast between the childless Edith and the notorious, but very fertile, Cleopatra. Married to her brother, she claimed that her son was Caesar's, and she later bore twins to Mark Antony. By letting Cleopatra into his narrative at all, the Anonymous risks criticizing Edith. He does give voice to those who did just that with allusion to women whose lives were governed by sexual passion, allowing a glimpse of the way in which claims of sexual impropriety were used to undermine women, including Edith. However, further references to *De bello civili* put to rest any lingering doubt that the Anonymous may be writing, subversively, against the interests of Edith, whom he insists be seen as a figure of concord.

Edith as concord is evident in the Anonymous's echoing of Lucan. When the Anonymous writes that the nobles were able "agnouere suum regem magnumque patronum" (to recognize their own illustrious patron, their own king), he recalls a chilling scene in *De bello civili* when two warring camps of Romans are facing each other.[59] The men on the opposing sides of the Roman civil war find themselves horrified that they are about to kill each other. Lucan moralizes that they could have chosen to stop what he calls the civil Erinys, and then Caesar would have had to make friends with Pompey. Erinys is one of the Furies; she is associated with murder within a family or a clan. Lucan asks that Concord be present and that she allow the men, who recognize their own (agnovere suos), to turn away from the brink of war. In the *Vita Ædwardi* the Anonymous circles around this highly appropriate passage from *De bello civili.* In a later poem Erinys and Concord reappear together when the Anonymous laments the horror that is going to unfold when Tostig and Harold fall out and civil war envelopes England. In that poem Edith is clearly figured as Concord.[60] Although the Anonymous lets us hear the voices of those who would censor Edith, he silences them over the course of the *Vita Ædwardi* by developing the image of Edith as Concord and leaving Cleopatra, like Dido, behind.

---

59 Lucan, *De bello civili* 4.187–94.

60 *VE* 1.5. On the theme of discord and concord see Jordan, "Chronology and Discourse," esp. 136–53.

Allusions to Statius's *Thebaid*, meanwhile, allow the strife between Harold and Tostig to cloud the joy of Edward's coronation. The Anonymous's phrase "despecto vertice" takes us to Statius's poem, when the Argives, supporting Polynices, head off to war against Thebes, whose throne has been wrongfully retained by Eteocles. The Argives depart despite their seer's prophesying their destruction. In his catalogue of their seven leaders and their troops Statius describes Capaneus looking down on the dead Hydra.[61] The monstrous giant snake, with its triple crown, is said to be covered with bronze, silver, and gold and with moving snakes. The Anonymous echoes this imagery and language in his poem, with both the Hydra and Edward's boat striking terror. As with the earlier allusions to the *Aeneid*, prophecy is at issue, but now we have not an inverted allusion to the future glory of Rome but a sombre recollection of the destruction of both brothers in the struggle for the throne of Thebes. Although the killing of the Hydra is one of Hercules's twelve famous labours, in this poem we have Edward's boat compared to the lifeless Hydra, gazed on by a soon-to-be-dead and notoriously arrogant Argive leader. In the context of other allusions to Statius's epic within the *Vita Ædwardi* and of the Anonymous's explicit references to the *Thebaid*, this echo carries meaning. The building centrality of the imagery of monstrosity, especially snake-like monstrosity, both to the poetry of the *Vita Ædwardi* and to the *Thebaid* further anchors this allusion into the passage under discussion here.

De bello civili and the *Thebaid* recur together as the poem draws to a close, definitively undermining any golden age and inscribing these two intertexts into the *Vita Ædwardi* as firmly as the *Aeneid*. The poem ends with these lines:

> Pax antiqua suos rediens sic uisitat Anglos,
> aufugiunt rixae, discedunt bella, furorque
> omnis frigescit, tellus pontusque quiescit,
> ac passim laetis celebrantur festa choreis.
>
> (Thus ancient peace returns to visit her Englishmen, disputes flee, wars depart, and all wrath fades away. Earth and sea fall calm, and everywhere people are united in joyful dances.)[62]

---

61 Statius, *Thebaid* 4.165–73.

62 *VE* 1.1 (Summerson, "Tudor Antiquaries," 172).

As Keynes and Love discuss, the vision of a peaceful reign is here undone with the words "furor" and "tellus pontusque," which take us to the opening of Lucan's dark epic where he refers to Romulus's murder of Remus when the two brothers, the founders of Rome, could not share rule.[63] This phrase also appears twice in book 11 of the *Thebaid*.[64] Most relevant here, given Edith's position, is its occurrence in a line where Pietas, like a sister or a mother, despairs over fraternal strife.[65] The Anonymous will return to this book and indeed this very passage as the discord between Harold and Tostig takes over his story. The space that this book of the *Thebaid* makes for the women who try futilely to stop the violence enveloping the brothers and the Theban kingdom, and then are left to mourn its consequences, will come to preoccupy the Anonymous as he writes for Edith.

Returning to *De bello civili*, the passage to which "furor" and "tellus pontusque" lead is the same to which the Encomiast alluded subversively in the final section of the *Encomium* where it undermines the superficial claim of unity between Harthacnut, Edward, and Emma.[66] Setting up a tension between Virgil and Lucan to comment on Anglo-Saxon court politics is not the Anonymous's innovation. For the Encomiast, this reference to Lucan appeared as an in-joke, accessible to the same learned audience that could have appreciated his subtle readings of Servius and Macrobius, but it was not part of his political message for a wider audience. The Anonymous sees what the Encomiast has done (he is an expert reader of this earlier text), but in the *Vita Ædwardi* this tension between Virgil and Lucan has become central to the text's political meaning, a move that requires a different kind of audience and which will be explored in the next chapter.

The final words of the poem, "festa choreis," come from the late antique poet Paulinus of Nola, while other phrases recall further Christian poets.[67] A striking feature of the poetry of the *Vita Ædwardi* is the care with which the Anonymous excludes allusions to religious verse from his classicizing poetry and vice versa. In the religious poems the literary debts lie with Christian Latin poetry and the Bible. In revealing himself to be so in

63 Lucan, *De bello civili* 1.96.

64 Statius, *Thebaid* 11.67 and 468.

65 Keynes and Love, "Godwine's Ship," 217–18.

66 *Enc.* 3.14. Keynes and Love, "Godwine's Ship," 217. See chapter 2 herein.

67 Paulinus of Nola, *Carmina* 14.109.

control of his language, so alert to the mechanics of intertextuality, he invites us to ask why he alludes to Paulinus at the close of such a consciously classicizing poem. The reference proves to be as apt as those he made to the epic poets. The phrase comes from Paulinus's poem to Saint Felix, whose feast day met with rejoicing in Rome, a city described by the poet as transformed from one that once held primacy only by virtue of its imperial power and military victories to one that now holds primacy by virtue of its possession of the tombs of the apostles.[68]

This message of transformation, underpinned by allusion to Virgil, is one that the Anonymous hears clearly as he attempts to replace his vision of Edward as a second Aeneas with a vision of Edward as a saint. In this context Paulinus's emphasis on the value of the saintly life of a confessor (as Felix was) rather than a martyr also has direct appeal to Anonymous and reveals how, from the very beginning of the *Vita Ædwardi*, he is thinking about Edward's potential for sanctity.[69] Sanctity is not an option that he reserves solely for book 2. We see in this first poem a movement that is mirrored in the *Vita Ædwardi* as a whole, where the Anonymous turns away from the Roman story world to an explicitly religious framework, in this case hagiography, when all hopes of dynastic triumph are extinguished.

The Ship, Godwine, and the Death of Alfred

The reading developed here of the Anonymous's dense allusions may seem to load more meaning onto the description of the ship and the celebrations of which it was a part than they can hold. However, the ship stood in for one of the most shocking events of eleventh-century English history, the death of the Ætheling Alfred, an event that had deeply troubled the Encomiast two decades earlier. Poetic and political weight are evenly matched. William of Malmesbury and John of Worcester both claim that Godwine made a gift of just such a heavily ornamented ship not to Edward but to Harthacnut in order to expiate himself from a role in the murder of the new king's half-brother.[70] Keynes and Love have shown that William's and John's versions of the ship were transpositions of the Anonymous's

68 Paulinus of Nola, *Carmina* 14.85–8.

69 Paulinus of Nola, *Carmina* 14.1–12 and 14.21–4.

70 William of Malmesbury, *GRA* 2.188; and John of Worcester, *Chronicon*, s.a. 1040.

account of Godwine's gift to Edward.[71] The Anonymous's allusive blackening of Godwine's character as the bearer of the Trojan horse and murderer of Priam, king of Troy, his echoes of Lucan and Statius, together with his emphasis on the *probitas* that Godwine displays in giving this lavish gift, expose very clearly the ship's symbolic valency. Neither John nor William loses sight of this symbolism, even when transposing the gift from Edward to Harthacnut. The ship is a visible sign of Godwine's guilt; in such a context the ironic use of Virgil and the dark notes from Lucan and Statius become much more conspicuous. The Anonymous's lingering description of the ship emerges not so much as an audacious attempt to rewrite Godwine's past in order to present him as the foundation of Edward's rule, but as an insistence that such a rewriting is not possible, that stability could never have been found in a kingdom that rested on the Godwines.

The Anonymous's detailed ekphrasis of Godwine's gift to Edward participates in a network of claims and counterclaims about Alfred's murder that reverberated throughout the eleventh century, spilling into arguments about the causes of the Conquest. The *Vita Ædwardi*, while itself coy about Godwine's role in it, leaves no doubt about the murder's continued political reverberations. The Anonymous explicitly identifies rumours about the killing as the root of the conflict between the Godwines and Edward in 1051. The Norman archbishop of Canterbury, Robert of Jumièges, is said to have persuaded Edward that the earl was going to attack him just as he had attacked his brother.[72] For William of Poitiers, the murder in part justifies the Conquest; condemning Godwine for Alfred's death, he praises William the Conqueror for avenging the Norman prince by killing Harold Godwineson. William of Poitiers enables us to see that the Anonymous's indirectness about Godwine is not only political manoeuvring but also part of a larger silence in the face of an event, Alfred's death, so dreadful that it challenges the understanding of the nature of history as exemplary. Poitiers follows his gruesomely detailed account of the torture and murder of Alfred, in which Godwine is the prime mover, with these words: "Libuit inhumanum scelus hoc perpetuo silentio sepelire: sed in historiarum serie res quoque minus pulchras, cum necessario incidunt, non a charta semouendas putamus, ut ab imitatione facti semouendae sunt" (One would wish to bury this inhuman crime in perpetual silence; but since unseemly events occur in the course of history, we consider that

71 Keynes and Love, "Godwine's Ship," 218–23.
72 *VE* 1.3.

they should not be removed from the written page, so that imitation of the deed may be proscribed).[73]

In the *Vita Ædwardi*, a text that takes refuge in praise of Edith because exemplary history seems impossible, there is no place for this murder, which nonetheless cannot be forgotten. Much closer to the event, the Encomiast had earlier masked his own reluctance to include it in dynastic history by claiming that his tact and obfuscation stemmed from concern for Emma's feelings. When he does finally tell the story, he does so out of chronological order, claiming to be prompted by his concern that his reader is wondering why the episode has not yet been told. He is clearly conscious that the murder hangs over his text and that it cannot in the end be kept in silence.[74] That both Poitiers and the Encomiast draw attention to the murder as disrupting history also reminds us that the Anonymous has chosen to deal with this episode in poetry, outside of history. Where Poitiers could tell the story within history because William's avenging of the murder was exemplary, it could not be made so in England.

Ovidian Metamorphosis and Political Change (Poem 2)

The Anonymous's poem of a Virgilian golden age subverted is followed by a prose panegyric of Edith, as least as far as we can tell from Barlow's reconstruction of the missing text, which draws on Osbert of Clare and on Richard of Cirencester.[75] This panegyric, which provides much of the biographical information about the queen that will be discussed in the next chapter, is unsettlingly juxtaposed to a bleak poem that moves anxiously back and forth between the hope of a paradisal future and the fear of chaos. The threat of civil war and fratricide, which lay below the surface of the last poem, now erupts menacingly into the open.

The poem begins with the depiction of Godwine in language that immediately evokes Aeneas as a pivot between Trojan ancestors and Roman descendants, thus advancing and further complicating the thematics of the previous poem. Godwine is an earl, happy in his pious children, and blessed in his ancient lineage – "Felix prole pia dux stripe beatus auita" (O happy earl, in bairns and forebears blessed). The line recalls Anchises's

73 William of Poitiers, *GG* 1.4; and William of Jumièges, *Gesta Normannorum ducum* (hereafter cited as *GND*) 4.18 and 7.16.

74 *Enc.* 3.3–7.

75 Barlow, *VE*, xxxix–xliv.

promise to Aeneas, when he visits his father in the underworld, that Rome will be "felix prole virum" (blessed with descendants of heroes).[76] Moving from the dead-end prophecy of Edward's sails, the poem's opening lines confidently project a *translatio imperii* from the House of Wessex to the House of Godwine in which the earl's children will ensure peace for the English. In the next lines Edith stands as the perfect meeting point between her father and her husband, "patre ... digna suo" (worthy of her father) and "regi condigna marito" (very worthy of her spouse, the king), although in reality her childlessness undermines this position. The poet then praises Edith as a figure of good counsel, who, in a role powerfully deployed by queens, creates peace and prevents the breaking of pacts.[77] The language that the Anonymous uses, "federa pacis" (pacts of peace), returns to the same passage of Lucan's *De bello civili* around which he circled in the previous poem where the two sides recognized each other, and the possibility of averting war still existed.[78] Thus the Anonymous ties his first two poems closely together and develops the theme of Edith as a paragon whose advice can hold the kingdom back from disaster.

Leaving Edith in this idealized position, the Anonymous returns to an image that the muse presented to the poet in the prologue: Godwine as a fount of the streams of Paradise. However, the apparent obedience of the poet to his muse's thematic and formal prescriptions (he even echoes the language that she used when assigning this theme) quickly recedes as the streams become dark and uninterpretable. The Anonymous's shocking image of monstrous transformation takes over the poem:

Sic de fonte tuo, paradise, latentibus uno
deriuas orbi signis in quattuor amnes
sufficienter aquas, uegetent ut uiscera terrę,
atque statum uitę foueant hominum pecorumque;
seque uno laudant utero generata potenter,
pignora dissimili partu generis uariati
corpore, uoce, loco, spatio quoque, tempore, motu.
Aera conscendit pars hec herendo supernis,
spemque sui generis nido fouet arboris altę.
Illa profunda petit tranans inimica uoratrix,

76 Virgil, *Aeneid* 6.784.
77 Stafford, "Royal Women," esp. 145–7 and 149–50.
78 Lucan, *De bello civili* 4.205.

dampna suę stirpis faciens truncumque parentem
pendit ab ore tenens, dum certo tempore uitę
flatus uiuificans animal de non animata
matre creat; studet inde suis resoluta rapinis.
Felicem mundum si seruent flumina cursum
quęque suum, proprias sic fecundantia terras,
fędere seruato, statuit quod celicus ordo!

(Thus from your single fount, O Paradise,
You part in secret water for all lands,
Four ample streams to stir the earth's recess
And nourish the estate of men and beasts.
Themselves they loudly praise, born from one womb,
Issue of various kind, unlike in birth,
In flesh and voice, place, space, and time and motion.
The one part mounts the skies, to heaven twined,
And tends its race's hope in tree-top nest.
The other, gulping monster, seeks the depths,
Attacks its roots and mouths the parent trunk,
And holds, until, as doomed, the breath of life
Creates a creature from a lifeless dam;
And losing grip, pursues again its prey.
O happy world, if each would keep its course
And water its own lands, with pacts observed,
As the celestial order has ordained!)[79]

Four streams pour forth from Godwine. While one stream ascends and tends the nestlings in the top of a tree (the future hope of the people), another stream, transformed into a serpent-like monster, attacks the parental roots and trunk. Then from the now lifeless mother a new living creature is created. The difficulty of interpreting this passage, in part, turns on the questions of whether the four rivers should be equated with specific children of Godwine, and whether when they become just two streams (one of which cannot be distinguished from the tree itself), we are to think of Tostig and Harold, whose strife so preoccupies the Anonymous. The number of

79 *VE* 1.2.

rivers of Paradise as in Genesis 2, however, rather than concern for specific children of Godwine, drives the reference to four in the *Vita Ædwardi*. More generally, the monster is deliberately enigmatic; it is hard to visualize when the stream becomes the tree and when the tree in turn becomes the serpent. The central image's resistance to interpretation must be considered part of the Anonymous's meaning. He keeps this whole episode on a deliberately opaque level with the monstrous making meaning on a figurative rather than a literal level. This indeterminacy makes the metamorphosing streams more frightening, with the danger, the enemy, not clearly recognizable but certainly of the Godwine family.[80]

Gender also intervenes to thwart interpretation. Although the poet holds Edith apart from this amorphous monster, the female gender of both the nurturing and the devouring extensions of the streams or tree brings her firmly back within the frame. Likewise, the monster's femininity shakes any confident reading of the two parts of the tree or stream as Harold and Tostig. This feminizing inevitably prompts questions about the relationship of Edith to the *voratrix*. Earlier in the poem Edith was denoted as "probitatis amatrix." The linking rhyme enforces a contrast between Edith and the monster, rather than a parallel. This works in much the same way that the allusions to Dido and Cleopatra did when the spectre of female rule and promiscuity was raised and then ultimately dismissed. Edith as *voratrix* is set aside, but this does not efface the centrality of children to this monstrous but clearly dynastic tree. Edith's lack of a child lies alongside the jealous feuding of Godwine's sons at the heart of the impending but as yet unknown chaos. The emphasis in this whole passage of metamorphosis on fertility, birth, and mothering brings a distinctively female perspective to the collapse of the West Saxon dynasty and the fall of the House of Godwine, both of which could have been prevented by the birth of a male child. The Anonymous insists that Edith's counsel, rather than Edith's child, is all that holds back chaos now.

Just as the horror of the serpent-tree bursts forth unexpectedly into the poem, calm suddenly reasserts itself as the possibility is proffered that each stream will keep to its own course. The Anonymous now describes an Edenic landscape. Yet even here Paradise is disrupted. The tree that stands in the midst of this pastoral idyll is not only gloomy; it evokes yet another monster. The Anonymous writes:

80 Barlow (ed. *VE*, 26–7), Jordan ("Chronology and Discourse," 142–4), and Otter ("Closed Doors," 79–82) all consider the poem to be obscure and difficult to interpret.

aerię toruo spectabunt lumine quercus
subiectas late terras deuictaque regna.

(The giant oaks, with gloomy eyes, survey
The lands laid out, the kingdoms overcome.)[81]

The collocation of an "aeria quercus" with "turvo ... lumine" recalls the terrifying Cyclops from which Aeneas and his men flee.[82] That Harold and Tostig are referred to here will be confirmed when the next classicizing poem opens with the two brothers figured as *robora* (oak trees). Monstrosity is always close to the surface in this poem. As the allusion to the Cyclops suggests, the evocation of a paradise is more wishful thinking than the reality that the Anonymous can no longer keep at bay. Alarm spills back into the poem as the Anonymous goes on to paint a picture of the "antiquum ... chaos" (entailing uprooted and broken trees) that will return "si" envy breaks out. The poem ends not on an optimistic note but with impending primeval disorder. This disorder is expressed in the future indicative but still remains dependent on the "si." Envy can yet be restrained. The Anonymous's stance, that Harold and Tostig have not yet destroyed each other, militates against a post-1066 composition for this portion of the *Vita Ædwardi.*

From Cnut's *stirps* that are felled in the opening prose of the first chapter of book 1, to Edward's famous death-bed vision of England as a tree, cut down and unable to return to its roots and flower again, in the final chapter of book 2, images of trees haunt the *Vita Ædwardi*, in prose as well as poetry, hagiography as well as history. All three dynasties, West Saxon, Danish, and Godwine, which vie for the throne before the Conquest, are cut down. In this thematic context the grotesqueness of the tree of the second poem, with its intertwined images of motherhood and parricide, cannot be excised from the *Vita Ædwardi.* Ovid provides a way to integrate its threatening and purposeful resistance to interpretation into a reading of the text as a whole. In the *Metamorphoses* the Anonymous found not a single narrative, not a story to use as an interpretative framework, but shape-shifting as a way of understanding and imagining how hope threatened to come to nothing – the hope that had been placed in the expectation of a Godwine on the throne through the birth of a son to

81 *VE* 1.2.
82 Virgil, *Aeneid* 3.677–80.

Edith and Edward, and then placed in the sons of Godwine as protectors and heirs of the kingdom. Shape-shifting conveys a sense of the unreal, that the change that has happened and which continues to unfurl, threatening collapse, is so horrible as to be uncontainable within the realm of the real, hence its monstrosity. As Carolyn Walker Bynum points out, the word *monstrum* comes from the verb *monstrare* 'to show', and thus the monstrous demands wonder and presents itself as a source of knowledge and insight.[83] The Anonymous finds in metamorphosis, in a shape-shifting that has to be read and reread to be grasped, a way of pointing to the horrible reality of English political life on the eve of the Conquest. In so doing he turns both the monstrous and metamorphosis into political discourses.

While Ovid's *Metamorphoses* provides a way of thinking about this passage, there is also a specific Ovidian allusion in play. In depicting his monstrous tree, the Anonymous has a particular passage from the opening of book 12 in mind. Book 12 marks the beginning of Ovid's account of the story of Troy and Rome. The Greeks, keen to set off to war but held back by stormy winds, are amazed by the strange sight of a serpent climbing a tree. At the top of the tree the mother (*mater*) has built a nest (*nidus*) for her now damned (*damna*) nestlings, whom the serpent seizes and devours in its mouth (*os*). Coiled around the tree branches, the serpent then changes into stone. The Greek augur steps forward to interpret the slaughter, whose meaning Ovid tells us is clear, as a joyful portent of their coming conquest of Troy:

> Thestorides "vincemus"; ait "gaudete, Pelasgi!
> Troia cadet, sed erit nostri mora longa laboris.
>
> (Thestorides said, "We shall conquer. Rejoice, ye Greeks,
> Troy shall fall, but our task will be of long duration.")[84]

The Anonymous's own metamorphosing tree pushes beyond Ovid; his intertwining of the fate of ancestors and descendants with a dynasty's drive for self-destruction is baroque compared to Ovid's simplicity and interpretability. Yet the connection between the two images is compelling,

83 Walker Bynum, *Metamorphosis*, 71–2.
84 Ovid, *Meta*. 12.19–20.

not only confirming the Roman poet's profound influence on the Anonymous's poetic imagination but also pointing to some of the meaning of the tree. The Trojan context of Ovid's portent is not at all incidental to the Anonymous. The whole story of Troy, in Virgil's telling, has been a driving intertext for the Anonymous, and this specific poem began by casting, or rather miscasting, Godwine's progeny as symbolic descendants of Aeneas founding a dynasty.

The Trojan parallel does not, however, entirely account for the Anonymous's stream-tree-serpent, which exceeds its Ovidian model in its attempt to encompass the unfolding, self-inflicted, collapse of the Godwine dynasty. In depicting the tree, the Anonymous makes recourse to Norse mythology, alluding to Yggdrasil, the world tree, an ash that links earth (*Miðgarðr*) with the home of the gods (*Ásgarðr*) and whose roots spread out through the universe. The Yggdrasil is best known from the *Grímnismál*, a poem of the *Poetic Edda*, which was preserved in the late-thirteenth-century Codex Regius.[85] In this account the tree is eaten alive – its foliage by harts, and its roots by serpents, in a detail that brings us back to the *Vita Ædwardi*. Also like the Anonymous's tree, it is situated within a divine landscape of primal rivers – flowing from the antlers of a hart, rather than a Paradisal fount. While the allusion to Norse mythology does not operate as a strongly invoked story world (as Troy is here) or as a structuring poetics (as metamorphosis is here), it does have a strong impact on the poem. On the level of political message, the calling up of Yggdrasil casts the Scandinavian ties of the Godwines as a source of danger. On the level of poetry, the mixing of Roman, Christian, and Norse story worlds underscores the difficulty of narrating, fitting into history, the Godwine family, with its many allegiances. In the end this horror is no text-bound story but a reality that threatens to engulf the Anonymous's patron and which he presents himself as writing to hold back.

Just as the Anonymous's metamorphosing streams take the reader by surprise, impressing on him or her the horror of the double dynastic collapse that preceded the Conquest, the Anonymous's Ovidian poetry stands out in high relief when seen against the backdrop of eleventh-century European Latin poetry. Since it was only in the later eleventh century that Ovid came to be fully a part of medieval literary culture, and it was not until the middle of the following century that his poetry was securely part

85 *Grímnismál* 26–35. I am grateful to James Williams and Amy Mulligan for pointing out this allusion.

of the curriculum, the Anonymous's use of the poet places him at the forefront of a revolution in Latin poetry that saw it engage fully with secular life, including women and love, and with ideas of fiction. The poets most known for their early Ovidianism are a group often called the Loire school, among whom were Marbod of Rennes (1035–1123) and Baudri of Bourgueil (1045/6–1130), along with Hildebert of Lavardin and Godfrey of Reims whose Boethian parody we have already noted is shared by the Anonymous. This Ovidian poetics flowered fully in the twelfth century when it fed into the beginnings of French vernacular poetry. Twelfth-century Latin and French poetry's enthusiastic embrace of Ovidian myths of metamorphosis and love, potentially antithetical to Christian doctrine, fed into and fostered debates about the aesthetic and moral value of *fabulae*, which in turn stimulated the development of theories of fiction.[86]

The work of Gerald Bond and Jean-Yves Tilliette on the Ovidianism of Baudri's poetry has revealed that the engagement of Baudri with Ovid's exploration of myth and sexuality stimulated his own thinking about fiction. Both myth and sexual love in their literal form were proscribed to this monk, and so he casts his retellings of pagan stories and his erotic poetic flirtation with the nun Constance in what would become the language of fiction (it remains open whether or not Constance is herself a fiction of Baudri).[87] Our poet shares Baudri's attraction to pagan myth, to the Roman story world, but he utterly rejects themes of sexual love that would undo his representation of the chastity of Edith and Edward's marriage. Fascinatingly, nowhere have I found stray echoes of Ovidian erotics in the Anonymous's work, even though the *Metamorphoses*, like the amatory verse, is shot through with explorations of sexuality. If the Anonymous were not a thoughtful reader of Ovid, we might find the ancient poet's erotics flowing incongruously into the *Vita Ædwardi*. His ability, so knowingly, to suppress the sexual is a sign of his full assimilation of the ancient poet. In the Anonymous's verse we find an early and astonishingly confident appropriation of Ovid. Moreover, the radicalness of his embrace

86 Tilliette, "Hermès"; Tilliette, "*Troiae ab oris*"; Bond, *Loving Subject*, 42–69; Wetherbee, "From Late Antiquity," 128–31. See Tilliette, "Hermès," 121–2, on the problematic but heuristically useful notion of the Loire School. On the less-known Godfrey see Boutemy, "Autour de Godefroid"; J.R. Williams, "Godfrey"; Tilliette, "Retour d'Orphée"; and Broecker, in his edition of Godfrey's poems, *Gottfried von Reims*, 14–24.

87 For an overview of the issue of Constance's fictionality see Tilliette, "Hermès," 138–44.

of Ovid remains even though he rejects the erotic. Writing at the end of the eleventh century, Conrad of Hirsau worried about the teaching of Ovid to schoolboys; this revealed that the "transformation of substances," the theme of the *Metamorphoses*, was considered to be "idol-worship," which was as potentially challenging to the confines of Christian poetry as was sex.[88] And, of course, the monstrous mother of the Anonymous's poem, giving birth and devouring her young, has much to do with sex and reminds us that Macrobius's rejected fables, which William of Conches would redeem, were precisely about the sexual misadventures of the gods; they were described in terms of the monstrous – "per turpia et indigna numinibus ac monstro similia" (shameful to and unworthy of the gods, and even resembling a monstrosity).[89] The Anonymous negotiates the fabulous space of the erotic and the monstrous with a sure step, as he keeps Edith and Edward chaste.

The Anonymous's sophisticated and subtle Ovidianism demands that we place him alongside Baudri, a positioning that is confirmed by the linguistic parallels between the two poets. For instance, with respect to this current poem, the Anonymous's Ovidian-inspired exclamation finds an echo in the younger poet. The Anonymous writes: "heu quanta ruina sequeter! / Antiquumque chaos rursum miser orbis habebit" (O what ruin comes! / The wretched world again old Chaos keeps).[90] Baudri, writing a generation later, included the following line in his poem to the William the Conqueror's daughter, the Countess Adela of Blois: "Antiquumque cahos uideas in parte sequestra" (Following next in the sequence, you will see the primeval chaos).[91] The combination of "antiquum chaos" with "sequeter" / "sequestra" shows that Baudri had the Anonymous as much as Ovid in mind here.[92] The image goes back to Ovid's account of the fear

88 Conrad of Hirsau, *Dialogus super auctores*, pp. 114–16 (trans. 56). Wetherbee, "From Late Antiquity," 130.

89 Macrobius, *In somnium Scipionis* 1.2.11. On William of Conches's commentary on Macrobius see Minnis and Scott, *Medieval Literary Theory*, 118–19. For William's text see Dronke, *Fabula*, 71.

90 *VE* 1.2.

91 Baudri of Bourgueil, *Carmina* 134.101.

92 The collocation of "antiquum" and "chaos" is not unusual. However, only Baudri and the Anonymous use the expression "antiquumque chaos" and in the same metrical position. The two poets often use the same language or similar language, which is generally shared, but not widely, by other earlier classical and Christian poets. For example, see in the Adela poem "in thalami" (134.99 and *VE* 1.4).

that the primeval chaos preceding creation would return if the too hot sun dried up the earth and forced streams to contract back into the womb of mother earth, *viscera matris*.[93] Streams seeking a womb are, of course, grimly suited to the Anonymous's morbid tree. For the Anonymous this ancient chaos also recalls the opening section of Lucan's *De bello civili* – lines that he had already brought into play at the end of the previous poem – where the collapse of Rome threatens a reversion to "antiquum … chaos."[94] The dual invocation of Ovidian metamorphosis and Lucanesque civil strife acts as a figure for the way in which the Anonymous will explore the politics, rather than the erotics, of fiction.

Religious Interlude (Poems 3 and 4)

In each of the two central chapters of book 1, which tendentiously narrate the events of 1051 when Edward briefly succeeded in banishing the Godwines, religious rather than classicizing poetry counterpoints the prose. In recounting how open conflict broke out between the Godwines and Edward, the Anonymous deploys both prose and poetry to exculpate Godwine from any blame. Blame is pinned instead on Robert of Jumièges, while Godwine is lauded again as the father of the English. The theme of good counsel, which the last poem associated with Edith, weaves through the prose of both chapters. Edward, in unwisely accepting Robert's counsel, is deprived of the good counsel of Godwine and Edith, whereas the counsel of wise men results in Edward receiving Godwine back. In the first poem, which addresses the situation between the banishment and the reconciliation, Godwine, in his innocence, is compared to three falsely accused biblical figures: Susanna, Joseph, and Christ. In the second poem, Godwine is David to Edward's Saul. Saul, the anointed king of Israel who had lost God's favour, was reliant on the military might of David, his son-in-law. Although envy drove Saul to try to kill David, David never attempted to kill the king, God's anointed, even when he was at war with him. Despite the reversal of the son and son-in-law relationship, the resonance for Edward and Godwine is obvious.[95]

93 Ovid, *Meta.* 2.272–300.

94 Lucan, *De bello civili* 1.74.

95 In contrast, Licence, "Date and Authorship," reads this poem as representing Godwine, in his refusal to attack an anointed king, as a positive exemplum for Tostig with regard to Harold.

In terms of understanding the classicizing verse of the *Vita Ædwardi*, there are several points to be made about the Anonymous's religious poetry. Our sense that the poet's allusions to the Roman story world are thematically rather than linguistically driven is confirmed by their virtual absence from these two poems. These poems instead draw on the language of late antique and early medieval Christian poetry. The obvious intrusion of the Roman story world, when the Anonymous draws a contrast between Godwine, as the fount of Paradise, and the Scylla that soiled him, actually proves this point. References to rocky Scylla had become common in Christian Latin poetry, and so here the Anonymous stays within its parameters, while deliberately juxtaposing Christian and pagan images. Thematically, within the poetry, this juxtaposition contributes to a developing paradigm of condemning Godwine from a secular perspective and exonerating him from a religious perspective. Yet both the recourse to the classical story world and the reference to Godwine as the fount of Paradise (whose streams were threateningly changeable in the previous poem) destabilize the apparent transparency of this religious poem.

In the opening of the next poem, which continues the narrative in a celebratory mode as the Godwines and Edward are reconciled, there is a calculatedly mischievous allusion to Lucan's *De bello civili*. The poet, "rejoicing at this settlement" (pro tanto fędere rerum), addresses the muse. Yet this clause repeats the language of the opening of book 2 of *De bello civili* in which, all preliminaries now aside, war finally breaks out.[96] Thus, while the poet rolls out his portrayal of Godwine as David, and Edward as Saul, the image of civil war is held in the frame. There is, meanwhile, no flinching in the face of the utter shock of likening Edward to Saul. The Anonymous goes so far as to remind us that David restrained himself from killing Saul even when the latter was at his most exposed, defecating in a cave.

The multivocality of the *Vita Ædwardi* is forcefully underscored in these two religious poems, with Edward unreservedly condemned, but fully redeemed by the turn to hagiography in book 2, and Godwine seemingly exonerated but in a language that is so tainted within the *Vita Ædwardi* as to be hardly consoling. In presenting this perspective, the Anonymous again defies his muse, as he did when he invoked Thebes and civil war. This act of defiance is made complete because he calls on the muse directly in these two poems, unlike in the others.

96 Lucan, *De bello civili* 2.2.

Doublespeak and Pagan Error (Poem 5)

With the death of Godwine, who is mourned as a father figure when the next chapter opens, the Anonymous comes to the most fraught phase of his narrative: the thus far unspoken, but everywhere intimated, rivalry between Harold and Tostig. In prose he expresses a new determination to present his account as exemplary history, a mode thus far conspicuously absent, writing:

> Et quoniam occasio se intulit, de his duobus fratribus uitam et mores actusque eorum notitię subsequentium pro captu ingenioli nostri innotescere cupimus. Quod nos agere uelle non putamus absque re, tum pro operis serie, tum ut exempla imitabilia habeant ii qui in eorum successerint posteritate.
>
> (And since the occasion offers, we wish, to the best of our small powers, to inform posterity about the life, character, and deeds of these two brothers. And we do not think our wish to do this unreasonable, both on account of the plan of the work, and also so that their posterity shall have models for imitation.)[97]

This is a very pure expression of the principles of exemplary history, not moderated in any way to suit the unexemplary status of Harold and Tostig. This turn to exemplarity catches the reader by surprise because the prologue professes an aim to praise Edith through her family, just as the *Encomium* had done a generation before. As the Anonymous goes on to offer his account of the two brothers, an artifice surfaces that warns the reader to attend carefully. The Anonymous's prose in this chapter takes the form of a rigid, almost brittle, structural and stylistic paralleling that attempts to figure Harold and Tostig as equals. Yet, although Harold emerges as more suited to be king (his fault is to be too scrupulous in taking counsel rather than not taking it at all), the Anonymous is unable to contain Tostig, his patron's favourite, within his rigid paradigm of equality. The tension between the superabundance of his account of Tostig clashes with his recognition that Harold should rule, leading to doublespeak. The glaring gap between form and content of this prose section alerts the reader to a gap between ideal and reality: Tostig and Harold cannot be the subject of exemplary history any more than they can be equals.

---

97 *VE* 1.5.

The Anonymous follows the artful balance of his prose with a rich and complex poem that simultaneously and not accidentally explores the enmity between Harold and Tostig (so conspicuously suppressed in the prose) and the relationship of Christian and Roman story worlds. As a result the whole chapter is shaped around a purposeful series of doublings: Tostig doubles Harold, verse doubles prose, and pagan doubles Christian. Within the poem the Anonymous deploys the stories of pairs of murderous brothers – Eteocles and Polynices, Thyestes and Atreus, Cain and Abel – and in the midst of this he implicates fathers by reworking the story of Tantalus and Pelops. This multiplicity of stories, both pagan and Christian, picked up and abandoned one after the other, expresses a crisis of tellability, which is also figured in his abandonment of his muse. Unable to sing of a Virgilian golden age, even superficially, he now beseeches Ill Fortune, Discordant Vice, Holy Faith, and Mary. Throughout the poem it may seem that the Roman story world slips beyond the Anonymous's grasp, that he knows only the vague outlines and not the details of the stories he deploys, and that he is crashing around.[98] He was, however, an expert and bold reworker of his classical inheritance, who demanded a similar level of learning and openness to innovation on the part of his reader.

The multiplicity of the intertexts that are brought to bear in this one poem requires that we begin with an overview of the explicitly invoked stories before turning to the allusions. In a move that echoes his earlier Ovidian experiment, the first lines feign optimism before the Anonymous allows his poem to be overwhelmed by horror. United by a pact of peace ("unito federe pacis"), the two brothers are compared to oak trees, to Hercules, Atlas, and Mercury, and to angels holding up the English kingdom. There is a quiet echo here of the same passage from book 4 of *De bello civili*, upon which the Anonymous called in the first and second poems.[99] Thus he creates a textual unity by weaving specific sections from his ancient poets into the fabric of his whole set of poems. As a result, particular moments from Lucan and Statius especially become central to the meaning of the *Vita Ædwardi*, and their recurrence makes that centrality hard to overlook. The poet then quickly changes direction, invoking the pyres of Thebes, which are lit to burn the bodies of the warring brothers Eteocles and Polynices, as he pleads to know why Fortune has

98 Southern, "First Life," 396.
99 Lucan, *De bello civili* 4.187–94.

troubled Harold and Tostig. Next he steps outside of the Roman story world to recall Eve's son Cain killing his brother Abel and to condemn the especially evil nature of murder among those of the same flesh. The poet then reaches back into the Roman story world to unleash his most disturbing intertext yet, the House of Atreus, which is consumed over three generations by cannibalism as Tantalus feeds his young son Pelops to the gods, and then Pelops's son Atreus feeds his nephews to their father, his brother. The Anonymous then abandons the Roman story world, stepping out of his poem to press metapoetic questions about the truth or value of pagan stories compared to biblical stories. Although he does find value in the pagan, he finishes his poem with the greater truth of the New Testament as he calls on Faith to lead them to a better life, and on the Virgin, referred to as Concord, to bring peace. From beginning to end, the poem teeters between disaster and the possibility that it will be averted. All is contingent on Harold and Tostig keeping peace with each other, and the Anonymous very carefully maintains the stance that there has as yet been no collapse of the brothers' alliance. Within this high tension the Roman world turns out, for all its interpretative utility, to be just stories, while the Christian world represents a reality, active in the present, to whose God one can pray for intervention to stop the looming madness.

Most of this poem relies on an overt use of the classical, alongside the Christian, story world to expose the looming disaster that will be caused by Harold and Tostig's feuding. At first these two frameworks appear to figure themselves and the two brothers as united, as attention to allusion reveals. The brothers are said to be "nubigenę … terrę" (of a cloud-born land), which dovetails with their explicit comparison to angels via the well-known pun on Angles and angels ("Angligenos") in subsequent lines. The angelic connotation of *nubigenus* is attested by Goscelin (a monk of Saint-Bertin who made his home in England across the Conquest) in his *Historia minor sancti Augustini*, where cloud-born saints are angel-like.[100] The unusual word also appears with similar connotations in the work of Folcard, another Saint-Bertin monk in England, in a preface to his rewriting of the life of Saint Bertin addressed to Abbot Bovo.[101] Commonly,

100 Goscelin, *Historia minor sancti Augustini* 61 (as cited in Barlow, *VE*, 58).
101 Folcard, *Vita sancti Bertini*, 604.

however, the adjective *nubigenus* calls to mind flooding rivers and threatening centaurs. For example, Gozechinus of Liège and Mainz, writing contemporaneously with the Anonymous, recalls the destructive fury of the flooded Meuse when Aeolus, the god of winds, reigns "in convivium deorum cum nubigenis amnibus, fratribus suis."[102] Statius made recourse to the same imagery; the exiled Polynices travels through a storm, frightened, listening to "nubigenas e montibus amnes," and, in the *Aeneid* and the *Metamorphoses*, *nubigenus* is used for centaurs killed by Hercules.[103] These examples, drawn from contemporary prose and the poetic intertexts in which the Anonymous casts his own story, suggest that cloud-born Harold and Tostig might be read less as angels and more as threatening, centaur-like, swollen rivers. The rivers of Paradise that run from Godwine are about to bring havoc down on England.

This sense of impending collapse that undermines the security projected on the surface of these opening lines is reinforced by a seemingly blundering comparison of the brothers Harold and Tostig to Atlas and Mercury jointly holding up the heavens. Atlas is unproblematic, but Mercury appears to make no sense since he did not hold up mountains in ancient mythology. The Anonymous's denotation of Mercury as "Cyllenius heros," which evokes his birth on Mount Cyllene, might be taken as pointing to the source of the Anonymous's confused association of him with mountains. In fact, it reveals that he is further undermining his own image of Harold and Tostig as two Hercules securing the kingdom. The epithet "Cyllenius heros" appears at the end of a hexameter line in the *Ecloga* (as it does here), where Theodulus associates Mercury with witchcraft and leading people out of Hades.[104] Theodulus's *Ecloga*, written at an uncertain date after the first decade of the tenth century, was, by the eleventh century, a well-known school text that paralleled pagan myths with Christian truths. The brothers, one Atlas, one a problematic Mercury, emerge as not so indistinguishable after all, a message that the Anonymous asserts more and more forcefully as the poem continues.[105]

---

102 Gozechinus, *Epistola ad Walcherum* 6.

103 Statius, *Thebaid* 1.365; Virgil, *Aeneid* 7.674 and 8.293; and Ovid, *Meta.* 12.211.

104 Theodulus, *Ecloga* line 197.

105 R.P.H. Green, "Medieval Textbook"; M. Irvine, *Textual Culture*, 356–68; and Wetherbee, "From Late Antiquity," 121–2. See further, chapter 5 herein.

Thebes

The Anonymous leaves behind the superficial harmony of the poem's opening lines with a searching question:

> Quid super his geminis turbato felle minaris,
> infelix fortuna, nimis liuore gemello
> Thebanis accincta rogis hinc inde ministras
> funereas intenta faces furialibus armis?
>
> (Why then, Ill Fortune, menace these two men
> With thickened gall, with more than double spite,
> And, set for Theban pyres, intent on dreadful war,
> From both sides furnish torches for the dead?)[106]

Until this anguished authorial intervention, allusion held the *Thebaid* as a steady, anxious beat in the background of the poetry of the *Vita Ædwardi.* Theban allusions, and the bleak picture of Harold and Tostig's end that they presage, can no longer be evaded as the framework becomes explicit. Thus even a reader unfamiliar with the story, not able to recognize the echoes, is now impelled to seek explanation, and no reader can seek refuge any more in the strained balance of the chapter's prose.

The language of the Anonymous's Theban allusions takes us to the last two books of Statius's epic. Having lost her patience with the years of war between the Argives (who take up the exiled Polynices's cause) and the Thebans (who defend Eteocles's unlawful retention of the throne), the Fury Tisiphone goads these brothers into single combat. As she pushes them towards mutual destruction, their father, Oedipus (who killed his own father), their mother, Jocasta (who was also Oedipus's mother), their sister Antigone, their wives, Polynices's father-in-law Adrastus (also king of the Argives), and Pietas (family love) plead with them to cease. Despite the power of their pleas these family members and Pietas are ultimately ineffectual, and the two brothers engage in one-to-one combat in which they dramatically die together. Polynices, attempting to strip the wounded Eteocles of his regalia, is killed as the dying king plunges his sword into his brother's heart. Polynices in turn collapses on top of Eteocles, crushing

106 *VE* 1.5.

his brother to death under the weight of his armour. In the aftermath a distraught Oedipus visits the corpses accompanied by a dutiful Antigone. The throne passes to Creon, brother of Jocasta, who, despite Antigone's entreaties, sends Oedipus into exile. The new king is subsequently defeated by Theseus, outraged that Creon has not allowed the burial of the Argive dead; kingship thus passes from Thebes to Athens, and an ancient dynasty, founded when Cadmus sowed serpents' teeth, falters and collapses.

The Theban legend provides an obvious parallel to the demise of the House of Godwine, pinning the blame squarely on Harold and Tostig. But many aspects of Statius's telling invite the Anonymous to move beyond the surface in order to explore the dimensions of the collapse of the Godwine dynasty from which even the most unsympathetic accounts, both Norman and English, shy away. Mention of Thebes implicates the father of these fratricides: it was Oedipus's curse that let loose the murderous envy that would destroy the brothers. And, uncomfortably, the wider story of Oedipus hangs ominously over the whole poem. Godwine comes into the frame for further severe censure. In addition, Edward, described as being more like a father than a husband to Edith, is implicated by Oedipus.[107] In their old age both the Anonymous's Edward and Statius's Oedipus are compared to lions. The Anonymous portrayed the younger Edward of the coronation as lion-like in his anger, "leonini uidebatur terroris." In the prose paired with this current poem, the status as lion of the kingdom is clearly passed to Harold who threatened thieves and robbers with "leonino terrore et uultu."[108] Statius develops an extended simile of Oedipus as a lethargic and weary old lion who springs to attack when approached, only to remember his decrepitude and the strength of younger lions.[109] Although the Anonymous does not make overt reference to Oedipus, anyone who knows the tale of Thebes cannot help but look to Godwine and Edward, neither of whom the Anonymous shirks from criticizing in earlier poetry.

In the context of a poem written for Edith, which attends so assiduously to her emotions, it is hard to overlook the relevance of the prominence that Statius gives to the roles played by female figures as he horribly and slowly unfolds his tragedy in book 11.[110] It is Tisiphone who incites the

107 *VE* 2, prologue; see also 1.2 and 2.11.
108 *VE* 1.1 and 1.5.
109 Statius, *Thebaid* 11.741–7.
110 Newlands, *Statius*, 113–17.

brothers, and, among the parade of family members pleading for restraint, Antigone, the sister of Eteocles and Polynices and the dutiful daughter of Oedipus, stands out. It is hard not to imagine Edith being invited to identify with Antigone. Statius tells how this Theban woman addressed her exiled brother Polynices from the city walls, futilely begging him not to attack. From this perspective, Edith is again cast as a peacemaker trying to stop Tostig's jealousy of Harold from spilling over into warfare. Such associations fit in well with her being figured later in this poem and elsewhere in the *Vita Ædwardi* as Concord. Like Antigone, she fails to restrain her favourite brother, who had been unjustly denied the kingdom. And when we see Edith consoling Edward, plunged into grief by Tostig's rebellion and Harold's response, Antigone, accompanying her father to view the bodies, is not far away.[111]

In unwrapping the place of women within the story of Thebes and arguing that by invoking Theban fratricide the *Vita Ædwardi* makes a place for Edith within its narrative of the end of Edward's reign, it is important to see that the *Vita Ædwardi* is not isolated in its interest in the women left grieving after the spent violence of Thebes. Contained among the several passionate laments from the *Thebaid* and the *Aeneid* that are excerpted in the *Cambridge Songs* (*Carmina Cantabrigiensia*) are the sorrowing words that Argia speaks over the body of her dead husband, Polynices, and in which she asks after Antigone and Jocasta.[112] Copied at St Augustine's Canterbury in the mid-eleventh century, the *Cambridge Songs* were likely brought together for Emperor Henry III. They may have been brought back to England by Bishop Ealdred of Worcester after an extended visit to Cologne, where he went in search of Edward the Exile, whom the Confessor hoped to recognize as heir.[113] The *Cambridge Songs* include verse composed in Germany, France, and Italy, as well as classical and late antique verse. This includes neumed metra from the *Consolatio*, among which is Boethius's evocation of how the Muses taught him to seek solace in poetry. Women's voices, perspectives, and experiences are prominent throughout the manuscript, not only in its classical and late antique excerpts but also in poetry about nunneries and queens, themes that are

111 Newlands, *Statius*, 127–31.

112 *Carmina Cantabrigiensia* 28 and 32.

113 For a full discussion of the *Cambridge Songs* with extensive references see Tyler, "German Imperial Bishops."

central to the *Vita Ædwardi*. Among the songs is Wipo's poem on the death of Henry III's father, Conrad II.[114] The dynastic connections between the Imperial and West Saxon houses are evident in this poem that also records, with grief, the death of Gunnhild, daughter of Emma and Cnut, and half-sister of Edward. The positioning of Argia's lament for Polynices directly before Wipo's poem, which is in turn followed by an excerpt from the *Aeneid* in which Aeneas mourns the death of Hector, illustrates that the *Songs* share the *Vita Ædwardi*'s impulse to juxtapose classical poetry and contemporary history.[115] Although Ziolkowski has seen the *Cambridge Songs* as only accidentally preserved in an Anglo-Saxon manuscript, the dynastic and ecclesiastical ties between the courts of Henry III and Edward the Confessor (which will be explored further in the next chapter) suggest that Thebes and its women were a part of a shared interest in the Roman story world among lay audiences.[116]

The *Thebaid*, although beginning to become part of the school curriculum in the eleventh century, was considerably less well known than either the *Aeneid* or *De bello civili*, only gaining in popularity in the twelfth century.[117] Conrad of Hirsau's meagre grasp of only part of the *Thebaid*'s plot in his summary of the text for his *Dialogus super auctores* illustrates that even some of the best educated in this period did not know it first-hand.[118] However, in addition to a copy surviving from Rochester (London, British Library, Royal 15.C.x), and fragments of a glossed copy from Worcester (Worcester, Cathedral Library, Q.8, fols. 164–71), a glossed Statius was left to Exeter Cathedral by Bishop Leofric, as his donation list records, when he died in 1072.[119] Leofric's copy brings us close to court, including Edith. Trained in Imperial Lotharingia, Leofric was among the clerics who returned to England with Edward the Confessor, whom he served as a royal chaplain. After becoming bishop, Leofric continued to move in court circles; the charter recording the consecration of Exeter Cathedral asserts Leofric's continuing close ties with king and queen, describing Edward as

114 *Carmina Cantabrigiensia* 33.

115 *Carmina Cantabrigiensia* 34.

116 *Carmina Cantabrigiensia*, ed. Ziolkowski, xxx–xxxi and xxxix.

117 L.D. Reynolds, *Texts and Transmission*, 394–6; M. Irvine, *Textual Culture*, 356–8; Munk Olsen, "Production of the Classics," 3; and Wetherbee, "From Late Antiquity," 125.

118 Conrad of Hirsau, *Dialogus super auctores*, 119–20 (trans. 61–2).

119 Robertson, *Anglo-Saxon Charters*, 228–9.

leading Leofric on his right arm, and Edith on his left arm, to the altar.[120] The Anonymous's recourse to the *Thebaid* reveals either that his audience was well read or that writing in the face of impending disaster led him to stretch his audience, to introduce new models. From either vantage point, the *Vita Ædwardi* and Edith's situation become an instigation for the wider circulation of not just stories of Thebes but the *Thebaid*.

Within the pages of the *Vita Ædwardi* we can see something of the process of that reception of the *Thebaid*, which alerts us further to the place of the Anonymous's prosimetrum on the cutting edge of mid-eleventh-century literary culture. As the Anonymous develops his Theban theme, Lucan's *De bello civili* seems to move into the background. However, the language of the Anonymous's poetry reveals that he has very much in mind Lucan's shaping of the Theban legend. As civil war looms, Lucan writes:

> Vestali raptus ab ara
> Ignis, et ostendens confectas flamma Latinas
> Scinditur in partes geminoque cacumine surgit
> Thebanos imitata rogos.
>
> (From the Vesta's altar the fire vanished suddenly; and the bonfire which marks the end of the Latin Festival split into two and rose, like the pyre of the Thebans, with double crest.)[121]

The Anonymous follows him in describing Harold and Tostig as "Thebanis accincta rogis" at the beginning of a hexameter. And when he returns to Thebes later in the poem, his description of the flames recalls the same passage from Lucan's poem:

> Hec quoque tempestas scindit nequissima flammas
> fratribus impositis per mutua uulnera lapsis.
>
> (A wind, most wanton, parts in twain the flames above
> The pyre for brothers killed by mutual blows.)[122]

120 *Electronic Sawyer*, S1021.
121 Lucan, *De bello civili* 1.549–52. Barlow notes the allusion to Lucan.
122 *VE* 1.5.

Lucan both explicitly invokes Thebes as a framework for understanding civil war and designates the story not as *historia* but as *fabula*.[123] Knowing that the Anonymous's Theban language is as much Lucan's as it is Statius's leads to two points. First, the dual debt suggests that while the Anonymous knew the *Thebaid*, his language was shaped by Lucan's epic, which was the better known and more fully studied poem. From this perspective the Lucan-colouring of his Theban echoes looks like an early stage in the process of the full reception of Statius. Second and more profoundly, his mixing of Thebes and *De bello civili* reveals his alertness to the intertextuality of his own texts. That awareness of the intertextuality of Roman poetry profoundly informs his own poetics, with its reliance on allusion and his understanding of the value of made-up stories for understanding the present.

The attractiveness of the legend of Thebes as a model to think with amid bitter intra-dynastic fighting continued to draw lay audiences in the twelfth century. Orderic Vitalis, writing in Normandy some sixty years after the Conquest, saw Thebes as a story that lay people used to understand their experiences. For example, Orderic has Robert Curthose, who is furious with his father, refer to himself as a Polynices figure, going into exile in hopes of finding an Adrastus to aid him.[124] Almost a century after the *Vita Ædwardi*, Thebes was the first of the classical legends to move into the written vernacular in the form of a romance, when a poet associated with the Angevin court of Henry II and Eleanor of Aquitaine rendered Statius's poem into French. Ziolkowski has identified the way in which the popularity of Statian poetry, evinced in the *Cambridge Songs*, contributed to the emergence of courtly romance, such as the *Roman de Thèbes*; and now we can situate the *Vita Ædwardi* as part of that process.[125] The central place of women in book 11 of the *Thebaid*, picked up in the *Cambridge Songs* as well as the *Vita Ædwardi*, suggests that the role of female patronage played in this early popularity should not be discounted. The desire to see history through women's eyes, and especially Edith's eyes, which is so evident throughout the *Vita Ædwardi* and which has been identified as one of the impetuses for the emergence of the romance genre in the twelfth century, appears to have promoted the Anonymous's innovative use of the *Thebaid*.[126]

123 Lucan, *De bello civili* 4.549–51 and 6.355–9.

124 Orderic, *HE* 3.100–1, 4.122–3 and 6.86–7.

125 *Carmina Cantabrigiensia*, ed. Ziolkowski, 263; and Newlands, *Statius*, 131 and 133.

126 Field, "Romance as History," 165–6.

Seneca and the House of Atreus

Statius and Servius's commentary on the *Aeneid* also intertwine the story of the Theban brothers with the even more horrible story of the House of Atreus.[127] The Anonymous understands his own poem within this well-established pattern. At first glance, however, it appears that he has only an uncertain grasp of the barest outline of this classical story of a family torn apart by cannibalism. However, when we look closely at how he has reworked the story to expose what he had artfully obscured on the surface (which son of Godwine was the guiltier), the Anonymous emerges as a confident wielder of classical myth, alert to the way that poets have always reworked this inheritance.

According to classical myth, Atreus holds the kingdom coveted by his jealous exiled brother Thyestes. Although he has the throne, Atreus is devoured by the fear that his brother has seduced his wife and thus his sons are actually Thyestes's. In revenge he invites the exile back and feeds him a feast of his own sons' flesh; the father thus unwittingly eats his own children. The Anonymous, however, reverses the roles and gives us Thyestes as the murderer of his nephews. While Barlow, like Southern, considers this a mistake, the change casts Tostig, the exile not chosen for the throne, as the one who feeds Harold his own children.[128] The reworking accords with a gruesome story recounted by Henry of Huntingdon. According to Henry, Tostig, who was enraged that Harold was favoured by Edward, went to Hereford where his brother was preparing a banquet for the king: "Vbi ministros fratris omnes detruncans, singulis uasis, uini, medonis, ceruisie, pigmenti, morati, cisere, crus humanum, uel caput, uel brachium imposuit" (In which place he dismembered all his brother's servants, and put a human leg, head, or arm into each vessel for wine, mead, ale, spiced wine, morat, and cider).[129] Tostig's subsequent warning to the king that he will only find salted food when he arrives ensures that the gruesome feast is for his brother. The source of Henry's story, which is not recounted elsewhere, is unknown.[130] As well as indicating that Henry did not make up the tale, the parallel with the *Vita Ædwardi* suggests two observations. First, that a story about Tostig and cannibalism circulated across the

127 Statius, *Thebaid* 1.247, 1.279, 2.436, and 11.128; and Servius on *Aeneid* 1.347 and 6.608.

128 Barlow, *VE* 146; and Southern, "First Life," 396.

129 Henry of Huntingdon, *HA* 6.25.

130 Henry of Huntingdon, *HA*, ed. Greenway, 383n148.

Conquest, and thus the Anonymous knew what he was doing in assigning Thyestes, the brother excluded from the throne, the part of parricide. Second, that the Anonymous's playing with the story reveals a command of his intertext and an expectation that his audience would also understand his point or be engaged enough to want to learn the stories that would allow them to. The association in the classical world of cannibalism with tyrants meanwhile suggests further that the Anonymous saw Tostig as unfit to rule (though he does not say this explicitly in prose). Later in the *Vita Ædwardi*, when explaining the causes of the Northern Rebellion, the Anonymous records Tostig's harsh response to the misdeeds of the Northumbrians. While the Anonymous may seem unjudgmental of Tostig, in an account that very much takes his side on the surface, clemency was an important political virtue. William of Poitiers, for example, praises William the Conqueror's display of clemency towards his rebellious paternal uncle.[131] Tostig comes in for criticism such as we have already seen levelled at Edward and Godwine. Meanwhile, this episode at Hereford took place in 1063 and marked a deterioration in relations between Harold and Tostig, reminding us that long before the Northern Rebellion enmity between the brothers had come to the surface. The Anonymous's anxious warning against fratricide and civil war had meaning well before the end of 1065.

The skill with which the Anonymous manipulates the story of Thyestes is all the more striking because it was hardly known before the expanded circulation of Seneca's *Tragedies* in the twelfth century. Orosius's treatment is typically terse; he mentions Thyestes but only to identify the brothers as parricides in a list of tales that he will not tell.[132] Although the grim cannibalism of the House of Atreus was often referred to in classical poetry, the level of detail that would allow the Anonymous to reverse so expertly the roles of the brothers is generally absent. Among classical poets likely to be known to the Anonymous, Horace, Ovid, and Lucan simply assume knowledge.[133] Servius is similarly compressed.[134] Hyginus's *Fabulae* do not account for all the details known by the Anonymous.[135] Moreover, none of these possible sources begins to convey the emotional power that the Anonymous so clearly finds in the story and which is such

131 *VE* 1.7; William of Poitiers, *GG* 1.28. Blurton, *Cannibalism*, 1–9 and 59–65.

132 Orosius, *Historiae* 1.12.

133 Horace, *Carmina* 1.6.8, 1.28.7, and 2.13.37; Horace, *Epodes* 17.65; Horace, *Ars Poetica* 91; Ovid, *Meta.* 6.401–11 and 15.462; and Lucan, *De bello civili*, 1.544 and 7.451.

134 Servius on *Aeneid* 1.568 and 11.262.

135 Hyginus, *Fabulae* 82–8.

a hallmark of Seneca's style. Between the late antique poets Claudian, Dracontius, and Sidonius Apollinaris, and around the time that the *Vita Ædwardi* was written, there appears to be not even passing reference to the story.[136]

A clue to the source of the Anonymous's knowledge of Thyestes may lie in the line with which he introduces this story. He writes: "Priscis nota satis tua sic contagia ludis" (your plagues are notes in the ancient plays). *Ludus* denotes a wide range of activities including games, sport, jokes, and jests, as well as stage plays.[137] Thyestes's unwitting cannibalism of his own children is the subject of a violently moving play, a *ludus*, by Seneca the Younger. Except for small excerpts, Seneca's *Tragedies* are hardly attested before the end of the eleventh century when the earliest full codex appeared in the 1093 catalogue of the northern Italian monastery of Pomposa, in a text likely to derive from one at Monte Cassino. The abbot of Pomposa, Jerome, defended the reading of classical literature in his monastery, arguing that it acted as a deterrent, offering negative exempla that contrasted with the Christian way.[138] Looking further we find that key elements of the story as told by the Anonymous are shared only with Seneca. The Anonymous moralizes that although Christianity had not yet come to teach brotherly love, Error knew that their crime was wrong, and the skies, their stars absent, fell black in revulsion. While Servius records that the sun disappeared in horror at the outcome of Atreus's and Thyestes's struggle for the throne, it is Seneca who repeatedly writes that the stars as well as the sun ceased to shine. Indeed he develops this into a memorable image at the end of the play as the Chorus becomes terrified of the now perpetual night. Seneca brings the absence of the stars to the fore by enumerating the constellations that are no longer visible.[139] Also, the Anonymous may have been influenced by the central place of *pietas* (in the sense of family love) as the force that would be able to stop the destruction unleashed by Atreus's act, in *Thyestes*. He wrote:

Tu post crimina sex pietatem septima ledis
altius, errores per se quę diluit omnes.

136 Claudian, *De bello Gildonico* 400; Dracontius, *Orestes* 203, 308, 486, 684, and 970; and Sidonius Apollinaris, *Carmina* 9.106–8 and 23.277.

137 Isidore, *Ety.* 18.16.

138 L.D. Reynolds, *Texts and Transmission*, 379; and Schmidt, "Rezeption," 65.

139 Seneca, *Thyestes* 789–884.

(Your seventh, most deadly crime destroys that love
Which by itself can wipe all errors out.)[140]

Seneca's chorus trusts too much in pietas:

Nulla vis maior pietate vera est;
iurgia externis inimica durant,
quos amor verus tenuit, tenebit.

(no force is greater than true love of family.
Disputes among strangers persist in rancour,
But those it has held, true love will hold.)[141]

When Atreus decides to kill Thyestes's son Tantalus, named after his grandfather (and thus Atreus's father), this choice of young Tantalus is attributed to Atreus's perverted notion of *pietas*.[142] The role of Pietas in the Anonymous's poem may owe itself to both *Thyestes* and the *Thebaid*, as well as to its value in the *Aeneid*.

Although the Anonymous appears to know the story of Seneca's *Thyestes* and to allude openly to a play, there are no verbal echoes from the play in the poems of the *Vita Ædwardi*. While the differing metres employed in the two texts contribute to this lack of echoes, their absence also prompts questions about how the Anonymous and presumably also his audience knew *Thyestes*. Perhaps the text was so newly known that, while it had shaped the Anonymous's imagination, it had not shaped his language. Or perhaps, while he vividly remembered the story (as we see in his handling of the darkening stars), writing in England he no longer had access to the text. Even just knowing the story in the mid-eleventh century marks the Anonymous as exceptional in his poetic culture. If the poet knew the story and his audience did not, the openly made reference suggests that he would have been prompted to tell the story, and thus the *Vita Ædwardi* becomes an occasion for the spread of new learning. The story of Thyestes was so new that it was surely a talking point that attracted attention to itself rather than acting as a shield for the devastating portrait of the Godwines entailed by its deployment.

140 *VE* 1.5.
141 Seneca, *Thyestes* 549–51.
142 Seneca, *Thyestes* 718.

Considering the Anonymous within the context of other poets who also appear to have some knowledge of Seneca's plays in the later half of the eleventh century further underscores both his precocity and his connections to the Loire school. Looking at the eleventh and early twelfth centuries, Otto Zwierlein finds traces of knowledge of Seneca in the poetry of Marbod and Petrus Pictor. In his poem "De Machabaeis" Marbod includes the phrase "turpis coenae culpa ... Micenae," which is a reference to the story of Thyestes, among a list of other themes that occur in Seneca's *Tragedies*. What is more, in a move that is familiar from the *Vita Ædwardi*, he refers to them as *ludi* and goes on to make additional references to the theatre. He appears to be familiar with the range of Seneca's plays rather than having had recourse to excerpts in florilegia, as his younger contemporary Hildebert may have had.[143] Meanwhile, later in the eleventh century, Petrus Pictor, a canon of Our Lady, Saint-Omer, whose poetry was influenced by the poets of the Loire school, also appears to have had some limited knowledge of the *Tragedies*.[144] The Anonymous's reference is, however, fuller and more sophisticated than that of these two poets. Not only is the *Vita Ædwardi* an early witness to interest in the story of Thyestes, but its witness is among the most detailed and most demanding. The Anonymous does not offer a fleeting reference that can be ignored if not recognized, but rather he requires that Edith and his wider audience learn, use, and rethink the story in order to understand the context and consequences of Tostig and Harold's disastrous falling out.

The next reference to the Roman story world that the Anonymous offers, the story of Tantalus and Pelops, picks up on the way in which the Theban allusions implicated fathers and father figures and suggests again the presence of Godwine and Edward in this poem. According to classical poets, Tantalus feeds his son Pelops to the gods, hoping to gain their favour. Repulsed, the gods refuse to eat, with the exception of Ceres, who absent-mindedly consumes the boy's shoulder, which she subsequently restores in ivory. In the Anonymous's retelling, Ceres is replaced by Concord, a move that evokes Edith, who is figured as and associated with Concord throughout the verses of the *Vita Ædwardi*. The poet has thus prominently placed Edith in the midst of a story that involves a father horrifyingly sacrificing his son in order to gain favour with the gods. But he has carefully changed the story to absolve Edith of any guilt in the

143 Marbod, "De Machabaeis," col. 1296; and Zwierlein, "Spuren," 183–95 (esp. 191).

144 Petrus Pictor, *Carmina* 14; and Zwierlein, "Spuren," 179–83.

conflict between father and son. Within the *Vita Ædwardi*'s rendering of the myth, Concord is cast as the healer of Pelops, without any mention that she had actually eaten the shoulder, as did Ceres. Concord's redress of a father's terrible transgression against a son must have some bearing on the relations among Godwine and his children. Although not stated by the Anonymous, Pelops is the father of Atreus and Thyestes, so we have a multigenerational tale of cannibalism, in which fathers are as implicated as are brothers in the repeated slaughter of the family's children.

Although the story of Pelops is less obscure than that of his sons (it is told more fully by Ovid than that of Thyestes, and Statius makes repeated though very compressed references to the story), it is likewise not widely known.[145] Servius, who unlike Ovid mentions Ceres, seems to be the most likely source of the Anonymous's detailed knowledge.[146] In the opening lines of *Cligès*, where Chrétien de Troyes makes his famous claim for a *translatio studii* into the vernacular, the French poet says that he has written a vernacular version of "le mors de l'espaule" (the bite of the shoulder).[147] This suggests that the story was familiar in the late twelfth century and re-emphasizes a link between the story world of the *Vita Ædwardi* and that of twelfth-century romance. Yet again the Anonymous's engagement with a story from classical antiquity is early. In replacing Concord with Ceres, which is clearly not a mistake but a purposeful reworking, he shows himself to be sufficiently assured to take control of classical myth and legend, and that he deploys them with an eye to exonerating Edith. In his hands the process of interpreting the present through the past involved reworking the past to fit the present, and vice versa. Some of the attractiveness of the Roman story world to the Anonymous lies precisely in this malleability, a quality that is not available to him when he is invoking biblical frameworks.

The Anonymous's extended and conspicuously learned, indeed showy, engagement with the cannibalism of the House of Atreus is of profound importance to our understanding of the *Vita Ædwardi* both as a literary text and as an historical source. By figuring the Godwines, especially but not exclusively Tostig, as cannibals, the Anonymous deploys two classical political discourses to portray them as unfit for rule and as deserving of conquest. Cannibalism was often a charge levelled against tyrants.

145 Ovid, *Meta.* 6.404–11; and Statius, *Thebaid* 1.246 and 11.126–7.

146 Servius on *Aeneid* 6.603.

147 Chrétien de Troyes, *Cligès* 4.

Meanwhile, the savagery of cannibals in the wonders of the East tradition, a genre well represented in the vernacular in Anglo-Saxon England, including in the *Letter of Alexander to Aristotle*, justified their conquest by more civilized peoples, opening doors to the Conqueror, who well before 1066 was a contender to succeed Edward.[148] Thus, the Anonymous presents Tostig as singularly unsuited to succeed Edward and levels searing criticism at father figures, most obviously Godwine, but also Edward. Edith (Concord) is, however, exculpated. The nature of the poetry demands that the *Vita Ædwardi* be re-evaluated as a source; it can in no way be read as a Godwinist account of the events leading up to the Conquest.

Metapoetics

After a brief return to Eteocles and Polynices (now lying dead on a single pyre) the Anonymous steps back to explore metapoetic questions. Although the confidence with which the Anonymous moulds the legends of Tantalus and his descendants to suit his purpose is striking, the intellectual assurance with which he asserts the value of pagan legend is even more striking:

> Hęcine gentilis sine re descripserit error?
> Doctrinę plenum figmentum tale probatur.
>
> (Would pagan error without fact write thus?
> The *figmentum* full of lessons earns our trust.)[149]

The truth value of pagan myth had, of course, been debated since the conversion of Roman elites to Christianity in late antiquity. Considering the Anonymous again in relation to the Loire school throws into sharp relief the depth of his engagement with questions of fiction. As Gerard Bond has shown, the Loire poets, practitioners of using the Roman story world, were posing similar questions and offering similarly generous answers a generation before William of Conches revised Macrobius. Baudri was not only using classical myths but also theorizing about them, for instance when, in addressing the nun Constance in his erotic poem, he makes the

148 Blurton, *Cannibalism*, 3–5.
149 *VE* 1.5.

case for the capacity of pagan stories to teach virtue.[150] After offering her examples of myths that can be read allegorically for their positive examples, including Hercules and Diana, he writes:

Sed uolui grecas ideo praetendere nugas
  Vt quaeuis mundi littera nos doceat,
Vt totus mundus uelut unica lingua loquatur
  Et nos erudiat omnis et omnis homo.

(But I wanted to put forward the Greek trifles as proof
That every literature of the world teaches us,
That the whole world speaks as with one tongue
And that each and every man educates us.)[151]

The Anonymous in his recuperation, not of Diana and Hercules, who can be read as figures of virginity and sexual continence, but of the horrifying and potentially corrupting myths about the cursed House of Tantalus and about Ovidian monsters, was making a more daring move than Baudri's, one that could not be redeemed by being refigured as Christian. In his long poem for William the Conqueror's daughter, the Countess Adela of Blois, Baudri, like the Anonymous, juxtaposes the biblical and pagan past with contemporary history. For both poets this move takes its cue from the dialogue between Christian Truth and pagan Falsehood that is found in Theodulus's *Ecloga*. At the end of the *Ecloga*, although Christian Truth wins out, Wisdom, with an admiring evocation of Orpheus, calls on Truth to show mercy to her conquered rival. Like Baudri, the Anonymous learned this lesson well. The continued currency of this well-known school text to increasingly affirming perceptions of classical myth and legend, such as Baudri's and the Anonymous's, is evinced by Bernard of Utrecht's late-eleventh-century commentary on the *Ecloga*; poets and commentators alike were pushing to justify fiction.[152]

The Anonymous's juxtaposing of pagan and Christian is a feature of his poetry but not of his prose. Thus, his use of the Roman story world is also related to his expectations of the roles of prose and verse in the telling of

---

150 Bond, *Loving Subject*, 57–8.
151 Baudri of Bourgueil, *Carmina* 200.121–5.
152 Bernard of Utrecht, *Commentum in Theodulum*. Otter, translation of *Carmina* 134 (106, note to lines 141–4); Baudri, *Carmina*, ed. Tilliette, 2:291–2, note to line 41; and Wetherbee, "From Late Antiquity," 121–5.

history, which was a pressing concern for historians in the eleventh century. As we saw in chapter 2, the Encomiast shared his anxieties about prose and verse with Wipo and William of Poitiers; all three writers positioned their work away from poetry. William, moreover, goes on to elaborate this as a rejection of the falsehood of the *Aeneid* and the *Thebaid*. These are precisely the two stories in which the Anonymous finds truth. William wrote:

> Scriptor Thebaidos uel Æneidos, qui libris in ipsis poetica lege de magnis maiora canunt, ex actibus huius uiri aeque magnum, plus dignum conficerent opus uera canendo. Profecto, si quantum dignitas materiae suppeditaret carminibus ediscererent condecentibus, inter diuos ipsorum stili uenustate transferrent eum. Nostra uero tenuis prosa, titulatura ipsius humillime regnantibus pietatem in cultu ueri Dei.

> (The authors of the *Thebaid* or the *Aeneid*, who in their books sing of great events and exaggerate them according to the law of poetry, could make an equally great and more worthy work by singing truthfully about the actions of this man [William the Conqueror]. Indeed, if by the beauty of their style they could equal the grandeur of their subject matter, they would rank him among the gods. But our feeble prose will bring humbly to the notice of kings his piety in the worship of the true God.)[153]

The combination of William's rejection of Statius and Virgil with his desire for straightforward prose emphasizes the deliberate multivalence of the Anonymous's choice for a prosimetrum and his equally deliberate, careful containment of pagan *fabulae* within poetry. William and the Anonymous actually share fundamental values about the writing of history; each would exclude *fabulae* like those found in the *Aeneid* and the *Thebaid*. The Anonymous has to step outside the boundaries of exemplary history to make sense of the final awful years of Edward's reign and so turns to the prosimetrum.

The Anonymous realizes as he concludes his poem that, though redeemed as a way of shaping and understanding experience, and even as consolation, the Roman story world offers no way forward, no solution to the impending chaos that he still depicts as an avoidable future, rather than from a retrospective viewpoint. Both the *Thebaid* and *Thyestes* end in desolation. In response, in the final lines of his poem on familial discord,

153 William of Poitiers, *GG* 2.22.

as the Anonymous turns away from pagan myth to Christian faith, his poem becomes a prayer, beseeching the guardian Spirit, holy Faith, and Mary to turn the baptized away from Hell and to bring peace lest "ignis … hostis" (hostile fire) should break out "de pignore regali seu stirpe fideli" (from the royal kin and loyal stock). Even within this overtly religious end to the poem, however, the poet continues his practice of paralleling Christian and Roman story worlds, suggesting that truth still remains in the latter. His depiction of Mary is especially interesting in this regard. He first refers to her as the "uia prima salutis" (first way of life), echoing the Sibyl's final words to Aeneas, that warn him of the terrible things to come but promise a road to safety, in the *Aeneid*.[154] Then his representation of Mary as Concord, who earlier had stood in for Ceres as restorer of Pelops, works similarly to insist that, while Christianity remains the Truth, classical myth need not be abandoned. Concord, who both brings peace to Olympus and is Christ's mother, is the meeting of the Christian and Roman story worlds, and she is, of course, Edith. The poem ends by powerfully situating Edith at the meeting point of two story worlds and as a figure of peace, still capable of averting disaster.

The Epithalamium (Poem 6) and Then the Loss of Poetry

The Roman story world is absent from the rest of book 1, which comprises two more chapters. After his poem of Theban darkness the Anonymous moves on, in chapter 6, to celebrate the peace made possible for England and Edward by Harold and Tostig's alliance. This return to optimism, in prose, exposes even further the different generic expectations that he so overtly deploys for verse and prose, and the fragmentation of history that results. In the peace created by the two brothers Edward builds Westminster Abbey and Edith builds Wilton Abbey. The Anonymous follows his account of their patronage with an epithalamium, a bridal song, to Wilton.[155] In this poem Wilton stands in for Edith, as the Anonymous returns to themes of progeny, childlessness, and motherhood, which were so to the fore in the earlier poems that drew on classical poets. Edith, represented metonymically by Wilton, becomes a surrogate mother to many more nuns than she could have had children. The poem abounds in Marian imagery that ties it closely to the end of the previous

154 Virgil, *Aeneid* 6.96.

155 My discussion of the epithalamium is indebted to Otter, "Closed Doors."

poem, in which Edith was figured simultaneously as Concord and the Virgin Mary. The link between the two poems and the lack of allusions to Virgil, Lucan, Statius, and Ovid in the epithalamium brings to a climax the Anonymous's theme of the relationship of the Roman and Christian story worlds. While Cleopatra, Dido, Antigone, and Ceres may offer tools for understanding, exploring, and even justifying Edith's situation, they do not present a way forward. Virginity on the model of Mary and closer association with Wilton are offered to Edith as protection in uncertain times and as consolation for the grief of childlessness. Regardless of the one who would succeed Edward, Edith's future lay with Wilton, according to the Anonymous, who offers her a way to survive her inevitable displacement from the role of queen, whether by Harold's wife Ealdgyth or the Conqueror's wife Matilda.[156] The future lies not with the vicissitudes of dynastic history seen through the lens of either Virgil or Statius but with Christian virginity. The absence of a poem after the next and final section of prose in chapter 7 renders more pronounced that the epithalamium is the final word in the dialogue between Christian and Roman. The primacy that the Anonymous claimed for poetry in his prologue makes its disappearance very striking.

In narrating the Northern Rebellion, which finally brought the simmering hostility between Tostig and Harold destructively out into the open, the Anonymous abandons the prosimetrical form that had grounded the whole of book 1. In so doing, he sets aside obedience to his muse's vision for the poetic form of his account of Edward's reign. The sudden disappearance of poetry in this final chapter of book 1, and the nature of its prose, has much to reveal about the Anonymous's use of the Roman story world and his understanding of the task of writing history. Poetry disappears because the horror that the Anonymous had contained within his admonitory classicizing verse has spilled into his prose, as the linguistic debt of his account of the Northern Rebellion to both Lucan's *De bello civili* and Statius's *Thebaid* makes clear. The struggle between Harold and Tostig is now explicitly a "civile bellum," and madness (*dementia*, *insania*, *furor*, and related words), so central to both the *Thebaid* and *De bello civili*, stalks England, ultimately killing Edward. Although the prose is full of the language of Lucan and Statius, the Roman story world itself is no longer an interpretative framework; rather the terrifying violence within

156 See chapter 5 herein.

England has become a story (not fiction, but grim fact) that absolutely eludes any attempts at exemplary history.

The context for the loss of poetry at the end of book 1 is Edith's loss of her role as counsellor once Tostig has been banished and Edward has died. Harold clearly has no time for Edith. The Anonymous dwells on the impact of the loss of Edith's good counsel, writing at length:

> At regina, quę hinc dissidio confundebatur fratrum, illinc regis mariti impotentia destituebatur, cum consilio, quo potissimum ex dei gratia eminebat si audiretur, non proficeret, lacrimis suis presagia futurorum malorum plenius edocebat, quibus inconsolabiliter fusis totum palatium in luctum deciderat. Irruentibus enim ante id aliquibus aduersis, ipsa presidio adesse solebat, quę et aduersa cuncta efficaci consilio depelleret, et regem eiusque frequentelam serenaret. Nunc uero peccatis exigentibus re in contarium lapsa, ex uisis presentibus quique futura colligebant mala.
>
> (The queen was, on the one hand, confounded by the quarrel of his brothers, and, on the other, bereft of all support by the powerlessness of her husband, the king. And when her counsels came to nought – and by God's grace she shone above all in counsel if she were heard – she plainly showed her foreboding of future evils by her tears. And when she wept inconsolably, the whole palace went into mourning. For when misfortunes had attacked them in the past, she always stood as a defence, and had both repelled all the hostile forces with her powerful counsels and also cheered the king and his retinue. Now, however, when, owing to sin, things had turned against them, all men deduced future disasters from the signs of the present.)[157]

Throughout the poetry, especially that drawing on the Roman story world, Edith stood out as Concord, and, now that her advice no longer keeps violence at bay, there is no poetry. The conjunction of the loss of poetry with the loss of Edith's counsel suggests that the Anonymous saw the Roman story world as an active political discourse with which Edith could negotiate the dangerous politics of the Anglo-Saxon court on the eve of Edward's death.

157 *VE* 1.7.

The poems of book 1, which are so admonitory in tone, demand to be read differently after Stamford Bridge and the Conquest. The stories of Thebes, civil war, and metamorphosis serve to assert Edith's innocence. From the end of 1066 these dark poems take on the character of prophecy, the very role that the Anonymous now assigns to Edith, and a mode that has fascinated him from his celebration of Edward's golden ship (with its allusion to the prophecy of Aeneas's shield). The function of the poetry, especially the classicizing poetry, and Edith's position at court are very tightly fused. Admonition becomes prophecy as Edith is transformed from counsellor to prophetic woman, from queen to dowager. The potential for admonition to be read retrospectively as prophecy also enables the first book of the *Vita Ædwardi* to have meaning and an active political purpose even after the multiple disasters of 1066. Book 1 is neither discarded nor hastily rewritten, as was the ending of the *Encomium*; rather it is joined to book 2, and its representation of Edith as a good counsellor is redeployed to protect her position in post-conquest England. The Anonymous's preoccupation with Edith as counsellor until those who listened to her are dead lends further weight to the reality of his real-time narration across the events of 1065–6 and to his conceptualization of the text as one that could inform the advice given by his patron amid the infighting of a highly factional court.

The Value of the Roman Story World (Prologue 2)

The Roman story world, though stripped of its role within the narrative once fraternal strife has become reality, returns on the level of metanarrative in the prologue to book 2. With Edward, Harold, and Tostig all dead and a Norman on the throne (though William and Hastings are not mentioned), the disconsolate poet confronts his muse, lamenting that the biblical and classical frameworks urged on him by the muse have collapsed. Although he explicitly says that his song has become one of horror, be that of Thebes, Roman civil war, or metamorphosis, Virgil is not left behind. In the context of his own and Edith's grief, the poet recounts Harold and Tostig's renowned defeat of the Welsh king Gruffydd and their presentation of the golden prow of his ship to the king:

Hinc reduces Angli clara cum laude triumphi
  sub tantis ducibus hoc retulere decus.
Nam fractis ratibus, quarum par non fuit usus
  huius uel regnum oceanique ducum,

proram cum puppi, pondus graue scilicet auri,
artificum studio fusile multiplici,
Ædwardo regi donant sua signa trophei,
direptas gazas nobilumque uades.

(In blaze of glory, ably led, the English
Return, and bring back this fine ornament:
They smashed a fleet – for their [i.e., the Welsh] control and lore
Was not the equal of the Ocena's chiefs –
And take a prow and stern of solid gold,
Cast by the smiths' assiduous skill, and this,
With looted treasures and the hostages,
As proof of victory they give King Edward.)[158]

The golden prow becomes a nostalgic and melancholy symbol of how, when the two brothers worked together, Edward's kingdom flourished. But as the reader has now come to expect, the Anonymous's poetry is rarely monovalent, and the account of Gruffydd's ship, an oddly historical intrusion into a poem concerned with poetics, will prove no exception.

The Trojan Welsh

The Anonymous depicts the Welsh as "gentem Caucaseis rupibus ingenitam" (a race bred in Caucasian rocks), and so he invokes Dido's furious claim that Aeneas, about to abandon her to take up his imperial destiny, was no Dardan but rather came from the remote Caucasus.[159] The reference to Gruffydd as coming from the Caucasus is a pointed undermining of his and the wider Welsh identity as descendants of Troy, which is attested as far back at the *Historia Brittonum* (in origin a ninth-century text).[160] Other recollections of the *Aeneid* intensify the belittling of the Trojan Welsh. Gruffydd is said to be "impar congressu" (unequal to the fight), a slight that humiliatingly recalls the death of Troilus, the son of King Priam, who, too young to fight, is killed by the famous Greek warrior Achilles at Troy.[161] The Anonymous drives home his point, writing

158 *VE* 2, prologue.
159 Virgil, *Aeneid* 4.365–7. This passage is discussed in Tyler, "Trojans," 16–19, where there are further references.
160 For recent discussion see Coumert, *Origines*, 441–99.
161 Virgil, *Aeneid* 1.475.

that the fleeing Gruffydd was afraid to "conferre manum" (to fight hand-to-hand) with the troops of Harold and Tostig. Virgil uses the phrase "conferre manum" repeatedly in his epic. Most distinctively, it recurs three times in the final book as Aeneas and Turnus are held back from and then finally partake in the decisive hand-to-hand combat, in which Aeneas's slaughter of Turnus ensures the conquest of Italy and his marriage to Lavinia.[162] Not only is Gruffydd, figured as Turnus, not a Trojan, but he is portrayed as their bitter enemy. Multiple allusions come together to deny any credence or dignity to Gruffydd's claim to Trojan origins. John Gillingham's identification of the use of classicism by twelfth-century historians to represent the Welsh as barbarians and the English as civilized Europeans is relevant here.[163] However, the *Vita Ædwardi* shows the phenomenon taking place decades earlier. The Anglo-Saxons, like their Norman successors, were attempting to use that touchstone of civilization, Virgil, to paint the Welsh as uncivilized, born in Caucasian rocks.

This return to Virgil is much more than a simple gesture of consolation made towards the grieving queen, and its implications extend beyond Anglo-Welsh relations. First, the Anonymous recounts the defeat of Gruffydd not in hexameters but in elegiac distiches, which he has so far reserved for metapoetic dialogue rather than for narrative. Second, and more fundamentally, the Anonymous has placed the Welsh king's defeat out of chronological order. He earlier drew attention to this achronology when recording the building of Westminster and Wilton amid the peace brought to the kingdom by the defeat of the Welsh and the Scots by Harold and Tostig. He wrote: "Sed hanc historiam, quoniam prolix<i>or est et uarie multiplex et longis euoluenda relationibus, ad certiorem notitiam ex industria reseruamus" (But we deliberately reserve this *historia* for a more faithful treatment in the future. It is rather protracted and complicated, and can be explained better in a longer report).[164] In light of this aside, the reader is alert for the story of the defeat of the Welsh and is perhaps surprised to find this *certiorem* account transposed to poetry and out of order. Chronology was a defining feature of historical narration, while *ordo artificialis* was a marker of fiction, as any reader of Servius's commentary on the *Aeneid* knew, and was especially associated with

162 Virgil, *Aeneid* 12.345, 12.480, and 12.678.

163 Gillingham, *English in the Twelfth Century*, 41–58; and Gillingham, "Civilizing the English?"

164 *VE* 1.6.

poetry.[165] In this regard, it is highly significant that the Anonymous has moved the Trojan Welsh not only out of chronology but out of prose. The Welsh claim to Trojan origins is here flagged as fictional, but this does not mean that the Anonymous has dismissed them. Far from it, he is fascinated by the space, both political and theoretical, made by the recognition of the fictionality of Trojan origins, especially now that William the Conqueror is on the throne. The description of Gruffydd's ship also carries implications for how we read Edward's own golden ship, drawing it more deeply into the fiction of Troy.

Given the Anonymous's love of structure and pairings, the Welsh ship cannot help but remind the reader of Godwine's ostentatious gift to Edward, also complete with golden prow. Furthermore, his description of Gruffydd's prow contains echoes of Edward's ship and also of Svein's and Cnut's fleets from the *Encomium* that are not found in the earlier ekphrasis of Edward's ship.[166] The echoes of Svein's and Cnut's fleets remind us yet again that the Anonymous knew, like the Encomiast, that Virgil's ships, and indeed the story of Troy itself, were *fabulae*. Literal descent from Troy was thus rejected, a move with profound literary consequences because it opens up a space for theorizing about fiction, which the Anonymous, like the Encomiast before him, enthusiastically engages. The links between the ships of the *Encomium* and of the *Vita Ædwardi* thus not only have a bearing on the renegotiation of the Anglo-Danish character of the beginning of Edward's reign, but also become a space for theorizing about fiction.

The echoes between Edward's ship and Gruffydd's are initially harder to interpret than those that link Edward's ship and the Anglo-Danish fleet. At this point, Geoffrey of Monmouth's *Historia regum Britanniae* can help. The place of Arthur's Trojan ancestors in Geoffrey of Monmouth's calculatedly fictional work, which appeals to a shared Welsh and Norman descent from which the English are excluded, can alert us to what is at stake in the Anonymous's poetic denunciation of the Trojan Welsh.[167] His depiction of the conquest of Europe by the Trojan-descended Arthur and

165 Servius on *Aeneid* 1.4. D.H. Green, *Medieval Romance*, 96–102.

166 Tyler, "Wings Incarnadine," 97–9.

167 From the extensive bibliography on Geoffrey of Monmouth I have drawn particularly on Gillingham, "Context and Purposes"; Ingledew, "Book of Troy"; D.H. Green, *Medieval Romance*, esp. 169–75; and Aurell, "Geoffrey of Monmouth."

the prophecy of his return provoked furious accusations that the *Historia* was fiction rather than history, most notably by William of Newburgh at the end of the twelfth century.[168] Even before Geoffrey wrote, William of Malmesbury was associating both Arthur's and Norman claims to Trojan origins with fable.[169] Thus the rejection of Troy was not all about the Welsh, but, coming as it does in the second prologue written after the Conquest, it is also about the Normans. Edward's Norman parentage and exile would have invested him in Norman claims to Trojan origins and provided a conduit for these claims to be known in the English court. The Anonymous's derision of Gruffydd, set alongside his earlier parody of Edward as a parallel to Aeneas, raises the possibility that Edward celebrated himself as sharing in the Trojan descent of the Normans and that, while his rule marked the end of the West Saxon dynasty, it marked the beginning of the Norman rule of England. Only from this perspective can he be in any way a second Aeneas; only from this perspective can the sails of his ship be construed as forward looking. Edward's Virgillian ship then becomes a figure for both the failure of the West Saxon dynasty and the triumph of the new Norman dynasty, whose illustrious forebears are discreetly shown to be nothing but fable.

The wider literary implications of the *Vita Ædwardi*'s Trojan turn is evident in Jean-Yves Tilliette's article "*Troiae ab oris.*" Here he identifies the mid-eleventh century as the point at which stories of classical pagan mythology, most especially the Trojan foundation of Rome, captured the imagination of poets and later fed into the emergence of Troy as a powerful political discourse in the late eleventh and twelfth centuries. Earlier Troy, known especially from the *Aeneid*, remained as unelaborated prose origin legends. For Tilliette, the explosion of interest in Troy is a key moment in French literary history, led by the poets Godfrey of Reims, Baudri of Bourgueil, and Hildebert of Lavardin.[170] However, this meeting of poetic imagination and political utility occurred a generation earlier not in France but in England, where the Anonymous's response to a very political and typically English rejection of literal descent from Troy had profound literary consequences, opening up a space for theorizing about fiction, where politics and fictionality were inextricably related.

168 William of Newburgh, *Historia rerum Anglicarum* 1, prologue.
169 William of Malmesbury, *GRA* 1.8 and 3.287. See further in chapter 6.
170 Tilliette, "*Troiae ab oris.*"

Back to Boethius

That all this mixing of fiction and politics is situated within a reprise of the Boethian dialogue between the muse, Clio, and the poet demands a return to the question of the value of poetry, especially classicizing poetry, that was raised in the first prologue. The language of the muse's rebuke of the moaning poet makes this conjunction of Boethius and the Roman story world very clear. The muse tells the poet:

> Hic meror ratione caret, *dementia* mentem
> impedit, et luctus nescit habere modum.
> Te proprius nostris admouit nostra papillis
> delectum *pietas*, amplius ut biberes,
> altius et saperes non a ratione dolere,
> sed pressus nostro uincere *consilio*.
>
> (This sadness lacks a reason, *dementia* stops
> The mind, and sorrow does not know its bounds.
> Our *pietas* drew you, our dear-beloved,
> Still closer to our breasts, that you might drink
> More deeply, learn to grieve with temperance,
> And, when oppressed, to conquer through our *consilio*.)[171]

The Anonymous reminds his reader of the identity of the muse as a re-working of Lady Philosophy, by the reference to her nursing the poet, which recalls the *Consolatio*.[172] His Muse's rejection especially of Lucan and Statius is evident in her use of the word *dementia*, which runs through *De bello civili* and the *Thebaid* and from there into the *Vita Ædwardi*. These texts, having lost their power to warn Harold and Tostig against turning on each other, are simply a source of despair and must be set aside. *Pietas* is to be found in rationality, that virtue so espoused by Lady Philosophy – not in the pages of Lucan or Statius, nor with Aeneas, who in the wake of the Conquest can only be evoked to denote what Gruffydd, Edward, and William are not.

The identity of the muse as Clio, one of the poetic muses banished by Lady Philosophy, insists, however, that we not find in these lines a simple

171 *VE* 2, prologue.

172 Boethius, *Consolatio* 1.2 (prose).

rejection of poetry, which was never Boethius's own message. The Anonymous is responding to, exceeding, and even challenging Boethius's Lady Philosophy. The prosimetrical form is not about certainty but about seeking understanding, as Boethius and those medieval poets who followed him knew.[173] The Anonymous's language and preoccupations draw his poetry towards that of Hildebert. For example, in this final dialogue between muse and poet his awe at the workmanship of the prow and stern of Gruffydd's ship, expressed in the phrase "artificum studio," binds his poem to Hildebert's famous ekphrasitic poem on Rome ("Par Tibi, Roma"), which uses the same phrase to marvel at the human skill that went into making statues of pagan gods. Hildebert's deeply allusive poem, which along with its pair invokes pagan and Christian responses to the city, is marked by a celebration of human creativity, even while it deeply recognizes its transience. The links with Hildebert remind us not to shy away from attributing the kind of sophisticated questioning of the Latin literary tradition that we find in Hildebert to the Anonymous.[174] Indeed, in this poem the Anonymous himself has challenged the idea of direct descent from Rome, in figuring Trojan origins as fiction. This one echo between the two poets forms a part of a whole linguistic tissue indicating that at the very least the Anonymous worked within the same school as Hildebert, who like the Anonymous also radically transformed Boethius's Lady Philosophy.[175] Perhaps the younger French poet had even read the Anonymous's work.[176] So we must ask what the Anonymous is saying by figuring Clio as Lady Philosophy and by having her, in the face of the Conquest, urge the Anonymous to write a hagiography of Edward in support of Edith. What kind of abandonment of the Roman story world does this constitute?

The answer lies in returning to the terms in which Clio urges rationality on the poet, quoted above. While these lines emphatically reject being led by poetry, by the Roman story world, into despair or nostalgia, they equally emphatically figure poetry as constitutive of social and political

173 See above, page 141.

174 Hildebert, *Carmina minora* 36 ("artificum studio" is in line 36) and 38. Tilliette, "*Tamquam lapides*"; Jaeger, "Charismatic Body"; and Smolak, "Beobachtungen."

175 The phrase "artificum studio" occurs at the beginning of a pentameter line only in the *Vita Ædwardi* and Hildebert's Rome poem. It occurs at the beginning of a hexameter in the early-twelfth-century *Liber maiolichinus de gestis pisanorum illustribus*. In the form "artificis stadium" it occurs at the beginning of a pentameter in Baudri's humorous poem (*Carmina* 12.20), engaged with human invention, in praise of a wax tablet.

176 See chapter 5 herein.

order. Chief among the political virtues expounded in the poetry of book 1 of the *Vita Ædwardi* are *pietas*, the giving and taking of good *consilium*, and the avoidance of madness, *dementia*. Their repetition here, in the prologue to book 2, opens up a further dimension of Anonymous's metapoetics; poetic efficacy and political stability are portrayed as sharing the same foundations, thus revealing that the Anonymous understands poetry as having a role in achieving the latter. Indeed, throughout book 1 his poetry used both the Roman and the Christian story worlds to warn against allowing the madness of fratricide and civil war to bring chaos. It is not a rejection of poetry, or the Roman story world – which he has explicitly associated with *figmenta* (fiction) – that causes the Anonymous to abandon poetry. Once Harold and Tostig have killed each other, and both the West Saxon and the Godwine dynasties have collapsed in the face of the Conquest, although poetry can still protect Edith's position, presenting her as innocent, its role is diminished; it cannot prevent civil war, and the time for advising restraint and for offering Edith the model of concord has passed. There is no longer a point to either the admonitory poetry or the prose attempts at exemplary history, and both disappear.

Finally the Boethian framework also bears on the question of the *Vita Ædwardi*'s date of composition. In the preface to book 1 there is an easy identification of the Lady Philosophy–inspired muse with Edith, both of whom support the struggling poet, and we can easily see how the *Consolatio* might have been attractive to the Anonymous as he sought to understand his own relationship to an authoritative, educated female patron. However, by the beginning of book 2, Edith herself is in need of consolation, and the space between her and the figure of the muse becomes wider as a result. The relationship between muse and Edith will be explored further in the next chapter. Here it is sufficient to point out that the *Consolatio* was a much less complicated model for the Anonymous to turn to before Edith lost her place at court upon the banishment of Tostig, the death of Edward, and the accession of Harold. Thus the Anonymous's choice of the *Consolatio* as a model suggests that he did indeed write as events unfolded.

Conclusion

What does the Anonymous's handling of Virgil, Lucan, Ovid, and Statius reveal about his attitude to the Roman story world, including its fictionality and its political utility? The rich and carefully integrated poetry of the *Vita Ædwardi*, shaped by metapoetic reflection and a deep and innovative understanding of the poetic art, political meanings, and the complex intertextuality of Virgil, Lucan, Statius, and Ovid, shows us a poet drawn to and thoroughly steeped in classical Latin poetry. Although he recognized that the Christian story world was closer to the truth and ultimately took refuge in the hope that religious belief affords Edith both in this world, as the wife of a saintly king, and in the afterlife, he remained deeply invested in the power of the Roman story world to structure secular experience. In the mythical, legendary, and historical poetry of pagan Rome, he found a tool to help him narrate the events of Edward's reign and to understand, interpret, and even, most important, shape them. He also offered this story world to the queen as an effective political language, not just for consolation.

The final turn of both the poetry of book 1, with its climax in epithalamium, and the whole of the hagiographic narrative of book 2 to religious discourse does not represent a rejection of the newly found confidence in the value of the Roman story world for structuring secular experience in order to record and interpret secular experience as well as to intervene in it. It is, rather, a recognition that such a use of the Roman story world could not be made to work in the face of the catastrophic political collapse of 1066. In the face of the end of both the West Saxon and the Godwine dynasties, there was no place for panegyric punctuated by sombre warning. In this context, only virginity, hers and her husband's, held a future for Edith. Secular and religious poetry are not opposed to each other; in the *Vita Ædwardi* each engages with the same themes and images; both types of poetry pull in the same direction, giving access to the same truths. But within the Anonymous's Christian frame of reference, as death succeeds life, so the religious must supersede the secular; the necessity of this movement is only heightened by the events of 1066, not created by them. Whereas in book 1 the hostility of Harold and Tostig was ultimately held responsible for the Conquest, in book 2 the catastrophe was God's punishment for the nation's sin.[177] The Anonymous abandons the Roman story world and the secular, whether in poetry or in history.

177 *VE* 2.11.

5 Reading through the Conquest

Introduction

The innovative and active use of the Roman story world, opened up in the previous chapter, drew a picture of the *Vita Ædwardi* as a sophisticated text that required educated readers in order to be able to do its political work. The central question posed in this chapter is, where does that sophistication lie? With the Anonymous? With Edith? With the text's wider audience? In his two prologues the Anonymous imagines a triple reception for his text: Edith, an audience that will engage with its praise and honouring of the queen, and a posterity that will receive and rework his, the earliest, account of Edward.[1] Here I will focus on these first two imagined audiences to argue that in order to understand how the *Vita Ædwardi* fits into literary history we must ascribe determining agency to its female patron and audience. To develop this argument I will consider the text's engagement with women and their perspectives in light of Edith's own learning, which she shared with other women educated in West Saxon royal nunneries. The text emerges as having been written for the royal nunnery at Wilton, whose women were both learned and closely associated with the court. To further support this argument I will look at two texts written by Goscelin for the women of this community around 1080, his *Vita* and *Translatio sanctae Edithae* and his *Liber confortatorius*. Of particular interest will be the links revealed by the *Liber confortatorius* between Wilton and the nunnery of Le Ronceray in Angers, whose religious and secular

1 *VE* 1, prologue; and *VE* 2, prologue.

members have long been recognized as the poetic correspondents of the Loire poets Marbod and Baudri. This chapter will contribute to a fuller understanding of the intellectual formation of the Anonymous, of the extent of the social networks within which the *Vita Ædwardi* was produced, and of the creative nature of female patronage in late Anglo-Saxon England.

The sophistication of the *Vita Ædwardi* does not push it away from Edith or from it being a social and political text intended to have a direct impact on her difficult situation. Edith's continued patronage of the Anonymous throughout the upheavals of 1065–7, alongside the Anonymous's tenacious determination to persevere with the text despite the collapse of its original subject matter and Virgilian theme, indicates that Edith saw literary culture as a productive way to intervene in the political arena and that she exerted considerable influence, direct and indirect, on the composition of the text. To be efficacious within such an arena, her text needed not only a patron and an author but also an audience. This audience had to be educated and invested in the events that the Anonymous recounted. Such an astute and engaged audience has the potential to have a direct impact on the text. Writing to explain and support Edith to the Wilton-educated women of the Anglo-Saxon elite directly shapes the Anonymous's remarkable use of the Roman story world and his demanding metapoetic reflection on the nature of fiction. The *Vita Ædwardi*, especially in the admonitory mode of book 1, shows history writing acting as a form of political counsel exercised by the learned at court. Thus the text shows strong continuities with the role that Janet Nelson attributed to history writing in the courts of Louis the Pious and Charles the Bald. In the case of the *Vita Ædwardi*, this place for history writing is inflected not only by the strong role of women in the Romanization of court culture but also by the Latin education of secular women, especially the queen.[2] Their own learning equipped them to participate directly, in collaboration with clerics, in this form of learned counsel.

The Case for Wilton

The surviving manuscript and what is known of the text's early use point away from Edith and Wilton. The manuscript (London, British Library, Harley 526, fols. 38–57) was probably copied in Canterbury, more likely

2 Nelson, "History-Writing," 435–42; and Nelson, "Gendering Courts," 197. See chapter 3 herein.

at Christ Church than at St Augustine's, around the year 1100.[3] The Anonymous himself takes special interest in the affairs of Christ Church, mentioning it on three occasions; Barlow suggests that he may have had some connection with the foundation.[4] Herman of Bury Saint Edmunds appears to have known the text by 1070 when he cites it in his *Miracula sancti Eadmundi*.[5] Sulchard's use of the *Vita Ædwardi* by 1084–5 provides evidence that the text had reached Westminster less than twenty years after its composition.[6] A copy of the text remained there until at least the fourteenth century when Richard of Cirencester, a monk of the abbey, incorporated excerpts from it in his *Speculum historiale de gestis regum Angliae*.[7] During his lifetime Edward promoted the building of a new abbey at Westminster, and he was interred there after his death. Even before the abbey encouraged his cult and canonization in the following century, any text about the king would have been of interest to its monks.[8] The Anonymous's description of the building and dedication of Edward's abbey and the king's burial there do not, however, amount to a particular concern for this foundation nor suggest that the Anonymous wrote with its monks in mind; he lavishes far more attention on Edith's parallel building program at Wilton, despite its more modest proportions.[9] Summerson shows that the Tudor antiquarian copy of the poem about Godwine's ship was likely to have been made from a manuscript other than Harley 526.[10] The absence of a Wilton copy of the manuscript needs to be contextualized within the general failure of books to survive from the foundation.[11]

The Anonymous's preoccupations are almost entirely with the court: its way of life and the events that took place there or that involved people known to have been a part of it.[12] Edith is praised for her solicitous concern that the otherworldly Edward was appropriately clothed in the splendour expected of a king and for her care in raising children of royal

3 *VE*, ed. Barlow, lxxix.
4 *VE*, ed. Barlow, xliv, xlvi, and lxxix.
5 Licence, "New Light"; and Licence, "Date and Authorship."
6 *VE*, ed. Barlow, xxx and xxxvii.
7 *VE*, ed. Barlow, xxxix.
8 *VE*, ed. Barlow, 150–63; and Bozoky, "Sanctity."
9 *VE* 1.6 and 2.11.
10 Summerson, "Tudor Antiquaries," 157–8.
11 Hollis, "Centre of Learning," 317–18.
12 *VE*, ed. Barlow, xxxii and xlvi.

descent.[13] The Anonymous's depiction of Edward's hunting prowess asserts a secular image of the king to put alongside his portrayal of the king's piety.[14] Within this court focus the Anonymous's engagement with the experiences and perspectives of women frequently makes itself evident. In particular, the Anonymous is aware of the political relationships that were created and fostered by the marriages of women abroad. He mentions the marriage of Emma and Cnut's daughter Gunnhild to the future Henry III in order to explain Henry's kinship with Edward.[15] Elsewhere among English sources this event is mentioned only in Heming's cartulary and by William of Malmesbury.[16] Likewise, the Anonymous mentions the connections that Tostig's marriage to Judith, daughter of Baldwin IV, forged between the earl and the Flemish count, and Flanders more broadly. He represents Judith in a manner rhetorically parallel to Edith in her promotion of her husband's piety and the chastity of her marriage to Tostig. In part, the Anonymous's notice of Judith may be taken to support the view that he, like the countess, came from Saint-Omer, but it also rests, perhaps more fundamentally, on an assumption of his audience's interest in her background and situation.[17] Meanwhile, mention of Edith's mother, Gytha, brackets the beginning and the end of book 1. She first appears as the sister of Cnut and as the wife of Godwine. She is thus the source of the claim in the second book's prologue that Harold and Tostig were boys of royal blood.[18] She then appears in the final chapter of the book as a figure of sympathy, the *merens mater* (sorrowing mother) of the exiled Tostig.[19]

The thematic centrality of motherhood, childbirth, and childlessness in the *Vita Ædwardi* also speaks to a female audience. Edith's role as a surrogate mother of the royal children at court and as a metaphorical mother of the nuns of Wilton compensates for her literal childlessness, which is explored obliquely but urgently in the poetry.[20] The placing of the

13 *VE* 1.2.

14 *VE* 1.6.

15 *VE* 1.1.

16 William of Malmesbury, *GRA* 2.188; and Heming, *Chartularium*, p. 267. See chapter 7 herein.

17 *VE* 1.3, 1.4, 1.5, 1.7, and 2.7. The use of *cælebs* for both Tostig and Edward (*VE* 1.1 and 1.5) illuminates the Anonymous's use of this word as "chaste," meaning "monogamous" rather than "sexless" when applied to a married man.

18 *VE* 1.1, and *VE* 2, prologue.

19 *VE* 1.7.

20 *VE* 1.2 and 1.6. See chapter 4 herein.

"Epithalamium to Wilton" as the culminating poem of book 1, moreover, puts bridal and maternal imagery at the high point of the text, after which political collapse overwhelms the Anonymous's narrative. It is certainly not the case, however, that the text ignores men. On the contrary, Godwine's and Edward's literal and metaphorical experiences of fatherhood are explored, with the themes of progeny being as much about fathers as about mothers.[21] But parenting in this text is insistently about fathering *and* mothering, and lineage is matrilineal *as well as* patrilineal. The Anonymous extols the Godwine children as distinguished by the virtues of father and mother ("paterna et materna probitate insignes").[22] Concern for women spills over into the Anonymous's deployment of the Roman and biblical story worlds. Dido, Cleopatra, Ceres, Concord, and the women of the House of Thebes are all invoked as he explores Edith's position amid dynastic collapse.[23] From the biblical world the Anonymous deploys both Mary and Susanna.[24] The reference to Susanna is especially interesting because her story of innocence in the face of a false accusation of sexual impropriety is applied to Godwine.[25] As with the monstrous Ovidian *genetrix* that was the metamorphosing stream, a male is figured as female, suggesting that women's experience rather than men's experience is the audience's frame of reference, though the text held obvious interest further afield, as its manuscript circulation illustrates.[26]

The focus of the *Vita Ædwardi* on the female experience reveals some contrasts with the *Encomium*, in which women outside Emma's immediate concern with the struggle for the succession after the death of Cnut do not figure. Ælfgifu of Northampton enters the story so that the legitimacy of Harold Harefoot can be denied; not only is he not Cnut's son, but he is not Ælfgifu's son either.[27] Emma's daughter Gunnhild and her marriage to Henry III, mentioned in the *Vita Ædwardi*, are simply skipped over. Despite the Encomiast's emotional empathy for Emma as a grieving mother when Alfred is killed, Emma is figured as a man, Octavian.[28] The

21 *VE* 1.1, 1.2, 1.4, 1.5, 1.6, and *VE* 2, prologue.
22 *VE* 1.1.
23 See chapter 4 herein.
24 *VE* 1.3 and 1.6.
25 See chapter 7 herein.
26 *VE* 1.2.
27 *Enc.* 3.1.
28 *Enc.* prologue, 3.2, and 3.6.

Anonymous's reversal of the Encomiast's use of men to think about women suggests that women, and not just Edith, were at the centre of his intended audience. Emma had to explain herself to the men of Harthacnut's court, whereas Edith faced a different audience – just as courtly and just as gendered but this time with a strong female component. To make the case for Edith, the Anonymous had to speak to other women as well as to men. His deep sympathy for and imaginative responses to Edith's childlessness suggest a man who has spent extended time in the company of women. His sustained engagement with women, as well as its court focus, also points away from the male monastic foundations (where the manuscript was later found) as his primary audience.

The pages of the *Vita Ædwardi*, in which Wilton emerges as a constant in Edith's life, suggest that we look to Wilton to find this community of women. The Anonymous recounts that the queen was educated there as a child and that she returned there when repudiated by Edward in 1051.[29] Perhaps like Wulfthryth when King Edgar set her aside in favour of Ælfthryth, she saw a future for herself there.[30] When describing how Edward summoned the leading men of England to himself at Britford for counsel in the midst of the Northern Rebellion, the Anonymous adds the orientating detail that this was near Wilton.[31] The queen's attention was focused on the nunnery in the mid-1060s during the building of the stone church, so extensively celebrated in verse and prose in the *Vita Ædwardi*. According to the Anonymous, she took a direct role in supervising the workmen and was certainly there for its dedication in 1065.[32] After the Conquest she retreated to Wilton and Winchester; perhaps she was even there as soon as Harold became king and his wife Ealdgyth replaced her as queen.[33] The queen's movements on either side of 1066, coupled with her text's evident interest in the nunnery, both point to Wilton as key in its composition and reception.

---

29 *VE* 1.2 and 1.3. ASC "D," s.a. 1052, and ASC "E," s.a. 1048, state that she was sent to Edward's sister, the abbess of Wherwell. Stafford, *QEQE*, 265; and *VE*, ed. Barlow, 37n84.

30 Hollis, "Goscelin's Writings," 231; and Hollis, "St Edith."

31 *VE* 1.7.

32 *VE* 1.6.

33 Keynes, "Giso," 243–4; Stafford, *QEQE*, 275; and Hollis, "St Edith," 253–4.

Edith: Patron and Reader

In his two prologues, in which the poet and the muse discuss the task of writing for the queen, and in a section of prose from book 1, the Anonymous purposefully portrays Edith as an active proponent and knowing reader of his text. He builds a picture of her as a patron in the strictest sense of the word as one who commissions and pays for a text.[34] The actual command to write comes from the muse; it would not do for Edith to be represented as telling him to write in praise of her. In the act of commissioning the text there is, however, much slippage between Edith and the muse, who share the role of watching over and helping the poet. The muse offers him *spes*, while Edith is herself *spes*. The Anonymous is not coy about Edith's material support for the production of her text: she is *opes* as well as *spes*. The use of mothering imagery for both figures creates further connection between muse and queen. The support offered by Edith is poetic as well as emotional and material, further blurring the relationship with the muse. In the first prologue, when the Anonymous puns on the dual anatomical and metrical meaning of *pedes*, saying that the queen will "fixit" his feet, the reader simultaneously imagines someone who will take care of physical and poetic feet. Although the poet complains to the muse that "longa quies calami dissoluit mentis acumen" (the pen's long rest destroys the mind's sharp point), it is actually Edith who "abiectos restituit calamos" (puts back the pens ... thrown away).[35] Edith, like the muse, is represented as involved in helping him to compose his poetry. The Anonymous's portrayal of the poet's dependence on Edith very powerfully enhances his representation of her agency and creativity.

Edith's active engagement with the text extends from its production to its reception. In the second prologue the Anonymous represents Edith as reading the texts and doing so with independence; he insists that she has no mediator.[36] Thus he offers us an Edith who could read and make sense of his demanding use of the Roman story world. In a prose section, which must be used carefully since it consists of text restored by Barlow from Osbert of Clare and Richard of Cirencester, the Anonymous precisely portrays Edith as the ideal reader of his text. Educated from childhood at

34 *VE* 1, prologue, 1.2; and *VE* 2, prologue. See the introduction herein.
35 *VE* 1, prologue.
36 *VE* 2, prologue.

Wilton, she is said to have read both religious and secular books ("lectione diuina uel seculari sedula") and written both poetry and prose ("ipsa per se prosa uel uersa eximia").[37] Edith, he tells us, is expert in reading and producing just the sort of text that he has produced – a prosimetrum, which follows secular history with an incipient hagiography. The Anonymous draws a compelling picture of the intertwined nature of his patron's learning and the form of his text.

In all his representations of Edith's learning and her engagement with the text the Anonymous is anxious to stress her capacity for agency; his patron is a mature reader who writes. Given the context of a text written to protect her position, we must assume that this was an attractive image to its intended audience. Artifice and promotion aside, Edith was widely famed for her education. The Anonymous's claim that she acquired a literary education from childhood at Wilton is well corroborated.[38] The author of the *Vita sancti Kenelmi*, arguably Goscelin, writes that Edith provided him with sources for his text.[39] Godfrey, who came to Winchester from Cambrai around 1070 and may have known of the queen, perhaps even directly, attributes learning in the liberal arts to her.[40] There can be no suspicion of posthumous flattery when William of Malmesbury records her education and learning amid an otherwise critical portrait.[41] If, as the Anonymous tells us, Edith did know Latin, French, English, Danish, and Irish (the first two perhaps learned at Wilton), she was a woman of exceptional linguistic capabilities that would not only have facilitated her central role in Edward's very international court but also have made her an exceptionally gifted student of Latin literary culture.[42] Regardless of whether she had full command of this range of languages, the Anonymous and the queen wanted their audience to see her this way; linguistic facility and the internationalism it signified were part of her image as the ideal queen. Edith's own learning thus directly enabled and encouraged the ambitious

37 *VE* 1.2. As the passage was restored from Richard of Cirencester, too much weight should not be put on specific language. See chapter 4 herein for a discussion of Barlow's edition.

38 *VE* 1.2. Stafford, *QEQE*, 258–9.

39 [Goscelin?], *Vita et miracula sancti Kenelmi*, preface. Love's introduction to the edition discusses authorship, xcvii–ci.

40 Godfrey of Winchester, *Epigrammata historica* 4. Rigg, *Anglo-Latin*, 17–20; and Stafford, *QEQE*, 26–7.

41 William of Malmesbury, *GRA* 2.197.

42 *VE* 1.2.

reach of the *Vita Ædwardi*, qualities that in turn accrued to her honour. Moreover, the Anonymous chose to announce this role within his text. In commissioning a text aimed at influencing opinion at court, she followed in her mother-in-law's footsteps; however, the coming together of this political impulse with her superior access to Latin literary culture, the result of her convent education, produces a much more intellectually demanding text, whose questions about fiction and the nature of historical reality are not confined to the prefaces but are shot through the entire *Vita Ædwardi*.[43]

Edith's instrumentality can also be seen to have an impact on how the Anonymous deploys his most cutting-edge Latinity and poetics. Edith appears to influence the Anonymous's use of both well-known texts and new texts and stories that he may well have introduced to her and her wider circle. With regard to Virgil, just as we saw with the *Encomium*, our foreign clerical author shows remarkable sensitivity to English views of Trojan origins.[44] Although the Anonymous uses a highly ironic and ostentatious figuring of Edward as a second Aeneas to celebrate the restoration of the House of Wessex in 1042, while marking its demise in 1066, he never alludes to Edward as a descendant of the Trojans, even though his Norman ancestry might suggest this.[45] The devastating critique that he offers of the Welsh claims to descent from Troy, and of the possibility that Trojan origins become newly politically charged after the Normans take the throne, shows the text reflecting a lay and courtly agenda rather than a clerical one.[46] Here we see evidence of the lay use of the Roman story world, in the context of competing origin legends, to negotiate momentous political change. England, where Trojan origins were considered suspect, was an ideal context for politics and the new poetics of the Loire to reinforce each other in making Troy a consciously fictional space. If we look more closely at the specific social context of the *Vita Ædwardi*, not only can we see even more clearly why Trojan origins might have been so charged at court, but we also see very clearly how Edith guided the handling of this inheritance from antiquity.

The Welsh king Gruffydd had been the most dangerous enemy of the West Saxon dynasty in the mid-eleventh century. His marriage to Ealdgyth, daughter of Ælfgar, Earl of Mercia, and sister of Edwin and Morcar, sealed

43 See chapters 2 and 3 herein.
44 See chapters 2, 3, and 4 herein.
45 *VE* 1.1. See chapter 4 herein.
46 *VE* 2, prologue. See chapter 4 herein.

an alliance that was aimed at checking the power of the Godwines as well as of the Crown. The Anonymous conveys their shared interest in defeating Gruffydd in his account of Harold and Tostig working together on behalf of Edward to successfully defeat and kill the Welsh king.[47] This conflict in itself would have been sufficient to make Welsh origin legends a subject of interest in the West Saxon court. However, Harold's marriage to Ealdgyth after Gruffydd's death may have occasioned heightened awareness of Welsh claims to Trojan ancestry. Ealdgyth is an obvious connection between the Welsh and the English court, and through Nest, her daughter with Gruffydd, she had her own stake in the Trojan inheritance of the Welsh.[48] Morever, Morcar's replacement of Tostig as earl of Northumbria, and Edith's own displacement as queen by Ealdgyth, Harold's new wife, would not have made the two women natural allies. Multiple factors – Edward's Norman heritage, the end of the West Saxon dynasty, the movement of Ealdgyth from one royal court to another, and the conquest of England by Trojan Normans – came together to make Trojan descent a contentious and pressing issue. Even when the Anonymous creates his narrative from classical material that was only just becoming familiar, he responds carefully to his patron, alert always to the perspectives brought by her gender. This is evident, for example, in his reworking of the Pelops story, where he replaced Ceres with Concord, a figure he had already associated with Edith, and in the way the invocation of the story of Thebes brings Antigone to mind.[49]

The Anonymous's deeply respectful stance towards Edith and his fiercely uncritical loyalty to her, which contrasts with his backhanded attitude to the men of her family, are especially evident in his distinctive use of Ovid. His exclusion of Ovidian erotics not only sheds light on his command of classical poetry but also reveals the depths of his allegiance to Edith. Ovidian erotics would have undermined the case he makes on her behalf for the chastity of her marriage. Such a move would also have constituted a disrespectful intrusion that would have been an attempt to assert his superior clerical learning at her expense. Any hint of erotic flirtation with Edith or the muse is also absent. He does not even play the game that we will see Baudri playing when, in writing to Adela, he announces his

47 *VE* 1.6, and *VE* 2, prologue.

48 Maund, *Ireland, Wales, and England*, 64–8; Maund, "Welsh Alliances"; and Davies, "Gruffudd."

49 See chapter 4 herein.

rejection of the dangers of courtly flirtation.[50] This absence of innuendo highlights the continence of the Anonymous's interaction with Edith; the nature of his relationship with her shapes his use of classical poetry. In this he works in a manner that is strikingly different from the clerical condescension and misogyny of some romance, including the Ovidian *Roman d'Éneas*, in which classical learning is used to create two audiences, insiders and outsiders. The first is an in-the-know clerical audience, and the second, a lay and female audience that is unaware of the way classical learning has been deployed to undermine them as romance sought to objectify them and place them firmly within male dynastic ambition.[51] Edith's own learning obviates the possibility of the Anonymous adopting such a stance towards her and, as a consequence, influences his poetics.

Finally, in considering Edith as patron, we must return to the slippage between muse and patron and between poet and the Anonymous noted earlier. The two extended dialogues between the poet and the muse expose the complex two-way dynamic between an exceptionally learned cleric and his likewise exceptionally learned female patron. Such a reading does not entail a reductive identification of muse with Edith and poet with the Anonymous but rather attends to the way in which the Anonymous follows Boethius in using historical detail to blur the boundary between himself and the persona of the narrator. Hildebert, Lawrence of Durham, Adelard of Bath, and Alan of Lille would all subsequently make a similar move in their own prosimetra.[52] For the Anonymous, this move involved an innovative fusing of the Muses of classical poetry with Boethius's Lady Philosophy.[53] Unlike the Muses onto whom Baudri displaces responsibility for his playful, often erotic verse, again in Ovidian language, the Anonymous's muse commands respect, though not obsequiousness.[54]

The struggle that emerges between muse and poet relates directly to the issue of which Roman story best explains the final years of Edward's reign: Virgil, Lucan, Statius, or Ovid. The muse tells him to write of a Virgilian golden age, which he does in his first poem but in a way that exposes the

50 Baudri, *Carmina* 134. See chapter 6 herein. I have benefited from discussing this issue with Emma Bérat; see her "Patron and Her Clerk," 29.

51 Krueger, *Women Readers*, 1–32; and see chapter 3 herein.

52 Balint, *Ordering Chaos*, 15–16.

53 See chapter 3 herein.

54 Baudri, *Carmina* 193 (lines 102–8) and 200 (line 163); Ovid, *Tristia* 2.354 (*iocusa musa*). Baudri, *Carmina*, ed. Tilliette, 278n39.

complete inappropriateness of this model for Edward's reign.[55] Instead, the poet finds a much closer fit between Edward's reign and the Roman civil war, the fall of Thebes, and the cannibalism of Tantalus's descendants. But he deftly poses all of this potential disobedience in the form of a warning against what might happen; this enables him to move beyond the muse's command without outright disobedience. In so doing, the Anonymous carefully negotiates his undoubtedly intellectual superiority to the queen. Her learning and the centrality of it to her image mean that he cannot flaunt his own learning at her expense. In the changed circumstances of 1066 the muse reasserts her power and offers hagiography rather than a golden age, and the poet steps back within the boundaries she has laid down. By exploiting the slippage between muse and patron the Anonymous has projected an image of the queen as having ultimate control over his text and especially over his use of the Roman story world.

The Women of Wilton

Although, as Otter has persuasively shown, the *Vita Ædwardi* has a powerful private consolatory dimension, its aim – which is reiterated verbatim in both prologues, "laus et honor sit ei" (may praise and honour be hers) – along with its need to be politically effective require a larger audience than the grieving queen.[56] The poet's refusal to recount the Battle of Stamford Bridge is couched in terms of fame, not of Edith's reaction:

> Quis demens scribet? quo mens languescit et horret
> auditus, tanti fama pudet sceleris.
> Et cui nunc scribam?
>
> (What madman writes of this, at which the mind
> Grows fain and ears are shocked? Fama feels shame
> At such a crime. For whom shall I write now?)[57]

Fame requires a public, and in these lines the Anonymous conveys a sense of the wider hunger for news about the events of 1066 (even if he claims to demur from feeding it) and a sense of his own place among the competing

55 *VE* 1, prologue and 1.1. See chapter 4 herein.
56 *VE* 1, prologue, and *VE* 2, prologue. Otter, "Closed Doors."
57 *VE* 2, prologue.

accounts of recent events. Given the foregrounding of women and Wilton within the text, and Edith's presence there, we will look to both its personnel and the educational tradition of this community to argue further that this foundation was the immediate audience intended by the Anonymous and his patron. Consideration of the relationship of the nunnery to the court will illustrate that there was nothing cloistered about this community. The Wilton women were ideally suited to promote the good reputation of Edith among the West Saxon aristocracy, if they could be convinced of it themselves.

Who were these Wilton women? Stephanie Hollis has recently considered their identities when Goscelin was writing there, c. 1080. I will draw on her work, as well as that of Pauline Stafford, Barbara Yorke, and Julia Crick, to argue that the Wilton community was made up of women who were players in Edith's story.[58] Although we need to look more widely than just at the years immediately before and after 1066 to find named women, this process, as well as providing insight into those who were certainly there at specific times, is suggestive of the kind of elite women attracted to the foundation. In addition to Edith herself, Harold Godwineson's daughter Gunnhild spent time there. The learning and piety of Margaret, daughter of Edward the Exile and sister of Edgar Ætheling, point to a nunnery education, perhaps at Wilton. Her sister Christina is found in the nearby royal nunnery of Romsey after the Conquest. In the next generation, after her marriage to the Scottish king Malcolm, Margaret sent her daughters Edith/Matilda and Mary first to Romsey and then to Wilton. Another Gunnhild, a sister of Edith, who had dedicated herself to the religious life, became a nun in Bruges after the Conquest. Perhaps that vocation predated her flight to the Continent and she, like her sister, had been educated at Wilton as a child.[59]

Two other women allow us to see the Wilton women closely engaged with the politics of Edward's reign. Thored, a follower of Cnut, whose son

58 This discussion of Wilton is indebted to the work of these four scholars, both for points of fact and for interpretations. Crick, "Wealth"; Stafford, "Queens, Nunneries," esp. 15–19; Stafford, *QEQE*, 274–9; Yorke, *Nunneries* 72–186 (esp. 89–91 and 157–60); Hollis, "Goscelin's Writings"; Hollis, "St Edith"; Hollis, "Edith as Contemplative"; and Hollis, "Centre of Learning."

59 Grierson, "England and Flanders," 109; Barlow, *Edward the Confessor*, 163–4; Huneycutt, *Matilda of Scotland*, 13–24; Barlow, *Godwins*, 120; Hollis, "Centre of Learning," 333–4; and Marritt, "Coincidences," 159 and 170. See further, chapter 6 herein.

Azor has been identified by Keynes as a "prominent member of King Edward's household," gave land to Wilton with the proviso that his daughters would be received into the community. Thus we see that women of an Anglo-Danish background, whose male relations flourished in royal service, found a place within Wilton's walls.[60] Looking at these women enables us to see not only a source – the Danish-speaking Edith – of the Anonymous's allusion to Yggdrasil, the Norse world tree, but also an appreciative audience that would have gotten the point.[61] The agency of his patron and the dynamics of reception ensured that the Anonymous brought learning to Wilton and learned himself. Women from the West Saxon dynasty, the Godwine dynasty, and families who served the king were the kind of politically implicated and culturally literate (across Latin and vernaculars) individuals who made up the Wilton community just before and after the Conquest.

Each of these Wilton women would have had her own version of the final years of Edward's reign consonant with her own loyalties. There is no reason to expect, for instance, that Harold's daughter Gunnhild would have been sympathetic to Tostig's champion, Edith. Similarly, the interests of the Ætheling's sisters, if they were there, would not have coincided with those of Edith or Gunnhild. William of Malmesbury's negative portrayal of Edith as a woman who was suspected of suspicious misconduct (probri suspitione) both before and after her husband's death is especially significant. He does this in his *Gesta regum Anglorum*, which was written at the bequest of the Wilton-educated Edith/Matilda, suggesting antipathy to the queen within a foundation eager to disassociate itself from the Godwine dynasty.[62] Edith's position at Wilton looks precarious. The Anonymous's delicate portrayal of the rivalry between Harold and Tostig, for instance, was well suited to the possibly divided alliances even among the Godwine women, let alone among the community as a whole. From this perspective the *Vita Ædwardi* addressed an urgent political crisis for the queen that would have been felt more acutely at Wilton than if she had retired elsewhere. His creation of a text, moreover, that embodies competing accounts of Edward's reign, mirrors the very stories that no doubt were circulating within and through Wilton.

60 Keynes, "Giso," 243–7 and 262–3; and Bolton, *Empire of Cnut*, 17–18.

61 *VE* 1.2. See chapter 4 herein.

62 William of Malmesbury, *GRA* 2.197. See chapter 7 herein.

Deeply enmeshed in politics, Wilton, like other royal nunneries, was not isolated from the court and the wider secular world. There was frequent exchange between the two, with women leaving the nunnery and men visiting. Edith moved between Wilton and the court during her life, including after 1066 when she made occasional appearances in the Conqueror's court.[63] The other royal women who may have been at Wilton in the years around the Conquest also moved in secular society. In his *Vita* and *Translatio*, written c. 1080 at the behest of the nuns of Wilton and explicitly recording their traditions, Goscelin looked back to the time of King Edgar. He described how the king's daughter, Saint Edith, received foreign diplomats there and how leading nobles implored her to take the throne after the murder of Edward the Martyr. He also records that Cnut was a frequent visitor and benefactor. Goscelin's depiction of the worldly cosmopolitan culture of Wilton may reflect his experience of the nunnery in his own day as much as it passes on information about the tenth-century saint.[64] The *Vita Ædwardi*, written for a community that saw itself as so open, could expect to find an audience well beyond its walls.

Even after 1066 Wilton remained a focal point for the Anglo-Saxon elite who had enjoyed close ties to the royal dynasty. A charter for 1072 records that the purchase of land by Bishop Giso of Wells from Azor Thoredsson (whose sisters were in the nunnery) was confirmed in the presence of Queen Edith and a group of Anglo-Saxon men, among whom were members of the queen's own household, including those who had served at court during the Confessor's reign. This meeting took place in an upper room of the church at Wilton and was made up of people who would have had their own experiences and judgments of Edward, Godwine, Harold, and Tostig, and indeed of the queen herself. The charter's record that the meeting took place with the permission of King William, Queen Matilda, Robert the Ætheling, and Archbishop Lanfranc associates Wilton with a sector of the displaced Anglo-Saxon elite who chose accommodation rather than resistance in the face of conquest. These were not men who had forgotten an Anglo-Saxon identity; the charters ends by commemorating the deaths of Archbishop Stigand and Bishop Leofric of Exeter, but they and Wilton were not a focus for rebellion.[65] Such a context highlights the

63 See chapter 4 herein.

64 Goscelin, *Vita sanctae Edithae* 11, 12, and 19. Hollis, "Goscelin's Writings," 233; Hollis, "St Edith," 277–82; and O'Brien O'Keeffe, *Stealing Obedience*, 160 and 182–4.

65 Keynes, "Giso," 243–7 and 262–3.

political utility of the *Vita Ædwardi*'s silence about William's victory and fits in with Edith's own readiness to make peace with the Conqueror. Her situation was more secure as a protected widow under William than as a dowager queen displaced from Harold's court.[66] Eleventh-century Wilton emerges as a foundation that fully participated in the political life of the kingdom throughout the reigns of Æthelred, Cnut, Edward, and William, and which sought a particular role in creating continuities across dynastic upheaval.

Wilton's Learning

The depths of learning required by the *Vita Ædwardi* point to an audience with a long-standing experience of education, one that did not spring up on the eve of the Conquest. The innovations of the *Vita Ædwardi* would have been lost on those with only an elementary level of Latinity and rest on a long West Saxon tradition of educating women in royal nunneries, stretching back at least as far as Alfred the Great.[67] Alfred himself founded Shaftesbury in 888 for his daughter Æthelgifu, and his widow, Ealhswith, founded Nunnaminster. The foundation of Wilton is uncertain; it may have been established as early as 830 by Elberga, the sister of King Egbert of Wessex. Edgar and Ælfthryth likely founded Romsey for her daughter from a previous marriage, and Ælfthryth was closely associated with the foundations of both Amesbury and Wherwell.

Looking back through the history of West Saxon nunneries, we see that the presence of so many royal women of different dynasties in Queen Edith's Wilton was the direct consequence of a deliberate strategy to control succession to the throne in the context of the tenth-century unification of England. Where in earlier centuries a West Saxon royal woman who wedded a Mercian or an East Anglian married out of the kingdom, that was no longer the case. Edward the Elder's daughters are especially interesting in this regard. Those who married were married outside of England, to the Continent and Viking-controlled York.[68] Those daughters who did not marry became religious women: Æthelhild and Eadflæd at Wilton, and Eadburh at Nunnaminster. Apart from those of Edward, all known royal

66 Stafford, *QEQE*, 275.

67 Discussion in this section continues to draw on work sited in footnote 59 (Crick, Stafford, Yorke, and Hollis) unless otherwise stated.

68 Stafford, "Queens, Nunneries," 5; MacLean, "Making a Difference," esp. 168–9; and Foot, "Dynastic Strategies."

daughters in the period were nuns. West Saxon nunneries were also places of retirement for widowed or divorced queens. Eadgifu, Edward the Elder's third wife, may have entered Shaftesbury after his death, and his second wife, Ælfflæd, appears to have retreated to Wilton when she was divorced. Wulfthyrth, Saint Edith's mother, became abbess of Wilton after being set aside by Edgar. That nunneries are the usual places for the burial of queens further testifies to the close association of royal women with the nunneries of Wessex, a role enshrined in *Regularis Concordia*, which established the queen as the protector of nunneries.[69] Even when the pressure of Viking attack obliged Æthelred to marry off his daughters to create alliances, one still became abbess of Wherwell. Regardless of whether or not it was the initial intention for nunneries to become centres of learning for both religious and secular women, like the Ottonian and Salian nunneries of the German Empire, the quality and range of learning evinced in the *Vita Ædwardi* testify to the major literary consequences of a political decision, which far outlasted the original marriage policy.

The glimpses we catch of the cultivation of history writing in royal nunneries indicate that learning enabled Anglo-Saxon royal women to play a role similar to that of German nuns as keepers of dynastic memory.[70] The quantity of historical writing surviving from tenth- and eleventh-century England does not compare with that emanating from the royal foundations of Essen, Gandersheim, Nordhausen, and Quedlinburg in Germany, although the different traditions of manuscript survival may be a large factor in influencing this picture. There is nothing in England to compare to the survival of manuscripts from Essen. Nor is there a figure like Hrostvita, the nun of Gandersheim, who herself wrote history.[71] However, it is remarkable, especially since little comes down to us from Anglo-Saxon nunneries, that much of the surviving historical and hagiographical writing from late Anglo-Saxon England can be connected to a nunnery. Both the Anglo-Saxon Chronicle and Asser's *Life of Alfred*, virtually the only historical writing from tenth-century England, may have been known in royal nunneries. Malcolm Parkes argues for a Nunnaminster scribe for parts of the "A" manuscript of the Anglo-Saxon Chronicle (as well as the Tollemache Latin Orosius).[72] James Campbell's suggestion

69 Stafford, *QEQE*, 95.

70 Leyser, *Rule and Conflict*, 72; Geary, *Phantoms of Remembrance*, 51–3; and Van Houts, *Memory and Gender*, 65–92.

71 Leyser, *Rule and Conflict*, 63–73; and Bodarwé, *Sanctimoniales litteratae*.

72 Parkes, "Palaeography" and "Fragment" and Robinson, "Scriptrix," 73. Dumville strongly disputes the association of the manuscript with Winchester, *Wessex and England*, 55–139.

that a copy of Asser was made for Shaftesbury may, meanwhile, hint that a commemorative role was expected for the foundation established by Alfred for his daughter.[73] Christine Fell thinks it likely that Edward the Martyr's post-conquest hagiographer drew on not only oral but also written sources from Shaftesbury.[74] Susan Ridyard makes the case that Osbert of Clare, writing a life of Eadburh in the first half of the twelfth century, drew on written sources from pre-conquest Nunnaminster.[75] Wilton provides the *Vita Ædwardi* and Goscelin's *Vita sanctae Edithae*, and Queen Edith's possession of documents (*indicia*) about the West Saxon royal saint Kenelm may also stem from her role as educated keeper of dynastic memory.[76]

Repeatedly renewed ties between the West Saxon and Saxon royal dynasties insured that the English were aware of the German institutions and the models they presented. As we saw, Matilda, the granddaughter of Edith, a daughter of Edward the Elder, and the wife of Otto I, requested information about her West Saxon ancestors from the ealdorman Æthelweard, prompting him to translate the Chronicle into Latin. Æthelweard was a major figure in Æthelred's court, and we should not assume that his knowledge of learned Saxon royal women was exclusive.[77] Later in the eleventh century Beatrice, granddaughter of Cnut and Emma, was raised at Quedlinburg after the death of her mother, Gunnhild. She went on to become abbess of both this foundation and Gandersheim. We need not doubt that Beatrice was known to her Anglo-Saxon family. The *Inventio et miracula sancti Vulfranni*, written in Normandy in the mid-1050s, mentions that she became a nun. Elisabeth van Houts identifies Robert of Jumièges (Edward's chaplain and then archbishop of Canterbury) as the source of this text's up-to-date knowledge of the English court. If he knew about Beatrice, it is likely that Edward's court did too.[78] At least one Anglo-Saxon nunnery in the latter half of the eleventh century sought to follow Imperial customs. Cambridge, Corpus Christi College 163, contains a

73 J. Campbell, "England, France, Flanders," 195.
74 *Passio sancti Eadwardi*, ed. Fell, xvii–xx.
75 Ridyard, *Royal Saints*, 16–37.
76 *Vita Kenelmi*, preface.
77 See chapter 1 herein.
78 Wipo, *Gesta Chuonradi* 37; Bresslau and Kehr, *Urkunden Heinrichs III*, 135; and *Inventio et miracula sancti Vulfranni*, 18. Black, "Töchter Kaiser Heinrichs III," 52–3; Wolfram, *Conrad II*, 143; and Van Houts, "Historiography," 249.

copy of a Romano-Germanic pontifical (possibly one that Bishop Ealdred brought back from Cologne) that, while it contains ordines for the consecration of women, leaves out those for the consecration of men.[79]

Goscelin and Wilton

Goscelin was a monk of Saint-Bertin and a protégé of the Lotharingian Bishop Herman of Ramsbury and Sherborne, who had been Edward's royal chaplain and within whose diocese lay Wilton. In a period of exile Herman himself had converted to the monastic life at Saint-Bertin between 1055 and 1058. Details of Goscelin's early career are unknown. He may have come to England as early as 1058 or not until the early 1070s. A prolific hagiographer, he wrote for many monastic houses throughout southern England before he settled finally in St Augustine's Canterbury. Two texts with strong Wilton connections, written by Goscelin around 1080, help to uncover the learning of Wilton in the late eleventh century.[80] Goscelin's *Vita* and *Translatio Edithae* recounts the life of Edith, King Edgar's daughter and nun of Wilton. Not only is the text largely concerned with Wilton, but Goscelin attributes agency to the Wilton women who, he claims, instigated (with Bishop Herman) the composition of the work. He also identifies these women as his informants.[81] Stephanie Hollis has recently argued that Goscelin revised his first version of the life (Oxford, Bodleian Library, Rawlinson C. 938, fols. 1–29), which was addressed to Archbishop Lanfranc, for the nuns of Wilton (Cardiff, Public Library, I. 381).[82] At about the same time, Goscelin also produced his *Liber confortatorius* for Eve, the nun of Wilton whom he had tutored and who had recently left to become a recluse in Angers. In this section, I will argue that the learning evinced by these two texts indicates that some of the women of Wilton could have engaged with the *Vita Ædwardi*. This section will also contribute to our ongoing consideration of the milieu, learning, and identity of the Anonymous, as well as shedding further light on Goscelin.

79 Lapidge, "Origin of CCCC 163."
80 *VE*, ed. Barlow, 133–49. Stroud, "Eve"; and O'Brien O'Keeffe, "Goscelin."
81 Goscelin, *Vita sanctae Edithae*, prologue.
82 Hollis, "Goscelin's Writings," 234–6.

The Vita and Translatio Edithae

The *Vita* and *Translatio* of Edith, written together, combine hagiography with dynastic commemoration. While the focus is on Edith, she is explicitly and repeatedly contextualized as part of a dynasty of holy men and women that includes her father, Edgar; her mother, Wulfthryth; her brother Edward the Martyr; and her paternal grandmother, Ælfgifu. In the *Translatio* Cnut and Emma, and later William, are brought into the dynasty as Goscelin insists on their status as family: Emma through marriage to the saintly Edith's brother Æthelred, and Cnut and William more subtly, with the saint herself playing a role in their inclusion. Goscelin writes:

> [Germa]no sancte uirginis Edelredo regi, primo Edmundus, [deind]e Edwardus successere filii, his Cnutus Danorum [basileus m]edius intercidit; sic quippe regnorum dispensator al[tissimus d]isposuit, et prioris imperium cum ipsa matre sua Em[ma adop]tiuus optinuit, sicut et rex Willelmus posteriori success[sit: ille i]gitur externus rex Cnutus, sancte Edithe comperta pie[tate et sig]norum frequencia captus, tanto ei affectu et deuocione [erat addict]us acsi ipse uel frater Ethelredus uel nepos esset Edmundus.
>
> (To King Æthelred, the brother of the holy virgin, there succeeded his sons, first Edmund, then Edward, and between these came Canute, king of the Danes; for thus the almighty governor of the kingdoms determined; and Canute, a member of the royal family by adoption, gained the rule from Edmund, together with Edward's mother Emma, just as King William succeeded Edward. And so this foreign king Canute, captivated by what he had learned of the piety of the holy Edith and her frequent miracles, was as devoted to her in affection and reverence as if he had been her brother Æthelred or her nephew Edmund.)[83]

In Goscelin's hands Edith's sanctity becomes a means by which conquerors can be assimilated to the native ruling dynasty. In the version of the life for Lanfranc, Goscelin expresses a strong sense of engagement with the West Saxon dynasty, writing of Edith as imitating the holy women of her own family by following the examples of her own aunt Edith (of the monastery of Tamworth) and her grandmother Ælfgifu.[84]

---

83 Goscelin, *Translatio sanctae Edithae* 12.

84 Goscelin, *Vita sanctae Edithae* 8 (Wilton version).

Goscelin alerts his readers to the close relationship between his works and dynastic history when he writes that he takes what he hears about Edith "ut pro hystorie notitia pocius epitalamium odizare gestiamus" (that, in place of the facts of history, we may rejoice to rhapsodize the wedding song).[85] Although dynastic history, hagiography, and epithalamium are here combined in very different proportions, these forms were also the fundamental building blocks of the *Vita Ædwardi*. The *Vita sanctae Edithae* also shares its prosimetrical form with the *Vita Ædwardi* and is, moreover, the only one of Goscelin's many saints' lives to include poetry. The *Vita* and *Translatio* together include up to fourteen metres. Of the two surviving versions of the *Vita sanctae Edithae*, the one for Wilton, rather than the one for Lanfranc, contains more metres.[86] Prosimetrical texts are not common, and thus the fact that two prosimetra were produced for the Wilton women suggests their direct influence on the texts produced for and about them.

The commonality of the epithalamium to both texts underscores their shared discourses of virginity; both texts responded to the experiences of the Wilton women. Hollis argues that, in elaborating the image of the bride of Christ to frame Saint Edith's life, Goscelin was, with Anselm, at the vanguard of a new spirituality. Drawing on an ancient discourse going back to Origen's exegesis of the Song of Songs, this spirituality would be further elaborated in twelfth-century Cistercian mystical writing.[87] The Anonymous's own development of bridal mysticism in the Wilton epithalamium shows that he was as much at the forefront in new spiritual developments as he was open to new currents in the use of the Roman story world. Yet, as we saw with the deployment of the Roman story world, all agency does not lie with these two male incomers to Wilton. As Hollis has shown, this audience shaped the way in which Goscelin used bridal mysticism. Although in the *Vita sanctae Edithae* the saint is a worldly bride of Christ, in the *Liber confortatorius* when Goscelin presents the Saint Edith to Eve, who chose the ascetic life, he transforms the saint into a solitary contemplative.[88] Rather than thinking of bridal mysticism as something that Goscelin introduced to Wilton, we might reverse the terms of reference and think of it as something to which he was exposed there, and

85 Goscelin, *Vita sanctae Edithae*, prologue.
86 Hollis, "Goscelin's Writings," 240.
87 Fulton, *From Judgment*, 164; and Hollis, "Edith as Contemplative," 283.
88 Hollis, "Goscelin's Writings," 233.

which he and the nuns of Wilton might have continued to develop. There is, in any case, an observable dialogue between clerics and women involved with bridal mysticism at Wilton.

In thinking not just about what male clerics brought to Wilton but about what they found there, emphasis must be given to the particular attraction of the bride of Christ to a community that included women who were being educated for a secular life, alongside those who had a religious vocation; the imagery frames the life of the religious women in terms of the married woman. Indeed, although the *Vita sanctae Edithae* is focused on a woman who entered Wilton as a baby and remained a virgin, Goscelin never loses sight of those women who, like Queen Edith, were raised there to be good wives. He remembers the holiness of Saint Edith's grandmother, Ælfgifu, the mother of King Edgar, who in the Wilton version of the life "in thoro regis Ædmundi" (in the marriage bed of King Edmund) led a life of piety.[89] Like the Anonymous, Goscelin holds up Susanna, the figure of fidelity in marriage, as an example.[90] He is alert to the need to craft a flexible virginity that can encompass women like Saint Edith's mother, Wulfthryth, who, he writes, was taken from Wilton by Edgar and then returned after the birth of her daughter.[91] Wulfthryth is described at Edith's oblation, alongside King Edgar, as "tum rex cum sorore, de coniuge facta" (having been the king's wife and now his sister).[92] In representing the barren marriage of Edward and Edith as chaste, the Anonymous also casts the relationship of king and queen as non-conjugal, referring to Edith as Edward's mother and daughter.[93] The commonality of virginity in both lives suggests, as well, that the Wilton-educated Queen Edith may have been predisposed to see virginity as a way to redeem her childless marriage, and points to her guiding hand in this strategy of the Anonymous. The *Vita sanctae Edithae* and the *Vita Ædwardi* are united as much by the literary and religious culture of Wilton as by any possible personal or intertextual relationship between the authors.

The Anonymous's imagery of the bride of Christ and its evident currency for the Wilton women demand, like his more secular verse, that we

89 Goscelin, *Vita sanctae Edithae* 8.

90 *VE* 1.3; and Goscelin, *Vita sanctae Edithae* meter 2.

91 Goscelin, *Vita sanctae Edithae* 2 and 4.

92 Goscelin, *Vita sanctae Edithae* 5.

93 *VE* 1.2; and *VE* 2, prologue.

look at Queen Edith and her text in a wider European context. The ecclesiastical and genealogical connections of Edith as a member of her husband Edward's family strongly indicate the community's position as a portal for spiritual, intellectual, and aesthetic innovation – a portal created by the long tradition of educating Anglo-Saxon elite women and by the internationalism of Edward's court. In her discussion of Goscelin's use of bridal mysticism, Hollis, following Rachel Fulton, identifies John of Fécamp as an early, if tentative, proponent of the imagery in the context of a new focus on the humanity of Christ.[94] The Norman dukes supported John of Fécamp, an Italian, in his program of monastic reform. Abbot of Fécamp from 1028 to 1078, when he was especially close to the Confessor, he appears to have been associated with the promotion of a royal identity for the exiled ætheling in the 1030s when the latter was still in Normandy. After his return to England, Edward continued as a generous benefactor of Fécamp. John visited his abbey's English possessions in 1054, when he may have attended at court.[95] The possibility is thus strong that he had met Edith or that influence was passed from Edward to his queen and from her to Wilton. Although they are visible to us, these ties with John of Fécamp need not be the only route by which bridal mysticism travelled to England.

The text in which John so presciently if only fleetingly uses bridal imagery was *Libellus de scripturis et uerbis patrum collectus ad eorum presertim utilitatem qui contemplatiue uite sunt amatores*, written for Agnes of Poitou, who married Emperor Henry III subsequent to the death of Gunnhild. After the death of Henry III in 1056, when Agnes was regent for the young Henry IV, we find her in alliance with her stepdaughter Beatrice, Abbess of Quedlinberg and Gandersheim, and also Edward's niece. By 1061 Agnes had taken the veil and retired to a nunnery in Rome. She was, however, often found outside its walls back in Germany and throughout Italy.[96] Agnes is a well-known example of a medieval woman acting as a cultural ambassador. Even in her own time clerics commented, albeit unfavourably, on her bringing customs and fashions from Provence to the German court.[97] Edith, like Agnes, lived in and took part in creating a world that was very much open to the latest European religious and literary developments. The circulation of these developments was facilitated

94 Fulton, *From Judgment*, 155–70; and Hollis, "Edith as Contemplative," esp. 283.

95 Barlow, *Edward the Confessor*, 205; and Van Houts, "Edward," 70–5.

96 Black, "Töchter Kaiser Heinrichs III"; and Fulton, *From Judgment*, 155–6.

97 Bezzola, *Origines*, 1:284–6, and 290–4; Jaeger, *Origins*, 21; and Le Jan, *Femmes*, 30–7.

by the close ties that bound the ruling dynasties of western Europe. Her place at court, as well as her life-long connections with Wilton and its own traditions of openness to Continental learning, made Edith the ideal patron and reader for a text whose secular and religious poetry was so new. The currency of bridal mysticism across both the *Vita sanctae Edithae* and the *Vita Ædwardi* continues to strengthen the case for the wider community of women at Wilton as an early and ideal audience for Edith's *Vita*.

Goscelin as a Reader of the Vita Ædwardi

Goscelin's experience of writing for a learned community of women shapes his account of their saint, as we see in the way he reworks the *Vita Ædwardi* in order to write about the earlier saint. Goscelin's dependence on the *Vita Ædwardi* is most evident in his account of the building of Wilton.[98] Like the Anonymous, he is engaged not only by the distinctive spiritual life of Wilton but also by the fabric of its buildings. The *Vita Ædwardi* contains an extended account of the erection of a stone church at Wilton that Queen Edith funded in emulation of her husband's efforts at Westminster. This building replaced an earlier late-tenth-century structure whose construction is recounted by Goscelin. Although the earlier wooden church antedates the stone one by almost a century, Goscelin's description is the later one. In narrative terms the building of the earlier wooden church is modelled on the building of the later stone church. While some verbal similarities unite the two passages, more compelling are the overlapping thematic concerns and especially the overlapping shape of both narratives.

Whereas the Anonymous describes Westminster as being built at the command of Edward, he insists that Queen Edith was directly involved in the planning and execution of her church, writing (italics mine): "Quod clementius *intendens* per se, utpote que per spiritum dei misericordię uisceribus affluebat, hic regio opere lapideum monasterium inchoat, *feruentius*que instans operarios maturat" (Benignly she planned this herself, as one abounding in the bowels of mercy through the Holy Spirit, and began here royally to build a monastery in stone. Impetuously she urged the workmen to make haste).[99] Goscelin picks up on the language used here, writing that Saint Edith began her own building project "summo *feruore*

98 *VE* 1.6; and Goscelin, *Vita sanctae Edithae* 20–2 and metre 8.
99 *VE* 1.6.

… *intenta*" (eager with great fervour).[100] Queen Edith's active role in building the church – the Anonymous writes that she herself planned, built, and urged on the workmen – becomes in the *Vita sanctae Edithae* the saint's physical carrying of stone and care for the workmen: "Ipsa lapides in purpurea manica portare, operariis adesse, dapibus et leticia laborem illorum leuare, ac beneficiis magis quam uerbis rogitare" (She herself, in her purple sleeves, carried stones, was present beside the workmen, lightened their labour with food and cheerfulness, and urged them on with rewards rather than speeches).[101] Given that Saint Edith's church is wooden, the repetition of *lapid-* at just this point is particularly noteworthy. By reworking the passage thus, Goscelin insures that his Edith emerges as a gentle and considerate saint, in contrast to the Anonymous's more imperious queen.

The two narratives continue to progress in the same direction. The Anonymous tells that the queen was undeterred when, just before the dedication of the new church, fire destroyed all of the surrounding town. The dedication of Saint Edith's church was not threatened, but Goscelin continues to follow the plot of the *Vita Ædwardi* when at this point, between the church being finished and dedicated, he writes: "Hec domus sue requietionis est facta: tot annis, tot tempestatibus, tot periculis incendii immota, adhuc quoque tota deintus formose depicta, oculis potius quam relatione datur conspicua" (The house of her own laying to rest was completed: after so many years, through so many storms, unmoved by so many perils of fire, it is still so beautifully painted throughout the whole interior that it is more striking when seen than in any description).[102] The fire that threatened the queen's building becomes an explicitly absent threat in Goscelin's reworking, making his debt to the Anonymous all the more obvious. Both writers then move on to the arrival of the bishop, Dunstan (wrongly since he had already died) for Saint Edith's church and Herman for Queen Edith's, with multitudes of other clerics and people. The Anonymous's "concursu" is echoed in Goscelin's "concurrentibus."[103]

Both accounts are then organized around the imagery of the bride of Christ. Performing the dedication herself, Queen Edith is said to bestow new gifts on the bride, which is the church at Wilton. The narrative

100 Goscelin, *Vita sanctae Edithae* 20.
101 Goscelin, *Vita sanctae Edithae* 20.
102 Goscelin, *Vita sanctae Edithae* 20.
103 *VE* 1.6; and Goscelin, *Vita sanctae Edithae* 21.

immediately moves to an epithalamic poem in which, as Otter has argued, the church stands in for the queen.[104] Goscelin meanwhile continues to follow the movement of the *Vita Ædwardi* when his description of the church's dedication morphs into a marriage ceremony with Edith as the bride led by the bishop to her bridegroom, Christ. The Anonymous here focuses on the nuns of Wilton as a replacement for children, the result of a marital union between Christ and his bride, thus consoling Edith for her barren marriage. He then moves on to celebrate the church of Wilton as the biblical tabernacle of Psalm 83.[105] Goscelin follows the Anonymous's turn to poetry. Just like the second half of the Anonymous's epithalamium, his poem offers a biblical parallel for the church built by his heroine. He turns not to the Psalms but to Solomon's temple as described in Kings and Chronicles. In the *Vita sanctae Edithae* Dunstan then foresees the saint's imminent death, and two chapters later Edith is being buried. At this point Goscelin reaches back to pick up a detail from the Anonymous's account of Edward's patronage of Westminster, with both Saint Edith and Edward being said to have built their churches as their own sepulchres.[106]

Elsewhere, the Anonymous's portrait of the queen seems to have influenced the language of Goscelin's representation of her namesake, Saint Edith. In her command to depict Edith as standing at Edward's imperial side not just as his counsellor but as "corpore nam gemino unus habentur homo" (one person dwelling in a double form), the muse tells the poet that "hec tua spes et opes" (she is your hope and support). This phrase, uncommon in both verse and prose, appears also when Goscelin narrates the effort made to force Edith to rule the kingdom: "dum in hac una spes et opes omnium essent site" (since the hope and well-being of all were located in this one person).[107] Goscelin knew the *Vita Ædwardi*, and at a crucial moment in his own story the Anonymous's portrait of the queen shaped his of the saint, ironically as she refuses to rule, an option that was not available but perhaps deeply attractive to the other chaste princess of Wilton, Queen Edith. The evidence that Goscelin had read the *Vita Ædwardi* also allows us to see from a new perspective his self-representation within the *Liber confortatorius*. Goscelin, bereft of Eve and overwhelmed with

104 Otter, "Closed Doors," 68.

105 *VE*, ed. Barlow, 74n184.

106 *VE* 1.6; and Goscelin, *Vita sanctae Edithae* 22 and 24.

107 *VE* 1, prologue; and Goscelin, *Vita sanctae Edithae* 19.

sorrow, represents himself as a pelican in the wilderness; the language comes from Psalm 101:7. The context is similar to that of the Anonymous's invocation of the same pelican image from the Psalms.[108] The Anonymous too finds himself unable to write, confronted as he is by the disaster of the battles of Fulford and Stamford Bridge; he renounces his tablets, whereas Goscelin drops his pen. In modelling the saint on the queen and himself on the Anonymous, Goscelin reveals an admiration for the Anonymous, which was perhaps shared by the women of Wilton and by other poets, as we will see in chapter 7.

The influence of the *Vita Ædwardi* on the *Vita sanctae Edithae* raises the question of where Goscelin would have read the former. He might have consulted the *Vita Ædwardi* at Canterbury; however, he did not join the community of St Augustine's until the 1090s.[109] Given that he claims that he wrote the *Vita sanctae Edithae* at the behest of senior nuns and identifies not only oral testimony but information found in "patriis libris," it seems more likely that he encountered the *Vita Ædwardi* at Wilton, further supporting the case that it was written for this foundation.[110] It is also possible that he knew the Anonymous if they both were at Wilton, and especially if they were both monks of Saint-Bertin. If he did not know him, he would have known of him.

The Vita sanctae Edithae: Learning and Politics at Wilton

Returning more broadly to Wilton learning, the engagement of the prologue of the *Vita sanctae Edithae* with nuns and books extends beyond Goscelin's identification of his sources and introduces a text that is shot through with a concern for education. Alongside the demands made on the reader by the text, this provides, as Hollis has shown, great insight into the learning of the Wilton women over the course of the tenth and eleventh centuries.[111] Several dimensions of this learning are of particular importance as we assess how the *Vita Ædwardi* may have been received by women educated at Wilton. Goscelin keenly stresses the international

108 *VE* 2, prologue; and Goscelin, *Liber confortatorius* (hereafter cited as *LC*), p. 27 (trans. p. 22).
109 *VE*, ed. Barlow, 141.
110 Goscelin, *Vita sanctae Edithae*, prologues. Wright and Loncar's translation offers the reading "local books."
111 Hollis, "Centre of Learning," esp. 309.

nature of the education at Wilton, identifying Saint Edith's tutors as Radbod of Reims and Benno of Trier, and thus tying the abbey's learning traditions to those of both Northern France and the German Empire.[112] If Goscelin accurately reports the presence of Radbod of Reims, we have evidence of a link between Wilton and this intellectually vibrant environment that is independent of any ties forged by Goscelin and the Anonymous.[113] Benno of Trier meanwhile would have brought Wilton into contact with the educational traditions of Germany, where Imperial nunneries played a leading role.[114] In naming Osmund and Adelman as priests of Wilton in the generation after the death of Saint Edith, Goscelin asserts continued Continental ties.[115] The cultural milieu in which Goscelin wished to place Wilton towards the end of the eleventh century, and his desire to represent the nunnery as open to European intellectual currents, in both West Frankia and the German Empire, chime very closely with what we found in the poetry of the *Vita Ædwardi*. Goscelin describes Saint Edith not only reading but writing her own texts and working as a scribe.[116] Saint Edith's international education and her ability to read and write, whether represented or real, sit well beside the Anonymous's portrayal of a multilingual Queen Edith producing verse and prose.[117]

Despite the similarities between the *Vita Ædwardi* and the *Vita sanctae Edithae* and Goscelin's evident knowledge of the former, the two texts make very different demands on their readers, and the Anonymous and Goscelin were formed by very different, though not incompatible, intellectual traditions. Neither text is easy to read, and indeed Goscelin's prose style and the metrical virtuosity he seeks to display in the poetry of the *Vita sanctae Edithae* require and thus attest to excellent Latinity on the part of his readers, including the nuns of Wilton.[118] Goscelin does not, however, write classicizing verse in the manner of the Anonymous.[119]

112 Goscelin, *Vita sanctae Edithae* 7.
113 On Reims see chapters 2, 3, and 4 herein.
114 Riché, *Écoles*, 164–5; and Bodarwé, *Sanctimoniales litteratae*.
115 Goscelin, *Translatio sanctae Edithae* 4.
116 Goscelin, *Vita sanctae Edithae* 11.
117 See earlier, page 209, and *VE* 1.2.
118 *VE*, ed. Barlow, l–li; Hamilton, *Goscelin of Canterbury*, 375–484; Love, "Goscelin of Saint-Bertin," 241–4; and Wright's introduction to his translation (with Lorcar) of the *Vita* and *Translatio* of Edith, 18.
119 Barnes, "Goscelin's Greeks and Romans"; and Hollis, afterword to *Wilton Women*, 421.

Unlike the Anonymous's, his religious verse does not seem to be shaped by close study of the late antique Christian poets; he does not make meaning by alluding to them. He is not interested in the poetics of intertextual allusion that so fascinated the Anonymous. It is as though Goscelin's brilliance lies not in the production of highly allusive verse but in its music, in its extreme metrical variety. The poet Reginald of Canterbury, who was born in the Loire valley and who, like Goscelin, became a monk at St Augustine's, remembers him for his music in two poems, as does William of Malmesbury (perhaps drawing on Reginald).[120] In terms of function, the poetry of the *Vita sanctae Edithae*, unlike that of the *Vita Ædwardi*, is not at odds with the prose. Goscelin's work is not a text that as a whole means something radically different than when only the poetry or prose is taken into account. In Goscelin's work, poetry and prose work together in harmony. Goscelin may have followed in the footsteps of the Anonymous in producing a prosimetrical text, but he has his own ideas about the relationship of verse and prose. The much more complex social and political situation of Queen Edith within the community at Wilton throughout the Conquest pushed the prosimetrical form to its limits.

The learning displayed by Goscelin in the *Vita sanctae Edithae* and the *Translatio* is patristic rather than classical, and he incorporates the women of Wilton into this framework, comparing Benno to Jerome, and Wulfthryth and Saint Edith to the church father's learned female correspondents Paula and Eustochium.[121] It is striking that a major intertext for the *Liber confortatorius* is Jerome's letter to Eustochium extolling virginity, which unlike, for example, his *Contra Helvidium*, explicitly does not denigrate marriage or maternity.[122] Goscelin is very alert to the nature of the Wilton community. The only text to which he refers directly, apart from those "patriis libris" of the prologue, is Gregory's *Dialogues*, which he, like so many other hagiographers before him, uses as a model for miracle stories.[123]

120 Reginald of Canterbury, 15 (in Liebermann, "Raginald"); and William of Malmesbury, *GRA* 4.342. *VE*, ed. Barlow, 141–2.

121 Goscelin, *Vita sanctae Edithae* 14.

122 Jerome, *Epistulae* 22; and Jerome, *Contra Helvidium*. Hayward, "Spiritual Friendship," 349; and Hayward and Hollis, "Female Reader," 385.

123 Goscelin, *Vita sanctae Edithae*, prologue and 15, and *Translatio* 14. Hollis, afterword to *Wilton Women*, 423.

Classical references are not entirely absent from the *Vita sanctae Edithae*. When Edith resists the verbal and physical attempts to force her to take the throne, she is compared to Hercules slaying the Hydra and avoiding the sirens.[124] She acts like the strongest of men in refusing to take on the male role of kingship. The impact of this very vivid and memorable moment within the *Vita sanctae Edithae* would be lost if Hercules, the Hydra, and the sirens were unknown to the nuns of Wilton. Here it is important to pause and register the absence of classical intertexts elsewhere in the *Vita sanctae Edithae*, especially in the form of allusions and explicit references to Virgil, which are common in Goscelin's *Liber confortatorius* for Eve.[125] This absence does not indicate that Goscelin expected the Wilton women to be ignorant of classical literature, but rather that this was not the frame of reference he wished to invoke for the life of Saint Edith.[126] Goscelin is a man, like the Anonymous, who asserted control over his use of classical learning.

A serious problem, however, confronts the argument that the similarities between the *Vita sanctae Edithae* and the *Vita Ædwardi* result from both the responsiveness of their writers to the tastes and concerns of Wilton's educated women and from Goscelin's direct knowledge of the Anonymous's text. Neither in the *Vita* and *Translatio Edithae* nor in the *Liber confortatorius* does he mention Queen Edith and her generous benefaction to Wilton, despite the fact that in the *Translatio* Goscelin is much interested in recent and current Wilton history and personnel. Hollis attributes the hostility towards Edith to several factors, including her family's appropriation of the nunnery's land, a possible (rejected) attempt by the queen to become abbess, and an antagonism to the role of the queen as an overseer of nunneries. Goscelin's apparent antipathy to Queen Edith also needs to be situated in relation to his response to King Edward. While Goscelin works firmly within the mode of dynastic commemoration to assimilate both eleventh-century conquerors into the West Saxon dynasty, he shows remarkably little interest in Edward's holiness or in his restoration of the West Saxon dynasty. Where Edward is mentioned within the *Translatio*, his own prestige and potential sanctity are not at stake; rather, the focus is on showing how, via the biological connection between Emma, Edward, and William, the Norman duke came to claim the English throne.

---

124 Goscelin, *Vita sanctae Edithae* 19.
125 Hollis, afterword to *Wilton Women*, 422–3.
126 For Ovid and Virgil in *LC*, see pages 235 and 237–42 herein.

The absence of any reference to Edward's incipient sanctity furthermore stands out sharply given Goscelin's preoccupation with Saint Edith as a member of a dynasty that is especially noteworthy for its holy men and women, including her paternal grandmother, father, mother, and brother.[127]

Thus Goscelin, who knew Queen Edith, reveals that Wilton was deaf to her own presentation of herself as the chaste wife of the holy Edward.[128] This rejection of Queen Edith at Wilton reminds us that, although she retired there in 1066 and despite her lavish benefaction of a church, the community did not necessarily close ranks around her – quite the contrary. The Anonymous's lavish attention to his patron's relationship with Wilton may well have been intended to ease Edith's immediate situation as she tried to find a place at Wilton. The silence about the queen when Goscelin was writing for Wilton suggests that her version of events, however striking from a literary and theological perspective, was ultimately unpersuasive. Queen Edith's absence from the *Vita sanctae Edithae* and the *Liber confortatorius* is not evidence that the *Vita Ædwardi* was unknown at Wilton; indeed it seems clear that Goscelin had read it, and probably at Wilton. Rather it is evidence that the queen needed to defend herself to the very community in which she had been raised. The silence about the queen also reveals Goscelin's alertness to the concerns of the Wilton women, whose agency again comes into view.

The Liber confortatorius and the Learning of Wilton

The *Liber confortatorius*, written for Eve after what Goscelin experienced as the nun's painfully sudden and unannounced departure from Wilton for Saint-Laurent de Tertre, a hermitage in Angers, complements and extends the picture of Wilton learning as drawn from the pages of the *Vita* and *Translatio sanctae Edithae*.[129] Eve, the daughter of a Danish father and a

---

127 Goscelin, *Vita sanctae Edithae*, prologue. *VE*, ed. Barlow, li; Hollis, introduction to *Wilton Women*, 8; and Hollis, "St Edith," 253–4. See earlier, page 221.

128 See earlier, page 215.

129 Goscelin, *LC*, p. 30 (trans, p. 105). Key discussions of the *Liber confortatorius* on which I draw include Wilmart, "Éve et Goscelin [I]" and "Éve et Goscelin [II]"; Latzke, "Robert von Arbrissel"; Roy, "Sharpen Your Mind"; Whalen, "Patronage Engendered"; Van Rossum, "*Adest meliori parte*"; Otter's "Interpretative Essay" accompanying her translation of *LC*; and several essays in Hollis's *Writing the Wilton Women* (Hayward and Hollis, "Female Reader"; Barnes, "Goscelin's Greeks and Romans"; and Hollis, afterword to *Wilton Women*).

Lotharingian mother, likely came to Wilton in the early 1070s, first as a secular student, discovering a monastic vocation while there.[130] The timing of her arrival, her secular status, and Goscelin's interest in her parentage reveal that after the Conquest Wilton continued as a centre for the education of women and as open to the world, both secular and international; it had not become a relic of the West Saxon dynasty. The *Liber* reveals Goscelin's deep respect for both Eve's intellectual capacity and her Latinity. Not only does he write in a demanding style, but the books he recommends for her spiritual guidance include texts that are challenging in both their language and their content. The texts he enjoins her to read are all scriptural or patristic. Previous consideration of Goscelin's suggested reading list has especially focused on its inclusion of Augustine's *Confessiones* as the earliest evidence of knowledge of this text in England.[131] In his promotion of Augustine's *Confessiones* he reveals and passes on his knowledge of a text that would become key to twelfth-century developments in affective piety, conversion, and subjectivity, but which was not yet known in England. The recommendation of the *Confessiones* to a Wilton-educated woman is further evidence of the intellectual ambition of this foundation.

From the perspective of our engagement with the *Vita Ædwardi*, Goscelin's heavy emphasis on history writing in his recommendations for Eve stands out. The *Historia tripartita*, Eusebius's *Historia ecclesiastica*, and Orosius's *Historiae* all feature in his reading program. Orosius's *Historiae* is most significant because it provided a substantial account, albeit from a triumphalist Christian perspective, of both Greek and Roman pagan history. Familiarity with Orosius's text would have greatly facilitated a reader's ability to engage with the place of classical history, legend, and myth in the *Vita Ædwardi*.[132] Meanwhile, the presence of Boethius's *Consolatio* suggests that the Anonymous's audacious reworking of Lady Philosophy and the prisoner as the muse and the poet would not have been lost on a Wilton audience.

Beyond the famous reading list, the texts of classical learning that leave their traces within the *Liber confortatorius* and the texts that Goscelin

130 Stroud, "Eve"; and O'Brien O'Keeffe, "Goscelin."

131 Goscelin, *LC*, pp. 80–1 (trans., p. 163). Webber suggests that Goscelin's knowledge of this text stems from Saint-Bertin, which may have provided the exemplar for the branch of the *Confessiones* that came to circulate in England. Webber, "Diffusion," 43; Olson, "Did Medieval Women Read?" 69–80; and Hollis, "Edith as Contemplative," 284 and 303.

132 See chapter 1 herein.

assumes Eve knows also shed light on the learning of Wilton.[133] Nowhere does Goscelin suggest that Eve should read classical pagan literature. That absence is a consequence not of his or her ignorance but rather of his writing for someone who has chosen to follow the strictest form of monastic life, that of a recluse. The Roman story world in fact is a language and interpretative framework that Goscelin and Eve already share. He everywhere presupposes not only that she knows some of the most famous stories from the classical world but also that she is accustomed to using them to understand her own experience. In this regard she is like Jerome's beloved correspondents Paula and Eustochium, to whom we have already seen Goscelin compare Wulfthryth and Saint Edith, and whom Goscelin now commends to Eve as models of pious and ambitious learning.[134]

The learning of Paula and Eustochium has specific bearing on the value of the Roman story world to Eve.[135] On the one hand, in his famous letter on virginity Jerome warns Eustochium that Horace, Virgil, and Cicero are not compatible with the Psalter, the Gospels, and Paul. On the other hand, however, it would be a mistake to read this as an outright rejection of classical learning. In the preface to his commentary on Zephaniah, addressed to the two women, Jerome holds up both pagan and Christian women as exemplary and reminds them that Greek and Roman history is filled with virtuous women who demanded and read whole books.[136] Jerome also begins and ends his life of Paula by celebrating her descent from Agamemnon, who destroyed Troy, and her marriage to a descendant of Aeneas.[137] Goscelin picks up on this duality. In the same chapter in which he offers Paula and Eustochium to Eve for imitation, he includes Homer among his largely scriptural examples of advice for the young nun. He refers to the insights that he has gained from reading Homer, and quotes the Latin epitome of the *Iliad*, the *Ilias Latina*, written in the first century AD. In referring to the ancient pagan poet, he turns to the language of fiction ("fumus fabularum" and "fingitur") and thus asserts both the fictionality and the value of the Roman story world.[138]

---

133 Hollis, afterword to *Wilton Women*, 423–4.

134 Goscelin, *LC*, pp. 31, 35, and 81 (trans., 107, 110, and 164); and *Vita sanctae Edithae* 14. See earlier, page 230.

135 Ferrante, *Glory of Her Sex*, 47–52.

136 Jerome, *Commentarius in Sophoniam*, prologue.

137 Jerome, *Epistulae* 108.

138 Goscelin, *LC*, p. 82 (trans., p. 165); and Baebius Italicus, *Ilias Latina*. Verbaal, "Homer," 329.

Not surprisingly, Virgil's *Aeneid*, with Goscelin referring to this text both allusively and explicitly, is most prominent within the *Liber confortatorius*.[139] Significantly, his use of this intertext looks forward to twelfth-century scholars such as Bernard Silvestris, who developed Fulgentius's late antique allegorical readings of Aeneas as one who undertook a spiritual journey.[140] Elsewhere Goscelin turns to Virgil when he describes Eve as a soldier, even though it is Christ, not Latium, for whom she fights.[141] In writing to Eve about exile, he invokes the Trojan journey to Italy. He also finds in Virgil's epic good advice about how to live life in this world. Of course, the Christian life, whose goal is heaven, transcends the earthly, and thus he assures Eve that the confines of her cell exceed those of Octavian's empire, and her life is better than that of emperors.[142] Goscelin's depiction of Eve's cell as Octavian's empire cannot help but recall for us the Encomiast's figuring of Emma as this first emperor of Rome.[143] Throughout the eleventh century English women used Virgil to understand themselves in remarkably powerful ways: not as Lavinia but as Aeneas and Octavian.

Goscelin's classical learning is more adventurous than just reading Virgil. His use of the latter part of Seneca's letters, the section that was hardly known before the twelfth century, shows him steeped in learning that would become central to the flourishing of discourses of monastic friendship in the following century.[144] Goscelin's early reference to Seneca may point to the wider authority of this antique pagan author at Wilton, providing further context for thinking about the Anonymous's knowledge of *Thyestes* and his likely reference to the play.[145] The *Ilias Latina* might be overlooked as evidence of new learning since it has never been admired for its literary sophistication. However, it was only from the late eleventh century that it became integrated into the schoolroom curriculum. Goscelin shares with Eve his knowledge of the text and makes

139 Barnes, "Goscelin's Greeks and Romans," esp. 409–10.

140 Goscelin, *LC*, pp. 88–9 (trans., 172); and Minnis and Scott, *Medieval Literary Theory*, 150–4.

141 Goscelin, *LC*, pp. 36 and 47 (trans., pp. 112 and 125).

142 Goscelin, *LC*, pp. 47 and 77–8 (trans., pp. 126 and 160). Barnes, "Goscelin's Greeks and Romans," 407.

143 *Enc.* argument; and see chapter 3 herein.

144 L.D. Reynolds, *Medieval Tradition*, 120–4; L.D. Reynolds, *Texts and Transmission*, 369–75; Barnes, "Goscelin's Greeks and Romans," 402, 405, and 408–9; and Hollis, afterword to *Wilton Women*, 427.

145 See chapter 4 herein.

ostentatious reference to Homer.[146] Like the Anonymous, Goscelin was preoccupied with defending pagan learning and finding value in what it taught. Although he condemns pagan philosophers, saying that their learning and righteousness led them away from Christ, he asserts their value when he teaches Eve that Greeks and Romans, like monks, understood the virtue of the rejection of worldly luxury and the rewards of physical abstinence. Such philosophy, he writes, brought peace to those pagans who pursued it, and even allowed the Romans to conquer the world.[147] On the evidence of the *Vita Ædwardi* and the *Liber confortatorius* pagan learning and its status were a question not just for highly educated foreign clerics who wrote for the Wilton community but for the women themselves, who were accustomed to interpreting their political as well as spiritual lives through the teaching of pagan philosophers and poets. These women share the view that *fabulae* (fiction) brought understanding and insight.

Finally, the affinities between the reading cultures of the *Vita Ædwardi* and the *Liber confortatorius* extend beyond the high level of Latinity that both assume to the way in which the Anonymous and Goscelin envisage their texts being read. Goscelin places reading at the centre of Eve's spiritual formation and tells her: "sed occupa, reuolue, relege, donec affatim capias" (but take hold, return, read again, until you understand abundantly).[148] The language of this injunction looks in two directions. On the one hand, it is remarkably similar to that used by the Anonymous when he wrote that Edith "leget atque relecta reuoluet" (will read, reread, and brood) the *Vita Ædwardi*, which further confirms Goscelin's reading of the *Vita Ædwardi*.[149] On the other hand, Goscelin's injunction also recalls John of Fécamp's advice that Agnes read his *Libellus* frequently and with reverence and devotion.[150] In a sense, Goscelin stands in the middle of the affective piety to which John was inviting Agnes and of an intense study of the text to which the Anonymous was inviting Edith; the objects were different, but the expectations of careful, reflective, and repeated reading

146 Goscelin, *LC*, p. 82 (trans., p. 165). M. Irvine and Thompson, "*Grammatica*," 38; Wetherbee, "From Late Antiquity," 122; Barnes, "Goscelin's Greeks and Romans," 412; and Verbaal, "Homer," 329.

147 Goscelin, *LC*, pp. 73–5 (trans., pp. 155–7). Hollis, afterword to *Wilton Women*, 424.

148 Goscelin, *LC*, p. 81 (trans., p. 164).

149 *VE* 2, prologue.

150 John of Fécamp, "Letter to the Empress Agnes," 214–15. Fulton, *From Judgement*, 155–6. See page 224 herein.

are shared. Wilton women not only fitted into a wider European development of demanding reading culture for secular as well as religious women but were on its leading edge. Looking from John and Goscelin, we can see that the Anonymous assumes that Queen Edith has experienced monastic habits, suited to the *lectio divina*. The convergence of reading and mediation in the *lectio divina* means that the Anonymous could count on an audience whose understanding of reading entailed the close reflective scrutiny that the *Vita Ædwardi* required.[151] A nunnery, which educates lay and religious women, provides a perfect environment for monastic habits to shape secular reading. Turning to Goscelin, the similarities between the *Vita sanctae Edithae* and the *Vita Ædwardi* suggest that both the reading culture he encountered at Wilton and the texts, specifically the *Vita Ædwardi*, he read there shaped his expectations of Eve's learning.

Goscelin, Ovid, and Eve

Despite the intimacy between the *Vita Ædwardi* and the *Liber confortatorius* (as well as the *Vita* and *Translatio sanctae Edithae*), there are strong divergences between Goscelin's texts and the Anonymous's. Thus far in discussing Goscelin, I have moved quickly over Ovid. Likewise, I have not alluded to the vexed question of whether or not the *Liber confortatorius* reveals Goscelin's experience and expression of inappropriate romantic feeling for the young nun Eve. Looking at Ovid and the erotic together in these three texts written for Wilton will allow us to consider not only the different educational formations of their authors but also, critically, the role that the Wilton women played in shaping their own literary culture.

Goscelin portrays an emotionally close relationship between himself and the young nun that exceeds that of a father or a mother for a daughter. The possibility that there was an erotic dimension to either Goscelin's actual relationship with Eve or his own feelings, as expressed in *Liber confortatorius*, has much engaged scholars. Along the way it has been suggested that because Goscelin fell in love with Eve, he was not allowed to see her before she left Wilton for Angers, and there was hostility between Goscelin and Osmund, Herman's successor.[152] Recent scholarship has

151 Leclercq, *Love of Learning*, 15–17 and 184; and Rector, "*En sa chamber.*"

152 Reviewed by Hayward, "Spiritual Friendship," esp. 341–6.

done much to allay scholarly squeamishness about Goscelin's feelings towards Eve. Rebecca Hayward situates the emotions of Goscelin's addresses to Eve firmly within the tradition of the passionate male monastic friendship, discussed especially by Stephen Jaeger in *Ennobling Love*. She argues that in using this discourse, rather than sexualizing Eve, Goscelin acknowledges as his equal the nun who had recently chosen the hermetic life of a soldier of Christ over the life of a bride of Christ at Wilton.[153] Van Rossum underscores the little attention paid by Goscelin to Eve's virginity; he accepted this as a given, but preferred to draw attention away from sexuality and femininity.[154] Stroud and O'Brien O'Keeffe's work, meanwhile, has taken away the taint of paedophilia by making Eve older, a teenager rather than a child, when Goscelin is first attracted to her physical beauty.[155] However, the tension that is inherent in using the public discourse of ennobling love for the relationship between a man and a woman is not thus entirely eluded, as Otter's reading of the text continues to maintain.[156] This tension is most unambiguously evident in Goscelin's description of how he gazed on Eve at the dedication of a church, more than in his use of language of love.[157] Goscelin's assertion of the chaste nature of the friendship that is nurtured by a letter that passes between them meanwhile reveals his own awareness that, at least from the outside, his relationship with Eve might appear inappropriate, and that using the discourse of ennobling love for a relationship with a woman requires careful negotiation, as do perhaps his own emotions.[158]

Rebecca Hayward very aptly draws a distinction between the playfulness with which Baudri approaches the problem of the potential snares entailed in a spiritual friendship with a woman, and Goscelin's seriousness.[159] In his verse letter to Constance, Baudri plays up the issue in order to acknowledge and overcome it. He delicately spins out Ovidian erotic innuendo, while urging the nun to maintain a life of perpetual virginity. In so doing, he tests the limits of his ability to resist the erotic as a way of asserting the depths of his own chastity. Yet elsewhere Baudri avoids Ovidian

153 Hayward, "Spiritual Friendship"; and Van Rossum, "*Adest meliori parte*," chapters 3 and 4.
154 Van Rossum, "*Adest meliori parte*," 145 and 151–9.
155 Stroud, "Eve"; and O'Brien O'Keeffe, "Goscelin."
156 Otter's "Interpretative Essay" in her translation of *LC*, 154–61 and 166–7.
157 Goscelin, *LC*, pp. 28–9 (trans., p. 104).
158 Goscelin, *LC*, pp. 27 and 29 (trans., p. 101).
159 Hayward, "Spiritual Friendship," 347–8 and 352–3.

erotics when writing to women; it is a discourse reserved, like that of spiritual friendship in more religious writers, for men writing to men and may perhaps add weight to the argument that Constance is herself one of Baudri's fictions rather than a real correspondent.[160] Baudri emerges as remarkably like the Anonymous, deeply imbued with Ovid but entirely capable of excluding his erotics when it would be inappropriate. With Baudri's and the Anonymous's control in mind, let us return to Goscelin and Ovid.

W.R. Barnes, in his essay on "Goscelin's Greeks and Romans," finds no evidence in his close study of language that Goscelin knew Ovid. One allusion to the *Metamorphoses*, used without any alertness to its context, does not make Goscelin a reader of Ovid's poetry.[161] Likewise, Hayward writes that he "did not draw on Ovid's texts on love as a way of representing the close friendship of men and women in a religious context."[162] Yet, Otter convincingly argues that Goscelin drew on Ovid's *Tristia* and also on his *Amores* to shape a self-representation of himself as a lover, kept apart from his beloved by exile and rejection.[163] Otter's view is supported by Goscelin's prominent reference to the loyal friendship of Orestes and Pylades. As Barnes notes, Goscelin's version of this story does not derive entirely from Ambrose's or Augustine's accounts.[164] Orestes and Pylades do figure frequently in the *Tristia*, almost always in poems that the poet addresses to loyal friends. Perhaps Ovid's frequent references to the pair brought them to the fore as Goscelin wrote to Eve.[165] The potential compatibility of Barnes's and Otter's assessments of Goscelin's knowledge of Ovid, which only appear to be contradictory, simultaneously opens up to view some of the issues involved in the reception of Ovid and the agency of the women of Wilton.

---

160 Baudri, *Carmina* 200 and 201. Dronke, *Women Writers*, 84–91; Bond, "*Iocus Amoris*," 168; and Bond, *Loving Subject*, 142–3. See further chapters 4 and 7 herein.

161 Barnes, "Goscelin's Greeks and Romans," 402; and Hollis, afterword to *Wilton Women*, 422–3.

162 Hayward, "Spiritual Friendship," 348.

163 Otter, notes to her translation of *LC*, 21 and 48; and Otter, "Interpretative Essay," 157–61.

164 Barnes, "Goscelin's Greeks and Romans," 406.

165 Goscelin, *LC*, p. 44 (trans., p. 120); and Ovid, *Tristia* 1.5.22, 1.9.27–8, 2.395, 4.4.69, 4.4.87, and 5.4.25. Barnes, "Goscelin's Greeks and Romans," 406. Ovid's single reference to Pylades by name (*Tristia* 1.9.27) may contribute to Goscelin's failure to remember it.

Goscelin appears to be familiar with the *Tristia* but not to know it in detail. Indeed, the passages that Otter cites as convincing parallels to the *Tristia* do not show close linguistic echoes.[166] I would suggest that while Goscelin has encountered the text, been moved by it, and been drawn to it, it has not formed his language. The general absence of Ovidian language in his later work suggests that he would never come to know it completely, perhaps in part because the hagiographical nature of this work militated against the acquisition and display of Ovidian learning. He may also have deliberately decided not to follow the rising popularity of Ovid. We can be certain that he would have been aware of the Ovidian revolution around him. The verse of Reginald of Canterbury, Goscelin's friend and fellow monk at St Augustine's, reveals that the younger man knew Ovid more fully.[167] There were those, of course, who turned away from classicism and especially Ovid. Guibert of Nogent conveys a clear sense of the way in which composing verse in imitation of Ovid could lead a young monk to sexual temptation.[168] In England in the 1090s Herman of Bury Saint Edmunds scorned Ovid.[169] Closer to Wilton, we find Gervinus, abbot of Saint-Riquier. The chronicler Hariulf recounts Gervinus's recognition of the sexual danger posed by the pagan poetry he had learned to cultivate as a student and canon at Reims. Hariulf's use of the language of desire, *voluptas*, strongly suggests that the poetry in question is Ovid's, and his account of how Edith was furious when the pious monk refused her kiss of greeting illustrates their interaction.[170] Barnes flags the gap between Goscelin and the classicizing of the twelfth-century renaissance.[171] The *Liber confortatorius* and his friendship with Reginald show that Goscelin was neither ignorant of nor hostile to classicism, even though, apart from the confusion of his stance in writing to Eve, he seems to have deliberately cultivated a different literary and spiritual formation.

In this context of uncertainty around pagan poetry, and Ovid in particular, it is interesting in the *Liber confortatorius*, a text much more personal

166 Otter, "Interpretative Essay," 160.

167 Reginald of Canterbury, *Vita sancti Malchi*, ed. Lind, 19, and notes to book 4 (pp. 194–206).

168 Guibert of Nogent, *Monodiae*, 1.17.

169 Herman the Archdeacon, *Miracula*, 37. I am grateful to Tom Licence for drawing this example to my attention.

170 Hariulf, *Chronicon*, 4.13 and 22.

171 Hollis, afterword to *Wilton Women*, 424–5.

than Goscelin's usual hagiographic output, to see Ovid intruding on his understanding of his relationship with Eve. However, he has not assimilated this text or, like the Anonymous and Baudri, worked out the implication of writing to a woman in an Ovidian mode. His use of the *Tristia*, which presents him with poetry of both friendship and a romantic love lost as a consequence of exile, spills out of his control. This lack of control either reveals the conflicted nature of his feelings for Eve or perhaps contributes to making it appear conflicted.

The presence of Ovid within the *Vita Ædwardi* raises the intriguing possibility that Goscelin came to know Ovid at Wilton. His incipient and only partly understood Ovidianism may represent his response to the women of Wilton. Goscelin's own text encourages us to think in terms of the impact of Wilton literary culture on the monk. Although the Wilton library does not survive, it was evidently well enough equipped to include texts that were otherwise unavailable to Goscelin at Sherborne.[172] He fondly recalls that Eve, in her youth, "libros optatos dedisti" (gave [me] books that I wished for).[173] In choosing to record this detail, Goscelin deliberately announces a two-way relationship between his learning and that of the women of Wilton. His *Liber confortatorius*, moreover, makes clear that Eve benefited from the oversight of a *magistra*, a female teacher, from within the community and about whom Goscelin wrote with respect.[174] Perhaps among the books Eve lent to Goscelin was the *Vita Ædwardi* itself; we cannot know, and this suggestion remains no more than speculation, but it is not idle – the *Vita Ædwardi* has emerged as intimately related to the *Vita sanctae Edithae* and the *Liber confortatorius*.

The very different poetry and learning of Goscelin and the Anonymous illustrate just how attractive Wilton was to men of outstanding learning and how the women pushed both men to produce radically new texts whose experimentalism depended on the learning of their female readers. The ambitious demands made on their readers by both the Anonymous and Goscelin reveal the remarkable intellectual, spiritual, and poetic openness of the Wilton women in those very decades in which the twelfth-century renaissance was gathering pace. Their ambition as well as the high

172 Hollis, "Wilton as a Centre of Learning," 316–18.

173 Goscelin, *LC*, p. 28 (trans., p. 102).

174 Goscelin, *LC*, pp. 28 and 37 (trans., pp. 103 and 113). Hollis, "Centre of Learning," 315–16.

calibre of the scholars they attracted produced three of the most distinctive texts of the late eleventh century. To attract one such scholar could be viewed as an accident; to attract two suggests that there was something that drew them. Queen Edith's and Eve's exceptional educations and intellects point to the outstanding learning possible among the women, secular and religious, of Wilton. The dazzling innovation of the texts written for them highlights the decisive role of female patronage in the very different ways that each of these texts radically challenged and expanded the boundaries of literary culture.

Following Eve to Angers

To conclude this chapter, with its focus on understanding the audience of the *Vita Ædwardi*, we will follow Eve to the Continent. Ever since the *Liber confortatorius* attracted the scholarly attention of André Wilmart in the 1930s, there has been speculation about why she left Wilton around 1080 to become a recluse at Saint-Laurent du Tertre; a group of hermitages, it included both men and women and was attached to the nunnery of Le Ronceray in Angers. What pushed her away from Wilton? What drew her to Saint-Laurent? What kind of agency did she exert in both the decision to leave and the choice of destination?[175] Here I will ask what light the poetry of the *Vita Ædwardi* sheds on Eve's departure for Angers and, conversely, what light her destination sheds on this poetry. This approach entails examining the possible links between Wilton and Le Ronceray. I will argue that these links manifest themselves in the form of a shared monastic and literary culture and in terms of specific social ties.

In addition to the *Liber confortatorius* and our knowledge of Wilton in the late Anglo-Saxon period, several other sources will be central to the discussion. In 1102, Geoffrey, abbot of Vendôme, wrote letters to a hermit, Hervé, about the life that the latter shared with Eve after she left Saint-Laurent for Saint-Eutrope; one of these letters is addressed to both Eve and Hervé.[176] Saint-Eutrope, also located in Angers, was a hermitage of the priory of Lévière, a foundation of La Trinité in Vendôme. Shortly

175 Key scholarship for Eve's departure from Wilton and her time in Angers includes Wilmart, "Ève et Goscelin [1]" and "Ève et Goscelin [2]"; Latzke, "Robert von Arbrissel"; Van Rossum, "*Adest meliori parte*," 35–65; and Hollis, "Goscelin Writings and the Wilton Women," 228–31.

176 Geoffrey of Vendôme, *Epistolae* 4.48–50.

after Eve's death (by 1125 or even by 1120) Hilary of Orléans wrote a long poem commemorating her life.[177] Meanwhile, poetry written by Marbod and Baudri to and about the women of Le Ronceray, alongside information about the community that is derived primarily from its extensive contemporary cartulary, will allow us to compare that community and its literary life to those of Wilton.[178] Goscelin records his despair at Eve's departure, rather than her reasons, which appear unknown to him. Uninformed about her departure in advance, Goscelin considered it sudden.[179] Eve herself may have laid careful plans, as the connections and similarities between Wilton and Le Ronceray suggest.[180]

Le Ronceray was founded in 1028 by Count Fulk of Anjou and his wife Hildegarde. It housed aristocratic women, and its community brought together nuns and young virgins with widows and married women who were living separately from their husbands. Young women who lived as part of the community were not necessarily consecrated to the monastic life. One Fulk of Plessis-Macé entrusted his daughter to the nuns before going to Jerusalem. If he did not return, she was to be allowed either to marry or to become a nun. The nunnery may even have supported an external school for boys. The nuns of Le Ronceray were served by four priests who lived under the authority of the abbess. Le Ronceray, with its aristocratic lay and secular women, its reputation for scholarship, and its close ties to the local aristocracy and clergy, recalls the openness and worldliness of Wilton.[181]

At the end of the eleventh century and during the first half of the twelfth century, there is ample evidence of not only the receipt of poetry but also

---

177 Hilary of Orléans, *Versus et ludi* 1. On the date of Eve's death, see Hollis, "Goscelin Writings and the Wilton Women," 230.

178 Marbod, "Ad amicam repatriare parantem," "Puella ad amicum munera promittentem," "Rescriptum ad amicam," "Rescriptum rescripto eiusdem," "Ad puellam adamatam rescriptum," "Ad puellam iniuste accusantem," "Ad eandem resipiscentem," "Ad amicam zelantem," and "Ad amicam gementem"; Baudri, *Carmina* 138–42, 153, 200; and Marchegay, ed., *Cartularium*. Tuten, "Lady Constance."

179 Goscelin, *LC*, pp. 29–30 (trans., pp. 104–5).

180 Van Rossum ("*Adest meliori parte*," 62) and Hollis ("Goscelin's Writings," 228, and afterword to *Wilton Women*, 429) suggest that knowledge about connections between Angers and Wilton before 1080 would enable us to understand better Eve's decision to go to Angers and that we would be less likely to attribute it to her relationship with Goscelin.

181 Verdon, "Moniales"; and Avril, "Fondations," 27–33, 38–40, and 45–8.

the composition of poetry by the women of Le Ronceray. Peter Dronke argues that the poems that Marbod addressed to women, when he was schoolmaster and archdeacon of Angers cathedral, were likely written to Le Ronceray. Dronke further thinks that the recipients were among the community's secular women.[182] Like Wilton, learning was not the reserve of the religious members of the community. The poetic exchange between Baudri and Constance takes its place among Baudri's more chaste verse addressed to Emma, Le Ronceray's *grammatica*, and to Beatrice and Agnes. His poems also refer to two further nuns, pupils of Emma, named Orieldis and Godehild.[183] Women with these names also appear in the Le Ronceray cartulary in the first decades of the twelfth century.[184] In the next generation Hilary of Orléans, whose poem is among the sources for Eve's life, was one of the canons of Le Ronceray, and he wrote to other members of the nunnery.[185] Marbod's poems claim that he was replying to women who had written to him.[186] Baudri records that Beatrice had written to him, and Emma's own excellence as a poet is indicated by Baudri's fear of her criticism of his verse.[187]

In considering the relationship between Wilton and Le Ronceray, chronology is revealing. Marbod's more frivolous poetry, including his poetic epistles to the women of Le Ronceray, is attributed to his time as a secular cleric in Angers from 1069 until his departure in 1096 to become bishop of Rennes.[188] Baudri's poetry dates largely to the period when he was the abbot of Bourgueil, 1078/82–1107.[189] Thus the *Vita Ædwardi* is anterior to both poets' exchanges with Le Ronceray. Moreover, the Anonymous's claim that Edith herself wrote poetry suggests that the nuns and ladies of Wilton were recipients, active patrons, *and* producers of poetry, earlier than their counterparts in Angers.[190] In this regard, it should be remembered that, compared to Wilton, Le Ronceray was a

182 Dronke, *Love-Lyrics*, 1:213–14; and Dronke, *Women Writers*, 85.

183 Baudri, *Carmina* 138–42, 153, and 200.

184 Marchegay, ed., *Cartularium*, including nos. 69, 101, 124, 133, 192, 208, 209, 247, 253, 267, 269, 293, 313, 333, 336, 383, 387, 416, 426, 446, 450, and 468. Tuten, "Lady Constance."

185 Hilary of Orléans, *Versus et ludi* 1–4.

186 Dronke, *Women Writers*, 85.

187 Baudri, *Carmina* 139 and 140.

188 Bond, *Loving Subject*, 71–2.

189 Baudri, *Carmina*, ed. Tilliette, xv; and Otter's translation of *Carmina* 134, p. 60.

190 *VE* 1.2.

recent foundation whose educational and poetic culture, however exceptional and lively, did not have the long history attested at Wilton. The foundation of Le Ronceray was part of a broader intensification of female religious life in France that gathered pace from the eleventh century onwards. When the nunnery was founded, it was the only one in the diocese of Angers.[191] In contrast, royal nunnery culture was long and densely established within Wessex.

As we shall explore further in the next chapter, the nuns of Wilton continued to stay in touch with the poets of the Loire and elsewhere well into the twelfth century, when Baudri, Hildebert, and Serlo of Bayeux recognized the foundation both for its poets and for its attraction of poets. They were writing to Muriel, a nun, probably of Norman origins, at Wilton who, it appears, had earlier been a nun at Le Ronceray.[192] The literary ties to Baudri and Hildebert that the poetry of the *Vita Ædwardi* evinces may point to direct links between Wilton and Angers as early as the 1060s, indicating that at the time of Eve's departure for Angers Wilton was embedded within social and cultural networks that included Le Ronceray. Hollis and Hayward raise the question of what networks made Eve's journey possible: were they those of the convent, with its English abbess, or those of the diocese, with its bishop the continental Osmund?[193] Sustained ties between Wilton and the poets of the Loire suggest that the women themselves were active agents in Eve's placement.

Eve's desire to live an anchoritic life does not render the social status and cultural life of Le Ronceray irrelevant. Her intellectual ambition and impressive learning indicate that the contrary was the case. In this regard the evidence that those who sought out the eremitic life at Saint-Laurent du Tertre remained integrated in the life of the abbey is highly relevant. Saint-Laurent du Tertre, a dependent cemetery chapel, was located in close proximity to Le Ronceray, and Goscelin's description of Eve's life as an anchorite indicates that, far from being isolated, she was nurtured by the abbess and the sisters of the nunnery and visited by bishops and priests.[194] Goscelin writes:

191 Avril, "Fondations," 27; and Venarde, *Women's Monasticism*, 17–51.

192 See chapter 7 herein.

193 Hollis, "Goscelin's Writings," 228 and 230–1; and Hayward, "Spiritual Friendship," 343. Van Rossum, "*Adest meliori parte*," 63, also raises the possibility of connections between the two nunneries.

194 Comte and Siraudeau, *Documents d'evaluation*, 43–4 and plan 6; and Van Rossum, "*Adest meliori parte*," 47–8 and 55–6.

Quod autem te, o dulcissima, hic populus colligit, quod huius piissime matris cunctarumque sororum affectus in te redundant, quod te partum et pontificum dignitas uisitat, quod hec benedicta domina, que tibi hunc locum parauit, que Christum secuta, nunc est uerius comitissima, te colit et affectat ... fert consolationem.

(But the fact that this people welcomes you, O sweetest one, the fact that the affection of this very pious mother and all the sisters overflows on you, the fact that the dignity of fathers and bishops visits you, the fact that this blessed lady, who obtained this place for you, who followed Christ, and who is now more truly a very close companion, loves you and has affection for you ... brings consolation.)[195]

The women of Le Ronceray are to the fore in this account of Eve's exile, and Goscelin himself identifies a *benedicta* (blessed woman) as being responsible for her having a cell at Saint-Laurent du Tertre. This is further evidence that women, on both sides of the channel, were at the heart of this network (most visible poetically but presumably more multifaceted) that brought Eve to her new hermitage. The fact that Goscelin has information about Eve's life in Angers indicates that ties between Wilton and Le Ronceray were ongoing.[196] It also seems likely that among the anchorites of Saint-Laurent du Tertre were other nuns of Le Ronceray with whom Eve may have mingled. The life of Saint Girard records the presence in the hermitage of a nun named Petronilla. Given that there was not another religious foundation for women in the city or region at the time, Petronilla is likely to have come from Le Ronceray.[197]

Not only were there close relations between the nunnery and its dependents at Saint-Laurent du Tertre, but poetry appears to have been involved. Baudri wrote an epitaph for an Angevin recluse named Benedicta, who died c. 1100, and who may have been among the men and women of Saint-Laurent du Tertre. Latzke has identified Baudri's Benedicta with Goscelin's *benedicta*.[198] If this is the case, we can draw Eve and the famous poet closer

195 Goscelin, *LC*, p. 92 (trans., p. 176).

196 Van Rossum, "*Adest meliori parte*," 56–8 and 62.

197 *Vita Sancti Girardi* 15. Wilmart, "Ève et Goscelin [I]," 415; Verdon, "Moniales," 247; and Van Rossum, "*Adest meliori parte*," 63.

198 Baudri, *Carmina*, 171, Tilliette's notes to this poem (2:265); and Wilmart, "Ève et Goscelin [I]," 414–15; Latzke, "Robert von Arbrissel," 140–1; Van Rossum, "*Adest meliori parte*," 56; and Otter's note 10, p. 113, to her translation of *LC*.

together. Regardless, his epitaph for Benedicta recalls the chaste encouragement that Baudri offered to Emma and her young charges, suggesting that despite the erotics of his exchange with Constance he would not have been an inappropriate interloper among Eve's visitors at Saint-Laurent du Tertre. Moreover, as the bishop of Dol in Brittany, Baudri wrote a life of Robert of Arbrissel, the eremitic cleric and founder of Fontevraud, who put spiritual friendship between men and women at the heart of his radical vision of monastic life. Marbod condemned Robert's encouragement of men and women sleeping in the same room together in order to strengthen their devotion to chastity. But the practice recalls Baudri's poetic exchange with Constance: desire is courted and explored, only to be rejected in favour of virginity. When Eve left Saint-Laurent du Tertre for Saint-Eutrope, she joined Hervé, a disciple of Robert, in a single cell.[199] The worlds of Baudri and Eve were contiguous, if not overlapping. The posthumous celebration of her life by Hilary is evidence that even after she had left Saint-Laurent, she remained known to the nunnery and its poets.[200] The social ties that linked the poetry of the *Vita Ædwardi* to Baudri and Hildebert may have brought Eve to Angers.

When we look at Eve's relationship with Goscelin from the perspective of her companionship with a disciple of Robert of Arbrissel, rather than in isolation, it looks as though the two monastics, one female and one male, participated in and contributed to the earliest phase of a new movement that Robert of Arbrissel and others would develop, amid much censure, in the next century.[201] The *Vita Ædwardi* places Wilton similarly on the cutting edge of new developments that would change the face of both Latin and French poetry. Eve's destination allows us to see the *Vita Ædwardi* not as an isolated fluke but as testimony to Wilton's place within the European mainstream and at the heart of the most exciting new spiritual and intellectual developments. That the *Vita Ædwardi*, the *Vitae Edithae*, and the *Liber confortatorius* are all the products of the same institution underscores the interconnections between, rather than separation of, Ovidianism and new forms of spiritual life. The embrace and then rejection of Ovid that we see in Gervinus, Marbod, and Guibert, and perhaps

199 Baudri, *Carmina* 200 and 201; *Vita prima beati Roberti de Arbrissello*; and Marbod, *Epistola* 6, lines 5–14. Wilmart, "Ève et Goscelin [I]," 429–30; Latzke, "Robert von Arbrissel"; Van Rossum, "*Adest meliori parte*," 35–41 and 57; Hollis, introduction to *Wilton Women*, 10; and Dalarun, *Robert of Arbrissel*.

200 Hilary of Orléans, *Versus et ludi* 1–4.

201 Dalarun, *Robert of Arbrissel*, 231.

Goscelin too, touched the women of Wilton as they also took hold of and nurtured the newest religious and literary movements. Developments at Wilton do not anticipate what will happen on the Continent but grow out of and feed directly into the changes reshaping European literary culture as a whole. When we look at Wilton and Le Roncerary together, the importance of active female patronage to the earliest steps of the new literature of the twelfth century comes into even sharper focus.

The Anonymous

Although we have been focusing on the implications of reading the *Vita Ædwardi* as a Wilton text for our understanding of this congregation of women, the exercise also contributes to our understanding of the Anonymous. As we saw in chapter 4, he is customarily identified, following Barlow as a cleric of Saint-Omer, either as a monk of Saint-Bertin or as a canon of the Church of Our Lady, although Barlow considers that he may have been from another Flemish or Lotharingian foundation. If he did come from Saint-Omer, he may have had first-hand knowledge of the Godwines, especially Tostig, and we might consider that the Godwine connections with the city brought him to Edith's notice.[202] Here I will bring together what the Anonymous's poetry suggests about his social networks, alongside a consideration of learned Flemish, Lotharingian, and French clerics who were known to have connections with Edward's court or with Wilton, in order to try to situate a likely Germanic-speaking Flemish cleric whose poetic culture is that of Reims and the Loire.

To begin, we can consider the Anonymous in comparison with two monks of Saint-Bertin, Goscelin and Folcard, who were known to have been writing in England in the 1060s. We have already looked extensively at the relationship between the work of the Anonymous and the work of Goscelin and have seen that, although they share vocabulary and imagery, they are definitively not the same writer.[203] That Goscelin was a reader of the *Vita Ædwardi* reminds us, however, that there are reasons other than common authorship for texts to show linguistic and thematic affinities – including education, literary exchange, and social networks. The intellectual formation of Goscelin and the Anonymous was strikingly different,

202 *VE*, ed. Barlow, xliv–lix; and see chapter 4 herein.

203 A view with which Keynes and Love ("Earl Godwine's Ship," 204–7) and Licence ("Date and Author") concur.

yet they appear to come from the same foundation, one imitated the other, and they are linked within a social network of writers.

Building on Barlow's suggestion that Folcard was also a candidate for authorship of the *Vita Ædwardi*, Licence has now made a stronger, and important, case for Folcard.[204] Licence considers in far greater detail than did Barlow the shared language, themes, and narrative shapes in the work of these two writers. Of particular interest for this present study are the similarities between the way in which Folcard presents his relationship with Queen Edith in the prologue to his life of John of Beverley, written for Ealdred, archbishop of York, and the way in which the Anonymous depicts his relationship with her.[205] Folcard tells us that Queen Edith had commended him to Ealdred after he was driven out of his own monastic community, perhaps Saint-Bertin, which, as we have seen, suffered a very disrupted history in the mid-eleventh century. Edith becomes Folcard's *maris stella* (star of the sea) in a move that creates slippage between her and the Virgin Mary (often figured as the star of the sea), and in a manner comparable (though not as sophisticated) to the slippage in the Anonymous's representation of the queen and his muse.[206] There are important differences between Folcard's *Vita sancti Johannis* and the *Vita Ædwardi*, however. Folcard's literary debt in writing about John of Beverley lies primarily with Bede, and not surprisingly there are no classicizing moves in the prologue. Meanwhile, his engagement with paganism is about religious belief in early medieval Northumbria, not about the capacity of classical epic to access truth.

Also of relevance is a poem, possibly by Folcard. Hariulf, the late-eleventh- and early-twelfth-century chronicler of the abbey of Saint-Riquier, attributes a short poem about Saint Vigor to one "Fulcardus," who may be our Folcard.[207] As Licence illustrates, there are some strong linguistic and narrative links between this poem and the poetry of the *Vita Ædwardi*, both of which are written in hexameters with a strong presence of leonine verses. A striking difference, however, is that the poem in praise of Saint Vigor, evangelist of Neustria and foe of pagans, is not written in the allusive style that is so characteristic of the Anonymous's use of both classical and late antique Christian poets. The poetics of Folcard's Saint

204 *VE*, ed. Barlow, xliv–lix (esp. lii–lix); and Licence, "Date and Authorship." I am grateful that Licence and I were able to exchange drafts of his article and this chapter.

205 Folcard, *Vita sancti Johannis*, 239–42.

206 See chapter 3 herein.

207 Hariulf, *Chronicon* 4.20.

Vigor poem are distinct from those of the Anonymous's *Vita Ædwardi*, despite the metrical similarities. This distinction in poetics is not necessarily an impediment to this "Fulcardus" being identified as the Anonymous. As we have seen, the Anonymous was very self-consciously in control of his deployment of allusion and thus would have been able to write in a more direct mode if the context required it. Unfortunately, Hariulf's *Chronicon* does not let us see that context. On the opposite side of the scales, we should note that poetics is part of what clearly distinguishes Goscelin and the Anonymous. The poetics of Fulcardus, as far as can be judged from the short poem about Saint Vigor, show more affinity with those of Goscelin (who was himself a metrical experimenter) than with those of the Anonymous.

The prologue to Folcard's *Vita sancti Bertini*, written at the behest of Bovo, abbot of Saint-Bertin, probably around 1050, while Folcard was still a member of that community, allows us to see another side of his literary production.[208] This text is securely attributed to the same Folcard who was later in England. At the end of the prologue, which is addressed to Bovo, in his role as reviser of the *Vita sancti Bertini* Folcard casts his abbot as an "alter Aristarchus" (second Aristarchus). Aristarchus of Samothrace (217–145 BC) was head of the library in Alexandria and known for his grammatical and literary scholarship, among which was a critical edition of Homer. He is remembered as a sharp critical editor by Horace and Ausonius, as well as by Cicero. In invoking Aristarchus, Folcard makes lavish allusion to Horace's widely known and deeply influential *Ars Poetica*, echoing many of its phrases as he invites Bovo to revise his text.[209]

---

208 Folcard, *Vita sancti Bertini*, 604.

209 Folcard writes: "In qua coërcenda limæ laborem & moram exosus, nec longa die nec multa litura sum usus; idoneum fuit consilium tuis primum offerre auribus, si tamen tu idem, venerabilis pater; te in hoc velis præbere idoneum, ut scilicet *recidas* omne, quod trahitur ultra profectum; *parum claris lucem* inferas, *incompositis atrium signum allinas*, & ubi tua opera indiget, servo tuo alter *Aristarchus fias*." These lines are as printed in the *Acta sanctorum Bollandiana* (hereafter cited as *AASS*), though they are in need of editing.

He draws on Horace:

vir bonus et prudens versus reprehendet inertis,
culpabit duros, *incomptis allinet atrum*
traverso calamo *signum*, ambitiosa *recidet*
ornamenta, *parum claris lucem* dare coget,
arguet ambigue dictum, mutanda notabit,
fiet Aristarchus. (*Ars Poetica* lines 445–50)

As we saw in chapter 3 when considering the intellectual context of the Encomiast, Bovo's own text, the *Inventio et elevatione sancti Bertini*, engaged with questions of credibility and invention, and the abbot's prefatory letter flagged his debt to Reims and its learning.[210] Bovo would have been a receptive reader of the invocation of Aristarchus. And perhaps we should also see Folcard quietly figuring himself here as a second Homer. From Ovid's *Ex Ponto* and Ausonius's poetry he may have known of Aristarchus specifically as a critic of Homer.[211] Goscelin, as we saw earlier, was a reader of the *Ilias Latina* and acknowledged that he had learned from Homer's *fabula*. Thus we might identify an interest at Saint-Bertin in the ancient Greek poet. The value that Folcard and Goscelin place on classical pagan poetry strengthens the case for associating the Anonymous with Saint-Bertin.[212]

In any case, what we see here in the reference to Aristarchus is Folcard making the kind of explicit intertextual move that we have come to see as a hallmark of the Anonymous's style. And since the *Vita sancti Bertini* antedates the *Vita Ædwardi* we cannot see Folcard as an imitator of the Anonymous, as Goscelin was. The differences between the prologues to Folcard's *Vita sancti Bertini* and *Vita sancti Johannis* underscore the importance of patronage and audience to shaping his work: he responds to Bovo and Ealdred differently. If Folcard is the Anonymous, we see this responsiveness very clearly in his figuring of Edith as the Virgin Mary for Ealdred, and as Clio and Lady Philosophy when addressing the queen herself and writing for Wilton.[213]

Although we have identified some interest in classical pagan poetry at Saint-Bertin, this does not account for the Anonymous's Ovidianism, which he must have acquired elsewhere, perhaps facilitated by links with the archbishopric of Reims. Here our gap in knowledge of Folcard's career between c. 1050 when he wrote for Bovo and sometime in the 1060s

---

210 See chapter 3 herein.

211 Ovid, *Ex Ponto* 3.9.23; Ausonius, "Citario" 3; and Ausonius, "Ludus Septem Sapientum" 12.

212 See earlier, page 234.

213 Licence sees the attribution of the *VE* to Folcard, whom he connects with York and Ealdred, as drawing the text away from Edith and her voice. He also reads the text as supportive of the Godwines. However, given the very strong female perspectives and the hostility to the Godwine men, which literary analysis of the text reveals, and how little we know about Folcard's location in 1065–7, this seems unlikely. Both Barlow and Licence see the queen addressed by Folcard as being more likely Edith than the Conqueror's queen Matilda.

(perhaps as early as 1061) when he wrote for Ealdred comes into play. If Folcard is the Anonymous, this gap was critical in the development of his poetics. Although his *Vita sancti Bertini* makes clear that Folcard was looking early to classical models, his classicism at that stage was not as developed as the classicism in the *Encomium* and the *Vita Ædwardi*. Turning to the prose of the *Vita Ædwardi*, the Anonymous's interest in history writing, rather than a preoccupation with hagiography, also sets him apart from other Flemish writers of the eleventh century, including what we know of Folcard, and points away from a formation solely at Saint-Bertin. Further literary and historical research, focused on the missing years of Folcard's career, may lead to a definitive argument for his authorship of the *Vita Ædwardi*; such an attribution would help us to understand better the *Vita Ædwardi*, and the *Vita Ædwardi* would in turn offer new insights into Folcard and his career.

The career of Goscelin's bishop, Herman of Ramsbury and Sherborne, is instructive in considering the variety possible among the men who were considered monks of Saint-Bertin, which is particularly instructive for understanding the nature of the poetics of *Vita Ædwardi*. As a result of his monastic profession there while he was in exile in the mid-1050s, Herman is a monk of this foundation, and his earlier period as royal chaplain to Edward had brought him into court circles.[214] Likely a Lotharingian, he is a candidate for the authorship of the *Vita Ædwardi*, but, more important, he illustrates that we should not be surprised to find the experience of Saint-Bertin coupled with an intellectual formation that took place elsewhere. Within the *Vita Ædwardi* the Anonymous refers to him as very learned; if this were a self-reference on the part of the author, it would nicely balance his representation of Edith as the ideal reader of his text.[215] Herman was specifically close to the queen; he dedicated her church at Wilton, and Edith's generosity appears to stand behind the improvement of his diocese, after his return from Saint-Bertin, when Sherborne was added to it in 1059. The queen is recorded in the Domesday Book as owning Sherborne in the time of King Edward.[216]

214 See chapter 3 herein.

215 *VE* 1.6.

216 *VE*, ed. Barlow, xlviii–xlix, l, and lvi. I am grateful to Tom Licence for discussing Herman with me and especially pointing out the connection of Sherborne to Edith.

If Herman was the Anonymous, we need to account for his knowledge of Ovid and of Seneca's *Thyestes*. Yet Herman was in England from the mid-1040s and thus was not likely to have moved in circles where this poetry was becoming a prominent aesthetic and intellectual challenge. His three-year exile on the Continent was spent at least partially at Saint-Bertin, and it seems unlikely that he would have spent enough time elsewhere to become such an accomplished poet of verse showing affinities with the Loire school. Goscelin's inexperienced handling of Ovid suggests that the Anonymous was someone with sustained experience of the sophisticated poetic culture on display in the *Vita Ædwardi*. Poetry emanating from the German Empire from the mid- to late eleventh century provides a useful comparison, especially that of Sextus Amarcius. Deeply drawn to classical poetry and the Roman story world that it depicts, in his *Sermones* he confronts many of the same pressing questions about the moral status of pagan poetry that we have observed among Loire poets. The answers that Amarcius finds, however, although they affirm the value of the ancients when they accord with Christian teaching, are much less subtle than those of Marbod, Baudri, Hildebert, and the Anonymous. The Ovidianism, the theorizing about fiction, and the newly dynamic relationships with lay patrons that mark Loire poetry (and also, without the Ovidianism, the *Encomium*) do not characterize the work of Amarcius and that of other writers from the Empire.[217] Herman stands as a marker that origins outside Flanders do not rule out connections with Saint-Bertin. Like Herman, the Anonymous could have spent time at Saint-Bertin, perhaps even under this bishop's auspices. The mobility of clerics who found preferment in the Confessor's court is remarkable and adds to the difficulty in identifying the Anonymous or understanding where his poetics were formed.

The *Vita Ædwardi*'s poetry also prompts us to look at French clerics who served the king or came into contact with him. Edward's physician, Baldwin, a monk of Saint-Denis, was one whose career illustrates the movement of clerics between France and the Empire. Born in Chartres, he was prior of Lièpvre, a cell of Saint-Denis, located in the western reaches of the Empire.[218] Another is Hélinand, a Pontieuse whom Guibert of Nogent

217 Sextus Amarcius, *Sermones*. Notes to Manitius's edition of the *Sermones* provide ample evidence of Amarcius's engagement with classical poetry.

218 Gransden, "Baldwin"; and Herman the Archdeacon, *Miracles*, ed. Licence, xxxi–xxxii.

records was sent by Walter, Count of Mantes and Edward's nephew (he was the son of Edward's sister Goda and Drogo), to be the king's chaplain. The king often sent him as an envoyé to Henry I of France. By 1052 Hélinand had become bishop of Laon, and in 1070 he became for a time archbishop of Reims, a position he was accused of buying. Although Guibert of Nogent accuses Hélinand of being uneducated, the Reims connections are worth considering because they illustrate links between the Confessor's court and the cathedral where Godfrey, one of the most daring and imaginative of the Loire poets, was chancellor and schoolmaster from 1076/7.[219] Goscelin's emphasis on the presence of foreign clerics as chaplains at Wilton, including Radbod of Reims, should encourage us not to discount the possibility of a cleric at Wilton with connections to this archiepiscopal see in the 1060s. [220]

The connection to Reims recurs when we look at the career of Gervinus, abbot of Saint-Riquier in Picardy, whom we earlier saw rejecting Ovid and Edith's kisses. A further connection between Gervinus and Edward emerges because the French abbot knew Baldwin, the Confessor's physician. Before his monastic conversion Gervinus had been a canon at Reims. He also illustrates the close links between Northern France and Flanders, which may account for the distinctive profile of the Anonymous, seemingly a Germanic speaker whose poetic culture draws him towards Reims and the Loire. In the minority of the French king Philip I, Gervinus attested a charter alongside the king's guardian, Count Baldwin V. In the next generation Hariulf himself would move from Saint-Riquier to become abbot at Oudenburg near Bruges.[221] In view of the close links between Flanders and France, we should remind ourselves too of the linguistic complexity of the county that encouraged bilingualism across Dutch and French and which could facilitate individual movement between Flanders and France.[222] Finally, the demonstrable links between Wilton and Angers, which we will continue to trace into the twelfth century in the next chapter, suggest that the Anonymous may have enjoyed ties to the Loire, either directly or through Reims.

---

219 Guibert of Nogent, *Monodiae* 3.2. Barlow, *English Church*, 19n5; Licence, "Robert of Jumièges," 320–1; and see chapters 2 and 6 herein.

220 See chapter 4 herein.

221 Hariulf, *Chronicon*, 4.13 and 4.22. *CHP*, ed. Barlow, xlii. I am grateful to Tom Licence for pointing out the connection between Baldwin and Gervinus.

222 See earlier, chapter 3 herein.

Looking forward to two poets of the next generation, Petrus Pictor and Reginald of Canterbury further reveal how intertwined and complex could be the poetic and social networks of England, France, and Flanders in which the *Vita Ædwardi* was embedded. Petrus Pictor allows us to begin in Saint-Omer, where he was a canon in the early twelfth century. He has been identified by the editor of his poetry as the only Flemish poet whose work was influenced by the Loire school. There are affinities between his poetry and that of the Anonymous, including Ovidian allusion, connections with Hildebert (although in this case it is Petrus who draws from Hildebert), and possible knowledge of Seneca's *Tragedies*. In comparison with other known Loire poets and the Anonymous, his work, however, is derivative. Critical to understanding the poetry of the *Vita Ædwardi* and the Anonymous's formation is the fact that Petrus spent long periods outside of Flanders, and it was this that shaped his poetics.[223]

Reginald, a monk of St Augustine's, Canterbury, was probably born in the mid-eleventh century in Faye-la-Vineuse, a village on the Poitou-Anjou border – less than thirty miles due south of Bourgueil. Before coming to England he was associated with the abbey of Noyers, near Tours. Reginald was at Canterbury by 1100, where he became a friend of Goscelin. His poetry suggests that he was a reader of the *Vita Ædwardi*, a text known to his friend and perhaps already in Canterbury when he arrived. Linguistic and thematic affinities run through his work (but most especially two poems for Goscelin), the *Vita Ædwardi*, and the Loire poets. The connections to the *Vita Ædwardi* suggest that Reginald was drawn particularly to the Anonymous's poems in which he asked searching questions about the value of the pagan Roman story world and the nature of fiction and the Wilton epithalamium. Reginald shares the Anonymous's mythological interests, including in the unusual Thyestes story.[224] As Sylvia Parsons and

223 Petrus Pictor, *Carmina*, ed. Van Acker, vii–xlviii. Zwierlein, "Spuren," 179–83. See chapter 3 herein.

224 The poems to Goscelin include one of praise for his friend and a second on the begetting (a theme so central to the *VE*) of musical voices (both are edited by Liebermann, whose numbers are given here). In the praise poem Reginald refers to Goscelin as a "Cillenius heros" (15. 50) (aptly since Mercury is the god of oratory, the inventor of the lyre, and patron of literature), using an epithet that the Anonymous had applied to Tostig (*VE* 1.5). Beare ("Goscelin," 264–5) writes that the echo demonstrates that Goscelin wrote *VE* and that here Reginald honours him with the echo. Although shared knowledge of Theodulus's *Ecloga* probably contributes to the repetition (see chapter 3 herein), it is striking that it occurs here, in the context of other linguistic parallels in the *VE*, in the second poem addressed to Goscelin. The Anonymous's

David Townsend insightfully open up, Reginald's *Vita Malchi* engages deeply with classical Latin poetry, especially Virgil's *Georgics*, as it recounts the chaste marriage between a former monk, Malchus, and Malcha. Although Malcha's name is a reflection of her husband's, she is not nameless as in the life by Jerome that is Reginald's starting point, but rather "an active collaborator in the formation of the couple's unique quasi-monastic praxis."[225] The theme of chaste marriage and Reginald's classicizing poetics make evident what may have drawn Reginald to the *Vita Ædwardi* and suggest the influence and circulation of the Anonymous's poetry. We might imagine that Goscelin, who had experienced emotional crisis in his own chaste friendship with Eve and knew of Reginald's literary interests, would have shared his appreciation of the *Vita Ædwardi* with him, and that Reginald in turn drew on the *Vita Ædwardi* in writing poetry for his friend. Not only do the Anonymous and Reginald compose within a similar intellectual milieu, but it is possible to see how the *Vita* came to be transmitted to Reginald through a highly visible social network.

As we know from the poems that accompanied his *Malchus*, Reginald sent out at least ten copies of his epic to recipients who included Goscelin, Lambert (abbot of Saint-Bertin), Stephen (abbot of Noyers), and Hildebert, alongside clerics resident in England; six copies were sent to Arnulf (the learned French monk who became prior of Christ Church, Canterbury, and then bishop of Rochester).[226] Hildebert wrote back, praising Reginald's use of "figmenta ... fabularum," noting appreciatively the younger poet's echoing of some of his own poetry and encouraging a literary friendship.[227] In the previous chapter we noted links between the

---

epithalamium (*VE* 1.6) and this second poem on music share "genitura" (16.28) and "de ventre creates" (16.55) at the end of hexameters; within the corpus of the *PoetriaNova*, the former is rare in this position prior to the *VE*, and the latter only recurs in the thirteenth century in a poem of John of Garland. The expression "laus et honor," which occurs in both *VE* prologues, repeats twice in this poem (16.72 and 16.75), although without metrical identity with the *VE* instances. Elsewhere, in a poem to Aimericus, abbot of Faye-la-Vineuse, Reginald writes "quod amicus amico" (published by Wright, *Satirical Poets*, 2:262–3) where the Anonymous had "quid amicus amico" (*VE* 1.5). For the reference to Thyestes (*Vita Malchi* 4.364–6) and for general discussion of the poem, including fiction, see Rigg, *Anglo-Latin*, 25–6.

225 Parsons and Townsend, "Gender," 433–7.

226 These poems are published by Liebermann, ed., in "Raginald von Canterbury." Rigg, *Anglo-Latin*, 27–9.

227 Hildebert, *Epistolae* 3.15. Rigg, *Anglo-Latin*, 27.

language of Hildebert's poetry and that of the *Vita Ædwardi*; if they are not simply the result of working within the same circle, Reginald may have been a point for its transmission to Hildebert, if the latter did not come to know it during his exile in England or via his connections with Muriel, a nun of Wilton whom we will meet again in chapter 7. Of specific interest, given the possibility that Folcard is the Anonymous, is that, in sending his *Malchus* poem to Arnulf, Reginald invoked Aristarchus. References to Aristarchus are rare and thus a distinctive move, whether made in poetry or prose, and suggest that not only did Reginald know the *Vita Ædwardi*, but he knew its author if it was Folcard. The reference to Aristarchus is not a mere linguistic parallel but indicates a shared understanding of the place of the active critic within literary culture. We should not conclude, however, that that shared understanding was limited to Folcard and Reginald, and that the reference to Aristarchus is definitive in identifying Folcard as the author of the *Vita Ædwardi*. Folcard and Reginald are part of a multigenerational and international network of prose and poetry writers who flourished in England on either side of the Conquest and who were exploring the value of classicism. Aristarchus may have had a currency within that network.

The circulation of Reginald's *Malchus* poem illuminates aspects of how the Anonymous, whoever he was, may have fitted into a literary culture that extended from the Loire, across Northern France, England, and Flanders (but strikingly not Lotharingia or elsewhere in the Empire). Reginald's distribution of the *Vita Malchi* reveals that poetic networks and friendships included poets who wrote within the same school (Hildebert and Reginald) and poets who did not (Goscelin and Reginald). Unlike Goscelin's, Reginald's poetics is profoundly formed by his encounter with classical poets, including Ovid; so we find, separating these two friends, distinctive poetic cultures that mirror those of Goscelin and the Anonymous. Reginald's distribution of his poetic *Vita Malchi* enables us not only to see the social networks that facilitated the circulation of poetry in the late-eleventh century but to recognize the diversity of poets and readers encompassed by these networks. At the same time it alerts us to the way in which literary imitation and a shared poetics of allusion within social networks make it difficult to identify securely individual authors when they are not explicitly named. The Anonymous, with his links to Saint-Bertin and the Loire school, sits comfortably within this world, even if his identity remains not yet entirely secure.

Returning to Queen Edith's Wilton

Eve, Goscelin, the Anonymous, Reginald, and their international poetic networks have taken us far from Queen Edith's Wilton and her use of the Roman story world to explain herself to other royal women there. Yet Goscelin, in writing to Eve, speaks to her in the most worldly of terms about the spiritual and physical exile that they have both experienced. The frame of reference that he offers to Eve is that of royal women married to foreign rulers. He writes:

> Filie regum et principum in deliciis a lacte nutrite, nichil scientes preter gloriam et felicitatem natalitie terre, nubunt in exteras nationes, et aliena regna, barbaros mores et ignotas linguas disciture, seuisque dominis ac repugnantibus a naturali usu legibus seruiture, sicut nuper filia marchisi Flandrensium nupsit Cunuto regi Danorum. Tales semel ualedixere parentibus et natalibus patrie, ultra non ualentes aut nolentes patriam respicere, maritali affectu plus omnibus ualente.
>
> (Daughters of kings and princes, brought up from the time of suckling in luxuries, knowing nothing except the glory and happiness of their native lands, marry into foreign peoples and strange kingdoms. They will have to learn barbarous customs and unknown languages and severe harsh lords and laws repugnant to natural usage, just like the daughter of the Count of Flanders, who recently married Canute, King of the Danes. Such ones say goodbye once and for all to parents and origins in their homeland, not able or willing to look again on their homeland, as marital affection works more strongly than other things.)[228]

Cutting across national, linguistic, and cultural boundaries shapes Eve's spiritual journey as it shaped the lives of her secular counterparts at Wilton. Just as Goscelin encouraged Eve to use the Roman story world to think with, he encouraged her to use the experience of royal women who married abroad to create dynastic alliances to understand her spiritual life. Living in the Wilton of Queen Edith and the Anonymous ensured that royal women and international horizons were formative for the young nun. The international ambitions of the nunnery's royal women attracted exceptional poets and writers. As a result, Wilton became a focal point in

228 Goscelin, *LC*, p. 41 (trans., p. 117).

an international poetic network. The literary experimentalism of the *Vita Ædwardi* did not find just vague inspiration in the circumstances of Edith and the women of Wilton. Invested in literary culture not as a distraction amid political turmoil but in an urgent effort to impose order, they were active patrons and readers. Such women would have been tremendously attractive to a poet whose expectations of patronage had been shaped by emulation of Virgil, Ovid, or Horace.[229] The Anonymous's serious engagement with the learning and the gender of the Wilton women leads him to move beyond the Encomiast's figuring of Emma as his Octavian. Edith as Lady Philosophy is figured as a critical interlocutor in the intellectual, aesthetic, political, and religious project to make a secure place for the Roman story world in the literary culture of western Europe. As we shall see in the next chapter, the marriages of Wilton's royal women and the continued vitality of the poetic culture of which it was a part ensured that this community would continue to exert a major influence on literature within and beyond the expanding Anglo-Norman realm.

229 Haye, "*Nemo Mecenas.*" See earlier, chapter 3 herein.

6 The Women of 1066

Introduction

Looking at the Conquest and its impact on literary culture through the experience of the royal women of England is a move sanctioned not only by Edith's *Vita Ædwardi* but also by the usually male-dominated Anglo-Saxon Chronicle. As Pauline Stafford has recently showed, in the account of 1067 found in "D" the Anglo-Saxon Chronicle steps aside from its usual preoccupation with men, to use women to think with about the Conquest. In this chapter we will follow the lead of the chronicler of "D" and focus on the English royal women of three dynasties – West Saxon, Godwine, and Norman – for whom 1066 was a momentous year, inaugurating new lives for them far away from their homelands. The lives of the woman of these three dynasties, and the poetry and the history written for them, offer insight into the ways in which they created literary, political, and social networks that intertwined throughout the Conquest.[1] Moving from Queen Edith to Countess Adela of Blois, this chapter will reveal the channels whereby the learning of Anglo-Saxon royal women, particularly those of Wilton, played an integral role in developments in European literary culture across England, Northern France, Flanders, and also Scandinavia.

Within the entry for 1067, records of rebellion, harsh taxation, harrying, betrayal, and deadly battle bracket an account of the flight from England of the Godwine and West Saxon women and the arrival of William the Conqueror's wife, Matilda. First, the chronicler follows Edward the Exile's

1 This discussion of the women of ASC "D" 1067 and of the entry's form draws directly on Stafford's incisive article "Chronicle D, 1067." See also Cubbin's edition of "D," lxxiv and lxxix; and Wormald, *Anglo-Saxon Deerhurst* (Deerhurst Lecture, 1991), 9–17.

widow, Agatha, and her children, Edgar the Ætheling, Margaret, and Christina, as they flee to Scotland, where they found sanctuary with King Malcolm ("Malcholmes cyniges gryð"). At this point the entry contains an extended life of Margaret, including a few lines of rhymed verse, recounting how she married Malcolm against her will, preferring a life of a virgin dedicated to God. Then the chronicler turns his attention to women of the House of Godwine; Gytha (widow of Godwine and mother of Harold and Edith) departs for Saint-Omer accompanied by "manegra godra manna wif mid hyre" (the wives of many good men). Only once they are gone does the chronicle recount the arrival of Matilda of Flanders for her consecration as queen by Archbishop Ealdred.

The entry, as Stafford shows, "is not a transparent recording of events, but a shaping of them," which foregrounds the "symbolic" value of women, who "in some respects… stand [in for] the defeated England and the victorious Normans."[2] By beginning and ending the entry with the violence of men (Anglo-Saxon, Norman, and Welsh), the chronicler uses the order of narration to juxtapose the contrasting male and female experiences of conquest. This story is not simply one that focuses around women; rather its interest lies with the women who crossed from one kingdom into another. By ignoring the Anglo-Saxon women who stayed behind, perhaps finding accommodation with the Normans, it portrays the Conquest as complete rupture. Queen Edith and Harold's daughter Gunnhild, both at Wilton, are passed over. No mention is made of either of Harold's wives, Edith Swanneck or Ealdgyth. The dispersal of women, which catches the imagination of the chronicler, will send Anglo-Saxon women to Scotland, Flanders, Denmark, and Kiev Rus' and bring Norman women to England; as a result it will have consequences for the history of European literature. The ability of these women to move in Europe will rely on and extend their linguistic expertise across multiple vernaculars and reinforce the value of Latin as the pre-eminent language of elite women's literary culture that was not delimited by political boundaries. And, as this chapter will show, the movement of women ensured that with regard to literary culture, as in politics, 1066 was a point of both rupture and new connections.

The entry's subversion of the rigid chronology of the annal form further emphasizes the symbolic meaning of these women. Matilda of Flanders

2 Stafford, "Chronicle D," 212 and 214.

did not arrive in England until 1068. The presence of annal numbers in the margins of the "D" manuscript makes all the more evident the deliberate displacement of this event to 1067. This blatant artfulness, especially evident in its treatment of women, reminds readers of the entry that it is just one more version of the events set in train by the Conquest. It appears, further, that this entry was composed and recomposed over the course of the final decades of the eleventh century and into the early twelfth century. The brief life of Margaret was incorporated into the entry, probably after her death in 1093 or after the marriage of her daughter Edith/Matilda to the Norman king Henry I in 1100. This marriage of Anglo-Saxon and Norman dynasties altered the political significance of Margaret's life. The entry's composition reveals that the fate of these royal women remained a site that had to be returned to and reworked in order to negotiate the evolving relationship between the past and the present in post-conquest England.[3] As this and the following chapter will argue, the lives of these women and their daughters were continually reinterpreted, in the poetry and the history, which they themselves often commissioned, as England came to terms with the meaning of the Conquest.

The Godwine Women

Following the Chronicle, this chapter will approach women in dynastic groupings, though intermarriage quickly mingles women across these lines. We will begin with the Godwines, and, before following the women whom the Chronicle tells us fled to the Continent, we will turn to those about whom the Chronicle is silent because they stayed: Queen Edith and her niece, Harold Godwineson's daughter Gunnhild. In considering the kind of women who may have formed the audience for the *Vita Ædwardi*, we have already looked at these two women's places in Wilton after the Conquest. Here they will come into focus for what they reveal about the connections between Wilton and the new Norman elite and particularly the literary implications of these connections.

Edith

Edith's quick settlement with the Normans served her political interests and those of the new king, in whose court she appeared. Although it does

3 Stafford, "Chronicle D," 210–14.

not show Edith wishing for William to be king, as William of Poitiers's *Gesta Guillelmi* does, the *Vita Ædwardi* was suited to accommodation.[4] If, as some scholars argue, the *Vita Ædwardi* influenced the Bayeux Tapestry, and if Odo, bishop of Bayeux, Earl of Kent, and half-brother of William, was the tapestry's patron, then the *Vita Ædwardi* very quickly reached Norman court circles (by 1075).[5] Among the courtiers of both king and bishop were men who could have appreciated its innovative poetry and its place among the competing narratives of 1066. Samson, a clerk in William's chapel, had been sent by Odo to study at Liège. He was also taught by the poet Marbod. Marbod was among those who benefited from Odo's largesse, and he appears to have been known to the Conqueror. Marbod, Samson, and Hildebert all wrote verse for the bishop.[6] The tapestry shares with the *Vita Ædwardi* a capacity to convey multiple perspectives on events, including potentially pro-English ones. This multi-vocality reminds us that Edith's text did not need to be sycophantic towards the Conqueror for it to have been written at least partially (when it was completed after the Conquest) with an eye to forging relations with the Normans. The capacity to tell more than one story at once has frustrated attempts to use both the *Vita Ædwardi* and the tapestry as stable historical sources.[7]

Gunnhild II

As the daughter of Harold, Gunnhild may initially have been less sympathetic to the Normans than her aunt was. However, she too appears to have made quick accommodation with England's new rulers, leaving Wilton with Count Alan Rufus, a Breton supporter and second cousin of King William I. Alan, among the ten richest men in England in 1086, remained close to the Conqueror and then to his successor, William Rufus, during their reigns, and thus Gunnhild, like her aunt Edith, moved in the highest Norman circles. Sharpe has argued that her relationship with Alan Rufus produced a daughter, Matilda, and, although never formalized as a

4 William of Poitiers, *GG* 2.8. Stafford, "Chronicle D," 222; and see chapter 5 herein.

5 *VE*, ed. Barlow, 116–17n296; and Heslop, "Regarding the Spectators," 225.

6 Heslop, "Regarding the Spectators," 232–7; and Bulst, "Studien zu Marbods Carmina," 181–4.

7 Pastan and White, "Problematizing Patronage," 2; and Heslop, "Regarding the Spectators," esp. 224.

marriage, it legitimated his possession of her mother Edith Swanneck's land, as recorded in the Domesday Book. Later in life, after Alan's death in 1093, Gunnhild received two letters from Archbishop Anselm, encouraging her to return to the life of a nun. These letters, the second of which is famous for Anselm's excoriation of Gunnhild for her intention to take up with Alan Niger, Alan Rufus's younger brother, offer tantalizing views of her life at Wilton, her changing political value, and possibly her learning.[8] The debate, unresolved to this day, about whether or not Gunnhild originally intended to be a nun illustrates how the political valence of Anglo-Saxon royal women changed at the Conquest. The same potential to act as transmitters of legitimacy to conquered lands that led them to seek refuge in nunneries would soon propel them out into marriage with Norman men.

Anselm admits that Gunnhild had never been consecrated but says that she willingly wore a habit for many years. His claim that she left Wilton because she had been denied the abbacy, if true, adds weight to the view that her original vocation was as a nun and may further encourage the view that she was literate. Her return to Wilton after Alan Rufus's death and before joining Alan Niger, as well as the absence of a marriage to Rufus, also suggests that she had originally been intended for the monastic life. In writing to Gunnhild, Anselm uses language that he usually reserved for nuns (see also letters 184 and 185) rather than for married women; she is a *sponsa Christi* (a bride of Christ), which vocation was familiar to her

8 Anselm, *Epistolae* 168 and 169. I am following the revisionist narratives of Gunnhild's life that were recently put forward by Sharpe and O'Brien O'Keeffe. Sharpe convincingly challenges Southern's widely accepted account of her life and of the connection between her elopement with Alan Rufus and Edith/Matilda's own departure from Wilton to marry Henry I. In considering how this narrative fits in with Anselm's insistence in the 1090s that Gunnhild had long worn the habit of a nun, he suggests that Anselm was referring to a period from 1066 to 1072. Sharpe does not appear to consider the possibility that she was being educated at Wilton before the Conquest (and thus stayed there, rather than fleeing there) or that she had actually intended to become a nun. O'Brien O'Keeffe importantly underscores that we have only Anselm's tendentious account of Gunnhild's elopement, which may conceal an abduction and which is not a reliable source for her choice to become a nun. Southern, *Anselm and His Biographer*, 185; Searle, "Women and the Legitimisation," 167–9; Keats-Rohan, "Bretons and Normans"; Keats-Rohan, "Alan Rufus"; Sharpe, "King Harold's Daughter"; O'Brien O'Keeffe, "Leaving Wilton"; and O'Brien O'Keeffe, *Stealing Obedience*, 185–209.

from Wilton, who has scorned her proper husband.[9] Anselm recounts too that, after Rufus's death and before she joined with Niger, he and Gunnhild conversed together with delight, and that she followed up their meeting by sending a letter. Anselm's positive characterization of their meeting suggests that it affirmed her religious vocation and revealed her ability to speak in the idiom of a nun.[10]

Harold Godwineson may have seen the presence of a daughter at the head of Wilton as part of his strategy for claiming the West Saxon crown. Even later in the eleventh century and into the twelfth century, although the meaning of her symbolic value as Harold's daughter had changed, it continued to be recognized. The translation by William of Malmesbury of Coleman's Old English life of Saint Wulfstan recalls that on a visit to the nunnery the bishop heard that Gunnhild, depicted as no more than an ordinary member of the community, had been afflicted by blindness, and he had her brought to him. Wulfstan, who had been Harold's confessor, is moved to heal her by the memory of what he owed her father.[11] After 1066 it was no longer to her dynasty's advantage for her to lead a religious life, and likewise it was no longer to Wilton's advantage to have her as abbess. Gunnhild could evidently find higher standing outside the nunnery.

Gunnhild's learning may have extended to speaking French. As Richard Sharpe points out, it is likely that the conversation between Gunnhild and Anselm took place in French.[12] While she may have learned this language in Alan Rufus's household, equally she may have learned this language at Wilton, where Edith herself may have learned French.[13] Possession of French would thus have facilitated, rather than resulted from, her liaison with Alan Rufus. The ability of the Latinate women of Wilton, perhaps also including Eve, to move across linguistic borders between French and English enabled them to make their way in new ecclesiastical and secular circles. Thus the linguistic expertise of the Wilton women would ensure that the nunnery's literary culture spread out not only beyond the cloister but also across the divide between Anglo-Saxon and Norman.

9 O'Brien O'Keeffe, "Leaving Wilton," esp. 211–18; and O'Brien O'Keeffe, *Stealing Obedience*, 197–203.

10 Anselm, *Epistolae* 168, 169, 184, and 185.

11 William of Malmesbury, *Vita Wulfstani*, 2.11. Hollis, "Centre of Learning," 338.

12 Sharpe, "King Harold's Daughter," 26.

13 See chapter 5 herein.

Gytha I

Our sense of the learning of the women of the house of Godwine becomes stronger when we return to the Anglo-Saxon Chronicle's 1067D entry and take up the women recorded as fleeing in the face of the Conquest. The flight to the Continent of Harold and Edith's other close female relatives shows that the same international ties that shaped England's literary culture in the eleventh century provided refuge for the Godwine women. Edith's Danish mother, Gytha, linked to rebellion after the Conquest, chose a course that ran counter to that of her daughter's and granddaughter's accommodation to Norman rule. We see from this that even within her natal family Edith confronted a variety of opinions about the causes and rightful responses to William's victory. Gytha went first to the Flemish town of Saint-Omer, benefiting from the Godwines' long-standing connections there, and then continued on to the Danish court of her nephew King Svein Estrithson. Her life thus extends from the Danish to the Norman Conquest and beyond, with post-conquest Danish claims to the English throne stemming from her, just as Norman claims had stemmed from Emma. Svein, supported by Edgar Ætheling and other English rebels, attacked England in 1069, and the Danes continued to pose a threat throughout William's reign.[14]

Useful to Svein as evidence of Danish claims to the English throne, Gytha is likely to have acted as a source, among other people, of information about the events of 1066 and its consequences for the men of her family, who were all kinsmen of Svein. When Svein became one of Adam of Bremen's informants about eleventh-century Anglo-Saxon England, her views of England may then have influenced the writing of a famous and highly literate eleventh-century historian. Adam's classical (as well as biblical) learning is on display in the prologue to his *Gesta Hammaburgensis ecclesiae pontificum*. Like the Encomiast, Adam participated in contemporary debates about the relationship of history to fiction, an issue that he articulates, in a Macrobian fashion, by claiming that his detractors would liken his work to the dream created by Cicero for Scipio or to the false dreams imagined by Virgil. Pauline Stafford has, furthermore, emphasized

14 Körner, *Battle of Hastings*, 138–45; Barlow, *Godwins*, 119; A. Williams, "Godwine"; Stafford, "Chronicle D," 219–20; and Bolton, "English Political Refugees," 19–21.

Adam's interests in the ways in which intermarriage created the complex bonds between England, Denmark, Germany, and Normandy.[15]

Gunnhild I

The women who fled with Gytha neatly demonstrate the elite aristocracy's participation in a world where daughters were raised either for the religious life or for dynastic marriage. Both types of women played important roles as cultural ambassadors across northern Europe in the years after 1066. Gytha was accompanied to Flanders and Denmark by her daughter Gunnhild, who was dedicated to the religious life from childhood and who died later in Bruges, the location of the Flemish comital court. She left a psalter glossed in Old English to Saint Donatian's in Bruges. Her religious vocation suggests that she had been educated, like her sister Edith, at Wilton or another royal nunnery. We may thus catch a glimpse of another member of the audience of the *Vita Ædwardi*.[16] The literacy indicated by a psalter with vernacular glosses is of a different order than that for which Edith was renowned; it accords, however, with Goscelin's reference to vernacular writing in "patriis literis" during the abbacy of Brihtgifu (1065–7).[17] Gunnhild's journey to Denmark and return to Flanders, in possession of a psalter, suggest that she may have shared her sister Edith's education as well as her linguistic prowess. The Scandinavian visit points to Danish as a language that the two women could have learned from their family and been familiar with at Wilton – where we find not only Anglo-Danish women but also Eve, whose father was a Dane.[18]

The glosses on Gunnhild's psalter hold interest when considering the influence of the early English use of the vernacular on the Continent. The earlier eleventh-century Dutch glosses, likely by an English or a Norman scribe, which we previously noted in a Saint-Bertin copy of Orosius, are now joined by an early Dutch gloss written as a pen trial in a Rochester

15 Adam of Bremen, *Gesta*, prologue, 1.48, 1.61, and 2.54. Mortensen, "Vernacular Interviews," 56–7; Bolton, "English Political Refugees," 21–5; and Stafford, *QEQE*, 22–4.

16 Grierson, "England and Flanders," 109; and Barlow, *Godwins*, 120.

17 Goscelin, *Translatio sanctae Edithae* 16. Hollis, "St Edith and the Wilton Community," 273.

18 See chapter 5 herein.

manuscript from the second half of the eleventh century. This pen trial takes the form of a brief poem in the vernacular and Latin (generally referred to by the opening words of the vernacular lines: "Hebban olla vogala") about two birds building a nest together (Oxford, Bodleian Library, Bodley 340, fol. 169v). The recent suggestion that the poem is in the Kentish dialect of Old English rather than in Dutch, even though strained, illustrates how the linguistic proximity of Dutch and Old English would have eased the movement of political exiles, as well as clerics, between England and the Low Countries, as well as opening up channels for literary exchange that shaped both Latin and vernacular learning. The importance that Latin played in such exchanges, and its intimate relationship with the vernacular, is represented by its presence alongside the Dutch of this little poem. The occurrence of this linguistic experimentation in a manuscript of Ælfric's *Catholic Homilies*, meanwhile, cautions against divorcing the internationalism of eleventh-century English literary culture from what has been more traditionally studied as Anglo-Saxon literature.[19]

Gytha II

Harold's daughter Gytha also left England with her grandmother and namesake. She went on to marry Vladimir Monomakh; on his father's side he was prince of Smolensk and then of Kiev, while on his mother's side he was related to the Byzantine emperor Constantine IX. This English woman's ties to the ruling dynasty of Denmark made her an attractive marriage prospect on a much wider European stage. The earlier marriages of Vladimir's aunts illustrate clearly that Gytha's marriage did not remove her to the periphery. Anna of Kiev married the Capetian king Henry I (whom the *Vita Ædwardi* remembers as a kinsman of Edward) in 1051. Anna is likely to have been educated, even signing her name in Cyrillic script in a French charter. Her sister, Elisabeth, married the Norwegian king Harold Hardrada, who was killed alongside his ally Tostig at the Battle of Stamford Bridge in 1066.[20]

---

19 De Grauwe, "*Olla vogala*"; Milis, "French Low Countries," 346–7; Dronke, "Latin and Vernacular Love-Lyrics"; Kwakkel, "*Hebban olla vogala*"; Van Oostrom, *Stemmen op schrift*, 93–107; and Van Houts, "Contrasts and Interaction," 4–5. And see chapter 3 herein. The language of the texts is much more securely Dutch than Kentish; I am grateful to Richard Dance for discussion of this point.

20 Bogomoletz, "Anna of Kiev"; Dimnik, "Kievan Rus'," 254–60; and Raffensperger, *Reimagining Europe*, 108–9.

Judith

Tostig's wife Judith, who fled to Flanders with her husband after his banishment in 1065, appears to have stayed there initially. The daughter of Count Baldwin IV of Flanders, she had married Tostig when he was in exile there in 1051 along with other members of his family. We later find Judith in Denmark, like her in-laws the Godwine women. She then went on to marry Welf IV, Duke of Bavaria. The influence, of the Anglo-Saxon gospel books that were made for her, on Bavarian manuscript illumination is visible testimony to the cultural impact of the flight of royal women from Conquest England, here in artistic rather than literary terms.[21] At the same time, her kinship with both William the Conqueror (her mother was the daughter of Duke Richard II of Normandy) and Matilda of Flanders (whose half-aunt she was) illustrates that the cultural world of the Anglo-Saxon royal women was not sealed off from that of their Continental counterparts. Her kinship and marriage illustrate too that within the highest elite circles English and Norman were not exclusive identities, as we have already seen with Emma and Edward.

The West Saxon Cadet Line

Agatha

The West Saxon princesses who fled north to Malcolm III's court continue to let us trace the internationalism, learning, and the intertwined worlds of court and cloister that the Godwine women exemplified. Despite his West Saxon ancestry, Edgar Ætheling had proven too young and too lacking in political support to claim the throne in the face of either Harold's or William's challenges. The 1067D entry in the Chronicle recounts that his mother, Agatha, and two sisters, Margaret and Christina, accompanied him when he fled to Scotland. Agatha, whose Rus' name was Agafia, was another daughter of Jaroslav I; he also fathered Anna (wife of Henry I of France) and Elisabeth (wife of Harold Hardrada). Agatha married Edward the Exile (Æthelred's grandson) when his banishment after Cnut's

21 Grierson, "England and Flanders," 109–11; McGurk and Rosenthal, "Gospel Books of Judith"; and Barlow, *Godwins*, 120.

conquest led him to the court of her father. The couple appears to have travelled from there to the Hungarian court, where a fourth sister was married to King Andrew. Agatha and her children came to England when Edward the Confessor, in his search for an heir, recalled his nephew Edward. Although Edward the Exile died within the year, his widow and children were welcomed into the Confessor's court.[22] Agatha may have shared in the literacy of her sister Anna, and she must have come to command several languages in her move from the Rus' to the Hungarian to the West Saxon and finally to the Scottish court. Edward's marriage to Agatha brought him and his children into an influential Eastern dynasty with powerful connections throughout Europe. The horizons of the West Saxon dynasty stretched far to the East.

Margaret

In considering the kind of women who were at Wilton when the *Vita Ædwardi* was written, we have already touched on the possibility that Margaret, like her sister Christina (a nun of Romsey), was convent educated.[23] Although she was not a patron of classicizing learning (her learning was of a more pious nature), Margaret remains an important figure in our exploration of cross-conquest continuities in the cultivation of the Roman story world by English royal women.[24] Turgot, a monk of Durham and bishop of St Andrew's, wrote a life of Margaret for her daughter Edith/Matilda. Both the Anglo-Saxon Chronicle entry for 1067D and Turgot's life represent her genealogy as bringing West Saxon lineage and piety to the Scottish royal dynasty.[25] A letter from Lanfranc, archbishop of Canterbury, also singles out the royal lineage ("regali stirpe progenita") that she brought to her marriage with Malcolm.[26] The attractiveness of this

---

22 Barlow, *Edward the Confessor*, 163–4; Hooper, "Edgar the Ætheling," 199–200; Huneycutt, *Matilda of Scotland*, 14; and Raffensperger, *Reimagining Europe*, 104–6 (crucial for its recent identification of the previously shadowy Agatha as a daughter of Jaroslav I).

23 See chapter 5 herein.

24 Gameson, "Gospels of Margaret."

25 [Turgot?], *Vita sanctae Margaretae*. Huneycutt ("Perfect Princess"), on the manuscripts and Edith/Matilda's commission of the life. Harrison ("Mortuary Roll," 67–71) and Huneycutt (*Matilda of Scotland*, 10–12) flag the uncertain identification of Turgot as the author of Margaret's life. For a strong statement in favour of Turgot see Bartlett, "Turgot." The life is discussed further in chapter 7 herein.

26 Lanfranc, *Epistolae* 50.

ancient lineage to the Scottish royal throne is evident not only in the pressure that Malcolm put on Margaret to marry him but also in the West Saxon dynastic names given to many of their children.[27] Since the poetry of the Chronicle is so focused on the lives of kings, the inclusion of a poem about Margaret in the entry for 1067D highlights her significance in perpetuating the ancient lineage.[28]

Both lives of Margaret, alongside Lanfranc's letter, portray her piety in ways that recall the learning and spiritual life of Wilton. The verse and the prose of the brief life in the Chronicle insist that she resisted marriage to Malcolm in order to use her *mægðhad* (maidenhood) to please the Lord. Deploying the language of virgins as the brides of Christ, so familiar at Wilton, the poet draws on the semantic range of the Old English word *hlaford*, which, alongside a secular lord, can denote a husband as well as God. Turning to Turgot's Latin, we see Margaret as a reader formed by monastic habits, as were Edith and Eve earlier. He claims that she not only read scripture but fully occupied her time with it: "Inerat ei ad intelligendum quamlibet rem acuta ingenii subtilitas, ad retinendum multa memoriæ tenacitas, ad proferendum gratiosa verborum facilitas" (She had a keen acuteness of intellect for judging whatever matter there was to be understood, a tenacity of memory for retaining many things, and a favoured facility for expressing things in words).[29] And in a manner that brings to mind Goscelin's relationship with Eve, though without the attendant sexual anxiety, Turgot and Margaret enjoy a spiritual intimacy. Turgot writes: "Plane sacrorum voluminum religiosa, nec parva illi aviditas inerat, in quibus sibi acquirendis familiaris ejus caritas & caritativa familiaritas me ipsum me fatigare plerumque cogebat" (Certainly she was more than a little full of holy passion for sacred books, and my intimate affection for her along with affectionate intimacy with her caused me to tire myself out trying to procure many books for her).[30] Elsewhere he describes how he saw both her exterior works and her inner conscience.[31]

Lanfranc too sought a relationship of spiritual equality. He eventually gave in to Margaret's request, sent to him by letter, that he act as her

27 Huneycutt, *Matilda of Scotland*, 10.
28 Bredehoft, *Textual Histories*, 99–118 (and, arguing that the Margaret poem is actually substantially longer, *Authors, Audiences*, 189–94).
29 [Turgot?], *Vita sanctae Margaretae* 1.6.
30 [Turgot?], *Vita sanctae Margaretae* 2.10.
31 [Turgot?], *Vita sanctae Margaretae* 3.17.

spiritual father, but not until he had refigured this as a relationship of mutual support.[32] Meanwhile, the letters of Theobald d'Étampes (a Caen-educated teacher and theologian) confirm that he sought to become one of her chaplains, illustrating the attraction of her learning to educated clerics and suggesting that Turgot's presentation of her debating with scholars at the Scottish court was not unfounded.[33] The Latin learning of Margaret, like that of Edith and Eve before her, thus plays a role in the respect she commands from clerics.

The survival of Margaret's gospel book also corroborates Turgot's picture of her religious reading. The gospel book, moreover, brings to the fore again the wider network of women who may have shared some degree of her learning. Like Tostig's wife Judith, Margaret appears to have been responsible for the movement of books, which were in both cases illuminated gospels (though Margaret's is a partial lectionary) covered in gold. Margaret and Judith, whose marriages turned them into international cultural ambassadors, are likely to have known each other through Edward's court.

In Turgot's representation, Margaret's learning endowed her with an extraordinary authority, not only in her individual relations with clerics but also in her civilizing of the barbarian Scottish court and church. Her experience in the courts of Europe is clearly an advantage, as she raises the standard of court fashion, especially Malcolm's, and attracts foreign merchants to Scotland. Turning to spiritual matters, which are represented as her chief concern, she read to her illiterate husband, who, in awe of her learning, held her books for her, kissed her favourite ones, and occasionally had them decorated with treasure.[34] Turgot reports that she fostered church reform and presided over a synod, where Malcolm acted as her "adjutor ... præcipuus" (distinguished helper), carrying out whatever she commanded, including acting as her interpreter because she did not understand Gaelic. (Turgot raises this point not to diminish her linguistic skills but to emphasize the superiority of English, the language shared by the king and queen.) It is unlikely that she herself convened a synod, but the claim indicates the power that Turgot attributes to her piety and learning.[35]

32 Lanfranc, *Epistolae* 50.

33 [Turgot?], *Vita sanctae Margaretae* 2.10. Evans, "Theobald."

34 [Turgot?], *Vita sanctae Margaretae* 2.11.

35 [Turgot?], *Vita sanctae Margaretae* 2.13. Huneycutt, *Matilda of Scotland*, 13–14.

An even more unlikely scene served a similar purpose in Goscelin's *Vita Edithae* when Goscelin depicted the leading noblemen seeking out Saint Edith as successor to her murdered brother Edward the Martyr.[36] Both portraits underscore the extraordinary political and moral authority that learned women commanded: a lesson well-known to the women of Wilton and one that Margaret may have learned directly from her great-aunt, Queen Edith.

Margaret actively passed this lesson on to her daughter, Edith/Matilda, both in person (Turgot says she took a direct role in raising her children) and through her textual representation. The value of Latin, and of a reputation for piety, to a woman expected to cross cultural and linguistic borders may have encouraged Margaret to send two of her daughters south to Romsey and then to Wilton to be educated before they married (she sent Edith/Mathilda and Mary, the future wife of Eustace III, Count of Boulogne). Margaret, whose life saw her move across courts in which Hungarian, German, English, French, and finally Gaelic were spoken, more than any of the women whose lives and reading we have traced, would have been keenly aware of the communicative and European-wide currency of Latin. The wanderings of the women of the West Saxon cadet line descended from Edmund Ironside gave a further boost to the cultivation of Latin among educated English royal women. In the figure of Margaret we see a powerful coming together of this international experience with West Saxon traditions of nunnery education, which she passed on to her daughter Edith/Matilda, the subject of the final chapter.

The Norman Women

In the 1067D Chronicle entry the flight of the Anglo-Saxon royal women is answered by the arrival of William's wife, Matilda of Flanders, and her consecration as queen – an act that turns a Capetian granddaughter, a Flemish princess, and a Norman duchess into an English queen. Looking at Matilda and her relationships with poets allows us to consider how the literary culture of the Anglo-Saxon royal women compares to that of their Continental counterparts in Normandy, Flanders, and France. Matilda knew and was known to poets, some working within the Loire school. She

36 Goscelin, *Vita sanctae Edithae* 19. See chapter 5 herein.

did not, however, act as their patrons, and any classicizing poetry written for or about her is conspicuously absent, though in the next generation her daughter Adela of Blois will attract the attention of such poets.

Matilda and Her Mother

Matilda's mother, Adela, Countess of Flanders, was the daughter of Robert the Pious, Capetian king of France.[37] Adela, a strong supporter of religious foundations for both men and women, was herself literate. Although the *Gesta Normannorum ducum* of William of Jumièges claims that Adela was raised from the cradle in the Flemish court, her education may also reflect her Capetian origins, which are emphasized in the *Genealogia comitum Flandrensium*.[38] Adela's father, especially remembered for his pious learning, was educated at Reims by one of the leading scholars of his day, Gerbert of Aurillac (later Pope Sylvester II). In his *Epitoma vitae Regis Rotberti pii* written in the early 1040s, Helgaud of Fleury presents Robert as a "rex sapientissimus litterarum" and a champion of monks. His son Henry I and his grandson Philip do not, however, share his reputation for learning, and none of these early Capetians is remembered for literary patronage.[39]

Two texts allow us to gain an impression of Adela's learning. Gervase, archbishop of Reims, writing to her husband, Count Baldwin V of Flanders, in a prefatory letter to a life of Saint Donatian of Bruges that was produced at their request, singles out Adela as "litterarum disciplinis inbutam" (imbued with the knowledge of letters) and notes her Capetian descent.[40] Meanwhile, Adela commissioned a copy of Odilo of Cluny's *Epitaphium domine Adelheide*, as recorded in a short poem appended to the text. Adelheid was the wife of Otto I, mother of Otto II, and grandmother of Otto III. Picking up on Odilo's hope, expressed in his preface, that the example of Adelheid might reach the ears of empresses and queens, the poem attests to the value of the *Epitaphum* as an exemplum for the countess. Adela's seeking out of this particular text merits further consideration. Odilo presents Adelheid as a politically powerful figure in all

37 Huyghebaert, "Femmes Laïques," esp. 371, 376–7, and 381–6; Huyghebaert, "Adela van Frankrijk"; and Van Houts, "Flemish Contribution," 112 and 126.

38 William of Jumièges, *Gesta Normannorum ducum* 6.6; and *Genealogia comitum Flandrensium*, 7.

39 Helgaud, *Epitoma vitae Robertii pii* 3; Rosenthal, "Early Capetians," 371 and 374.

40 Gervase of Reims, *Ex miraculis sancti Donatiani Brugensibus*, 855.

three reigns, as well as being a defender of monasteries and the poor. Moreover, she was not only literate but, in her old age, constantly sought further instruction in divine letters from the abbot of the monastery founded by her at Selz.[41] Adela's commissioning of the *Epitaphum* raises two points. First, it suggests that she used her literacy actively to provide herself with an attractive model of female power, both political and spiritual. Second, the commissioning of a copy of an already extant text draws attention to the dearth of lay literary patronage in Flanders. Even when there were literate elite women, Flemish clerics sought patronage among the Anglo-Saxon royal women.[42] The Encomiast's depiction of Emma being warmly welcomed to Bruges by Adela as well as by Baldwin also illustrates the closeness of the English, Flemish, and French courts and thus further emphasizes the distinctive nature of the queenly patronage of Emma and Edith.[43]

Adela's education presented an important model for her daughter Matilda to take to Normandy.[44] Although we find Matilda praised by poets and even in their company, we do not find evidence of her patronage; she is said to be learned, but this does not appear to be a defining feature of her character. Orderic, in a long, rather conventional catalogue of virtues, notes simply that Queen Matilda was "litterarum scientia" (learned in letters).[45] Her death is commemorated in four epitaphs. Godfrey of Winchester, who was fulsome about Queen Edith's cultivation of the seven liberal arts, is silent about Matilda's learning. Godfrey, as prior of Winchester, was positioned to know first-hand about Matilda, as argued earlier for Edith.[46] The poem (which Orderic Vitalis records) inscribed on Matilda's tomb in the Holy Trinity Caen similarly makes no mention of any learning.[47] Holy Trinity was Matilda's own foundation where her daughter Cecilia became abbess in the early twelfth century; thus this epitaph shows how those closest to her chose to remember her.[48] Since Matilda took care to ensure that Cecilia was well educated, as we will

41 Odilo of Cluny, *Epitaphium domine Adelheide*, prefatory letter, 10, and 19. The poem for Adela can be found in Pertz's edition of the *Epitaphium*, 635.

42 Van Houts, "Flemish Contribution," esp. 112 and 126–7.

43 *Enc.* 3.7.

44 Musset, "Reine Mathilde," 192–3.

45 Orderic Vitalis, *HE*, 4 (2:224–5) and 7.9 (4:44–7).

46 Godfrey of Winchester, *Epigrammata historica* 1 and 6. See chapter 5 herein.

47 Orderic Vitalis, *HE* 7.9 (4.44–7).

48 Musset, "Reine Mathilde," 205.

discuss, the absence of a reference to her own learning or literary patronage is particularly revealing of its marginality to her public image. As van Houts has suggested, one cause of this absence of patronage is that neither she nor her mother, Adela, needed the type of propagandist sought by Edith and Emma before her. However, Matilda's distance from the cultivation of literary culture as part of her image will prove more deeply rooted and less accidental.[49]

Fulcoius of Beauvais, who also wrote epitaphs for Matilda, provides an opportunity to consider Matilda's place in the emergence of classicizing poetry for lay patrons.[50] A married cleric who rose to be an archdeacon, Fulcoius enjoyed the patronage of Archbishop Manasses of Reims, who was likewise a patron of Godfrey of Reims. In its overt and reflective use of the Roman story world and in its poetic language Fulcoius's verse shows strong connections to the *Vita Ædwardi* and the poetry of the Loire school, although it lacks their linguistic and intellectual sophistication. Through the course of his poetic career Fulcoius fashioned a Virgilian poetic persona for himself. Like many poets of the eleventh century, his encounter with classical poetry shaped his own self-understanding and his search for patronage.[51] This persona is most developed in his long epistle to the German emperor Henry IV, son of Henry III, in whose court the *Carmina Cantabrigiensia* (*Cambridge Songs*), with their classical excerpts, may have been compiled. Fulcoius greets Henry IV:

> Cesare Henrico redierunt aurea secla.
> Alter Virgilius redit alter et Octouianus.
>
> Golden ages have returned with the Emperor Henry.
> Another Virgil and another Octavian return.[52]

Here his stance is reminiscent of the Encomiast's towards Emma.[53] These lines also bring to mind the muse's original command that the poet of the

---

49 Van Houts, "Flemish Contribution," 125–6.

50 Fulcoius, *Epitaphia* 9 and 10.

51 Fulcoius, *Epistulae*, ed. Colker, 191–208; Van Houts, "Latin Poetry," 46; Haye, "Christliche und pagane Dichtung"; Haye, "*Nemo Mecenas*"; and Moser, *Cosmos of Desire*, 22–9.

52 Fulcoius, *Epistulae* 1, lines 98–9. See chapter 4 herein.

53 *Enc.*, argument.

Vita Ædwardi sing of a "secula … aurea."[54] Even Fulcoius's religious verse is deeply shaped by his attraction to Virgil, whom, even as he rejects him, he figures as one who prepared the way.[55] However, he does not call on this Virgilian persona in writing about Matilda. In two epitaphs Fulcoius remembers Matilda as "prudens et fortis, sobria, justa" (intelligent, powerful, sober, and just) and emphasizes her royal descent. One of the Matilda epitaphs is among the most substantial in the surviving collection of forty-nine, and yet it does not share in the classicizing that marks some of Fulcoius's memorial poems.[56]

Orderic Vitalis's claim that Guy, bishop of Amiens, likely author of the *Carmen de Haestingae proelio*, accompanied Matilda to England (on the same journey recounted by the Anglo-Saxon Chronicle) draws further attention to her simultaneous proximity to classicizing poets and distance from patronage of their verse.[57] Written shortly after the Conquest, Guy's *Carmen* celebrates William's victory at Hastings.[58] In the poem he draws on Carolingian panegyric while he shares the growing eleventh-century preoccupation with using the Roman story world to narrate lay experience, as suggested by Orderic's characterization of his verse as written in imitation of Virgil and Statius.[59] Guy's classicizing is, however, of a different order from that of the Loire poets; he wrote a much more direct type of verse, generally easy to read and straightforward in its approach to the history, legend, and myth of Rome, and he was not an Ovidian. In its directness it shows affinities with *chansons de geste*, rather than the poetry of the Loire. From the opening lines of Guy's epic poem, William is heralded as a second Julius Caesar, and the poem is marked by other simple references to Vulcan and Hercules, which provide a contrast to the complex and knowing reworking of Roman myth that we found in the *Vita Ædwardi*.[60] The poem's preoccupation with the French among William's men, its occasional criticism of the Conqueror, and the time Guy spent in the French court points to a Northern French audience away from the

54 *VE* 1, prologue.
55 Fulcoius, *De nuptiis*, lines 1–34 (esp. 23–4).
56 Fulcoius, *Epitaphia* 9 (esp. line 3) and 10.
57 Orderic Vitalis, *HE* 4 (2:214–15). Van Houts, "Latin Poetry," 54; and Guy of Amiens, *CHP*, ed. Barlow, xvii–xviii.
58 Van Houts, "Latin Poetry," 56; and Guy of Amiens, *CHP*, ed. Barlow, xl.
59 Orderic Vitalis, *HE* 3 (2:184–7). Guy of Amiens, *CHP*, ed. Morton and Muntz, lxvi–lxxi; and Guy of Amiens, *CHP*, ed. Barlow, xlvii.
60 Guy of Amiens, *CHP*, lines 32, 152, and 482.

ducal court.[61] Guy appears to have acted as a spiritual adviser to Matilda without writing poetry for her.

Matilda's Daughters

Although not a literary patron, Matilda of Flanders appears to have attended carefully to the education of at least two of her daughters: one destined for the cloister, Cecilia, and the other, Adela, for dynastic marriage. In seeing to the education of her daughters, she was bringing new expectations to Normandy. For both daughters, 1066 and their father's conquest of England would be a turning point. On the eve of the Conquest William and Matilda promised Cecilia to the nunnery Holy Trinity, which Matilda had founded in 1059. On the occasion of her consecration at Fécamp in 1075 Fulcoius offered her father a consolatory poem, drawing on the biblical figure of Jephthah who had himself offered up a daughter in return for victory.[62] Likely conceived shortly after the Conquest, Adela was celebrated by Godfrey of Reims as the first of the conqueror's children to be born in the purple (that is, after he became king).[63]

Cecilia was taught by Arnulf of Chocques (in Flanders). A little after 1063, while he was still young, Arnulf entered the monastery of Saint-Stephen, William's foundation in Caen. There he was taught by Lanfranc and William Bona Anima. Matilda is likely to have been responsible for introducing this fellow Fleming into the ducal court. As well as serving as Cecilia's tutor, he became a chaplain to Robert Curthose. In considering the type of cleric close to the ducal family, we should observe that he did not share the deep religious piety of his teachers; drawn to the secular life, he was know as "malcouronne" (ill tonsured). We can glimpse Arnulf's teaching through the writing of his pupil Raoul de Caen. The latter's *Gesta Tancredi*, an account of the Normans on the First Crusade, reveals that Raoul had studied classical literature including Virgil, Horace, Ovid, and Lucan, alongside the historians Livy, Caesar, and Sallust. In his preface Raoul praises his teacher's knowledge of the liberal arts and calls on him to correct his prosimetrical work. Interestingly, Cecilia's education was not

---

61 Van Houts, "Latin Poetry," 39–40 and 55–6; and Guy of Amiens, *CHP*, ed. Barlow, xxiv–liii.

62 Fulcoius, *Epistulae* 11. Van Houts, "Latin Poetry," 42.

63 Godfrey of Reims, "Ad Ingelrannum," line 135. Barlow, *William Rufus*, 441–5; Van Houts, "Latin Poetry," 47–8; and LoPrete, *Adela of Blois*, 23–4.

entrusted to a cleric with a narrow, pious range, focused on patristic learning. Arnulf's desire for new learning may in part stand behind Orderic's emphasis that Cecilia was not only educated but "erudita multipliciter."[64]

Judging by the poetry sent to Cecilia by Baudri and Hildebert, Arnulf of Chocques's education laid the foundation for her receptivity to the classicizing poetry of the Loire school. In writing to her, Baudri projects her dual role as daughter of a king, whom he hails as *augustus*, and bride of Christ. Baudri's exclamation that she surpasses all the girls of Rome evokes both the classical and the religious associations of that city. Ovidian and Virgilian echoes contribute to the transposing of the images of the bride of Christ into a much more courtly image than the one we are familiar with from the poetry of Wilton. The striking attractiveness of her body is openly acknowledged, in contrast to the Anonymous's discreetly respectful stance towards Edith.[65] Hildebert's more sophisticated poem fully invokes the Roman story world, legendary and mythological. Hildebert creates a persona for himself who, although worthy of comparison with Cicero, can hardly speak in Cecilia's presence because Nature has distinguished Cecilia from all the other goddesses. He casts a leering Ovidian eye when he writes:

maiestate tua stupui, totamque vaganti
percurrens oculo, sum ratus esse deam.

(I was stupefied by your majesty; running over it all
with a wandering eye, I considered you a goddess.)[66]

Like Baudri, he portrays Cecilia as the bride of Christ, and yet, also like his fellow poet, he does not hesitate to describe her in ways that frankly acknowledge not just her beauty but her sexual attraction.[67] The flirtatious nature of these poems suggests that the nunnery of Holy Trinity, like that of Le Ronceray and of Wilton, was open to the secular world.[68]

---

64 Ralph of Caen, *Gesta Tancredi*, prologue; Orderic Vitalis, *HE* 5.2 (3:9–10); David, *Robert Curthose*, 217–20; Foreville, "École de Caen," esp. 84–9; Musset, "Reine Mathilde," 202–3; Spear, "School of Caen," esp. 57; and Van Houts, "Matilda (d. 1083)." I am grateful to Elisabeth van Houts for discussing Cecilia's education with me.

65 Baudri, *Carmina* 136.

66 Hildebert, *Carmina Minora* 46.

67 Latzke, "Fürstinnenpreis," 60–2; and Van Houts, "Latin Poetry," 46–7.

68 Musset, "Reine Mathilde," 201–2; Spear, "School of Caen," 65–6; and Walmsley, "Early Abbesses," 435–7.

Baudri's poem for Cecilia also shows that the nuns of Holy Trinity were among the poetic correspondents of Baudri and Hildebert, as were the nuns of Wilton and of Le Ronceray. Furthermore, he reveals that they were part of a network of relationships between the nuns of these three foundations. At the end of his poem Baudri asks Cecilia to remember him to her *soror*, who was from Bayeux and then Angers. Tilliette suggests that this unnamed woman had been a sister at Le Ronceray, where Baudri may have met her. Since Le Ronceray was the only nunnery in Angers, this identification seems secure.[69] Earlier in chapter 5 we were able to see that the social networks of nuns united in their patronage of Loire school poetry may have lain behind Eve's move from Wilton to Angers. The mortuary roll of Matilda, founding abbess of Holy Trinity, was circulated to 253 monastic communities, including many of the major West Saxon royal nunneries (Nunnaminster, Wherwell, Amesbury, Shaftesbury, Wilton, Romsey, and Barking), illustrating the links of these foundations to Holy Trinity. The inclusion among the three poems added by Nunnaminster of a poem by a niece of Abbess Matilda points to specific personal ties between the newly founded Holy Trinity and the long-established nunnery culture of Wessex.[70] From this perspective we see not just random instances of contact between Hildebert and Baudri and nuns but rather a network of women who are in touch with each other and are also the correspondents of these poets. Some of the agency in the production of poetry for nuns shifts towards the women if we see that the cultivation of poetry took place across nunneries whose sisters were known to each other.

The presence of such ties between women points to the active nature of their literary culture and to the determining role that the education of patrons, recipients, and audiences played in the nature of the poetry. It is not incidental that Baudri effuses about Cecilia's learning, attributing it to her "sollicitudo legendi" (care for reading).[71] The Ovidian playfulness of both of the poems to Cecilia suggests that she was a sophisticated recipient of their classicizing verse and that her education at the hands of Arnulf, perhaps arranged by her mother, was formative. The selection of a tutor versed not only in Christian learning but also in classical learning points to a particular vision about the nature of nunneries and their openness to

69 Baudri, *Carmina* 136. Tilliette's notes to *Carmen* 136 (2:218); and Van Houts, "Latin Poetry," 47. See chapter 5 herein.

70 Delisle, *Rouleaux des morts*, 177–279 (for the West Saxon nunneries, 187–90, 278, and 279).

71 Baudri, *Carmina* 136, line 7.

court culture, and to a desire for both to be part of the latest cultural developments.

The self-presentation of the two men who wrote prose history for William the Conqueror also emphasizes that Cecilia was the first member of the ducal family to attract the literary attention of sophisticated poets like Baudri and Hildebert. William of Poitiers, as we have seen in comparing his *Gesta Guillelmi* with the *Encomium* and the *Vita Ædwardi*, wrote a classicizing prose. However, he ostentatiously situates his account of the Conqueror's life away from poetry and its fictions and chooses to liken William to a historical Caesar rather than to reflect on the value of the pagan Roman story world.[72] William of Jumièges, whose monastic education in Normandy did not involve classical learning, writes explicitly in his dedicatory letter to the Conqueror that he could not produce the elegant and weighty style used by the rhetoricians.[73] William of Poitiers's choice of prose and William of Jumièges's non-classicizing style corroborate the absence of classicizing verse for the Conqueror. Marbod and Hildebert were known to his brother Odo, but they did not write for the duke. Fulcoius, although he wrote a poem for the duke when Cecilia became a nun, was disparaging (in his poem figuring the German Henry IV as Octavian) about Norman ignorance of the "vates" (poets).[74] Guy of Amiens wrote about the duke but not for him.[75]

At this point it remains only to return to Cecilia and to consider chronology. She was not professed as a nun until 1075 and ruled as abbess from 1113 to 1127. Baudri wrote to her while she was a nun, and Hildebert while she was abbess – that is, well after the composition of the *Vita Ædwardi.* The patronage by Edith of classicizing poetry, for an audience that included the women of Wilton, was in advance of the development of similar poetry for nuns of Le Ronceray and Holy Trinity.

Adela, Countess of Blois

Recent work by van Houts and Bond has brought Adela of Blois into focus as an active patron of classicizing poetry written by the poets of the

72 William of Poitiers, *GG* 1.20 and 2.39. See chapters 2 and 4 herein.

73 William of Jumiègs, *GND*, prefatory letter. Van Houts's edition of *GND*, 1.xxxii–xxxv (for date) and 1.lix–lx (William's learning).

74 Fulcoius, *Epistulae* 1, line 217.

75 See earlier, page 277.

Loire school. Bond, in particular, revealed her politically astute use of poetry and, later in life, history writing to craft a powerful courtly persona, which evolves as she matures from a fiancée to young wife and mother to co-ruler and then to regent. In emphasizing that her patronage pre-dates that of Edith/Matilda, the wife of her brother, by some twenty years, Bond seeks to locate innovative secular engagement with Latin poetry in France rather than in England.[76] Recognition of the links between the *Vita Ædwardi* and the poetry of the Loire allows us to consider Adela's patronage in the context of not only what came after it but also what came before. In this section I will situate Adela's literary patronage within the social and literary lineages that bound together the women of the West Saxon, Godwine, and Norman dynasties. These lineages contributed to the creation of a literary culture, one of whose hallmarks was the use of the Roman story world as a politically and artistically powerful tool.

Adela's advanced literacy is repeatedly attested by cleric after cleric who responded to the opportunities she provided for patronage, figured her as learned, and wrote to her with a sophistication that assumes learning. Although we do not know for certain where she acquired her learning, it has been suggested that she was educated, like her sister Cecilia, by Arnulf of Chocques. Regardless of whether she was taught by Arnulf or other tutors, within the court or within the cloister, Adela's education, like that of her older sister, equipped her to use, enjoy, and reflect on the Roman story world.[77]

Adela was still a young woman when she was betrothed (around 1080) and then married (by 1085) to the Thibaudian Count Stephen of Blois-Chartres-Meaux.[78] The Thibaudian lands, which virtually encircled the Capetian Île de France, extended from the borders of Lotharingia in the north to Anjou in the south and almost to Normandy in the west.[79] The inclusion within her husband's patrimony of parts of the Loire valley and such important centres of learning as Reims and Chartres may have provided opportunities for Adela to continue to broaden her learning after her marriage. Adela's marriage also brought her political power. Not only was she sought as a bride because of her father, but as regent she herself

76 Van Houts, "Latin Poetry," 47–50; and Bond, *Loving Subject*, 129–57.

77 See earlier, page 278; and LoPrete, *Adela of Blois*, 29–34.

78 LoPrete, *Adela of Blois*, 34–9.

79 Parisse, *Atlas de la France*, 41–8; Bouchard, "Kingdom of the Franks," 122–3 and 137–8; and LoPrete, *Adela of Blois*, 67–9.

came to wield power during her husband's absences on crusade and then during the minority and young adulthood of his successor, her son, Thibaud IV.[80] Thus she was among the most powerful and most admired lords in Northern France. Her engagement with the history, philosophy, legend, and myth of Rome shaped her rulership and her education of her children.[81] From the beginning of Adela's project to use literary patronage to bolster her political power, the Roman story world was invoked. In a poem written when Adela could still be called a *virgo* Godfrey of Reims praises her as a goddess and attributes William's victory at Hastings to the need for her to be born to a royal father. He criticizes his fellow poet Ingelrannus as inadequate to the task of Adela's praise, which is worthy of the poets of antiquity.[82] Hildebert also, in two short poems, places her among the pagan goddesses of classical antiquity.[83]

Adela and Baudri: Countess and Poet

In Baudri's long poem to Adela (1,368 lines), written between 1099 and 1102, the classicism of Godfrey's earlier verse is fully developed.[84] We discussed Baudri's poem earlier in order to illustrate the affinities between the *Vita Ædwardi* and the poetry of the Loire.[85] Here we return to consider the light it sheds on Adela's place within the cultivation of classicizing poetry for English royal women in the decades after the Conquest. The poem is built around the conceit of the description of Adela's bedchamber, with the poet describing the room to his poem, which he is sending to the countess in his place. Its walls are decorated with tapestries, its ceiling with the constellations and planets, and its floor with a *mappa mundi*. Around her bed stand statues of Philosophy and the Seven Liberal Arts, who are joined by Medicine. This program of decoration draws heavily on the contemporary schoolroom curriculum, especially Martianus Capella's *De nuptiis philologiae et Mercurii*, and both classical and Christian poetry exert a strong influence on Baudri's poetry. Mary Carruthers has suggested

80 LoPrete, *Adela of Blois*, 71–231.

81 LoPrete, "Mother and Countess."

82 Godfrey of Reims, "Ad Ingelrannum," line 134. Latzke, "Fürstinnenpreis," 58; Van Houts, "Latin Poetry," 47–8; and Bond, *Loving Subject*, 145–6.

83 Hildebert, *Carmina Minora* 10 and 15.

84 Van Houts, "Latin Poetry," 49.

85 See chapter 4 herein.

that the poem could have been offered to Adela to use in educating her children.[86] Within the poem Baudri represents Adela not only as learned but specifically as more learned than her father; again, we are reminded of the leading role that royal women, rather than royal men, played as literary patrons throughout the eleventh century.[87] In a manner reminiscent of the Anonymous's depiction of Edith, Baudri describes Adela as both audience for and writer of verse.[88] As with the *Vita Ædwardi*, the active patronage of the poem's addressee is made part of the subject of the poem, with Baudri claiming that Adela commissioned it.[89]

Baudri's classicizing in his poem for Adela is very overt, with explicit references to classical figures as well as dense allusions to the poetry of Virgil, Ovid, Statius, and Lucan. Like the *Vita Ædwardi*, it would have provided many opportunities for literary discussion among its audience. Here I want to emphasize a familiar theme, the presentation of the Roman story world, alongside the biblical one, as a framework with which to understand contemporary political events – specifically the conquest of England by Adela's father. The tapestries that are said to decorate Adela's walls offer explicitly conflicting accounts of the same time period. The first depicts biblical events that Baudri denotes as *historia*.[90] The second depicts the story world of Greece and Rome, from Saturn to the fall of Troy and the founding of Rome. In this section, which most captures the poet's imagination and attention (he gives it more space than the biblical material), Baudri focuses on myth and legend, for which he uses the language of fiction: *fabula*, *umbras*, *ambages*, and *fictitia*.[91] Then he switches gears to the more historical Rome, which he denotes as *res Romana*.[92] This period, however, interests him less, and he simply says that the tapestry depicts the hundred kings of Rome. A third tapestry, said to be designed and executed by Adela herself and detailed at much greater length (over 300 lines), depicts the Conquest.[93] William in his fearsomeness is

86 Throughout, my discussion draws on the excellent notes provided in Tilliette's edition of Baudri's poems (*Carmina* 134) and Otter's translation; key additional recent discussions include Ratkowitsch, *Descriptio picturae*, 17–127. Carruthers, *Craft of Thought*, 213–20; and Heslop, "Regarding the Spectators," 235–7.

87 Baudri, *Carmina* 134, lines 37–8.

88 Baudri, *Carmina* 134, lines 39–42.

89 Baudri, *Carmina* 134, lines 53–4.

90 Baudri, *Carmina* 134, line 146.

91 Baudri, *Carmina* 134, lines 144, 170, and 178.

92 Baudri, *Carmina* 134, lines 205–6.

93 Baudri, *Carmina* 134, lines 235–572.

simultaneously compared to the Trojan Hector and the Greek Achilles, and the account culminates with William as the highest of the Caesars.[94] As Sandy Heslop has shown, the William tapestry evokes Virgil's account of the wall paintings, telling the story of Troy, which adorn Dido's Temple of Juno. Thus they pull together the Trojan foundation of Rome with William's English conquest, representing the latter as a parallel and continuation of the former.[95] In drawing on Dido's temple, Baudri also returns to passages of the *Aeneid* that had earlier fascinated the Anonymous.[96]

Baudri's exploration of fiction is not limited to the characterization of the classical past but rather encompasses the representation of recent events and involves recurrent metapoetic questioning. Although he introduces the tapestry account of the Conquest as "veras historias" (true histories), he destabilizes the possibility of the representation being straightforwardly true, repeatedly drawing attention to the status of his poetry as ekphrasis and thus to the levels of mediation involved.[97] Baudri explicitly presents the issue of credibility and mediation when he comments:

Veras crediderim uiuasque fuisse figuras,
  Ni caro, ni sensus deesset imaginibus.

(Truly, I would have believed the figures real and living
Had not the pictures lacked language and sense and flesh.)[98]

Then he goes on, addressing the poem that he is sending into Adela's chamber, to question the truth of his own account of the tapestry as well as of Adela's account:

Haec quoque, si credas haec uere uela fuisse,
  In uelis uere, cartula nostra, legas.
Sin autem, dicas: "Quod scripsit debuit esse,
  Hanc diuam talis materies decuit.

94 Baudri, *Carmina* 134, lines 445–6 and 558.
95 Heslop, "Regarding the Spectators," 237–40.
96 See chapter 4 herein.
97 Otter, notes to her translation of Baudri's *Carmina*, 61–3; and Heslop, "Regarding the Spectator," esp. 233 and 236.
98 Baudri, *Carmina* 134, lines 563–4.

Ipse coaptando quae conueniant speciei
  Istius dominae scripsit et ista decent."

(All this, if you believe it, was shown on that marvellous hanging;
  If you believe me, my book, you'll see it all when you go.
Or, if you don't, say, "What he wrote should have been real;
  All this is fitting – no more – for one so great, so divine.
Baudri has merely adjusted the beauties and splendours that should be
  Due to a lady like her; all that he's written is right.")[99]

These lines problematize the layers of narration involved in his poem. By describing the tapestry, he is representing a representation. What is especially interesting here is that this theorizing about fiction relates to an account of the Norman Conquest that he has denoted as "veras historias."[100]

In raising the issue of fiction at this point, he gestures towards many dimensions of the larger debate about fiction. First, there are competing accounts of the Conquest between Norman and English sides and from within either side. The way that the poem shares narrative elements with Guy of Amiens's *Carmen de Hastingae proelio*, William of Poitiers's *Gesta Guillelmi*, and the Bayeux Tapestry reminds the reader, regardless of whether or not Baudri knew these works directly, that this account is but one of many different versions – stories – of the Conquest.[101] Like the author of the *Vita Ædwardi*, Baudri reveals an awareness, which he incorporates into the theme of his poem, of his own account being one mediation of events that could be told from many different perspectives. Second, by raising these questions in the context of writing a poem about the Conquest (which is in effect what Baudri does for almost a quarter of this long poem), he enters the debate about the capacity for poetry to render a truthful account of history – a debate that we have seen running through the *Encomium*, the *Vita Ædwardi*, and the *Gesta Guillelmi*. Baudri then overtly locates the value of his account in its having narrated not what actually happened but what should have happened. Furthermore, by juxtaposing the Conquest tapestry with the biblical and classical tapestries, he presents the possibility of different kinds of truth. Although biblical truth

99 Baudri, *Carmina* 134, lines 567–72.
100 Baudri, *Carmina* 134, line 234.
101 Baudri, *Carmina*, ed. Tilliette, 2:172n96.

is clearly prioritized, it is also the least engaging or challenging section of the poem; as a *historia* it remains flat and unimaginative. Baudri combines two different accounts of the past, and an account of the Conquest as it should have been, with reflection on mediation and the possibility of pagan truth. His integration of these elements forcefully makes the point that intellectual and aesthetic theorizing about fiction was closely bound up with social and political experiences of arguing about contemporary politics, in this instance the Norman Conquest.

When it comes to thinking about the place of Adela's agency in commissioning Baudri's poem and to attending to the way in which poets respond to the learning of their patrons, Baudri's direct attribution of the design of all the tapestries to Adela is striking. Thus she is not just a passive recipient of the poem but is figured as actively participating in its creation. He writes:

> Astiterat dictans operantibus ipsa puellis
> Signaratque suo quid facerent radio.

> (She herself oversaw and instructed the girls in their working,
> Told them exactly what she wanted their shuttles to do.)[102]

Adela is responsible for creating an account of the Conquest and is imagined as engaged in the habit of juxtaposing the biblical and the classical with the contemporary. She herself is seen to compare her father to Hector, Achilles, and Caesar, and she herself participates in the multilayered fictionality in which the tapestry is embedded. Baudri figures her as, like Emma and Edith before her, taking control of how the Roman story world is deployed. He writes that she was responsible for the way the needlework "nobis iteret historias ueteres" (tells us once again histories told of old) and for the way the "elementa nouo moderamine iuncta / et librata suis singula ponderibus" (elements mixed in new combinations / Every one in its place, held by its proper weight).[103] The written word is relevant here. Throughout his long poem Baudri refers to the *tituli* that identify and explain the pictures of the tapestries, floors, and ceilings of Adela's chamber. By particularly dwelling on those that accompany this tapestry, Baudri effaces the distinction between himself as poet and master of

102 Baudri, *Carmina* 134, lines 103–4.
103 Baudri, *Carmina* 134, lines 98–100.

words, and Adela as weaver; she too takes on the role of wordsmith. As his account of the tapestry closes, he writes:

> Littera signabat sic res et quasque figuras,
> Vt quisquis uideat, si sapit, ipsa legat.
>
> (Each of the objects and figures were designated by letters;
> Literate viewers could read them as they observed.)[104]

Both Baudri and Adela use language in the crafting of their accounts of the Conquest. Baudri goes a step beyond the Anonymous in making his patron his co-creator. Although in the final lines of the poem, when he refers to his entire work as a *fabula* and a *fabella*, he renders Adela's composition a fiction and makes it his own creation, he still figures her as a collaborator in this exploration of fictionality.[105] Creativity is a central dimension of the image of ideal patronage that Baudri offers the countess.

The control that Baudri represents as belonging to Adela as designer of the tapestries makes evident his respect for her own creative capacities and is related to his generally deferential stance towards her. This deference spills over into his treatment of the potential for sexual tension between female patron and male poet. Baudri critiques the role of the sexually intrusive male cleric who flirts with women at court, playing out this issue by thematizing the subject of the male gaze.[106] This anxiety around sexual tension between poet and patron has an impact as well on his Ovidianism. Early in the poem he acknowledges that Adela's beauty attracts the male eyes but immediately responds that her dignity renders her as hard as granite ("tam duram silicem").[107] He goes on to represent himself as reduced not just to a peasant but, as we realize when we follow up the Ovidian allusion, to a peasant girl; that is, he is feminized when he simply catches sight of her. He blushes and turns away lest he find himself speechless.[108]

The politics of the gaze is further kept in view when Baudri compares Adela to Medusa, Circe, and Diana in quick succession.[109] Baudri reveals

---

104 Baudri, *Carmina* 134, lines 565–6.
105 Baudri, *Carmina* 134, lines 1351–4.
106 Bérat, "Patron and Her Cleric," 29.
107 Baudri, *Carmina* 134, line 70.
108 Baudri, *Carmina* 134, lines 75–6; and Ovid, *Meta.* 5, 583–4.
109 Baudri, *Carmina* 134, lines 79–88.

that the gaze is specifically at stake in these lines because he attributes Circe's ability to transform men into animals to her stare, rather than, more conventionally, to her magic potions. While Thomas Moser reads the invocation of these three mythical females as contributing to Baudri's turning of "the countess into an eroticized object of male desire," on the contrary these allusions function to mark repeatedly the dangerous transgression entailed in sexualizing Adela, either in verse or through one's actions. In identifying Medusa, Circe, and Diana as seductresses Moser conflates the three and overlooks their particular relevance to Adela.[110]

Ovid records, with approval, that Minerva turned Medusa's beautiful hair into snakes as punishment when Neptune ravished the beautiful woman in the virgin goddess's temple. Anyone who subsequently looked on her was turned to stone. Perseus succeeded in cutting off her head by looking at her only indirectly in the mirrored surface of his shield.[111] Baudri's knowledge of Medusa extends beyond Ovid. His poetic reworking of Fulgentius's *Mitologiae* explains that, before Medusa was killed by Perseus, she had ruled her father's kingdom after his death, surpassing him and other kings in her ability to amass wealth. In Fulgentius's and Baudri's versions Perseus conquers Medusa because he desired her riches for himself. Later Baudri glosses Medusa as "neqeat ... videre" (she is not able to see) and offers an allegorical reading in which Perseus represents *sapientia* slaying a cause of fear.[112] The complexity of Baudri's Medusa is not easily resolvable.[113] Bond sees the double appearance of Medusa in *Carmina* 134 and 154 as evidence that Baudri was eliciting Adela's response as an allegorical reader, because otherwise she would have been offended by the allusion.[114] However, even when read allegorically as blindness, Medusa remains potentially insulting. I would like to emphasize rather the way that Medusa recalls the dangers that face politically powerful ruling women, a theme to which the historian Hugh of Fleury will return in addressing Adela later in her life.[115] The Medusa of *Carmen* 154 encourages us to read the reference to Medusa in the Adela poem as less about a seductive woman and more about how a powerful woman deflects the sexual advances of men, which would threaten her dominion (a theme all too familiar to Dido).

110 Moser, *Cosmos of Desire*, 59–63.
111 Ovid, *Meta.* 4.769–803 and 5.1–249.
112 Baudri, *Carmina* 134, lines 283 and 285.
113 Baudri, *Carmina* 154, lines 251–98.
114 Bond, *Loving Subject*, 150.
115 See pages 294–8.

The comparison of Adela to Circe also poses challenges to the reader. Baudri's rewriting of Circe's story so that it fits his theme of the gaze assures us that he particularly wanted to include this mythical figure in his poem. Ovid's Circe was not just a sexually voracious woman who made Ulysses her husband ("thalamoque receptus/coniugii") but also a successful queen, a courtly figure who ruled in her own right.[116] In reading Baudri's poem, we should also entertain the possibility that he has redeemed as well as rewritten Circe and Medusa, presenting them from a woman's rather than a man's standpoint. In rewriting these stories, he takes a playful approach to the myths of Rome and participates in and continues their fiction. In the next chapter, when we look at Abbess Willetrudis's reworking of the biblical story of Susanna, we will return to the subject of women resisting the male gaze.[117]

The reference to Diana maintains Baudri's exploration of the gaze and the risk that men take when they are attracted by the beauty of powerful women. According to Ovid's telling, when the hunter Actaeon accidently caught sight of Diana bathing, she turned him into a stag, whereupon he was promptly devoured by his own hunting dogs.[118] The Actaeon story was another that Baudri allegorizes in *Carmen* 154.[119] Although the virgin goddess was not a ruler, like Medusa and Circe, her role as protector of young children and women in childbirth gives her specific significance for Adela.

The allusions to Medusa, Circe, and Diana are multivalent, simultaneously figuring Adela as a mother and a powerful ruler, and as gazed on and as gazer, while warning her of the danger that sexuality poses to women who seek to assert political control. In interpreting Baudri's use of classical allusion in this passage, we need to read from the standpoint of his primary intended audience, Adela, a learned and authoritative women whose favour he sought. From this perspective we find not eroticization but a warning to both countess and courtier poet of the threat posed by the erotic, and a strong assertion of Baudri's own rejection of the sexual objectification of his patron. Indeed, Baudri's admittance to Adela's *thalamus*, her bedchamber in the sense of her private quarters, becomes dependent on his averted eyes as he claims that he barely saw her ("vix ipsam uidi").[120]

116 Ovid, *Meta.* 14.247–415.

117 See chapter 7 herein.

118 Ovid, *Meta.* 3.155–252.

119 Baudri, *Carmina* 154, lines 1119–38.

120 Baudri, *Carmina* 134, line 87.

The use of the term *thalamus* here and in Ovid's account of Circe further ties the poet's entry into her bedchamber to his recasting of Ovid's goddess. He seeks to commend himself to the countess by using the Roman story world to present her with models of power rather than objectification. His respect and his lack of intrusion, not his sexual advances, gain him admittance. In the final lines of the poem, moreover, we see the poet's body, not Adela's, as he first solicits a cloak and a shirt from the countess and then tries to get her to look at him: "Si me respicies, id michi sufficiet" (All I want is a look – that is sufficient for me).[121] The clothed woman and the naked supplicating man is an arresting image not only of sexual restraint but of a reversed sexual vulnerability that can helpfully be contextualized through a brief comparison with some of Baudri's, Marbod's, and Hildebert's other verses for women.

Generally, Baudri suppressed the erotic in his verse for women, as would seem appropriate given that all his correspondents except Adela were nuns. Two exceptions stand out: his poem to Constance and his poem to Cecilia.[122] Marbod's deeply misogynist streak draws him to objectify women in a way that Baudri avoids. This stance is evident in his poems to a young woman, perhaps a laywoman being educated in Le Ronceray, his poem to the Breton countess Ermengarde, and his poems on good and bad women.[123] Hildebert's poems provide a remarkable parallel to Baudri's poems to Adela and Cecilia. He is similarly more reserved towards Adela, even though she is married, than he is towards her sister Cecilia, whose body he does not hesitate to look up and down. He assures the countess that he seeks favours neither of her hand nor of her neck but of her mind: "mente fave."[124] Looking at these three poets suggests that the combination of Adela's political power and her Latinity had an impact on the way she was presented by Baudri and Hildebert; she was off limits in a way that her sister, though a nun, was not. Baudri was highly conscious of the potential for erotic tension between poet and laywoman, but he was equally clear that in the case of Adela this was no route to

121 Baudri, *Carmina* 134, line 1362.

122 Baudri, *Carmina* 134, lines 136 and 200. Bond, "*Iocus Amoris*," 168; and see chapter 5 herein.

123 Marbod, "M. episcopus E. comitissae"; Marbod, *Liber decem capitulorum* 3 and 4, and Marbod's poems published in Bulst, "Liebesbriefgedichte Marbods." Bulst, "Liebesbriefgedichte Marbods," 300–1; Dronke, *European Love Lyric*, 1.213–14, Dronke, *Women Writers*, 85; and Moser, *Cosmos of Desire*, 43–6.

124 Hildebert, *Carmina Minora* 10 and 15, line 4.

patronage; thus the poem is shot through with what Otter has identified as the uneasy Ovidianism of its "latent eroticism."[125] This perception of Adela's role in enforcing the restraint shown by her poets may indicate that she is not the subject of Godfrey of Reims's poem "Satyra de quadam puella virgine," as Bond has suggested. This perception is further strengthened by the terms of Godfrey's praise of Adela in his poem to Ingelrannus that shies away from any but the most general reference to her beauty.[126] The *Vita Ædwardi* fits in here too; the Anonymous knows Ovid, but he also knows that the erotic does not suit his story of Edith and Edward's chaste marriage and that he dare not intrude on the queen.[127] Active patronage by a politically powerful and Latinate laywoman desexualizes the relationship with the poet.[128]

Adela, like Edith before her, earned the praise of her poets for her chaste devotion to her husband and her fertility. Where Edith's chastity was intimated to be virginity, and her numerous children were spiritual, Adela, mother of as many as nine children, is adorned by their nobility.[129] Indeed, Carruthers argues that Adela's maternity invites Baudri to pun in a literal way on her fertility, which we might see as taking the place of erotic punning.[130] In light of Adela's evident fertility, Baudri's depiction of Lady Philosophy, a statue that stands beside Adela's bed, as both mother and teacher (*magistra*) of the Seven Liberal Arts explicitly recalls the countess herself (953–70) and provides a further point of noteworthy contact with the *Vita Ædwardi*, where Edith and Lady Philosophy were associated in the figure of the muse.[131] Philosophy, like Adela early in the poem, is both beautiful and awe inspiring. Although her breasts are described as pouring forth milk (an image that the Anonymous also took from Boethius to describe his muse), Baudri hastens to tell us that Philosophy is fully clothed.

125 Otter's introduction to *Carmen* 134.

126 Bond, *Loving Subject*, 147–8. Tilliette ("*Troiae ab oris*," 421–2) disagrees with Bond, and Broecker does not accept the identification (Godfrey of Reims, *Gottfried*, ed. Broecker, 198–203).

127 See chapter 5 herein.

128 My thinking on the place of the erotic in the poetry of Baudri, Hildebert, Marbod, Godfrey, and the Anonymous has benefited from discussion with Emma O'Loughlin Bérat; see her "Patron and Her Clerk."

129 Baudri, *Carmina* 134, line 62; and *VE* 1.6.

130 Carruthers, *Craft of Thought*, 217–18.

131 Baudri, *Carmina* 134, lines 953–70; and *VE* 1, prologue, and 2, prologue. See chapter 5 herein, and Otter's note to lines 954–64.

Positive images of fertility come into view again in the extended description of Medicine, who joins Philosophy and the Seven Liberal Arts among the statues around Adela's bed.[132] Baudri finishes his description of Medicine, which is his final view of her bedroom, with the image of Hippocrates and Galen warm in her womb.[133] Thus he draws his poem to a close with images of mothers of male and female children who take on roles that (as LoPrete demonstrates) Adela as mother took on for herself, acquiring both tutors and physicians for her children.[134]

Baudri's interest in fertility continues as he turns to address the countess directly in the final lines of the poem. He includes a subtle and, given the poet's sexual restraint, complex image. As Carruther's translation draws out (and Otter concurs), Baudri imagines that he has inseminated the parchment book, which swells with his poem, a child growing in the womb.[135] Blurring the line between the book and Adela, Baudri, in the persona of the poet, hopes that Adela, for whom he has laboured, will not be sterile for him (1350). This language is sexual but in a creative way that does not objectify Adela; it further links her role as mother to his poem and picks up on the poet, rather than the countess, as naked. She is figured in maternal language as part of the process of producing the poem, which would be lifeless without her. Adela's patronage results in a poem in which pregnancy and maternity are not terrible dangers to be endured or escaped through holy virginity (as in the misogynist tradition that touches the *Vita Ædwardi* epithalamium and will shape Serlo of Bayeux's poem to Muriel, nun of Wilton, to be discussed in the next chapter); they are positive images of creativity that stand in for poetic composition.[136] Indeed, Baudri's designation of the poem as a *fabula* at this point underscores the creativity of the poem in its use of the language of fiction.[137] Throughout the poem Baudri's handling of Ovid's eroticism, the myths to which he chooses to refer (Medusa and Circe among many others), and his representation of Adela as the originator of the Conquest tapestry show her as having a direct impact on the way he deployed the Roman story world. If

132 Baudri, *Carmina* 134, lines 1255–1342.

133 Baudri, *Carmina* 134, lines 1337–8.

134 LoPrete, "Mother and Countess," 317–20 and 325.

135 Carruthers, *Craft of Thought*, 218; and Otter's note to lines 1347–50.

136 *VE*, 1.6; and Serlo of Bayeux, "Versus ad Muriel sanctimonialem," lines 233–40, on which see further in chapter 6 herein.

137 Baudri, *Carmina* 134, line 1346.

it is correct to suggest, as I did in the previous chapter, that Baudri knew the *Vita Ædwardi*, we can see Adela as a direct heir of Edith, despite the change of dynasty.[138]

Adela and Hugh of Fleury: Countess and Historian

Hugh of Fleury's *Historia ecclesiastica*, written for Adela in two stages over 1109 and 1110, provides further perspectives on the intellectual and political contexts in which she encountered and used the Roman story world and on the way in which her experience had an impact on the wider network of Anglo-Norman royal women.[139] In the prefatory letter to Adela, Hugh identifies the text as a history of emperors from the time of Octavian to Louis the Pious.[140] However, his work is actually a more ambitious universal history that draws on a range of sources to interweave pagan, biblical, Christian, and imperial history. Although Hugh does not claim that Adela commissioned the text, he closely associates it with her. The later recension of the *Historia* sent to Bishop Ivo of Chartres continues to identify the text as the history written for Adela.[141] A desire to please her and to teach her shapes his work everywhere.[142]

The extensive preface seeks directly to engage the countess, appealing to her both as ruler and as learned woman. Hugh boldly addresses her as the foremost prince of her day and mounts an audacious defence of women's learning. He not only praises Adela's intellect, but, in a claim that recalls Baudri's that she was more learned than her father, Hugh writes emphatically: "Sed tam compendiosum et honestum volumen non illiteratis principibus, quibus ars litteratoria spretui est, sed vobis merito dedicavi, ne nominis vestri monimentum ulla valeat umquam vetustate corrumpi, quae posterorum memoriae solet inimicari" (But I dedicated such a compact and honorable volume not to uneducated princes, for whom the literary

138 See chapter 5 herein.

139 There is no full modern edition of Hugh's *Historia*. The fullest printed edition is Rottendorf's. For discussion of the manuscripts see Waitz's introduction to his partial edition, 337–49. For further discussion of manuscripts of the two versions see Wilmart, "Histoire ecclésiastique," and Lettinck, "Édition critique."

140 Neither the preface nor the epilogue addressed to Adela are edited by Rottendorf; see Waitz, 349–51 and 353.

141 The letter to Ivo is edited by Wilmart, "Histoire ecclésiastique," 297. Lettinck, "Edition critique," 390.

142 Ferrante, *Glory of Her Sex*, 97–8, drawing on an unpublished paper of LoPrete.

art is to be scorned, but deservedly to you, so that the monument of your name would never be tarnished by age).[143]

Hugh finds more learning and opportunity for patronage with Adela than with her male peers and provides evidence that secular women were seen as literary patrons for generations before their fathers, brothers, and sons were, even when these men, like Adela's brothers and sons, had some education.[144] Telling in this regard is his expressed hope that his *Libellus de regia potestate et sacerdotali dignitate*, dedicated to Adela's brother Henry I, would reach not the king himself but his ministers.[145] In his prefatory letter to the *Historia*, addressing Adela, Hugh draws a distinction between two kinds of audiences for his work: educated and uneducated. To the latter it offers an accessible summary, and to the former, who read a great deal, it offers a brief reminder of what they already know. He goes on to refer those who are not satisfied with his short work to the rich and magnificent volumes that were his sources. He clearly classifies Adela among these educated readers, and while there is no doubt that an element of flattery is involved, the move accords with Baudri's poem and with Hildebert's advice to her that, as a ruler, she should read Seneca's Letter to Nero on clemency.[146] LoPrete suggests that Hugh's work may have been intended for Adela to use in teaching her children, just as Carruthers suggested for Baudri's poem.[147] Indeed, the straightforward Latin of Hugh's text lends itself to instruction, whether being read by a student or extemporaneously translated. Adela acted as a meeting point between the educated and the uneducated reader, a role that could extend beyond her interactions with her children.

In defending himself for writing for women, Hugh appeals to three examples: Jerome's many works for Paula and Eustochium; Gregory the Great's putative gift of a copy of the *Dialogi* for the Lombard queen Theodelinda; and Christ's teaching of women, who proved themselves to be more devout than even the apostles.[148] Paula and Eustochium, whom we have seen Goscelin invoke repeatedly for the women of Wilton, though

143 Hugh of Fleury, *HE*, epilogue (Waitz, 353).

144 David, *Robert Curthose*, 6; J.A. Green, *Henry I*, 22–3; and LoPrete, "Mother and Countess," 320.

145 Hugh of Fleury, *Libellus de regia potestate*, prologue.

146 Hildebert, *Epistolae* 1.3.

147 LoPrete, "Mother and Countess," 320; and Carruthers, *Craft of Thought*, 213.

148 Hugh of Fleury, *HE*, prefatory letter (Waitz, 349–51).

they appear widely as examples of a pious widow and a virgin, were no mere commonplace for Hugh or Adela. Jerome's many letters to these two women, alongside the prefaces to the biblical commentaries that they requested from him, attest to their advanced learning, as does Jerome's repeated requests that they check his work.[149] They model an authoritative female literacy, ranging across pagan and Christian writers, which Hugh urges Adela to take up. If we take seriously Hugh's depiction of Adela as learned and thus among those who could turn to the books themselves rather than relying on Hugh's brief narrative, we should not be surprised to find her familiar with Jerome's letters or encouraged by Hugh's letter to become familiar with them. Perhaps as Adela, once a lover of classicizing poetry, was widowed and began to contemplate the monastic life for herself, these two fourth-century nuns and their own deep classical learning, never wholly left behind, spoke directly to her.

Writing for Adela shapes how Hugh tells the history of antiquity.[150] Like his model, Justinus's third-century *Epitome* of the lost Phillipic history by Pompeius Trogus, Hugh begins his history with the reign of the Assyrian king Ninus and his wife Semiramis, who after the death of her husband famously ruled by dressing as a man until she was killed by her son. Although he follows Justinus almost word for word, he makes one critical change: he leaves out the incest between mother and son in order to transform the queen from a figure of lasciviousness into one of a powerful ruling woman.[151] Van Houts's argument – that the Semiramis poem found in a manuscript associated with the Norman duchess Gunnor satirized the marriage of Emma and Cnut – illustrates just how that wanton Semiramis could function as political discourse and a negative exemplum aimed at women.[152] It is hard not to read the invocation and reworking of this myth by Hugh as a pointed piece of political advice to a countess who continued to rule as regent even after her son had reached adulthood. In an echo of Baudri's own sexual restraint in writing to Adela, there is no suggestion of sexual impropriety, but the warning about her position remains clear. Hugh similarly modifies the story of the Amazons, removing the

149 Jerome, *Epistulae* 22, 30, 31, 33, 39, 46, and 108. Ferrante, *Glory of Her Sex*, 47–52; and see chapter 5 herein.

150 Ferrante, *Glory of Her Sex*, 97–8.

151 Hugh of Fleury, *HE* (Rottendorf, 1–2); and Justinus, *Epitome* 1.2.

152 *Semiramis*, ed. Dronke. Samuels, "Semiramis in the Middle Ages," 33–6; Van Houts, "*Jezebel* and *Semiramis*," esp. 21; and see chapter 3 herein.

points that they had sex with foreign men in order to conceive children and that they murdered the male offspring to insure a female-ruled kingdom. Ultimately these legendary women are subdued by Hercules, but the removal of sex and infanticide transforms them into a space in which the dynamics and dangers of female political power can be explored.[153] Given the learning that Hugh has attributed to Adela and the fact that the stories of Semiramis and the Amazons were not recherché, we can ask if she herself would have been conscious of this transformation: it seems likely that she was, that is, that Adela herself not only occasioned but participated in debates about the nature of *historia*.

In seeking to use history to offer political advice to Adela, Hugh discovers that writing for a woman requires a rewriting of the past because history in its preoccupation with ruling men did not speak to ruling women. Not only does his rewriting underscore the overriding value of the exemplarity (rather than the fact) of history writing, but it also emphasizes how seriously he took Adela as the dedicatee of his work. His address to Adela was no mere token or pitch for reward but a serious attempt to write (and rewrite) history for the countess. Significantly, he did not see his revisionist work as suited only for her eyes; not only did he send it to Ivo of Chartres, but some years later he rededicated the work for King Louis VI of France. Hugh's history would come to circulate widely; over thirty manuscripts or fragments survive, including one copied by William of Malmesbury.[154] From this perspective we see clearly how female patronage and readership could transform the nature of history itself.

In addition to any discussions that might have been provoked by Hugh's modifications of Semiramis and the Amazons, at other points he flags the issue of the truth value of the pagan world and the nature of history writing in ways that would have chimed with what Adela read in Baudri's poetry. After listing the judges of Israel and referring to Paris's abduction of Helen and the reign of Agamemnon, he notes that at this time renowned grammarians made up stories ("celebres apud Grammaticos fabulae sunt inuentae").[155] These *fabulae* range from Triptolemus and Ceres, through the Minotaur, Medusa, Oedipus, Ganymede, and finally the Danae. A brief mention of the fall of Troy and Aeneas's journey to

153 Hugh of Fleury, *HE* (Rottendorf, 29–30); and Justinus, *Epitome* 2.4.

154 Hugh of Fleury, *HE* (Oxford, Bodleian Library, Selden B 16). Thomson, *William of Malmesbury*, 66–7, and see chapter 7 herein.

155 Hugh of Fleury, *HE* (Rottendorf, 4).

Italy is placed ambiguously between these myths and the resumption of biblical history with Saul and David.[156] Later Hugh will follow his account of pagan philosophers, whom he treats with respect, with an assertion of the priority of the biblical prophets.[157] Finally, when we step back and consider the form of the *Historia ecclesiastica* up to the birth of Christ in the reign of Octavian, we find the repeated juxtaposition of biblical and pagan history that recalls the Old Testament and the Greek tapestries which Baudri imagined for Adela's bedroom, as well as the Anonymous's juxtaposition of biblical and pagan truth, and the questions he posed about different kinds of historical truth.[158]

Although Hugh's history ends before the arrival of the Normans in Francia, his epilogue illustrates his understanding of the intimate relationship between the Roman Imperial history that has been his subject and the history of Adela's own family.[159] Celebrating Adela's paternal genealogy from Rollo, Hugh compares William the Conqueror to Julius Caesar (as we found in the pages of William of Poitiers, Guy of Amiens, and the poets of the Loire) and to Claudius as the only emperors who dared attempt the subjection of Britain. Hugh's Romanizing reference to Adela's own lineage comes in the context of his suggestion that, if Adela so desired, he would write for her a history of the Franks, including her ancestors, the Danes and the Normans. Thus he appeals to her as a keeper of her own family's history and urges on her a role that Anglo-Saxon and Imperial women had fulfilled for centuries. Hugh appears never to have written such a history for Adela, but he did write precisely such a work for her niece, Empress Matilda.[160] Matilda, daughter of Adela's brother Henry I and his Wilton-educated wife Edith/Matilda, was then the young wife of the German emperor Henry IV. In preparation for this marriage the Anglo-Norman princess had been sent to be educated in the household of the Bishop of Trier so that she would be able to speak German; since she was literate, she appears also to have been taught Latin there.[161] In the preface to his history for Matilda, Hugh directs her to the *Historia* that he

156 Hugh of Fleury, *HE* (Rottendorf, 4–5).

157 Hugh of Fleury, *HE* (Rottendorf, 24–7).

158 See chapter 4 herein.

159 Hugh of Fleury, *HE*, epilogue (Waitz, 353).

160 Hugh of Fleury, *Liber qui modernorum*. Lettinck, "Édition critique," 391–2. Lettinck thinks that the epilogue that occurs in the first version only of the *HE* was never sent to Adela. It was modified and included in the preface to book 6 of the second version of the *HE* and also modified for the preface to the *Liber qui modernorum*.

161 Chibnall, *Empress Matilda*, 11 and 25.

wrote for Adela, if she wishes to know more about history before the time of Louis the Pious.[162] This expectation that she could acquire a text written for her aunt reveals that the two were seen as connected by literary and dynastic lineage.[163] The obligation of family commemoration united women across the generations of one family, encouraging the circulation of texts between them, just as their international marriages insured that these lineages would create literary as well as dynastic connections across the courts of northern Europe, including but extending well beyond the Anglo-Saxon and the Norman.

The suggestion that Adela used both Baudri's poem and Hugh's history to teach her children naturally raises the question of whether she passed her literary learning and awareness of its political utility on to her own daughters. Unfortunately little is known of them, including how many she had and which were her step-daughters.[164] Among her granddaughters, however, we see the continued importance of aristocratic ties to both the old Anglo-Saxon royal nunneries and the new ducal foundation at Caen. Isabel, daughter of Adela's first-born son, William, succeeded her great aunt Cecilia as abbess of Holy Trinity, though we can only wonder what, if any, literary education she received.[165] Isabel's cousin, Mary of Blois, daughter of King Stephen and Matilda of Boulogne, was a nun first at Stratford and then at Lillechurch before entering Romsey, where she became abbess. Mary was the granddaughter of Adela of Blois on her father's side and of the Wilton-educated Mary, daughter of Margaret of Scotland, on her mother's side. In Mary of Blois's assumption of the abbacy of Romsey we see the coming together of Anglo-Saxon and Norman lineages, such as those celebrated in the marriage of Edith/Matilda and Henry I, within the convent walls. Mary, the only heir of Boulogne, was later forced to leave Romsey to wed Matthew of Flanders, recalling Margaret of Scotland's marriage to Malcolm, when she would have preferred to remain a bride of Christ. After bearing him two daughters, Mary returned to the monastic life, becoming a nun at Sainte-Austreberthe near Montreuil, and thus brought her knowledge of an ancient Anglo-Saxon nunnery to this newer foundation on the Continent.[166]

162 Hugh of Fleury, *Liber qui modernorum*, 376–7.
163 Ferrante, *Glory of Her Sex*, 96.
164 LoPrete, *Adela of Blois*, 551–3.
165 Orderic Vitalis, *HE* 7.9 (4:46–7).
166 Thompson, "Mary."

Conclusion

Many striking parallels mark the literary patronage of Edith and Adela, as well as the *Vita Ædwardi* and Baudri's *Carmen* 134. Both were powerful Latinate women who pushed the Roman story world into new spaces as they looked for tools with which to interpret and articulate their political ambitions. These women were also asked to engage in urgent metapoetic reflection on the truth value of the classical past, both fictional and historical. Thus we can see that secular pressure, exerted especially by women, for new frameworks with which to shape their experience, alongside a consciousness of the subjective mediated nature of historical narration, contributed to eleventh- and twelfth-century debates about the nature and ethics of fiction. Nunneries played an important part in the ability of women to reach out to the classical past. Edith and Adela were raised within families that supported nunneries. If Adela was educated in part at Holy Trinity, as some suggest, then she shared a convent education with Edith. Regardless, it was with her generation that the ducal family began to educate its daughters in a manner similar to that already experienced by elite Anglo-Saxon women.

Another defining feature of their literary patronage was its internationalism. The *Vita Ædwardi* is the result of a multilingual English woman, with a Danish mother and a Norman husband, attracting into her service a cleric who had ties to Flanders and to the poetry of the Loire. The poetry and history for Adela similarly cannot be labelled as the cultural heritage of any one country or region; she was the daughter of a Norman duke and an English king and a franco-Flemish mother; she was educated in Normandy, perhaps by a Flemish cleric. Her education, along with that of her sister Cecilia, at once drew on traditions that her mother had brought to Normandy and was part of her parent's new regal self-fashioning. We should not imagine that her parents were unaware of the Anglo-Saxon royal nunneries and their close ties to court. They knew Edith from her appearances at William's court and in Winchester.[167] She, after all, did not leave England in 1067. The Anglo-Saxon Chronicle "D," with which we began this chapter, later draws attention to the care that William lavished on her burial, placing Edith in Westminster beside her husband Edward.[168]

167 Stafford, *QEQE*; and see chapter 5 herein.

168 ASC "D" s.a. 1067.

Moreover, Edith was related to Matilda and William through both her marriage to Edward the Confessor and her brother Tostig's marriage to Judith. Meanwhile, Adela's predecessors among the women of the Thibaudian comital family are not known as literary patrons. The arrival of an educated and powerful royal woman from outside the Thibaudian lands attracted poets and historians, thus stimulating the development of literary innovation.

The recognition that the *Vita Ædwardi* was the product of a poet from the Loire school allows us to reassess the relationship of Adela's and Edith's patronage and indeed to see both, in their own right, from new perspectives. The men who wrote for them worked within the same poetic movement, as the close thematic and linguistic parallels between Baudri's poetry and the *Vita Ædwardi* attest. These poets, along with Hugh of Fleury, were pushed towards daringly imaginative new uses of the Roman story world by powerful Latinate women who could appreciate their expertise and reward them accordingly. The conjunction of an educated woman, political exigency, and a receptive audience occurred first in Anglo-Saxon England, where a Loire poet found early patronage, well before Adela attracted the attention of Godfrey, Baudri, and Hildebert. However, internationalism makes the point that it is a misapprehension to frame the emergence of this new secular Latinate literary culture in terms of the priority of France or England, as Gerald Bond does when he writes that Adela's antecedence to Edith/Matilda makes this an essentially French development.[169] The active female patronage of mobile women contributed to the creation of networks of poets across Northern France, Normandy, Flanders, and England and was an essential element in the development of secular literary culture in Europe. Perceiving the connections between Edith and Adela offers insights into the dynamics of female patronage, underscores the importance of Latinity, agency, and political necessity as instruments of change, and reveals the truly European nature of the literary culture they fostered.

169 Bond stresses the priority of France over England (*Loving Subject*, 1–17, and also 156).

7 Edith Becomes Matilda

Introduction

The transformation of the Anglo-Scottish princess Edith, woman of Wilton, into the Anglo-Norman queen Matilda enabled the West Saxon dynasty to return to the throne (albeit through a woman) and brought the literary culture of the Anglo-Saxon royal nunnery directly into the Norman court. Edith was born in 1080 to the Anglo-Saxon princess and Scottish queen Margaret and her husband King Malcolm III; her baptismal name, evoking as it did both Ediths of Wilton (the saint and the queen), signals the continued prestige of the West Saxon royal dynasty within late-eleventh-century Britain. Her married name, which recalls that of the Conqueror's wife, did not, however, represent an entirely new marital identity: Matilda of Flanders was the princess's godmother, and Matilda's son Robert Curthose was her godfather. This choice of godparents reveals starkly that her political capital was recognized from her birth. It was not enough, however, to be born into the West Saxon line; she had to be raised as an Anglo-Saxon princess, and this provides the context for her Wilton education. Seeking her hand as soon as he became king in 1100, Henry I clearly desired this planned union of genealogies. During their marriage she bore two children, Matilda and William, and wielded extensive political power, especially when her husband's ducal responsibilities detained him in Normandy. Henry I publically commemorated her Anglo-Saxon identity, and thus the descent of their children, when he had her buried in 1118 in Westminster near the graves of Edward the Confessor and Edith.[1]

---

1 This introduction draws particularly on Chibnall, *Empress Matilda*; Huneycutt, *Matilda of Scotland*; and King, *King Stephen*. Throughout the chapter I am especially

The hope that the marriage of Henry I and Edith/Matilda would result in an Anglo-Norman dynasty appeared dashed when their only son, William, drowned in the sinking of the *White Ship* in 1120. By then, Edith/Matilda had been dead for over two years, leaving no possibility of a further son of her union with Henry. Without any legitimate male heir, Henry married Adeliza of Louvain shortly after the *White Ship* disaster. This marriage had no issue, and in 1127 Henry I recognized as heir his daughter, Matilda, now the widow of the German emperor Henry V. Once again, the possibility of Anglo-Norman rule returned, but this time it involved the momentous challenge of accepting a woman, not just as a conduit of ancestry but as a ruler. The result was a long period of civil war, with Stephen, son of Adela of Blois, claiming the throne in opposition to the empress. Resolution only came when the Empress Matilda's son, Henry II, was recognized as Stephen's heir.

From Edith/Matilda's christening to Henry II's assumption of the throne in 1154 female lineage was under intense scrutiny. Not only did any links to the Anglo-Saxon past come through Margaret and Edith/Matilda, but during the long period of civil war even the links back to the Conqueror were traced through women: Henry II was the son of his granddaughter, and Stephen was the son of his daughter. Before the empress was widowed, Stephen appeared to have been Henry I's favoured successor, and he himself was keenly aware of the strong impulse to create an Anglo-Norman dynasty. In 1125 he married Matilda of Boulogne, the daughter of Mary, who like her sister Edith/Matilda had been educated in an Anglo-Saxon royal nunnery.

The empress's claim to the throne and the wider importance of descent, be it Anglo-Saxon or Norman, through the maternal line made female lineage an urgent political issue for the whole of the first half of the twelfth century and one that would leave its mark on the literary culture that English royal women made part of their political power. The preoccupation of the hagiography, poetry, and historiography written for Edith/Matilda with her lineage reveals her actively using it to enhance her political position; in so doing, she might seem to follow in the footsteps of her sister-in-law Adela of Blois.[2] Whereas Adela commemorated her father, however, the importance of maternal descent ensured that female lineage

---

indebted to Huneycutt's publications on Edith/Matilda. For the burial of Edith/Matilda see *Liber Monasterii de Hyda* 31, and J.A. Green, *Henry I*, 140.

2 Bond, *Loving Subject*, 156.

newly came to be the subject of history and poetry alike. Where the *Encomium*, the *Vita Ædwardi*, and Baudri's poem, and even Hugh's history for Adela, largely preserved stories about men (even if from a female perspective), the texts written for Edith/Matilda wrote women into history and poetry. Scholars since Bezzola have been alert to Edith/Matilda's literary patronage, with Huneycutt in particular arguing compellingly that this patronage, which followed Anglo-Saxon queenly practice, was an important dimension of her political power.[3] The focus of this chapter will build on Huneycutt's work to reveal the ways in which the queen was following a specifically Anglo-Saxon model, with its distinct investment in classicism, internationalism, and the agency of women patrons and readers. Edith/Matilda's active literary patronage, which aimed to make known, enhance, and preserve her royal lineage, changed the landscape not only of early twelfth-century English literary culture but of western Europe more widely.

Turgot's Life of Saint Margaret

In the previous chapter we used Turgot's life of Saint Margaret for the insight it offered on its subject, the saintly Scottish queen. The text also provides grounds for considering the use of texts by Margaret's daughter in the exercise of her queenship. In the prologue Turgot elaborates his claim that he wrote Margaret's *Vita* at the request of the newly married Edith/Matilda. Drawing out his account of its inception and emphasizing her commanding role in its production through wordplay, he writes: "et postulando jussistis, & jubendo postulastis" (in requesting you have commanded, and in commanding you have requested). Indeed the prologue is largely taken up with his professions of Edith/Matilda's authority. By using style to move beyond simple topos, Turgot adds weight to his claim and incorporates Edith/Matilda's active patronage into the meaning of his own work. Turgot's other major preoccupation within the prologue is with Edith/Matilda's desire to know more about her mother's virtues and to have her life written down in a form to which she can repeatedly return and read on her own. The queen's desire not only to hear about her mother but also to read about her – to use her learning to gain access to

3 Bezzola, *Origines*, 2.2:422–6; and Huneycutt, *Matilda of Scotland*, esp. 125–43 and her earlier articles, "Perfect Princess" and "Proclaiming Her Dignity."

the mother from whom she was separated at an early age – is identified by Turgot as integral to the genesis of his account.[4] A woman, educated in an Anglo-Saxon royal nunnery, is the driving force behind the production of both an incipient saint's life and a chapter in West Saxon dynastic history.

The emphasis placed on Edith/Matilda wanting to know about her mother, rather than on either Turgot or Margaret herself as originators of the text, disrupts the usual dynamic of authority in what is, as Huneycutt has argued, a mirror for a princess. Although Margaret's life is shaped into a model for Edith/Matilda to follow, and Turgot represents himself in his prologue as having known Margaret better than her daughter did, the text's claim is not generated by Margaret's imperative to Turgot to teach her children, but by Edith/Matilda's desire to know more about her mother. The text thus offers a reading of Margaret's life that is particularly revealing about her daughter, including her intention to use her mother as a guide for her own queenship and to assert the value of her own lineage that is traced through the female rather than the male line.[5] Whereas Adela's authority derived from her father and her husband, Edith/Matilda's derives from her mother. Whereas Queen Edith's story was one of the men in her family, Edith/Matilda's is one of her mother. We are able to see how a daughter's request for an account of her mother opens up new dimensions for English historiography. The centrality of the imitation of models in the construction of the self in the twelfth century gives this commission further weight.[6] As a woman faced with the daunting role of healing genealogically and symbolically the rupture of the Conquest, Edith/Matilda looked within her own family for a precedent. That act of looking within her family to her mother, who had grown up in the Confessor's court and perhaps also in a royal nunnery, signals the importance of the Anglo-Saxon past to her sense of self and her recognition of literary culture as a way to perpetuate this now defeated dynasty.

A mirror for a princess written at the behest of its intended recipient offers a particularly good vantage point on her self-fashioning as a queen. Two distinctive elements come into the foreground in the life: pious learning and genealogy.[7] Edith/Matilda was taught as a young bride that

4 [Turgot?], *Vita sanctae Margaretae*, prologue.

5 Huneycutt, "Perfect Princess," 87–9.

6 Walker Bynum, "Did the Twelfth Century Discover the Individual?" esp. 9, as discussed by Huneycutt, "Perfect Princess," 88.

7 Huneycutt, "Perfect Princess," 92 and 93.

learning was both a source of authority for a woman and the particular domain of the queen rather than the king. The young queen learned these lessons well. Her spiritual authority, grounded in piety and learning, enabled her to smooth over the fissures caused by the investiture controversy and her husband's conflict with Archbishop Anselm. In the secular realm Edith/Matilda directly exercised considerable political power, even chairing king's councils during her husband's absences from England.[8] Turgot's representation of Margaret as the dual and equal inheritor of the virtues of the Anglo-Saxon king Edgar and the Norman duke Richard I, even though she herself was Norman only by association (her grandfather Edmund Ironside did not share Edward the Confessor's Norman mother), expresses not the reality of Margaret's lineage but the aspiration that her daughter's marriage would unite the Norman and Anglo-Saxon dynasties.[9]

The genealogical chapters of the *Vita sanctae Margaretae* hold further interest because they embody an expectation that learned women access their own family history through books. Turgot suggests to Edith/Matilda that if she wants to know more about Duke Richard, she should read the *Gesta Normannorum*, a reference to either Dudo's *De Moribus* or William of Jumièges's *Gesta Normannorum ducum*, a copy of which was possessed by Durham when Turgot was a prior in the early twelfth century.[10] Likewise there appear to be echoes of the *Vita Ædwardi* portrait of Edward the Confessor within the account of Margaret's genealogy. Unless its depiction of the Confessor as a second peaceful Solomon, slow to anger and otherworldly, was already a commonplace when Turgot wrote, the possibility arises that Turgot knew the Anonymous's work; perhaps it is not too much to speculate that he knew the text through Margaret or her daughter.[11] That Margaret's genealogy incorporates references to the writing of dynastic history indicates that Edith/Matilda's early formation sowed the seeds of her later patronage of William of Malmesbury. A generation later, Robert of Torigni, when continuing the *Gesta Normannorum ducum*, not only used Margaret's *Vita* as a source of information on both mother and daughter but went so far as to suggest that he might add the text to his own

8 Huneycutt, "Proclaiming Her Dignity," 162; and *Matilda of Scotland*, 73–124.

9 [Turgot?], *Vita sanctae Margaretae* 1.4–5. Huntington, "St Margaret," 158–60.

10 Huneycutt, *Matilda of Scotland*, 164n12, suggests that the reference is to Dudo. The presence of the *GND* in the Durham library makes it more likely that it is to this text that Turgot refers (*GND*, ed. Van Houts, 1:xcviii).

11 *VE* 1.1.

work as a "noticia rerum gestarum" (record of events).[12] This interlinking creates a cross-generational textual interdependence that closely associates both women with the writing of history.

Turgot intervenes in the debate about classicism that has been so prominent in writings for English royal women. Asserting the Christian credentials of his narrative, he invokes Jerome. The Durham monk closes his prologue by making a bid for the credibility of his account, which he positions far away from lying, flattery, and fiction, by recalling the warning of the orator against the crow's adorning himself with the feathers of the swan. His orator, however, is not Cicero, as we would normally expect. Very aptly, given that he is writing about Margaret for Edith/Matilda, the allusion is to Jerome's life of the saintly Paula that was written for her daughter, Eustochium: "Profiteor me nihil addere, nihil in maius extollere, more laudantium; sed ne rerum excedat fidem, multa detrahere; et ne apud detractores, et 'genuino me semper dente rodentes,' fingere puter, et 'cornicem Aesopi' alienis coloribus adornare" (I profess that I am adding nothing, extolling nothing more, in the way of flatterers, but leaving much out in order not to stretch credulity, so I am not thought by my detractors, "always gnawing at me with real teeth," to be making it up and adorning "Aesop's crow" with alien colors).[13]

Thus Jerome's anxiety about his own debt to the pagan classics is brought to bear on Turgot's writing for Edith/Matilda. Given the prominence of Paula and Eustochium in writings for women, including those of Wilton, Turgot may well have expected his patron to recognize gentle censure of her learning and literary sensibilities.[14] She did not, as we shall see, heed his advice.

The Anselm Correspondence

Even before Edith/Matilda and Archbishop Anselm corresponded directly, she had figured in his letters.[15] Earlier we discussed Anselm's letters to Gunnhild in which he exhorted her to return to the religious life at Wilton.[16] When we consider the letter collection as a whole, we find that Anselm

12 Robert of Torigni, *GND* 8.10 and 25. Van Houts's discussion in the introduction, *GND*, 1:lxxxvii–lxxxviii.

13 Jerome, *Epistulae* 108.15.

14 See chapters 4 and 5 herein.

15 Southern, *Saint Anselm*, 394–403 and 459–81.

16 Anselm, *Epistolae* 168. See chapter 6 herein.

kept himself closely informed about the major Anglo-Saxon royal nunneries. In writing to their abbesses, sending greetings via other clerics and asking after them, he mentions Shaftesbury, Nunnaminster, and Romsey, as well as Wilton.[17] His acute awareness of the capacity for these nunneries to act as repositories of Anglo-Saxon loyalties and cultural memory is evident when he rebukes the nuns of Romsey for venerating as a saint Waltheof, the Anglo-Saxon rebel executed on the order of William the Conqueror, and for sheltering his son within their foundation.[18]

Wilton, with its close connection to both Anglo-Saxon royal dynasties, and thus its continued political importance, particularly concerned him. Although he counselled Gunnhild to return to the monastic life, he was eventually persuaded to allow Edith/Matilda to marry despite the fact that she had worn a veil at Wilton. The legitimacy of the fusion of the Anglo-Saxon and Norman dynasties rested on the resolution of the issue of Edith/Matilda's veiling, lending it a singular political weight. Edith/Matilda benefited from political expediency, whereas the absence of a desire for a continuation of the Godwine dynasty in elite clerical circles offered Gunnhild no such possibility. Multiple versions circulated of the story of Edith/Matilda's veiling, which denied that the future Norman queen had freely chosen the religious life. Lanfranc considered the distinction crucial in determining which residents of Anglo-Saxon convents were nuns and which were free to marry.[19] Eadmer, Anselm's close confidant, attributes her veiling to the pressure of her aunt Christina rather than to her own vocation, and Herman of Tournai, reporting Wilton's own traditions in the 1140s, claims that the abbess ordered the princess to be veiled to protect her from the lustful intentions of William Rufus. Her father's angry response to her veiling, in Herman's account, points to the convent's memory that the princess had been sent there to be educated and prepared for marriage. Anselm's and Herman's reports of Rufus's interest in the young woman illustrate that her political value as a bearer of West Saxon blood was widely acknowledged.[20]

---

17 Anselm, *Epistolae* 183, 185, 208, 236, 237, 276, 337, and 403.

18 Anselm, *Epistolae* 236 and 237.

19 Lanfranc, *Epistolae* 53.

20 Anselm, *Epistolae* 177; Eadmer, *Historia novorum*, pp. 121–5; Herman of Tournai, *De restauracione*, 16. For William of Malmesbury's version, see pages 346, 348, and 351. Southern, *Anselm and His Biographer*, 183–6; Searle, "Women and the Legitimisation," 166–7; Sharpe, "King Harold's Daughter," 14–19; and O'Brien O'Keeffe, *Stealing Obedience*, 173–8 and 188–90.

After the question of her marriage had been resolved, the pre-eminent place of Edith/Matilda among Anselm's network of female correspondents illustrates the value that the queen placed on literary culture in the exercise of spiritual and political power and the way in which she used it to influence the archbishop.[21] Among the recipients of his numerous surviving letters, Edith/Matilda was his most frequent female correspondent. Anselm sought to support, direct, and occasionally rebuke her, while relying on her to negotiate with the king, especially when conflict with Henry I led to his exile. The other women to whom he wrote included both nuns and those connected closely to the ruling Anglo-Norman dynasty. The abbesses of the West Saxon royal nunneries are conspicuous in that group, and Matilda, first abbess of Queen Matilda I's foundation at Caen, also appears.[22] Adela of Flanders (the Capetian mother of Matilda of Flanders), Ida of Boulogne (whose son Eustace of Boulogne would marry Edith/Matilda's sister Mary), Adela of Blois, the nun Adelaide (another daughter of the Conqueror), Clemence (wife of Count Robert II of Flanders, nephew of Queen Matilda I), and Gunnhild all receive letters or are mentioned in them.[23]

This roll call of names attests to the social network that lay behind the emergence of a literary culture shared between the women of the Anglo-Norman realm and fed, from among other sources, by the West Saxon tradition of nunnery education. Anselm's letters witness the continued prominence of these foundations after the Conquest, and his recognition of Wilton's particular role in preparing women for marriage and the religious life. Anselm made frequent recourse to the imagery of the bride of Christ in addressing nuns (or, in Gunnhild's case, should-be nuns). Strikingly, in his letter to Matilda, abbess of Wilton, he couples this discourse with extolling as good examples the married women who are true to their earthly husbands. Anselm recognized the dual secular and religious constituency of this nunnery.[24]

---

21 These letters number eleven and include those within the two main letter collections and those preserved outside them (Anselm, *Epistolae* 243, 246, 288, 296, 317, 321, 329, 346, 347, 385, and 406). Five additional letters are written in Edith/Matilda's name to the archbishop (Anselm, *Epistolae* 242, 320, 384, 395, and 400). Vaughn's book-length study of Anselm's letters to female correspondents is problematic (*St Anselm and the Handmaidens of God*); see van Houts's and Luscombe's reviews.

22 Anselm, *Epistolae* 298.

23 Anselm, *Epistolae* 10, 82, 86, 114, 131, 167, 180, 244, 247, 248, 249, 287, 298, 340, and 448.

24 Anselm, *Epistolae* 168, 169, 184, and 185.

Of all these women, Edith/Matilda is the one who takes the most advantage of the exchange of letters to project an image of herself as not only pious but also on the vanguard of new learning. Preserved along with Anselm's letters are five produced in her name. Regardless of the author of these letters (Edith/Matilda or, more likely, a cleric in her service), they carefully craft an image of the queen as emotionally close to the archbishop, her spiritual adviser.[25] She seeks to support him spiritually, forging a two-way relationship reminiscent of those that flourished between the Anonymous and Queen Edith and between Goscelin and Eve. Returning to the Roman story world, these letters, moreover, reveal her desire to claim classical learning for herself.[26]

Her first letter to Anselm is an extended and ornately written exhortation to him to turn away from excessive fasting. She quotes ostentatiously from Cicero's *De senectute*, naming both author and text, and goes further, directly engaging in the debate about the value of classical learning. After presenting the archbishop with biblical examples of those who fasted, she turns to Gentile examples of frugality, singling out Pythagoras, Socrates, and Antisthenes among the philosophers. Having juxtaposed Old Testament and pagan examples, she moves "ad novae legis gratiam" (to the grace of the new law), citing examples of the importance of eating to Christ, the Apostles, and Gregory.[27] In a later letter she repeats the gesture of invoking both pagan and Christian models in praising the style and content of a letter she has received from Anselm. She writes that his letters "non his desunt Frontonica gravitas, Ciceronis fluvii aut Quintilliani acumina. In his sane doctrina quidem redundat Pauli, diligentia Ieronimi, elucubratio Gregorii, explanatio Augustini" (do not lack the seriousness of Fronto, the fluency of Cicero, or the wit of Quintilian; the doctrine of Paul, the precision of Jerome, the learning of Gregory, and the interpretation of Augustine are indeed overflowing in them).[28]

The classical references in this list reflect Edith/Matilda's literary culture, not Anselm's own, or that which she wished a cleric to associate with her. His reply to her letter responds almost point by point to her appeal but without echoing her classical allusions. Instead he holds up to her the Church, Christ's bride, as in need of the queen's protection.[29] In general he

25 Huneycutt, *Matilda of Scotland*, 112.
26 Huneycutt, *Matilda of Scotland*, 131–2.
27 Anselm, *Epistolae* 242.
28 Anselm, *Epistolae* 384.
29 Anselm, *Epistolae* 243.

keeps explicit classical references and allusions to a minimum in his letters. The classicism of Edith/Matilda's letters does not take its cue from the archbishop, who prized biblical and patristic learning above all and who, when he turned to antiquity, sought out philosophers, not orators and poets.[30] The inclusion of Edith/Matilda's letters within Anselm's major letter collection, brought together at Canterbury either by Anselm or his disciples, illustrates that the image of the queen as classically learned was deliberately preserved for others.[31] Edith/Matilda asserted the classical learning of her Wilton education as a strong element in her image. Among those who knew of this classically educated queen of the letters was William of Malmesbury, who made a copy of the Anselm collection (copying some letters himself and supervising the whole production).[32]

Another of Edith/Matilda's letters to Anselm, meanwhile, resembles the epistolary poetry of Baudri and the nun Constance. Like Constance she substitutes a piece of parchment sent by her correspondent for his physical presence: "Cartulam quidem a vobis missam loco patris amplector, sinu foveo, cordi quoad possum propius admoveo, verba de dulci bonitatis vestrae fonte manantia ore relego, mente retracto, corde recogito, recogitata in ipso cordis arcano repono" (I embrace the parchment sent by you in the place of a father, I press it to my breast, I move it as near to my heart as I can, I reread with my mouth the words flowing from the sweet fountain of your goodness, I go over them in my mind, I ponder them again in my heart, and when I have pondered over them I place them in the sanctuary of my heart).[33]

While sharing in the sensuality of the Baudri and Constance exchange, Edith/Matilda does not engage in their erotic game playing; she invokes the relationships of father and daughter, lord and handmaid, shepherd and sheep, rather than of lovers. Punning and repetition also bind together the letters of Anselm and the queen in a way that further recalls the exchange between Baudri and Constance. In one letter she echoes language found in an earlier letter sent to her by Anselm in which he too writes punningly of an absent presence and of desire for an absent body.[34] Anselm meanwhile greets the physicality of her reception of his letters (clutched to her breast)

30 Southern, *Saint Anselm*, 39–66.

31 See note 21 in this chapter.

32 London, Lambeth Palace Library 224. Southern, *Saint Anselm*, 400–2; and Thomson, *William of Malmesbury*, 87.

33 Anselm, *Epistolae* 320, and see also 384.

34 Anselm, *Epistolae* 288 and 320. On Constance and Baudri, see chapter 4 herein.

with approval. He writes that in her letter "satis ostenditis quanto me affectu diligatis, cum cartulam meam taliter, sicut scripsistis, suscipitis et tractatis" (you clearly displayed with what affection you love me when you received and treated my parchment in the way you describe).[35] He goes on to quote her own words back to her, writing, "eos qui mei sunt genere, vestros esse adoptione et dilectione" (those who are mine by kinship are yours by adoption and love).[36] The echoing between their letters is two-way imitation expressing the mutual respect between queen and archbishop. Finally, her account of her sensual reading of Anselm's letter displays her personal literacy and reveals that, like Edith and Eve before her, she was schooled in the ruminative monastic reading practices cultivated in the nunnery and that she wants Anselm to know this.[37] Even if the letters are written on her behalf, they attest that the learning, which she so conspicuously displayed, was part of the way in which she forged a mutually beneficial relationship with the archbishop, who confirmed the legitimacy of her marriage and crowned her queen.

Poetry for the Queen

William of Malmesbury depicted Edith/Matilda as engaged in the patronage of poetry above all other art forms.[38] The quantity of verse either for or about the queen bears out his picture. Van Houts identifies five poems addressed to the queen in her lifetime and one that takes her as its subject but addresses her daughter the Empress Matilda.[39] The Ovidian language and style of all six poems alerts us to their place within the sphere of influence of the Loire school; moreover, two are by Hildebert and one is by Marbod. Hildebert spent a period of exile in England, 1099–1100, and it is tempting to speculate that he knew Edith/Matilda directly, especially since he seems also to know Muriel, nun and poet of Wilton.[40] During her queenship Hildebert sent Edith/Matilda a series of letters whose tone and substance show the two to have been close.[41] In their use of classicizing

35 Anselm, *Epistolae* 321.
36 Anselm, *Epistolae* 320 and 321.
37 Anselm, *Epistolae* 320.
38 William of Malmesbury, *GRA* 5.418.
39 Van Houts, "Latin Poetry," 50–1. See also Huneycutt, *Matilda of Scotland*, 138–9.
40 Wilmart, "Muriel," 378–9; and Barlow, *William Rufus*, 412.
41 Hildebert, *Epistolae* 1.7, 1.9, 3.11, and 3.12.

language, in their careful deployment of the Roman story world, and in their engagement with female lineage the Edith/Matilda poems reveal the impact that an educated woman could have on the poets writing for her.

Of the two poems written by Hildebert for the queen, the longer, which takes Edith/Matilda and Henry I as its dual focus, is known as "Anglia terra ferax."[42] Alongside praising Edith/Matilda through her men (her father, her husband, her son, and her son-in-law the Roman emperor Henry V), the poem is remarkable for its insistence on the importance of her saintly mother Margaret in forming her character. The poem is also interesting for the way in which Hildebert, whom we have seen leering in his poem for Cecilia, pointedly desexualizes Edith/Matilda despite the debt of its language to Ovid.[43] Not only do we encounter her modesty and chastity, but he displaces Edith/Matilda and writes instead of Anglia, whose cheeks are adorned not with beauty but with genius, an intellectual quality. Her breasts, meanwhile, are not physical but rather the location of law, which flourishes under Henry's rule ("pectora legis erunt").[44] Hildebert's linking of the queen with Henry as a just king is echoed also in the anonymous "Septem maiores," which praises her doubly royal descent and celebrates her intercessory role in persuading Henry to reject iniquitous laws. Like Hildebert's "Anglia terra ferax," its language reveals its poet's familiarity with Ovid, but never does this lead him to stray into the sexual.[45] A further anonymous poem, "Filia praeteriti," maintains this studied sexual distance.[46] Although the poet celebrates her beauty, he does not

42 Hildebert, *Carmina minora* 4 and 37. *Carmen* 4 is a short four-line poem warning of the transience of wealth in the face of death. Latzke, "Fürstinnenpreis," 53–4.

43 Hildebert, *Carmina minora* 46. See chapter 6 herein. For Ovidian language see for example "terra ferax" (line 1; *Amores* 2.16.7, *Meta.* 1.314, and *Fasti* 1.68), "rege sub hoc" (line 15; *Meta.* 4.633 and 14.623), "pignora multa" (line 28; *Fasti* 3.74), and "sceptra manu" (line 30; *Meta.* 1.596).

44 Hildebert, *Carmina minora* 46, lines 31–2.

45 "Septem maiores" shows an Ovidian layer to its language, which is not deployed as tightly controlled allusion in the frequent manner of Marbod, Hildebert, and Baudri. For example: "addimus" (line 3; *Heroides* 4.175 and 16.113); "fama per" (line 16; *Ponto* 4.4.16); "premi" (line 16; *Amores* 1.5.19; *Ponto* 2.3.2 and 4.9.22; *Fasti* 6.368; and *Tristia* 2.450); "quid mihi cum" (line 19; *Amores* 2.19.57; *Heroides* 6.47 and 14.65; *Tristia* 3.11.55 and 5.13.9); "filia regis erat" (line 20; *Fasti* 3.468); and "publica cura" (line 26; *Fasti* 5.290).

46 "Filia praeteriti." The poem in not in the canon accepted by Scott (it is not included in his *Carmina minora* edition, and see his "The Poems of Hildebert"). Van Houts treats it as anonymous ("Latin Poetry," 51).

glance at her body. When simplicity adorns the mind, and honesty the face, beauty becomes a moral not a physical virtue.[47]

The most interesting of these Ovidian poems for Edith/Matilda, because it picks up the theme of sexuality and pushes it to the limits, is Marbod's "Ad reginam Anglorum."[48] Strikingly, although the poem is attracted to Ovidian eroticism, often when it is most sexually explicit, Marbod elaborately performs his rejection of this erotic discourse as inappropriate to Edith/Matilda (in a manner reminiscent of Baudri's poem to Adela). Thus Marbod, who of all the Loire poets writes the most sexually aggressive verse, exposes and makes part of his poem the complex dynamics between poet and patron that attend the production of Ovidian poetry when the learned patron resists objectification.

The poem begins by overtly situating itself within an Ovidian framework, with Marbod recalling the classical poet's experience of exile and hardship:

> Est operae pretium tentasse pericula ponti,
> Et dubiae sortis pertimuisse minas.
>
> (It is the value of this work to have attempted the dangers of the sea,
> to have feared the threats of a dubious fate.)[49]

The cause of this exile is not the loss of political favour but Marbod's desire to see the queen's face. Unlike Ovid, he is not exiled away from women whom he loves but rather drawn towards Edith/Matilda. Like the Anonymous author of the *Vita Ædwardi*, he finds support in his proximity, real or imagined, to the queen.

> Reginam vidisse juvat, quam nulla decore
> Corporis ac vultus aequiparare queat.
>
> (It helps to have seen a queen to whom none
> can be compared in beauty of body and face.)[50]

---

47 "Filia praeteriti," lines 33–4.

48 Marbod, "Ad reginam Anglorum." Latzke, "Fürstinnenpreis," 54–6; and Moser, *Cosmos of Desire*, 35–9.

49 Marbod, "Ad reginam Anglorum," lines 1–2.

50 Marbod, "Ad reginam Anglorum," lines 3–4.

These lines introduce the main theme of the poem: Edith/Matilda's modesty and her incomparable beauty. Drawing on language from Christian Latin poets, Marbod comments first on the queen's modesty, her *pudor novus*, which although it compels her to cover her body under a loose-fitting dress, cannot hide her beauty.[51] Rather than intrude on her body, Marbod goes on to describe, in highly erotic Ovidian language, the bodies of other women who, even though they resort to artifice, never approach the natural beauty of the queen. Marbod's verse recalls the *Amores* and the *Ars amatoria*, and especially the figure of Ovid's mistress, the married Corinna.[52] He shows no restraint, describing the artifice of these women as adulterous, and lingering over their breasts and thighs.[53] He then returns to the subject of the queen whose fear of appearing beautiful is recounted in lines that again take up the language and imagery of biblical and late antique Christian poetry. Edith/Matilda is finally gently rebuked for trying to hide her light (not her body) that is a gift from God.[54]

Latzke argues that Edith/Matilda is virtually incidental to this poem, a type rather than an individual, and, in Moser's reading, Marbod urges propriety and sexual continence on the queen.[55] However, Marbod is responding to and conveying an image of the queen consonant with that expressed by Turgot and found in the letter exchange with Anselm; it is highly specific to, and created by, Edith/Matilda herself. The agency in Marbod's representation of the queen lies with his subject. The queen's modesty and chastity represent virtues inculcated by both her saintly mother and her Wilton upbringing. The emphasis on the modesty of her attire is doubly fitting given the controversy over the time she spent in the habit of a nun. The games Marbod plays with Ovidian erotics meanwhile also and equally rely on her Wilton education. The learning of Wilton equipped her not only to appreciate this poem but to stamp her image on it and to prevent the poet from even imagining taking liberties with her.

51 Marbod, "Ad reginam Anglorum," lines 5–6.

52 For examples of Ovidian language: "pericula Ponti" (line 1; *Meta.* 14.439 and *Tristia* 5.2.29); "pertimuisse minas" (line 2; *Heroides* 9.74); "purpureas ... genas" (line 12; *Amores* 1.4.22); "fronte capillos" (line 17; *Amores* 1.7.49); and "formosa videri" (line 19; *Meta.* 4.319 and 9.462).

53 Marbod, "Ad reginam Anglorum," lines 11–16.

54 Marbod, "Ad reginam Anglorum," lines 22–4.

55 Latzke, "Fürstinnenpreis," 54–6; and Moser, *Cosmos of Desire*, 35–9.

While it is possible to argue that the mere introduction of the erotic into a poem calls up Edith/Matilda's own body, however deep might be the concealing folds of her dress, a strong counter-argument can be made. Powerful queens, with enough Latin to not only construe but also interpret and fully understand Latin verse, were not ideal for the sexual objectification that marks so much clerical poetry about women; indeed, Marbod thematizes this very situation. Moreover, he places the Roman story world at the heart of a struggle over the representation of women. Marbod might want to invoke Corinna in depicting the queen, but her own poetic expertise makes this impossible. The strong possibility that Edith/Matilda's Latinity was such that she could recognize what Marbod was doing turns what could have been a lascivious move into an acknowledgment of her control over the way he could deploy his classicism. Indeed, taking into account Edith/Matilda's poetic education makes it impossible to read this poem as eroticizing the queen. The consonance of her image across the poetry of Hildebert, Marbod, and the anonymous poets suggests that she played a determining role in her actively cultivated poetic image. Although William of Malmesbury mentions Edith/Matilda's patronage of poetry, we do not have evidence that these poems specifically responded to a request from her.

The importance of her maternal lineage to the Empress Matilda's status insured that Edith/Matilda remained in the sight of her poets even after her death. Hildebert's poem "Augustis patribus augustior" for her daughter, the empress, addressed her as her mother's daughter, above all else.[56] He thus reveals contemporary perceptions that the cultivation of learning and literature was a specifically maternal inheritance of England's royal women. Ovidian erotics are again ostentatiously inverted, as they were for her mother, to project a chaste modesty whose beauty is not the product of artifice.[57] The classicizing framework of the poem is especially obvious in the claim that the empress "redolet … Sabinam" (is redolent of a Sabine woman).[58] These women were abducted by the first Roman men, who would otherwise have been wifeless. Later they attempted to stem war between their fathers and husbands – that is, from a medieval perspective,

56 Hildebert, *Carmina minora* 35. Latzke "Fürstinnenpreis," 50–3.
57 Hildebert, *Carmina minora* 35, line 8.
58 Hildebert, *Carmina minora* 35, line 7.

performing the role of women given in dynastic marriage.[59] Ovid remembered them as unadorned figures of austere married chastity – a fitting image for the empress, praised as her mother's daughter.[60]

The thematic repetition between Hildebert's poem for the empress and those written for her mother asserts the primacy of the mother-daughter lineage and embodies it within poetic culture. This mother-daughter relationship is so strong that it not only pushes to the margins definitions of Matilda in terms of her relationship to kings (be they fathers, sons, husbands) but even pushes the empress herself to the margins as the highest praise is reserved for her mother:

> Neve simul caderet muliebris gloria sexus
> te peperit, partu tota renata tuo.
> Non semel orta parens iacet urna, regnat in aula,
> hic homini, sursum collaterata Deo.

> (And lest the glory of the womanly sex should decline
> she, completely reborn in your birth, gave birth to you.
> Not born only once, the parent who lies in the urn, rules in the court,
> here beside men, above, beside God.)[61]

In these lines the mother outshines the daughter.

Not only does Edith/Matilda displace her daughter in the poem, as illustrated by scholarly disagreement about which woman is actually its subject, but she appears to displace the poet himself.[62] The poem opens with a conventional profession that the empress exceeds the capacity of poets to praise her, yet "una loqui te lingua potest" (one [tongue] may utter you).[63] This one tongue may be the empress's mother in whose mouth

---

59 Livy, *Ab urbe condita* 1.9–13.

60 See, for example, Ovid, *Amores* 1.8.39 and 2.4.15; and Ovid, *Meta.* 14.832.

61 Hildebert, *Carmina minora* 35, lines 13–16. The translation is Ferrante's (*Epistolae* project) with some changes to make clear the relationship between Edith/Matilda and her daughter.

62 Scott (ed., *Carmina minora* 35, p. 21) and van Houts ("Latin Poetry," 51) see the subject of the poem as Edith/Matilda. Latzke ("Fürstinnenpreis," 50–3) and Chibnall (*Empress Matilda*, 47) prefer the empress, whom van Houts acknowledges as a possibility.

63 Hildebert, *Carmina minora* 35, line 5. The line is difficult to construe. The translation here is that suggested by Ferrante, *Epistolae* project.

Hildebert goes so far as to put the final lines of his poem.[64] Edith/Matilda is here imagined, even after death, as actively shaping classicizing poetry, rather than being passively represented by it , and then passing this role on to her daughter. The daughter is, as yet, just an echo of her mother without a distinct poetic persona.

Muriel of Wilton

Our view of Edith/Matilda as a knowing reader of Latin verse and thus an agent in its production is supported by returning to look at the poetry written for Muriel, the nun of Wilton.[65] This small corpus also provides a space from which to consider the place of Normandy within the poetic developments that we have traced across Northern France and England. Muriel was at Wilton in the late eleventh and the early twelfth century. She was thus very likely to be a contemporary of and known to Edith/Matilda.[66] Three poems written to Muriel, by Baudri, Hildebert, and Serlo of Bayeux, survive. Although none of Muriel's own verse has been preserved, other poetry that is possibly from early-twelfth-century Wilton has been.

Baudri may have been the earliest of the three to write to Muriel.[67] Tatlock suggests that his poem was written before, and perhaps well before, 1095. Tilliette suggests that, if we accept Baudri's claim that Muriel was the first women to whom he wrote, we must date the poem early, certainly prior to 1102 and perhaps many years before that (as would be consonant with Wilton's longer educational tradition than Le Ronceray's).[68]

64 "nondum me totam celesti sede recepi,
magne Deus, requie semibeata fruor.
pars iacet in tumulo, pars Anglica regna gubernat,
divisamque tenent aula, sepulchra, polus.
quam tenet aula iuva: quam clausa sepulchra reforma:
quam polus exaudi, sisque corona tribus."

(Hildebert, *Carmina minora* 35, lines 21–6)

65 Tatlock, "Muriel"; and Stevenson, "Anglo-Latin Women Poets," 95–100. Dronke thinks that Muriel was a nun at Le Ronceray (*Women Writers*, 85), and Signori agrees with him ("Muriel"). Tilliette, in his edition of Baudri's poem to Muriel, does not find Dronke or Signori persuasive (*Carmina*, 2:218–19n1).

66 Van Houts, "Latin Poetry," 50.

67 Baudri, *Carmina* 137.

68 Tatlock, "Muriel," 318; and Baudri, *Carmina*, ed. Tilliette, 2:220n13. See chapter 5 herein.

The language of Baudri's poem to Muriel everywhere reveals his knowledge of Ovid. However, in this context his linguistic debt to Ovid does not take the form of allusions to particular stories or situations recounted by the poet. As is typical of his poems for nuns, except Constance, he does not use Ovid to establish an erotic subtext.[69] Quite the contrary, while he acknowledges that her beauty, noble birth, and riches make her an attractive bride, the physical Muriel is hardly present. Nor does he lecture her on virginity beyond praising her rejection of "carnis spurcitia" (filth of the flesh).[70] Rather, the abundant riches of her intellect impress him.[71] Their relationship is a pure meeting of poetic talent (and he is very specific about her mastery of poetics); in Baudri's account their poems become intimate before they embark on compassionately correcting each other's verse.[72]

Hildebert's more classicizing poem is the product of his period of banishment to England or at least imagines itself within that experience.[73] The poem goes beyond its Ovidian language to cast itself as the outpouring of an exiled poet, clearly recalling Ovid's *Tristia*.[74] Muriel is not, however, a woman whose caresses he misses. Rather she is a modern-day Sibyl who speaks the words of the gods and whose poetry alleviates the heavy burden of his exile.[75] Even more than Baudri, perhaps because he is writing to her later in life, Hildebert seeks not the physical but the intellectual Muriel.[76] Indeed the poem pauses so little over her physical presence that we cannot know whether Hildebert visited her or simply came to know her verse, or indeed whether he knew her by reputation (perhaps via Le Ronceray) before coming to England. The similarities between Baudri's and Hildebert's poems, both of which insist on her excellence as a poet, suggest a common experience, whether literary or first hand, of Muriel herself and of a shared poetic culture.

The poem of Serlo, in contrast to that of Baudri and of Hildebert, frames Muriel within a different poetic tradition and in so doing sheds light on

69 Bond, "*Iocus Amoris*," 168; and Moser, *Cosmos of Desire*, 52.
70 Baudri, *Carmina* 137 line 17.
71 Baudri, *Carmina* 137 line 43.
72 Baudri, *Carmina* 137 lines 11–12, 25–6, and 45–6.
73 Hildebert, *Carmina minora* 26; and Wilmart, "Muriel," 378–9.
74 Hildebert, *Carmina minora* 26, lines 21–32.
75 Hildebert, *Carmina minora* 26, lines 1 and 25–32.
76 Hildebert, *Carmina minora* 26, lines 2–20.

the place of Normandy in relation to the Loire school.[77] Serlo was not an Angevin prelate, like the other two, but a canon of Bayeux. He enjoyed the patronage of Bishop Odo, half-brother of William the Conqueror, but was not part of the ambitious striving after new ways of using and conceptualizing the value of the Roman story world that was fed by the schools of Angers, Tours, Orléans, and Reims.[78] Serlo's long and conventional poem finds its roots in the essentially misogynist tradition that encouraged women to become brides of Christ in order to avoid the twin horrors of marriage to a potentially abusive mortal spouse and of maternity. The theme, which goes back to patristic writers, is spelled out in unpleasant detail in Jerome's letter to Helvidius. Jerome's avowed refusal to explore this theme in his letter to Eustochium about virginity is of interest in considering Serlo and Muriel. As we have seen, this letter to Eustochium, with its avoidance of such misogyny, was an important intertext for Goscelin's *Liber confortatorius* when he wrote to the Wilton nun Eve.[79] Serlo's focus on marriage and maternity as deterrents positions him away from Wilton and its traditions, rooted in its mixed community of secular and religious women. Hildbebert's letter to the recluse Athalisa is a well-known example of this misogynist mode. Fascinatingly, it is not a position he adopts in writing to Muriel; rather, his poetic correspondence with her recognizes a relationship of another order altogether.[80] Returning to Serlo's poem, while never encroaching on Muriel's body, he does dwell in lurid detail on the sad consequences of marriage for women.[81] In this respect the poem is strikingly different from the epithalamium in the *Vita Ædwardi*, which works with bridal mysticism but deploys it in a manner that conveys respect for religious *and* married women.[82]

The Roman story world is also at stake in the gap between Serlo and his Loire contemporaries. His modesty topos takes the form of worrying about how his poem will compare with those others that are read in the *faecunda versibus urbs*. In particular, Serlo thinks that her Virgil will

77 Serlo, "Versus ad Muriel sanctimonialem," pp. 233–40 (Wright's edition is not lineated).

78 Bates, "Character and Career," 13–14; Bates, "Patronage"; and Heslop, "Regarding the Spectators," 232–3.

79 See chapter 5 herein.

80 Jerome, *Epistulae* 22; Jerome, *Contra Helvidium*; and Hildebert, *Epistolae* 1.21. See also Marbod, *Liber decem capitulorum* 4, lines 47–51. Newman, *Virile Woman*, 19–45, esp. 28–34.

81 Serlo, "Ad Muriel," 234–8.

82 *VE* 1.6; and see chapter 5 herein.

deride his verse.[83] This invocation early on overtly acknowledges the classicizing literary culture of Wilton. At the same time, he exposes his own awareness of his distance from the poetic culture of the Loire; he is no inheritor of Virgil, and he is rightly concerned that his poetry will not impress nuns accustomed to the poetry of the Loire. When Serlo does call up the Roman story world, it is not to explore its possibilities for understanding contemporary experience or its value as fiction. Rather, antiquity simply becomes a source of bad examples of women overcome by sexuality.[84] There is no complex relationship between classical fiction and Christian truth to be teased out. In Serlo's hands, past and present, pagan and Christian, are juxtaposed to offer examples of equally bad behaviour rather than to be mutually illuminating. Serlo's anxious reference to Virgil also chimes with the absence of an Ovidian layer, either linguistic or thematic, to this poem. His poem for Muriel points back to the poetry of the previous centuries rather than forward to a period of Ovidian experimentation. Serlo further stands apart from Hildebert and Baudri because, while he does represent Muriel as an active partner in a correspondence, requesting a poem from him, he does not represent her as a fellow poet. He makes no claim to an exchange of poems with Muriel, nor does he position her as the superior poet, as we have seen Baudri do – not only with Muriel but also with the nuns of Le Ronceray.[85] Serlo's poetic circle is not influenced by the active participation of women as learned readers and even as poets themselves.

In the absence of Muriel's own poetry we must look elsewhere to assess the poetic culture of Wilton. Jane Stevenson has argued that a poem about the biblical Susanna (found attributed to a Willetrudis) in a thirteenth-century German manuscript is by the early-twelfth-century abbess of Wilton. Stevenson compellingly makes the case that the poem is particularly

83 Serlo, "Ad Muriel," 233. Boutemy, "Muriel," 245.

84 Quam rabies torret, quæ nil quod diligat horret,
Decipiturque cito, sic fit Jove digna marito.
Purpura quas vestit, Venus has magis urere gestit;
Quæ nupsit tauro, gemmis radiabat et auro.
Quid tua nupta, Nero? Sed cur mala pristina quæro?
Hoc plures ævo maculantur crimine sævo;
Hæ magis elati quæ florent culmine fati.
(Serlo, "Versus ad Muriel sanctimonialem," 237)

85 See chapter 5 herein.

valuable as the work of a female poet.[86] Rather than taking the position of the old judges who secretly watch the naked Susanna in her orchard and then wrongly accuse her of adultery, as in the Bible, the female poet tells a story of men ordering the beautiful woman to be stripped naked and then violently assaulting her with their gaze.[87] Willetrudis leaves the reader in no doubt about the moral depravity of these men. This position stands in contrast to other medieval poets who, though they exonerate Susanna, nonetheless find sympathy with the men, who are rendered incapable of controlling their lust in the face of her beauty. Petrus Pictor, the Saint-Omer canon whose connections to the Loire school we have already considered, for example, is backhanded in making Susanna a figure of the virtuous wife in his satirical poem on married women. A husband boasts that his wife is like Penelope, Susanna, and Anna, only to be cuckolded by her many times over as she uses religious devotion as a cover for visits to her lover.[88] In Willetrudis's poem the responsibility for the men's transgression lies with them, and the violence of what they have done is deliberately heightened. Susanna is of particular relevance to a Wilton audience because she is a figure not of virginity but of the faithful wife. In light of the controversy over Edith/Matilda's veiling, the insistence of the lecherous judges in the biblical account that Susanna be unveiled in court so that they "satiarentur decore eius" (might be satisfied with her beauty) takes on further significance.[89] Susanna's poetic commemoration by Willetrudis, who addresses her "sorores," would suit Wilton's dual function as nunnery and convent school.[90] Not surprisingly, given her wide currency as a model for wives, we see Susanna appear and reappear in Wilton texts. The Anonymous makes recourse to her when protesting, in religious poetry, Godwine's innocence in 1051.[91] Later, Goscelin, in the second metre of his *Vita sanctae*

86 The material about Susanna is drawn largely from Stevenson, "Anglo-Latin Women Poets," 97–100, and *Women Latin Poets*, 130–8. I have quoted the text as Stevenson edited and translated it in her publications. I have also consulted a digital facsimile of the manuscript (Munich, Bayerische Staatsbibliothek, clm 12513, fols. 23–35). Other medieval Latin poems about Susanna are discussed by Mozley, "Susanna." Where I have consulted other secondary and primary texts, these are indicated. For the biblical account see Daniel 13.

87 Willetrudis, "Susanna" line 170 ("ac visu dignae violant pudibunda Susannae").

88 Petrus Pictor, *Carmina* 16, lines 1–13. Petrus Pictor is not discussed by Stevenson or Mozley. See chapter 5 herein.

89 Daniel 13:32.

90 Willetrudis, "Susanna" line 18.

91 *VE* 1.3.

Edithae, writes that "Susannam celebrat conubii fides" (fidelity in marriage celebrates Susanna).[92]

If the Susanna poem is the work of Wilton's Willetrudis, there is a remarkable resonance between its awareness of women's experiences of and resistance to sexual objectification and that displayed within the poetry for Edith/Matilda, giving further weight to the view that her education at the hands of learned nuns, who protected her from William Rufus, shaped her interaction with the poets who sought her patronage and who did not dare gaze on her in their verse. The place of women poets and patrons within the Loire school made new demands on poetry, pushing it in radical directions, which included new thinking about the representation of women and new departures in the use of the Roman story world.

The presence of poetry in the entries made by Wilton, as well as Nunnaminster, Shaftesbury, and Amesbury, in early-twelfth-century funeral rotuli attests further to the continued cultivation of verse among English nuns.[93] When a message announcing the death of a brother or a sister was sent out to the other communities who were in confraternity with the deceased's foundation, it became customary for a response, often in verse, to be added, resulting in long rotuli. In addition to recording their prayers for the dead man or woman, the receiving community often included prayers for their own dead, creating a confraternity of the dead as well as of the living. The rotuli announcing the deaths of Abbess Matilda of Caen in 1113 and Vitalis of Savigny (chaplain to William to Conqueror and follower of Robert of Arbrissel) in 1122 circulated throughout France and England.[94] Amesbury, Nunnaminster, and Shaftesbury all contributed verse about Matilda; Wilton meanwhile contributed one about Vitalis.[95] This last poem, written in leonine hexameters like the poem on Susanna, contains phrases found also in Ovid and Hildebert. The entry that includes the poem remembers most prominently its own abbess Willetrudis

92 Goscelin, *Vita sanctae Edithae* metre 2.

93 The insight offered by these rotuli into the composition of verse in the English royal nunneries is discussed by Stevenson, "Anglo-Latin Women Poets," 95–7, and *Women Latin Poets*, 119–22. They are collected and edited by Delisle, *Rouleaux*.

94 Delisle, *Rouleaux*, 177–344.

95 Delisle, *Rouleaux*, 187–90 and 328–9. As one of the Nunnaminster poems is explicitly by a woman, and among the surviving Nunnaminster manuscripts from this period there is a colophon identifying the scribe as a *scriptrix*, we need not pause to doubt that the nuns themselves could have composed the verses they entered in the rotuli. Stevenson, "Anglo-Latin Poets," 96; and P.R. Robinson, "Twelfth-Century *Scriptrix*."

among its own deceased.[96] Marbod, Baudri, and Hildebert all composed poetry for mortuary rolls.[97] The very ordinary poem from the Vitalis rotulus hints at the wider literary culture of which Wilton was a part, gesturing towards Ovid and the Loire poets.

William of Malmesbury and Edith/Matilda

William of Malmesbury's *Gesta regum Anglorum* was begun in the confident and happy expectation that Edith/Matilda and Henry I's son, William, would reign, thus uniting the Anglo-Saxon and Norman dynasties. After her death and that of her son, William of Malmesbury continued, amid the uncertainty about the succession, with unwavering loyalty to the ideal of a union of the Anglo-Saxon and Norman dynasties (an ethnic mix that, he tells us, he shared and which made him better able to give an impartial account of the Conquest).[98] William thus found himself devoted to the cause of the Empress Matilda, not just as a powerful woman but as a ruling woman.[99]

The second half of this chapter looks at the *Gesta regum* through the lens of the roles played by Edith/Matilda and the empress in its production and reception. William's prefatory letters to the queen's brother, David, king of the Scots, and her daughter, the empress, alongside the prologue to book 1 do not vaguely invoke the queen's patronage; rather her direct agency is asserted.[100] William recalls that the queen approached him, wanting to know about her ancestors. Although she died well before he had completed the earliest version of the *Gesta regum*, Edith/Matilda's initial patronage of the *Gesta regum* has been accepted by scholars, as has William's eagerness to get it to the empress.[101] Of course, it was not written exclusively for these two women, which is made plain by the rededication to Robert of Gloucester, Henry I's learned and powerful son whose illegitimacy

96 "Mora longa" is common in Ovid; "parcite vestras" (compare to "parcite vestris" of the roll) appears in Ovid, *Ars* 2.557; "reddite nostris" appears in Ovid, *Meta*. 13.372; and "ut prece sanctorum" appears in Hildebert, *De mysterio missae* 582). Delisle, *Rouleaux*, 328–9.

97 Sheerin, "Sisters in Literary Agon," 94 and 99. See Hollis ("Barking's Monastic School," 53–4) on Nunnaminster poetry in a roll for Abbess Matilda of Caen.

98 William of Malmesbury, *GRA* 3, preface.

99 William of Malmesbury, *GRA Epistola* 2.

100 William of Malmesbury, *GRA Epistolae* 1 and 2, and 1, prologue.

101 Thomson, *William of Malmesbury*, 36–7; and William of Malmesbury, *GRA*, ed. Thomson, 2.18.

kept him from the throne.[102] Yet, the impact of the roles of these two women on the text's production and reception has not been appreciated. There is a tendency to weight its later dedication to Robert of Gloucester equally and to draw the text into the orbit of his much celebrated literary patronage, despite the fact that less is known about his connections with William.[103] This tendency has little foundation when one takes into account Edith/Matilda's learning and the evidence of William's alertness to women readers of the *Gesta regum*.

Throughout the *Gesta regum*, in which he frequently steps back to consider his reader, William shows himself to be particularly aware of the reception of his text. His anxiety about his reader's response to his criticism of Malcolm's support for the Ætheling Edgar, Morcar, and Waltheof is telling with respect to Edith/Matilda, the empress, and David as readers. He writes: "quorum singillatim exitus si commemorauero, fortasse superfluus non ero, licet fastidii discrimen immineat, dum relatori, si forte secundum dictores suos mentiatur, difficilis sit regressus ad ueniam" (If I record the ends of these men one by one, I shall perhaps not go too far, though there is some risk of becoming tedious, and the narrator who by chance in following his authorities tells an untruth has a hard path back to his reader's good graces).[104] William's palpable desire to displace his criticism of Malcolm draws our attention to Edith/Matilda and the empress as ideal readers of the *Gesta regum*, rather than Robert of Gloucester. Focusing on Edith/Matilda and the empress is not to deny a wider audience for the *Gesta regum*, one made up largely of men. However, when we see Edith/Matilda in the context of the long-established tradition of educating Anglo-Saxon royal women, and we take seriously evidence of her agency in Turgot's *Vita sanctae Margaretae*, the Anselm correspondence, and the poetry written for her, her fundamental role in shaping both the form and the content of the *Gesta regum* emerges strongly.[105]

William's sophisticated and self-conscious conceptualization of history writing has long been recognized, with scholars appreciating his debt to

102 William of Malmesbury, *GRA Epistola* 3.

103 Thomson, *William of Malmesbury*, 37; and William of Malmesbury, *GRA*, ed. Thomson, 2:6.

104 William of Malmesbury, *GRA* 3.248.

105 Thomson's view of Edith/Matilda's impact on the *Gesta regum* is shaped by a downplaying of her active role in the production of Latin texts; see William of Malmesbury, *GRA*, ed. Thomson, 2:8–9 and 2:275.

Bede, his classicizing, his overtly even-handed account of the Conquest, his source criticism alongside his fascination with *mira* and *mirabilia*, and their implications for his notions of fiction and its relationship to history.[106] Joan Ferrante has meanwhile demonstrated that writing for Edith/Matilda led William to include and foreground women within his text in an unprecedented manner.[107] Here I will argue that writing at the instigation of a woman and with the rule of a woman so firmly in mind profoundly shaped his understanding and experience of *historia*, both as events and as a narrative account. The *Gesta regum* stands at the heart of a network of texts and social relationships that defined the literary culture of English royal women across the eleventh and twelfth centuries.

The Gesta regum

William's *Gesta regum* is a history of the kings of England, in five books, from the *Adventus Saxonum* up to the end of the reign of Henry I. Book 1 recounts the period from the heptarchy to the sole monarchy of the West Saxons over England, a political and military settlement that William celebrates and locates early, in the reign of Ecgberht (d. 839).[108] Book 2 covers the history of the West Saxon dynasty to its end in 1066, a year marked by Edward the Confessor's death, Harold's brief reign, and the Conquest. Book 3, which revisits some of the material at the end of book 2, is devoted to William the Conqueror, and books 4 and 5 cover the reigns of his two sons, the despised William Rufus and the much-admired Henry I, respectively. Within this framework William includes much additional information about the Church, the history of other European polities, the Crusades, and various marvellous stories. The importance of Rome, politically, culturally, and ecclesiastically, is signalled from the start when, after only a few lines devoted to the arrival of the Angles and the Saxons, William explains that to make the story clear he must go back in time to Julius Caesar's conquest of Britain, an event that has left a still legible mark both in the written record and on the landscape.[109]

---

106 Gransden, *Historical Writing*, esp. 167–8 and 175–8; Thomson, *William of Malmesbury*, esp. 14–39; Otter, *Inventiones*, 96–102; and Barrow, "William of Malmesbury."

107 Ferrante, *Glory of Her Sex*, 100–4.

108 Rather than placing it in the reign of Edward the Elder (d. 924). William of Malmesbury, *GRA* 1.105.

109 William of Malmesbury, *GRA* 1.1.

The *Gesta regum* was written in several stages over many years. Thomson, the most recent editor of the *Gesta regum*, argues that it was begun before Edith/Matilda's death and then set aside, though not for long. In Thomson's view the copy presented to David and the empress, likely when they were both in England in 1126, represents an early version. The manuscripts show that William continued to work on the *Gesta regum* whose last version, revised and finished after Henry I's death in 1135, was dedicated to Robert, earl of Gloucester. Comparison of the manuscripts shows that some material was excised with the empress's sensibilities in mind. By the time William presented a copy to Robert, further research had also made new information available.[110]

In the context of this present chapter it is particularly important to note that the early version presented to David and Matilda lacks its final folios; in discussing the episodes contained in them, we have thus to rely on the later text as presented to Robert of Gloucester. This loss is of particular importance to my discussion because the explanation of Henry I's philandering, the portrait of Edith/Matilda, and the account of the *White Ship* disaster would have been found, if they were included in the earlier manuscript, in those lost folios.[111] We are also missing any epilogue, such as that addressed to Robert, which might have been addressed to either David or Matilda.[112] If the copy given to the empress and David followed a similar pattern to that given to Robert with an epilogue, the entire text of the *Gesta regum* was enveloped within the dynastic context of its female patronage and reception.

The prefatory letters accompanying the version of the *Gesta regum* presented to David and the empress, along with the prologue to book 1, spell out the circumstances of the commissioning of the *Gesta regum*.[113] In these letters William writes that he met and spoke with the queen, who had oversight of Malmesbury, and emphasizes her agency in the text's production.[114] In telling the story of the inception of the *Gesta regum* to her daughter, William situates it within exemplary history for kings *and*

110 William of Malmesbury, *GRA*, ed. Thomson, 2:xvii–xxxiv.

111 William of Malmesbury, *GRA* 5.412, 5.418, and 5.419.

112 William of Malmesbury, *GRA Epistolae* 1–3 and 5.448–9. Thomson thinks that he did include such an epilogue (William of Malmesbury, *GRA*, ed. Thomson, 2:xviii).

113 *GRA Epistolae* 1 and 3, and 1, prologue. On how both letters came to be attached to the single manuscript preserved in Troyes, see William of Malmesbury, *GRA*, ed. Thomson, 2:6–8.

114 Huneycutt, *Matilda of Scotland*, 65.

queens, with its recollection of figures from the past for imitation or as cautionary tales. He specifically states that knowledge of this genre had encouraged the learned queen to seek to know more about her family, when the two were discussing Aldhelm, who, like the queen, was of the West Saxon line. Thinking herself not worthy of a *volumen gestorum regum* (volume of the history of the kings) written "more antiquo" (in the traditional manner), she at first requested only a brief account. But this left her dissatisfied, and she sought a *grandiuscula narratio* (somewhat fuller narrative), thus inducing William to consider a "plenam de antecessoribus eius ... historiam" (full history of ... her predeccessors).[115] In seeking out her daughter, the empress, to receive the finished version, he mourns her mother's absence, thus inscribing Edith/Matilda again as his ideal reader. In the prefatory material William represents Edith/Matilda's agency not conventionally but as intimately linked to the production, content, genre, and reception of the *Gesta regum* and seeks to pass this legacy on to her daughter.

In the prologue to book 1 William moves on from the prefatory letters to flesh out his understanding of the genealogy of his *Gesta regum* as exemplary history.[116] The narrative of book 1 is drawn, as William announces, largely from Bede. William looks to Bede not merely for content, as he also finds in the Northumbrian monk his own good exemplum, his own ancestor, for his task as a history writer. He audaciously claims to be the first to write English history since the *temporum series* (chain of our history) was broken after Bede. Bede, however, could not stand as a straightforward model for William in the latter's aim to write secular history for a woman. From Bede William inherited an Augustinian model of salvation history, ultimately based on biblical models, in which conversion, rather than worldly rulership, was the guiding narrative. His need to pull Bede towards the more secular history that he was writing emerges when he recalls that his predecessor too was the beneficiary of royal patronage. He not only recounts that Bede wrote at the behest of Ceolwulf, but also reminds his audience that Ceolwulf was a king learned enough to accept and correct the first draft of the *Historia ecclesiastica*. Here too is a secular patron, like William's own, who can intervene in the production of history.

115 William of Malmesbury, *GRA Epistola* 2.
116 William of Malmesbury, *GRA* 1, prologue.

Bede's writings are also critical for William's conception of the nature of *historia*. He incorporates his debt to Bede into the closing chapters of the *Gesta regum* when he writes, echoing the Northumbrian historian, that he has followed the "vera lex ... historiae." However, he has reshaped Bede for his own purposes. Where Bede understood this law as putting "ea quae fama uulgante collegimus ad instructionem posteritatis literis mandare studuimus" (to writing what I have collected from common report for the instruction of posterity), William glosses it as working from "a fidelibus relatoribus uel scriptoribus" (trustworthy report or written source).[117] Just as William modifies Bede's understanding of the law of history, he will need to move beyond the confines of salvation history, however exemplary it might be for kings, to produce genuinely secular history, whose guiding narrative is royal genealogy, not conversion. Bede's model of *historia* also posed specific problems when writing secular history that not only was for a woman but also included women. The Northumbrian monk's full portraits of the Abbess Hild and of Æthelthryth, successful in her quest for chastity within marriage, are exceptions.[118] Usually his women are unrealized figures, exchanged in the dynastic marriage.[119] William's simultaneous admiration for and struggle with Bede was intimately related to his patron's gender and her secular status. Moreover, in setting his patron up as expert in exemplary history, he implicates her fully in his consciousness of the generic limitations of Bede as a model for her history.

William of Malmesbury's Classicism

William's knowledge of Roman literary culture, both historiographic and poetic, also provided him with models for writing secular history. The depth of his classical learning is evident from the prominence of classical texts in his *Polyhistor*, in his unrivalled collection of Cicero's works, in his wide knowledge of Roman historians, and in the rich texture of allusions to Roman poets, especially Virgil, Lucan, and Statius, which marks the prose of the *Gesta regum*.[120] In the prologue he sets up his turn to Rome as

117 Bede, *HE*, preface; and William of Malmesbury, *GRA* 5.445.

118 Bede, *HE* 4.19 and 4.23.

119 Bede, *HE* 2.9, 2.14, and 2.20.

120 N. Wright, "William of Malmesbury"; N. Wright, "Industriae Testimonium"; and Thomson, *William of Malmesbury*, 14–75. Thomson's notes to the *GRA*, both within the edition and within the commentary, include William's classical allusions; those in the commentary are gathered in a useful list, *GRA* 2:458–63. In the discussion below I have relied on the allusions noted in Thomson's edition.

a matter of style: he aims to add Roman salt ("Romano sale") to a history recorded largely in English.[121] His inability to begin his history with the arrival of the Anglo-Saxons, without a backwards reference to the Roman conquest of Britain, and his inclusion in full of Hildebert's moving and sophisticated elegy "Par tibi, Roma" to the glory of Rome are only the most overt manifestations of the place of Rome in his intellectual and aesthetic landscape.[122] Although in texts for monastic audiences he frequently expresses a conventional anxiety about the pagan classics, this issue does not intrude when he writes for secular patrons and audiences. This anxiety, it appears, relates more to his understanding of the nature of the monastic vocation than to the morality of classical learning.[123] In writing for a secular patron he is free to fashion a different position for himself in relation to his classical inheritance. This self-fashioning recalls the similarly fundamental impact that the reading of Virgil, Ovid, and Horace had on authorial personae and the search for lay patronage in the eleventh century, as we saw first in the *Encomium*.[124]

William's prefatory letter to the empress brings his Roman literary inheritance directly to bear on the writing of secular history for a woman. In drawing to a close his account of Edith/Matilda's role in the production of the *Gesta regum*, he writes "maius itaque moueri fecimus de regibus opus" (we came "to set on foot a great enterprise"), echoing Virgil's own words as he invokes the muse Erato when he set out to tell the events of the last six books of the *Aeneid*.[125] In so doing, William might be seen as using allusion to make two points: first, to cast himself as a second Virgil; second, to recall the union of the Latin and Trojan stock, brought together by the defeat of Turnus and the momentous marriage of Aeneas and Lavinia, because directly after the invocation of the Muses, Virgil turns his attention to King Latinus and Lavinia. From this perspective William figures Edith/Matilda as a second Lavinia, who brings the line of English kings into union with the Normans. Yet, although the allusion is there and is sharply appropriate, William does not make it foundational, and thus he creates a space between his work and poetry. The shortcomings of Virgil's poem as

121 William of Malmesbury, *GRA* 1, prologue.

122 William of Malmesbury, *GRA* 1.1–3 and 4.351. Tilliette, "*Tamquam lapides*"; and Smolak, "Beobachtungen." Also see chapter 6 herein.

123 Thomson, *William of Malmesbury*, 10–12 and 29–33.

124 Haye, "*Nemo Mecenas*"; and see chapter 3 herein.

125 William of Malmesbury, *GRA Epistola* 2; and Virgil, *Aeneid* 7.45.

a model of history, both because it is panegyric and because its women provide no models for his patron, could not but have occurred to William and the women for whom he wrote. Like the Encomiast, when writing for a powerful woman, he does not find Lavinia an attractive model.[126]

What I want to pursue now is the possibility that Edith/Matilda's own knowledge of the Roman story world, which I have argued for in this chapter, was among the factors that drew her to William as author of the *Gesta regum*. For this ambitious work why did Edith/Matilda choose William, certainly a young man when he began to discuss history with the queen?[127] The unrequited classicism of her letters to Anselm and her attraction of and to Hildebert and Marbod illustrate that the Roman story world was part of her public image. As a queen whose court attracted scholars from all over Europe, which William himself acknowledged, she was well placed, like Emma and Edith before her, to find an author whose education and literary formation could express her own aspiration.[128]

Approaching the extensive classicism of the *Gesta regum* from the perspective of the way in which Anglo-Saxon royal women used the Roman story world, especially that of the poets, illustrates how William contributed to the debate (begun in the *Encomium*) about the relationship of Roman epic to history writing. As shown by Neil Wright's important studies of William's use of classical poets, all of William's work, and most particularly the *Gesta regum*, is shot through with references to Virgil, Lucan, and Statius; Ovid figures too.[129] William clearly recognizes the close connection between history and poetry within the Roman tradition of rhetorical historiography. When faced with his inadequacy in recounting the counsels and enterprises of Henry I's reign, he consoles himself that the task would have exceeded both Cicero and Virgil, writing: "Vix haec auderet uel Cicero in prosa, cuius adorat sales tota Latinitas, uel si quis uersuum fauore Mantuanum lacessit poetam" (Scarcely would Cicero hazard them in prose, whose brilliance makes him the idol of the Latin world, nor any rival of the bard of Mantua (if such there be) in verse).[130] His statement of the two possibilities, prose or poetry, however, only serves to flag his own definitive choice to write prose history, shaped

126 See chapter 3 herein.
127 Thomson, *William of Malmesbury*, 4 and 37.
128 William of Malmesbury, *GRA* 5.418.
129 N. Wright, "William of Malmesbury"; and N. Wright, "Industriae Testimonium."
130 William of Malmesbury, *GRA* 5, prologue.

by his study of Cicero alongside his interest in Roman, late antique, and medieval historians.[131] The contrast between the *Gesta regum* on the one hand and the *Encomium* and the *Vita Ædwardi* on the other is telling in this regard. The Encomiast and the Anonymous directly presented their queens with Roman epics as frameworks for interpreting events. This use of epic to understand history became a site for exploring the relationship of poetry to history writing and for questioning the boundaries between the two.[132] Although William is deeply engaged by the potential fictionality of his text, he purposefully does not work this out in metapoetic reflection on his own use of the Roman story world or by positioning himself as a second Virgil.[133] His aim to teach Edith/Matilda and her daughter about their Anglo-Saxon and Norman heritage as exemplary pushes him away from the panegyric that governs Virgil's poem and retrospectively emphasizes the distance between the *Encomium* and the *Vita Ædwardi* and exemplary history. In simultaneously writing in the language of the poets while keeping his poetic classicism separate from the questions that he poses about the fictionality of his own text, William makes a strong statement about the nature of *historia*.

The body of the *Gesta regum* contains a diversity of responses to the classical heritage from which both the strength and the nuance of William's intervention in the debate about the Roman story world and history writing are clear. Two issues in particular come to the fore: his concern to maintain a clear distinction between his own text and panegyric, and his awareness of the mediated and textual nature of our knowledge of the great figures of classical antiquity. Whereas the Encomiast, William of Poitiers, and the poets who wrote for women of the Conqueror's family invoked Julius Caesar and Caesar Augustus (Octavian) as uncomplicated models for conquerors and rulers of empires, William's recourse to these figures is much more circumspect. Chronologically his narrative begins with the historical Julius Caesar's imposition of Roman rule on Britain, and it is this Julius Caesar whom he recalls in his account of William the Conqueror. Distinctively, however, this is not the Julius Caesar of the poets but a man whom William of Malmesbury admires as a writer of history. William explicitly compares the moustaches of the Anglo-Saxons (which so surprised the Normans) to those described by Julius Caesar as being

131 Thomson, *William of Malmesbury*, 66–70.

132 See chapters 2 and 4 herein.

133 Otter, *Inventiones* 1–19, 98–9, and 109; and Otter, "Functions of Fiction," 116–19.

worn by the British in his *Gallic Wars*. He returns to Caesar's writing when he compares the battle tactics of William the Conqueror to those used by the Roman general against the Germans, which William knew from the pages of the *Gallic Wars*.[134] Recourse to Caesar's own writings, to draw parallels, is far away from William of Poitier's flattery of William as a second Julius Caesar. William of Malmesbury knew the *Gesta Guillemi*, and no doubt had it in mind when he referred to the distinction between his own work, which would steer a middle course, and the partisan Norman accounts of the Conqueror.[135] In the way that Malmesbury counters Poitiers's use of Julius Caesar, he reveals that he read the *Gesta Guillemi* more as panegyric than as history.

Later in the *Gesta regum*, in recounting the reign of William Rufus, Malmesbury returns again to the figure of Julius Caesar, this time in the form of Lucan's villainous instigator of the Roman civil war. However, he makes no simplistic comparison between Lucan's Julius Caesar and Rufus. Instead, he writes: "Et fortassis erit aliquis qui, Lucanum legens, falso opinetur Willelmum haec exempla de Iulio Cesare mutuatum esse. Sed non erat ei tantum studii uel otii ut litteras umquam audiret" (Some people, as they read their Lucan, might perhaps wrongly suppose that William borrowed the inspiration for these actions from Julius Caesar; but he never had either the interest or the leisure to pay any attention to literature).[136] Given the sophistication of William's reading of Lucan, which Wright has convincingly demonstrated, we are justified in reading this comment as packed and complex.[137] In reaching out to an ancient epic considered to be as much history as poetry, he simultaneously draws attention to the way in which texts can provide multiple representations of the past, to the capacity of those texts to teach, and to his own rejection of the panegyric trope of comparing a ruler to Julius Caesar.[138] Finally, the explicit reference to Lucan in his judgment of Rufus creates a bond between William and his reader, drawing him or her in as one who, like Edith/Matilda, shares his knowledge of the ancient poet.

Meanwhile, unlike his contemporary poets, Malmesbury avoids hailing William the Conqueror, or any of his sons, as a second Caesar Augustus in

134 William of Malmesbury, *GRA* 1.1, 3.239, and 3.254.

135 William of Malmesbury, *GRA* 3, preface. *GRA*, ed. Thomson, 2:219 and 2:466.

136 William of Malmesbury, *GRA* 4.320.

137 N. Wright, "Industriae Testimonium," 519–21.

138 Von Moos, "*Poeta* und *Historicus*."

the fashion of the German emperors. After offering his positive assessment of Henry III, he restricts any notion of the German ruler as a latter-day Roman emperor to his extensive quotation of Henry III's verse epitaph.[139] This manner of conceiving of modern rulers is thus labelled as the stuff of poetry, which, he reminds his reader when quoting Hildebert's long poem on Berengar of Tours, is the realm of excessive praise.[140] When Malmesbury produces his devastating portrait of Henry V, his acceptance that Henry V "antiquis Caesaribus in nullo virtute deiectior" (in no manly virtue fell short of the Caesars of Antiquity) is shortly followed by a cutting reference to his source. William dismisses this now lost text by the bishop of Bangor, David the Scot, as written "magis in regis gratiam quam historicum deceret acclinis" (with more prejudice in favour of the king than is proper for an historian).[141] Given its presence in the final folios of the *Gesta regum*, now lost from the copy presented to the empress, we do not know if William saw fit to present her with his devastating portrait of her first husband. Its inclusion in the copy he gave to her half-brother and fierce supporter of the Angevin cause, Robert of Gloucester, however, articulates his commitment to history as a mode far removed from panegyric.

William's controlled and overtly historical and textual handling of the figures of Caesar Augustus and of Julius Caesar suggests that he would have been a sceptical reader of the *Encomium*. Thomson does not include the *Encomium* among William's medieval sources. However, the nature of William's criticism of Emma suggests that he had indeed read her text. Like the Anglo-Saxon Chronicle, he attributes Emma's difficult relationship with Edward to her withholding of financial support, and locates the enmity between mother and son in her marriage to Cnut, commenting bitingly that "magis Cnutonem et amauerat uiuum et laudabat defunctum" (she had loved Cnut more [than Æthelred] while he was alive and dwelt more on his praises after his death).[142] Praises for Cnut after his death is an apt characterization of the *Encomium*, which promised to praise Emma, like Octavian, by praising her family; in addition, Cnut is presented, unproblematically, as a second Aeneas and as a Caesar.[143] William, like the Encomiast, understood that the offering of straight praise as history pushed

139 William of Malmesbury, *GRA* 2.194.
140 William of Malmesbury, *GRA* 2.284.
141 William of Malmesbury, *GRA* 5.420.
142 William of Malmesbury, *GRA* 2.196.
143 See chapter 3 herein.

beyond the limits of the capacious and undefined boundaries of *historia*. As Roman as its flavour was, perhaps the *Encomium* was not included in William's chain of English history, broken from Bede to himself, not because it was not written by an Englishman but because it was not history. William seems to have understood well the Encomiast's prefatory explorations of fictionality.

William's treatment of the European myths of Trojan descent exposes further his resistance to mistaking poetry for history. Unsurprisingly, William does not cast the Anglo-Saxons as descendants of the Trojans. His reliance on Bede and his awareness of the West Saxon dynasty's own consciousness of descent from Woden ruled out any claims to descent from Aeneas, as we saw in reading the *Encomium* and the *Vita Ædwardi*.[144] Both earlier texts were marked by the avoidance and even ridicule of claims that the Danes, the Normans, or the Welsh might trace their lineage back to Troy. William's exceptional knowledge of Virgil would have made him a very discerning reader of the Anonymous's demolition of Welsh and Norman beliefs in a Trojan identity, and he continues to develop the theme of looking to Troy as a model but not as an origin, which is found in earlier English texts. The *Gesta Normannorum ducum* was well known to William, and so we must see the absence of any hint that the Normans sprang from a Trojan line as deliberate.[145] More interesting still, in considering his view of the Trojans, is his treatment of the Franks. William's admiration for the Franks is readily apparent in the pages of the *Gesta regum*.[146] Even when they are in political disarray amid Carolingian disintegration, William remains conscious of their descent from Charlemagne, that great figure of *translatio imperii*. Frankish kingship was for William a key constitutive influence on English kingship. For example, according to William, Ecgberht's period of exile in Francia in the ninth century is central to his ability to rule well over all of England.[147]

Among his main sources of Frankish history was Hugh of Fleury's *Historia ecclesiastica* written for Adela of Blois.[148] William himself copied the *Historia* into his compendium of historians that began with Dares's supposedly eyewitness account of the Trojan war (Oxford, Bodleian

144 See chapters 3 and 5 herein.

145 William of Jumièges, *GND* 1.3. William of Malmesbury, *GRA*, ed. Thomson, 2.466.

146 William of Malmesbury, *GRA* 1.9, 1.67–8, 1.92, 1.97, 2.106, 2.110, and 2.112.

147 William of Malmesbury, *GRA* 2.106.

148 See chapter 6 herein.

Library, Archivum Seldenianum B.16).[149] Drawing on Hugh for his lineage of the Carolingians, William, in the *Gesta regum*, makes an important omission when it comes to the Trojans. Where Hugh traced the Franks back to Troy, William pointedly leaves out any mention of such illustrious ancestors, tellingly writing: "Sane, quoniam ad id locorum uenimus ut Karoli Magni mentio ultro se inferret, uolo de linea regum Francorum, de qua multa fabulatur antiquitas, ueritatem subtexere" (Now, having reached the point at which mention of Charlemagne naturally came up, I should like to add a true account of the lineage of the Frankish kings, the subject of so many hoary myths).[150] Thomson, who notes the divergence from Hugh, views William's refusal to give Trojan origins to the Franks as a result of his seeing them as a Germanic people descended from Woden, like the Anglo-Saxons and the Normans.[151] His use of the language of *fabula*, *veritas*, and *texere* suggests that William's concern to draw a clear distinction between the stuff of history and poetry was the overriding issue here, and that Troy was the unspoken referent. In the context of debates about Trojan origins at court and of the social networks that linked English royal women across the Anglo-Saxon and Anglo-Norman dynasties, William's labelling of Frankish claims to Trojan descent as fiction merits special attention. He has done this in a book written at the behest of Edith/Matilda, Adela's sister-in-law, and presented to the empress, who when still a young bride was directed by Hugh to seek a copy of the *Historia ecclesiastica* written for her aunt.[152] William was not merely indulging in scholarly debate when he took up the subject of the Trojans, but participating in international courtly controversies that engaged his female patrons and about which they were well informed.

The Roman epics also troubled William as a writer of history for women. Recollection of the Encomiast's casting of Emma as Octavian flags their inadequacy as a place to find positive images of powerful women.[153] Virgil's insufficiently imagined Lavinia hardly registers. Dido is the female figure from the *Aeneid* who most captures William's attention, as she did many before and after him. The way he refers to her reveals the challenge entailed in using Roman epic not to flatter, console, or rebuke but rather

149 Thomson, *William of Malmesbury*, 28 and 66–7.
150 William of Malmesbury, *GRA* 1.67.
151 William of Malmesbury, *GRA* 1.5. Thomson, *William of Malmesbury*, 151–2.
152 See chapter 6 herein.
153 See chapters 2 and 3 herein.

to provide *exempla*, when the audience included powerful women. In William's account of the death of Harold, shot in the eye by an arrow, his words are Virgil's describing how Cupid's arrow (fatally as it turns out) wounds Dido when she first sees Aeneas. Thus Harold is feminized, and his illegal rule of England portrayed as being as doomed and unnatural as Dido's female rule of Carthage. William uses the very same words only a book later in reporting the accidental death of William Rufus, shot by an arrow while hunting in the New Forest.[154] The effeminacy of Rufus's court, so sharply criticized by William, thus comes to mind at the point of his death, as his rule is broadly likened to that of a woman.[155] William's use of the same well-known image for both deaths is not merely felicitous language but rather makes a political point, juxtaposing two rulers, one Anglo-Saxon, the other Norman, whom he considers unfit to rule. Fascinatingly, he relies on his readers' recognition of allusion to the unforgettable character of Virgil's Dido. His ideal reader seems shaped by Edith/Matilda's love of poetry.

Dido reappears like a spectre in William's distinctive recounting of the tragic sinking of the *White Ship*.[156] The passage is dense with echoes especially to both Virgil and Lucan, but also to Statius.[157] Here, as William struggles to make sense of the death of a prince whose longed-for birth united the Anglo-Saxon and Norman dynasties, we come closest to the way the Anonymous used the epic poets in an attempt to give meaningful shape to the senseless events that threatened the stability of the kingdom. Similar too is the way the clashing of the paradigms resembles the Anonymous's switching around from Virgil to Lucan to Statius, which expressed the author's lack of sense of where his narrative was going.[158] According to William, the cause of the drowning of the prince, who had turned back even though he was free of the wrecked ship, was the voice of his half-sister calling out "femineo ululatu" (with feminine shrieks), which through allusion adds Dido's death cries to the chaos of the scene.[159] This

154 William of Malmesbury, *GRA* 3.243 and 4.333. William of Malmesbury, *GRA*, ed. Thomson, 2:235 and 2:287; and Heslop, "Regarding the Spectators," 239.

155 William of Malmesbury, *GRA* 4.314.

156 William of Malmesbury, *GRA* 5.419.

157 N. Wright, "William of Malmesbury," 150–2; and William of Malmesbury, *GRA*, ed. Thomson, 2:382–4.

158 See chapter 4 herein.

159 Virgil, *Aeneid* 4.667. N. Wright, "William of Malmesbury," 151.

invocation of the grief-driven suicide that ended Dido's reign heightens the irony of the prince being killed by the actions of one of his father's many illegitimate children, who could not rule even when they were as illustrious as Robert of Gloucester. These allusions to Dido further underscore the problematic nature of the Roman story world when one looks for exemplary figures for women who exercise and transmit political power. William's memorable portraits of women, from Hengest's daughter to Edith/Matilda herself, are not underpinned by references to Roman epic women.[160] His very conventional reference to Matilda, marchioness of Tuscany, as an Amazon when she leads troops into battle in support of Urban's claim to the papal throne, is isolated, reinforcing the sense that, while classical poetry is a language that William shares with Edith/Matilda, it limitations when writing for a woman were obvious.[161]

Genealogy: Dynastic and Textual

Genealogy, in the form of Edith/Matilda's request for more information about her ancestors, is, as we have seen, the explicit raison d'être of the *Gesta regum*.[162] As genealogy is so foundational to William's narrative, the empress becomes an ideal recipient. After the death of her mother and her brother, she, as the only descendant of the West Saxon dynasty with a claim to the throne, is the only reader for whom the *Gesta regum* makes full sense. For any other reader it can be no more than exemplary history; for her it is exemplary history fused with dynastic lineage. The late dedication to Robert of Gloucester sits oddly with this genealogical preoccupation, accentuating how, while other learned readers can gain from learning about the illustriousness of the Anglo-Saxon past, they remain outsiders. Both prefatory letter and dedicatory epilogue addressed to Robert draw attention to, rather than minimize, the earl's particularly outsider status – the former by tracing his virtues back to his Norman father, uncle, and grandfather, and the latter by tracing them back to his Norman, Flemish, and French forebears; Anglo-Saxon descent is conspicuous in its absence. Likewise, William's evasiveness about Robert's absence from the *Gesta regum* hangs over the epilogue, even though William tries to cover it by saying he will go on to write a further history about current events for

160 William of Malmesbury, *GRA* 1.7–8 and 5.418.
161 William of Malmesbury, *GRA* 3.289.
162 William of Malmesbury, *GRA Epistola* 1.

him.[163] William fulfils his promise; Robert, in his role as supporter of the empress, is the main focus of William's subsequent *Historia novella*, which was intended for Robert from the outset, not dedicated to him as an afterthought.[164] He writes one kind of history for Edith/Matilda and her daughter, and another kind, annals rooted in the here and now rather than the *longue durée* with all its genealogical weight, for Robert of Gloucester. Geoffrey of Monmouth's dedication of the *Historia regum Britanniae*, with its glorification of the British over the Anglo-Saxons, further underscores Robert's lack of investment in the Anglo-Saxon past.[165] His role in the sacking of Wilton in the civil war illustrates that he had no special regard for the Anglo-Saxon nunneries that preserved so much of that past.[166]

The prominence of genealogy as an impulse for the production of the *Gesta regum* presents itself in William's development of the image from the *Vita Ædwardi* in which a green tree appeared to Edward the Confessor on his deathbed.[167] Edward prophesies that there will be remission of suffering for the English people only "si arbor uiridis a medio sui succidatur corpore, et pars abscisa trium iugerum spatio a suo deportetur stipite, cum per se et absque humana manu uel quouis amminiculo suo connectetur trunco, ceperitque denuo uirescere et fructificare ex coalescentis su<c>i amore pristino" (when a green tree, if cut down the middle of its trunk, and the part cut off carried the space of three furlongs from the stock, shall be joined again to its trunk, by itself and without the hand of man or any sort of stake, and begin, once more to push leaves and bear fruit from the old love of its uniting sap).[168] With this vision in mind, William writes: "Plures ergo prouintiae spectabant nutum pueri, putabaturque regis Eduardi uaticinium in eo complendum; ferebaturque spes Angliae, modo arboris succisa, in illo iuuenculo iterum floribus pubescere, frutus protrudere, et ideo finem malorum sperari posse" (Thus many provinces looked to the boy's lightest wish, and in him it was supposed King Edward's prophecy was to be fulfilled: the hope of England, it was thought, once cut down like a tree, was in the person of that young prince again to blossom

163 William of Malmesbury, *GRA Epistola* 3, and 5.446–9.

164 William of Malmesbury, *Historia novella*, preface.

165 Geoffrey of Monmouth, *Historia regum Britanniae*, prologue.

166 *Gesta Stephani* 73.

167 For the image in subsequent decades see Osbert of Clare, *Vita beati Eadwardi* 22; and Aelred of Rievaulx, *Vita Edwardi regis*, Patrologiae cursus completus (hereafter cited as PL) 195, cols. 771D–774A. Stein, *Reality Fictions*, 73–5.

168 *VE* 2.11.

and bear fruit, so that one might hope the evil times were coming to an end).[169] That William records, rather than occludes, the dashed hopes that Edward's vision would be fulfilled exposes how fully this vision of the flowering green tree governed his understanding of the purpose of writing history. He may have been able to rededicate the book to Robert of Gloucester, but he could not turn around its genealogical momentum. Thus his recounting of the vision unfulfilled becomes a figure for the thwarting of his own narrative. William is unable to change course; he cannot pass over the tree in silence. Instead he incorporates into his narrative both his and the kingdom's distress that it did not bloom.[170] He continues to write a history whose ultimate goal is a ruler who brings together the Norman and West Saxon dynasties, and thus a woman reader, the empress, remains central to his vision of history. The urgency, so evident in his letters to the empress and to her uncle David, with which he seeks out the empress as a reader lies in large part because he has written a text and fundamentally developed an understanding of history that was specific to her mother as a transmitter of Anglo-Saxon dynastic claims – a role that he now urges her daughter to assume.[171]

William's green tree, taken from the *Vita Ædwardi* and then developed, is thus simultaneously about dynastic and textual genealogy. The appropriation and development of Edward's vision within the *Gesta regum* illustrates how firmly imbricated William's work was within the textual culture of English royal women throughout the eleventh and twelfth centuries; he had read many of the works written for them. William's reading, as Thomson has shown, was unparalleled in England: dissatisfied by his monastery's holdings, he bought his own books and travelled widely to consult other libraries.[172] His insatiable desire to know about the past makes it almost inevitable that he would be acquainted with the poetry and history produced for these English royal women; little slipped beyond his grasp. However, these women played a more instrumental part in his reading. Most basically, Edith/Matilda's financial support may have facilitated his access to these books, among others.[173] Even more fundamentally, his reading of the texts written for and about Emma, Edith,

169 William of Malmesbury, *GRA* 5.419.

170 *VE* 2, prologue.

171 William of Malmesbury, *GRA Epistola* 1–2.

172 Thomson, *William of Malmesbury*, 14–96.

173 Thomson, *William of Malmesbury*, 18 and 36–7.

Wilton, Margaret, Adela, and Edith/Matilda demonstrates that he worked at the culmination of a textual culture that was created by the learning and active patronage of English royal women. The *Gesta regum* reveals that he was both profoundly shaped by and critical of that textual culture, especially in its recourse to poetry.

As we saw above, William's criticism of Emma for praising Cnut too much may point to his knowledge of the *Encomium*, as do further elements such as his Emma-oriented presentation of her marriage to Cnut and the doubts he casts on Harold Harefoot's parentage.[174] Although he did not share the Encomiast's sympathies for Emma, William would have been a perceptive reader of his Virgilian exploration of fictional history writing. The late-medieval St Augustine's provenance of the eleventh-century *Encomium* manuscript may indicate that it was at St Augustine's in the twelfth century, where William could have read it. If there was a copy at Glastonbury (a distinct possibility given that the fifteenth-century Breamore copy of the Edwardian recension may have been copied from Glastonbury), William may have found it there. The Glastonbury library had a direct impact on his later revisions to the *Gesta regum*.[175] In turning to the next generation, we are on a securer footing because William certainly knew the *Vita Ædwardi*.[176] The text's Wilton associations would have marked it as a text of particular relevance to Edith/Matilda. William's learning, particularly of classical Latin poetry and of Hildebert, would have enabled him to recognize the distinctive polyphony of the Anonymous's contradictory verse and prose accounts of Edward's reign. However, for all his reliance on the *Vita Ædwardi*, his unsympathetic view of Edith shows him to have been a critical reader of her text, as apparently were many others within Wilton.[177] In this context his disdain for poetic history would have been reaffirmed by the *Vita Ædwardi*.

Another Wilton text on which William draws in the composition of the *Gesta regum* is Goscelin's *Vita* and *Translatio sanctae Edithae*.[178] The *Vita*, surviving in a version for Lanfranc, archbishop of Canterbury, as well as in a version for Wilton, may also have been known to William at

---

174 William of Malmesbury, *GRA* 2.181 and 2.188. See chapters 2 and 3 and page 334.

175 Keynes, introduction, xlv and li; William of Malmesbury, *GRA*, ed. Thomson, 2: xxvii–xxxiv; and Bolton, "Newly Emergent," 216–18.

176 See chapters 4 and 5.

177 William of Malmesbury, *GRA* 2.197 and 2.199.

178 See chapter 5 herein.

Canterbury.[179] William admired the work of Goscelin greatly; he not only drew on his works but also included a chapter in his praise in the *Gesta regum*.[180] His own visits to Canterbury would have acquainted him with the work and reputation of Goscelin, who was at St Augustine's from the 1090s onwards; he appears not to have died before 1107.[181] Perhaps the young William had met the elderly Flemish monk and discussed Wilton.[182] However, knowing that Edith/Matilda had been raised at Wilton could have influenced his turn to Goscelin's *Vita sanctae Edithae* when he sought to foreground women in his account of Anglo-Saxon royal saints. It is possible not only that Edith/Matilda knew the *Vita sanctae Edithae* but that William knew that she knew it. His inclusion of a version of the story of the Colbeck dancers within the *Gesta regum* is fascinating in regard to his sense of working within a literary tradition that he partly owed to Wilton.[183] Not only was the story recorded in Goscelin's *Translatio sanctae Edithae*, but Goscelin also claimed that the Wilton abbess Brihtgifu had had it committed to writing in English.[184] The Colbeck dancers is a story that William, familiar with Goscelin's writing, might have expected Edith/Matilda to know. William was also well placed to recognize the way that Goscelin drew on the *Vita Ædwardi* in writing the *Vita sanctae Edithae* and to recognize that there already existed an interrelated body of works for Wilton that created a Wilton textual culture. In this regard it is notable that William himself records in the *Historia novella* that the empress was at Wilton while negotiations were taking place between her and King Stephen at Winchester.[185] Although she was not educated there, this still prestigious royal foundation was a natural place for her to stay.

William and Edith/Matilda's common textual culture extended beyond Wilton. Perhaps Edith/Matilda was instrumental in providing him with access to Turgot's *Vita sanctae Margaretae*, which Thomson thinks William

179 Hollis, "Goscelin and the Wilton Women," 237–8.

180 William of Malmesbury, *GRA* 4.342. William of Malmesbury, *GRA*, ed. Thomson, 2:298–9.

181 *VE*, ed. Barlow, 133–45.

182 On William's birth date and his youthful connections with Canterbury see Thomson, *William of Malmesbury*, 5, 47, and 199–201.

183 William of Malmesbury, *GRA* 2.74–5.

184 Goscelin, *Translatio sanctae Edithae*, 16.

185 William of Malmesbury, *Historia novella*, 491.

may have used.[186] His obvious admiration for the poetry of Hildebert, two of whose poems he incorporates into the *Gesta regum* and whom he singles out for the excellence of his style, was shared by Edith/Matilda.[187] The poems about Edith/Matilda and her daughter were among a collection of Hildebert's verse, known to William. William was a reader of both "Anglia terra ferax" and "Augustis parentibus augustior," poems that celebrate the three-generational mother-daughter lineage linking Margaret, Edith/Matilda, and the empress, and which may have shaped his understanding of the *Gesta regum* as an inter-generational text. He also, not incidentally, was a reader of Hildebert's poem on Muriel.[188] His use of Hugh of Fleury's *Historia ecclesiastica* in writing about the Franks in the *Gesta regum* also marks his familiarity with the textual culture of English royal women, including Adela and the empress.[189]

Tracing these textual genealogies and the place of William and Edith/Matilda within them has important implications for our appreciation of how female patronage influenced William's writing and conceptualization of history. Earlier texts written for women enabled William to include women in his history. His use of texts for royal women is significant in illustrating his place within a textual genealogy created by a cross-generational network of women. Furthermore it shows that he wrote within a literary culture shaped by and for these women and that his work participated in a long debate, instigated and participated in by these very women, about the place of the Roman story world in interpreting, structuring, and recording their history. William was not only highly dependent on women's dynastic commemoration when it came to mending the chain of history, but he recognized that dependency.

Women, History, and Romance

William's *Gesta regum* evinces an abiding concern to make space within history for women, revealing how seriously he took his intention to write an exemplary history for a woman. A desire to include royal women, often

186 William of Malmesbury, *GRA*, ed. Thomson, 2:275 and 2:364. See also pages 304–7.

187 William of Malmesbury, *GRA* 3.284 and 4.351. See also page 330.

188 Thomson, *William of Malmesbury*, 71–2; and William of Malmesbury, *GRA*, ed. Thomson, 2:260.

189 See pages 335–6.

in stories from which they had previously been excluded, marks William's text from his account of the *Adventus Saxonum* to his portrait of Edith/Matilda herself. As Thomson notes, William wrote about "no fewer than ninety-one of them," and Ferrante strongly draws forth their importance.[190] His addition of difficulties in childbirth to the story of Æthelflæd, Lady of the Mercians, sharply illustrates that writing for a female audience made him view history afresh. His explanation that her dangerous first pregnancy accounted for her having only one child, a daughter, brings him close to Edith/Matilda. The queen, who had herself experienced difficulty in childbirth, had only two children, the second of which was her son.[191] William was well aware that gynaecology could make history: perhaps Edith/Matilda would have gone on to have further children rather than ceasing to have or desire children, as William records, if her reproductive health had been better.[192] An extra son would have prevented the succession crisis that followed Henry I's death. The variety of women and female experiences that William includes offers critical insight into the relation of Edith/Matilda's initial act of patronage to the kind of history William eventually produced.

William is particularly attentive to the role of inter-dynastic marriage in not just creating alliances but also uniting peoples.[193] In his account the very beginning of Anglo-Saxon history is marked by such a marriage. In telling the story of the invitation of the British king, Vortigern, to the Germans to come to defend and settle Britain, he supplements the information that he has gathered from Bede and the *Historia Brittonum* with legendary material in order to include the marriage of the daughter of the German invader Hengest to Vortigern. Telling a romance-like story that occurs also in Geoffrey of Monmouth's *Historia regum Britanniae* and from there in Wace's *Roman de Brut*, William recounts how the beauty of this daughter attracted the lust of Vortigern.[194]

190 Ferrante, *Glory of Her Sex*, 100–4; and William of Malmesbury, *GRA*, ed. Thomson, 2:381.

191 William of Malmesbury, *GRA* 2.125 and 5.418. The Anglo-Saxon Chronicle, the *Merician Register*, John of Worcester, and Henry of Huntingdon do not mention the pregnancy.

192 Huneycutt, *Matilda of Scotland*, 74.

193 Ferrante, *Glory of Her Sex*, 100.

194 William of Malmesbury, *GRA* 1.7–8 and 2.21; Geoffrey of Monmouth, *Historia regum Britanniae* 100 and 102; and Wace, *Roman de Brut*, lines 6931 and 6961.

Later William returns again and again to the early-tenth-century marriages of Edward the Elder's daughters into the leading imperial, royal, and comital families of Europe. Within the pages of the *Gesta regum* we can see how William struggles to find out what happened to all these women and how, as he finds out more information, he supplements his first attempts. The earlier version of the *Gesta regum*, which he presented to the empress, included three separate discussions of some of these women, who would have been of particular interest to both Edith/Matilda and her daughter given the latter's marriage to Henry V.[195] The romance quality of his story of Hengest's daughter, combined with his wider preoccupation with dynastic marriage, flags the common ground between William's *Gesta regum* and Anglo-Norman romance with its particular concern for the way in which marriage to a native heiress can legitimize claims to land taken by conquest. William's *Gesta regum* provides an early and very specific space within which to observe the links between female patronage and the proximity of history and romance, two genres that were defining themselves in relation to each other in the twelfth century.[196]

William's method of offering a balanced version of the reign of Edgar, one that presents him as pious, politically powerful, but sexually incontinent, entails bringing Edgar's women fully into history, even if it leads William to produce accounts that have more in common with romance than the Anglo-Saxon Chronicle. Like Gaimar, whose turn to romance appears obvious, William tells how Edgar's pursuit of the beautiful Ælfthryth was thwarted by his ealdorman Æthelwold, who married her in the king's stead. When she discovers what has happened, Ælfthryth reveals her beauty directly to the king, who kills her husband and marries her himself.[197] He recounts in detail other stories of Edgar's women. In one, which is told

195 William of Malmesbury, *GRA* 2.112, 2.126, 2.135, and 2.217. His most coherent account of their fates is a later insertion, contained in the version presented to Robert of Gloucester. Thomson suggests that the absence of *GRA* 2.126 from the version presented to the empress reflects a lack of Continental interest in these women (*GRA*, 2:xviii–xix). I would suggest the opposite: William's repeated efforts to find out what happened to them, which continued after he had presented a copy to the empress, reveal his sense of their particular importance in a history initiated by a woman. Thomson's commentary to each of these chapters reveals the efforts to which William went to gather information on Edward's daughters, *GRA* 2:86, 2:109–10, and 2:123.

196 Searle, "Women and the Legitimisation"; Field, "Romance as History," esp. 165–6 and 169; and Green, *Medieval Romance*, 134–201.

197 William of Malmesbury, *GRA* 2.157; and Gaimar, *Estoire*, lines 3599–974. See the concluding chapter herein.

from the vantage point of the women involved, Edgar is tricked into bedding a servant girl, whom he subsequently loved and remained faithful to (until Ælfthryth).[198] He tells the story of the marriage of Saint Edith's mother, Wulfthryth, to Edgar with an eye to Edith/Matilda's own marriage to Henry I. Although in his previous chapter William recounted Edgar's abduction and rape of a nun, he insists that Wulfthyrth was not a professed nun – merely wearing the veil for protection – when she was forced into marriage with the king.[199]

In William's hands, Edgar's women, who (save for one reference to Ælfthryth) are absent from the Anglo-Saxon Chronicle, emerge to play a variety of roles and to be seen from a variety of perspectives.[200] They are not stock characters but more individualized. Including Edgar's women was not a simple task, however; it pushed William to the edge of what he considered history. He flags his uncertainty about the veracity of these stories, which he has presented as a group, repeatedly attributing his information on Edgar's amorous adventures to people who sought to find fault with the king. Once finished, he signals the movement back to a more reliable historical account with these words: "Sed haec quomodocumque se habeant, illud constat" (But however that may be, this … is certain).[201] William made a decision (and drew attention to it) to step outside what he considered sound history in order to include women within the *Gesta regum*.

Emma and Edith, both of whose texts William may have known, were in no danger of slipping outside of history. William does not need to step beyond written sources to produce his less-than-flattering accounts of these two women.[202] Likewise, in his praise of Margaret he can draw on written sources like the Chronicle and Turgot's life and on the memories of those, such as her own daughter, who knew her.[203] More interesting in considering the challenge posed by women to the writing of history is Emma and Cnut's daughter Gunnhild, who was left out of the *Encomium* and mentioned only in passing in the *Vita Ædwardi*, despite her prestigious

198 William of Malmesbury, *GRA* 2.159.
199 William of Malmesbury, *GRA* 2.158–9.
200 ASC "D," s.a. 965.
201 William of Malmesbury, *GRA* 2.160.
202 For Emma, see William of Malmesbury, *GRA* 2.165, 2.180, 2.188, and 2.196. For Edith, see William of Malmesbury, *GRA* 2.197 and 2.199.
203 William of Malmesbury, *GRA* 2.228, 3.249, and 4.311.

marriage to Henry III.[204] William's fascination for her is easily understood within the context of the empress's marriage to Henry V. However, precisely because of that earlier neglect, William knows little about Gunnhild and has to rely on quasi-legendary material rather than the Continental historical writing such as Wipo, Adam of Bremen, the *Inventio et miracula sancti Vulfranni*, or various German and Italian chronicles that record her activities.[205] He himself acknowledges the non-historical nature of her memory when he writes that the lavishness of her wedding remained the subject of popular song in his own time. His account clearly displays its affinities with romance. He tells his readers that her beauty was great and that, when she was charged with adultery after some years of marriage, she was defended against her accuser, a gigantic man, by a pageboy who took him on in single combat. Exonerated, Gunnhild divorced her husband and became a nun. None of these details matches the life of the historical Gunnhild, who died young in Italy, leaving Henry III with a daughter who was entrusted to the nuns of Quedlinburg.[206] William's keenness to include just the sort of woman who would interest both Edith/Matilda and Matilda led him to include material whose historical veracity he himself flags as doubtful. Typically for William, he draws attention to this problem, and thus at the same time he reveals his own awareness that the historical record only inadequately represents the lives of women.[207]

The story of Gunnhild, like that of the Colbeck dancers, alerts us furthermore to the presence within the *Gesta regum* of a significant body of German legendary material relating to the reign of Henry III.[208] Gunnhild's appearance among these stories underscores that the transmission of this material was, in part, the result of and facilitated by the marriages of English royal women into the Imperial family, a matter of particular concern to both Edith/Matilda and the empress. The preponderance of stories about women and of the relations between men and women within these stories illustrates that William's turn to Germany was in part motivated by his immediate audience.[209] Dynastic marriage combined with female

204 *VE* 1.1.

205 See chapter 3 herein.

206 William of Malmesbury, *GRA* 2.188; *VE* 1.1; and Heming, *Chartularium*, p. 267. See chapter 5 herein, and Tyler, "Polyglot Royal Women."

207 See page 346.

208 See page 342.

209 *GRA* 2.174–5, 2.188, and 2.190–1.

patronage, in this context, becomes a strong impetus for the internationalization of literary culture.

The mention of the death of the historical Gunnhild within the *Carmina Cantabrigiensia* (*Cambridge Songs*) encourages us to return to them. Not only do they share the interest of the *Vita Ædwardi* in lamenting voices, including women, from classical Latin epic, but they also share William's interest in fabliau-type stories about men and women. To convey a sense of Henry III's excellent good humour, William tells one story about the emperor's sister carrying her clerkly lover on her back through the snow so that his footprints would not be detected, and another about the romantic dalliances of a clerk from the Imperial chapel.[210] William recounts another story of a beautiful young nun from Cologne who, in the convent as a result of her parents' choice rather than her own vocation, was struck by lightning, along with her lover.[211] Fabliau and stories, including about the nuns of Cologne, featured too among the *Carmina Cantabrigiensia.* Rather than being an isolated collection, in England only by chance, the songs indicate that the literary ties between Germany and England that nourished William extended back to well before the Conquest and that women always had a central place within them. Given the presence of the *Carmina Cantabrigiensia* in Canterbury at St Augustine's, William may have encountered them there.[212] The obvious relevance of William's runaway Cologne nun for Edith/Matilda, whose own veiling at Wilton was so controversial and who must have known about Harold's daughter Gunnhild and her liaisons with the counts of Richmond, underscores yet again the impact that the queen exerted on the content of the *Gesta regum.*

Writing for a woman, especially one educated at Wilton, also compels William to seek out self-consciously the lives of nuns and female saints. In praising the royal saints of the West Saxon dynasty, he apologizes for how little he knows about the women but insists that this will not deter him from including them: "Nomina quoque puellarum regii generis aliquarum oris mei perstringet preconium, prefata breuitatis uenia quam non fastidii nausia sed miraculorum facit inscitia" (There are some virgins too of royal lineage on whose names I will touch with words of praise, having first

210 William of Malmesbury, *GRA* 2.190–1.

211 William of Malmesbury, *GRA* 2.175.

212 See chapter 4 herein; *Carmina Cantabrigiensia*, ed. Ziolkowski, xxvi, xxxi, 213, and 279; and Tyler, "German Imperial Bishops." The relevant poems are 6, 14, 20, 26, and 35.

begged pardon for my brevity, which is the fruit of ignorance of their miracles and not lack of interest).[213] In the *Gesta pontificum*, the religious history of England on which he worked alongside the *Gesta regum*, William gives voice to his frustration at his inability to find out more about the female communities at Amesbury, Wherwell, and Romsey. Poignantly, he does not consign these communities to oblivion but registers their absence from the historical record and his own intention to continue pursing them. He writes of the saints of Romsey: "quarum gesta, quia nescio, non tam pretereo quam ad maiorem scribendi diligentiam reseruo, si forte congnouero" (as I am ignorant of their story, I am not so much passing it over as reserving it for more careful treatment if I ever learn it).[214] Looking for women to incorporate into his *historia* has taught him to look at the historical record in new ways and to acknowledge its primary investment in the lives of men.

Edith/Matilda is the last woman who fully engages William's attention in the *Gesta regum*. His portrait of her is ambivalent, offering censure alongside praise to such a degree that it may appear at odds with her initial act of patronage or with her daughter as substitute ideal reader.[215] The even-handedness of William's treatment of Edith/Matilda, however, presents no barrier to it being sent to the empress, nor does it undermine William's claim that the *Gesta regum* began with her mother. William praises Edith/Matilda for her beauty and for her exceptional piety, evident in her hair shirt, her care for the poor, and her attention to divine services. In keeping with the poets, William commemorates Edith/Matilda for her illustrious ancestry on both sides and singles out her affinity with her mother. But William also sharply criticizes her for her liberality to poets and to foreigners who "famam eius longe per terras uenditarent" (advertise her fame in other countries). Her liberality was so lavish as to become the vice of prodigality, which led her to wrong her tenants, depriving them of their livelihoods. Despite her faults, William concludes by assuring his reader that she now resides in heaven.[216]

The terms of his criticism of Edith/Matilda disclose further how writing for a woman has deeply shaped his practice of history. First, he is

213 William of Malmesbury, *GRA* 2.214.

214 William of Malmesbury, *Gesta pontificum* 2.78.7.

215 William of Malmesbury, *GRA*, ed. Thomson, 2:380–1. We cannot be certain that the account of Edith/Matilda was included in the version sent to the empress because it is found in the folios that were lost from its end.

216 William of Malmesbury, *GRA* 5.418.

following precisely his by-now-established method for recounting the lives of the kings of England: history demands that both the good and the bad be revealed about a subject. So with regard to the holy Edgar, as we have seen, he feels obliged to explore his reputation for lust.[217] Even in recording the life of William Rufus, whom he clearly despises, he finds that history writing dictates that he say something good about the king.[218] His censure of Edith/Matilda therefore signals that he takes her seriously as the subject of history and that he takes other women, especially the empress, seriously as readers of history. He does not offer flat, objectified stereotypes of women written for men; they are not all Ælfthryth, seductress and evil stepmother, or holy Margaret. Rather they are fully and variously imagined and incorporated into history so that other women can follow or avoid their examples. Women become part of history not solely because they keep it or are recounted in it but also because they are taught by it.

This sense that the whole nature of *historia*, both as events that happened and as their recording, is at stake in his portrait of Edith/Matilda is further brought into focus when we look at the particulars of William's criticism of her. He disapproves of her generosity to poets and foreigners who spread her fame. The problem with both poetry and fame, as William said with regard to David's account of Emperor Henry V, is that they are not history but flattery that can be bought.[219] Although in William's words we can certainly capture the sound of a complaint that Edith/Matilda had not lavished greater material benefit on the foundation of Malmesbury when she was queen and its protector, the nature of history is uppermost in his mind. In the manner of his depiction of Edith/Matilda, William makes a strong point about himself as a historian. Although he may have profited from his relationship with the queen, and his prefatory letter discloses that he hoped the empress and David would look favourably on Malmesbury, he was no mere flatterer. Praise such as that offered by the Encomiast and the Anonymous is not what William would consider history and not what he wanted to present to her daughter. Edith/Matilda was not a naive consumer of history, passively accepting what was presented to her. On the contrary, she knew other texts and genres and other writers, as William himself makes clear, and thus was free to make choices

217 William of Malmesbury, *GRA* 2.157–9. See herein pages 345–6.
218 William of Malmesbury, *GRA* 4.320.
219 William of Malmesbury, *GRA* 5.420.

about whom she patronized and what she wanted from their texts. William wants the queen and her daughter to choose history over poetry.

Edith/Matilda's own agency is to the fore in the account of her veiling that William includes in her biographical sketch. As its repeated retelling and refashioning by twelfth-century clerics illustrates, the veiling was of critical political importance and became a crucial site for the negotiation of Anglo-Saxon and Norman sovereignty.[220] In William's pages we find a version that is very close to the queen herself and one that projects the central role of women in transmitting dynastic legitimacy. According to William, Edith/Matilda veiled herself in order to be able to reject the unworthy husbands with which her father presented her before her marriage to Henry I. William expresses a powerful woman's perspective on, and more crucially intervention in, the politics of dynastic marriage. In opposition to her father she makes a politically astute choice, which enables the Anglo-Saxon and Norman lines to come together and which will in the long run allow the green tree to flower. William's Edith/Matilda takes charge of genealogy and thus of the future of English history. In this episode William shares with the romance genre an interest in women's choices, though not yet in women's interiority. The preoccupation of *Roman d'Eneas* with Lavine's falling in love with Eneas provides a point of comparison, especially since William insisted earlier on Henry I's long-held affection for Edith/Matilda, on the *amor* that brought him to seek her hand.[221] William's women everywhere display affinities with the women of romance as the historian turns to legendary material to recover and imagine what male-dominated history had forgotten.

Crucial divergences, however, separate William from the world of romance. Edith/Matilda is not represented as manoeuvred to fit in with a man's dynastic vision, as Lavine was.[222] The *Gesta regum* did not teach royal women to cultivate love in order to redeem dynastic marriage for themselves, as the *Roman d'Eneas* did. Rather, affection, women's choices, and political ambition are represented as going together to the benefit of all concerned, including England. Where the *Roman d'Eneas* expanded on women's lives in order to persuade them to concede to male ambition, William's exemplary history incorporated women into history so that they

220 See earlier on page 308.

221 William of Malmesbury, *GRA* 5.393; and *Roman d'Eneas* lines 7856ff.

222 See chapter 3 herein.

could be taught to rule well themselves and the kingdom. The empress, seeking to rule the kingdom in her own right (with William's approval), was the ideal recipient of the *Gesta regum*, including the criticism, as well as the praise, of her mother.

This comparison of the *Gesta regum* with the *Roman d'Eneas* recalls our earlier discussion of the *Encomium*, which similarly gave a very different role to Emma than that of a second Lavinia. Yet the *Gesta regum* and the *Encomium*, for all their shared debt to Roman history and epic, must not be conflated here. The Encomiast could only figure a powerful woman, Emma, as a man, Octavian.[223] In the historical circumstances of the 1120s in which there was no male heir of the marriage of Edith/Matilda and Henry I, and in which William longed for the rule of a woman, the empress, no such substitution was necessary. Likewise, although the Encomiast represented family relation to Emma as key for legitimate succession to the throne, she herself passed on neither Anglo-Saxon nor Danish lineage. In William's eyes what distinguished the empress from her rival Stephen was not Norman ancestry, as they shared this, but her Anglo-Saxon ancestry, passed on to her by her mother.[224] The *Gesta regum* is profoundly marked by William's support of descent in the female line and of female rule.

Edith/Matilda's patronage of the *Gesta regum* and William's desire that it engage and instruct her daughter have changed history up to this present day. William is among the most influential sources of late Anglo-Saxon and Anglo-Norman history whose inclusion of women has informed modern understandings of the period. Even when he is forced to write fiction (that is to use romance), almost always knowingly, he saves these women from oblivion and insists that history cannot be told without them. As a direct result, they are not forgotten, and we remember them, even when we are frustrated, as in the case of Emma and Cnut's daughter, Gunnhild, by the absence of historicity.[225] In the process of fulfilling Edith/Matilda's request, William discovered something about the

223 See chapter 3 herein.

224 The possibility that the issue of the marriage of Stephen and Matilda (granddaughter of Margaret of Scotland), which took place in 1125, could result in an English king of joint Anglo-Saxon and Norman descent cannot have shaped the *Gesta regum*, a full version of which was presented to the empress in 1126. See page 327 herein.

225 See pages 346–7 herein.

limitations of the historical record, which he then made, by virtue of his frequent insertions of meta-narrative, part of his own understanding of history, including the enabling place of fiction within it. As well as offering his readers, male as well as female, examples from which to form themselves, he instructed them in the value of history intertwined with fiction. In so doing, he found himself, from a different starting point, asking similar questions to those posed by the Encomiast, the Anonymous, William of Poitiers, and Baudri of Bourgeuil when they scrutinized their own uses of the Roman story world to interpret the political upheaval of eleventh-century England. Throughout the eleventh and twelfth centuries English royal women were the drivers of radical thinking about history and fiction, modes that would come to claim a separateness for themselves but which secular patronage – and especially active female patronage – pushed close together in one of the most exciting periods of historical writing.

Conclusion: Endings and Beginnings

A book of this nature, which traces a literary culture that has been passed down through direct genealogical or marital links from one queen to the next and looks at the wider influence of that culture, could in theory go on without end. We could ask in what ways the practices of Anglo-Saxon educated queens were passed on to figures such as Henry II's wife Eleanor of Aquitaine.[1] Or we could look at Barking, an Anglo-Saxon nunnery with close ties to Wilton, where Henry II's illegitimate daughter Matilda became abbess circa 1175. Goscelin wrote saints' lives for this foundation, as he did for Wilton, and much later in the twelfth century a nun of Barking wrote a French version of the life of Edward the Confessor that derives ultimately from the Anonymous's *Vita Ædwardi.*[2] My book finishes, however, with a brief consideration of how Edith/Matilda's daughter, the empress Matilda, and her successor, Adeliza of Louvain, discontinue and transfer into French, respectively, the legacy of Latin learning that was bequeathed to them by the royal women of the West Saxon dynasty. The aim is to bring into sharp focus just how deep, influential, and distinctive the Latinate learning of English royal women was from the beginning of the eleventh century to the middle of the twelfth century.

1 For recent minimalist views of Eleanor of Aquitaine's patronage see Broadhurst, "Henry II of England," 71–83, and Gillingham, "Cultivation of History," 26, 28, 36–7, 39; for a classic maximalist view see Lejeune, "Rôle littéraire."

2 For a recent collection of essays on Barking see Brown and Bussell, *Barking Abbey*.

The Empress

The empress Matilda, as we have seen, was fully, or more accurately potentially fully, integrated into the textual culture that united the English royal women across the eleventh and twelfth centuries. Like her aunt Adela of Blois, she was the recipient of a text from Hugh of Fleury, who addressed his history of the Franks from Louis the Pious up to the present to her as a newly married princess. In its preface he figures her conquering grandfather as a modern-day Claudius and Julius Caesar. Hildebert wrote classicizing poetry about her, celebrating her as above all her mother's daughter. What is strikingly absent from these texts is a sense of her own agency and deep literary learning, reminding us that this was no empty topos when deployed in praise of the empress's predecessors. Hugh's chronicle seems to be sent speculatively to the empress, in marked contrast to the texts for Emma, Edith, Adela, and Edith/Matilda. The praise he includes of her Norman ancestors is tacked on at the end of the preface to a work devoted to the Franks, and it is not part of the work as a whole. Although through her great-grandmother (Robert the Pious's daughter, Adela) the empress too is a Frank, Hugh makes no effort to associate her with the Capetian dynasty.[3] He did not write his chronicle with the empress as a patron of dynastic history in mind; she is secondary. The passivity, which in this instance can be attributed to her youth, continues. Hildebert's poem virtually conflates the empress with her mother, leaving no sense that the younger woman has carved out a distinctive place for herself within the literary culture that she inherited from Edith/Matilda.[4] William of Malmesbury's attempt to present the *Gesta regum* to the empress, while seriously made, has an air of desperation; his *Gesta regum* above all called for a female reader of the West Saxon dynasty, which left him with the empress. But he nowhere appeals to her own learning or even claims that she asked to receive the *Gesta regum*. Indeed, he approaches her, rather tentatively, through her uncle King David of Scotland; there is no direct contact, such as we have seen as characteristic of the relationship of author and active patron. The dedication of the final version to Robert of Gloucester is a recognition that he and other writers had tried and failed to shape the empress into a reader like her mother.[5] The empress was

3 Hugh of Fleury, *Liber qui modernorum*, pp. 376–7. See chapter 6 herein.
4 Hildebert, *Carmina minora* 35. See chapter 7 herein.
5 See chapter 7 herein.

repeatedly approached by historians and poets and chose not to patronize them. They sought to fit her into a genealogy of literary patronage stretching back to Emma and having roots in the tenth-century establishment of royal nunneries. Whereas Edith/Matilda had consciously modelled herself on her mother, Margaret, using historiography to achieve this in her commission of a life of her mother, the empress turned away. Although the empress's generosity to religious houses is recorded, she is not remembered for her literary patronage.[6]

When we catch a glimpse of the empress, much later in life in 1164, participating in Latin textual culture, she is intervening between her son, Henry II, and Thomas Becket. In a letter to the archbishop, the prior, Nicholas, of the Augustinian hospital of Mont-Saint-Jacques in Rouen, recounts how he sought the help of the empress in negotiating the increasingly intractable conflict between Henry and Becket. She asks that the Constitutions of Clarendon, which restricted ecclesiastical legal jurisdiction in favour of the crown, be read to her in Latin, which she evidently understands, and then be explained in French ("praecepit nobis eas latine legere, et exponere gallice").[7] The Latin of the constitutions is not the demanding prose of William of Malmesbury or the poetic language of Hildebert, such as her mother read; rather it is direct documentary prose, which the empress asks to have explicated in the vernacular. This episode points to a different way of interacting with texts than that of her mother. The empress is associated with historical writing of a straightforward chronicle type, more of a piece with William of Malmesbury's *Historia novella*, written for Robert of Gloucester, than the *Gesta regum*. She may have brought chronicles back with her when she returned from Germany, and she was likely known to Robert of Torigni, who, in his continuations of the *Gesta Normannorum ducum*, praises her lavishly and suggests that she knew Turgot's life of her grandmother Margaret.[8] However, she is not an active literary patron who deeply shapes both the content and the form of texts she commissions. Neither do we find classicizing or a turn to the Roman story world for interpretative frameworks and reflection on the truth of fiction in work written for her. She is not

6 Chibnall, *Empress Matilda*, 177–94.

7 Duggan, ed., *Correspondence* 41; Stubbs, ed., *Select Charters*, 163–7. Chibnall, *Empress Matilda*, 169–71; and Van Houts, "Latin and French," 68.

8 Robert of Torigni, *GND* 8.11, 8.25–7, and 8.33. Van Houts, "Latin and French," 54–7, 62–3, and 67–9.

approached as if she were a poetic or an intellectual collaborator, or even an informant.

Educated from childhood in the household of the bishop of Trier, the empress did not experience the Anglo-Saxon royal nunnery education that had so formed her mother and other Anglo-Saxon elite women (nor did she have a similar German nunnery education). Indeed, in a letter, Hildebert laments the lack of direct contact between mother and daughter, despite his episcopal efforts.[9] What we know of her education comes not from Latin historians or poets but from a vernacular writer, Benoît de Sainte-Maure, who, in reference to her learning German, emphasizes her vernacular education.[10] This gap between types of education, however, is only part of the story. Nicholas offers a portrait not of an exceptionally learned woman but of a politically powerful one. Her mother, her grandmother, her aunt, Edith, and Emma were all politically powerful and astute women who participated in governing the kingdom. There was, however, no question of their ruling it in their own right, and in different circumstances they all turned to history writing to further their own cases. Recognized by her father as his heir, Empress Matilda was in a different position: she envisaged and fought for a future where she ruled in her own name. This ambition and this understanding of herself did not leave time for the cultivation of dynastic poetry and history.

The *Vita Ædwardi*, like Goscelin's Wilton texts, Baudri's poem for Adela, and Turgot's life of Margaret, announced that it required ruminative readers, whose reading drew on the habits of monastic *lectio divina*.[11] The training and leisure required to be such an enquiring, self-conscious, and reflective reader would rarely be available to a ruler; it is marked as clerical or, in the case of the secular elite, as female. Edith/Matilda was not satisfied with the brief account of her ancestors that William had originally produced; the result of her persistence is a very long history, written in elegant Latin, which reached out to include Hildebert's linguistically and conceptually challenging poem on Rome. For all of Robert of Gloucester's cultivation of letters, the annals that William wrote specifically for and

9 Hildebert, *Epistolae* 3.14. Chibnall, *Empress Matilda*, 55; J. Green, *Henry I*, 198; and see chapter 7 herein.

10 Benoît de Sainte-Maure, *Chronique des duc de Normandie* lines 43255–63. Chibnall, *Empress Matilda*, 25.

11 See chapters 5, 6, and 7 herein.

about him when he was fully engaged in war with Stephen on behalf of the empress are brief and persuasive.[12] Their intellectual framework is designed to cement the earl's support for his half-sister at a critical time, rather than to explore and analyse multiple perspectives (as in the *Vita Ædwardi*) or centuries of history (as in the *Gesta regum*). After Edith/Matilda, secular history writing takes on a more accessible style, marked by its inclusion of documents, not poetry, and its use of romance syntax that enabled it to be easily read aloud in French for a lay audience or comprehended quickly and orally by the learned among them. Its audiences and producers were largely male, many with experience of court administration.[13] Seen from this perspective, the empress, chastised in the *Gesta Stephani* for being unfeminine, is revealed as a woman who used textual culture in a more instrumentalist manner, as a tool for governing the kingdom.[14] Perhaps the comment made of Henry II, who was well educated but with little time for literature, would fit her too. Gerald of Wales lamented that in addressing his work to Henry and his son Richard I he had written for "principibus parum literatis et multum occupatis" (princes too little lettered and too much occupied).[15] Henry II himself is associated with the direct promotion of history writing in French, specifically with Wace's *Roman de Rou* and Benoît of Sainte-Maure's *Chronique des ducs de Normandie*, not in Latin.[16]

Recognizing that the empress, sought by poets and historians alike, chose not to deploy literary culture politically offers critical insight into the history writing of eleventh- and twelfth-century England. The Latin historiographical culture that Emma initiated and Edith refracted through an Anglo-Saxon nunnery education stops with the empress because she was interested in exercising power as men do; also she was not nunnery educated (either at Wilton or in Germany). From this perspective we see

---

12 William of Malmesbury, *GRA Epistola* 1, and 4.351; and William of Malmesbury, *Historia novella*. See chapter 7 herein.

13 Gillingham, "Cultivation of History," 28–32, 36, and 39; Bainton, "Literate Sociability," esp. 23–4; and Mortensen, "Comparing and Connecting."

14 *Gesta Stephani* 58–60. Chibnall, *Empress Matilda*, 62–3 and 97.

15 Gerald of Wales, *Itinerarium Kambriae*, first preface. Gillingham, "Cultivation of History," 31. Gillingham argues persuasively that Henry II was not a patron of Latin historical writing. However, the same could be said of earlier kings. What has changed is that queens are no longer patrons of Latin historical writing as they had been in earlier generations.

16 Wace, *Roman de Rou*; Benoît, *Chronique*. Gillingham, "Cultivation of History," 28–30.

politics having a very visible impact on literary culture, throwing into high relief that the secular Latin historiography that flourished from the *Encomium* to the *Gesta regum* was the realm of royal women. This history's use of the Roman story world to negotiate conquest, its rigorous exploration both of the relationship of history and poetry and of the place of fiction within history, and its exploitation of learned Latin's symbolic value in complex multilingual court societies are all directly related to the way in which women used literary patronage to wield political power on an international stage.

Adeliza of Louvain

Although English royal women ceased to be the patrons of Latin historical writing with the death of Edith/Matilda, the never-static international literary culture created by these women across the eleventh and early-twelfth centuries did not disappear in 1118. The interlinked historiographical and poetic culture fostered by Edith/Matilda fed into the appearance of written French in a context within which written vernacular literature, unlike in Anglo-Saxon England, would be produced by female authors, such as Clemence of Barking and Marie de France, and be associated with female patronage.[17] French was a written language well before the twelfth century, with examples surviving from the mid-ninth-century Oaths of Strasbourg onwards. However, this early written French was sporadic, attested in fewer than a dozen manuscripts and largely in the form of short texts.[18] It was not until the twelfth century that French, in Northern *langues d'oïl* forms, began to be used, in Anglo-Norman court circles in England, for extended texts.[19] Adeliza of Louvain, Henry I's second wife, whom he married in 1120, is closely associated with this development, including the first known use of written French for history writing.[20]

17 Tyson, "Patronage of French Vernacular History," 185 and 220–1; and Field, "Romance as History," 166.

18 Careri, Ruby, and Short, *Livres et écritures*, xvii–xviii.

19 Clanchy, *Memory to Written Record*, 199–225; Short, "Patrons and Polyglots"; Wogan-Browne, *Saints Lives*, 1–18; Tyler, "Old English to Old French"; and O'Donnell, Townend, and Tyler, "European Literature," 635. See chapter 3 herein.

20 The account of Adeliza here draws directly on O'Donnell, Townend, and Tyler, "European Literature," 627–34, and on O'Donnell and Tyler, "From the Severn to the Rhine." In the joint article by O'Donnell, Townend, and Tyler the section including Adeliza was written by Thomas O'Donnell, and I have benefited in this chapter from further discussion with him about Adeliza.

Adeliza is said to have commissioned a French life of Henry I from one David. In so doing, she was continuing to cultivate history for dynastic commemoration, following a model set by her Anglo-Saxon predecessors but doing it in the vernacular. David's French life of Henry does not survive. We know of it from Gaimar who, writing in the late 1130s, boasted that his own *Estoire des Engleis* was far more exciting than David's dull history; it was written at the behest of a noble woman, Constance Fitz-Gilbert, and drew on both the Anglo-Saxon Chronicle and Geoffrey of Monmouth's *Historia regum Britanniae*.[21] If Gaimar's claim about David's history is not a piece of fiction (in step with Geoffrey's claims about a Welsh book, perhaps), Gaimar's own work may offer insight into vernacular history writing in Adeliza's court.

Despite his disparagement of David, we can register how firmly Gaimar had his eye on developments at court in his claim that Constance herself had a copy of David's book, and wonder how many features of his text reflected what he knew of history writing there for the queen. As writers from the Encomiast to William of Malmesbury had done when writing for queens, Gaimar gives great emphasis to Constance's active patronage of his text.[22] Like William of Malmesbury, he includes women in his history by adding romance episodes to a narrative that draws heavily on the Anglo-Saxon Chronicle; it is easy to see that female patronage also challenged Gaimar's understanding of *historia* (or rather *estoire*) and of the nature of the historical record.[23] Although the surviving text of the *Estoire des Engleis* begins with the *adventus Saxonum* (coming of the Saxons), Gaimar claims that his full two-volume work (the first volume of which has not survived) spanned the Trojan origins of the Britons up to the death of William Rufus. While we cannot read David's life, Gaimer's text shows us that history, written in French, which ostentatiously displayed its links to the royal court, continued to promote the Roman story world. Especially in light of the texts patronized by English royal women, we can suspect that classicism in some guise was a central element of David's own work. In Gaimar's acceptance of Trojan origins for the British we see a

21 Gaimar, *Estoire*, lines 6488–9. Short's commentary on these lines and Short, "Epilogue."

22 Gaimar, *Estoire*, lines 6435–98.

23 See for example Gaimar's accounts of Haveloc (lines 27–818) and Æthelthryth, lines 3587–974. Gransden, *Historical Writing*, 209–12; Press, "Precocious Courtesy"; and Gaimer, *Estoire*, ed. Short, xiv–xv and xl–xli.

new resolution of the debate that went back at least to the *Encomium* and which powerfully shaped the idea of fiction.[24]

The disputed patronage of the Anglo-Norman *Voyage of Saint Brendan*, which scholars (like the manuscripts themselves) attribute to both Edith/Matilda and Adeliza, underscores the very close links between the development of French as a written literary language in England and the literary culture of English royal women. The *Voyage of Saint Brendan*, a French reworking, by an unknown Benedeit, of the Latin *Navigatio sancti Brendani* is a key text for French literary history because of its early date (in the first quarter of the twelfth century), its substantial length, and its affinities with romance. Although generically it remains a tale of a sea voyage, its emphasis on wonder and adventure shares qualities with later romance, as does its octosyllabic verse form.[25] The difficulty of determining whether Edith/Matilda or Adeliza commanded its composition not only suggests how influential the Anglo-Saxon model of queenly literary patronage had become but also exposes something of what was at stake for literary scholars trying to work outside the boundaries of nationalizing literary history.[26]

Scholars, initially myself too, have often favoured Edith/Matilda's candidacy.[27] Although of the surviving four manuscripts of the prologue only one identifies Edith/Matilda as commissioner, that manuscript is textually distinct from the two main groups of manuscripts and may go back to an early exemplar.[28] As the daughter of the Scottish king, Edith/Matilda might be thought to have had a particular interest in an Irish saint, given the close ties between Scotland and Ireland. The romance aspects of William of Malmesbury's stories about women responded to Edith/Matilda as patron and reader, as perhaps also did the romance elements of the *Voyage of Saint Brendan*. If Edith/Matilda was the patron of the Anglo-Norman *Voyage of Saint Brendan*, then the royal women of Anglo-Saxon England took a very direct role in encouraging the beginning of French written literary culture, including the new genre of romance. From that perspective the *Voyage of Saint Brendan* becomes a tangible instance of the way in

24 Gaimar, *Estoire*, lines 6528–30.

25 *Navigatio sancti Brendani*. Benedeit, *Brendan*, ed. Short and Merrilees, 18–22.

26 Benedeit, *Brendan*, lines 10 and 13. For an account of the *Brendan*, including its patronage, see O'Donnell, Townend, and Tyler, "European Literature," 631–3.

27 Huneycutt, *Matilda of Scotland*, 139–43; and Tyler, "Old English to Old French," 176.

28 Benedeit, *Brendan*, ed. Short and Merrilees, 7–8.

which the long experience of English as a confident written language was instrumental in creating an environment in which French became a written literary language.

Edith/Matilda's linguistic experience is directly relevant to this story. Not only was she exposed from an early age to a number of European vernaculars (English, French, Gaelic, and perhaps even the German, Hungarian, and Russian of her mother's youth), but we can infer that she was aware of written English from childhood. Goscelin referred to vernacular texts at Wilton, and through William of Malmesbury she would have learned of a range of texts and documents written in English, especially the Anglo-Saxon Chronicle, if she did not already know of them.[29] She was someone who would at least have known of the Chronicle, perhaps even directly. Thus she was well placed to understand at first hand the full potential of the written vernacular word and that, in the international and multilingual contexts of the Anglo-Norman court, this potential was ebbing away from English and could be turned towards French. William of Malmesbury himself signals the importance of French literary culture within the Anglo-Norman court when he includes the first reference to the *Chanson de Roland*'s being sung by the Normans in his *Gesta regum* account of the Battle of Hastings.[30] And from the perspective of the internationalism of the literary culture of English queens, the nature of French is highly relevant. French, unlike English, was not bound to a single polity but was itself an international language – of France, the Low Countries, the western German Empire, Norman Sicily and, with the Crusades, Outremer.[31] According to this story of French, one of the pivotal moments in the development of written French, the production of the *Voyage of Saint Brendan*, not only is claimed for England but is the culmination of the educational traditions and internationalism of the Anglo-Saxon royal nunneries.

Yet, pushing hard for Edith/Matilda as the patron of the *Voyage of Saint Brendan* – however attractive that might seem for an account, such as this current book, which argues for Anglo-Saxon England's central place in European literary history – would in the final analysis shut down rather than open up the dynastic literary culture of the Anglo-Saxon royal nunneries. The Latin literary culture of the English court across the eleventh

29 See chapters 6 and 7 herein.

30 William of Malmesbury, *GRA* 3.242. William of Malmesbury, *GRA*, ed. Thomson, 2:233–4.

31 See most recently Gaunt, "French Literature Abroad."

and twelfth centuries demands to be situated in a distinctively international context in which England, France, Flanders, Normandy, and the Empire (including both Lotharingia and Germany) met.

Adeliza was the daughter of Godfrey, count of Lower Lotharingia and duke of Brabant. Three of the four surviving prologues of the *Voyage of Saint Brendan* claim that she commissioned it.[32] If our focus is the active literary patronage that is so characteristic of Anglo-Saxon queens, Adeliza is a much better candidate than Edith/Matilda. Benedeit does, after all, insist that such patronage stands behind the *Voyage of Saint Brendan* when he writes twice in the opening lines of his poem that the queen commanded him to make his translation.[33] And for all its Irish subject matter, the *Navigatio sancti Brendani*, from which the *Voyage of Saint Brendan* is translated, was especially popular in Lower Lotharingia in the early-twelfth century and apparently not known in Britain or Ireland.[34] Adeliza, rather than Edith/Matilda, is thus more likely to have known the *Navigatio* and sought its translation into French. Her commissioning of the *Voyage of Saint Brendan* is not, moreover, an isolated act; among surviving early French texts, as well as being the putative patron of David's history, she is also the dedicatee of Phillipe de Thaon's *Bestiaire*.[35]

As with Edith/Matilda, Adeliza's linguistic experience also needs to be taken into account. She was a francophone woman from a part of the Empire where Romance and Germanic languages intermingled and where ethnicity, polity, and language were obviously not identical and where social standing had a strong role to play in language choice. The place of French as a high-status language in Lotharingian elite circles may have been a factor in Adeliza's desire to have a written French translation of the *Navigatio*.[36] Adeliza was a queen with an elite experience of the interaction of French and a Germanic language, in this case Dutch rather than English, which was not framed by conquest. In this regard it is worth noting that Edith/Matilda's request for information about her West Saxon ancestors entailed a *translatio* of history from English, a language whose

32 Benedeit, *Brendan*, ed. Short and Merrilees, 4.

33 Benedeit, *Brendan*, lines 10 and 13.

34 Selmer, "Study of Latin Manuscripts," 179, and his edition of the *Navigatio*, xxviii. But note that the existence of an eleventh-century copy at Saint-Évroult points to a route, via this Norman monastic house, for the *Navigatio* to have become known to Edith/Matilda.

35 Phillipe de Thaon, *Bestiaire*, line 18.

36 Haubrichs, "Volkssprache"; and Haubrichs, "*Pêle-mêle.*"

sound distressed William of Malmesbury, into Latin in order to save it from oblivion.[37] From this perspective written English may have been more obviously a model for French in the context of the patronage of Adeliza than of Edith/Matilda. Although for both Adeliza and Edith/Matilda French was an international language, French and English likely had different symbolic values for each woman. If Adeliza was the original patron of the *Voyage of Saint Brendan*, we have, moreover, another example of the catalyzing impact of the movement of royal women on literary culture, this time from Brabant to Anglo-Norman England.

Although Adeliza takes the radical step of asking repeatedly for written French texts, and even if we have no reason to expect that she received the intensive education characteristic of Wilton, we cannot attribute her turn to the vernacular as a mark of her exclusion from Latin literary culture. French is not so much a replacement for Latin as a wholly new direction, a vernacular language that was both international and written. She held Wilton and thus was well placed to know of the nunnery's reputation for Anglo-Saxon royal learning.[38] Serlo of Wilton, a Latin poet who had studied in Paris and who also wrote French verse, may have been in her service.[39] Some manuscripts of Phillipe de Thaon's *Bestiaire* begin not with its French dedication but with a Latin poem in praise of Adeliza. The terms of its praise evoke the classicizing of the Loire poets, even if the poem itself is far from their sophistication. Adeliza is compared to Juno, Venus, and Minerva, and the gifts granted to her by Nature, such a prominent figure in Hildebert's poems about Cecilia, are said to exceed even Ovid's skill.[40] The flat-footedness of this poem, in stark contrast to the Loire poets, manifests an awareness of the cultural currency of the Roman story world when addressing an English queen. This clumsy imitation speaks of an effort to perpetuate an image of Adeliza consonant with the one so deliberately cultivated and projected by Emma, Edith, Adela, and Edith/Matilda as connoisseurs of the Roman story world. Adeliza's patronage of

37 William of Malmesbury, *GRA* 1, prologue; and William of Malmesbury, *Gesta pontificum* 4.186. It is interesting to note that William refrains, in the *GRA*, from making his sharpest criticisms of English, perhaps in deference to his patron.

38 Huneycutt, *Matilda of Scotland*, 64.

39 Rigg, *Anglo-Latin*, 70–1; and Rigg, "Serlo of Wilton."

40 Phillipe de Thaon, *Bestiaire*, ed. Walberg, ci–cii; and O'Donnell, Townend, and Tyler, "European Literature," 631. See chapter 6 herein.

French literary culture, on which Benedeit's prologue insists, was built explicitly on models forged by Anglo-Saxon queens.

The direct passing on of an English inheritance to a now francophone world is too limited a narrative: in Adeliza's circles, as in Emma's, the English queen was the active focal point of international literary culture. The marrying in of Emma and Adeliza, the marrying out of so many royal women after 1066, and the links between the Anglo-Saxon, Norman (Holy Trinity), and Angevin (Le Ronceray) nunneries insured that the movement of women was critical both to English court culture and to its being a major constitutive dimension of secular western European literary culture in the High Middle Ages. And even after the end of our story of English queens consciously following Anglo-Saxon models of literary patronage, Phillipe de Thaon's rededication of the *Bestiaire*, originally for Adeliza, to Henry II's wife Eleanor of Aquitaine reminds us that the promotion of French history writing by these Angevin monarchs drew in part on the attitudes towards the written vernacular that were current in England. Opening up the eleventh- and twelfth-century Latin literary culture of English queens brings into view the overlapping of Anglo-Saxon, Norman, Flemish, German, Lotharingian, and Northern French literature in the English royal court that put Anglo-Saxon England, though politically dead, at the heart of early-twelfth-century European literary culture.

Bibliography

Editions and Translations

Adam of Bremen. *Gesta Hammaburgensis ecclesiae pontificum*. Edited by Bernhard Schmeidler. MGH SS rer. Germ. 2. Hannover and Leipzig: Hahn, 1917. Translated by Francis Tischan as *The History of the Archbishops of Hamburg-Bremen*, 2nd ed. (New York: Columbia University Press, 2002).

Acta sanctorum Bollandiana. Brussels and elsewhere, 1643–.

Adelard of Bath. *De eodem et diverso*. Edited and translated by Charles Burnett. In *Adelard of Bath, Conversations with His Nephew: On the Same and the Different, Questions on Natural Science, and On Birds*, 2–79. Cambridge: Cambridge University Press, 1998.

Aelred of Rievaulx. *Vita sancti Edwardi regis et confessoris*. PL 195:771–4. Translated by Jane Patricia Freeland in *Aelred of Rievaulx: The Historical Works*, 125–243. Kalamazoo, MI: Cistercian Publications, 2005.

Æthelweard. *Chronicon Æthelweardi*. Edited and translated by Alistair Campbell. London: Nelson, 1962.

Alan of Lille. *De planctu Naturae*. Edited by Nicholas M. Häring as "Alan of Lille, *De Planctu Naturae*," *Studi Medievali* 19 (1978): 797–879. Translated by James J. Sheridan as *The Plaint of Nature* (Toronto: Pontifical Institute of Mediaeval Studies, 1980).

Alexander of Paris. *Le roman d'Alexandre*. Edited by E. C. Armstrong, et al. In *The Medieval French Roman d'Alexandre*, vol 2. Princeton: Princeton University Press, 1937.

Die ältere Wormser Briefsammlung. Edited by Walther Bulst. MGH Briefe d. dt. Kaiserzeit 3. Weimar: Hermann Böhlaus Nachfolger, 1949.

The Anglo-Saxon Chronicle. Translated by Dorothy Whitelock, David C. Douglas, and Susie I. Tucker. London: Eyre and Spottiswoode, 1961.

The Anglo-Saxon Chronicle MS A. Edited by J.M. Bately. Vol. 3 of *The Anglo-Saxon Chronicle: A Collaborative Edition*. Cambridge: D.S. Brewer, 1986.

The Anglo-Saxon Chronicle MS C. Edited by Katherine O'Brien O'Keeffe. Vol. 5 of *The Anglo-Saxon Chronicle: A Collaborative Edition*. Cambridge: D.S. Brewer, 2001.

The Anglo-Saxon Chronicle MS D. Edited by G.P. Cubbin. Vol. 6 of *The Anglo-Saxon Chronicle: A Collaborative Edition*. Cambridge: D.S. Brewer, 1996.

The Anglo-Saxon Chronicle MS E. Edited by Susan Irvine. Vol. 7 of *The Anglo-Saxon Chronicle: A Collaborative Edition*. Cambridge: D.S. Brewer, 2004.

Annales Bertiniani. Edited by F. Grat, J. Vielliard, and S. Clémencet as *Les annales de Saint-Bertin*. Paris: Société de l'histoire de France, 1964. Translated by Janet Nelson as *Annals of Saint-Bertin* (Manchester: Manchester University Press, 1991).

Annales Hildesheimenses. Edited by Georg Waitz. MGH SS rer. Germ. 8. Hannover: Hahn, 1878.

Anselm. *Epistolae*. Edited by F.S. Schmitt. In vols. 4 and 5 of *Sancti Anselmi Cantuariensis archiepiscopi opera omnia*. Edinburgh: Nelson, 1949 and 1951. Translated by Walter Fröhlich as *The Letters of St Anselm of Canterbury*, 3 vols. (Kalamazoo, MI: Cistercian Publications, 1990–4).

Asser. *Vita Alfredi*. Edited by William Henry Stevenson with an introduction by Dorothy Whitelock, as *Asser's Life of King Alfred*. Oxford: Clarendon Press, 1959. Translated by Simon Keynes and Michael Lapidge, in *Alfred the Great: Asser's Life of King Alfred and Other Contemporary Sources* (Harmondsworth, UK: Penguin, 1983).

Ausonius. "Citario Siculo Syracusano grammatico Burdigalensi Graeco." Edited by Karl Schenkl. In *D. Magni Ausonii opuscula*. MGH Auct. Ant. 5/2:65. Translated by H.G. Evelyn White, in *Ausonius*, 1:119 (Cambridge, MA: Harvard University Press, 1921).

– "Ludus septem sapientum." Edited by Karl Schenkl. In *D. Magni Ausonii opuscula*. MGH Auct. Ant. 5/2:104–11. Translated by H.G. Evelyn White, in *Ausonius*, 1:119 (Cambridge, MA: Harvard University Press, 1921).

– "Nomina musarum." Edited by Karl Schenkl. In *D. Magni Ausonii opuscula*. MGH Auct. Ant. 5/2:251. Translated by H.G. Evelyn White, in *Ausonius*, 2:280–1 (Cambridge, MA: Harvard University Press, 1921).

Baebius Italicus. *Ilias Latina*. Edited by Marco Scaffai. Bologna: Pàtron, 1982.

Baudri of Bourgueil. *Carmina*. Edited and translated by Jean-Yves Tilliette as *Poèmes*, 2 vols. Paris: Belles Lettres, 1998–2002. No. 134 translated by Monika Otter as "Baudri of Bourgueil, 'To the Countess Adela,'" *JML* 11 (2001): 60–141; and nos. 200 and 201, translated by Bond, in *Loving Subject*, 170–81 and 182–93.

– *Vita prima beati Roberti de Arbrissello*. PL 162:1043–58. Translated by Bruce L. Venarde, in *Robert of Arbrissel: A Medieval Religious Life*, 6–21 (Washington, DC: Catholic University of America Press, 2003).

Becker, Gustav, ed. *Catalogi bibliothecarum antiqui*. Bonn: Max. Cohen, 1885.

Bede. *Historia ecclesiastica*. Edited and translated by Bertram Colgrave and R.A.B. Mynors as *Bede's Ecclesiastical History of the English People*. OMT. Oxford: Clarendon Press, 1993.

Benedeit. *Voyage of St Brendan*. Edited by E.G.R. Waters as *The Anglo-Norman Voyage of St Brendan by Benedeit. A Poem of the Early Twelfth Century*. Oxford: Clarendon Press, 1928. Also edited by Ian Short and Brian Merrilees as *The Anglo-Norman Voyage of St Brendan* (Manchester: Manchester University Press, 1979). Translated by Glyn S. Burgess, in *The Voyage of Saint Brendan*, edited by W.R.J. Barron and Glyn S. Burgess, 74–102 (Exeter: University of Exeter Press, 2005).

Benoît de Sainte-Maure. *Chronique des ducs de Normandie*. Edited by Carin Fahlin. 4 vols. Uppsala: Almqvist and Wiksell, 1951–4, 1967, and 1979.

Beowulf. Edited by R.D. Fulk, Robert E. Bjork and John D. Niles. In *Klaeber's Beowulf and the Fight at Finnsburg*, 4th ed. Toronto: University of Toronto Press, 2008. Translated by R.M. Liuzza as *Beowulf* (Peterborough, ON: Broadview Press, 2000).

Bernard of Utrecht, *Commentum in Theodolum*. In Huygens, *Accessus ad auctores*, 55–69.

Bernard Silvestris. *Cosmographia*. Edited by Peter Dronke as *Bernardus Silvestris: Cosmographia*. Leiden: Brill, 1978. Translated by Winthrop Wetherbee as *The Cosmographia of Bernardus Silvestris* (New York: Columbia University Press, 1973).

Boethius. *De consolatione philosophiae*. Edited by Ludwig Bieler as *Anicii Manlii Severini Boethii Philosophiae consolatione*. 2nd ed. CCSL 94. Turnhout: Brepols, 1984. Translated by S.J. Tester, in *The Theological Tractates, The Consolation of Philosophy*, Loeb Classical Library (Cambridge, MA: Harvard University Press, 1973).

– *In Ciceronis topica*. Edited by J.C. Orelli and G. Baiterus. In *Ciceronis Opera*, vol. 5, part 1. Zurich: Fuesslini, 1833. Translated by Eleonore Stump as *Boethius's In Ciceronis topica* (Ithaca, NY: Cornell University Press, 1988).

Bovo. *Relatio de inventione et elevatione sancti Bertini*. Edited by Oswald Holder-Egger. MGH SS 15/1:525–34. Hannover: Hahn, 1887.

Bresslau, Harry, and Paul Kehr, eds. *Die Urkunden Heinrichs III*. MGH DD 5. Berlin: Weidmann, 1931.

Carmina Cantabrigiensia. Edited and translated by Jan M. Ziolkowski as *The Cambridge Songs (Carmina Cantabrigiensia)*. New York: Garland Publishing, 1994.

Chrétien de Troyes. *Cligès*. Edited by Charles Méla and Olivier Collet. Paris: Livre de Poche, 1994. Translated by W.W. Comfort as *Chrétien de Troyes, Arthurian Romances* (London: Dent, 1914).

Chronica monasterii Casinensis. Edited by Hartmut Hoffmann. MGH SS 34. Hannover: Hahn, 1980.

Chronicon Novaliciense. Edited by Ludwig Bethmann. MGH SS 7:73–133. Hannover: Hahn, 1846.

Cicero. *De inventione*. Edited by Eduard Stroebel. Bibliotheca scriptorum Graecorum et Romanorum Teubneriana. Berlin and Leipzig: Teubner, 1915. Translated by H.M. Hubbell, in *De inventione, De optimo, Genere, Oratorium, Topica*, Loeb Classical Library (Cambridge, MA: Harvard University Press, 1949).

– *Topica*. Edited and translated by Tobias Reinhardt. Oxford: Oxford University Press, 2003.

Claudian. *De bello Gildonico*. Edited by John Barrie Hall. In *Claudii Claudiani carmina*. Bibliotheca scriptorum Graecorum et Romanorum Teubneriana. Berlin and Leipzig: Teubner, 1985. Translated by Maurice Platnauer, in *Claudian*, 1:98–137, Loeb Classical Library (Cambridge, MA: Harvard University Press, 1922).

Conrad of Hirsau. *Dialogus super auctores*. In Huygens, *Accessus ad auctores*, 71–131.

Dares Phrygius. *De excidio Troiae historia*. Edited by F.O. Meister. Bibliotheca scriptorum Graecorum et Romanorum Teubneriana. Leipzig: Teubner, 1873. Translated by R.M. Frazer, in *The Trojan War: The Chronicles of Dictys of Crete and Dares the Phrygian* (Bloomington: Indiana University Press, 1966).

Delisle, Léopold, ed. *Rouleaux des morts du IXe au XVe siècle*. Paris: Société de l'histoire de France, 1866.

Donatus. *Vita quae Donati aucti dicitur*. Edited by Giorgio Brugnoli and Fabio Stok. In *Vitae Vergilianae Antiquae*, 71–135. Rome: Istituto Polygraphico, 1997.

Dracontius. *Orestes*. Edited by Friedrich Karl Vollmer. In *Blossii Aemilii Dracontii carmina*. MGH Auct. Ant. 14:197–226. Berlin: Weidmann, 1905.

Dudo of Saint-Quentin. *De moribus et actis primorum Normanniæ ducum*. Edited by Jules Lair. Caen: F. Le Blanc-Hardel, 1865. Translated by Eric Christiansen as *History of the Normans* (Woodbridge, UK: Boydell and Brewer, 1998).

Duggan, Anne J., ed. and trans. *The Correspondence of Thomas Becket, Archbishop of Canterbury: 1162–1170*. 2 vols. OMT. Oxford: Clarendon Press, 2000.

Eadmer. *Historia novorum in Anglia*. Edited by M. Rule. RS 81. London: Her Majesty's Stationery Office, 1884. Translated by Geoffrey Bosanquet as *Eadmer's History of Recent Events in England* (London: Cresset Press, 1964).

Encomium Emmae Reginae. Edited and translated by Alistair Campbell, with a supplementary introduction by Simon Keynes. Cambridge: Cambridge University Press, 1998.

Epistola Alexandri ad Aristotelem. Edited by W. Walther Boer. Meisenheim am Glan: Anton Hain, 1973. Translated by Richard Stoneman, in *Legends of Alexander the Great*, 3–19 (London: Dent, 1994).

"Filia praeteriti." PL 171:1444–5. Translated by Ferrante, in *Epistolae* as Hildebert's.

Folcard. *Vita quarta sancti Bertini*. *AASS*, Sept., 2:604–13.

– *Vita sancti Johannis episcopi eboracensis*. Edited by James Raine. In *Historians of the Church of York*, 1:239–60. RS 71. London: Her Majesty's Stationery Office, 1879.

Fulcoius. *Epistulae*. Edited by Marvin L. Colker. As "Fulcoii Belvacensis epistulae." *Traditio* 10 (1954): 191–273.

– *Epitaphia*. Edited by M.H. Omont as "Épitaphes métriques en l'honneur de différents personnages du XIe siècle, composées par Foulcoie de Beauvais, Archidiacre de Meaux." In *Mélanges Julien Havet: Recueil de travaux d'érudition dédiés à le mémoire de Julian Havet (1853–1893)*, 211–36. Paris: Ernest Leroux, 1895.

– *De nuptiis Christi et Ecclesiae*. Edited by Mary Isaac Jogues Rousseau. In *Fulcoii Belvacensis Utriusque de nuptiis Christi et Ecclesiae libri septem*. Washington, DC: Catholic University of America Press, 1960.

Gaimar, Geffrei. *Estoire des Engleis: History of the English*. Edited and translated by Ian Short. Oxford: Oxford University Press, 2009.

Genealogia comitum Flandrensium. Edited by Georg Heinrich Pertz. MGH SS 9:317–25. Hannover: Hahn, 1851.

Geoffrey of Monmouth. *Historia regum Britanniae*. Edited by Michael D. Reeve and translated by Neil Wright as *The History of the Kings of Britain*. Woodbridge, UK: Boydell Press, 2007.

Geoffrey of Vendôme. *Epistolae*. PL 157:184–8.

Gerald of Wales. *Itinerarium Kambriae*. Edited by James F. Dimock. In *Geraldi Cambrensis Opera*. vol 6. RS 21. London: Her Majesty's Stationery Office, 1868. Translated by Lewis Thorpe, in *The Journey through Wales and the Description of Wales* (Harmondsworth, UK: Penguin, 1978).

Gervase of Reims. *Ex miraculis sancti Donatiani Brugensibus*. Edited by Oswald Holder-Egger. MGH SS 15/2:854–8. Hannover: Hahn, 1888.

Gesta Stephani. Edited and translated by K.R. Potter, with a new introduction and notes by R.H.C. Davis. OMT. Oxford: Clarendon Press, 1976.

Godfrey of Reims. Edited by Elmar Broecker as *Gottfried von Reims: Kritische Gesamtausgabe*. Frankfurt: Peter Lang, 2002.

– "Ad Ingelrannum archdiaconum de moribus eius." In Broecker, *Gottfried von Reims*, 179–85.

– "Godefridus ad Lingonensem episcopum." In Broecker, *Gottfried von Reims*, 206–25.

– "Sompnium Godefridi de Odone Aurelianensi." In Broecker, *Gottfried von Reims*, 186–97.

Godfrey of Winchester. *Epigrammata historica*. In Wright, *Anglo-Latin Satirical Poets*, 2:148–55.

Goscelin. *Historia minor sancti Augustini*. PL 150:743–64.

– *Liber confortatorius*. Edited by C.H. Talbot as "The *Liber confortatorius* of Goscelin of Saint Bertin." *Analecta Monastica*, 3rd. series, Studii Anselmiana 37 (1955): 2–117. Translated by W.R. Barnes and Rebecca Hayward, in Hollis, *Writing the Wilton Women*, 99–207. And translated by Monika Otter as *Goscelin of St Bertin: The Book of Encouragement and Consolation ("Liber confortatorius")* (Cambridge: D.S. Brewer, 2004).

Translatio sanctae Edithae. Edited by André Wilmart as "La légende de Ste Édith en prose et vers par le moine Goscelin." *AB* 56 (1938): 265–307. Translated by Michael Wright and Kathleen Loncar, in Hollis, *Writing the Wilton Women*, 69–93.

– *Vita sanctae Edithae*. Edited by André Wilmart as "La légende de Ste Édith en prose et vers par le moine Goscelin." *AB* 56 (1938): 5–101. Translated by Michael Wright and Kathleen Loncar, in Hollis, *Writing the Wilton Women*, 21–67 (Wilton version of chapters 8–12 of *Vita* are at 63–7).

[Goscelin?]. *Vita et miracula sancti Kenelmi*. Edited and translated by Rosalind C. Love. In *Three Eleventh-Century Anglo-Latin Saints' Lives*, 49–89. OMT. Oxford: Clarendon Press, 1996.

Gozechinus. *Epistola ad Walcherum*. Edited by R.B.C. Huygens. In *Apologiae duae: Gozechini epistola ad Walcherum; Burchardi... apologia de barbis*. CCCM 62:11–43. Turnhout: Brepols, 1985. Translated by Jaeger, in *Envy of Angels*, 349–75.

Grímnismál. Edited by Gustav Neckel. In *Die Lieder des Codex Regius nebst verwandten Denkmälern I: Text*, 56–68. Revised by Hans Kuhn. 5th ed. Heidelberg: Carl Winter, 1983. Translated by Andy Orchard, in *The Elder Edda: A Book of Viking Lore*, 49–59 (Harmondsworth, UK: Penguin, 2011).

Guibert of Nogent. *Monodiarum suarum libri tres*. Edited by Edmond René Labande as *Autobiographie*. Paris: Belles Lettres, 1981. Translated by Paul J. Archambault as *A Monk's Confessions: The Memoirs of Guibert of Nogent* (University Park: Penn State University Press, 2006).

Guy of Amiens. *Carmen de Hastingae proelio*. Edited and translated by Frank Barlow. OMT. Oxford: Clarendon Press, 1999. Also edited and translated by C. Morton and H. Muntz (Oxford: Clarendon Press, 1972).

Hariulf. *Chronicon Centulense*. Edited by Ferdinand Lot as *Chronique de l'abbaye de Saint-Riquier (Ve siècle–1104)*. Paris: Alphonse Picard et Fils, 1894.

Helgaud of Fleury. *Epitoma vitae regis Rotberti Pii.* Edited and translated by Robert-Henri Bautier and Gillette Labory as *Vie de Robert le Pieux*. Paris: Centre National de la Recherche Scientifique, 1965.

Heming. *Hemingi chartularium ecclesiae Wigorniensis*. Edited by Thomas Hearne. 2 vols. Oxford: [Sheldonian Theatre], 1723.

Henry of Huntingdon. *Historia Anglorum*. Edited and translated by Diana Greenway as *Historia Anglorum: The History of the English People*. OMT. Oxford: Clarendon Press, 1996.

Herman of Tournai. *Liber de restauracione monasterii sancti Martini Tornacensis*. Edited by Georg Waitz. MGH SS 14:274–317. Hannover: Hahn, 1883. Translated by Lynn H. Nelson as *The Restoration of the Monastery of Saint Martin of Tournai* (Washington, DC: Catholic University of America Press, 1996).

Herman the Archdeacon. *Miracula sancti Eadmundi*. Edited and translated by Tom Licence. In Herman the Archdeacon and Goscelin of Saint-Bertin, *Miracles of St Edmund*. OMT. Oxford: Clarendon Press, 2014.

Hilary of Orléans. *Versus et ludi*. Edited by Walther Bulst and M.L. Bulst-Thiele. In *Hilarii Aurelianensis: Versus et ludi; Epistolae; Ludus Danielis Belouacensis*. Leiden: Brill, 1989.

Hildebert. *Carmina minora*. Edited by A. Brian Scott. Rev. ed. Munich and Leipzig: K.G. Saur, 2001. (4, 10, 15, 35, and 46 are translated by Ferrante, in *Epistolae*.)

– *De mysterio missae*. PL 171:1177–96.

Epistolae. PL 171:141–312. (1.3, 1.7, 1.9, 3.11, and 3.12 are translated by Ferrante, in *Epistolae*.)

Hildebert of Lavardin. *De querimonia*. Edited by Peter Orth. In *Hildeberts Prosimetrum "De Querimonia" und die Gedichte eines Anonymous*. Vienna: Österreichische Akademie der Wissenschaften, 2000. Translated by Balint, in *Ordering Chaos*, 174–90.

Hill, Joyce, ed. *Old English Minor Heroic Poems*. Durham, UK: Department of English Language and Medieval Literature, University of Durham, 1983.

Historia Apollonii regis Tyri. Edited by G.A.A. Kortekaas. Groningen: Bouma's Boekhuis, 1984. Translated by Elizabeth Archibald, in *Apollonius of Tyre*, 112–81.

Horace. *Ars Poetica*. Edited by D.R. Shackleton Bailey. In *Horatius: Opera*, 310–29. 4th ed. Bibliotheca scriptorum Graecorum et Romanorum Teubneriana. Berlin: de Gruyter, 2008. Translated by H.R. Fairclough, in *Satires, Epistles, Art Poetica*, 450–89, revised ed., Loeb Classical Library (Cambridge, MA: Harvard University Press, 1929).

– *Carmina*. Edited by D.R. Shackleton Bailey. In *Horatius: Opera*, 1–134. 4th ed. Bibliotheca scriptorum Graecorum et Romanorum Teubneriana. Berlin: de Gruyter, 2008. Translated by Niall Rudd, in *Odes and Epodes*, 22–261, Loeb Classical Library (Cambridge, MA: Harvard University Press, 2004).

– *Epodes*. Edited by D.R. Shackleton Bailey. In *Horatius: Opera*, 139–64. 4th ed. Bibliotheca scriptorum Graecorum et Romanorum Teubneriana. Berlin: de Gruyter, 2008. Translated by Niall Rudd, in *Odes and Epodes*, 270–319, Loeb Classical Library (Cambridge, MA: Harvard University Press, 2004).

Hugh of Fleury. *Historia ecclesiastica*. Edited by Bernard Rottendorf as *Chronicon*. Münster, 1638. Edited by Georg Waitz, *Historia ecclesiastica*. MGH SS 9:349–64. Hannover: Hahn, 1851. (Prefatory letter and epilogue are translated by Ferrante, in *Epistolae*.)

– *Libellus de regia potestate et sacerdotali dignitate*. Edited by Ernest Sackur. MGH Ldl, 2:465–94. Hannover: Hahn, 1892.

– *Liber qui modernorum regum Francorum continet actus ad 1108*. Edited by Georg Waitz. MGH SS 9:376–95. Hannover: Hahn, 1851.

Huygens, R.B.C., ed. *Accessus ad auctores: Bernard d'Utrecht, Conrad d'Hirsau*. Leiden: Brill, 1970.

Hyginus. *Fabulae*. Edited by P.K. Marshall. 2nd ed. Munich: K.G. Saur, 2002. Translated by R. Scott Smith and Stephen M. Trzaskoma, in *Apollodorus' Library and Hyginus' Fabulae: Two Handbooks of Greek Mythology*, 95–192 (Indianapolis, IN: Hackett Publishing Company, 2007).

Inventio et miracula sancti Vulfranni. Edited by J. Laporte. Société de l'Histoire de Normandie, Mélanges 14. Rouen: Impr. Lainé, 1938.

Isidore of Seville. *Etymologiae sive origines*. Edited by W.M. Lindsay. 2 vols. Oxford: Clarendon Press, 1911. Translated by Stephen A. Barney et al. as *The Etymologies of Isidore of Seville* (Cambridge: Cambridge University Press, 2006).

Jerome. *Commentarius in Sophoniam*. Edited by M. Adriaen. In *Opera Exegetica*. Part 6a:655–711. CCSL 76A. Turnhout: Brepols, 1970. Translated by Ferrante, in *Epistolae*.

– *Contra Helvidium*. As *De perpetua virginitate Beatae Mariae, contra Helvidium*. PL 23:183–206. Translated by W.H. Fremantle, in *A Select Library of Nicene and Post-Nicene Fathers of the Christian Church*, 2nd ser., vol. 6, 334–46 (New York: Christian Literature Co., 1912).

– *Epistulae*. Edited by Jérôme Labourt as *Correspondance*. 8 vols. Paris: Belles Lettres, 2002–3. (Letters 22, 30, 31, 33, 39, 46, and 108, translated by Ferrante, in *Epistolae*.)

Jezebel: A Norman Latin Poem of the Early Eleventh Century. Edited and translated by Jan Ziolkowski. New York: Garland Publishing, 1989.

John of Fécamp. "Letter to the Empress Agnes." Edited by Jean Leclercq and Jean-Paul Bonnes. In *Un maître de la vie spirituelle au XI*[e] *siècle: Jean de Fécamp*, 211–17. Paris: J. Vrin, 1946. Translated by Ferrante, in *Epistolae*.

John of Worcester. *Chronicon*. Edited by R.R. Darlington and P. McGurk, and translated by Jennifer Bray and P. McGurk, as *The Chronicle of John of Worcester*. Vol. 2, *The Annals from 450–1066*. OMT. Oxford: Clarendon Press, 1995.

Justinus. *Epitome*. Edited by Otto Seel as *M. Juniani Justini epitome historiarum Philippicarum Pompei Trogi*. Bibliotheca scriptorum Graecorum et Romanorum Teubneriana. Stuttgart: Teubner, 1972.

Kelly, Susan, ed. *The Charters of Abingdon Abbey*. 2 parts. Anglo-Saxon Charters 8. Oxford: Oxford University Press (for the British Academy), 2000–1.

Lambert of Saint-Omer. *Liber floridus*. Edited by Albert Derolez. Ghent: Story-Scientia, 1968.

Lanfranc. *Epistolae*. Edited and translated by Helen Clover and Margaret Gibson as *Letters of Lanfranc, Archbishop of Canterbury*. OMT. Oxford: Clarendon Press, 1979.

Liber Monasterii de Hyda. Edited and translated by Elisabeth van Houts and Rosalind C. Love as *The Warenne (Hyde) Chronicle*. OMT. Oxford: Clarendon Press, 2013.

Livy. *Ab urbe condita*. Edited by Jean Bayet et al. as *Histoire Romaine*. 34 vols. Paris: Belles Lettres, 1947–84. Translated by B.O. Foster et al. as *History of Rome*, 14 vols., Loeb Classical Library (Cambridge, MA: Harvard University Press, 1919–59).

Lucan. *De bello civili libri X*. Edited by D.R. Shackleton Bailey. 2nd ed. Bibliotheca scriptorum Graecorum et Romanorum Teubneriana. Berlin: de Gruyter, 2013. Translated by J.D. Duff as *The Civil War, Books I–X*, Loeb Classical Library (Cambridge, MA: Harvard University Press, 1928).

Macrobius. *Commentarium in somnium Scipionis*. Edited by James Willis. 2nd ed. 2 vols. Bibliotheca scriptorum Graecorum et Romanorum Teubneriana. Stuttgart: Teubner, 1963. Translated by William Henry Stahl as *Commentary on the Dream of Scipio* (New York: Columbia University Press, 1952).

– *Saturnalia*. Edited by Robert A. Kaster. Oxford: Oxford University Press, 2011. Translated by Robert A. Kaster as *Saturnalia*, 3 vols., Loeb Classical Library (Cambridge, MA: Harvard University Press, 2011).

Marbod. "Ad amicam gementem." In Bulst, "Liebesbriefgedichte Marbods," 294.

– "Ad amicam repatriare parantem." In Bulst, "Liebesbriefgedichte Marbods," 289–90.

– "Ad amicam zelantem." In Bulst, "Liebesbriefgedichte Marbods," 293–4.

– "Ad eandem resipiscentem." In Bulst, "Liebesbriefgedichte Marbods," 293.

– "Ad puellam adamatam rescriptum." In Bulst, "Liebesbriefgedichte Marbods," 292.
– "Ad puellam iniuste accusantem." In Bulst, "Liebesbriefgedichte Marbods," 292.
– "Ad reginam Anglorum." PL 171:1660. Translated by Ferrante, in *Epistolae*.
– "De Machabaeis." PL 171:1293–1302.
– *Epistolae*. PL 171:1465–92. *Epistola* 6, translated by Bruce Venarde, in *Robert of Arbrissel: A Medieval Religious Life*, 92–100 (Washington, DC: Catholic University of America Press, 2003).
– *Liber decem capitulorum*. Edited by Rosario Leotta. In *De ornamentis verborum; Liber decem capitulorum*, 29–72. Florence: SISMEL, 1998. Nos. 3 and 4 translated by Alcuin Blamires, in *Women Defamed and Women Defended: An Anthology of Medieval Texts*, 100–3 and 228–32 (Oxford: Oxford University Press, 1992).
– "M. episcopus E. comitissae." PL 171:1659–60.
– "Puella ad amicum munera promittentem." In Bulst, "Liebesbriefgedichte Marbods," 290.
– "Rescriptum ad amicam." In Bulst, "Liebesbriefgedichte Marbods," 290–1.
– "Rescriptum rescripto eiusdem." In Bulst, "Liebesbriefgedichte Marbods," 291.

Marchegay, Paul, ed. *Cartularium monasterii Beatae Mariae caritatis Andegavensis*. Vol. 3 of *Archives d'Anjou: Recueil de documents et mémoires inédites sur cette province, publié sous les auspices du Conseil general de Maine et Loire*. Angers: Cosnier et Lachèse, 1854.

Martianus Capella. *De nuptiis philologiae et Mercurii.* Edited by James Willis. Bibliotheca scriptorum Graecorum et Romanorum Teubneriana. Leipzig: Teubner, 1983. Translated by William Harris Stahl, Richard Johnson, and E.L. Burge as *Martianus Capella and the Seven Liberal Arts*, 2 vols. (New York: Columbia University Press, 1971–7).

Matthew Paris. *La estoire de seint Aedward le rei.* Edited by Kathryn Young Wallace. London: Anglo-Norman Text Society, 1983. Translated by Thelma S. Fenster and Jocelyn Wogan-Browne as *The History of Saint Edward the King by Matthew Paris* (Tempe, AZ: Arizona Center for Medieval and Renaissance Studies, 2008).

"Maxims II." Edited by Elliott Van Kirk Dobbie. In *Anglo-Saxon Minor Poems*, 55–7. *ASPR* 6. New York: Columbia University Press, 1942. Translated by T.A. Shippey, in *Poems of Wisdom and Learning in Old English*, 76–9 (Cambridge: D.S. Brewer, 1976).

"Menologium." Edited by Elliott Van Kirk Dobbie. In *Anglo-Saxon Minor Poems*, 49–55. *ASPR* 6. New York: Columbia University Press, 1942. Translated by Christopher A. Jones, in *Old English Shorter Poems*, vol. 1, *Religious and Didactic*, 174–89, Dumbarton Oaks Medieval Library (Cambridge, MA: Harvard University Press, 2012).

Navigatio sancti Brendani. Edited by Giovanni Orlandi and Rossana E. Guglielmetti. Florence: Edizioni del Galluzzo, 2014. And edited by Carl Selmer. Notre Dame, IN: University of Notre Dame Press, 1959. Translated by John J. O'Meara and Jonathan M. Wooding, in *The Voyage of Saint Brendan*, edited by W.R.J. Barron and Glyn S. Burgess, 26–64 (Exeter: University of Exeter Press, 2005).

Odilo of Cluny. *Epitaphium domine Adelheide auguste*. Edited by Herbert Paulhart as *Die Lebensbeschreibung Kaiserin Adelheid von Abt Odilo von Cluny*. Mitteilungen des Instituts für Österreichische Geschichtsforschung, Ergänzungsband 20.2. Graz and Cologne: Verlag Hermann Böhlaus Nachfolger, 1962. And edited by Georg Heinrich Pertz. MGH SS 4:633–49. Hannover: Hahn, 1841.

Old English "Apollonius of Tyre". Edited by Peter Goolden. Oxford: Oxford University Press, 1958. Translated by Elaine Treharne, in *Old and Middle English, c. 890–c. 1450: An Anthology*, 3rd ed., 275–99 (Oxford: Blackwell, 2010).

Old English Bede. Edited and translated by Thomas Miller. As *Old English Version of Bede's Ecclesiastical History of the English People*. 2 vols. EETS O.S. 95 and 96. London: Oxford University Press, 1890 and 1891.

Old English Boethius: An Edition of the Old English Versions of Boethius's "De Consolatione Philosophiae." Edited and translated by Malcolm Godden and Susan Irvine. 2 vols. Oxford: Oxford University Press, 2009.

Old English Orosius. Edited by Janet Bately. EETS, S.S. 6. London: Oxford University Press, 1980.

Old English Pastoral Care. Edited by Henry Sweet. As *King Alfred's West Saxon Version of Gregory's Pastoral Care*. EETS, O.S. 45. London: Oxford University Press, 1871. Preface translated by Elaine Treharne, in *Old and Middle English, c. 890–c. 1450: An Anthology*, 3rd ed., 13–17 (Oxford: Blackwell Publishing, 2010).

Orderic Vitalis. *Historia ecclesiastica*. Edited and translated by Majorie Chibnall. 6 vols. OMT. Oxford: Clarendon Press, 1968–80.

Orosius. *Historiarum adversum paganos libri septem*. Edited by Karl Zangemeister. CSEL 5. Vienna: Gerold, 1882. Translated by A.T. Fear as *Seven Books of History against the Pagans* (Liverpool: Liverpool University Press, 2010).

Osbert of Clare. *Vita beati Eadwardi regis*. Edited by Marc Bloch as "La vie de S. Édouard le Confesseur par Osbert de Clare." *AB* 41 (1923): 5–131 (edition 64–131).

Ovid. *Amores*. Edited by Antonio Ramirez de Verger. In *Carmina amatoria*, 2nd ed., 1–140. Bibliotheca scriptorum Graecorum et Romanorum Teubneriana.

Munich: Saur, 2006. Edited and translated by Grant Showerman and revised by G.P. Goold, in *Heroides; Amores*, 2nd ed., 313–511, Loeb Classical Library (Cambridge, MA: Harvard University Press, 1977).

– *Ars amatoria*. Edited by A. Ramirez de Verger. In *Carmina amatoria*, 2nd ed., 153–262. Bibliotheca scriptorum Graecorum et Romanorum Teubneriana. Munich: Saur, 2006. Translated by J. Mozley, in *The Art of Love and Other Poems*, 12–175, Loeb Classical Library (Cambridge, MA: Harvard University Press, 1979).

– *Ex Ponto, libri quattour*. Edited by John A. Richmond. Bibliotheca scriptorum Graecorum et Romanorum Teubneriana. Leipzig: Teubner, 1990. Translated by A.L. Wheeler and revised by G.P. Goold, in *Tristia; Ex Ponto*, 264–489, 2nd ed., Loeb Classical Library (Cambridge, MA: Harvard University Press, 1988).

– *Fastorum libri sex*. Edited by E.H. Alton, Donald E. Wormell, and Edward Courtney. 4th ed. Bibliotheca scriptorum Graecorum et Romanorum Teubneriana. Stuttgart: Teubner, 1997. Translated by James G. Frazer and revised by G.P. Goold. 2nd ed. Loeb Classical Library. Cambridge, MA: Harvard University Press, 1989.

– *Heroides*. Edited and translated by Grant Showerman and revised by G.P. Goold. In *Heroides; Amores*, 1–311, 2nd ed., Loeb Classical Library. Cambridge, MA: Harvard University Press, 1977.

– *Metamorphoses*. Edited by William S. Anderson. 2nd ed. Bibliotheca scriptorum Graecorum et Romanorum Teubneriana. Leipzig: Teubner, 1982. Translated by Frank Justus Miller and revised by G.P. Goold, Loeb Classical Library, vol 1, 3rd ed. (Cambridge, MA: Harvard University Press, 1977). Vol 2, 2nd ed. (Cambridge, MA: Harvard University Press, 1984).

– *Tristia*. Edited by John Barrie Hall. Bibliotheca scriptorum Graecorum et Romanorum Teubneriana. Stuttgart: Teubner, 1995. Translated by A.L. Wheeler and revised by G.P. Goold, in *Tristia; Ex Ponto*, 2–261, 2nd ed., Loeb Classical Library (Cambridge, MA: Harvard University Press, 1988).

Passio sancti Eadwardi regis at martyris. Edited by Christine Fell as *Edward King and Martyr*. Leeds: University of Leeds, School of English, 1971.

Patrologiae cursus completus, series latina. Edited by J.-P. Migne. 221 vols. Paris, 1844–64.

Paulinus of Nola. *Carmina*. Edited by Guilelmus de Hartel and revised by Margit Kamptner. In *Sancti Pontii Meropii Paulini Nolani carmina*. 2nd ed. Vol. 2. CSEL 30. Vienna: Verlag der österreichischen Akademie der Wissenschaften, 1999. Translated by P.G. Walsh as *The Poems of St. Paulinus of Nola* (New York: Newman Press, 1975).

Petrus Pictor. *Carmina*. Edited L. Van Acker. CCCM 25. Turnhout: Brepols, 1972.

Phillipe de Thaon. *Le Bestiaire*. Edited by Emmanuel Walberg. Lund and Paris: H.J. Möller and H. Welter, 1900.

Priscian. *Praeexercitamina Prisciani grammatici ex Hermogene versa*. Edited by Karl Halm. In *Rhetores Latini Minores*, 551–60. Bibliotheca scriptorum Graecorum et Romanorum Teubneriana. Leipzig: Teubner, 1863.

Ralph of Caen. *Gesta Tancredi*. Edited by Edoardo D'Angelo as *Radulphi Cadomensis Tancredus*. Turnhout: Brepols, 2011. Translated by Bernard S. Bachrach and David S. Bachrach as *The Gesta Tancredi of Ralph of Caen: A History of the Normans on the First Crusade* (Farnham: Ashgate, 2007).

Reginald of Canterbury. *Poemata*. In Wright, *The Anglo-Latin Satirical Poets*, vol. 2, 259–67.

– *Vita sancti Malchi*. Edited by Levi Robert Lind as *The Vita Sancti Malchi of Reginald of Canterbury: A Critical Edition with Introduction, Apparatus Criticus, Notes, and Indices*. Urbana: University of Illinois Press, 1942. Book 4 translated by Sylvia Parsons as "A Verse Translation of Book 4 of Reginald of Canterbury's *Vita Sancti Malchi*." In *Anglo-Latin and Its Heritage: Essays in Honour of A.G. Rigg on His 64th Birthday*, edited by Siân Echard and Gernot R. Wieland, 67–91. Turnhout: Brepols, 2001.

– Various poems. Edited by Felix Liebermann. In "Raginald von Canterbury." *Neues Archiv der Gesellschaft für ältere deutsche Geschichtskunde* 30 (1888), 519–56.

Rhetorica ad Herennium. Edited by Gualtiero Calboli. Bologna: Pàtron, 1969. Translated by Harry Caplan. Loeb Classical Library. Cambridge, MA: Harvard University Press, 1954.

Richer of Saint-Rémi. *Historiae*. Edited by Hartmut Hoffmann. MGH SS 38. Hannover: Hahn, 2000. Translated by Justin Lake. 2 vols. Dumbarton Oaks Medieval Library. Cambridge, MA: Harvard University Press, 2011.

Robert of Torigni. *Gesta Normannorum ducum*. See William of Jumièges.

Robertson, A.J., ed. *Anglo-Saxon Charters*. 2nd ed. Cambridge: Cambridge University Press, 1956.

Roman d'Eneas. Edited by J.-J. Salverda de Grave as *Eneas: Roman du XII*[e] *siècle*. Paris: Champion, 1925–9. Translated by John Yunck as *Eneas: A Twelfth-Century French Romance* (New York: Columbia University Press, 1974).

Sawyer, P.H., ed. *The Charters of Burton Abbey*. Anglo-Saxon Charters 2. Oxford: Oxford University Press (for the British Academy), 1979.

Semiramis. Edited and translated by Dronke. In *Poetic Individuality*, 66–75.

Seneca. *Thyestes*. Edited by Otto Zwierlein. In *Seneca Tragoediae*. Oxford: Clarendon Press, 1986. Translated by John G. Fitch, in *Oedipus; Agamemnon; Thyestes; Hercules on Oeta; Octavia*. Loeb Classical Library (Cambridge, MA: Harvard University Press, 2004).

"Septem maiores." In Boutemy, "Notice sur le recueil poétique," 304–5.

Serlo of Bayeux, "Versus ad Muriel sanctimonialem." In Wright, *Anglo-Latin Satirical Poets*, vol. 2, 233–41.

Servius. *Servii grammatici qui feruntur in Vergilii carmina commentarii*. Edited by G. Thilo and H. Hagen. 3 vols. Leipzig: Teubner, 1881–7.

Sextus Amarcius. *Sermones*. Edited by Karl Manitius. MGH, QQ zur Geistesgesch 6. Weimar: Hermann Böhlaus Nachfölger, 1969. Translated by Ronald E. Pepin as *Satires*, Dumbarton Oaks Medieval Library (Cambridge, MA: Harvard University Press, 2011).

Sidonius Apollinaris. *Carmina*. Edited by C. Luettjohann. In *Epistulae et carmina*. MGH Auct. Ant. 8:173–264. Berlin: Weidmann, 1887. Translated by W.B. Anderson, in *Poems and Letters*, 2–327, Loeb Classical Library (Cambridge, MA: Harvard University Press, 1936).

Simon of Ghent. *Gesta abbatum sancti Bertini Sithiensium*. Edited by Oswald Holder-Egger. MGH SS 13:635–63. Hannover: Hahn, 1848.

Statius. *Thebaid*. Edited by D.E. Hill as *Thebaidos libri xii*. 2nd ed. Leiden: Brill, 1996. Translated by J.H. Mozley. 2 vols. Loeb Classical Library (Cambridge, MA: Harvard University Press, 1928).

Stubbs, William. *Select Charters and Other Illustrations of English Constitutional History*. 9th ed., revised by H.W.C. Davis. Oxford: Clarendon Press, 1913.

Theodulus. *Ecloga*. Edited by R.P.H. Green. In *Seven Versions of Carolingian Pastoral*, 26–35. Reading, UK: Department of Classics, University of Reading, 1980.

[Turgot?]. *Vita sanctae Margaretae*. *AASS*, June, 10:328–35. Translated by Huneycutt, in *Matilda of Scotland*, 162–78.

La vie d'Édouard le confesseur: Poème anglo-normand du XIIe siècle. Edited by Ö. Södergård. Uppsala: Almqvist and Wiksell, 1948. Translated by Jane Bliss as *La vie d'Édouard le confesseur by a Nun of Barking Abbey* (Liverpool: Liverpool University Press, 2014).

Virgil. *Aeneid*. Edited by R.A.B. Mynors. In *Opera*, 103–422. Oxford: Clarendon Press, 1969. Translated by H. Rushton Fairclough. Revised ed. 2 vols. Loeb Classical Library (Cambridge, MA: Harvard University Press, 1934).

Vision of Leofric. Edited and translated by Peter A. Stokes. In "The Vision of Leofric: Manuscript, Text and Context." *RES* 63 (2012): 529–50.

Vita Ædwardi. Edited and translated by Frank Barlow as *The Life of King Edward Who Rests at Westminster*. OMT. 2nd ed. Oxford: Clarendon Press, 1992. The full extent of poem 1.1 is edited and translated in Summerson, "Tudor Antiquaries," 170–2.

Vita sancti Girardi. *AASS*, November, 4:493–502.

Wace. *Roman de Brut*. Edited and translated by Judith Weiss as *Wace's Roman de Brut: A History of the British*. Rev. ed. Exeter: Exeter University Press, 2002.

– *Roman de Rou*. Edited by Hugo Andresen as *Maistre Wace's Roman de Rou et des ducs de Normandie*. 2 vols. Heilbronn: Henninger, 1877–9. Translated by Glyn S. Burgess as *The History of the Norman People: Wace's Roman de Rou* (Woodbridge, UK: Boydell Press, 2004).

Warner of Rouen. *Moriuht: A Norman Latin Poem from the Early Eleventh Century*. Edited and translated by Christopher McDonough. Toronto: Pontifical Institute of Mediaeval Studies, 1995.

Whitelock, Dorothy, ed. *Anglo-Saxon Wills*. Cambridge: Cambridge University Press, 1930.

"Widsith." Edited by George Philip Krapp and Elliott Van Kirk Dobbie. In *The Exeter Book*, 149–53. *ASPR* 3. New York: Columbia University Press, 1936. Translated by Robert E. Bjork, in *Old English Shorter Poems*, vol 2., *Wisdom and Lyric*, 44–55, Dumbarton Oaks Medieval Library (Cambridge, MA: Harvard University Press, 2014).

Willetrudis. "Susanna." Munich, Bayerische Staatsbibliothek, clm 12513, fols. 23–35.

William of Conches. "Selections from William of Conches's Commentary on Macrobius." In Dronke, *Fabula*, 68–78.

William of Jumièges, Orderic Vitalis, and Robert of Torigni. *Gesta Normannorum ducum*. Edited and translated by Elisabeth M.C. van Houts. 2 vols. OMT. Oxford: Clarendon Press, 1992–5.

William of Malmesbury. *Gesta pontificum Anglorum: The History of the English Bishops*. Vol. 1, *Text and Translation*, by M. Winterbottom. Vol. 2, *Introduction and Commentary*, by R.M. Thomson. OMT. Oxford: Clarendon Press, 2007.

– *Gesta regum Anglorum: The History of the English Kings*. Edited and translated by R.A.B. Mynors, R.M. Thomson, and M. Winterbottom. 2 vols. OMT. Oxford: Clarendon Press, 1998–9.

– *Historia novella*. Edited and translated by K.R. Potter. London: Nelson, 1955.

– *Vita Wulfstani*. Edited and translated by M. Winterbottom and R.M. Thomson. In *Saints Lives*, 1–155. OMT. Oxford: Clarendon Press, 2002.

William of Newburgh. *Historia rerum Anglicarum*. Edited and translated by P.G. Walsh and M.J. Kennedy as *The History of English Affairs*. 2 vols. Warminster: Aris and Phillips, 1998–2007.

William of Poitiers. *Gesta Guillelmi*. Edited and translated by R.H.C. Davis and Marjorie Chibnall. OMT. Oxford: Clarendon Press, 1998.

Wipo. *Gesta Chuonradi*. Edited by Harry Bresslau. In *Wiponis opera*, 3rd ed. MGH SS 61:3–62. Hannover and Leipzig: Hahn, 1915. Translated by Theodor

E. Mommsen and Karl F. Morrison, in *Imperial Lives and Letters of the Eleventh Century*, 52–100 (New York: Columbia University Press, 1962).
– *Tetralogus*. In *Wiponis opera*, 3rd ed. MGH SS 61:75–86. Hannover and Leipzig: Hahn, 1915.
Wolfhere. *Vita Godehardi episcopi posterior*. Edited by Georg Heinrich Pertz. MGH SS 11:196–218. Hannover: Hahn, 1854.
The Wonders of the East. Edited and translated by Andy Orchard. In *Pride and Prodigies*, 175–203.
Wright, Thomas, ed. *The Anglo-Latin Satirical Poets and Epigrammatists of the Twelfth Century*. Vol 2. RS 59. London: Her Majesty's Stationery Office, 1872.
Wulfstan. *Institutes of Polity*. Edited by Karl Jost as *Die "Institutes of Polity, Civil and Ecclesiastical." Ein Werk Erzbischof Wulfstans von York*. Bern: A. Francke, 1959. Translated by Andrew Rabin, in *The Political Writings of Archbishop Wulfstan of York*, 101–24 (Manchester: Manchester University Press, 2015).
Ziolkowski, Jan, and Michael C.J. Putnam, eds. *The Virgilian Tradition: The First Fifteen Hundred Years*. New Haven, CT: Yale University Press, 2008.

Scholarship

Albu, Emily. *The Normans in Their Histories*. Woodbridge, UK: Boydell and Brewer, 2001.
Anlezark, Daniel. "Reading 'The Story of Joseph' in MS Cambridge, Corpus Christi 201." In *The Power of Words: Anglo-Saxon Studies Presented to Donald G. Scragg on His Seventieth Birthday*, edited by Jonathan Wilcox and Hugh Magennis, 61–94. Morgantown: West Virginia University Press, 2006.
Archibald, Elizabeth. *Apollonius of Tyre: Medieval and Renaissance Themes and Variations*. Cambridge: D.S. Brewer, 1991.
Ashley, Scott. "The Lay Intellectual in Anglo-Saxon England: Ealdorman Æthelweard and the Politics of History." In Wormald and Nelson, *Lay Intellectuals in the Carolingian World*, 218–45.
Aurell, Martin. "Geoffrey of Monmouth's *History of the Kings of Britain* and the Twelfth-Century Renaissance." *HSJ* 18 (2007): 1–18.
Avril, Joseph. "Les fondations, l'organisation et l'évolution des éstablissements de moniales dans le diocèse d'Angers (du XIe au XIIIe siècle)." In *Les religieuses en France au XIIIe siècle*, edited by Michel Parisse, 27–67. Nancy: Presses Universitaires de Nancy, 1989.
Bainton, Henry. "Literate Sociability and Historical Writing in Later Twelfth-Century England." *ANS* 34 (2012): 23–39.
Balint, Bridget K. *Ordering Chaos: The Self and the Cosmos in Twelfth-Century Latin Prosimetrum*. Leiden: Brill, 2009.

Banniard, Michel. "Language and Communication in Carolingian Europe." In *The New Cambridge Medieval History* II*: c. 700–c. 900*, edited by Rosamond McKitterick, 695–708. Cambridge: Cambridge University Press, 1995.

Banniard, Michel. *Viva Voce: Communication écrite et communication orale du IV*[e] *au IX*[e] *siècle en Occident latin*. Paris: Institut des Études Augustiniennes, 1992.

Barlow, Frank. *Edward the Confessor*. Berkeley and Los Angeles: University of California Press, 1970.

– *The English Church, 1000–1066*. 2nd ed. London: Longman, 1979.

– *The Godwins: The Rise and Fall of a Noble Dynasty*. Harlow, UK: Longman, 2002.

– *William Rufus*. 2nd ed. New Haven, CT: Yale University Press, 1990.

Barnes, W.R. "Goscelin's Greeks and Romans." In Hollis, *Writing the Wilton Women*, 401–17.

Barratt, Alexandra. "Small Latin? The Post-Conquest Learning of English Religious Women." In *Anglo-Latin and Its Heritage: Essays in Honour of A.G. Rigg on His 64th Birthday*, edited by Siân Echard and Gernot R. Wieland, 51–65. Turnhout: Brepols, 2001.

Barrow, Julia. "William of Malmesbury's Use of Charters." In *Narrative and History in the Early Medieval West*, edited by Elizabeth M. Tyler and Ross Balzaretti, 67–89. Turnhout: Brepols, 2006.

Bartlett, Robert. *The Making of Europe: Conquest, Colonization and Cultural Change, 950–1350*. London: Allen Lane, 1993.

– "Turgot (*c.*1050–1115)." *ODNB*. Oxford University Press, 2004. http://www.oxforddnb.com/view/article/27831, accessed 19 October 2015.

Baswell, Christopher. "Latinitas." In *The Cambridge History of Medieval English Literature*, edited by David Wallace, 122–51. Cambridge: Cambridge University Press, 1999.

– *Virgil in Medieval England: Figuring the Aeneid from the Twelfth Century to Chaucer*. Cambridge: Cambridge University Press, 1995.

Bates, David. "The Character and Career of Odo, Bishop of Bayeux (1049/50–1097)." *Speculum* 50 (1975): 1–20.

– "Le patronage clérical et intellectuel de l'évêque Odon de Bayeux 1049/50–1097." In *Chapitres et cathédrales en Normandie*, edited by Sylvette Lemagnen and Philippe Manneville, 105–14. Caen: Musée de Normandie, 1997.

Baumgartner, Emmanuèle. "La formation du mythe d'Alexandre au XIIe siècle: *Le roman d'Alexandre* et l'exotisme." In Harf-Lancner, Mathey-Maille, and Szkilnik, *Conter de Troie et d'Alexandre*, 137–58.

Bäuml, Franz H. "Varieties and Consequences of Medieval Literacy and Illiteracy." *Speculum* 55 (1980): 237–65.

Baxter, Stephen. *The Earls of Mercia: Lordship and Power in Late Anglo-Saxon England*. Oxford: Oxford University Press, 2007.

– "Edward the Confessor and the Succession Question." In Mortimer, *Edward the Confessor*, 77–118.

– "MS C of the Anglo-Saxon Chronicle and the Politics of Mid-Eleventh-Century England." *EHR* 122 (2007): 1189–227.

Beare, Rhona. "Did Goscelin Write the Earliest Life of Edward the Confessor?" *Notes and Queries* 55 (2008): 262–5.

Bédague, Jean-Charles. "Naissance et affirmation d'une collégiale: Notre-Dame de Saint-Omer, du début du IXe au début du XIIIe siècle" (unpublished thesis, École nationale des chartes, Paris, 2009). A summary can be found at http://theses.enc.sorbonne.fr/2009/bedague. Accessed 15 October 2015.

Bell, Susan Groag. "Medieval Women Book Owners: Arbiters of Lay Piety and Ambassadors of Culture." In *Women and Power in the Middle Ages*, edited by Mary Erler and Maryanne Kowaleski, 149–87. Athens: University of Georgia Press, 1988.

Bennett, Judith. "Confronting Continuity." *Journal of Women's History* 9 (1997): 73–94.

Bérat, Emma O'Loughlin. "The Patron and Her Clerk: Multilingualism and Cultural Transition." *New Medieval Literatures* 12 (2010): 23–45.

Bezzola, Reto. *Les origines et la formation de la littérature courtoise en Occident (500–1200)*. 3 parts in 5 vols. Paris: Champion, 1966–8.

Black, Mechtild. "Die Töchter Kaiser Heinrichs III und der Kaiserin Agnes." In *Vinculum Societatis: Joachim Wollasch zum 60 Geburtstag*, edited by Franz Neiske et al., 36–57. Sigmaringendorf: Glock und Lutz, 1991.

Bliese, John. "Study of Rhetoric in the Twelfth Century." *Quarterly Journal of Speech* 63 (1977): 364–83.

Bloch, Marc. "La vie de S. Édouard le Confesseur par Osbert de Clare." *AB* 41 (1923): 5–131.

Blurton, Heather. *Cannibalism in High Medieval English Literature*. Basingstoke, UK: Palgrave MacMillan, 2007.

Bodarwé, Katrinette. *Sanctimoniales litteratae: Schriftlichkeit und Bildung in den ottonischen Frauenkommunitäten Gandersheim, Essen und Quedlinburg*. Münster: Aschendorf, 2004.

Bogomoletz, Wladimir V. "Anna of Kiev: An Enigmatic Capetian Queen of the Eleventh Century." *French History* 19 (2005): 299–32.

Bolton, Timothy. *The Empire of Cnut the Great: Conquest and the Consolidation of Power in Northern Europe in the Early Eleventh Century*. Leiden: Brill, 2009.

– "English Political Refugees at the Court of King Sveinn Ástriðarson, King of Denmark (1042–76)." *Mediaeval Scandinavia* 15 (2005): 17–36.

– "A Newly Emergent Mediaeval Manuscript Containing *Encomium Emmae Reginae* with the Only Known Complete Text of the Recension Prepared for King Edward the Confessor." *Mediaeval Scandinavia* 19 (2009): 205–21.

Bond, Gerald A. "'*Iocus Amoris*:' The Poetry of Baudri of Bourgueil and the Formation of the Ovidian Subculture." *Traditio* 42 (1985): 143–93.

– *The Loving Subject: Desire, Eloquence and Power in Romanesque France.* Philadelphia: University of Pennsylvania Press, 1995.

Borsa, Paulo, Christian Høgel, Lars Boje Mortensen, and Elizabeth Tyler. "What is Medieval European Literature?" *Interfaces: A Journal of Medieval European Literatures* 1 (2015): 7–24.

Bouchard, Constance Brittain. "The Kingdom of the Franks." In Luscombe and Riley-Smith, *New Cambridge Medieval History*, 4.2:120–53.

Bouet, Pierre. "Dudon de Saint-Quentin et Virgile: *L'Énéide* au service de la cause normande." In *Recueil d'études en hommage à Lucien Musset*, 215–36. Cahier des Annales de Normandie 23. Caen: Musée de Normandie, 1990.

Boutemy, André. "Autour de Godefroid de Reims." *Latomus* 6 (1947): 231–55.

– "Muriel: Note sur deux poèmes de Baudri de Bourgueil et de Serlon de Bayeux." *Le Moyen Âge*, 3rd ser., 6 (1935): 241–51.

Bozoky, Edina. "The Sanctity and Canonisation of Edward the Confessor." In Mortimer, *Edward the Confessor*, 173–86.

Bredehoft, Thomas. *Authors, Audiences and Old English Verse.* Toronto: University of Toronto Press, 2009.

– *Textual Histories: Readings in the Anglo-Saxon Chronicle.* Toronto: University of Toronto Press, 2001.

Breisach, Ernst, ed. *Classical Rhetoric and Medieval Historiography.* Kalamazoo, MI: Medieval Institute Publications, 1985.

Bresslau, Harry. *Jahrbücher des deutschen Reichs unter Konrad II.* 2 vols. Leipzig: Duncker and Humblot, 1879–84.

Broadhurst, Karen M. "Henry II of England and Eleanor of Aquitaine: Patrons of Literature in French?" *Viator* 27 (1996): 53–84.

Brooks, Nicholas. "Why Is the *Anglo-Saxon Chronicle* about Kings?" *ASE* 39 (2010): 43–70.

Brown, Jennifer N., and Donna Alfano Bussell. *Barking Abbey and Medieval Literary Culture: Authorship and Authority in a Female Community.* Woodbridge, UK: York Medieval Press, 2012.

Bulst, Walther. "Liebesbriefgedichte Marbods." In *Liber Floridus: Mittellateinische Studien*, edited by Bernhard Bischoff and Suso Brechter, 287–301. St Ottilien, Germany: Eos Verlag der Erzabtei, 1950.

– "Studien zu Marbods Carmina varia und Liber decem capitulorum." Nachrichten Göttingen philol.-hist. Kl. n.s. Fachgruppe 4: Neuere Philologie und Literaturgeschichte 2 (1937–9): 173–241.

Butterfield, Ardis. *The Familiar Enemy: Chaucer, Language and Nation in the Hundred Years War*. Oxford: Oxford University Press, 2009.

Campbell, James. "Anglo-Saxon Courts." In Cubitt, *Court Culture in the Early Middle Ages*, 155–69.

– "England, c. 991." In *The Battle of Maldon: Fiction and Fact*, edited by J. Cooper, 1–17. London: Hambledon, 1993.

– "England, France, Flanders and Germany: Some Comparisons and Connections." In *Essays in Anglo-Saxon History*, 191–207. London: Hambledon Press, 1986.

Campbell, Miles W. "The *Encomium Emmae Reginae*: Personal Panegyric or Political Propaganda?" *Annuale Mediaevale* 19 (1979): 27–45.

Careri, Maria, Christine Ruby, and Ian Short. *Livres et écritures en français et en occitan au XIIe siècle: Catalogue illustré*. Rome: Viella, 2011.

Carruthers, Mary. *Craft of Thought: Meditation, Rhetoric, and the Making of Images, 400–1200*. Cambridge: Cambridge University Press, 1998.

Cary, George. *The Medieval Alexander*. Cambridge: Cambridge University Press, 1956.

Chase, Colin, ed. *The Dating of Beowulf*. Toronto: University of Toronto Press, 1981.

Chibnall, Marjorie. *The Empress Matilda: Queen Consort, Queen Mother and Lady of the English*. Oxford: Blackwell, 1991.

Clanchy, Michael. *From Memory to Written Record: England, 1066–1307*. 3rd ed. Oxford: Wiley-Blackwell, 2013.

Comparetti, Domenico. *Vergil in the Middle Ages*. Translated by E.F.M. Benecke, with an introduction by Jan M. Ziolkowski. Princeton: Princeton University Press, 1997.

Comte, François, and Jean Siraudeau. *Angers: Documents d'évaluation du patrimonie archéologique des villes de France*. Tours: Centre national d'archéologie urbaine, 1990.

Coumert, Magali. *Origines des peuples: Les récits du haut moyen âge occidental (550–850)*. Paris: Institut d'Études Augustiniennes, 2007.

Courcelle, Pierre. *La consolation de philosophie dans la tradition littéraire: Antécédents et postérité de Boèce*. Paris: Études Augustiniennes, 1967.

– *Lecteurs païens et lecteurs chrétiens de l'Énéide*. Vol 1. Paris: Boccard, 1984.

Cowdrey, H.E.J. *The Age of Abbot Desiderius: Montecassino, the Papacy, and the Normans in the Eleventh and Early Twelfth Centuries*. Oxford: Oxford University Press, 1983.

Crick, Julia. "The Wealth, Patronage and Connections of Women's Houses in Late Anglo-Saxon England." *Revue Bénédictine* 109 (1999): 154–85.

Cubitt, Catherine. "Ælfric's Lay Patrons." In *A Companion to Ælfric*, edited by Hugh Magennis and Mary Swan, 165–92. Leiden: Brill, 2009.

– ed. *Court Culture in the Early Middle Ages: The Proceedings of the First Alcuin Conference*. Turnhout: Brepols, 2003.

Curtius, Ernst Robert. *European Literature and the Latin Middle Ages*. Translated by Willard R. Trask. London: Routledge and Kegan Paul, 1953.

Dalarun, Jacques. *Robert of Arbrissel: Sex, Sin and Salvation in the Middle Ages*. Translated by Bruce L. Venarde. Washington, DC: Catholic University of America Press, 2006.

D'Alverny, Marie Thérèse. "Les muses et les spheres célestes." In *Classical, Medieval and Renaissance Studies in Honor of Berthold Louis Ullman*, edited by Charles Henderson, 2:7–20. Rome: Edizioni di Storia e Letteratura, 1964.

Damian-Grint, Peter. *The New Historians of the Twelfth-Century Renaissance: Inventing Vernacular Authority*. Woodbridge, UK: Boydell and Brewer, 1999.

David, Charles Wendell. *Robert Curthose: Duke of Normandy*. Cambridge, MA: Harvard University Press, 1920.

Davies, Mike. "Gruffudd ap Llywelyn, King of Wales." *Welsh History Review* 21 (2002): 207–48.

de Carlos, Helena. "Poetry and Parody: Boethius, Dreams, and Gestures in the Letters of Godfrey of Rheims." *Essays in Medieval Studies* 18 (2001): 18–30.

de Grauwe, Luc. "Zijn *olla vogala* Vlaams, of zit de Nederlandse filologie met een koekoeksie in (harr) nest(en)?" *Tijdschrift voor Nederlandse taal- en letterkunde*, 120 (2004): 44–56.

de Moreau, Éduard. *Histoire de l'église en Belgique*. 2nd ed. Brussels: L'Édition Universelle, 1945.

Denoël, Charlotte. "*Vie* de saint Omer." *La France romane: Au temps des premiers Capétiens (987–1152)*. Entry 242. Paris: Musée du Louvre Éditions (Hazan), 2005.

Derolez, Albert. *The Autograph Manuscript of the Liber Floridus: A Key to the Encyclopedia of Lambert of Saint-Omer*. Turnhout: Brepols, 1998.

– "Le 'Liber Floridus' et l'énigme du manuscrit Cotton Fragments vol. 1." *Mittellateinisches Jahrbuch* 17 (1982): 120–9.

Desmond, Marilyn. "*Dominus/Ancilla*: Rhetorical Subjectivity and Sexual Violence in the Letters of Heloise." In *The Tongue of the Fathers: Gender and Ideology in Twelfth-Century Latin*, edited by David Townsend and Andrew Taylor, 35–54. Philadelphia: University of Pennsylvania Press, 1998.

– *Reading Dido: Gender, Textuality, and the Medieval Aeneid*. Minneapolis: University of Minnesota Press, 1994.

Dickey, Mary. "Some Commentaries on the *De Inventione* and *Ad Herennium* of the Eleventh and Early Twelfth Centuries." *Mediaeval and Renaissance Studies* 6 (1968): 1–41.

Dimnik, Martin. "Kievan Rus', the Bulgars and the Southern Slavs, c. 1020–c. 1200." In Luscombe and Riley-Smith, *New Cambridge Medieval History*, 4.2:254–76.

Dronke, Peter. *Fabula: Explorations into the Uses of Myth in Medieval Platonism*. Leiden: Brill, 1974.

– "Latin and Vernacular Love-Lyrics: Rochester and St Augustine's Canterbury." *Revue Bénédictine* 115 (2005): 400–10.

– *Medieval Latin and the Rise of European Love-Lyric*. 2nd ed. 2 vols. Oxford: Oxford University Press, 1968.

– *Poetic Individuality in the Middle Ages: New Departures in Poetry, 1000–1150*. Oxford: Clarendon Press, 1970.

– *Verse with Prose from Petronius to Dante: The Art and Scope of the Mixed Form*. Cambridge, MA: Harvard University Press, 1994.

– *Women Writers of the Middle Ages: A Critical Study of Texts from Perpetua (†203) to Marguerite Porete (†1310)*. Cambridge: Cambridge University Press, 1984.

Dumville, David. "Kingship, Genealogies and Regnal Lists." In *Early Medieval Kingship*, edited by P.H. Sawyer and I.N. Wood, 72–104. Leeds: University of Leeds, School of History, 1977.

– *Wessex and England from Alfred to Edgar: Six Essays on Political, Cultural and Ecclesiastical Revival*. Woodbridge, UK: Boydell Press, 1992.

Evans, Gillian. "Étampes, Theobald d' (c.1060–c.1125)." *ODNB*. Oxford University Press, 2004. http://www.oxforddnb.com/view/article/53483, accessed 19 October 2015.

Fenster, Thelma, and Daniel Lord Smail, eds. *Fama: The Politics of Talk and Reputation in Medieval Europe*. Ithaca, NY: Cornell University Press, 2003.

Ferguson, Margaret W. *Dido's Daughters: Literacy, Gender, and Empire in Early Modern England and France*. Chicago: University of Chicago Press, 2003.

Ferrante, Joan M. *To the Glory of Her Sex: Women's Roles in the Composition of Medieval Texts*. Bloomington and Indianapolis: University of Indiana Press, 1997.

Field, Rosalind. "Romance as History, History as Romance." In *Romance in Medieval England*, edited by Maldwyn Mills, Jennifer Fellows, and Carol M. Meale, 163–73. Cambridge: D.S. Brewer, 1991.

Fleischmann, Suzanne. "On the Representation of History and Fiction in the Middle Ages." *History and Theory* 22 (1983): 278–310.

Foehr-Janssens, Yasmina. "La reine Didon: Entre fable et histoire, entre Troie et Rome." In *Entre fiction et histoire: Troie et Rome au moyen âge*, edited by Emmanuèle Baumgartner and Laurence Harf-Lancner, 127–46. Paris: Presses Sorbonne Nouvelle, 1997.

Foot, Sarah. "Dynastic Strategies: The West Saxon Royal Family in Europe." In *England and the Continent in the Tenth Century: Studies in Honour of*

Wilhelm Levison (1876–1947), edited by D. Rollason, C. Leyser, and H. Williams, 237–53. Turnhout: Brepols, 2010.

– "The Making of *Angelcynn*: English Identity before the Norman Conquest." *TRHS* 6th series, 6 (1996): 25–49.

– *Veiled Women*. Vol. 1, *The Disappearance of Nuns from Anglo-Saxon England*. Vol. 2, *Female Religious Communities in England, 871–1066*. Aldershot, UK: Ashgate, 2000.

Foreville, Raymonde. "L'école de Caen au XIe siècle et les origines normandes de l'université d'Oxford." In *Études médiévales offertes à M. le doyen Augustin Fliche*, 81–100. Montpellier: Publications de la Faculté des lettres de Montpellier, 1952.

Fowler, Dan. "The Virgil Commentary of Servius." In *The Cambridge Companion to Virgil*, edited by Charles Martindale, 73–8. Cambridge: Cambridge University Press, 1997.

Frank, Roberta. "Skaldic Verse and the Date of *Beowulf*." In Chase, *The Dating of Beowulf*, 123–39.

Fulton, Rachel. *From Judgment to Passion: Devotion to Christ and the Virgin Mary, 800–1200*. New York: Columbia University Press, 2002.

Galloway, Andrew. "Word-Play and Political Satire: Solving the Riddle of the Text of *Jezebel*." *Medium Ævum* 68 (1999): 189–208.

Gameson, Richard. "L'Angleterre et la Flandre aux Xe et XIe siècles: Le témoignage des manuscrits." In *Les échanges culturels au moyen âge*, edited by Régine Le Jan, 165–206. Paris: Publications de la Sorbonne, 2002.

– "Gospels of Margaret of Scotland and the Literacy of an Eleventh-Century Queen." In *Women and the Book: Assessing the Visual Evidence*, edited by Lesley Smith and Jane H.M. Taylor, 148–71. London: British Library, 1997.

– "'Signed' Manuscripts from Early Romanesque Flanders: Saint-Bertin and Saint-Vaast." In *Pen in Hand: Medieval Scribal Portraits, Colophons, and Tools*, edited by Michael Gullick, 31–74. London: Red Gull Press, 2006.

Gaunt, Simon. "French Literature Abroad: Towards an Alternative History of French Literature." *Interfaces: A Journal of Medieval European Literatures* 1 (2015): 25–61.

Geary, Patrick. *Phantoms of Remembrance: Memory and Oblivion at the End of the First Millennium*. Princeton: Princeton University Press, 1994.

Georgianna, Linda. "Coming to Terms with the Norman Conquest: Nationalism and English Literary History." In *Literature and Nation*, edited by Brook Thomas, 33–53. (REAL, Yearbook of Research in English and American Literature, 14.) Tübingen: Gunther Narr Verlag, 1998.

Gibson, M.T., and Lesley Smith. *Codices Boethiani: A Conspectus of Manuscripts of the Works of Boethius*. Vol. 1, *Great Britain and the Republic of Ireland*. London: Warburg Institute, University of London, 1995.

Gillingham, John. "Civilizing the English? The English Histories of William of Malmesbury and David Hume." *Historical Research* 74 (2001), 17–43.

– "The Context and Purposes of Geoffrey of Monmouth's *History of the Kings of Britain.*" *ANS* 13 (1991): 99–119.

– "The Cultivation of History, Legend, and Courtesy at the Court of Henry II." In Kennedy and Meecham-Jones, *Writers of the Reign of Henry II*, 25–52.

– *The English in the Twelfth Century: Imperialism, National Identity and Political Values*. Woodbridge, UK: Boydell and Brewer, 2000.

Glauche, Günter. *Schullektüre im Mittelalter. Entstehung und Wandlungen des Lektürekanons bis 1200 nach den Quellen dargestellt*. Munich: Arbeo-Gesellschaft, 1970.

Gneuss, Helmut. "The Origin of Standard Old English and Æthelwold's School at Winchester." *ASE* 1 (1972): 63–83.

Gneuss, Helmut, and Michael Lapidge. *A Bibliographical Handlist of Manuscripts and Manuscript Fragments Written or Owned in England up to 1100*. Toronto: University of Toronto Press, 2014.

Godden, M.R. "The Alfredian Project and Its Aftermath: Rethinking the Literary History of the Ninth and Tenth Centuries." *Proceedings of the British Academy* 162 (2009): 93–122.

– "The Anglo-Saxons and the Goths: Rewriting the Sack of Rome." *ASE* 31 (2002): 47–68.

– "Did Alfred Write Anything? The Integrity of the Alfredian Canon Revisited." *Medium Ævum* 76 (2007): 1–23.

– "The Old English *Orosius* and Its Context: Who Wrote it, for Whom, and Why?" *Quaestio Insularis: Selected Proceedings of the Cambridge Colloquium in Anglo-Saxon, Norse and Celtic* 12 (2011): 1–30.

– "The Old English *Orosius* and Its Sources." *Anglia* 129 (2011): 297–320.

Goldberg, Eric J. *The Struggle for Empire: Kingship and Conflict under Louis the German, 817–876*. Ithaca, NY: Cornell University Press, 2006.

Gransden, Antonia. "Baldwin, Abbot of Bury St Edmunds, 1065–1097." *ANS* 4 (1981), 65–76 and 187–95.

– *Historical Writing in England, c. 550 to c. 1307*. London: Routledge and Kegan Paul, 1974.

– "Prologues in the Historiography of Twelfth-Century England." In *England in the Twelfth Century: Proceedings of the 1988 Harlaxton Symposium*, edited by Daniel Williams, 55–81. Woodbridge, UK: Boydell and Brewer, 1990.

Green, D.H. *The Beginnings of Medieval Romance: Fact and Fiction, 1150–1220*. Cambridge: Cambridge University Press, 2002.

– *Medieval Listening and Reading: The Primary Reception of German Literature, 800–1300*. Cambridge: Cambridge University Press, 1994.

– *Women Readers in the Middle Ages*. Cambridge: Cambridge University Press, 2007.

Green, Judith A. *Henry I: King of England and Duke of Normandy*. Cambridge: Cambridge University Press, 2009.

Green, R.P.H. "The Genesis of a Medieval Textbook: The Models and Sources of the *Ecloga Theoduli*." *Viator* 13 (1982): 49–106.

Gretsch, Mechthild. "Historiography and Literary Patronage in Late Anglo-Saxon England: The Evidence of Æthelweard's *Chronicon*." *ASE* 41 (2012): 205–48.

Grierson, Philip. "The Relations between England and Flanders before the Norman Conquest." *TRHS*, 4th ser., 23 (1941): 71–112.

Grundmann, Herbert. "Die Frauen und die Literatur im Mittelalter: Ein Beitrag zur Frage nach der Entstehung des Schrifttums in der Volkssprache." *Archiv für Kulturgeschichte* 26 (1936): 129–61.

Guenée, Bernard. *Histoire et culture historique dans l'Occident médiévale*. Paris: Aubier, 1991.

Hagedorn, Suzanne. *Abandoned Women: Rewriting the Classics in Dante, Boccaccio, and Chaucer*. Ann Arbor: University of Michigan Press, 2004.

Hamilton, Thomas J. "Goscelin of Canterbury: A Critical Study of His Life, Works and Accomplishments." 2 vols. PhD diss., University of Virginia, 1973.

Hanawalt, E.A. "Dudo of Saint-Quentin: The Heroic Past Imagined." *HSJ* 6 (1994): 111–18.

Hanning, Robert W. *The Vision of History in Early Medieval Britain, from Gildas to Geoffrey of Monmouth*. New York: Columbia University Press, 1966.

Harf-Lancner, Laurence, Laurence Mathey-Maille, and Michelle Szkilnik, eds. *Conter de Troie et d'Alexandre*. Paris: Presse Sorbonne Nouvelle, 2006.

Harrison, Julian. "The Mortuary Roll of Turgot of Durham (d. 1115)." *Scriptorium* 58 (2004): 67–83.

Haubrichs, Wolfgang. "Volkssprache und volkssprachige Literaturen im Lotharingischen Zwischenreich (9–11 Jh)." In *Lotharingia: Eine Europäische Kernlandschaft um das Jahr 1000 / une région au centre de l'Europe autour de l'an mil*, edited by Hans-Walter Herrmann and Reinhard Schneider, 181–244. Saarbrücken: Kommissionsverlag, 1995.

– "Von *pêle-mêle* zum *vis-à-vis* Sprachinseln, Bilingualität und Sprachgrenzen zwischen Maas und Rhein in Mittelalter und Neuzeit." In *Mehrsprachigkeit im Mittelalter*, edited by Michael Baldzuhn and Christine Putzo, 69–107. Berlin: de Gruyter, 2011.

Haug, Walter. *Vernacular Literary Theory in the Middle Ages: The German Tradition, 800–1300, in Its European Context*. Translated by Joanna M. Catling. Cambridge: Cambridge University Press, 1997.

Haye, Thomas. "Christliche und pagane Dichtung bei Fulcoius von Beauvais." In *Latin Culture in the Eleventh Century: Proceeding of the Third International Conference on Medieval Latin Studies*, edited by Michael W. Herren, C.J. McDonough, and Ross G. Arthur, 1:398–409. Turnhout: Brepols, 2002.

Haye, Thomas. "*Nemo Mecenas, Nemo Modo Cesar*: Die Idee der Literaturförderung in der Lateinischen Dictung des hohen Mittelalters." *Classica et Mediaevalia* 55 (2004): 203–27.

– "Spiritual Friendship and Gender Difference in the *Liber confortatorius.*" In Hollis, *Writing the Wilton Women*, 341–53.

Hayward, Rebecca, and Stephanie Hollis. "The Female Reader in the *Liber confortatorius.*" In Hollis, *Writing the Wilton Women*, 385–99.

Heningham, Eleanor K. "The Genuineness of the *Vita Æduuardi Regis.*" *Speculum* 21 (1946): 419–56.

– "The Literary Unity, the Date, and the Purpose of the Lady Edith's Book: 'The Life of King Edward Who Rests in Westminster.'" *Albion* 7 (1975): 24–40.

Herren, Michael W., C.J. McDonough, and Ross G. Arthur, eds. *Latin Culture in the Eleventh Century: Proceedings of the Third International Conference on Medieval Latin Studies, Cambridge, September 9–12, 1998*. 2 vols. Turnhout: Brepols, 2002.

Heslop, T.A. "Regarding the Spectators of the Bayeux Tapestry: Bishop Odo and His Circle." *Art History* 32 (2009): 223–49.

Hexter, Ralph. Review of *Historia Apollonii regis Tyri*, edited by G.A.A. Kortekaas. *Speculum* 63 (1988): 1986–90.

Heyworth, Melanie. "*Apollonius of Tyre* in Its Manuscript Context: An Issue of Marriage."*Philological Quarterly* 86 (2007): 1–26.

Hinds, Stephen. *Allusion and Intertext: Dynamics of Appropriation in Roman Poetry*. Cambridge: Cambridge University Press, 1998.

Hofmann, Heinz, ed. *Latin Fiction: The Latin Novel in Context*. London: Routledge. 1999.

Hofstetter, Walter. "Winchester and the Standardization of Old English Vocabulary." *ASE* 17 (1998): 139–61.

Hollis, Stephanie. Afterword to *Writing the Wilton Women*, 419–30.

– "Barking's Monastic School, Late Seventh to Twelfth Century: History, Saint-Making and Literary Culture." In Brown and Bussell, *Barking Abbey*, 33–55.

– "Edith as Contemplative and Bride of Christ." In *Writing the Wilton Women*, 281–306.

– "Goscelin's Writings and the Wilton Women." In *Writing the Wilton Women*, 217–44.

– Introduction to *Writing the Wilton Women*, 1–13.

– "St Edith and the Wilton Community." In *Writing the Wilton Women*, 245–80.

– "Wilton as a Centre of Learning." In *Writing the Wilton Women*, 307–38.

– ed. *Writing the Wilton Women: Goscelin's Legend of Edith and Liber confortatorius*. Turnhout: Brepols, 2004.

Hooper, Nicholas J. "Edgar the Ætheling: Anglo-Saxon Prince, Rebel and Crusader." *ASE* 14 (1985): 197–214.

Howe, Nicholas. "The Cultural Construction of Reading in Anglo-Saxon England." In *The Ethnography of Reading*, edited by Jonathan Boyarin, 58–79. Berkeley: University of California Press, 1993.

– *Migration and Mythmaking in Anglo-Saxon England*. New Haven, CT: Yale University Press, 1989.

Huneycutt, Lois L. "The Idea of the Perfect Princess: The *Life of St Margaret* in the Reign of Matilda II (1100–1118)." *ANS* 12 (1990): 81–98.

– *Matilda of Scotland: A Study of Medieval Queenship*. Woodbridge, UK: Boydell Press, 2003.

– "'Proclaiming Her Dignity Abroad': The Literary and Artistic Network of Matilda of Scotland, Queen of England, 1100–1118." In McCash, *The Cultural Production of Medieval Women*, 155–74.

Huntington, Joanna. "St Margaret of Scotland: Conspicuous Consumption, Genealogical Inheritance, and Post-Conquest Authority." *Journal of Scottish Historical Studies* 33 (2013): 149–64.

Huyghebaert, Nicolas. "Adela van Frankrijk, gravin van Vlaanderen, stichteres van de abdij van Mesen (ca. 1017–1079)." *Iepers kwartier: Driemaandelijks tijdschrift voor heemkunde* 15 (1979): 65–132.

– "Les femmes laïques dans la vie religieuse des XIe at XIIe siècles dans la province ecclésiastique de Reims." *I Laici nella "societas christiana" dei secoli xi e xii*. Miscellanea del Centro di Studi Medioevali 5 (Milan, 1968): 346–90.

Ingledew, Francis. "The Book of Troy and the Genealogical Construction of History: The Case of Geoffrey of Monmouth's *Historia regum Britanniae*." *Speculum* 69 (1994): 665–704.

Innes, Matthew. "Memory, Orality and Literacy in an Early Medieval Society." *Past and Present* 158 (1998): 3–36.

– "Teutons or Trojans? The Carolingians and the Germanic Past." In *The Uses of the Past in the Early Middle Ages*, edited by Yitzhak Hen and Matthew Innes, 227–49. Cambridge: Cambridge University Press, 2000.

Insley, Charles. "Assemblies and Charters in Late Anglo-Saxon England." In *Political Assemblies in the Earlier Middle Ages*, edited by P.S. Barnwell and Marco Mostert, 47–59. Turnhout: Brepols, 2003.

– "The Family of Wulfric Spott: An Anglo-Saxon Merican Marcher Dynasty." In *The English and Their Legacy, 900–1200: Essays in Honor of Ann Williams*, edited by David Roffe, 115–28. Woodbridge, UK: Boydell and Brewer, 2012.

Irvine, Martin. *The Making of Textual Culture: "Grammatica" and Literary Theory, 350–1100*. Cambridge: Cambridge University Press, 1994.

Irvine, Martin, and David Thompson. "*Grammatica* and Literary Theory." In Minnis and Johnson, *The Cambridge History of Literary Criticism*, 15–41.

Irvine, Susan. "The Anglo-Saxon Chronicle and the Idea of Rome in Alfredian Literature." In *Alfred the Great*, edited by Timothy Reuter, 63–77. Aldershot, UK: Ashgate, 2003.

– "Ulysses and Circe in King Alfred's *Boethius*: A Classical Myth Transformed." In *Studies in English Language and Literature: Doubt Wisely; Papers in Honour of E.G. Stanley*, edited by M.J. Toswell and E.M. Tyler, 387–401. London and New York: Routledge, 1996.

– "Wrestling with Hercules: King Alfred and the Classical Past." In Cubitt, *Court Culture in the Early Middle Ages*, 171–88.

Jaeger, C. Stephen. "Charismatic Body – Charismatic Text." *Exemplaria* 9 (1997): 117–37.

– *Ennobling Love: In Search of a Lost Sensibility*. Philadelphia: University of Pennsylvania, 1999.

– *The Envy of Angels: Cathedral Schools and Social Ideals in Medieval Europe, 950–1200*. Philadelphia: University of Pennsylvania Press, 1994.

– *The Origins of Courtliness: Civilizing Trends and the Formation of Courtly Ideals, 939–1210*. Philadelphia: University of Pennsylvania Press, 1985.

Janson, Tore. *Latin Prose Prefaces: Studies in Literary Conventions*. Stockholm: Almquist and Wiksell, 1964.

– *Prose Rhythm in Medieval Latin from the 9th to the 13th Century*. Stockholm: Almquist and Wiksell International, 1975.

Jesch, Judith. *Women in the Viking Age*. Woodbridge, UK: Boydell and Brewer, 1991.

John, Eric. "The *Encomium Emmae Reginae*: A Riddle and a Solution." *Bulletin of the John Rylands University Library of Manchester* 63 (1980–1): 58–94.

Jordan, Victoria. "Chronology and Discourse in the *Vita Ædwardi Regis*." *JML* 8 (1998): 122–55.

Keats-Rohan, K.S.B. "Alan Rufus (d. 1093)." *ODNB*. Oxford University Press, 2004. http://www.oxforddnb.com/view/article/52358, accessed 19 October 2015.

– "The Bretons and Normans of England, 1066–1154: The Family, the Fief and the Feudal Monarchy." *Nottingham Medieval Studies* 36 (1992): 42–78.

Kelly, Douglas. *The Conspiracy of Allusion: Disruption, Rewriting and Authorship from Macrobius to Medieval Romance*. Leiden: Brill, 1999.

Kempshall, Matthew. *Rhetoric and the Writing of History*. Manchester: Manchester University Press, 2011.

Kennedy, Ruth, and Simon Meecham-Jones, eds. *Writers of the Reign of Henry II: Twelve Essays*. New York: Palgrave MacMillan, 2006.

Kershaw, Paul. "Eberhard of Friuli: A Carolingian Lay Intellectual." In Wormald and Nelson, *Lay Intellectuals in the Carolingian World*, 77–105.

Keynes, Simon. "The Æthelings in Normandy." *ANS* 13 (1991): 173–205.

– "The Declining Reputation of King Æthelred the Unready." In *Ethelred the Unready: Papers from the Millenary Conference*, edited by David Hill, 227–53. British Archaeological Reports, British Series 59. Oxford: [British Archaeological Reports], 1978.

– *The Diplomas of King Æthelred, "The Unready," 978–1016: A Study in Their Use as Historical Evidence*. Cambridge: Cambridge University Press, 1980.

– "Giso, Bishop of Wells (1061–1088)." *ANS* 19 (1996): 203–71.

– Introduction to *Encomium Emmae Reginae*, edited and translated by Alistair Campbell, xiii–lxxi. Cambridge: Cambridge University Press, 1998.

– "Manuscripts of the *Anglo-Saxon Chronicle*." In *The Cambridge History of the Book in Britain*, vol. 1, *c.400–1100*, edited by Richard Gameson, 537–52. Cambridge: Cambridge University Press, 2012.

– "Royal Government and the Written Word in Late Anglo-Saxon England." In *The Uses of Literacy in Early Medieval Europe*, edited by Rosamond McKitterick, 226–57. Cambridge: Cambridge University Press, 1990.

Keynes, Simon, and Rosalind Love, "Earl Godwine's Ship." *ASE* 38 (2010): 185–223.

King, Edmund. *King Stephen*. New Haven, CT: Yale University Press, 2010.

Körner, Sten. *The Battle of Hastings, England, and Europe, 1035–1066*. Lund: Gleerups, 1964.

Krueger, Roberta. *Women Readers and the Ideology of Gender in Old French Verse Romance*. Cambridge: Cambridge University Press, 1993.

Kwakkel, Erik. "*Hebban olla vogala* in historisch perspectief." *Tijdschrift voor Nederlandse taal- en letterkunde* 121 (2005): 1–24.

Lake, Justin. *Richer of Saint-Rémi: The Methods and Mentality of a Tenth-Century Historian*. Washington, DC: Catholic University of America Press, 2013.

– "Truth, Plausibility, and the Virtues of Narrative at the Millennium." *JMH* 35 (2009): 221–38.

Lapidge, Michael. "Abbot Germanus, Winchcombe, Ramsey and the Cambridge Psalter." In *Anglo-Saxon Literature: 900–1066*, 387–417 and 490.

– *Anglo-Latin Literature, 900–1066*. London: Hambledon Press, 1993.

– *The Anglo-Saxon Library*. Oxford: Oxford University Press, 2006.

– "The Hermeneutic Style in Tenth-Century Anglo-Latin Literature." In *Anglo-Saxon Literature: 900–1066*, 105–49 and 474–9.

– "The Origin of CCCC 163." *Transactions of the Cambridge Bibliographical Society* 8 (1981): 18–28.

– “Schools, Learning and Literature in Tenth-Century England.” In *Anglo-Saxon Literature: 900–1066*, 1–48 and 469.
– “The Study of Latin Texts in Anglo-Saxon England [1] The Evidence of the Glosses.” In *Latin and the Vernacular Languages in Early Medieval Britain*, edited by N.P. Brooks, 99–140. Leicester: Leicester University Press, 1984.
– “Three Latin Poems from Æthelwold’s School at Winchester.” In *Anglo-Latin Literature: 900–1066*, 225–77 and 484–6.
La Rocca, Cristina, and Luigi Provero. “The Dead and Their Gifts: The Will of Eberhard, Count of Friuli, and His Wife Gisela, Daughter of Louis the Pious (863–864).” In *Rituals of Power: From Late Antiquity to the Early Middle Ages*, edited by Frans Theuws and Janet L. Nelson, 225–80. Leiden: Brill, 2000.
Latzke, Therese. “Der Fürstinnenpreis.” *Mittellateinisches Jahrbuch* 14 (1979): 22–65.
– “Robert von Arbrissel, Ermengard und Eva.” *Mittellateinisches Jahrbuch* 19 (1984): 116–54.
Lawson, M.K. *Cnut: The Danes in England in the Early Eleventh Century*. London: Longman, 1993.
Leclercq, Jean. *The Love of Learning and the Desire for God: A Study of Monastic Culture*. Translated by Catharine Misrahi. New York: Fordham University Press, 1961.
Leersen, Joep. *National Thought in Europe: A Cultural History*. Amsterdam: Amsterdam University Press, 2006.
Lees, Clare A. “Engendering Religious Desire: Sex, Knowledge, and Christian Identity in Anglo-Saxon England.” *Journal of Medieval and Early Modern Studies* 27 (1997): 17–46.
Le Jan, Régine. *Femmes, pouvoir et société dans le haut Moyen Age*. Paris: Picard, 2001.
Lejeune, Rita. “Rôle littéraire d’Aliénor d’Aquitaine et de sa famille.” *Cultura Neolatina* 14 (1954): 5–57.
Lettinck, Nico. “Pour une édition critique de *l’Historia ecclesiastica* de Hugues de Fleury.” *Revue Bénédictine* 91 (1981): 386–97.
Lewis, C.P. “The French in England before the Norman Conquest.” *ANS* 17 (1995): 123–44.
Leyser, Karl J. *Rule and Conflict in an Early Medieval Society: Ottonian Saxony*. London: Edward Arnold, 1979.
Licence, Tom. “The Date and Authorship of the *Vita Ædwardi regis*.” *ASE* (forthcoming).
– “New Light on the Life and Work of Herman the Archdeacon.” In *Bury St Edmunds and the Norman Conquest*, edited by Tom Licence, 94–103. Woodbridge, UK: Boydell and Brewer, 2014.

– "Robert of Jumièges: Archbishop in Exile (1052–55)." *ASE* 42 (2013): 311–29.

Lifshitz, Felice. "The *Encomium Emmae Reginae*: A 'Political Pamphlet' of the Eleventh Century?" *HSJ* 1 (1989): 39–50.

LoPrete, Kimberly A. *Adela of Blois: Countess and Lord (c. 1067–1137)*. Dublin: Four Courts, 2007.

– "Adela of Blois as Mother and Countess." In *Medieval Mothering*, edited by J.C. Parsons and B. Wheeler, 313–33. New York: Garland, 1996.

Lord, Mary Louise. "Dido as an Example of Chastity: The Influence of Example Literature." *Harvard Library Bulletin* 17 (1969): 22–44 and 216–32.

Love, Rosalind. "'Et quis me tanto oneri parem faciet?': Goscelin of Saint-Bertin and the Life of St Amelberga." In O'Brien O'Keeffe and Orchard, *Latin Learning and English Lore*, 2:232–52.

Luscombe, David. Review of *St Anselm and the Handmaidens of God*, by Sally N. Vaughn. *Catholic Historical Review* 91 (2005): 360–1.

Luscombe, David, and Jonathan Riley-Smith, eds. *The New Cambridge Medieval History*. Vol. 4, *c. 1024–c. 1198*. Cambridge: Cambridge University Press, 2004.

MacLean, Simon. "Making a Difference in Tenth-Century Politics: King Athelstan's Sisters and Frankish Queenship." In *Frankland: The Franks and the World of Early Medieval Europe*, edited by Paul Fouracre and David Ganz, 167–90. Manchester: Manchester University Press, 2008.

Marritt, Stephen. "Coincidences of Names, Anglo-Scottish Connections and Anglo-Saxon Society in the Late Eleventh-Century West Country." *Scottish Historical Review* 83 (2004): 150–70.

Marshall, Peter K. *Servius and Commentary on Virgil*. Asheville, NC: Pegasus Press, 1997.

Martindale, Charles. *Redeeming the Text: Latin Poetry and the Hermeneutics of Reception*. Cambridge: Cambridge University Press, 1993.

Maund, K.L. *Ireland, Wales, and England in the Eleventh Century*. Woodbridge, UK: Boydell and Brewer, 1991.

– "The Welsh Alliances of Earl Ælfgar of Mercia and His Family in the Mid-Eleventh Century." *ANS* 11 (1988): 181–90.

McCash, June Hall. "The Cultural Patronage of Medieval Women: An Overview." In *The Cultural Production of Medieval Women*, 1–49.

– ed. *The Cultural Production of Medieval Women*. Athens: University of Georgia Press, 1996.

McGurk, Patrick, and Jane Rosenthal. "The Anglo-Saxon Gospel Books of Judith, Countess of Flanders: Their Text, Make-Up and Function." *ASE* 24 (1995): 251–308.

McKitterick, Rosamond. *The Carolingians and the Written Word*. Cambridge: Cambridge University Press, 1989.

– "Frauen und Schriftlichkeit im Frühmittelalter." In *Weibliche Lebensgestaltung im frühen Mittelalter*, edited by Hans-Werner Goetz, 65–118. Cologne, Weimar, and Vienna: Böhlau, 1991.
– *History and Memory in the Carolingian World*. Cambridge: Cambridge University Press, 2004.
– "Latin and Romance: An Historian's Perspective." In *Latin and the Romance Languages in the Early Middle Ages*, edited by Roger Wright, 130–45. London: Routledge, 1991.

Mehtonen, Päivi. *Old Concepts and New Poetics: Historia, Argumentum, and Fabula in the Twelfth- and Early Thirteenth-Century Latin Poetics of Fiction*. Helsinki: Societas Scientiarum Fennica, 1996.

Milis, Ludo J. "The French Low Countries: Cradle of Dutch Culture?" In Milis, *Religion, Culture and Mentalities in the Medieval Low Countries*, 327–51.
– "The Linguistic Boundary in the County of Guînes: A Problem of History and Methodology." In Milis, *Religion, Culture and Mentalities in the Medieval Low Countries*, 353–68.
– *Religion, Culture and Mentalities in the Medieval Low Countries: Selected Essays*. Edited by Jeroen Deploige, et al. Turnhout: Brepols, 2005.

Minnis, A.J., and A.B. Scott, eds. *Medieval Literary Theory and Criticism, c. 1100–c. 1375*. With the assistance of David Wallace. Rev. ed. Oxford: Oxford University Press, 1991.

Minnis, Alastair, and Ian Johnson, eds. *The Cambridge History of Literary Criticism*. Vol. 2, *The Middle Ages*. Cambridge: Cambridge University Press, 2005.

Mora-Lebrun, Francine. *L'"Énéide" médiévale and la naissance du roman*. Paris: PUF, 1994.

Morini, Carla. "The Old English *Apollonius* and Wulfstan of York." *Leeds Studies in English*, n.s. 36 (2005): 63–104.

Morse, Ruth. *Truth and Convention in the Middle Ages: Rhetoric, Representation and Reality*. Cambridge: Cambridge University Press, 1991.

Mortensen, Lars Boje. "Comparing and Connecting: The Rise of Fast Historiography in Latin and Vernacular (Twelfth–Thirteenth Century)." *Medieval Worlds* 1 (2015): 25–39.
– "The Diffusion of Roman Histories in the Middle Ages: A List of Orosius, Eutropius, Paulus Diaconus, and Landolfus Sagax Manuscripts." *Filologia mediolatina* 6–7 (2000): 101–200.
– "From Vernacular Interviews to Latin Prose (ca. 600–1200)." In *Oral Forms and Their Passage into Writing*, edited by Else Mundal and Jonas Wellendorf, 53–68. Copenhagen: Museum Tusculanum Press, 2008.

– "Stylistic Choice in a Reborn Genre: The National Histories of Widukind of Corvey and Dudo of Saint-Quentin." In *Dudone di San Quintino*, edited by P. Gatti and A. Degl'Innocenti, 77–102. Trento, Italy: Università degli Studi di Trento, 1995.

– "Working with Ancient Roman History: A Comparison of Carolingian and Twelfth-Century Scholarly Endeavours." In *Gli Umanesimi medievali: Atti del II Congresso dell'Internationales Mittellateinerkomitee, Firenze, Certosa del Galluzzo, 11–15 settembre 1993*, edited by Claudio Leonardi, 411–21. Florence: Edizioni del Galluzzo, 1998.

Mortimer, Richard, ed. *Edward the Confessor: The Man and the Legend*. Woodbridge, UK: Boydell and Brewer, 2009.

Moser, Thomas C. Jr. *A Cosmos of Desire: The Medieval Latin Erotic Lyric in English Manuscripts*. Ann Arbor: University of Michigan Press, 2004.

Mozley, J.H. "Susanna and the Elders: Three Medieval Poems." *Studi Medievali*, n.s. 3 (1930): 27–52.

Munk Olsen, Birger. *L'étude des auteurs classiques latins aux XIe et XIIe siècles*. Vol. 1, *Apicius–Juvénal*. Paris: Éditions du Centre National de la Recherche Scientifique, 1982.

– "Ovide au moyen âge (du IXe au XIIe siècle). In *Le strade del testo*, edited by Guglielmo Cavallo, 65–96. Bari: Adriatica Editric, 1987.

– "La popularité des textes classiques entre le IXe et le XIIe siècle." In *La réception de la littérature classique au Moyen Âge (IXe–XIIe siècle)*, 21–34. Copenhagen: Museum Tusculanum Press, 1995.

– "The Production of the Classics in the Eleventh and Twelfth Centuries." In *Medieval Manuscripts of the Latin Classics: Production and Use*, edited by Claudine A. Chavannes-Mazel and Margaret M. Smith, 1–17. London and Los Altos Hills, CA: Anderson-Lovelace, Red Gull Press, 1996.

– "Virgile et la renaissance du XIIe siècle." In *Lectures médiévales de Virgile: Actes du colloque organisé par l'École française de Rome*, edited by Jean-Yves Tilliette, 31–48. Rome: L'École française de Rome, 1985.

Murray, Alexander Callander. "Beowulf, the Danish Invasions, and Royal Genealogy." In Chase, *The Dating of Beowulf*, 101–11.

Musset, Lucien. "La reine Mathilde et la fondation de la Trinité de Caen (Abbaye aux Dames)." *Mémoires de l'Académie de Caen* 21 (1984): 191–210.

– "Rouen et l'Angleterre vers l'an mil: Du nouveau sur le satiriste Garnier et l'école littéraire de Rouen au temps de Richard II." In *Nordica et Normannica: Recueil d'études sur la Scandinavie ancienne et médiévale, les expéditions des Vikings et la fondation de la Normandie*, 467–71. Paris: Société des études nordiques, 1997.

Nees, Lawrence. *A Tainted Mantle: Hercules and the Classical Tradition at the Carolingian Court*. Philadelphia: University of Pennsylvania Press, 1991.

Nelson, Janet L. *Charles the Bald*. London: Longmans, 1992.

– "Dhuoda." In Wormald and Nelson, *Lay Intellectuals in the Carolingian World*, 106–20.

– "Gender and Genre in Women Historians of the Early Middle Ages." In *The Frankish World: 750–900*, 183–97. London: Hambledon Press, 1996.

– "Gendering Courts in the Early Medieval West." In *Gender and the Transformation of the Roman World*, edited by Julia Smith and Leslie Brubaker, 185–97. Cambridge: Cambridge University Press, 2004.

– "History-Writing at the Courts of Louis the Pious and Charles the Bald." In *Historiographie im frühen Mittelalter*, edited by Anton Scharer and Georg Scheibelreiter, 435–42. Munich: Oldenbourg, 1994.

– "Public Histories and Private History in the Work of Nithard." *Speculum* 60 (1985): 251–93.

Newlands, Carole E. *Statius: Poet between Rome and Naples*. London: Bristol Classical Press, 2012.

Newman, Barbara. *From Virile Woman to WomanChrist: Studies in Medieval Religion and Literature*. Philadelphia: University of Pennsylvania Press, 1995.

Niles, John D. "Locating *Beowulf* in Literary History." In *Old English Heroic Poems and the Social Life of Texts*, 13–58. Turnhout: Brepols, 2007.

Noble, Thomas F.X. "Secular Sanctity: Forging an Ethos for the Carolingian Nobility." In Wormald and Nelson, *Lay Intellectuals in the Carolingian World*, 8–36.

Nykrog, Per. "The Rise of Literary Fiction." In *Renaissance and Renewal in the Twelfth Century*, edited by Robert L. Benson and Giles Constable, 593–612. Cambridge, MA: Harvard University Press, 1982.

O'Brien, Bruce R. *Reversing Babel: Translation among the English during an Age of Conquests, c. 800–c. 1200*. Newark: University of Delaware Press, 2011.

O'Brien O'Keeffe, Katherine. "Goscelin and the Consecration of Eve." *Anglo-Saxon England* 35 (2006): 251–70.

– "Leaving Wilton: Gunnhild and the Phantoms of Agency." *Journal of English and Germanic Philology* 106 (2007): 203–23.

– *Stealing Obedience: Narratives of Agency and Identity in Later Anglo-Saxon England*. Toronto: University of Toronto Press, 2012.

O'Brien O'Keeffe, Katherine, and Andy Orchard. *Latin Learning and English Lore: Studies in Anglo-Saxon Literature for Michael Lapidge*. 2 vols. Toronto: University of Toronto Press, 2005.

O'Daly, Gerard. *The Poetry of Boethius*. London: Duckworth, 1991.

O'Donnell, Thomas, Matthew Townend, and Elizabeth M. Tyler. "European Literature and Eleventh-Century England." In *The Cambridge History of Early Medieval English Literature*, edited by Clare A. Lees, 607–36. Cambridge: Cambridge University Press, 2013.

O'Donnell, Thomas, and Elizabeth M. Tyler. "From the Severn to the Rhine: Geographies and Social Networks of English Literary Culture," forthcoming.

Olson, Linda. "Did Medieval Women Read Augustine's *Confessions*? Constructing Feminine Interiority and Literacy in the Eleventh and Twelfth Centuries." In *Learning and Literacy in Medieval England and Abroad*, edited by Sarah Rees Jones, 69–96. Turnhout: Brepols, 2003.

Ong, Walter J. "Orality, Literacy, and Medieval Textualization." *New Literary History* 16 (1984): 1–12.

Orchard, Andy. *A Critical Companion to Beowulf*. Cambridge: D.S. Brewer, 2003.

– "Literary Background to the *Encomium Emmae Reginae*." *JML* 11 (2001): 156–83.

– *Pride and Prodigies: Studies in the Monsters of the Beowulf-Manuscript*. Cambridge: D.S. Brewer, 1995.

Ortenberg, Veronica. *The English Church and the Continent in the Tenth and Eleventh Centuries: Cultural, Spiritual and Artistic Exchanges*. Oxford: Oxford University Press, 1992.

Otter, Monika. "Closed Doors: An Epithalamium for Queen Edith, Widow and Virgin." In *Constructions of Widowhood and Virginity in the Middle Ages*, edited by Cindy L. Carlson and Angela Jane Weisl, 63–92. Basingstoke, UK: Macmillan, 1999.

– "Functions of Fiction in Historical Writing." In *Writing Medieval History: Theory and Practice for the Post-Traditional Middle Ages*, edited by Nancy Partner, 109–30. London: Hodder and Arnold, 2005.

– "Intepretative Essay." In *Goscelin of St Bertin: The Book of Encouragement and Consolation ("Liber confortatorius")*, translated by Monika Otter, 151–67. Cambridge: D.S. Brewer, 2004.

– *Inventiones: Fiction and Referentiality in Twelfth-Century Historical Writing*. Chapel Hill: University of North Carolina Press, 1996.

– "1066: The Moment of Transition in Two Narratives of the Norman Conquest." *Speculum* 74 (1999): 565–86.

Oxford Dictionary of National Biography. Edited by H.C.G. Matthew and Brian Harrison. Oxford: Oxford University Press, 2004. Online edition with updates, http://www.oxforddnb.com.

Parisse, Michael. *Atlas de la France de l'an mil: État de nos connaissances*. Paris: Picard, 1994.

Parkes, Malcolm. "A Fragment of an Early-Tenth-Century Anglo-Saxon Manuscript and Its Significance." *ASE* 12 (1983): 129–40.

– "The Palaeography of the Parker Manuscript of the *Chronicle*, Laws and Sedulius, and Historiography at Winchester in the Late Ninth and Tenth Centuries." *ASE* 5 (1976): 149–71.

Parsons, John Carmi. "Of Queens, Courts, and Books: Reflections on Literary Patronage of Thirteenth-Century Plantagenet Queens." In McCash, *The Cultural Production of Medieval Women*, 75–201.

Parsons, Sylvia, and David Townsend. "Gender." In *The Oxford Handbook of Medieval Latin Literature*, edited by Ralph Hexter and David Townsend, 423–46. Oxford: Oxford University Press, 2012.

Partner, Nancy F. "The New Cornificius: Medieval History and the Artifice of Words." In Breisach, *Classical Rhetoric and Medieval Historiography*, 5–59.

– *Serious Entertainments: The Writing of History in Twelfth-Century England.* Chicago: University of Chicago Press, 1977.

Pastan, Elizabeth Carson, and Stephen D. White. "Problematizing Patronage: Odo of Bayeux and the Bayeux Tapestry." In *The Bayeux Tapestry: New Interpretations*, edited by Martin K. Foys, Karen Eileen Overbey, and Dan Terkla, 1–24. Woodbridge, UK: Boydell Press, 2009.

Poole, Russell. "Skaldic Verse and Anglo-Saxon History: Some Aspects of the Period 1009–1016." *Speculum* 62 (1987): 265–98.

– *Viking Poems on War and Peace: A Study in Skaldic Verse*. Toronto: University of Toronto Press, 1991.

Porter, D.W. "The Earliest Texts with English and French." *ASE* 28 (1999): 87–110.

Powell, Kathryn. "*Alexander the Great, Letter to Aristotle*." In *Blackwell Encyclopaedia of Anglo-Saxon England*, edited by Michael Lapidge, John Blair, Simon Keynes, and Donald Scragg, 27. Oxford: Blackwell, 1999.

Pratt, David. *The Political Thought of King Alfred the Great*. Cambridge: Cambridge University Press, 2007.

– "Problems of Authorship and Audience in the Writings of King Alfred the Great." In Wormald and Nelson, *Lay Intellectuals in the Carolingian World*, 162–91.

Press, Alan R. "The Precocious Courtesy of Geoffrey Gaimar." In *Court and Poet: Selected Proceedings of the Third Congress of the International Courtly Literature Society (Liverpool, 1980)*, edited by Glyn S. Burgess, A.D. Deyermond et al., 267–76. Liverpool: Francis Cairns, 1981.

Quint, David. *Epic and Empire: Politics and Generic Form from Virgil to Milton.* Princeton: Princeton University Press, 1993.

Raffensperger, Christian. *Reimagining Europe: Kievan Rus' in the Medieval World.* Cambridge, MA: Harvard University Press, 2012.

Ratkowitsch, Christine. *Descriptio picturae: Die literarische Funktion der Beschreibung von Kunstwerken in der lateinischen Großdictung des 12. Jahrhunderts.* Vienna: Österreichische Akademie der Wissenschaften, 1991.
Ray, Roger. "Bede, the Exegete, as Historian." In *Famulus Christi: Essays in Commemoration of the Thirteenth Centenary of the Birth of the Venerable Bede*, edited by Gerald Bonner, 125–40. London: SPCK, 1976.
– "Bede's *Vera Lex Historiæ.*" *Speculum* 55 (1980): 1–21.
– "Medieval Historiography through the Twelfth Century: Problems and Progress of Research." *Viator* 5 (1974): 33–59.
– "The Triumph of Greco-Roman Rhetorical Assumptions in Pre-Carolingian Historiography." In *The Inheritance of Historiography, 350–900*, edited by Christopher Holdsworth and T.P. Wiseman, 67–84. Exeter: University of Exeter, 1986.
Rector, Geoff. "*En sa chamber souvent le lit*: Literary Leisure and the Chamber Sociabilities of Early Anglo-French Literature (ca. 1100–1150)." *Medium Ævum* 81 (2012): 88–125.
Reuter, Timothy. "Assembly Politics in Western Europe from the Eighth Century to the Twelfth." In his *Medieval Polities and Modern Mentalities*, edited by Janet L. Nelson, 193–216. Cambridge: Cambridge University Press, 2006.
Reynolds, L.D. *The Medieval Tradition of Seneca's Letters.* Oxford: Oxford University Press, 1965.
– ed. *Texts and Transmission: A Survey of the Latin Classics.* Oxford: Clarendon Press, 1983.
Reynolds, Susan. *Medieval Reading: Grammar, Rhetoric and the Classical Text.* Cambridge: Cambridge University Press, 1996.
Riché, Pierre. "Les bibliothèques de trois aristocrates laïcs carolingiens." *Le moyen âge* 69 (1963): 87–104.
– *Écoles et enseignement dans le haut moyen âge: Fin du V*[e] *siècle–milieu du XI*[e] *siècle*. 3rd ed. Paris: Picard Éditeur, 1999.
– *Gerbert d'Aurillac: Le pape de l'an mil.* Paris: Fayard, 1987.
Riddy, Felicity. "Mother Knows Best: Reading Social Change in a Courtesy Text." *Speculum* 71 (1996): 66–86.
– "'Women Talking about the Things of God': A Late Medieval Sub-Culture." In *Women and Literature in Britain, 1150–1500*, edited by Carole M. Meale, 104–27. Cambridge: Cambridge University Press, 1993.
Ridyard, Susan. *The Royal Saints of Anglo-Saxon England: A Study of the West Saxon and East Anglian Cults.* Cambridge: Cambridge University Press, 1988.
Rigg, A.G. *A History of Anglo-Latin Literature, 1066–1422.* Cambridge: Cambridge University Press, 1992.

– "Serlo of Wilton: Biographical Notes." *Medium Ævum* 65 (1996): 96–101.

Roach, Levi. *Kingship and Consent in Anglo-Saxon England, 871–978: Assemblies and the State in the Early Middle Ages*. Cambridge: Cambridge University Press, 2013.

Robinson, Fred C. "Old English Literature in Its Most Immediate Context." In *Old English Literature in Context: Ten Essays*, edited by John D. Niles, 11–29. Cambridge: D.S. Brewer, 1980.

Robinson, P.R. "A Twelfth-Century *Scriptrix* from Nunnaminster." In *Of the Making of Books: Medieval Manuscripts, Their Scribes and Readers: Essays Presented to M.B. Parkes*, edited by P.R. Robinson and Rivkah Zim, 73–93. Aldershot, UK: Scholar Press, 1997.

Rosenthal, Joel. "The Education of the Early Capetians." *Traditio* 25 (1969): 366–76.

Roy, Gopa. "'Sharpen Your Mind with the Whetstone of Books': The Female Recluse as Reader in Goscelin's *Liber confortatorius*, Aelred of Rievaulx's *De Institutione Inclusarum* and the *Ancrene Wisse*." In Smith and Taylor, *Women, the Book and the Godly*, 1:113–22.

Salter, Elizabeth. *English and International: Studies in the Literature, Art and Patronage of Medieval England*, ed. Derek Pearsall and Nicolette Zeeman. Cambridge: Cambridge University Press, 1988.

Samuels, Irene. "Semiramis in the Middle Ages: History of a Legend." *Medievalia et Humanistica* 2 (1944): 32–44.

Sawyer, P.H. "The Charters of Burton Abbey and the Unification of England." *Northern History* 10 (1975): 28–39.

Schmeling, Gareth. "*The History of Apollonius, King of Tyre*." In Hofmann, *Latin Fiction*, 141–52.

Schmidt, Peter Lebrecht. "Rezeption und Überlieferung der Tragödien Senecas bis zum Ausgang des Mittelalters." In *Der Einfluss Senecas auf das europäische Drama*, edited by Eckard Lefèvre, 12–73. Darmstadt: Wissenschaftliche Buchgesellschaft, 1978.

Schwarzmaier, Hansmartin. *Von Speyer nach Rom: Wegstationen und Lebensspuren der Salier*. Sigmaringen: Thorbecke, 1992.

Scott, A.B. "The Poems of Hildebert of Le Mans: A New Examination of the Canon." *Mediaeval and Renaissance Studies* 6 (1968): 42–83.

Searle, Eleanor. "Fact and Pattern in Heroic History: Dudo of Saint-Quentin." *Viator* 15 (1984): 119–37.

– "Women and the Legitimisation of Succession at the Norman Conquest." *ANS* 3 (1981): 159–70 and 226–9.

Selmer, Carol. "A Study of Latin Manuscripts of the *Navigatio Sancti Brendani*." *Scriptorium* 3 (1949): 177–82.

Sharpe, Richard. "King Harold's Daughter." *HSJ* 19 (2007): 1–27.

Sharpe, Richard, J.P. Carley, R.M. Thomson, and A.G. Watson, eds. *English Benedictine Libraries: The Shorter Catalogues.* Corpus of British Medieval Library Catalogues 4. London: British Library in association with the British Academy, 1996.

Sheerin, Daniel. "Sisters in the Literary Agon: Texts from Communities of Women on the Mortuary Roll of the Abbess Matilda of La Trinité, Caen." In *Women Writing Latin: From Roman Antiquity to Early Modern Europe*, vol. 2, *Medieval Women Writing Latin*, edited by Laurie J. Churchill, Phyllis R. Brown, and Jane E. Jeffrey, 93–131. New York and London: Routledge, 2002.

Shopkow, Leah. *History and Community: Norman Historical Writing in the Eleventh and Twelfth Centuries.* Washington, DC: Catholic University of America Press, 1997.

Short, Ian. "Gaimar's Epilogue and Geoffrey of Monmouth's *Liber vetustissimus.*" *Speculum* 69 (1994): 323–43.

– "Patrons and Polyglots: French Literature in Twelfth-Century England." *ANS* 14 (1991): 229–49.

Signori, Gabriela. "Muriel and the Others … or Poems as Pledges of Friendship." In *Friendship in Medieval Europe*, edited by Julian Haseldine, 199–212. Stroud, UK: Sutton, 1999.

Simon, Gertrud. "Untersuchungen zur Topik der Widmungsbriefe mittelalterlicher Geschichtsschreiber bis zum Ende des 12. Jahrhunderts." *Archiv für Diplomatik, Schriftgeschichte, Siegel- und Wappenkunde* 4 (1958): 52–119, and 5–6 (1959–60): 73–153.

Singerman, Jerome E. *Under Clouds of Poesy: Poetry and Truth in French and English Reworkings of the Aeneid: 1160–1513.* New York: Garland Publishing, 1986.

Smalley, Beryl. *Historians in the Middle Ages.* London: Thames and Hudson, 1974.

Smith, Lesley, and J.H.M. Taylor, eds. *Women, the Book and the Godly: Selected Proceedings of the St Hilda's Conference, 1993.* Vol. 1. Cambridge: D.S. Brewer, 1995.

Smolak, Kurt. "Beobachtungen zu den Rom-Elegien Hildeberts von Lavardin." Herren, et al., *Latin Culture in the Eleventh Century*, 2:371–84.

Southern, Richard W. *Anselm and His Biographer: A Study of Monastic Life and Thought, 1059–c.1130.* Cambridge: Cambridge University Press, 1963.

– "Aspects of the European Tradition of Historical Writing: 1, The Classical Tradition from Einhard to Geoffrey of Monmouth." *TRHS*, 5th ser., 20 (1970): 173–96.

– "The First Life of Edward the Confessor." *EHR* 232 (1943): 385–400.

– *Saint Anselm: A Portrait in a Landscape*. Cambridge: Cambridge University Press, 1990.

Spear, David S. "The School of Caen Revisited." *HSJ* 4 (1992): 55–66.

Spiegel, Gabrielle M. "History, Historicism and the Social Logic of the Text." In *The Past as Text: The Theory and Practice of Medieval Historiography*, 3–28. Baltimore, MD: Johns Hopkins University Press, 1997.

– *Romancing the Past: The Rise of Vernacular Prose Historiography in Thirteenth-Century France*. Berkeley and Los Angeles: University of California Press, 1993.

Stafford, Pauline. "Ælfgifu (fl. 956–966)." *ODNB*. Oxford University Press, 2004. http://www.oxforddnb.com/view/article/179, accessed 19 October 2015.

– "Chronicle D, 1067 and Women: Gendering Conquest in Eleventh-Century England." In *Anglo-Saxons: Studies Presented to Cyril Roy Hart*, edited by Simon Keynes and Alfred P. Smyth, 208–23. Dublin: Four Courts Press, 2005.

– "The Portrayal of Royal Women in England, Mid-Tenth to Mid-Twelfth Centuries." In *Medieval Queenship*, edited by John Carmi Parsons, 143–67. Stroud, UK: Alan Sutton, 1994.

– *Queen Emma and Queen Edith: Queenship and Women's Power in Eleventh-Century England*. Oxford: Blackwell, 1997.

– *Queens, Concubines and Dowagers: The King's Wife in the Early Middle Ages*. London: Leicester University Press, 1983.

– "Queens, Nunneries and Reforming Churchmen: Gender, Religious Status and Reform in Tenth- and Eleventh-Century England." *Past and Present* 163 (1999): 3–35.

– *Unification and Conquest: A Political and Social History of England in the Tenth and Eleventh Centuries*. London: Edward Arnold, 1989.

Stein, Robert M. *Reality Fictions: Romance, History, and Governmental Authority, 1025–1180*. Notre Dame, IN: University of Notre Dame Press, 2006.

Stenton, Frank. *Anglo-Saxon England*, 3rd ed. Oxford: Oxford University Press, 1971.

Stephenson, Rebecca. "Byrhtferth's *Enchiridion*: The Effectiveness of Hermeneutic Latin." In Tyler, *Conceptualizing Multilingualism*, 121–43.

– "Scapegoating the Secular Clergy: The Hermeneutic Style as a Form of Monastic Self-Definition." *ASE* 38 (2009): 101–35.

Stevenson, Jane. "Anglo-Latin Women Poets." In O'Brien O'Keeffe and Orchard, *Latin Learning and English Lore*, 86–107.

– *Women Latin Poets: Language, Gender, and Authority from Antiquity to the Eighteenth Century*. Oxford: Oxford University Press, 2005.

Stock, Brian. *The Implications of Literacy: Written Language and Models of Interpretation in the Eleventh and Twelfth Centuries*. Princeton: Princeton University Press, 1983.

– *Listening for the Text: On the Uses of the Past*. Philadelphia: University of Pennsylvania Press, 1990.

Stok, Fabio. "Virgil between the Middle Ages and the Renaissance." *Journal of the Classical Tradition* 1 (1994): 15–22.

Stoneman, Richard. "The Latin Alexander." In Hofmann, *Latin Fiction*, 167–86.

– "The Medieval Alexander." In Hofmann, *Latin Fiction*, 238–52.

Stroud, Daphne. "Eve of Wilton and Goscelin of St Bertin at Old Sarum, c. 1070–1078." *Wiltshire Archaeological and Natural History Magazine* 99 (2006): 204–12.

Summerson, Henry. "Tudor Antiquaries and the *Vita Ædwardi Regis*." *ASE* 37 (2009): 157–84.

Swan, Mary, and Elaine Treharne M., eds. *Rewriting Old English in the Twelfth Century*. Cambridge: Cambridge University Press, 2000.

Tatlock, S.P. "Muriel, the Earliest English Poetess." *PMLA* 48 (1933): 317–21.

Thompson, S.P. "Mary, suo jure countess of Boulogne (*d.* 1182)." *ODNB*. Oxford University Press, 2004. Online ed., May 2014. http://www.oxforddnb.com/view/article/54455, accessed 19 October 2015.

Thomson, Rodney M. *William of Malmesbury*. Rev. ed. Woodbridge, UK: Boydell Press, 2003.

Thornbury, Emily V. "Aldhelm's Rejection of the Muses and the Mechanics of Poetic Inspiration in Early Anglo-Saxon England." *ASE* 36 (2007): 71–92.

Tilliette, Jean-Yves. "Hermès amoureux, ou les métamorphoses de la Chimère: Réflexions sur les *Carmina* 200 et 201 de Baudri de Bourgueil." *Mélanges de l'École française de Rome: Moyen âge* 104 (1992): 121–61.

– "Le retour d'Orphée: Refléxions sur la place de Godefroid de Reims dans l'histoire littéraire du XIe siècle." In Herren, et al., *Latin Culture*, 2:449–63.

– "*Tamquam lapides vivi*: Sur les 'élégies romaines' d'Hildebert de Lavardin (ca. 1100)." In "*Alla Signorina": Mélanges offerts à Noëlle de la Blanchardière*, edited by Claude Nicolet, 359–80. Rome: École française, 1995.

– "*Troiae ab oris*: Aspects de la révolution poétique de la seconde moitié di XIe siècle." *Latomus* 58 (1999): 405–31.

Townend, Matthew. "Contextualizing the *Knútsdrápur*: Skaldic Praise-Poetry at the Court of Cnut." *ASE* 30 (2001): 145–79.

– *Language and History in Viking Age England: Linguistic Relations between Speakers of Old Norse and Old English*. Turnhout: Brepols, 2002.

– "Norse Poets and English Kings: Skaldic Performance in Anglo-Saxon England." *Offa* 58 (2001): 269–75.

Treharne, Elaine M. *Living through Conquest: The Politics of Early English, 1020–1220*. Oxford: Oxford University Press, 2012.

Tuten, Belle S. "Who was Lady Constance of Angers? Nuns as Poets and Correspondents at the Monastery of Ronceray d'Angers in the Early Twelfth Century." *Medieval Perspectives* 19 (2004): 255–68.

Tyler, Elizabeth M., ed. *Conceptualizing Multilingualism in England, c. 800–c. 1250*. Turnhout: Brepols, 2011.

– "Crossing Conquests: Polyglot Royal Women and Literary Culture in Eleventh-Century England." In Tyler, *Conceptualizing Multilingualism*, 172–96.

– "'The Eyes of the Beholder Were Dazzled': Treasure and Artifice in the *Encomium Emmae Reginae*." *EME* 8 (1999): 247–70.

– "Fictions of Family: The *Encomium Emmae Reginae* and Virgil's *Aeneid*." *Viator* 36 (2005): 149–79.

– "From Old English to Old French." In Wogan-Browne, et al., *Language and Culture*, 164–78.

– "German Imperial Bishops and Anglo-Saxon Literary Culture on the Eve of the Conquest: *The Cambridge Songs* and Leofric's Exeter Book." In *Latinity and Identity in Anglo-Saxon England*, edited by Emily Thornbury and Rebecca Stephenson. Toronto: University of Toronto Press, 2016.

– "Talking about History in Eleventh-Century England: The *Encomium Emmae Reginae* and the Court of Harthacnut." *EME* 13 (2005): 359–83.

– "Trojans in Anglo-Saxon England: Precedence without Descent." *RES* 64 (2013): 1–20.

– "The *Vita Ædwardi*: The Politics of Poetry at Wilton Abbey." *ANS* 31 (2009): 136–56.

– "'When Wings Incarnadine with Gold Are Spread': The *Vita Ædwardi Regis* and the Display of Treasure at the Court of Edward the Confessor." In *Treasure in the Medieval West*, edited by Elizabeth M. Tyler, 83–107. Woodbridge, UK: York Medieval Press, 2000.

– "Writing Universal History in Eleventh-Century England: Cotton Tiberius B. I, German Imperial History-Writing and Vernacular Lay Literacy." In *The Life of the Universal Chronicle in the Middle Ages*, edited by Michele Campopiano and Henry Bainton. Woodbridge, UK: Boydell and Brewer, 2017.

Tyson, Diana B. "Patronage of French Vernacular History Writers in the Twelfth and Thirteenth Centuries." *Romania* 100 (1979): 180–222.

Ugé, Karin. *Creating the Monastic Past in Medieval Flanders*. Woodbridge, UK: York Medieval Press, 2005.

Vanderputten, Steven. "Crises of Cenobitism: Abbatial Leadership and Monastic Competition in Late Eleventh-Century Flanders." *EHR* 127 (2012): 259–84.

– "Individual Experience, Collective Remembrance and the Politics of Monastic Reform in High Medieval Flanders." *EME* 20 (2012): 70–89.

– *Monastic Reform as Process: Realities and Representations in Medieval Flanders, 900–1100*. Ithaca, NY: Cornell University Press, 2013.

Van Houts, Elisabeth. "Contrasts and Interaction: Neighbours of Nascent Dutch Writing; The English, Normans and Flemish (c. 1000–c. 1200)." *Queste* 13 (2006): 3–11.

– "Countess Gunnor of Normandy, c. 950–1031." *Collegium Medievale* 12 (1999): 7–24.

– "Edward and Normandy." In Mortimer, *Edward the Confessor*, 63–76.

– "The Flemish Contribution to Biographical Writing in England in the Eleventh Century." In *Writing Medieval Biography, 750–1250: Essays in Honour of Professor Frank Barlow*, edited by David Bates, Julia Crick, and Sarah Hamilton, 111–27. Woodbridge, UK: Boydell and Brewer, 2007.

– "Historiography and Hagiography at Saint-Wandrille: The 'Inventio et Miracula Sancti Vulfranni.'" *ANS* 12 (1990): 233–51.

– "Latin and French as Languages of the Past in Normandy during the Reign of Henry II: Robert of Torigni, Stephen of Rouen, and Wace." In Kennedy and Meecham-Jones, *Writers of the Reign of Henry II*, 53–77.

– "Latin Poetry and the Anglo-Norman Court." *JMH* 15 (1989): 39–62.

– "Matilda (d. 1083)." *ODNB*. Oxford University Press, 2004. Online ed., May 2008. http://www.oxforddnb.com/view/article/18335, accessed 19 October 2015.

– *Memory and Gender in Medieval Europe: 900–1200*. London: Macmillan, 1999.

– "A Note on *Jezebel* and *Semiramis*, Two Latin Norman Poems from the Early Eleventh Century." *JML* 2 (1992): 18–24.

– Review of *St Anselm and the Handmaidens of God*, by Sally N. Vaughn. *EHR* 119 (2004): 700–2.

– "Scandinavian Influence in Norman Literature." *ANS* 6 (1983): 107–21.

– "Women and the Writing of History in the Early Middle Ages: The Case of Abbess Matilda of Essen and Æthelweard." *EME* 1 (1992): 53–68.

Van Oostrom, Frits. *Stemmen op schrift: Geschiedenis van de Nederlandse literatuur vanaf het begin tot 1300*. Amsterdam: Bert Bakker, 2006.

Van Rossum, Irene. "*Adest meliori parte*: A Portrait of Monastic Friendship in Exile in Goscelin's *Liber confortatorius*." PhD diss., University of York, 1999.

Vaughn, Sally N. *St Anselm and the Handmaidens of God: A Study of St Anselm's Correspondence with Women*. Turnhout: Brepols, 2002.

Venarde, Bruce L. *Women's Monasticism and Medieval Society: Nunneries in France and England, 890–1215*. Ithaca, NY: Cornell University Press, 1997.

Verbaal, Wim. "Homer im lateinischen Mittelalter." In *Homer-Handbuch: Leben-Werk-Wirkung*, edited by Antonios Rengakos and Bernhard Zimmermann, 329–36. Stuttgart: J.B. Metzler, 2011.

Verdon, Jean. "Les moniales dans la France de l'Ouest aux XIe et XIIe siècles: Étude d'histoire sociale." *Cahiers de civilisation médiévale* 19 (1976): 247–64.

Vessey, D.W.T.C. "William of Tyre and the Art of Historiography." *Mediaeval Studies* 35 (1973): 433–55.

Von Moos, Peter. *Hildebert von Lavardin, 1056–1133: Humanitas an der Schwelle des höfischen Zeitalters*. Stuttgart: Anton Hiersemann, 1965.

– "*Poeta* und *historicus* im Mittelalter: Zum Mimesis-Problem am Beispiel einiger Urteile über Lucan." *Beiträge zur Geschichte der deutschen Sprache und Literatur* 98 (1976): 93–130.

Walker Bynum, Caroline. "Did the Twelfth Century Discover the Individual?" *Journal of Ecclesiastical History* 31 (1980): 1–17.

– *Metamorphosis and Identity*. New York: Zone Books, 2005.

Wallace, David. *Europe: A Literary History, 1348–1418*. 2 vols. Oxford: Oxford University Press, 2015.

Walmsley, John. "The Early Abbesses, Nuns and Female Tenants of the Abbey of Holy Trinity, Caen." *Journal of Ecclesiastical History* 48 (1997): 425–44.

Ward, John O. *Ciceronian Rhetoric in Treatise, Scholion and Commentary*. Turnhout: Brepols, 1995.

– "Commentator's Rhetoric: From Antiquity to the Renaissance; Glosses and Commentaries on Cicero's *Rhetorica*." In *Medieval Eloquence: Studies in the Theory and Practice of Medieval Rhetoric*, ed. James J. Murphy, 25–67. Berkeley and Los Angeles: University of California Press, 1978.

– "Some Principles of Rhetorical Historiography in the Twelfth Century." In Breisach, *Classical Rhetoric*, 103–65.

Webber, Teresa. "The Diffusion of Augustine's *Confessions* in England during the Eleventh and Twelfth Centuries." In *The Cloister and the World: Essays in Honour of Barbara Harvey*, edited by John Blair and Brian Golding, 29–45. Oxford: Clarendon Press, 1996.

Wetherbee, Winthrop. "From Late Antiquity to the Twelfth Century." In Minnis and Johnson, *The Cambridge History of Literary Criticism*, 99–144.

Whalen, George. "Patronage Engendered: How Goscelin Allayed the Concerns of Nuns' Discriminatory Publics." In Smith and Taylor, *Women, the Book and the Godly*, 1:123–35.

Whitelock, Dorothy. "The Prose of Alfred's Reign." In E.G. Stanley, ed., *Continuations and Beginnings: Studies in Old English Literature*, 67–103. London: Nelson, 1966.

Wickham, Chris. "Gossip and Resistance among the Medieval Peasantry." *Past and Present* 160 (1998): 3–24.
Wieland, Gernot F. "The Glossed Manuscript: Classbook or Library Book?" *ASE* 14 (1985): 153–73.
Williams, Ann. "Godwine, earl of Wessex (d. 1053)." *ODNB*. Oxford University Press, 2004. http://www.oxforddnb.com/view/article/10887, accessed 19 October 2015.
– "Leofric, earl of Mercia (d. 1057)." *ODNB*. Oxford University Press, 2004. Online ed., May 2005. http://www.oxforddnb.com/view/article/16470, accessed 19 October 2015.
Williams, John R. "The Cathedral School of Rheims in the Eleventh Century." *Speculum* 29 (1954): 661–77.
– "Godfrey of Rheims: A Humanist of the Eleventh Century." *Speculum* 22 (1947): 29–45.
Wilmart, André. "L'élégie d'Hildebert pour Muriel." *Revue Bénédictine* 49 (1937): 376–84.
– "Ève et Goscelin [I]." *Revue Bénédictine* 46 (1934): 414–38.
– "Ève et Goscelin [II]." *Revue Bénédictine* 50 (1938): 42–83.
– "L'histoire ecclésiastique composé par Hugues de Fleury et ses destinataires." *Revue Bénédictine* 50 (1938): 293–305.
– "Les livres de l'abbé Odbert." *Bulletin historique de la société des antiquaries de la Morinie* 14 (1929): 169–88.
Winterbottom, Michael. "The Style of Aethelweard." *Medium Ævum* 36 (1967): 109–18.
Wiseman, T.P. "Lying Historians: Seven Types of Mendacity." In *Lies and Fiction in the Ancient World*, edited by Christopher Gill and T.P. Wiseman, 122–46. Exeter: University of Exeter Press, 1993.
– *The Myths of Rome*. Exeter: University of Exeter Press, 2004.
Wogan-Browne, Jocelyn. "'Reading Is Good Prayer': Recent Research on Female Reading Communities." *New Medieval Literatures* 5 (2002): 229–97.
– *Saints Lives and Women's Literary Culture: Virginity and Its Authorizations*. Oxford: Oxford University Press, 2001.
Wogan-Browne, Jocelyn, with Carolyn Collette, Marianne Kowaleski, Linne Moody, Ad Putter, and David Trotter, eds. *Language and Culture in Medieval Britain: The French of England, c. 1100–c. 1500*. Woodbridge, UK: York Medieval Press, 2009.
Wolfram, Herwig. *Conrad II, 990–1039: Emperor of Three Kingdoms*. Translated by Denise A. Kaiser. University Park: Penn State Press, 2006.
Woodman, A.J. *Rhetoric in Classical Historiography*. London: Croom Helm, 1988.

Wormald, Patrick. "Archbishop Wulfstan and the Holiness of Society." In *Legal Culture in the Early Medieval West: Law as Text, Image and Experience*, 225–51. London and Rio Grande: Hambledon Press, 1999.

– *How Do We Know So Much about Anglo-Saxon Deerhurst?* Deerhurst Lecture 1991. Deerhurst, UK: Friends of Deerhurst Church, 1993.

– "*Lex Scripta* and *Verbum Regis*: Legislation and Germanic Kingship, from Euric to Cnut." In *Early Medieval Kingship*, edited by P.H. Sawyer and I.N. Wood, 105–38. Leeds: University of Leeds, 1977.

– *The Making of English Law: King Alfred to the Twelfth Century*. Vol. 1, *Legislation and Its Limits*. Oxford: Blackwell, 1999.

– "The Uses of Literacy in Anglo-Saxon England and Its Neighbours." *Transactions of the Royal Historical Society*, 5th ser., 27 (1977): 75–114.

– "Wulfstan (d. 1023)." *ODNB*. Oxford University Press, 2004. http://www.oxforddnb.com/view/article/30098, accessed 19 October 2015.

Wormald, Patrick, and Janet L. Nelson, eds. *Lay Intellectuals in the Carolingian World*. Cambridge: Cambridge University Press, 2007.

Wright, Neil. "'Industriae Testimonium': William of Malmesbury and Latin Poetry Revisited." *Revue Bénédictine* 103 (1993): 482–531.

– "William of Malmesbury and Latin Poetry: Further Evidence for a Benedictine's Reading." *Revue Bénédictine* 101 (1991): 122–53.

Wright, Roger. *A Sociophilological Study of Late Latin*. Turnhout: Brepols, 2002.

– "Translation between Latin and Romance in the Early Middle Ages." In *Translation Theory and Practice in the Middle Ages*, edited by Jeanette Beer, 1–32. Kalamazoo: Medieval Institute Publications (Western Michigan University), 1997.

Yorke, Barbara. *Nunneries and the Anglo-Saxon Royal Houses*. London: Continuum, 2003.

Ziolkowski, Jan. "Cultural Diglossia and the Nature of Medieval Latin Literature." In *The Ballad and Oral Literature*, edited by Joseph Harris, 193–213. Cambridge, MA: Harvard University Press, 1991.

Zwierlein, Otto. "Spuren der Tragödien Senecas bei Bernardus Silvestris, Petrus Pictor und Marbod von Rennes." *Mittellateinisches Jahrbuch* 22 (1987): 171–96.

Websites and Databases

The Electronic Sawyer: Online Catalogue of Anglo-Saxon Charters. http://www.esawyer.org.uk.

Epistolae: Medieval Women's Letters, edited by Joan Ferrante. http://epistolae.ccnmtl.columbia.edu.

Library of Latin Texts A and *B*. Turnhout: Brepols, 2014.

PoetriaNova: A CD-ROM of Latin Medieval Poetry (650–1250 A.D.), edited by Paolo Mastandrea and Luigi Tessarolo. Florence: SISMEL – Edizioni del Galluzzo, 2001.

The Production and Use of English Manuscripts, 1060 to 1220, edited by Orietta Da Rold, Takako Kato, Mary Swan, and Elaine Treharne. University of Leicester, 2010; last update 2013. http://www.le.ac.uk/ee/em1060to1220.

Prosopography of Anglo-Saxon England. http://www.pase.ac.uk.

Index

Toronto Anglo-Saxon Series

1 *Preaching the Converted: The Style and Rhetoric of the Vercelli Book Homilies*, Samantha Zacher

2 *Say What I Am Called: The Old English Riddles of the Exeter Book and the Anglo-Latin Riddle Tradition*, Dieter Bitterli

3 *The Aesthetics of Nostalgia: Historical Representation in Anglo-Saxon Verse*, Renée Trilling

4 *New Readings in the Vercelli Book*, edited by Samantha Zacher and Andy Orchard

5 *Authors, Audiences, and Old English Verse*, Thomas A. Bredehoft

6 *On Aesthetics in* Beowulf *and Other Old English Poems*, edited by John M. Hill

7 *Old English Metre: An Introduction*, Jun Terasawa

8 *Anglo-Saxon Psychologies in the Vernacular and Latin Traditions*, Leslie Lockett

9 *The Body Legal in Barbarian Law*, Lisi Oliver

10 *Old English Literature and the Old Testament*, edited by Michael Fox and Manish Sharma

11 *Stealing Obedience: Narratives of Agency and Identity in Later Anglo-Saxon England*, Katherine O'Brien O'Keeffe

12 *Traditional Subjectivities: The Old English Poetics of Mentality*, Britt Mize

13 *Land and Book: Literature and Land Tenure in Anglo-Saxon England*, Scott T. Smith

14 *Writing Women Saints in Anglo-Saxon England*, edited by Paul E. Szarmach

15 *Anglo-Saxon Manuscripts: A Bibliographical Handlist of Manuscripts and Manuscript Fragments Written or Owned in England up to 1100*, Helmut Gneuss and Michael Lapidge

16 *The King's Body: Burial and Succession in Anglo-Saxon England*, Nicole Marafioti

17 *From Lawmen to Plowmen: Anglo-Saxon Legal Tradition and the School of Langland*, Stephen Yeager

18 *The Politics of Language: Byrhtferth, Ælfric, and the Multilingual Identity of the Benedictine Reform*, Rebecca Stephenson

19 *Weaving Words and Binding Bodies: The Poetics of Human Experience in Old English Literature*, Megan Cavell

20 *Joinings: Compound Words in Old English Literature*, Jonathan Davis-Secord

21 *Imagining the Jew in Anglo-Saxon Literature and Culture*, edited by Samantha Zacher

22 *Latinity and Identity in Anglo-Saxon Literature*, edited by Rebecca Stephenson and Emily Thornbury

23 *England in Europe: English Royal Women and Literary Patronage, c. 1000–c. 1150*, Elizabeth M. Tyler

www.ingramcontent.com/pod-product-compliance
Lightning Source LLC
LaVergne TN
LVHW090145080826
844660LV00013B/681/J

* 9 7 8 1 4 4 2 6 4 0 7 2 6 *